SCHOOL LEADERSHIP & ADMINISTRATION

Important Concepts, Case Studies, & Simulations

TENTH EDITION

RICHARD A. GORTON
Gorton Associates, San Diego, CA

JUDY A. ALSTON
Ashland University

Mc Graw Hill Education

McGraw Hill Education

SCHOOL LEADERSHIP AND ADMINISTRATION: IMPORTANT CONCEPTS, CASE STUDIES, & SIMULATIONS

This book is printed on acid-free paper.

1 2 3 4 5 6 7 8 9 LCR 21 20 19 18

ISBN 978-1-260-08462-7
MHID 1-260-08462-0

Cover Image: ©*Andrea Danti/Shutterstock*

mheducation.com/highered

DEDICATION

As always, for Mom, Dad, Cynthia, and Cejae.

–Judy Ann Alston

PREFACE

Leadership is one of the hottest topics of conversation across the various disciplines and fields. The demand for well-trained educational leaders is greater than ever, and yet the challenges are just as great. The public expects more from schools than ever before, including greater accountability; improved performance on standardized tests; guarantees of school safety; more input from parents; better school-community relations; and an acceptance and appreciation of diversity, with equal opportunities for all students. Concurrently, many political, educational, and religious leaders are looking for answers to education's challenges by pursuing alternative routes to excellence–privatization, homeschooling, vouchers, charter schools, and various other efforts at reform.

School leaders are expected to make evidence-informed decisions, provide the instructional leadership for teachers, and create a collaborative school environment where teachers take part in school decisions. Morris and Brooks-Young (n.d.)[1] note that in order to be effective leaders for the twenty-first century, administrators must ensure that instructional needs, the expertise of teachers, and the ultimate needs of students are considered. These twenty-first century administrators should be the facilitators of a dialogue that asks:

- What outcomes do we want to accomplish in the classroom?
- What available tools and resources can and will support teachers in helping their students meet these outcomes?
- What preparation do we need to ensure teachers and students appropriately utilize tools and resources?
- How will we measure the effectiveness of these tools to gauge how well they support and improve teaching and learning?

While the challenges are countless, so are the rewards. The challenges are great for both the profession and for leadership preparation program faculty who are training individuals to fill the positions. For some years, administrator preparation programs have often been criticized as being too theoretical and insufficiently grounded in reality, and in-service programs have frequently been criticized for the reverse. What is needed is professional training that helps educational leaders form a vision of what can be, knowledge of what is known and being discovered, and practical understanding of how to apply the knowledge and carry out the vision in a time of extraordinary change.

This edition continues to spotlight the case studies, in-basket exercises, and simulations in Part II addressing the many forms of leadership (e.g., principal, teacher, collaborative) and how such leadership may be exercised. Since the school represents a microcosm of society, it should play an active role in trying to resolve or ameliorate its problems. Although the educational system has found it impossible to remain detached from the major controversies of the day, administrators and teachers have often been reluctant to assume leadership in seeking answers to societal problems. Our approach is intended to prepare students for the kinds of

[1] Morris, D., and Brooks-Young, S. (n.d.), Becoming a 21st Century Administrator. Creative Educator Accessed online http://creativeeducator.tech4learning.com/v08/articles/Becoming_a_21st_Century_Administrator

situations and problems they will encounter in administrative positions. This approach, therefore, incorporates key professional standards and competencies (such as the development of skills in communication, group leadership, conflict management, and the like) with action-based research methods and theoretical undergirding to assist in decision-making.

This tenth edition continues to reflect our own desire to be inclusive of all voices that are speaking, researching, and practicing in the educational leadership arena. In revising the book, we have taken into account the multiplicity of changes occurring in society in general and in education in particular. We have not made changes simply for the sake of change, and we want to assure instructors who have used previous editions that the strengths of these earlier editions have been retained. This edition does feature the new Professional Standards for Educational Leaders (PSEL), as well as updated background readings and web explorations.

The text is primarily focused toward school leaders, but it has global application with its principles for those who may be in areas such as higher education administration, military educational training programs, agency management, and government services administration.

We sincerely hope that this new edition will prove to be a light and guide for those who are seeking administrative/leadership positions as well as those who need a refresher every now and then.

ACKNOWLEDGMENTS

The authors are grateful to many people, including the scholars who stimulated our thinking, the practitioners who facilitated the field research for Part II of the text, and the students who pilot-tested various aspects of Part II.

Deep gratitude goes out to the many graduate students who, in their roles as teachers and administrators, provided the necessary slice of life to make this text come alive.

We thank the following professors who provided useful reactions to previous editions of this book as well as current revisions: Marna Beard, Robert Cheek, Joseph R. Higham, Gary Martin, Barbara Roquemore, Charles Waggoner, Ella Burton, Debra Touchton, Angela Robinson, Rodney Davis, Amy Klinger, Diane Alexander, Bonnie Fusarelli, and Keith Gurley.

Finally, we are thankful for the support of our loved ones, without whose patience and understanding this book would not have been possible.

RICHARD A. GORTON

JUDY A. ALSTON

McGraw-Hill Connect® is a highly reliable, easy-to-use homework and learning management solution that utilizes learning science and award-winning adaptive tools to improve student results.

Homework and Adaptive Learning

- Connect's assignments help students contextualize what they've learned through application, so they can better understand the material and think critically.
- Connect will create a personalized study path customized to individual student needs through SmartBook®.
- SmartBook helps students study more efficiently by delivering an interactive reading experience through adaptive highlighting and review.

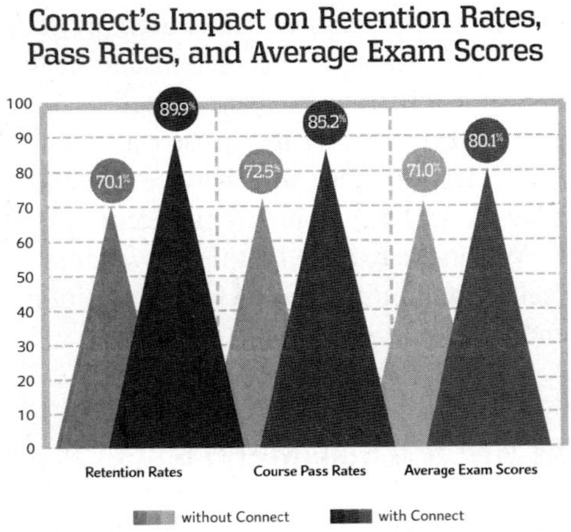

Using **Connect** improves retention rates by **19.8** percentage points, passing rates by **12.7** percentage points, and exam scores by **9.1** percentage points.

Over **7 billion questions** have been answered, making McGraw-Hill Education products more intelligent, reliable, and precise.

73% of instructors who use **Connect** require it; instructor satisfaction **increases** by 28% when **Connect** is required.

Quality Content and Learning Resources

- Connect content is authored by the world's best subject matter experts, and is available to your class through a simple and intuitive interface.
- The Connect eBook makes it easy for students to access their reading material on smartphones and tablets. They can study on the go and don't need internet access to use the eBook as a reference, with full functionality.
- Multimedia content such as videos, simulations, and games drive student engagement and critical thinking skills.

Robust Analytics and Reporting

©Hero Images/Getty Images

- Connect Insight® generates easy-to-read reports on individual students, the class as a whole, and on specific assignments.
- The Connect Insight dashboard delivers data on performance, study behavior, and effort. Instructors can quickly identify students who struggle and focus on material that the class has yet to master.
- Connect automatically grades assignments and quizzes, providing easy-to-read reports on individual and class performance.

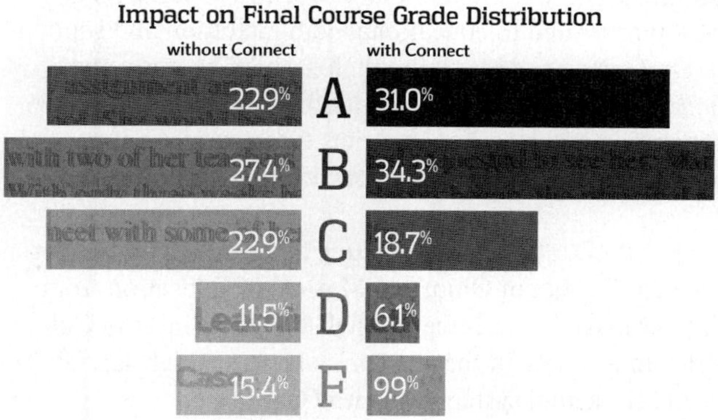

More students earn **As** and **Bs** when they use **Connect.**

Trusted Service and Support

- Connect integrates with your LMS to provide single sign-on and automatic syncing of grades. Integration with Blackboard®, D2L®, and Canvas also provides automatic syncing of the course calendar and assignment-level linking.
- Connect offers comprehensive service, support, and training throughout every phase of your implementation.
- If you're looking for some guidance on how to use Connect, or want to learn tips and tricks from super users, you can find tutorials as you work. Our Digital Faculty Consultants and Student Ambassadors offer insight into how to achieve the results you want with Connect.

www.mheducation.com/connect

MEET THE AUTHORS

RICHARD A. GORTON received his doctorate from Stanford University, majoring in school administration. His bachelor's degree in political science and his master's degree in counseling and guidance were conferred by the University of Iowa. Dr. Gorton's school experience includes teaching, counseling and guidance, and administration. He was Department Chairperson and Professor of Administrative Leadership and Supervision at the University of Wisconsin at Milwaukee. He is currently a consultant with Gorton Associates in San Diego, California.

A leader in state and national administrator organizations, Dr. Gorton has collaborated on a national study of "the effective principal." Because of his expertise and practical experience, he has frequently been called on as a consultant and workshop leader in the areas of teacher and administrator evaluation, in-service education, program evaluation, instructional supervision, student disciplinary problems, school–community relations, problem solving, and conflict resolution.

Dr. Gorton has published two textbooks, two monographs, and over 100 articles, book reviews, and abstracts on a variety of topics related to educational administration and supervision, as well as education in general. Dr. Gorton's other textbook, for which he was senior author, *School-Based Leadership: Challenges and Opportunities,* is used in numerous university courses devoted to administrator preparation and by school districts for in-service education. He has also served as senior editor for *The Encyclopedia of School Administration and Supervision.*

JUDY A. ALSTON received her Ph.D. at The Pennsylvania State University, a Master of Divinity from Methodist Theological School in Ohio, two Masters of Education from the University of South Carolina, and her bachelor's degree in English from Winthrop College in Rock Hill, South Carolina. Prior to teaching in the academy, she was a high school English teacher/teacher-leader in the public school system in South Carolina.

Currently Dr. Alston holds the position of Professor in the Department of Doctoral Studies and Advanced Programs at Ashland University.

Her research foci include gender and educational leadership with a focus on Black female school superintendents; urban education and educational leadership highlighting administrative reform in urban schools; diversity and educational leadership exploring how the intersections of class, race/ethnicity, gender, sexual diversity, and ability affect leaders; and spirituality and leadership. She is the author of numerous articles and book chapters in these areas of research, as well as the author of *Multi-leadership in Urban Schools*, and coauthor of *Herstories: Leading with the Lessons of the Lives of Black Women Activists*.

CONTENTS

CHAPTER 4

Communication 98

CHAPTER 5

Conflict Management 128

CHAPTER 9

Beginning Challenges 231

CHAPTER 10

Student Problems 265

PART

I

Major Concepts in Administration and the Social Sciences

Conceptual Tools for Effective School Leadership

INTRODUCTION

Standards and accountability affect all areas of education as well as for life outside of the discipline. The field of educational administration and leadership is no exception to this rule. This new 10th edition contains the 2015 Professional Standards for Educational Leaders (PSEL). These new standards replaced the former Interstate School Leaders Licensure Consortium (ISLLC) Standards. The National Policy Board for Educational Administration (NPBEA) notes that these new standards are "student-centric, outlining foundational principles of leadership to guide the practice of educational leaders so they can move the needle on student learning and achieve more equitable outcomes. They're designed to ensure that educational leaders are ready to meet effectively the challenges and opportunities of the job today and in the future as education, schools and society continue to transform" (NPBEA, 2015, p. 1). Each chapter in Part I has corresponding PSEL standards on which the instructors and students should focus during reading and discussion. In addition, case studies and simulations in Part II of the text are also aligned with standards for application during analysis, discussion, and role-play.

PROFESSIONAL STANDARDS FOR EDUCATIONAL LEADERS (2015)

(FORMALLY KNOWN AS ISLLC STANDARDS)

STANDARD 1: **Mission, Vision, and Core Values**

Effective educational leaders develop, advocate, and enact a shared mission, vision, and core values of high-quality education and academic success and well-being of each student.

EFFECTIVE LEADERS:

A. Develop an educational mission for the school to promote the academic success and well-being of each student.

B. In collaboration with members of the school and the community and using relevant data, develop and promote a vision for the school on the successful learning and development of each child and on instructional and organizational practices that promote such success.

C. Articulate, advocate, and cultivate core values that define the school's culture and stress the imperative of child-centered education; high expectations and student support; equity, inclusiveness, and social justice; openness, caring, and trust; and continuous improvement.

D. Strategically develop, implement, and evaluate actions to achieve the vision for the school.

E. Review the school's mission and vision and adjust them to changing expectations and opportunities for the school and the changing needs and situations of students.

F. Develop shared understanding of and commitment to mission, vision, and core values within the school and the community.

G. Model and pursue the school's mission, vision, and core values in all aspects of leadership.

STANDARD 2: **Ethics and Professional Norms**

Effective educational leaders act ethically and according to professional norms to promote each student's academic success and well-being.

EFFECTIVE LEADERS:

A. Act ethically and professionally in personal conduct, relationships with others, decision making, stewardship of the school's resources, and all aspects of school leadership.

B. Act according to and promote the professional norms of integrity, fairness, transparency, trust, collaboration, perseverance, learning, and continuous improvement.
C. Place children at the center of education and accept responsibility for each student's academic success and well-being.
D. Safeguard and promote the values of democracy, individual freedom and responsibility, equity, social justice, community, and diversity.
E. Lead with interpersonal and communication skill, social-emotional insight, and understanding of all students' and staff members' backgrounds and cultures.
F. Provide moral direction for the school and promote ethical and professional behavior among faculty and staff.

STANDARD 3: **Equity and Cultural Responsiveness**

Effective educational leaders strive for equity of educational opportunity and culturally responsive practices to promote each student's academic success and well-being.

EFFECTIVE LEADERS:

A. Ensure that each student is treated fairly, respectfully, and with an understanding of each student's culture and context.
B. Recognize, respect, and employ each student's strengths, diversity, and culture as assets for teaching and learning.
C. Ensure that each student has equitable access to effective teachers, learning opportunities, academic and social support, and other resources necessary for success.
D. Develop student policies and address student misconduct in a positive, fair, and unbiased manner.
G. Confront and alter institutional biases of student marginalization, deficit-based schooling, and low expectations associated with race, class, culture and language, gender and sexual orientation, and disability or special status.
H. Promote the preparation of students to live productively in and contribute to the diverse cultural contexts of a global society
I. Act with cultural competence and responsiveness in their interactions, decision making, and practice.
J. Address matters of equity and cultural responsiveness in all aspects of leadership.

STANDARD 4: **Curriculum, Instruction, and Assessment**

Effective educational leaders develop and support intellectually rigorous and coherent systems of curriculum, instruction, and assessment to promote each student's academic success and well-being.

EFFECTIVE LEADERS:

A. Implement coherent systems of curriculum, instruction, and assessment that promote the mission, vision, and core values of the school, embody high expectations for student learning, align with academic standards, and are culturally responsive.

B. Align and focus systems of curriculum, instruction, and assessment within and across grade levels to promote student academic success, love of learning, the identities and habits of learners, and healthy sense of self.

C. Promote instructional practice that is consistent with knowledge of child learning and development, effective pedagogy, and the needs of each student.

D. Ensure instructional practice that is intellectually challenging, authentic to student experiences, recognizes student strengths, and is differentiated and personalized.

E. Promote the effective use of technology in the service of teaching and learning.

F. Employ valid assessments that are consistent with knowledge of child learning and development and technical standards of measurement

G. Use assessment data appropriately and within technical limitations to monitor student progress and improve instruction

STANDARD 5: **Community of Care and Support for Students**

Effective educational leaders cultivate an inclusive, caring, and supportive school community that promotes the academic success and well-being of each student.

EFFECTIVE LEADERS:

A. Build and maintain a safe, caring, and healthy school environment that meets that the academic, social, emotional, and physical needs of each student.

B. Create and sustain a school environment in which each student is known, accepted and valued, trusted and respected, cared for, and encouraged to be an active and responsible member of the school community.

C. Provide coherent systems of academic and social supports, services, extracurricular activities, and accommodations to meet the range of learning needs of each student.

D. Promote adult-student, student-peer, and school-community relationships that value and support academic learning and positive social and emotional development.

E. Cultivate and reinforce student engagement in school and positive student conduct.

F. Infuse the school's learning environment with the cultures and languages of the school's community

STANDARD 6: **Professional Capacity of School Personnel**

Effective educational leaders develop the professional capacity and practice of school personnel to promote each student's academic success and well-being.

EFFECTIVE LEADERS:

A. Recruit, hire, support, develop, and retain effective and caring teachers and other professional staff and form them into an educationally effective faculty.
B. Plan for and manage staff turnover and succession, providing opportunities for effective induction and mentoring of new personnel.
C. Develop teachers' and staff members' professional knowledge, skills, and practice through differentiated opportunities for learning and growth, guided by understanding of professional and adult learning and development.
D. Foster continuous improvement of individual and collective instructional capacity to achieve outcomes envisioned for each student.
E. Deliver actionable feedback about instruction and other professional practice through valid, research-anchored systems of supervision and evaluation to support the development of teachers' and staff members' knowledge, skills, and practice.
F. Empower and motivate teachers and staff to the highest levels of professional practice and to continuous learning and improvement.
G. Develop the capacity, opportunities, and support for teacher leadership and leadership from other members of the school community.
H. Promote the personal and professional health, well-being, and work-life balance of faculty and staff.
I. Tend to their own learning and effectiveness through reflection, study, and improvement, maintaining a healthy work-life balance

STANDARD 7: **Professional Community for Teachers and Staff**

Effective educational leaders foster a professional community of teachers and other professional staff to promote each student's academic success and well-being.

EFFECTIVE LEADERS:

A. Develop workplace conditions for teachers and other professional staff that promote effective professional development, practice, and student learning.
B. Empower and entrust teachers and staff with collective responsibility for meeting the academic, social, emotional,

and physical needs of each student, pursuant to the mission, vision, and core values of the school.

C. Establish and sustain a professional culture of engagement and commitment to shared vision, goals, and objectives pertaining to the education of the whole child; high expectations for professional work; ethical and equitable practice; trust and open communication; collaboration, collective efficacy, and continuous individual and organizational learning and improvement.

D. Promote mutual accountability among teachers and other professional staff for each student's success and the effectiveness of the school as a whole.

E. Develop and support open, productive, caring, and trusting working relationships among leaders, faculty, and staff to promote professional capacity and the improvement of practice.

F. Design and implement job-embedded and other opportunities for professional learning collaboratively with faculty and staff.

G. Provide opportunities for collaborative examination of practice, collegial feedback, and collective learning.

H. Encourage faculty-initiated improvement of programs and practices

STANDARD 8: **Meaningful Engagement of Families and Community**

Effective educational leaders engage families and the community in meaningful, reciprocal, and mutually beneficial ways to promote each student's academic success and well-being.

EFFECTIVE LEADERS:

A. Are approachable, accessible, and welcoming to families and members of the community.

B. Create and sustain positive, collaborative, and productive relationships with families and the community for the benefit of students.

C. Engage in regular and open two-way communication with families and the community about the school, students, needs, problems, and accomplishments.

D. Maintain a presence in the community to understand its strengths and needs, develop productive relationships, and engage its resources for the school.

E. Create means for the school community to partner with families to support student learning in and out of school.

F. Understand, value, and employ the community's cultural, social, intellectual, and political resources to promote student learning and school improvement.

G. Develop and provide the school as a resource for families and the community.

H. Advocate for the school and district and for the importance of education and student needs and priorities to families and the community.

I. Advocate publicly for the needs and priorities of students, families, and the community.

J. Build and sustain productive partnerships with public and private sectors to promote school improvement and student learning.

STANDARD 9: **Operations and Management**

Effective educational leaders manage school operations and resources to promote each student's academic success and well-being.

EFFECTIVE LEADERS:

A. Institute, manage, and monitor operations and administrative systems that promote the mission and vision of the school.

B. Strategically manage staff resources, assigning and scheduling teachers and staff to roles and responsibilities that optimize their professional capacity to address each student's learning needs.

C. Seek, acquire, and manage fiscal, physical, and other resources to support curriculum, instruction, and assessment; student learning community; professional capacity and community; and family and community engagement.

D. Are responsible, ethical, and accountable stewards of the school's monetary and non- monetary resources, engaging in effective budgeting and accounting practices.

E. Protect teachers' and other staff members' work and learning from disruption.

F. Employ technology to improve the quality and efficiency of operations and management.

G. Develop and maintain data and communication systems to deliver actionable information for classroom and school improvement.

H. Know, comply with, and help the school community understand local, state, and federal laws, rights, policies, and regulations so as to promote student success.

I. Develop and manage relationships with feeder and connecting schools for enrollment management and curricular and instructional articulation.

J. Develop and manage productive relationships with the central office and school board.

K. Develop and administer systems for fair and equitable management of conflict among students, faculty and staff, leaders, families, and community.

L. Manage governance processes and internal and external politics toward achieving the school's mission and vision.

STANDARD 10: **School Improvement**

Effective educational leaders act as agents of continuous improvement to promote each student's academic success and well-being.

EFFECTIVE LEADERS:

A. Seek to make school more effective for each student, teachers and staff, families, and the community.

B. Use methods of continuous improvement to achieve the vision, fulfill the mission, and promote the core values of the school.

C. Prepare the school and the community for improvement, promoting readiness, an imperative for improvement, instilling mutual commitment and accountability, and developing the knowledge, skills, and motivation to succeed in improvement.

D. Engage others in an ongoing process of evidence-based inquiry, learning, strategic goal setting, planning, implementation, and evaluation for continuous school and classroom improvement.

E. Employ situationally appropriate strategies for improvement, including transformational and incremental, adaptive approaches and attention to different phases of implementation.

F. Assess and develop the capacity of staff to assess the value and applicability of emerging educational trends and the findings of research for the school and its improvement.

G. Develop technically appropriate systems of data collection, management, analysis, and use, connecting as needed to the district office and external partners for support in planning, implementation, monitoring, feedback, and evaluation.

H. Adopt a systems perspective and promote coherence among improvement efforts and all aspects of school organization, programs, and services.

I. Manage uncertainty, risk, competing initiatives, and politics of change with courage and perseverance, providing support and encouragement, and openly communicating the need for, process for, and outcomes of improvement efforts.

J. Develop and promote leadership among teachers and staff for inquiry, experimentation and innovation, and initiating and implementing improvement.

National Policy Board for Educational Administration (NPBEA). *Professional Standards for Educational Leaders* (Reston, VA: Author, 2015).

CHAPTER

1

Leadership

APPLICABLE PSEL STANDARDS

- **STANDARD 1: Mission, Vision, and Core Values**
  Effective educational leaders develop, advocate, and enact a shared mission, vision, and core values of high-quality education and academic success and well-being of each student.
- **STANDARD 2: Ethics and Professional Norms**
  Effective educational leaders act ethically and according to professional norms to promote each student's academic success and well-being
- **STANDARD 4: Curriculum, Instruction, and Assessment**
  Effective educational leaders develop and support intellectually rigorous and coherent systems of curriculum, instruction, and assessment to promote each student's academic success and well-being
- **STANDARD 5: Community of Care and Support for Students**
  Effective educational leaders cultivate an inclusive, caring, and supportive school community that promotes the academic success and well-being of each student.
- **STANDARD 7: Professional Community for Teachers and Staff**
  Effective educational leaders foster a professional community of teachers and other professional staff to promote each student's academic success and well-being.
- **STANDARD 9: Operations and Management**
  Effective educational leaders manage school operations and resources to promote each student's academic success and well-being.
- **STANDARD 10: School Improvement**
  Effective educational leaders act as agents of continuous improvement to promote each student's academic success and well-being.

It has been said, "The organization without effective leadership is in trouble."[1] Most administrators recognize that providing leadership is a major expectation for their role. This expectation is emphasized both in educational literature and at various professional meetings. But what constitutes leadership? How does the administrator exercise leadership? In response to these questions, literally hundreds of studies have been conducted, and thousands of articles and many books have been written. Although these efforts have, in many instances, provided insights into the subject of leadership, the concept remains elusive. In large part, this may be because leadership involves the effective utilization of all the other concepts in this text, and it is difficult to analyze as a distinct concept. This chapter reviews some of the relevant and seminal research on literature in leadership as well as describes and analyzes particular concepts that possess major relevance for the school administrator who wants to be an educational leader, with particular emphasis on the notion of group leadership.

DEFINITIONS AND NEED FOR LEADERSHIP

Theorists, researchers, and practitioners have defined *leadership* in a variety of ways.[2] Probably the most commonsensical definition was stated by Cowley in the 1920s: "The leader is the one who succeeds in getting others to follow him [or her]."[3] "Leadership is taking risks, making mistakes and learning from those mistakes. Leadership provides the very foundation for a sound educational program. When leadership is right, people are inspired to do their best." [4]

Individuals Can Lead; Groups Can Lead

As theorists and researchers began to analyze the term *leadership,* more elaborate and sophisticated definitions evolved. Stogdill, a respected authority on the subject, defined leadership as those activities engaged in by an individual or members of a group that contribute significantly to "development and maintenance of role structure and goal direction, necessary for effective group performance."[5] Stogdill's definition emphasizes that leadership need not be limited to one individual, such as the school administrator, and that the focus of leadership activities should be on increasing the performance effectiveness of the group.

Referring to Thomas Carlyle's "Great Man" theory of history, Bennis suggests that perhaps instead we should realize that to a great extent "our world has in fact been the product of 'Great Groups,' teams of creative persons who banded together to achieve remarkable successes that would not have been possible through a traditional hierarchical approach."[6] He emphasizes that a *shared dream* is at the heart of each "Great Group" and that individual egos are put aside in order to pursue the dream. Bennis writes that leadership is dispersed among Great Groups, not necessarily by formal rotation rules but by different group members assuming different types of leadership roles at different times and in different situations according to their individual abilities. Thus the group itself can be a leader at the same time that various members are leaders *within* the group. Certain traits characterize team or group leaders, according to Bennis: namely, providing direction and meaning, generating and sustaining trust, displaying an eagerness to take action, and spreading hope.[7]

Empowerment

The concept of *empowerment* has increasingly dominated the research on group leadership and group dynamics and has had an impact on the way leadership is defined. According to Taylor and Rosenbach, "Leadership involves assisting everyone working with the organization to collectively gain control over resources for the common good."[8] Conger and Kanungo define empowerment as "a process of enhancing feelings of self-efficacy among organizational members through identification of conditions that foster powerlessness and through their removal by both formal organizational practices and informal techniques of providing efficacy information."[9]

Conger stresses four ways in which effective leaders empower subordinates. First, they structure tasks so that staff members have success and are rewarded. Second, they use verbal persuasion to convince followers that they are able to successfully complete difficult tasks. Third, effective leaders reduce tensions and build excitement and pride in the organization. Finally, good leaders model empowerment through their own behavior, showing that they, too, are empowered when interacting with their superiors and thereby demonstrating what self-confidence can accomplish.[10]

Lilly, on the same subject of empowerment, writes that "power is the ability to get things done, rather than the ability to get one's way against resistance."[11] He distinguishes between *distributive* power and *collective* power. The former is adversarial and controlling, whereas the latter results from empowering all individuals involved. The use of collective power increases the power of all people as they reach the goals together that may have eluded them independently. According to Lilly, the powerful administrator is not independent but rather interdependent. Evidence that a group is truly empowered may be seen in a situation in which (1) people feel significant because everyone is making a contribution, (2) leaders model behavior that values the learning and competence of people in the organization, and (3) the work is viewed as exciting. Finally, leaders who empower their employees pull them, rather than push them, to a goal by embodying the vision toward which the rest of the group strives.[12] Effective leaders are themselves empowered and seek to do the same for their staff. They are willing to take risks and encourage their subordinates to be risk takers. To quote Morris, "Risk taking leaders do not wait for the future to occur. They create the future by actively engaging in it."[13]

Administrators, Managers, and Leaders

Another major contribution to the literature on leadership, one that the authors believe to hold significant implications for the educational administrator, was developed by Lipham.[14] Lipham made an important distinction between the *administrator* and the *leader.* He defined the administrator as "the individual who utilizes existing structures or procedures to achieve an organizational goal or objective."[15] He went on to say, "The administrator is concerned primarily with maintaining, rather than changing established structures, procedures, or goals."[16] Thus the administrator, according to Lipham, must be viewed as a stabilizing force.

In contrast, the *leader* as defined by Lipham, "is concerned with initiating changes in established structures, procedures or goals; he [or she] is a disrupter of the existing state of affairs." Leadership, to Lipham, is "the initiation of a new structure or procedure for accomplishing organizational goals and objectives."[17] Consequently, an administrator can be a leader by attempting to introduce change, but is not a leader simply because he or she happens to

WINDOW ON DIVERSITY

Leadership

CULTURALLY PROFICIENT LEADERSHIP CONTINUUM

1. **Cultural destructiveness:** See the difference, stomp it out–the elimination of other people's cultures.
2. **Cultural incapacity:** See the difference, make it wrong–belief in the superiority of one's culture and behavior that disempowers another's culture.
3. **Cultural blindness:** See the difference, act like you don't–acting as if the cultural differences you see do not matter, or not recognizing that there are differences among and between cultures.
4. **Cultural precompetence:** See the difference, respond inadequately–awareness of the limitations of one's skills or an organization's practices when interacting with other cultural groups.
5. **Cultural competence:** See the difference, understand the difference that difference makes–interacting with other cultural groups using the five essential elements of cultural proficiency as the standard for individual behavior and school practices.
6. **Cultural proficiency:** See the differences and respond positively and affirmingly–esteeming culture, knowing how to learn about individual and organizational culture, and interacting effectively in a variety of cultural environments.

ESSENTIAL ELEMENTS

These elements provide the standards for individual behavior and organizational practices:

- Name the differences: Assess culture.
- Claim the differences: Value diversity.
- Reframe the differences: Manage the dynamics of difference.
- Train about the differences: Adapt to diversity.
- Change for differences: Institutionalize cultural knowledge.

Source: Randall B. Lindsey, Kikanza Nuri Robins, and Raymond D. Terrell, *Cultural Proficiency: A Manual for School Leaders* (Thousand Oaks, CA: Corwin Press, 2007).

occupy what has been referred to as a "leadership position." It is not the *position* that determines whether someone is a leader; it is the nature of that individual's *behavior* while occupying that position.

Kotter has written that "management is about coping with complexity," a necessary response to the complexity of modern organizations, whereas leadership "is about coping with change" and is more necessary than ever before because of the vast changes taking place today; but he stresses that both management and leadership are necessary and should be considered "complementary systems of action." Although Kotter's discussion focused on the business world, his point applies to education as well.[18] Similarly, Conger and Kanungo also make a distinction between *leader* and *manager,* contending that motivation is the "very essence" of true leadership, coupled with the ability of leaders to build an emotional attachment with their followers. Leaders also use intuition, which is "insight, judgment, and executive ESP." Smith writes that good followers can be easily identified by these qualities. For example, followers listen, read the administrator's memos, brag about their colleagues, are kind to others, do not get involved in petty staff disputes, think in terms of "we" not "me," adjust their personal and school schedules to benefit others, think of themselves as part of a team or group, ask what they can do to help, recognize that "imitation is the sincerest form of flattery," share everything, and pitch in to help without being asked.[19] The leader's behavior, according to Conger and Kanungo's research, is characterized as charismatic and visionary. One important personality trait is the leader's understanding of the need for power and the approach to its use. The leader must also have the organizational vision necessary to direct the organization into its future and the ability to articulate this vision.[20]

As Lipham acknowledged, however, the administrator who adopts the role of leader will be unable to spend time on leadership only. Adequate attention must also be devoted to administering the school. There is considerable doubt whether an organization can successfully maintain itself if the administrator spends all or most of the time in initiating new procedures or goals. Nevertheless, it is equally clear that organizational improvement may suffer if the administrator spends all of his or her time maintaining the status quo. As Bennis aptly observes, "Managers are people who do things right; leaders are people who do the right things," and good managers successfully handle the routine daily jobs, but seldom question whether these jobs should be done in the first place.[21] If the organization is to improve its effectiveness and reach new heights, the administrator must initiate change in procedures and organizational goals–and if these changes achieve the desired ends, then the administrator has not only attempted to exercise leadership but also succeeded in exercising *effective* leadership, which seems to be needed more than ever in education.

Why Leadership Has Become So Important

Although the professional literature on school administration has long emphasized that one of the major responsibilities of the school administrator is to provide leadership, this emphasis has taken on new urgency in recent years. Beginning in the 1970s with the "effective school" research[22] and continuing into the early years of the twenty-first century, with various national and state reports recommending major changes in education,[23] the school administrator has frequently been cited as a pivotal figure in bringing about needed school reform and improvement. While some may doubt whether all, or, for that matter, many school administrators possess the necessary qualities for leadership,[24] there is general agreement that administrative leadership is needed if the schools are to improve significantly.[25]

New developments in leadership theory, for example, have focused on such matters as values and beliefs frequently embedded in the mission of the school or school district;[26] vision or "aesthetic motivation";[27] and the role of symbols, culture, and purpose.[28] Whether the focus is on defining a clear school purpose and mission, developing a definite set of staff expectations for improved student learning, providing an orderly school environment where serious learning can take place, or one of the other elements that school effectiveness research has identified,[29] *some* type of leadership contribution by the school administrator seems *necessary.*

Parks and Barrett stress that future administrators must be leaders of leaders by demonstrating the following abilities: recognizing, rewarding, and supporting the work of new leaders; coaching the leaders on values, missions, and goals of the school and school system; supplying necessary resources, such as release time, money, staff support, facilities, and equipment; providing tools for review and reflection of their work; promoting opportunities for leadership skill enhancement; giving credit to new leaders while maintaining responsibility; consulting often with and delegating freely to new leaders; and supporting these leaders' decisions.[30]

In the following sections, several theories of leadership containing the *most* useful ideas for the school administrator will be presented, including an exploration of the administrator's leadership role in working with groups. Leadership in this 21st century must also be for and about social justice. One major approach to leadership examines the *behavior* of effective leaders. Another approach emphasizes the *situation* in which the leader functions.

SEMINAL STUDIES IN LEADERSHIP AND TYPES OF LEADERSHIP

Trait Studies

Some of the first theories regarding leadership revolved around the study of traits. These studies attempted to identify traits that could be used to differentiate between leaders and those who are not. A hierarchical organizational structure housed its leaders at or near the top with trait theories, and the focus was on developing habits, approaches, viewpoints, or traits to become successful. In 1948 Stogdill noted that even though leaders exhibited some general managerial advantages over those who were not leaders relative to some traits, there were no characteristics or traits exhibited by leaders that were clearly superior. Current literature focusing on leadership traits include Stephen Covey's *Seven Habits of Highly Effective People* and John Wareham's *The Anatomy of a Great Executive.*[31]

Behavior Studies

From the 1930s, 1940s, and 1950s come the well-known behavior studies conducted at major midwestern research universities. In 1938, Lewin, Lippitt, and White, researchers at Iowa, conducted a group of studies called the "Leadership and Group Life" (also known as "The Iowa Studies") on the productivity of subordinates using three styles: autocratic, democratic, and laissez-faire.[32] The autocratic leader was very direct and had strong decision making skills, and power resided with this individual. The leader who was identified as laissez-faire gave complete decision-making power to the group. The researchers found a "democratic style" of leadership to be superior to the more autocratic or laissez-faire styles. The new democratic style was touted as more productive because this individual shared the decision making with the group. It was later generalized from this study to corporate settings.[33] The effective school leader in the twenty-first century will also employ this democratic style of leader behavior to foster a collaborative community of learners.

Another series of studies on leadership was done at The Ohio State University, beginning in the 1950s.[34] Researchers found two critical characteristics either of which could be high or low and were independent of one another: *Consideration* is the degree to which a leader acts in a friendly and supportive manner toward his or her subordinates; *initiating structure* is the degree to which a leader defines and structures his or her role and the roles of the subordinates toward achieving the goals of the group. The research was based on questionnaires to leaders and subordinates. These are known as the Leader Behavior Description Questionnaire (LBDQ) and the Supervisor Behavior Description Questionnaire (SBDQ).

The 1950s also found researchers at the University of Michigan conducting research on leader behavior, wherein three critical characteristics of effective leadership were found: task-oriented behavior, relationship-oriented behavior, and participative leadership. With task-oriented behavior, effective managers did not do the same kind of work as their subordinates. Their tasks were different, and included planning and scheduling work, coordinating activities, and providing necessary resources. They also spent time guiding subordinates in setting task goals that were both challenging and achievable. Those managers who displayed relationship-oriented behavior concentrated not only on the task but also on their relationship with their subordinates. They were more considerate, helpful, and supportive of subordinates, including helping them with their career and personal problems. They recognized effort with intrinsic as well as extrinsic reward, thanking people for effort. Overall, the effective managers preferred a general and hands-off form of supervision rather than close control. They set goals and provided guidelines, but then gave their subordinates plenty of leeway as to how the goals would be achieved. Finally, those who practiced participative leadership managed both at the group level and at the individual level, for example, using team meetings to share ideas and involve the team in group decisions and problem solving. By their actions, such leaders model good team-oriented behavior. The role of the manager is more facilitative than directive, guiding the conversation and helping to resolve differences. The manager, however, is responsible for results and is not absolved of responsibility. As such, the manager may make final decisions that take recommendations from the team into account. The effect of participative leadership is to build a cohesive team that works together rather than a set of individuals.[35]

Parallel to the university studies, in research conducted by Halpin, the behavior of aircraft commanders and school superintendents was studied, and two sets of behavior were found to be associated with effective leadership: initiating structure and consideration.[36] The leader who assumes an initiating structure leadership role will attempt to define the behavior expected from each member of the organization and will emphasize the importance of "getting the job done." In a sense, this behavior is similar to that of a *nomothetic* leader, first conceptualized by Getzels, in that work-related needs rather than the personal needs of the members of the group are emphasized.[37] The importance of this type of behavior has been documented in studies of principals in effective schools. For example, one study observed, "[The principal] sets clear expectations for the teachers, and all staff as professionals are accountable for the results of their efforts."[38] Another study reported, "These [effective] principals set high academic standards."[39] A related report on effective schools sees the principal framing and communicating goals, setting expectations, monitoring instructional progress, coordinating the curriculum, and supervising and evaluating the faculty.[40]

The second leadership variable identified by Halpin was a factor termed consideration. Whereas the "initiating structure" aspects of leadership are task-centered, the "consideration" aspects are people-centered. The administrator who assumes the consideration leadership role will attempt to develop a positive and satisfying relationship between leader and followers and will try to promote a spirit of cooperation among the different members of the group being led. This type of leadership has also been characterized by Getzels and his colleagues as *idiographic* leadership, in that it stresses the personal and emotional needs of the members of the group.[41] As emphasized by Finn, "Effective principals require the ability to work closely with others."[42]

In sum, consideration behavior on the part of a leader represents an attempt to meet the maintenance needs of a group, whereas initiating structure can be regarded as behavior designed to help a group achieve its objectives.

Some administrators may feel that they are leaders if they *either* initiate structure *or* provide consideration. Halpin emphasizes, however, that *both* types of behavior are important.[43] That is, the leader must initiate action and get things done; but in most situations, in order to achieve these objectives successfully, the leader must meet the personal and emotional needs of people to secure their continuing cooperation and commitment. This style of leadership has been referred to by Getzels and colleagues as *transactional leadership.*

For example, if an administrator emphasizes the initiation of structure in order to facilitate organizational achievement but neglects the needs of a group for consideration, cooperation in achieving the goals of the organization may not be attained. If, on the other hand, an administrator stresses the consideration dimension but pays insufficient attention to the initiation of structure needed to promote organizational achievement, the administrator may succeed in meeting a group's needs for maintenance but may fail to meet fully the organization's needs for achievement.[44]

In the 1960s, Blake and Mouton introduced their Managerial Grid with two dimensions (axes) of leadership orientation: concern for production (task) and concern for people (relationship). Here five leadership styles were identified via the two axes of the grid:

1. Authoritarian leader (high task, low relationship): People who get this rating are very much task-oriented and are hard on their workers (autocratic). There is little or no allowance for cooperation or collaboration. Heavily task-oriented people display these characteristics: They are very strong on schedules; they expect people to do what they are told without question or debate; when something goes wrong they tend to focus on who is to blame rather than concentrate on exactly what is wrong and how to prevent it; and they are intolerant of what they see as dissent (it may just be someone's creativity), so it is difficult for their subordinates to contribute or develop.
2. Team leader (high task, high relationship): These people lead by positive example and endeavor to foster a team environment in which all team members can reach their highest potential, both as team members and as people. They encourage the team to reach team goals as effectively as possible, while also working tirelessly to strengthen the bonds among the various members. They normally form and lead some of the most productive teams.
3. Country club leader (low task, high relationship): These people use predominantly reward power to maintain discipline and to encourage the team to accomplish its goals. Conversely, they are almost incapable of employing the more punitive coercive and legitimate powers. This inability results from fear that using such powers could jeopardize relationships with the other team members.
4. Impoverished leader (low task, low relationship): Leaders who use a "delegate and disappear" management style. Since they are not committed to either task accomplishment

or maintenance, they essentially allow their team to do whatever it wishes and prefer to detach themselves from the team process by allowing the team to suffer from a series of power struggles.

5. Organization non manager: A leader who maintains the status quo.

The team leader would be the most desirable place for a leader to be along the two axes and at most times would be with a 9 on task and a 9 on people.[45]

Updated in 1991, the New Managerial Grid[46] identifies seven new styles, which Blake and McCanse found to be the most important differences among leaders:

1. Control and dominate (dictatorial)
2. Yield and support (accommodating)
3. Balance and compromise (status quo)
4. Evade and elude (indifferent)
5. Prescribe and guide (paternalistic)
6. Exploit and manipulate (opportunistic)
7. Contribute and commit (sound)

SITUATIONAL LEADERSHIP AND CONTINGENCY MODELS

In addition to the emphasis on the characteristics of leadership and the behaviors of effective leaders, there is another major approach to leadership—an approach built less around the *person* and more around the *situation* in which the person functions. The nature of a particular situation is considered to be the most important variable determining how the leader operates. This school of thought rejects the premise that one approach to leadership is preferable to another. Instead, the proponents of situational leadership set forth two primary propositions that (1) the leadership approach employed by an individual should be relative to the situation and (2) different situations demand different kinds of behavior from the leader.[47] Figure 1.1

FIGURE 1.1
SITUATIONAL VARIABLES AND LEADERSHIP

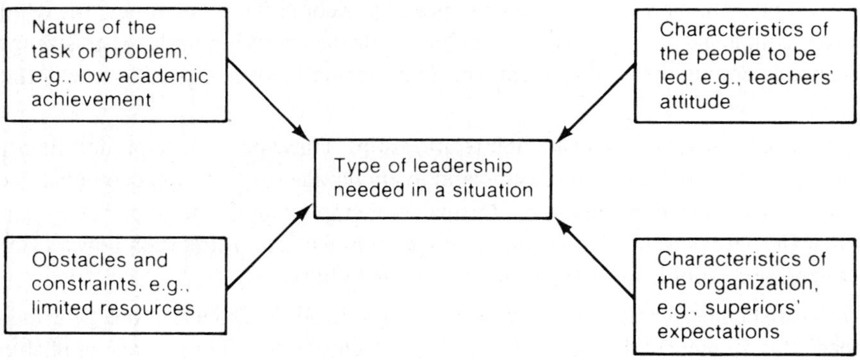

presents several major situational factors that could influence the type of leadership needed in a school or school district.[48]

As a conference on effective schools sponsored by the National Institute of Education made clear:

> There are very important contextual factors such as composition of the teaching staff, the student body, the community, the district situation, state mandates, and the principal's own past experience that seem to shape how the principals accomplish their role.[49]

Although the empirical evidence is not conclusive,[50] there is considerable observational experience to support the situational theory of leadership. For example, persons who are appointed or elected as leaders in one situation may not be chosen again when circumstances change. Individuals who are successful in leading a group in a given situation may not be successful with a different group or at another time.

The importance of situational leadership can easily be observed in educational administration. The individual for any specific administrative position is usually selected primarily by criteria of certain personal qualities and a style of leadership that meet the needs of the work situation. School boards, for instance, do not all look for the same type of leader to fill the position of superintendent. They want an individual who they feel will provide the type of leadership to meet the unique needs of the school district. In one situation, a school board may look for a superintendent who can successfully introduce basic changes in the schools, perhaps over the strong opposition of a number of people. At another time the board may want a superintendent who can play the role of harmonizer and who can ameliorate the conflicts between the school and its constituencies. On each occasion, the school board will seek someone who possesses the unique personal qualities and leadership style for a particular situation.

Circumstances change, and herein lies one of the fundamental problems of administration. The administrator who has been appointed for one situation via certain leadership characteristics may lack the necessary qualifications when a different set of circumstances arises. Perhaps a principal is hired because of organizational ability and a background in curriculum. For several years the principal operates a very efficient school and introduces several curricular innovations. Gradually, the principal gains recognition as an outstanding educational leader in the district. Things begin to change during the fifth year, however. Racial conflicts erupt; teachers become more militant and demand a colleague-like relationship with the administration; the community grows more critical of the school; and antagonism develops between teachers and parents.

Obviously, new characteristics and problems have been added to the situations in which this principal functions. The reasons for these changes are not immediately evident, but it is clear that a different set of personal qualities and a different leadership style are now required of the principal. Whether or not the administrator in this situation can meet the new requirements is undetermined. Success as an appointed leader, however, will greatly depend on the extent to which a principal possesses or develops the attitudes, skills, and approaches necessary to respond adequately to new circumstances.

In 1977, Hersey and Blanchard's Situational Leadership, originally called the "life cycle theory of leadership," became popular. Their theoretical model posits that the developmental levels of a leader's subordinates play the greatest role in determining which leadership styles are most appropriate (leader behaviors). According to this conceptualization, leader behaviors fall along two continua: (1) directive behavior and (2) supportive behavior. These two continua involve the following styles:

- Delegating style—allowing the group to take responsibility for task decisions; this is a low-task, low-relationship style.
- Participating style—emphasizing shared ideas and participative decisions on task directions; this is a low-task, high-relationship style.
- Selling style—explaining task directions in a supportive and persuasive way; this is a high-task, high-relationship style.
- Telling style—giving specific task directions and closely supervising work; this is a high-task, low-relationship style.

Hersey and Blanchard believed that leaders should be flexible and adjust their styles as followers and situations change over time.[51]

The situational theory of leadership maintains that no particular style of leadership or personal qualities of a leader is appropriate for every situation. The theory places a high premium on the administrator's adaptability and flexibility. A major problem with this theory, however, is that many administrators are influenced in their choice of a leadership style and in the way they behave as a leader by their own personality and need disposition, which tend to be rather consistent and unchanging over time and in different situations. Therefore, although the nature of the demands for leadership in education frequently changes, an administrator's basic personality may not make it possible to adapt individual leadership style to a new situation. Badaracco and Ellsworth have addressed this problem. They stress that leaders have certain personality traits that make it difficult to change styles to match the situation. They suggest leaders use their own personal philosophies of management and leadership to solve situational dilemmas or problems.[52]

One way to ameliorate this problem is for organizations and groups to select those administrators who are, or who can become, flexible and adaptable in their leadership responses to changing leadership demands. Another possibility is to select leaders who possess the type of personality characteristics and leadership style for the leadership demands of the situation, and then rotate these leaders to a new environment when the current situation changes. This approach is suggested by the contingency model, which attempts to incorporate the factors of personality, leadership style, and the nature of the situation by focusing on the interactive dynamics of these three variables.[53] A leading theorist of this school of thought is Fred Fiedler, who has researched and written extensively on the topic.[54] The approach is termed the contingency model because it is based on the assumption that effective leadership is contingent on a compatible relationship between the administrator's personal qualities and style and the demands of the situation.

Path-Goal Theory

The path-goal theory of leadership was developed to describe the way that leaders encourage and support their followers in achieving the goals they have been set by making the path that they should take clear and easy. In particular, leaders clarify the path so subordinates know which way to go, remove roadblocks that are preventing them from going there, and increase the rewards along the route. Leaders can take a strong or limited approach in these. In clarifying the path, they may be directive or give vague hints. In removing roadblocks, they may scour the path or help the follower move the bigger blocks. In increasing rewards, they may give occasional encouragement or pave the way with gold.

This variation in approach will depend on the situation, including the follower's capability and motivation, as well as the difficulty of the job and other contextual factors.[55]

House and Mitchell (1974) describe four styles of leadership:[56]

- Supportive leadership: Considering the needs of the followers, showing concern for their welfare, and creating a friendly working environment. This includes increasing the followers' self-esteem and making the job more interesting. This approach is best when the work is stressful, boring, or hazardous.
- Directive leadership: Telling followers what needs to be done and giving appropriate guidance along the way. This includes giving them schedules of specific work to be done at specific times. Rewards may also be increased as needed and role ambiguity decreased (by telling them what they should be doing). This may be used when the task is unstructured and complex and the follower is inexperienced. This increases the follower's sense of security and control and hence is appropriate to the situation.
- Participative leadership: Consulting with followers and taking their ideas into account when making decisions and taking particular actions. This approach is best when the followers are expert and their advice is both needed and they expect to be able to give it.
- Achievement-oriented leadership: Setting challenging goals, both in work and in self-improvement (and often together). High standards are demonstrated and expected. The leader shows faith in the capabilities of the follower to succeed. This approach is best when the task is complex.

Leaders who show the way and help followers along a path are effectively "leading." This approach assumes that there is one right way of achieving a goal and that the leader can see it and the follower cannot. This casts the leader as the knowing person and the follower as dependent.[57] It also assumes that the follower is completely rational and that the appropriate methods can be deterministically selected depending on the situation.

TODAY'S EFFECTIVE LEADERS

In their studies of more than 20,000 people on four continents, Kouzes and Posner identified the top four qualities constituents expected in leaders. These researchers found that leaders perceived as effective are honest, forward-looking, inspirational, and competent.[58] In addition, successful leaders keep their promises, align their actions to be consistent with the wishes of the people they lead, believe in the inherent self-worth of others, are capable of making a difference in the lives of others, admit their mistakes, arouse optimism about success, and create a climate for learning that is characterized by trust and openness.

In further research, Kouzes and Posner examined case studies and questionnaire surveys to see what practices marked personal-best examples of leadership. They found five basic practices that marked such leadership: challenging the process, inspiring in others a shared vision, enlisting the support of others and enabling them to act, setting an example by their own behavior, and encouraging the hearts of others to keep persevering in living out the shared vision.[59] Kouzes and Posner define leadership as "the art of mobilizing others to want to struggle for shared aspirations."[60] They consider the words "want to" essential to the definition. Ultimately the effective leader is one who employs what Randall Lindsey, Kikanza Nuri Robins, and Raymond Terrell have successfully introduced into the literature, culturally proficient leadership. Taking into consideration the leadership challenge, the culturally proficient leader is one who esteems culture, knows how to learn about individual and organizational culture, and interacts effectively in a variety of cultural environments (see "Window on Diversity-Leadership on p. 13).[61]

Transformational Leadership

In 1978 Bernard Bass coined the term "transformational leadership." Known as the "Father of Transformational Leadership," Bass defined the phrase in terms of how the leader affects followers, who are intended to trust, admire, and respect the transformational leader. He identified three ways in which leaders transform followers:

- Increasing their awareness of task importance and value.
- Getting them to focus first on team or organizational goals, rather than their own interests.
- Activating their higher-order needs.[62]

"Transformational leadership," as described by Leithwood, "is a form of consensual or facilitative power that is manifested through other people instead of over other people." It is composed of the following three elements: (1) a collaborative, shared decision-making approach; (2) an emphasis on teacher professionalism and empowerment; and (3) an understanding of change, including how to encourage change in others. Important skills necessary for transformational leaders are the abilities to see the complete picture, to concentrate on continuing school improvement, to foster a sense of ownership within the school community, and to create and work in teams.[63] Hoerr reveals that implementing the team approach is not an easy task. It requires more time, a redefinition of roles, and a shift in accountability because everyone plays an active part in deciding solutions.[64] Scholtes offers several guidelines for consideration in creating teams. The more complex an issue is, the more it will require several members or subgroups to divide it into workable components. Various disciplines and areas of expertise can be represented by different individuals. In addition, a group can better sustain the changes produced by a task requiring prolonged effort.[65] Poplin summarizes future effective leadership by writing, "While our new role of administrator/servant places leaders at both the top and bottom of the hierarchy, administrators of the future who can tolerate the ambiguity of the role will spark the change that can only happen inside institutions where everyone is growing."[66]

A contemporary view of transformational leadership is found in the research on spiritually based leadership theories. Dantley notes that "spirituality is that component of our total selves and community through which we make meaning and understanding of our world. It is our foundation of values, principles, influences and ethics that we exhibit in our interactions with others."[67] Here is found the linking of spirituality, transformational leadership, and leaders as moral agents, which is explored via Cornel West's notions of *deep-seated moralism, inescapable opportunism,* and *profound pessimism.* For educational leadership, Dantley expresses these notions as *principled leadership, pragmatic leadership,* and *purposive leadership:*[68]

1. Principled leadership: Based on idographic morality (leader's reflective journey regarding right and wrong) and nomothetic morality (using self-reflection for systemic transformation), principled leadership begins with a careful and critical reflection of one's position on issues of justice, democracy, and fairness. It is initiated when an individual questions the democratic efficacy of administrative decisions and procedures he or she is demanded to implement.
2. Pragmatic leadership: These leaders view their leadership role as one that not only promotes the acquisition of skills necessary for successful academic achievement but also emphasizes using those skills to bring about social, educational, political, and economic change. They understand that "schools can either reproduce or challenge the constructions that have been traditionally promulgated through educational institutions."
3. Purposive leadership: Purposive leadership is focused on "transforming school districts or implementing change in local school sites." This leadership becomes the impetus for innovative change.

Aligned with the notion of spirituality and leadership is the literature on servant leadership. Robert K. Greenleaf coined the term *servant leadership* in his 1978 essay," The Servant as Leader. "In this essay, he defines servant leadership as a way to serve and lead as a method of expanding service to individuals and institutions.[69] McClellan's critical servant leadership is an expansion of servant leadership by combining it with critical spirituality. It is the by-product of the infusion of two radical perspectives, which are critical theory and Cornel West's notion of prophetic spirituality.[70] Critical spirituality has three major components. The first component is a prophetic spirituality, which is a combative spirituality and frames the urgency for institutional and personal transformation. The second component is the impact of reflection on the leader(s). The third and final component is a spirit-filled resistance that proposes a project or praxis for self and institutional change.[71] Critical servant leadership is more than a theory or theoretical perspective. It is a way of being.

Distributed Leadership

Distributed leadership centers around a different model within the school where the distinctions between followers and leaders tend to blur.[72] It incorporates the activities and efforts of multiple groups in a school who work at guiding staff in the instructional change process.[73] The distributed leadership model involves distributing responsibility on all administrative levels, working through teams, and engendering collective responsibility.[74] In the distributed leadership model, the principal shares authority and power; teachers take leading roles, assume responsibility, and act independently as individuals or groups. However, the distributed leadership model "does not necessarily imply that the entire faculty controls decisions related to the school. Rather, principals create leadership positions that allow capable and willing teachers to work in a more focused leadership capacity."[75] According to James Spillane, distributed leadership is first and foremost about leadership practice rather than leaders or their roles, functions, routines, and structures. Furthermore, distributed leadership is a perspective–a conceptual or diagnostic tool for thinking about school leadership. It is not a blueprint for effective leadership nor a prescription for how school leadership should be practiced. It is leadership in a system of practice comprised of a collection of interacting components: leaders, followers, and situation. These interacting components must be understood together because the system is more than the sum of the component parts or practices.[76]

> In using a model of Distributed Leadership, the Massachusetts Department of Education makes the following assumptions:
>
> - The principal is the building administrator and the key leader in the building's leadership team, which may include assistant principals, department heads, guidance counselors, teacher leaders, and others. At the district level, the principal participates on the district-wide administrative team as a representative for his/her building and a steward of the district's mission, vision, and strategic goals.
> - Leading is not the same as doing. The key assumption for effective distributed leadership is not *which* functions or tasks can be delegated completely to an individual or group of individuals, but *what level of involvement in those functions or tasks is most appropriate and strategic* (e.g., most connected to core mission, greatest result for effort) for the building administrator to fulfill. Distributed leadership requires large and small-scale role changes across the district. Some changes will be harder to make than others, and may require either negotiation or planning on a person-to-person level. Certainly, the implementation of distributed leadership strategies will look different at every school and district. To be effective, any of the distributed leadership strategies must be integrated with existing systems and processes, rather than requiring new teams, additional meetings, etc. The focus of these systems and processes will necessarily reflect a deeper understanding and discussion of *people, potential, and results.*
> - Distributed leadership requires interdependence to work effectively. Those who lead, have primary responsibility for, or coordinate major functions (such as Curriculum and Instruction, or Operations) must connect their work with all important stakeholders, including those with subject matter or content expertise, to fulfill their objectives. These teams must collaborate and cooperate with full and shared knowledge of the goals, activities, and resources of other teams.
> - The Superintendent and Principal are responsible for establishing a high performance team culture in the district and the schools, respectively. As leaders, they need to remain involved in human resources development at the highest level (e.g., leading change, promoting effective work environments, coaching and mentoring staff, engaging in career development discussions, defining leadership development opportunities, hiring key positions, etc.). However, the more routine aspects of human resources management (e.g., benefits, policy implementation, coordinating HR activities with Central Office) may be handled locally by a Business Manager and his/her administrative support staff.
> - Distributed leadership focuses on maximizing underutilized resources both within and *outside* the district. True change requires the combined efforts of administrators, teachers, teacher-aides, support staff, parents, and even students to leverage all the available skills, experience, interest, and knowledge toward the enhancement of student achievement. This change must cascade from the district to the schools to the classroom to ensure equitable realignment of tasks system-wide.
> - Finally, there is not one model or one strategy that is a prerequisite for success. Each district and school must evaluate its own situation to develop a plan for distributed leadership that achieves the greatest return on investment.[77]

GROUP LEADERSHIP

The Group Dynamics Approach

To exercise leadership, an administrator will need to try to influence the various groups that are associated with the school or school district.[78] In some of these situations, the administrator may be heading a group, such as the faculty; in other circumstances, the administrator may be acting as an adviser to a group, such as the PTA; and in still other contexts, the administrator may be in an adversarial relationship with a group, as for example, a community pressure group. Regardless of the nature of the group or the relationship the administrator has to the group, to be an effective leader, the administrator must possess knowledge and skills in utilizing group dynamics concepts. In addition, ideas discussed in other concept chapters of this text must be well understood and properly applied. It is impossible to provide in this chapter a comprehensive treatment of a topic on which entire books have been written, but an attempt will be made to present important aspects of group dynamics that a school administrator should know.

Recognizing Possible Group Problems

When an administrator initially becomes the head of a group, individual or group problems are seldom considered. Usually there is a task or goal to be achieved, and although the administrator may be cognizant of certain problems, there is probably a lack of awareness of most difficulties that the group may encounter. Although not all groups experience problems, the administrator needs to realize that most groups encounter one or more of the following major types of difficulties:[79]

1. Lack of understanding by certain individuals as to why they are members of a group, and a consequent lack of commitment to the group.
2. Lack of understanding and/or acceptance by members of the group of the goal or task the group is supposed to address.
3. Difficulty in developing a constructive atmosphere that minimizes conflicting loyalties, competition, and individualistic needs, and promotes positive attitudes and collaborative efforts among the members of the group.
4. Difficulty in keeping people's attention and efforts focused on the task or goal to be achieved.
5. Inadequate group leadership, organization, or communication.
6. Lack of knowledge, skill, or resources from members of the group.
7. Inadequate follow-through on group decisions or assignments.

Because of the involuntary nature of the membership of many groups the administrator heads, certain members of a group may lack both commitment and understanding of how or why they have become members. The administrator may also experience a lack of leadership acceptance by the members of the group. As a consequence of their lack of understanding, commitment, and acceptance, certain members may express apathy or hostility, or both. The administrator may also find it difficult to develop among members the feelings of cohesiveness and collaborative effort that facilitate productivity.[80]

In most of these situations, because of bureaucratic restrictions, the administrator perhaps can do very little to avoid the problems described. The administrator can, however, be more aware of the involuntary nature of the membership of most of the group, the circumstances by which the administrator became the head of the group, and the possible implications of these two factors. More effort could also be devoted to developing an understanding on the part of the members regarding the reason or reasons they were included in the group and their potential contributions and roles. For example, the administrator can attempt to demonstrate the ability to lead and show an appreciation of the participation and contribution of each member. These steps may not eliminate all the problems a group could encounter, but they should be helpful in preventing many problems and ameliorating others.

In the final analysis, whether a group is ultimately successful depends as much on what happens to the group *after* it has been in operation as it does on the initial formation of the group and the way the group's head was selected.

Developing a Productive Group: The Importance of Cohesiveness and Trust An essential priority for an administrator in working with most groups, especially newly formed ones, is the development of cohesiveness and trust. Group cohesiveness is the degree to which the members of a group are attracted to the group, are willing to take personal responsibility for its tasks, and are willing to engage in cooperative actions to achieve its goals.[81] Group trust is the extent to which the members of a group feel secure with each other and are open toward each other.[82] Both factors are important contributors to the effective functioning of a group.

Group Members Must Feel Valued

In order to develop a high degree of group cohesiveness, the administrator should consider several needs. First, the members of a group need to feel that their membership is valued and that they can make an important contribution to its effectiveness.[83] This is particularly important for the members of an involuntary group, such as an appointed faculty committee, with the administrator as the head. The members of this type of group may not necessarily have wanted to join the group and may have mixed feelings about their identity and contribution. It is not unusual, however, for the members of other types of groups also to wonder about the extent to which they are valued. People generally possess needs for self-respect, affection, and recognition;[84] group interaction can either meet these needs or leave them largely unfulfilled. The administrator should try, to the extent possible, to meet these needs by showing the members of the group that their participation is necessary and valued and by encouraging group members to recognize and reward each other's contributions. It also should be emphasized that this kind of recognition and encouragement by the administrator must be conveyed periodically, rather than only occasionally, or its impact will be diminished over time.

Group Members Must Share Goals

A second major condition that will influence the cohesiveness of a group is the extent to which its members understand the goals of the group and the extent to which these goals are compatible with members' personal goals.[85] For example, a group will have a difficult time developing a very high degree of cohesiveness if members do not understand the goals of the group and/or do not agree with those goals. Although the administrator who is heading a group may feel that a particular goal is essential and that group members *should* understand and accept it, the members, in fact, may neither understand nor accept the goal, and for that reason may become apathetic or hostile in response to efforts to involve them in working toward the goal. Until the administrator can develop a better understanding and acceptance of the goal on the part of the members of this group, cooperative action and progress may be limited.

Group Members Must Have a Spirit of Cooperation and Teamwork

A third major condition that can influence the degree of a group's cohesiveness is the extent to which the leader and members can work cooperatively between and among themselves.[86] Cooperation, because it encourages acceptance and a feeling of esprit de corps, is necessary for the effective accomplishment of many tasks and goals. It does *not* result automatically with the forming of a group. The head of the group needs to help its members work cooperatively with each other. According to Johnson and Johnson, several understandings must occur in order for a group to develop cooperative interaction among its members.[87]

1. Individual members must understand the total problem or task to be addressed.
2. Individual members must see how each can contribute toward solving the problem or accomplishing the task.
3. Individual members must be aware of the potential contributions of the other group members and the need for coordination.
4. Individual members must understand and be sensitive to the other members' problems.
5. Individual members must be aware of and accept the need for cooperation in order to achieve the group goal.

The Need for Mutual Trust

While these five elements are important, the key to developing cooperative interaction and cohesiveness in a group, according to Johnson and Johnson, is the development and maintenance of a high level of trust among the members.[88] If a group has a high level of trust, its members will more openly express their feelings, concerns, opinions, and thoughts. If the trust level is low, then group members are more likely to be evasive, competitive, devious, defensive, or uncertain in their interaction with the other members. Cooperation and a positive identification with and commitment to a group are unlikely with a low level of trust among its members. For cooperative interaction and a high level of group cohesiveness to exist, there must be openness, sharing, and acceptance among the members of a group–all ingredients of a trusting relationship.[89]

The administrator has an important role to play in developing a high level of trust among the members of a group. Above all, the administrator must be trusting and cooperative, modeling such behavior if the members are to behave similarly. The administrator cannot expect them to behave in a trusting manner if the administrator does not demonstrate qualities of acceptance, openness, sharing, and nondefensiveness. The administrator will also need to *emphasize* the importance of openness and acceptance among the members of the group and reward these qualities when they surface. By developing a high level of trust among the members, the administrator should find it possible to obtain cooperative action, and the group should function with a higher level of cohesiveness. Grazian and Bagin offer the following suggestions for building a climate of trust:

1. Practice the two-way street of communication. Giving information is not the end; receiving feedback is.
2. Utilize face-to-face communication as often as possible. Do not rely too heavily on memos and e-mail.
3. Examine each instruction for clarity of understanding. Be as specific as possible.
4. Learn to listen. Ask questions to demonstrate interest in and respect for others when they speak.
5. Practice an open-door policy by getting out and talking with employees, agreeing to disagree, and listening to new ideas.
6. Concentrate on building credibility with the staff; trust is based on believing in someone.[90]

Effects of Group Size

Two additional conditions that can influence a group's cohesiveness are the size of the group and the similarity of background and interests of group members. In general, the larger the group, the less cohesive it is likely to be. As Tsouderos has observed, "With an increased membership there is a corresponding heterogeneity of the groups in terms of sentiments, interests, dedication to the 'cause,' etc., and a corresponding decline in a feeling of intimacy and frequency of interaction."[91] Although the administrator may not always have much discretion in deciding on the size of the group, frequently such discretion is possible. Therefore, the administrator should consider the impact of size on group cohesiveness whenever forming a group, such as a committee or task force, to address a particular problem or task.

Importance of Both Common and Diverse Backgrounds and Interests

The administrator should also consider, to the extent possible, the similarity of background and interests of individuals who might be appointed to a group. For the most part, the more the members of a group have similar backgrounds and interests, the more probable it is that they will like each other and be willing to work cooperatively together. On the other hand, in forming a group, the administrator should keep in mind that it is not always to the advantage of the group if everyone thinks the same way. Different backgrounds, experiences, and interests can generate ideas over and above those developed in situations in which all the members think the same way.[92] Therefore, while the administrator should select group members with a fairly high degree of similarity of background and interests in order to develop cohesiveness, the administrator should also provide sufficient diversity to stimulate new ideas. The administrator should not, however, provide for so much diversity in interests and thinking that it will be difficult for the members of the group to agree upon and become committed to the achievement of organizational goals.

Leadership in Group Meetings

Most groups are scheduled for periodic meetings of one kind or another. The role of the administrator in regard to these meetings will depend on whether or not the administrator is the head of the group. As the leader, responsibility for planning and conducting the meeting and for implementing the outcomes must be assured. This does not mean that the administrator is the only one who should perform these functions. It is the administrator's responsibility, however, to see to it that these functions are carried out in such a way that the meetings are productive and satisfactory to a majority of the group's members. While most administrators may believe that their group meetings are productive and satisfactory to the members, the members themselves may be perceiving these meetings differently. For example, in a survey of the principals and teachers in 11 school systems, Gorton and Herman found that most principals felt their faculty meetings were productive and satisfactory to the faculty, whereas a majority of teachers indicated the opposite.[93] In general, teachers expressed dissatisfaction with the planning of the meetings, the nature of problem solving during the meetings, and the lack of follow-up after the meetings.

The world of business has been giving a great deal of attention to what the Web site www.effectivemeetings.com calls "the meeting mania" sweeping across all types of organizations today. An emphasis on teamwork and shared leadership has resulted in efforts to make sure that everyone is informed and involved, and it is thought that meetings are the way to carry out this goal. However, some businesses are noticing a decline in productivity as the number of meetings increases. Meetings can eat up valuable time that could be spent on getting tasks done. On the other hand, meetings can be a valuable investment of time if they are conducted effectively. This is as true in the world of education as it is in business.

Hoerr observes that too many principals fall into the trap of using faculty meetings to inefficiently convey information. Rather than open up a dialogue or invite discussion of important topics, principals tend to read information to teachers. He suggests that information that doesn't require any discussion or learning–important as it may be–should be shared in writing. Reading off a sheet of paper to teachers can be insulting, and simply announcing something doesn't guarantee that it will be heard. Similarly, holding a meeting for the sake of holding a meeting not only wastes everyone's time but also reinforces the notion that meetings aren't worthwhile.[94]

A group leader must have a well-planned, wisely executed faculty meeting so that it can be beneficial to all in attendance. He notes that school leaders can do several things to make meetings more rewarding and worthwhile:

- *Take time to break the ice*–not just in August, but throughout the school year. Asking questions like "What teacher do you remember from your days as a student, and why?" or "What book would you recommend to a friend?" helps create a friendly, comfortable atmosphere. We need to take time to know and appreciate one another, because congeniality is the foundation of collegiality.
- *Spread the air time.* It's not a good sign when administrators do all the talking. Principals need to ensure that everyone gets a chance to contribute.
- *Vary the location of the meeting.* If space allows, holding meetings in teachers' classrooms fosters a climate of sharing. Ask the "host" teacher to talk a bit about how he or she decorated or designed the room for learning.
- *Focus meetings on particular topics.* Principals can set a tone of collaboration by announcing a meeting's topic beforehand and asking teachers to come with two or three suggestions.
- *Bring food!* Regardless of when meetings are held, munching on fruits, pretzels, or pastries makes them more pleasant.[95]

A FINAL NOTE

In all, for effective leadership in twenty-first-century schooling, school administrators must be attuned to the complexities of changing demographics as well as the needs of those persons who have been traditionally excluded from the core of educational reform.[96] School leadership in this new millennium must understand and embrace that cultural, racial, economic, linguistic, and other "borders" must be crossed to ensure that the ever-changing demographics of public schools are considered in efforts to create effective centers of learning that facilitate the academic success of all students. In order to have effective schools where all students achieve, we must find ways to manage our crossings for a successful existence in the "borderlands" between culture.[97] Strong leadership by today's school administrator is needed to understand and address the educational structures in which prejudice and discrimination affect student learning,[98] that is, tracking, standardized testing, curriculum, pedagogy, physical structure of the school, disciplinary policies, and limited roles of students, teachers, and parents and families.

Although many of the case studies, Suggested Learning Activities, and simulations presented in Part II of the text require the appropriate use of the ideas in this chapter on group leadership, the following exercises should provide the best opportunities for testing understanding and effective use of group leadership concepts: Cases 18, 22, 30, 31, 42, 50, 52, 67, 69, and 70.

NOTES

1. Fred E. Fiedler and Martin M. Chemers, *Leadership and Effective Management* (Glenview, IL: Scott, Foresman, 1974), p. 1.
2. Bernard M. Bass and Ralph M. Stogdill, *The Handbook of Leadership: Theory, Research, and Managerial Applications,* 3rd ed. (New York: Free Press, 1990). Also see A. G. Jago, "Leadership: Perspectives in Theory and Research," *Management Science* (March 1982), pp. 315–336; and Glenn L. Immegart, "Leadership and Leader Behavior," in Norman J. Boyan (Ed.), *Handbook of Research on Educational Administration* (New York: Longman, 1988), pp. 259–277.
3. W. H. Cowley, "Three Distinctions in the Study of Leaders," *Journal of Abnormal and Social Psychology* (April 1928), pp. 144–157.
4. Judy A. Alston, *Multi-leadership in Urban Schools* (Lanham, MD: University Press of America, 2002).
5. Bernard M. Bass and Ralph M. Stogdill, *Handbook of Leadership* (New York: Free Press, 1990), p. 411. Also see Alan Scharf, "How to Change Seven Rowdy People," *Industrial Management* (November–December 1989), pp. 20–22.
6. Warren Bennis, *Managing the Dream* (Cambridge, MA: Perseus Publishing, 2000), p. 135.
7. Ibid., chap. 12.
8. Robert T. Taylor and William E. Rosenbach, *Leadership Challenges for Today's Manager* (New York: Nichols Publishing, 1989), p. 207.
9. Jay A. Conger and Rabindra N. Kanungo, *Charismatic Leadership: The Elusive Factor in Organizational Effectiveness* (San Francisco: Jossey-Bass, 1988), pp. 3–5.
10. Jay A. Conger, *The Charismatic Leader: Behind the Mystique of Exceptional Leadership* (San Francisco: Jossey-Bass, 1989), pp. 109–117.
11. Edward R. Lilly, "The Determinants of Organizational Power Style," *Educational Review* (1989), pp. 281–290.
12. Warren Bennis, "Why Leaders Can't Lead," *Training and Development Journal* (April 1989), pp. 34–39.
13. Barry G. Morris, "The Executive: A Pathfinder," *Organizational Dynamics* (Spring 1988), pp. 62–75.

14. James M. Lipham, "Leadership and Administration," in Daniel Griffiths (Ed.), *Behavioral Science and Educational Administration: 63rd Yearbook of the National Society for the Study of Education* (Chicago: University of Chicago Press, 1964), pp. 119–141.

15. Ibid., p. 122.

16. Ibid.

17. Ibid. Christopher Hodgkinson denies the difference between administration and leadership, arguing for a value perspective on administration in *Educational Leadership: The Moral Art* (New York: State University of New York Press, 1991).

18. John P. Kotter, "What Leaders Really Do," in *Harvard Business Review on Leadership* (Boston: Harvard Business School Press, 1998), p. 37.

19. Wayne Smith, "Followership: The Art of Working Together," *Principal* (November 1994), p. 24.

20. Jay A. Conger and Rabindra N. Kanungo, "The Empowerment Process Integrating Theory and Practice," *Academy of Management Review* (July 1988), pp. 471–482.

21. Bennis, "Why Leaders Can't Lead," pp. 34–39.

22. For one of the first indications that the school administrator's leadership is important, see G. Weber, *Inner-City Children Can Be Taught to Read: Four Successful Schools* (Washington, DC: Council for Basic Education, 1971). Also see R. Edmonds, "Effective Schools for Urban Poor," *Educational Leadership* (October 1979), pp. 15–23; and J. V. Greer, "Cultural Diversity and the Test of Leadership," *Exceptional Children* (1988).

23. National Commission on Excellence in Education, *A Nation at Risk: The Imperative for Educational Reform* (Washington, DC: U.S. Department of Education, 1983); John Goodlad, *A Place Called School* (New York: McGraw-Hill, 2004); Theodore Sizer, *Horace's Compromise: The Dilemma of the American High School* (Boston: Houghton Mifflin, 1984, 2004); *Time for Results: The Governors' 1991 Report on Education* (Washington, DC: National Governors Association Center for Policy Research and Analysis, 1986); and University Council for Educational Administration, *Leaders for America's Schools: The Report of the National Commission on Excellence in Educational Administration* (Tempe, AZ: UCEA, 1987).

24. Nancy Pitner and W. W. Charters Jr., *Principal Influence on Teacher Behavior: Substitutes for Leadership* (Eugene: Center for Educational Policy and Management, University of Oregon, 1984). Also see Russell Gerstein et al., "The Principal as Instructional Leader: A Second Look," *Educational Leadership* (December 1982), pp. 47–50; and W. D. Greenfield, "Moral, Social, and Technical Dimensions of the Principalship," *Peabody Journal of Education* (Summer 1986).

25. JoAnn Mazzarella, "The Effective High School Principal: Sketches for a Portrait," *R and D Perspectives* (Winter 1985), pp. 1–8; Thomas Biester, *Effects of Administrative Leadership on Student Achievement* (Philadelphia: Research for Better Schools, 1984); and Wilma F. Smith and Richard L. Andrews, *Instructional Leadership: How Principals Make a Difference* (Alexandria, VA: Association for Supervision and Curriculum Development, 1989).

26. Terrence E. Deal, "The Culture of Schools," in Linda T. Sheive and Marian B. Schoenheit (Eds.), *Leadership: Examining the Elusive: 1987 Yearbook of the Association for Supervision and Curriculum Development* (Alexandria, VA: Association for Supervision and Curriculum Development, 1987); and Thomas J. Sergiovanni, *Value Added Leadership: How to Get Extraordinary Performance in Schools* (New York: Harcourt Brace Jovanovich, HBJ Leadership, 1990).

27. Warren Bennis and Burt Nanus, *Leaders: The Strategies for Taking Charge* (New York: Harper & Row, 1985).

28. Tom Peters, *Thriving on Chaos: Handbook for a Management Revolution* (New York: Alfred A. Knopf, 1987); and James M. Kouzes and Barry Z. Posner, *The Leadership Challenge*, 4th ed. (San Francisco: Jossey-Bass, 2007).

29. For a comprehensive review of these elements, see D. MacKenzie, "Research for School Improvement: An Appraisal of Some Recent Trends," *Educational Researcher* (April 1983), pp. 5–17.

30. David Parks and Thomas Barrett, "Principals as Leaders of Leaders," *Principal* (November 1994), pp. 11–12.

31. Fenwick W. English, *Theory in Educational Administration* (New York: HarperCollins, 1999).
32. K. Lewin, R. Lippitt, and R. K. White, "Patterns of Aggressive Behavior in Experimentally Created 'Social Constructs,'" *Journal of Science Psychology* (vol. 10, 1939), pp. 271-299.
33. Gary A. Yukl, *Leadership in Organizations,* 7th ed. (Upper Saddle, NJ: Prentice Hall, 2008).
34. R. M. Stogdill and A. E. Coons, *Leader Behavior: Its Description and Measurement* (Columbus, OH: Bureau of Business Research, The Ohio State University, 1957).
35. Accessed online, http://changingminds.org/disciplines/leadership/actions/michigan.htm, December 28, 2010.
36. R. R. Blake and J. S. Mouton, *The Managerial Grid III* (Houston, TX: Gulf, 1985).
37. Ibid.
38. National Institute of Education, *Making Our Schools More Effective* (June 1984), an ERIC report, Ed. 249576.
39. For a critical review of this literature, see Claude L. Graeff, "The Situational Leadership Theory: A Critical View," *Academy of Management Review* (April 1983), pp. 285-291; and Nancy J. Pitner, "The Study of Administrator Effects and Effectiveness," in Norman J. Boyan (Ed.), *Handbook of Research on Educational Administration* (New York: Longman, 1988), pp. 99-122.
40. Joseph L. Badaracco and Richard R. Ellsworth, *Leadership and the Quest for Integrity* (Boston: Harvard Business School Press, 1989), pp. 6-9.
41. Edwin P. Hollander, "Style, Structure, and Setting in Organizational Leadership," *Administrative Science Quarterly* (March 1971), pp. 2-3.
42. Fred E. Fiedler and Martin M. Chemers, *Leadership and Effective Management* (Glenview, IL: Scott, Foresman, 1974), pp. 73-120. Also, for an excellent analysis of research on Fiedler's contingency model, see Ellen Crehan, "A Meta Analysis of Fiedler's Contingency Model of Leadership Effectiveness," PhD dissertation, University of British Columbia, 1984.
43. Andrew Halpin, *Theory and Research in Administration*, 4th ed. (New York: Macmillian, 1971), p. 87.
44. J. W. Getzels, James Lipham, and Roald Campbell, eds. *Educational Administration as a Social Process: Theory, Research, Practice* (New York: Harper & Row, 1968), pp. 145-149.
45. Accessed online, http://changingminds.org/disciplines/leadership/actions/, December 28, 2010.
46. R. R. Blake and A. A. McCanse, *Leadership Dilemmas–Grid Solutions* (Houston, TX: Gulf Publishing, 1991).
47. Gary A. Yukl, *Leadership in Organizations,* 7th ed. (Upper Saddle River, NJ: Prentice Hall, 2008), p. 130.
48. Jacob W. Getzels and Egon G. Guba, *Role Conflict and Instructor Effectiveness at the Air Command and Staff School* (San Antonio, TX: Air Force Personnel Training and Research Center, 1956); Getzels et al., *Educational Administration as a Social Process: Theory, Research, Practice,* pp. 145-149.
49. Daniel Kunz et al., *Successful School Series* (1982), an ERIC report, Ed. 221640, p. 2.
50. Steven T. Bossert et al., *Making Our Schools More Effective: Proceedings of Three State Conferences* (June 1984), an ERIC report, Ed. 249576, p. 66.
51. Paul Hersey and Ken Blanchard. *Management of Organizational Behavior* Englewood Cliffs, NJ: Prentice Hall (1986).
52. Philip Hallinger et al., "School Effectiveness: Identifying the Specific Practices, Behaviors for Principals," *National Association of Secondary School Principals Bulletin* (May 1983), pp. 83-91.
53. Getzels et al., *Educational Administration as a Social Process: Theory, Research, Practice.*
54. In Chester E. Finn Jr., *A Principal's Leadership in Developing the Characteristics of Excellent Schools* (April 1983), an ERIC report, Ed. 233446, p. 47.
55. Accessed online, http://changingminds.org, December 28, 2010.
56. R. J. House, "A Path-Goal Theory of Leader Effectiveness." *Administrative Science Quarterly, 16,* 331-333.
57. Ibid.

58. A summary of both their 1987 and their 1995 studies of what people expect of leaders is given in James M. Kouzes and Barry Z. Posner, *The Leadership Challenge* (San Francisco: Jossey-Bass, 1995), pp. 20–30.

59. Ibid. Kouzes and Posner built the entirety of *The Leadership Challenge* around the findings they extracted from the personal-best reports of leaders.

60. Ibid., p. 30.

61. Randall B. Lindsey, Kikanza Nuri Roberts, and Raymond D. Terrell, *Cultural Proficiency: A Manual for School Leaders,* 3rd ed. (Thousand Oaks, CA: Corwin Press, 2009).

62. B. M. Bass, *Leadership and Performance Beyond Expectation* (New York: Free Press, 1985); and B. M. Bass, "From Transactional to Transformational Leadership: Learning to Share the Vision," *Organizational Dynamics* (Winter 1990), pp. 19–31

63. Kenneth A. Leithwood, "The Move toward Transformational Leadership," *Educational Leadership* (February 1992), pp. 8–12.

64. Thomas R. Hoerr, "Collegiality: A New Way to Define Instructional Leadership," *Phi Delta Kappan* (January 1996), p. 381.

65. Peter Scholtes, *Teams and Teamwork Serving Customers . . . Together! Creating Pride and Joy at Work* (Madison, WI: Scholtes Seminars and Consulting, 1996).

66. Mary S. Poplin, "The Leader's New Role: Looking to the Growth of Teachers," *Educational Leadership* (February 1992), pp. 10–11.

67. Michael Dantley, "Transforming School Leadership through **Cornel West's Notions of African American Prophetic Spirituality," paper presented at the annual meeting of the University Council for Educational Administration, October 2001.

68. Ibid. See also Linda C. Tillman "The Impact of Diversity in Educational Administration," in George Perreault and Fred C. Lunenburg (Eds.), *The Changing World of School Administration* (Lanham, MD: Scarecrow Press, 2002), pp. 144–156.

69. Robert K. Greenleaf, *Servant Leadership* (Mahwah, NJ: Paulist Press, 1977).

70. Patrice McClellan, "Wearing the Mantle: Spirited Black Male Servant Leaders Reflect on Their Leadership Journey," doctoral dissertation, Bowling Green State University (2006); and Patrice McClellan, "Toward Critical Servant Leadership in Graduate Schools of Education: From Theoretical Construct to Social Justice Praxis," in S. D. Horsford (Ed.), *New Perspectives in Educational Leadership: Exploring Social, Political, and Community Contexts and Meaning* (New York: Peter Lang Publishing, 2010).

71. Ibid.

72. Peter Gronn, "Distributed Properties: A New Architecture for Leadership," *Educational Management & Administration* (vol. 28, no. 3, 2000), pp. 317–338.

73. James P. Spillane, *Distributed Leadership* (San Francisco: Jossey-Bass, 2006).

74. Ron Ritchie and Philip A. Woods, "Degrees of Distribution: Towards an Understanding of Variations in the Nature of distributed leadership in schools," *School Leadership and Management* (vol. 27, no. 4, 2007), pp. 363–381.

75. John M. Loeser, "School Leadership," *Ebsco Research Starters* (2008), p. 3.

76. Accessed online, http://www.doe.mass.edu/cslp/leadership/models.pdf, March 14, 2008.

77. James P. Spillane, "Distributed Leadership," *The Education Forum* (vol. 69, no. 2, 2005), pp. 143–150.

78. Stephen J. Knezevich, *Administration of Public Education: A Sourcebook for the Leadership and Management of Educational Institutions,* 4th ed. (New York: Harper & Row, 1984), parts 3 and 4. Also see Van Morris et al., *Principals in Action: The Reality of Managing Schools* (Columbus, OH: Charles E. Merrill, 1984), chap. 3; a report by the National Association of Elementary School Principals, *Principals for 21st Century Schools* (1990), chap. 5; and Carl D. Glickman, Stephen P. Gordon, and Jovita M. Ross-Gordon, *Supervision of Instruction: A Developmental Approach,* 4th ed. (Boston: Allyn and Bacon, 1998).

79. Donelson R. Forsyth, *An Introduction to Group Dynamics* (Monterey, CA: Brooks/Cole, 1983), part 4.

80. Rodney W. Napier and Matti K. Gershenfeld, *Groups: Theory and Experience* (Boston: Houghton Mifflin, 2004), pp. 78–79. Also see Albert M. Koller Jr., "Developing and Managing a Winning Team," *Management* (November-December 1989), pp. 2-31; and Colin Leicester, "The Strategic Manager as Leader," *International Journal of Manpower* (April 1990), pp. 3-10.
81. Richard M. Steers, *Introduction to Organizational Behavior* (New York: HarperCollins, 1991), pp. 234–235.
82. Joseph Luft, *Group Processes: An Introduction to Group Dynamics* (Palo Alto, CA: Mayfield, 1984), p. 27.
83. Forsyth, *Group Dynamics,* p. 350.
84. Marilyn Bates et al., *Group Leadership: Strategies for Group Counseling Leaders* (Denver: Love, 1982), chap. 3.
85. Miriam Erez and Frederick H. Kanfer, "The Role of Goal Acceptance in Goal Setting and Task Performance," *Academy of Management Review* (July 1983), pp. 454–463.
86. For an excellent analysis of the research on the benefits of cooperation in a group, see Dean Tjosvold, "Cooperation Theory and Organizations," *Human Relations* (September 1984), pp. 743–767.
87. David W. Johnson and Frank P. Johnson, *Joining Together: Group Theory and Group Skills,* 10th ed. (Boston: Allyn and Bacon, 2008), pp. 104–105.
88. Ibid., p. 246.
89. Ibid., p. 247.
90. Frank Grazian and Don Bagin, "Communicating Better at Work," *Communications Briefings* (vol. 15, no. 1, 1995), p. 3.
91. J. Tsouderos, "Organizational Change in Terms of a Series of Selected Variables," *American Sociological Review* (April 1955), pp. 206–210.
92. Forsyth, *Group Dynamics,* pp. 349–368. Group leaders need to avoid the "groupthink" phenomenon. See Gregory Moorhead and John Montanari, "An Empirical Investigation of the Groupthink Phenomenon," *Human Relations* (May 1986), pp. 399–410.
93. Richard A. Gorton and Chuck Herman, "Faculty Meetings," in *National Forum of Educational Administration and Supervision,* (vol. 1, 1984–1985), pp. 29–34.
94. Thomas R. Hoerr, "Faculty Meetings Can Be Worthwhile," *Reading Comprehension* (vol. 65, no. 2, 2005), pp. 87–89.
95. Ibid.
96. Judy Alston, "The Many Faces of American Schooling: Effective Schools Research and Border Crossing in the 21st Century," *American Secondary Education* (Spring 2004), pp. 79–93; Colleen Capper (Ed.), *Educational Administration in a Pluralistic Society* (New York: SUNY Press, 1993).
97. Ibid.
98. Sonia Nieto, *Affirming Diversity: The Sociopolitical Context of Multicultural Education,* 4th ed. (Reading, MA: Addison Wesley, 2003).

CHAPTER

2

Decision Making

APPLICABLE PSEL STANDARDS

- **STANDARD 1:** **Mission, Vision, and Core Values**
  Effective educational leaders develop, advocate, and enact a shared mission, vision, and core values of high-quality education and academic success and well-being of each student.

- **STANDARD 2:** **Ethics and Professional Norms**
  Effective educational leaders act ethically and according to professional norms to promote each student's academic success and well-being.

- **STANDARD 3:** **Equity and Cultural Responsiveness**
  Effective educational leaders strive for equity of educational opportunity and culturally responsive practices to promote each student's academic success and well-being.

- **STANDARD 5:** **Community of Care and Support for Students**
  Effective educational leaders cultivate an inclusive, caring, and supportive school community that promotes the academic success and well-being of each student.

- **STANDARD 8:** **Meaningful Engagement of Families and Community**
  Effective educational leaders engage families and the community in meaningful, reciprocal, and mutually beneficial ways to promote each student's academic success and well-being.

National Policy Board for Educational Administration (NPBEA). *Professional Standards for Educational Leaders* (Reston, VA: Author, 2015). Used with Permission.

The ability to make effective decisions is vital to the successful performance of a school administrator. Herbert Simon has called it the "heart of executive activity," and Duncan considers it the one thing "generic" to the administrator's job.[1] In addition, reform proposals have called for numerous structural changes and strategic school governance revisions that further underscore the need to improve the process of decision making and develop successful decision-making skills. The empowerment of teachers has also resulted in new decision-making situations for administrators, as teachers are given more responsibilities in such matters as hiring, curriculum adoption, staff development and evaluation, and school policies, and have themselves become decision makers.

Although intuition and experience can provide a useful basis for decision making, they are seldom sufficient. The effective decision maker must also employ an analytical thought process with greater focus on explaining and predicting the everyday realities that affect educational decision making.

This chapter introduces an expansive view of decision making.[2] A set of theoretical constructs that have emerged from the early 1900s to the present are provided. These constructs, if appropriately applied, can improve a school administrator's decision-making capability. Through careful study and application of the nature and process of decision making, the reader should be able to develop and improve the skills necessary for making better decisions in schools and school systems.

THE NATURE OF DECISION MAKING

Over more than a century, the various models and theories associated with the process of decision making have been reflected in the research literature on management and educational administration. The aim has been to improve performance by making decisions that are cumulatively and successively built on assumptions of choice.

Rational Model

In one model, generally referred to as *rational* or *normative prescriptive,* decision making is viewed as a process that begins with a problem or need that the administrator then logically addresses by engaging in a series of sequential steps, culminating in an effective solution or decision.[3]

The rational or normative prescriptive decision-making approach is concerned with what should be done and with prescribing actions designed to produce the best solution. This theory assumes that choices are made by administrators to maximize certain desirable values and objectives via rational analysis within a highly structured, bureaucratic system.

It was this theory that provided a "scientific" base for the development of modern school systems in the late nineteenth and early twentieth centuries. The Industrial Revolution had posed new management questions for the world of business. The importance of efficiency in maximizing productivity began receiving much attention, and the growing influence of powerful urban business communities affected schools as well. School decision makers endeavored to apply levels of "scientific management" and Weber's ideal type bureaucracy.[4]

This rational view assumes that administrators function in a closed system, a bureaucracy, characterized by task specification, rigid adherence to written rules and regulations, and formal hierarchical control. Decision making in this structured context is seen through the lens of the decision maker, a supposedly rational administrator. The decision-making process emphasizes solutions to problems and an outcome that results from choice among alternatives in relation to clearly delineated objectives accomplished by following specific tasks and steps.[5]

Obviously, the school administrator's world does not operate in such a logical, sequential, and rational manner as the advocates of the rigidly bureaucratic decision-making tradition suggest. Various studies, both with school administrators and nonschool executives, have tended to confirm reservations about many aspects of this model of decision making. Such studies have revealed an organizational environment that is frequently more dynamic, complex, and uncertain for decision makers than the rational bureaucratic or normative prescriptive theory of decision making has recognized.[6] In addition, a number of these studies have raised severe doubts about how rational or sequential most administrators are in their thinking as they proceed to make a decision.[7] Nevertheless, to protect the image of the educational enterprise and of the school administrator from external interference, the appearance of rationality is frequently applied to the process of decision making. This, however, is wrought with ambiguities. Wise, for example, discusses the dangers of "hyperrationalization" in educational organizations as a result of attempts to impose rational standards on nonrational processes.[8]

Advantages and Disadvantages of the Rational Model Normative prescriptive theories have a number of advantages. They specify clearly what should be done in terms of goals, objectives, criteria, and outcomes. They provide the administrator with the challenge of deciding among knowable alternatives by placing highest priority on what is most effective and desirable. And they help to reach agreement on future plans of action. Normative tools, such as management by objectives (MBO), management information systems (MIS), and associated models for decision analysis, provide a structure for decision making that can assist the administrator in day-to-day managerial tasks. The use of staff time, organizational material, and financial resources can be efficiently and sensibly maximized by the decision maker using a rational decision-making process for budget development, personnel decisions, facility maintenance, scheduling, or plant management. Clearly, rational bureaucratic assumptions accurately reflect the context of many educational decisions.

On the other hand, in studies that critique the rational normative theory of decision making, researchers found that most administrators who participated in the studies did not spend much time seeking additional information about the nature of a problem to better understand its causes and consider possible alternative solutions. Instead, they ignored the need for a decision, apparently hoping the problem would go away, or they took quick action without carefully investigating the nature of the situation. In the latter instances, they typically considered only a narrow set of alternatives. In most cases, these alternatives were based primarily on experience rather than reason or analysis and were not carefully evaluated as to their advantages or disadvantages. The picture that emerges from these studies is that most administrators tend to "muddle through" when faced with a decision, and end up with an action that may have little relationship to the original situation that called for a decision.[9]

Shared Decision Making

A second model, *participatory, shared,* or *site-based decision making,* also builds on the assumption of choice. But whereas the rational bureaucratic theory suggests choices are made by the administrator to maximize attainment of objectives, the participatory model assumes choices are made to satisfy constraints. The theory reflects the democratic and nonhierarchical administrative norms dating to the work of Mary Parker Follett in the 1920s and constitutes a reaction to the impersonality and rigidity of scientific management.[10] After the *A Nation at Risk* report in 1983, serious attention was given to the quality management philosophy of William Edwards Deming, which came to be known in the United States as *total quality management* (TQM). Deming's principles of management had been used primarily for business applications in Japan and were credited with the remarkable recovery of Japanese industry after the damage it had suffered during World War II. Deming suggested that TQM techniques applied to any organization would make it more successful, and school leaders saw in these techniques a possible path to school improvement. Thornton and Mattocks have pointed out that Deming's famous 14 points, as applied to education, may be summarized under five general statements: "Create a consistency of purpose, adopt a cooperative philosophy, provide training for all, improve constantly and forever, and implement effective leadership."[11]

Participatory theories seriously question the definition of decision making as rational choice made solely by an administrator at the apex of an educational hierarchy. Instead, the focus is on consensual decision making, rooted in the values and beliefs of the participants. Assumptions and organizational preconditions for shared decision making include shared goals or values, influence based on professional expertise, open communication, and equal status among participants. Because many of these assumptions (such as shared goals and professional expertise within an organizational structure) are similar to the assumptions governing the rational bureaucratic model, participatory decision making has been viewed as a subset of the bureaucratic approach.

Descriptions of the way administrators make decisions versus how they should make decisions have contributed to the development of participatory decision-making theory. Led by the pioneering work of Herbert Simon and James March and more recent critiques of the rational approach to decision making, these critics believe that the organizational context in which decisions need to be made reflects much more complexity and uncertainty than the rational theory of decision making seems to acknowledge.[12] These critics also tend to see the decision maker as possessing limited control over the educational enterprise and as being influenced by personality, values, and previous experience more than by reason or intellect. The participatory view of decision making has the administrator rely far less on management controls and more on bonding staff by developing norms that are derived from a shared vision of what is important. These administrators are more likely to view the problem of coordination as cultural rather than as managerial.[13] In the process of participatory and/or group decision making, a consideration of diversity is crucial. In his book *The Difference: How the Power of Diversity Creates Better Groups, Firms, Schools, and Societies* Scott Page argues that group decision making is best when the group reflects unique perspectives and ways of thinking. According to Page, the key lies in bringing together individuals with different backgrounds and life experiences; the result will be a messy process, but one that out-performs groups of like-minded individuals chosen on the basis of extensive experience or high IQ.[14]

The benefits of using a participatory decision-making approach in terms of decision outcomes are not conclusive in the research literature. It is not clear, for example, what the direct effect of different obstacles to teacher participation is on decision outcomes and in decision making.[15] According to research by Straus, however, student achievement in mathematics and teacher morale were significantly higher in the five schools in their study that were using TQM as compared with the five not using TQM.[16] Many educators concur with Linda Jean Holman's assessment of site-based decision making as being the educational initiative that has had "more potential for effecting enduring change in the structure and operation of our schools" than has been true of any other in recent years.[17]

WINDOW ON DIVERSITY

Decision Making

According to a study by Margaret Neale of the Stanford Business School with regard to diversity and decision making, people tend to think of diversity as simply demographic, a matter of color, gender, or age. However, groups can be disparate in many ways. Diversity is also based on informational differences, reflecting a person's education and experience, as well as on values or goals that can influence what one perceives to be the mission of something as small as a single meeting or as large as a whole company. Furthermore, diversity among employees can create better performance when it comes to out-of-the-ordinary creative tasks such as product development or cracking new markets, and managers have been trying to increase diversity to achieve the benefits of innovation and fresh ideas. In the context of schooling and decision making, school leaders must also consider issues of diversity and ways in which they should respond. R. Roosevelt Thomas suggests that there are eight ways for leaders to respond to diversity:

1. *Exclude:* Aim to minimize diversity by keeping diverse elements out or by expelling them once they have been included.
2. *Deny:* Enable individuals to ignore diversity dimensions. They look at a green jelly bean and see only a jelly bean. This is viable only if the object of denial permits the practices: entities that celebrate being different are reluctant to allow denial.
3. *Suppress:* Encourage entities that are different to suppress their differences. For example, the treatment that "old timers" often give inquisitive newcomers who inquire, "Why do we do things this way?" A frequent response from the old timers is, "How long have you been here?"
4. *Segregate:* Practices such as clustering members of racial or ethnic groups in certain departments, isolating or piloting a change in a corner of the corporation, and so on.
5. *Assimilate:* Managers attempt to transform the element with differences into clones of the dominant group.
6. *Tolerate:* Adoption of the attitude, "We don't bother them, they don't bother us."
7. *Build relationships:* Assumption that a good relationship can overcome differences; happens when there are grounds for mutually beneficial relationships; focus on similarities.
8. *Foster mutual adaptation:* The parties involved accept and understand differences and diversity, recognizing full well that those realities may call for adaptation on the part of all components of the whole.

Source: M. Neale, "Diversity Can Improve Decision-Making," accessed online, http://www.retailgigs.com/articles/diversity-can-improve-decision-making-1156-article.html, December 28, 2010; and R. Roosevelt Thomas Jr., in *Beyond Race and Gender: Unleashing the Power of Your Total Work Force by Managing Diversity* (New York: AMACOM Books, 1991).

DECISION-MAKING ACTIVITY
WHO SHOULD BE HIRED?

Forrest Middle School is located in the Happy Valley School District (HVSD), and the total student enrollment is 1,500. Due to many years of ups and downs with regard to student enrollment, changing demographics, test scores, finances, and so on, the district has undergone many reforms in the past 15 years. The district has decided to try some major administrative reform, and it has chosen to try a distributed leadership model–the Alston Multi-leadership Model.

Taking on the role of the chief knowledge officer (CKO) in this school, and with school beginning in two weeks, you have the following situation:

> Seven teachers resigned two days ago and now you must hire seven replacements. Due to the many changes going on in HVSD, the chief operating officer (COO) and the chief financial officer (CFO) are unavailable to help you with this hiring, but they've agreed to sign off on your choices to fill the seven positions. Earlier in the year (between October and March–*note:* it is now August), the three of you conducted some interviews with 15 applicants. You only have the notes that all of you jotted down from those interviews along with applications and references to make your choice. Following is a summary of the information that you have about each applicant. Use this information to choose seven teachers to be hired on one-year contracts.

CASE DESCRIPTIONS

1. **Martha Atler:** 27, white, no religious affiliation. MS degree and four years of successful teaching experience (two years in middle-class predominantly White community and two years in a racially mixed community). She is reported to have ties to a military militia group.
2. **Robert Simpson:** 51, white, Protestant, a professed segregationist with a BA degree and 27 years teaching experience. Does not want to teach minority children. Married and father of two adult sons.
3. **Nannette Freeman:** 29, black, Muslim. Nannette has an MS degree with six years of fairly good experience. She is in good health and is an active member of several community activist organizations.
4. **Maxine Liberman:** 21, white, Jewish. BA from Vassar. Maxine has traveled extensively and is well versed in many areas. She has no prior teaching experience.
5. **James Crow:** 35, Native American, tribal religion. James has a BA degree and has worked for 11 years. He taught on several Indian reservations and for the Peace Corps. He is bitter about the conditions of his people.
6. **Mary Weaver:** 38, white, Pentecostal minister. Mary has a BA degree and has 15 years of experience. She has taught in church schools and in public schools. She feels strongly that a child's education should include a focus on morals as well as academics.
7. **Marie Vitale:** 32, Italian, Catholic. Marie has an MS degree and five years of teaching experience. She is reported to have lesbian tendencies.
8. **Bernice Johnson:** 22, black, Catholic. Bernice has a BA degree and one year of teaching experience in the middle-class community in which she was reared. She is a sports enthusiast.
9. **Julio Rodriguez:** 28, recently arrived from Mexico, Catholic. Received a chemical engineering degree from the University of Guadalajara. Originally certified through

the alternative certification program. Speaks limited English but feels able to communicate effectively with children.

10. **Herbert Brown:** 49, black, Baptist. He has an MS degree. Herbert was an active member of the Black Panthers of the 1980s and has taught for four years. His experience included Afrocentric freedom schools in the United States and Africa.
11. **Sister Robertann:** 40, white, nun. Sister Robertann is a strict disciplinarian who has taught in church schools for 19 years. She has a provisional certificate and permission from her order to teach in a public school system. She has been a religionist since she was 19 years old.
12. **Nguyen Nguyen:** 28, Vietnamese, Buddhist. BA degree with no teaching experience. Nguyen assisted in the literacy programs conducted in the factory where he was a part-time employee since age 16.
13. **Mary Jones:** 25, black, Methodist. Mary has a BS degree and one year of successful teaching experience. Single with one child. She was involved in a drug raid during her freshman year in college.
14. **Maria Garcia:** 39, Mexican American, Catholic. Maria is a former welfare recipient who received a BA degree by attending night school. She has worked for six years in a day care center. She is married and has 10 children, ranging in age from 9 to 21.
15. **Brian Nelson:** 25, white, no religious affiliation. Brian has a BA degree and has been asked to leave two schools in the two years that he has worked. He considers himself a liberal and feels that this contributed to his problems with his former principals.

Source: Adapted from Pamela M. Norwood and Deborah Carr Saldaña, "Who Should Be Hired?" in *Teaching about Culture, Ethnicity, and Diversity,* T. M. Singelis (Ed.), pp. 73–79, Thousand Oaks, CA: Sage Publications, 1998 and J. A. Alston, *Multi-leadership in Urban Schools: Shifting Paradigms for Administration and Supervision in the New Millennium* (Thousand Oaks, CA: Rowman & Littlefield, 2002).

Strategic Decision Making

The third model, the *strategic decision-making approach,* views decision choices as taking place in an environment made up of multiple interest groups, conflict, negotiation, limited resources, position authority, and informal power. This model incorporates structural elements found in the bureaucratic rational model (such as adherence to schedules and policies) with aspects of the participatory model (such as seeking consensus via the involvement of many people in the organization). The assumption governing this particular model is that choices the administrator makes are based on comprehensive knowledge and analysis of the internal and external environment.

For strategic decision making to be effective, constraints and obstacles, as well as opportunities and challenges that affect the decision choice, must be identified. Research studies dealing with strategic decision making go beyond the rational procedures prescribed in the bureaucratic model and the shared cooperative elements described in the participatory model. Instead, these studies view decision making in the context of multiple competing interests, problem situations, and influences of power and control.[18] The complexity of decision making is captured in this strategic decision model with many of the nonrational aspects of decision making reflected in the theoretical writings.

The strategic decision-making approach is utilized by the administrator interested in carrying out an educational vision and developing a long-range, overall plan that is flexible and subject to amendment. Decisions are governed by a shared philosophy and a shared purpose that ideally come from empathy and involvement with people committed to the same holistic purpose. The administrator may discover that, despite pure application of the strategic model, decision outcomes are influenced by unexpected events, behaviors, or value orientations. These realities of a world "thriving on chaos" or "organized anarchy" lead us to a description of the fourth model of decision making.[19] For lack of a more sophisticated term, we shall refer to this view as *differentiated decision making.*

Differentiated or Situational Decision Making

The differentiated model represents a shift from the traditional paradigm or way of thinking about decision making. This model takes into consideration various focal points or points of emphasis that require the administrator's attention and will affect the decision choice. The administrator can enter the decision-making process at different decision entry points, depending on the type of problem or situation. Hence, this model can also be referred to as "situational decision making." The process may begin with choosing among alternative solutions presented by groups of individuals, or the process may require the administrator to take a risk and decide against conventional mores in order to maximize a long-range educational goal. Many different situational variables influence the decision choices an administrator makes.

The new paradigm recognizes that some situations permit a linear, structured approach, and some may require group engagement or careful analysis of the external environment before the administrator takes that existential leap and decides. The decisions do not necessarily have to be goal based, but decision making can focus on the process itself, with the resulting actions having only a tenuous connection to the organizational outcome or the administrator's intention.[20] Ethical considerations, values, organizational culture, and climate are additional elements that influence decision making. The new paradigm of decision making recognizes the contextual ambiguity and uncertainty within organizations. It builds on the "garbage can model" of decision-making theory of the early 1970s, which describes a systematic, structured process, operating in an environment consisting of situations that severely limit decision-making capability and decision choices, thus affecting decision outcomes.[21] The new paradigm views effective and efficient performance by an administrator as the desired outcome of decision making.

There is limited research with practical implications for improved decision making in educational organizations faced with financial uncertainty, changing social patterns, technological advances, alternate delivery systems, and educational linkages. There are even fewer studies that provide empirical data and new theories with implications for practice on the symbolic nature of participatory decision making. This latter view of decision making is also incorporated in our new paradigm. The administrator intending to carry out a vision for the school must attempt not only to be performance conscious but also to determine the connectedness of individual and group participation, motivation, values, and goals to the decision choices. Even questions pertaining to the relationship between a particularly inspiring vision and the appropriate decision-making process must be considered in this paradigm for the twenty-first century. Empowering teachers, parents, or students, embarking on joint ventures with the community, and opening the educational system to change constantly demand reconceiving the paradigm of differentiated decision making.

Ethical Decision Making

In their article "Thinking Ethically," Claire Andre and Manuel Velasquez note that making good ethical decisions requires a trained sensitivity to ethical issues and a practiced method for exploring the ethical aspects of a decision and weighing the considerations that should influence our choice of a course of action. Furthermore, having a method for ethical decision making is absolutely essential. Finally, when practiced regularly, the method becomes so familiar that we work through it automatically without consulting the specific steps.[22]

A FRAMEWORK FOR ETHICAL DECISION MAKING

RECOGNIZE AN ETHICAL ISSUE

1. Is there something wrong personally, interpersonally, or socially? Could the conflict, the situation, or the decision be damaging to people or to the community?
2. Does the issue go beyond legal or institutional concerns? What does it do to people, who have dignity, rights, and hopes for a better life together?

GET THE FACTS

3. What are the relevant facts of the case? What facts are unknown?
4. What individuals and groups have an important stake in the outcome? Do some have a greater stake because they have a special need or because we have special obligations to them?
5. What are the options for acting? Have all the relevant persons and groups been consulted? If you showed your list of options to someone you respect, what would that person say?

EVALUATE ALTERNATIVE ACTIONS FROM VARIOUS ETHICAL PERSPECTIVES

6. Which option will produce the most good and do the least harm?

UTILITARIAN APPROACH: The ethical action is the one that will produce the greatest balance of benefits over harms.

7. Even if not everyone gets all they want, will everyone's rights and dignity still be respected?

RIGHTS APPROACH: The ethical action is the one that most dutifully respects the rights of all affected.

8. Which option is fair to all stakeholders?

FAIRNESS OR JUSTICE APPROACH: The ethical action is the one that treats people equally, or if unequally, that treats people proportionately and fairly.

9. Which option would help all participate more fully in the life we share as a family, community, society?

COMMON GOOD APPROACH: The ethical action is the one that contributes most to the achievement of a quality common life together.

10. Would you want to become the sort of person who acts this way (e.g., a person of courage or compassion)?

VIRTUE APPROACH: The ethical action is the one that embodies the habits and values of humans at their best.

MAKE A DECISION AND TEST IT

11. Considering all these perspectives, which of the options is the right or best thing to do?
12. If you told someone you respect why you chose this option, what would that person say? If you had to explain your decision on television, would you be comfortable doing so?

ACT, THEN REFLECT ON THE DECISION LATER

13. Implement your decision. How did it turn out for all concerned? If you had it to do over again, what would you do differently?

Source: "A Framework for Thinking Ethically." Markula Center for Applied Ethics at Santa Clara University, www.scu.edu/ethics.

THE PROCESS OF DECISION MAKING: IMPORTANT CONCEPTS AND STEPS

Decision making has been defined as "a process influenced by information and values, whereby a perceived problem is explicitly defined, alternative solutions are posed and weighted, and a choice made that subsequently is implemented and evaluated."[23] The process is usually viewed from the perspective of an individual administrator, but decision making also takes place in small committees and in large groups.

Site-Based Management

More recently, the philosophy of school-based management, designed to increase the autonomy of the local school staff, is gaining hold in school districts across the country.[24] Linda Jean Holman states, "If embraced in spirit as well as form, if genuinely supported by school boards, central office personnel, and campus-based administration, and if implemented at a pace neither too slow nor too abrupt, site-based decision making provides a vehicle whereby each school can adjust curriculum, scheduling, staffing, and budget to address its needs. Given time and sustained academic focus, the resulting empowerment and ownership should result in an improved instructional program and increased student achievement."[25] This approach gives greater flexibility to staff, offers increased participation opportunities, and has the ability to provide more immediate services to meet specific needs of students.

Some of the problems that arise in implementing school-based management are confusion of roles and responsibilities, along with difficulties in adapting to new roles. There could ensue a power struggle among administrators, teachers, and parents—especially if the administrator is unwilling to share decision-making authority. Some authorities argue that the individual administrator should not be making many decisions. Griffiths, for example, has asserted, "If the executive is personally making decisions, this means there exists malfunction in the decision process. It is not the function of the chief executive to make decisions; it is his [or her] function to monitor the decision-making process to make sure that it performs at the optimum level."[26]

Many school districts have successfully implemented a school-based management/shared decision-making (SBM/SDM) program that includes decentralizing decision making in order to enhance the leadership of school site administrators and to promote the empowerment of teachers at the work site. Evaluations of shared decision-making procedures are typically conducted by variously named groups of teachers, administrators, noninstructional personnel, parents, and students; supported by grade level or subject interest committees; and referred to a central decision-making body. Decisions are normally based on a majority vote with a great deal of opportunity for consultation and consensus resolution of issues, especially in cases where the principal has veto power.[27]

The Importance of Understanding Decision Making as a Process

Regardless of whether the decision making occurs individually or in groups, or whether the administrator's role is that of monitor of the process; decision maker; or, more likely, both, an administrator must possess a good understanding of the decision-making process in order to be effective in any of these roles. Careful reading and reflection on the following concepts and guidelines should help accomplish that objective.

Figure 2.1 identifies the major steps in decision making, and the sections that follow describe the concepts involved at each stage. Although the process recommended is based on the rational theory of decision making, every effort will be made in the discussion to present the complexities–as well as the less rational aspects–of decision making. It is, of course, impossible to have a purely rational process since the administrator cannot enjoy perfect knowledge. Hence, nonrationality becomes a necessity, with aspects of "muddling through." It is only when what at times may be a necessity becomes a virtue, replacing the search for knowledge and information in decision making, that effective performance suffers.[28]

Defining the Situation

The first step an administrator should take when faced with a decision is to define the nature of the situation that seems to require a decision. The importance of this step is underscored by Barnard's observation: "The fine art of executive decision making consists of not deciding questions that are not pertinent, in not deciding prematurely, in not making decisions that cannot be made effectively, and in not making decisions that others should make."[29] If this sage advice were followed more often, more effective administrative decision making would undoubtedly result.

FIGURE 2.1
MAJOR STEPS IN DECISION MAKING

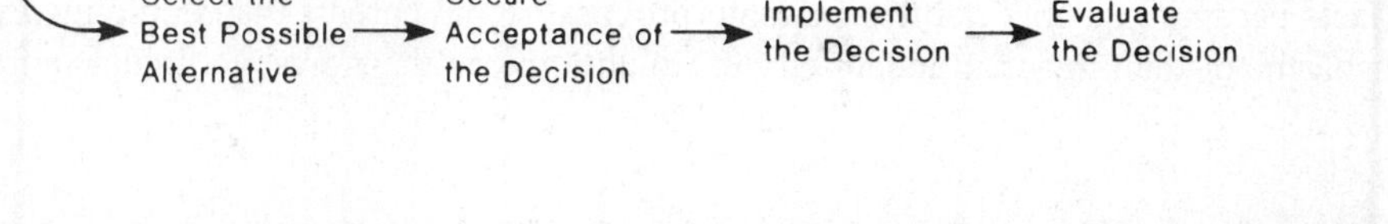

To make effective decisions, including the types of decisions referred to by Barnard, an administrator first needs to attempt to gain a better understanding of the question, problem, or set of circumstances that seems to require an administrative decision.

Except for routine situations, an administrator will not be in the position of possessing sufficient information or understanding at the time the need for a decision surfaces. Unfortunately, as research has shown, administrators often react too quickly on the basis of assumption, inadequate information, and/or someone else's perception of a situation and immediately begin looking for solutions before the situation has been sufficiently defined.[30]

Of course, in some situations the administrator will be forced to make an on-the-spot decision, and there will be circumstances when the press of time and a lack of available information influence the decision choice. In such instances, it will be important for an administrator to be decisive when the situation requires it and to avoid procrastinating in the hope that the perfect solution will at some point surface or that the problem will resolve itself.[31]

In most situations, however, particularly those involving important and long-range decisions, an administrator should take sufficient time to investigate and analyze the conditions necessitating a decision in order to reduce the possibility of an ineffective administrative decision.[32] This type of situational or problem analysis is most productively approached by the decision maker's seeking answers to questions such as the following:

1. What is known and unknown about the situation? What other factors must be clarified before a decision can be made?
2. Can anyone else provide additional information or a different perception of the situation? To what extent is the administrator's bias, or are the biases of others, influencing perception of the circumstances necessitating a decision?
3. Who will be affected by a decision?
4. How serious is the problem or question? How soon must a decision be made?

Effective situational and problem analysis is necessary in order to avoid making an incorrect decision based on an inadequate understanding of a situation or problem. Asking relevant questions is the key to effective situational and problem analysis. While there will be time constraints and possibly temptation to seek only the most accessible and interesting information about a situation,[33] the administrator should be trying to obtain the most relevant, accurate, and thorough information available on the situation or problem. A poorly understood problem or situation will almost guarantee an ineffective decision.

Identifying the Alternatives

Upon defining a problem or situation, the administrator will usually begin to perceive alternative courses of action. A typical mistake made by the inexperienced decision maker is to assume that only two alternatives exist.[34] For example, a principal faced with making a decision on a parents' proposal for greater involvement in school affairs may assume there are only two choices: to reject the parents' proposal or to accept their recommendation. But if the administrator examines the situation further, additional courses of action may appear. For instance, the administrator could decide to postpone a decision on the parents' proposal until more facts became available or offer a counterproposal to the parents that would incorporate less involvement than they had requested but would improve their present circumstances. Or the administrator could decide not to respond at all to the parents' proposal, hoping that the parents would take no further action.

What every administrator needs to avoid is the tendency to perceive alternatives in *either-or* terms. In most cases, an administrator will benefit from continuing to examine the problem, probing for that third or fourth alternative. This process requires careful analysis, imagination, and creativity, but it will usually result in an improved decision, one that may combine two previously identified alternatives or take a totally new approach.

Assessing the Alternatives

Administrators who fail to assess adequately the feasibility of the various alternatives under consideration may later encounter unanticipated consequences in the process of implementing their decisions.[35] This results, in part, from the ambiguity of information and uncertainty in estimating the consequences of selecting one alternative over another that is characteristic of much decision making.[36] But unanticipated consequences can also occur when an administrator makes certain assumptions about each of the alternatives that turn out to be unjustified. For example, a particular group may react differently than was anticipated, or a key individual may not possess the resources or competencies that are needed, or the extent of supplies required for implementation of the decision may exceed the original estimates. Usually the unanticipated consequences result from the administrator's failure to identify fully and to examine critically the assumptions inherent–although possibly unrecognized–in assessing the original alternatives. As noted previously, it is impossible to reach decisions or to take action without making certain basic assumptions. The real danger for an administrator, however, lies in making decisions without having examined the assumptions central to the feasibility of each alternative.

In attempting to assess the various alternatives, the administrator needs to anticipate their possible consequences, despite the uncertainty of the results. Such a process may be represented by the following sequence of thought: "If I choose alternative A, then result 1 will probably occur and result 2 will probably not. On the other hand, if I choose alternative B, then result 2 is likely to occur and result 1 is unlikely. If I choose alternative C, however, results 2 and 3 may come about while result 1 is unlikely."[37]

As the administrator evaluates each alternative, two important factors should be taken into consideration. The first concern is an assessment of one's own capability and that of the other individuals or groups who will participate in implementing a particular course of action. The second involves an assessment of the type of reception the decision will receive from those who will be most affected, for example, teachers, students, parents, and the general public.

The First Factor to Consider The initial question that an administrator must ask is, "To what extent do I possess the competency, resources, personal influence, or power necessary to implement this alternative?" For instance, an administrator may be interested in initiating a new program of individualized instruction. But before a decision is made to proceed with a plan, a personal inventory must be taken of the technical knowledge and skill for introducing the innovation, of the ability to obtain the necessary resources the new program will require, and of the extent to which personal influence or power is necessary for successfully implementing the decision. Although it may be difficult to evaluate one's own competency, personal influence, or resources objectively, these are the kinds of judgments required for an accurate feasibility assessment of a particular course of action.

A related question that the administrator should ask in assessing the feasibility of each alternative is, "To what extent do the other individuals or groups involved in implementing the decision possess the necessary competency or resources?" The effective implementation of most decisions depends on the capability or resources of people other than the administrator. Too frequently an administrator may assume that teachers, students, or other groups possess the skills, knowledge, or resources required for carrying out certain decisions. In the absence of these prerequisites, however, decisions are usually not implemented effectively, and the people involved may become quite frustrated. Therefore, it is essential that the administrator evaluate the degree to which coworkers possess the competency and resources necessary for successful implementation of a decision.

The Second Factor to Consider A second major factor to be considered by the administrator in assessing the feasibility of various alternatives is the type of reception the decision will be given by those most directly affected. Administrative decisions perceived as unsatisfactory may be resisted by those whose cooperation will be needed in the implementation stage.

The administrator should therefore determine how the affected individuals or groups regard the various alternatives. For example, with regard to each alternative, who can be counted upon for support? How solid would that support be? What would be the likelihood that a particular individual or group would reject or actively resist the course of action implied in each alternative? Which individuals or groups could exert sufficient influence or power to overturn a particular decision? Would it be possible for the administrator to change the attitudes of those who might reject or resist a decision? The answers to these questions should help the administrator ascertain the reception a particular decision will probably be given by those who will be most affected by it.

In trying to understand how various individuals or groups will react to each alternative, the administrator will frequently need to make judgments based on limited experience with those concerned. Although in a few circumstances it may be easy to predict the reactions of certain individuals or groups, it may be necessary in other instances to "float a trial balloon" to discover how a group would react to a particular decision.

Regardless of the specific circumstances, one cannot overemphasize the need for an administrator to assess objectively and thoroughly in advance the reactions that a particular decision may be given by others. In many situations these reactions may well determine the ultimate fate of any decision. Undoubtedly there will be circumstances when an administrator must or should make a particular kind of decision, regardless of the adverse reactions of those who will be affected by it. The administrator, however, should not ignore the attitudes and feelings of the people who will be affected by a decision. In most instances, such attitudes and feelings greatly influence the fate of any administrative decision and therefore need to be understood and considered carefully.

While the factors discussed thus far should play the major role in determining the feasibility of an alternative, an administrator needs to realize that other variables may unconsciously enter into the decision-making process. Each individual's decision making is affected by prior attitudes about the situation, group, or persons in question.[38] If the administrator's attitude is biased in some way, the administrator may distort the reality of a situation by not considering relevant facts, perceptions, or alternatives. As a result, a decision could be made about an individual or issue that might have been different had it been based on a more objective analysis of the circumstances. It will probably be impossible for an administrator to be completely objective in any situation. It is important, however, to be aware of personal biases and to avoid letting them significantly affect the decision-making process.

Selecting a Desirable Alternative

If an administrator has followed the previously described guidelines, the best available alternative will usually become apparent.[39] If it does not, then the administrator's steps should be retraced and the assumptions reviewed, beginning with the question of whether the problem has been adequately defined. Of course, in most situations there is no ideal alternative, and in some circumstances it is a matter of selecting the least undesirable alternative. Through diagnosis, objective assessment of alternatives, and a little imagination—which never hurts—the best course of action will generally surface.

Implementing the Decision

Although some administrators seem to behave as though once they have made a decision, implementation will occur automatically and spontaneously, the process of implementation is more involved than has been frequently recognized.[40] The initial and perhaps most important step in implementing a decision is, as previously discussed, to secure its acceptance from those who will be most affected. Whether the administrator can gain acceptance of the decision depends on many factors, one of which is the perceived legitimacy of the administrator's position within the organization as a decision maker for the issue, question, or problem under consideration. (We discuss additional factors that determine whether an administrator's decision is accepted in Chapter 3, "Authority, Power, and Influence.") If the individuals or groups who will be affected by a decision perceive the administrator as having the right to make that decision, based on the administrator's position in the organization, the likelihood of having that decision accepted is greatly enhanced. If, on the other hand, those individuals or groups who will be affected by the decision do not perceive the administrator as possessing any more right than anyone else to make the decision in the situation, the possibility of securing acceptance of the administrator's judgment may be severely jeopardized.

The key factor in the acceptance of the principal's decisions is not self-perceived legitimacy but how others perceive the legitimacy of that administrator as a decision maker. If teachers, parents, students, and other reference groups do not believe the principal has the right to make certain decisions, his or her personal belief in that right is not enough to engender agreement.

However, even if those affected by the decision do not perceive the administrator as possessing a basic right to make a determination, they may accept the decision if they are persuaded that there is little or nothing they can do to change it or thwart its implementation. For example, although the faculty adviser to the student newspaper may feel that the principal has no right to censor the publication, the decision to screen the content of the newspaper before it is published may be reluctantly accepted if there is little that can be done to stop the principal. If the adviser thinks support can be obtained from the on-site representative of teachers' association, the city newspaper, or the civil liberties union, the adviser may resist the principal's original decision—or at least try to modify its implementation. Also, proponents of teacher and principal empowerment may argue that the administrator is resisting the teacher's expanded role as an inquiring, risk-taking, and contributing professional. The administrator could provide opportunities and the necessary assistance to maintain that teacher's self-esteem without taking ownership of the issue or task, listen with empathy and compassion, and possibly ask for help to solve this problem. Of course, if negative attitudes continue to persist, the administrator will need to take additional steps in resolving the problem.[41]

Encountering Resistance The administrator encountering negative reactions to a decision can either modify or abandon the original decision, try to enforce the decision against the will of others, or try to change their attitudes. If there is a need to change the attitudes of those who will be affected by the decision, the administrator should recognize that negative attitudes can result from some of the following phenomena:

1. The individual's or group's feeling about the administrator as a person, or about the way in which the decision was made.
2. An incorrect understanding of the way in which the decision will affect the individual or group.
3. Inadequate skill or competency on the part of those who are to carry out the decision.
4. A perception by the individual or group that the decision will cause more personal disadvantages than advantages.
5. An honest disagreement about the merits of the decision, despite the fact that those involved may not feel they would be adversely affected.

An administrator should realize that the reasons people resist a decision or react negatively are complex in nature and need to be analyzed fully. Therefore, when faced with resistance, the administrator should try to diagnose the source of the resistance by thoroughly investigating the various and sometimes subtle reasons an individual or a group is not accepting the decision. Unfortunately, an administrator is sometimes thrown off balance by a negative reaction to the decision and responds directly to that reaction, rather than trying to explore and understand the reasons for it. The administrator is unlikely to be successful in counteracting resistance from others until the underlying causes of the resistance are dealt with.

Rowe and Mason suggest that hidden factors such as the administrator's decision style and that of the staff may affect overall performance. They found that where style is aligned with the requirements of the job, performance is often successful, and where it is not aligned, performance does not meet the person's potential. The authors contend that decision style reflects one's mental predisposition regarding personal objectives, what situations one avoids, what kinds of jobs one enjoys, what things one dislikes, how one communicates, and how one approaches problems and makes decisions. Patterns among these predispositions can be uncovered through the use of a decision style inventory developed by these authors.[42] The administrator attempting to deal with the underlying causes of resistance to a particular decision needs to better understand people's mental predispositions, perceptions, and consequent actions, as well as the differences in the way people approach their jobs through the use of such a decision style inventory.

Implementation Steps If the administrator can obtain acceptance of the decision from those who will be most affected, or if there is a need to proceed in spite of their adverse reactions, the administrator should then attempt to secure the resources and personnel necessary to initiate action. Depending on the nature of the decision, there may be the need only to instruct one individual about what must be done. On the other hand, there may be a need to design and carry out a complicated plan involving many resources, a large number of people, retraining programs, and variables of time and role redefinition. Although the steps that must be taken have been designated by the various terms and have been applied in contexts other than the implementation of a decision, the basic activities include the following:

1. **Planning:** Working out in broad outline the things that need to be done and the methods for doing them to accomplish the purposes set for the enterprise.
2. **Organizing:** Establishing the formal structure of authority through which work subdivisions are arranged, defined, and coordinated for the specific objective.
3. **Staffing:** Selecting and training the staff and maintaining favorable conditions of work.
4. **Directing:** Making decisions and embodying them in orders and instructions; serving as the leaders of the enterprise.
5. **Coordinating:** Interrelating the various parts of the work.
6. **Reporting:** Keeping those to whom the executive is responsible informed as to what is taking place; keeping the executive and the subordinates informed through records, research, and inspection.
7. **Budgeting:** Fiscal planning, accounting, and control.
8. **Evaluating:** Formative and summative.[43]

CONSTRAINTS AND VALUES

The process of decision making described in the previous section is a logical, rational process that, if followed, should result in improved decision making. Several situational constraints and personal variables exist, however, that can affect the success of the decision maker's efforts. In addition to the technical expertise required in decision-making and decision-analysis procedures, personal values and ethical factors always will impact an administrator's decision choice. Decisions that are ethically unsound will not have a long commitment from the people required to implement the decision in the work setting. Organizational ethics include the development of the administrator as a moral person, the influence of a moral organizational environment, and a policy that reflects ethical performance goals.[44]

None of the constraints or personal variables diminishes the need for the administrator to follow the decision-making guidelines previously stated. Nevertheless, these constraints and personal factors must be considered if the administrator is to minimize negative effects. Nutt draws attention to a particular kind of decision made in and for organizations, which he calls a "tough decision" in his comprehensive book entitled *Making Tough Decisions.* This type of decision is characterized by situational constraints and personal variables that must be taken into account, including such related dilemmas as ambiguity, conflict, and uncertainty. The author recommends that administrators investigate future conditions and use sound procedures to gather and analyze information to inform the decision choice they ultimately make. Decision makers who simply focus on conflict management must make assumptions that negate ambiguity and uncertainty, treating tough decisions as if they were easy, frequently resulting in ineffective decision choices. One particular situational constraint, future projection, or the ability of the administrator to anticipate future events and outcomes that may affect the final decision, requires the administrator to possess specific forecasting skills and techniques.[45]

Many of the difficult decisions an administrator must make deal with future conditions—whether to implement a new multicultural curriculum or install a preschool and after-school care program, for example. A strategic decision-making process requires the administrator to identify the obstacles or barriers as well as the opportunities or benefits associated with the decision.[46] In addition, thoughtful planning and technical expertise must be utilized by the administrator as a professional decision thinker. This implies expanding the strategic framework to include in the decision choice a concern for the personal values of the staff and community and acknowledging a responsibility to outside constituent groups and the greater society at large.

Situational Constraints

All administrators, even in the best of situations, operate under certain situational constraints. Although the types of constraints may vary from one situation to another, the most typical situational constraints under which administrators operate in a decision-making context are the following:[47]

1. Amount of time available to make a decision.
2. Availability of resources necessary to implement any particular alternative.
3. Amount of information available to make a decision.
4. Ambiguity of the situation, including the alternatives and potential consequences.
5. Degrees of organizational autonomy given for decision making.
6. Expectations of others regarding the nature of the decision-making process and the ultimate decision.
7. Amount of tension in the situation.

Each of the factors can act as an important situational constraint on the decision maker and can influence the effectiveness of the final decision on a matter or on its implementation. Whether or not the impact of these factors will be negative seems to depend as much on the type of person the administrator is as it does on the nature of the factors. For example, what is perceived as sufficient time, resources, information, and autonomy by one administrator in order to make a particular decision may not be deemed adequate by another administrator in the same situation. A situation characterized by one individual as possessing too much ambiguity, tension, and pressure by an external group for a quick decision may not bother or affect another administrator in the same set of circumstances. These differences reflect variations in personality and capabilities.[48]

Administrators can also differ in their perceptions of potential constraints. One administrator may perceive strong expectations by a certain reference group to make a quick decision the same week, whereas another administrator in the same situation may not sense the same degree of pressure and may plan to take a month or more to make the decision. In reality, both administrators may be misperceiving the expectations of the reference group, and the effectiveness of the decision may be impaired. Therefore, it is essential for an administrator to test initial perceptions about a potential constraint and to evaluate their validity to make sure they correspond reasonably with reality.

It also needs to be emphasized in discussing the role of situational constraints in decision making that, assuming the administrator is perceiving them accurately, they need to be analyzed critically to ascertain their potential for modification. There will, of course, be circumstances in which the amount of time available to make a decision may be a real and significant constraint. If an administrator is frequently experiencing this problem, however, and it is seriously affecting the decision making, then an analysis of overall time spent and an evaluation of the order of priorities need to be conducted. Effective decision making about matters that are out of the ordinary takes time, and although there will be situations in which the administrator must make a quick decision, the necessary time should be set aside for careful and thoughtful decisions on crucial matters.

Realistically, an administrator will not be able to eliminate or even modify every type of constraint; but if an administrator is to be effective as a decision maker, an effort must be made to analyze the causes and nature of the constraints and attempt to decrease their impact on decision making.

Personal Thoughts	*Type of Attitude or Value*
1. "I wonder about the risks involved in pursuing this particular alternative."	Risk orientation
2. "If Hank recommends it, I am sure that it would make a good decision."	Attitude toward people
3. "I question whether adopting a 'far-out' innovation like the open classroom is good education."	Educational philosophy
4. "This is the type of decision that an educational leader should make."	Concern about status
5. "It seems to me that if we choose that alternative, we can no longer 'call the shots' in that area."	Concern about authority and control

Personal Variables

In addition to situational constraints that can affect the decision-making process, numerous personal variables or value considerations can influence the decision maker and, ultimately, the final decision. These can perhaps be best illustrated by the thoughts expressed by several administrators, along with the attitude or value orientation each represents.

These five examples, of course, are only illustrative of a wide range of possible values and attitudes any administrator might possess and that could play a major role in influencing the type of decision made.

As Lipham and Hoeh have perceptively observed:

> Values serve as a perpetual screen for the decision maker, affecting both his [or her] awareness of the problematic state of a system and his [or her] screening of information relative to the problem. Second, values condition the screening serve as a perceptual screen for the decision maker, affecting both his [or her] awareness of the possible alternatives. . . . Finally, values serve as the criteria against which higher order goals are assessed and projected.[49]

Although an administrator probably cannot avoid the influence of values and attitudes in making decisions, the administrator should attempt to become more aware of the ethical nature of those values. In his study of chief school administrators, Dexheimer discovered that they were more inclined to engage in nonethical forms of accommodations in critical decision-making activities than in ethical forms.[50] Although it appears that the study has not been replicated with similar or other administrative positions, Dexheimer's discovery points up the need for every administrator to consider carefully whether the attitudes and values influencing a particular decision are morally and ethically defensible. This will be a challenging task for the decision maker because most individuals not only lack awareness of their values, attitudes, and how they are affected by them but also lack criteria and standards for evaluation.

The emphasis on organizational ethics is found predominantly in writings on business ethics and organizational culture. Studies and articles range in content, from business student attitudes before and after taking a course in ethical decision making, to identifying ethical business practices after students have completed a course on business ethics, to models for building ethical organizations.[51] The findings could have implications for an administrator in an educational setting who desires more information on value development and ethical conduct in general.

A problem related to the influence of attitudes and values in decision making is the extent to which they can play a dominant role in compromising the objectivity of the decision maker and short-circuiting the decision-making process. For example, the administrator whose attitude is, "If Hank recommends it, I am sure that it would make a good decision," reveals a strong, positive attitude or bias toward the person Hank. Because of the administrator's attitude in this situation, it will probably be difficult to be objective about evaluating Hank's recommendation or any competing alternative. As a result, the administrator may not engage thoroughly in the various steps of the decision-making process—steps that should include identifying and evaluating objectively all possible alternatives.

Although the administrator's attitude in the previous example is a positive one, at least toward Hank, in another situation involving someone else it may be negative, with the same potential results of compromised objectivity and a superficial decision-making process. Of course, it is not axiomatic that such a decision will be a poor one, and it is recognized that the press of time on an administrator may require taking a shortcut through the decision-making process. Unfortunately it is because of the bias of the decision maker and such shortcuts that poor decision making frequently results. Therefore, an administrator should make every effort to become more aware of attitudes and values and their influence on the type of decision choices, attempting to reduce that influence when it could compromise objectivity or result in a less thorough and thoughtful decision-making process.

Involving Others

Involving people in the decision-making process—be they individuals, groups, or both—who will be either affected by the decision or in some way responsible for implementing a decision is not a new concept in the social science and school administration literature.[52] Frequently referred to as *participatory decision making* (PDM), this approach has generated considerable research revealing that PDM can be effective under certain conditions but is a more complex process than typically has been recognized.[53] The process of shared decision making is the cornerstone of site-based management (SBM), school-site budgeting (SSB), and total quality management (TQM), which have been implemented in many school systems. The following sections will identify appropriate and inappropriate conditions for participatory decision making; the complexities associated with the process will be analyzed and discussed.

The rationale for involving persons other than just the administrator in the decision-making process consists of the following elements:

1. It increases the number of different viewpoints and ideas that might be relevant to the decision being made.
2. It makes for better utilization of the available expertise and problem-solving skills that exist within the school community.
3. It may improve school morale by showing the individuals involved that the administrator values their opinions, giving them greater feelings of professional pride and job satisfaction.
4. It can aid acceptance and implementation of a decision because the people who are involved are more likely to understand the decision and be more committed to its success.
5. It is consistent with a democratic principle of our society that holds that those who are affected by public institutions such as the school should have some voice in how they are run.[54]

Therefore, although frequently given the sole responsibility for making a particular decision, administrators may find it desirable to involve others in the process of arriving at the best determination. The old adage "two heads are better than one" can be applied to administrative decision making with appreciable advantage under certain conditions.

An administrator should not involve others in the decision-making process, however, if the administrator has already decided the outcome. It is certainly appropriate for an administrator to have some tentative ideas about a decision before involving others, but unless those ideas are tentative and there is a willingness to be flexible and open-minded in considering the ideas of others, it would be better not to involve others in the decision-making process. It can be a very frustrating and disillusioning experience for people to be involved with an administrator whose mind is already made up[55] and who is involving other people only because of trying to project a "democratic" image or to be able to say at a later date, "Well, they were involved, weren't they?" As Lammers has observed, encouraging and allowing participation by others in decisions over which they have little control may be just as damaging, if not more so, than no participation at all.[56]

Variables Influencing Extent of Involvement

Whether an administrator should involve others in decision making seems to depend on a number of factors. Perhaps the most important initial factor is the administrator's attitude toward the people who might be potentially involved in decision making. Unless the administrator's attitude toward other people is one of trust, confidence, and respect, it is unlikely that involvement in administrative decision making will result. According to David, "Strong councils are usually led, though not always chaired, by strong principals (and sometimes teachers) who exercise leadership by mobilizing others. They encourage all parties to participate. And they model inquiry and reflection."[57]

A second major factor that initially seems to influence the administrator regarding whether to involve others in the decision-making process is the degree of organizational autonomy the administrator has been given by superiors for making decisions. Palmer discovered that the more autonomy administrators were given for making decisions, the more likely they were to consult and involve others in the decision-making process.[58] One implication of Palmer's study is that a certain degree of administrative autonomy and independence from superiors may be a necessary prerequisite for involving others in administrative decision making.

Involvement Considerations

Assuming that an administrator has reasonable autonomy within the organization, is open-minded, and believes that involving others may help in arriving at the best decision, three basic questions must be considered: (1) *When* should others be involved in decision making? (2) *Who* should be involved? (3) *How* should they be involved?

When Others Should Be Involved With regard to the first question, Bridges has proposed that other individuals or groups should be involved in those administrative decisions that they feel will significantly affect their lives.[59] He theorizes, based on earlier conceptual work by Barnard, that most people possess a zone of indifference. By implication, they also possess a "zone of concern." When a particular issue or problem falls within a group's zone of concern, the members will expect to be involved by the administrator in the decision-making process. If the members are permitted to be involved, they will be self-motivated in their participation because the final determination may affect them in some significant manner. If excluded from the decision-making process, they may feel deprived, and dissatisfaction with the administrator or the decision is likely to result.[60]

Deciding Who Will Be Decision Makers David writes that determining who will make what decisions is critical. Sound decisions are made by those who are both informed and concerned about the issue; in addition, an understanding of the circumstances in which the decision will be implemented is essential. Otherwise, there is no assurance that these decisions will be any better than those made by administrators many steps removed. School professionals are often the best group to make some decisions, whereas parents or students are the best to make others. In other situations, representatives of several constituencies or a formal schoolwide body would be the appropriate decision-making team.[61]

How Involvement Works Progress requires that a school faculty and staff redefine themselves as a community capable of setting and reaching its goals and managing its own resources. This redefinition requires establishing new working relationships among all participants. The principal must not control, monitor, or direct, but must respect the team as a responsible community of adults. Initially, these people must together set in place the framework within which collective action can occur. David cites three operating principles that form the foundation of involvement in decision making:

1. Responsibility and authority go hand in hand.
2. Children and adults learn best in trusting communities in which every person is both a learner and a resource for learning.
3. All adult members of the school staff care for the institution and community as a whole as well as for their primary roles in it.[62]

The goal for the administrator should be to involve people in the process of decision making when their involvement could improve the quality, acceptance, or implementation of the decision, and when the involvement is based on people's desired level of involvement. Also, obviously, not everyone wants to be involved, and not all the decisions under the province of an administrator will be of concern to other individuals and groups.[63] On the other hand, it would be unwise for the administrator to assume that people want to have certain decisions made for them or that they are not concerned about particular issues or problems. Untested assumptions frequently result in unanticipated consequences. The administrator should not rely on assumptions but should actively seek feedback from appropriate others regarding the extent to which they are concerned about various issues and problems and the degree to which they feel their participation is desirable in making decisions.

Involvement Prerequisites

In many situations, the lack of feasibility will preclude participation in the decision-making process by everyone who may desire to do so. Consequently, the administrator will need to determine which individuals or groups should help make a decision in a particular area.

Objectivity would appear to be an important consideration. Individuals who are interested in being involved but who show a particular bias or an ax to grind are not likely to be helpful. Effective decision making requires an open mind and an unbiased examination of the facts and alternatives.

The most desirable criterion for selecting those who should be involved in decision making seems to be the extent to which they possess the expertise for contributing to an improved decision. Numerous individuals or groups may be interested in participating in decision making, but they may not all possess the expertise necessary to make a positive contribution. As Bridges has pointed out, the interested party should "not only [have] some stake in the outcome but also the capability of contributing to the decision affecting the outcome."[64] Interest and motivation are necessary but not always sufficient conditions for involvement in administrative decision making; the degree to which an individual or group possesses the relevant expertise should also be a consideration. Utilizing the latter criterion, the administrator should identify those students, teachers, parents, or other individuals or groups who can offer special insights, knowledge, or skills for improved decision making. They are the people who can be of considerable assistance to the administrator in arriving at effective decisions.

Levels of Involvement

Having determined that a certain group possesses the necessary motivation, objectivity, and expertise for participating in decision making, an administrator still faces the question of at what level to involve the group. Five alternative levels of involvement, each with its underlying assumptions, are presented in Figure 2.2. As Figure 2.2 shows, the question of how an administrator might involve others in school decision making is a complex one. Several alternatives are usually available, each of which is based on certain assumptions. While there is no formula for easily determining the most appropriate level of involvement

FIGURE 2.2
ALTERNATIVE LEVELS OF INVOLVEMENT

Level 1. The administrator makes a tentative decision and utilizes the reactions of other individuals or groups to assess the soundness of her [or his] decision. The administrator reserves for herself [or himself], however, the final determination on whether or not to proceed with her [or his] original decision.

Assumptions

a. The administrator has probably already reached the best decision for the situation.
b. It is unlikely that anyone else could offer a better alternative.
c. There is a possibility that the administrator might yet improve her [or his] decision by obtaining the reactions of others.
d. The administrator must make the final determination herself [or himself].

Level 2. The administrator describes the problem situation to other individuals or groups and ask them to investigate the various alternatives and to make a recommendation to her [or his] on several possible courses of action, listing the advantages and disadvantages of each. The procedures to be used by the individuals or groups investigating the alternatives are specified by the administrator. She [or he] will utilize their recommendations to help her [or his] make up her [or his] mind on the best course of action to follow.

Assumptions

a. The administrator has already adequately defined the nature of the problem.
b. Other people could provide help in identifying the available alternatives.
c. Because of the other participants' inexperience or need for direction, the administrator should specify the procedures they should follow in arriving at their recommendations.
d. The administrator must make the final decision herself [or himself].

Level 3. The administrator describes the problem situation to other individuals or groups and ask for help in better defining the nature of the problem, question or issue, and that she be presented with a recommendation on the best course of action to follow. The administrator specifies the procedures which must be used in arriving at the recommendation and reserves the right to veto the recommended alternative if she [or he] doesn't believe it to be in the best interests of the school.

Assumptions

a. Other people could help the administrator to better define the nature of the situation for which a decision is required.
b. Other people could provide help for the administrator in identifying the best available alternative.
c. Because of the other participants' inexperience or need for direction, the administrator should specify the procedures to be followed in arriving at their recommendation.
d. The administrator must make the final decision herself [or himself].

FIGURE 2.2 *Concluded*

Level 4. The administrator describes the problem situation to other individuals or groups and ask for their help in better defining the nature of the problem, question, or issue, and requests their recommendation on the best course of action to follow. At this level of involvement the administrator specifies no particular procedures to be used in arriving at a recommendation. However, she [or he] still reserves the right to reject any recommended which she [or he] believes to be incompatible with the best interests of the school.

Assumptions

a. Other people could help the administrator to better define the nature of the problem and to arrive at a recommendation for the best course of action.
b. The other participants possess sufficient experience and self-direction to determine for themselves the procedures to be used in reaching a recommendation.
c. The administrator must make the final decision herself [or himself].

Level 5. The administrator describes the problem situation to other individuals or groups and ask for their help in defining the nature of the problem, question, or issue, and requests them to determine the best alternative. At this level of involvement, the administrator delegates to the other participants the prerogative of determining the procedures to be used in arriving at the best decision and she [or he] indicates her [or his] willingness to accept whatever decision is finally made.

Assumptions

a. Other people could help the administrator to better define the nature of the problem and arrive at a decision on the best course of action.
b. The other participants are as competent as the administrator to make the final decision.
c. The administrator can be delegate the responsibility for making the final decision, and she [or he] can accept and support whatever decision is reached by the other participants.

by others, the administrator should try to be certain that the assumptions made in reaching this decision are tenable. Although it will be impossible to avoid making assumptions, the administrator should refrain from making those that could restrict valuable input from other people or provide more involvement than others could constructively handle. The initial conceptual work in this area was developed by Robert Tannenbaum and Warren H. Schmidt.[65] The authors have adapted and modified the original model for the purpose of administrative decision making and have added the basic assumptions that undergird each level of involvement.

There is research suggesting that an administrator's choice of the level at which to involve other people is typically based on the individual's attitude toward encouraging the involvement of others in school decision making, the perception of the administrator's immediate superior's attitude toward this question, and the perception of the expectations of others for a certain level of participation in school decision making.[66] The same research indicates that the administrator's own attitude about involving others and the perception of the immediate superior's attitude are the two most important factors influencing the administrator in deciding how to involve others.

In view of the research presented earlier in this book, however, showing that a growing number of students, teachers, and parents are dissatisfied with their current level of involvement in school decision making, it would seem important for every administrator to give greater consideration to these expectations for more meaningful participation. The challenge for the school administrator is to involve these groups in ways that will permit them to derive satisfaction from their participation and, at the same time, make a contribution to improved decision making in the schools.

Types of Involvement

The most typical approach is for an administrator to analyze a problem or situation calling for a decision with another person or persons in a conference or group setting. Such discussions can be helpful in clarifying the administrator's thinking and obtaining reactions from others.

The Quality Circle One systematic example of this approach is the *quality circle.*[67] A quality circle is a small group of employees such as teachers, secretaries, or any other group performing a common task. They meet weekly or biweekly to analyze problems that impair the effectiveness of the group or reduce the desired quality of a product or outcome of the group or, perhaps, to offer fresh ideas to improve some aspect of their work.[68] A group leader, perhaps an administrator, facilitates group discussion and helps the group identify and analyze problems, identify and assess alternative solutions, select the most desirable and feasible solution, and develop a decision implementation plan. The decision-making process followed in a quality circle is very similar to the process outlined in Figure 2.1.[69]

Although research on the effectiveness of the quality circle is limited, the approach is utilized in a number of schools apparently with some success.[70] The assumption that group decisions will be better than the decisions of the most knowledgeable group member is not always proved in the empirical research literature. It is traditionally believed that under most circumstances, the knowledge of the most competent group member represents the upper limit of what a group might reasonably be expected to achieve. However, findings from studies that focused more on contextually relevant and consequential problems to be solved by groups rather than on ad hoc groups using artificial problems and trivial rewards for solving problems demonstrated that groups outperformed their most proficient group member 97 percent of the time. This finding presents a strong argument for involving groups in problem-solving activities to improve the effectiveness of the decision choice.[71]

In addition, the keys to the success of the quality circle seem to be a strong commitment from the school board, the district administration, and members of the quality circle to this type of participatory decision making, as well as a committed group leader equipped with group leadership skills.[72] (These skills are discussed in Chapter 1.) Also, training in group interaction processes and problem-solving methods is essential for the members of the quality circle.[73]

Although the quality circle or other types of group interaction methods of decision making can, under the right conditions, improve the effectiveness of a decision, such conditions are not always present. For example, the people whom the administrator is trying to involve in a quality circle may not feel secure in responding to the administrator or to the other members of the group, and, when that occurs, such feelings and thoughts are frequently not revealed. Also, while it is true that in a quality circle or in other types of group decision-making situations the people involved may stimulate each other's thinking, it is also true that often in a group discussion it is difficult to engage in the thorough, reflective thinking that is important for creative decision making. In addition, in group discussions certain individuals or personalities may dominate, and social relationships may become more important than solving a problem or making the best decision.[74] It should be noted that these problems are not inevitable with the quality circle or any other kind of group interaction approach, but their occurrence has led to the consideration of two alternative ways of involving people in the decision-making process.[75]

The Delphi Technique The first of these is known as the *Delphi technique.* It is basically a process for generating ideas, reactions, or judgments that could be helpful to the decision maker and includes the following major steps: (1) defining the problem, decision, or question to which reactions of others are sought; (2) identifying those individuals and/or groups whose opinions, judgments, or expert knowledge would be valuable to obtain in the process of making a decision; (3) asking for their responses, usually through the completion of a questionnaire; and (4) summarizing the results of the questionnaire, distributing the results back to the people surveyed, and asking them to review the results and to indicate any changes in their initial responses. This last step is repeated until there is a reasonable consensus on the problem or decision.

The advantage of the Delphi technique is that it is an excellent approach to involving a large number of people in the decision-making process. The step of writing responses to questions helps people think through the complexity of a problem and submit specific, high-quality ideas. The anonymity and isolation of the respondents tend to minimize the influence of status factors and conformity pressures.[76] One disadvantage of the Delphi technique is that the lack of opportunity for interaction among people asked for their input into the decision-making process can lead to a feeling of detachment and noninvolvement. Furthermore, the lack of opportunity for verbal clarification of responses can cause communication and interpretation problems, and summarizing responses does not address the problem of conflicting or incompatible ideas.

The Nominal Group Technique Another approach to involving people in the decision-making process, the *nominal group technique* (NGT), has been developed to avoid or to minimize the possible disadvantages of the Delphi technique. NGT is a good method to use to gain group consensus, for example, when various people (program staff, stakeholders, community residents, etc.) are involved in constructing a logic model and the list of outputs for a specific component is too long and therefore has to be prioritized.[77] The nominal group technique, developed by Andre L. Delbert and Andrew H. Van de Ven in 1968, has been employed in a variety of settings. Its main steps include the following: (1) presenting to a group, verbally or in writing, a question, problem, or task to be addressed by the members of the group; (2) requesting each member in the group to take a period of time, for example, 10 minutes, to jot down individual ideas (without talking to anyone else in response to the question, problem, or task); (3) asking each member of the group at the end of the time period to present one of the ideas, recording these ideas on a blackboard or flip chart (at this stage it is important that there be no evaluation of the ideas by anyone); (4) continuing the presentation of ideas in round-robin fashion until all the ideas are recorded; (5) discussing briefly each idea, in the sequence in which it is recorded, as to clarity or rationale; and (6) voting privately in writing by rank-ordering or rating the ideas, and then mathematically pooling the outcome of the individual votes.

While the entire process may seem complicated, it is in fact fairly simple after one has acquired some experience with the various steps. Although NGT does have some disadvantages in that it does not provide as much social interaction as some people may want and it requires the people involved to hold in abeyance their evaluation of the ideas being presented until later in the process, it nevertheless has tended to be very productive in producing higher-quality ideas than either the group discussion or Delphi technique approaches.[78]

Administrators must also consider their roles in regard to the participation of others in the decision-making process. For example, the administrators could be confined to presenting the initial circumstances calling for a decision and later receiving a group's final recommendation, *or* could attempt to play the role of a resource person for those who are helping reach a decision. The administrator might, alternatively, attempt to influence the final recommendation of the group by playing a dominant role in the group's deliberations. The question of *which* role the administrator should play while involving others in school decision making is an important one, and the three examples provided are only illustrative of the many possibilities. The administrator's final resolution of this question is sure to influence the nature of the participation by others in the decision-making process.[79]

PREREQUISITES FOR SUCCESS

Assuming that the administrator has selected appropriate participants and methods of involvement, several other factors determine whether their involvement will result in the mutual satisfaction of both the administrator and participants and whether they will reach a better decision than if the administrator had decided unilaterally. The administrator must recognize that involving others in decision making increases the complexity and difficulty of making a decision. It increases the number of situational variables with which the administrator will be working and requires a greater degree of competency than if the administrator alone made the decision. To be successful in involving others, an administrator must become competent in the group dynamics and interaction skills we discussed in more detail in Chapter 1. Strategic decision making is a popular approach that may be used for training administrators or top executives in business. Most of these training programs focus upon sensing opportunities and problems, diagnosing the situation and generating alternatives, and, of course, making that all-important choice. The popularity of various types of training programs at any given moment is reflected in the administration theory currently under discussion. Beginning with the decade of the 1990s and continuing to the present, the emphasis has been on training administrators in participatory and group decision making as a result of research on strategic decision making and teacher empowerment. The group process, collaboration, and teamwork produce better decisions if more people are helping to generate options.[80]

Furthermore, the administrator needs to be certain that the individuals or groups involved are given sufficient training for participation in decision making and adequate information to make a decision. Frequently administrators have attempted to involve students, parents, or teachers in decision making and have become discouraged and discontented because these individuals and groups did not participate fully or productively. When confronted by this type of behavior, the administrator should try to diagnose its cause or causes, which might include a lack of skills for participation or insufficient information about the problem.

The administrator also needs to make sure that those involved understand the reason they are being involved and the purpose, authority, and scope of their participation. Involvement of others tends to run into difficulty when there has not been agreement on the purpose, scope, and authority of that involvement.

The administrator may wish to embark on a strategic planning approach that measures the impact of the decision choices on organizational purposes and performance. This technique of decision analysis is frequently used by administrators and planners to determine the lowest practical level to which a class of decisions should be delegated. Various classes or types of decisions and factors determining the strategic value of the decision category and the impact in measurable, weighted criteria are the major elements of this technique.

Dougherty discusses some of the factors that may need to be considered when making a particular decision pertaining to a specific goal or method, such as involving others in decision making: (1) *Futurity* refers to the length of time after the decision is made before an evaluation of the decision outcome can be made; (2) *reversibility* is the ease with which a decision can be reversed; (3) *scope* means the extent of the organization affected by the decision; (4) *human impact* indicates the degree of the impact on the people affected by the decision; and (5) *frequency* refers to how often the decision would normally be made. The strategic value of each decision category is then numerically calculated. Decision analysis can also be utilized to determine the maximum level of involvement feasible. Any number of criteria can be used to make this determination, including "facts available," "competence," "advice available," and "present" or "proposed levels of decision making."[81]

Finally, if the administrator is involving others on a committee whose decision will be only advisory to the administrator, then this needs to be made clear to the committee at the outset. The administrator also needs to provide rewards to those involved throughout the decision-making process to keep their spirits up and to show appreciation for their efforts. The time, effort, and contributions of the participants in the decision-making process should not be taken for granted by the administrator if a high level of sustained performance is desired.

ASSESSING DECISION-MAKING EFFECTIVENESS

If school administrators are to improve as decision makers, they will need to devote time to assessing the effectiveness of the process they followed in making decisions and the quality of the outcomes of those decisions. Such assessment is a challenging task for a variety of reasons. Most school administrators are busy people, and unless a high priority is given to assessing the effectiveness of decision making, the assessment task is not likely to be accomplished. Also, it is difficult for most decision makers to remain objective about their decisions. After all, once an administrator makes a decision, there is naturally an inclination to have a vested interest in the appearance, if not the reality, of effectiveness. (Involving others in the assessment who do not have that vested interest could increase the objectivity of the evaluation.) An assessment of the decision's effectiveness may threaten to reflect negatively on the administrator. Perhaps the most serious obstacle to the school administrator's self-assessment of decision-making effectiveness is the fact that, unless a decision results in significantly negative consequences, there is seldom any pressure from superiors or anyone else for the administrator to evaluate a decision's effectiveness. Nor are there incentives or rewards for evaluating whether a better decision could have been made.

Despite these difficulties, it is important for the school administrator to assess periodically the effectiveness of decision making if improvement is to continue in this area. Experience in making decisions is not, in itself, a sufficient basis for improvement without reflection upon and assessment of that experience. The checklist presented in Figure 2.3 is proposed for assessing the effectiveness of the decision-making process.[82]

We realize that administrators will not have the time or the need to assess the effectiveness of every choice. If they are to continue to improve decision-making skills, however, periodic assessment of the process and quality of their decisions will be essential and–in the case of decisions with negative consequences–*imperative.*

FIGURE 2.3
CHECKLIST FOR ASSESSING DECISION-MAKING EFFECTIVENESS

	Check one response for each question		
	Yes	No	Uncertain
1. Did you sufficiently investigate the nature of the problem or situation (including causes) that required a decision?	____	____	____
a. Did certain facts later surface that you should have ascertained at the outset?	____	____	____
b. Could facts, if known earlier in the decision-making process, have improved the quality of the final decision?	____	____	____
c. Are there additional questions you could have or should have asked when the situation first presented itself that could have provided information leading to a better decision?	____	____	____
d. Do you have a good reason for not asking those questions?	____	____	____
2. Did you try to identify more than one or two alternative courses of action to resolving a situation?	____	____	____
a. Did you assume without much thought that only one or two alternatives existed and select the first one that "looked good"?	____	____	____
b. Reflecting upon the decision process you followed and thinking about the consequences of the decision you made, can you see that there may have been another alternative course of action that might have better resolved the situation or problem?	____	____	____
c. Do you know why the alternative course of action wasn't considered at the time?	____	____	____

■ **FIGURE 2.3** *Continued*

	Check one response for each question		
	Yes	No	Uncertain
3. Did you adequately assess the advantages and disadvantages of the alternatives you considered before making a final decision?	_____	_____	_____
a. Did certain unanticipated consequences develop that adversely affected the consequences of the final decision?	_____	_____	_____
b. Were there problems that occurred that you did not adequately anticipate in choosing the course of action you did?	_____	_____	_____
c. Do you understand now why you didn't sufficiently identify or anticipate those problems?	_____	_____	_____
4. Did you involve to an appropriate extent those individuals and/or groups who could have contributed to an effective decision?	_____	_____	_____
a. Were there people whom you should have involved and whom you would involve if you had to do it over again?	_____	_____	_____
b. Were there people whom you did involve in the decision-making process whom you wouldn't involve if you had to do it over again?	_____	_____	_____
c. Have you analyzed how you would have changed the ways in which you involved other people in the decision-making process?	_____	_____	_____
5. Did the decision generate resistance?	_____	_____	_____
a. Could that resistance have been anticipated, and steps taken to prevent or reduce it? (Resistance does not automatically mean that the decision was a poor one, but it does have implications for the implementation of the decision, and it may mean that there was room for improvement in the process you followed.)	_____	_____	_____

Continued

FIGURE 2.3 *Concluded*

	Yes	No	Uncertain
b. Has the decision been fully implemented by the people who were supposed to implement it?	____	____	____
c. If the decision has not been fully implemented, do you understand why not?	____	____	____
d. Are there certain steps you could have taken (or still could take) to improve implementation?	____	____	____
6. Were the objectives that the decision was intended to achieve accomplished?	____	____	____

(Check one response for each question)

A FINAL NOTE

Having a process that allows you to habitualize decision making allows you to maximize your mental efforts when unexpectedly called upon.[83] Effective decision making is a complex process requiring considerable analysis and thought by the administrator. It does not occur in a vacuum but is influenced by situational constraints and the personal values and expertise of the individual making the decision. The process and product of decision making can frequently be improved by the involvement of others, although certain conditions must be met before that involvement will be helpful. Although decision making may be the most important administrative process, its effectiveness will depend to a large degree on the understanding and skill with which the administrator utilizes the other administrative practices presented in the following chapters.

Most of the case studies, suggested learning activities, and simulations presented in Part II of the text require the appropriate application of the ideas formed in this chapter on decision making. The following exercises, however, should provide the best opportunities for testing your understanding and effective use of decision-making concepts: Cases 19, 20, 21, 24, 34, 64, 66, 67, and the in-basket exercises.

NOTES

1. Herbert A. Simon, *The New Science of Management Decisions* (New York: Harper & Row, 1960); and W. Jack Duncan, *Great Ideas in Management* (San Francisco: Jossey-Bass, 1989), p. 69.
2. The major source of insight for the conceptual framework of decision making is found in an excellent article by Suzanne Estler, "Decision Making," in Norman J. Boyan (Ed.), *Handbook of Research on Educational Administration* (New York: Longman, 1988), pp. 305–319.
3. Richard Draft, *Organizational Theory and Design* (San Francisco: West, 1986), pp. 348–349. For classic treatment of rational decision making and problem solving, see Charles H. Kepner

and Benjamin B. Tregore, *The Rational Manager* (New York: McGraw-Hill, 1976).

4. Max Weber, *The Theory of Social and Economic Organization* (Oxford, England), A. M. Henderson and T. Parsons, Trans. (Oxford University Press, 1947). Also see Frederick W. Taylor, *The Principles of Scientific Management* (New York: Harper Bros., 1911).
5. Karen S. Cook and Margaret Levi (Eds.), *The Limit of Rationality* (Chicago: University of Chicago Press, 1990).
6. For example, see Jon Saphier, Tom Bigda-Peyton, and Geoff Pierson, *How to Make Decisions That Stay Made* (Alexandria, VA: Association for Supervision and Curriculum Development, 1989).
7. For example, see Henry Mintzberg, *The Nature of Managerial Work* (New York: Harper & Row, 1973); H. Fraser and M. Anderson, "Administrative Decision Making and Quasi Decision Making: An Empirical Study Using the Protocol Method," *Planning and Changing* (Winter 1983), pp. 204–213; Ray Cross, "A Description of Decision-Making Patterns of School Principals," *Journal of Educational Research* (January–February 1980), pp. 154–159; and Paul C. Nutt, "Types of Organizational Decision Processes," *Administrative Science Quarterly* (September 1984), pp. 414–450. For further discussion, see J. G. March, "Emerging Developments in the Study of Organizations," *The Review of Higher Education* (1982), pp. 1–18; J. M. Meyer and B. Rowan, "The Structure of Educational Organizations," in J. W. Meyer (Ed.), *Environments and Organizations* (San Francisco: Jossey-Bass, 1978).
8. A. Wise, "Why Educational Policies Often Fail: The Hyperrationalization Hypothesis," in J. V. Baldridge and T. Deal (Eds.), *The Dynamics of Organizational Change in Education* (Berkeley, CA: McCutchan, 1983), pp. 9–113.
9. This label was originally coined by C. E. Lindblom, in "The Science of 'Muddling Through,'" *Public Administration Review* (Spring 1959), pp. 79–88.
10. N. Gross, "The Scientific Approach to Administration," in D. E. Griffiths (Ed.), *Behavioral Science and Educational Administration. The 63rd Yearbook of the National Society for the Study of Education* (Chicago: University of Chicago Press, 1964), part 2, pp. 33–72. See also Pauline Graham (Ed.), *Mary Parker Follett: Prophet of Management* (Cambridge, MA: Harvard Business School Press Classic, 1994).
11. Bill Thorton and T. C. Mattocks, "The Implementation of TQM: Procedures and Pitfalls for Small Schools," *The AASA Professor* (vol. 22, no. 4, Summer 1999); Accessed online, http://www.aasa.org/TAP/summer99thornton.htm, October 14, 2000. See also W. Edwards Deming, *Out of the Crisis* (Cambridge, MA: MIT Center for Advanced Engineering Study, 1986); and George J. Michel et al., "What Are the Principal's Skills in School Communications?" Paper presented at the meeting of the Management Institute, Hilton Head, SC, February 1995, pp. 17-21, an ERIC report, Ed. 383084.
12. Herbert A. Simon, *Administrative Behavior,* 3rd ed. (New York: Harper & Row, 1976). Simon's original work on this topic was published in the first edition of this book in 1947; James G. March, "Decision Making Perspectives," in Andrew H. Van de Ven and William F. Joyce (Eds.), *Perspectives on Organizational Behavior* (New York: John Wiley, 1981), pp. 205–245; Rudi K. Bresser and Ronald C. Bishop, "Dysfunctional Effects of Formal Planning: Two Theoretical Explanations," *Academy of Management Review* (October 1983), pp. 588–599; Donald A. Schon, *The Reflective Practitioner: How Professionals Think in Action* (New York: Basic Books, 1984); and M. M. Kennedy, "How Evidence Alters Understanding and Decision," *Educational Evaluation and Policy Analysis* (1984), pp. 207–226. Also see Warren J. Pelson et al., *Tough Choices: The Decision-Making Styles of America's Top 50 CEO's* (Homewood, IL: Dow Jones–Irwin, 1989).
13. William A. Firestone and Bruce L. Wilson, "Using Bureaucratic and Cultural Linkages to Improve Instruction: The Principal's Contribution," *Educational Administration Quarterly* (1985), pp. 7–30.
14. Scott Page, *The Difference: How the Power of Diversity Creates Better Groups, Firms, Schools, and Societies* (Princeton, NJ: Princeton University Press, 2007).

15. D. L. Duke, B. K. Showers, and M. Imber, "Teachers and Shared Decision Making: The Costs and Benefits of Involvement," *Educational Administration Quarterly* (1980), pp. 93–106; W. K. Hoy and C. G. Miskel, *Educational Administration: Theory, Research and Practice,* 2nd ed. (New York: Random House, 1982); and Colin Eden and Jim Radford (Eds.), *Tackling Strategic Problems: The Role of Group Decision Support* (Newbury Park, CA: Sage, 1990).

16. Jeanette Ann Straus, "The Impact of Total Quality Management on Student Achievement and School Improvements Team Performance in an Urban Elementary Setting," PhD dissertation, Old Dominion University, 1996.

17. Linda Jean Holman, "Should Site-Based Committees Be Involved in the Campus Staffing Process?" *NASSP Bulletin* (March 1995), p. 65.

18. M. Gittell, *Limits to Citizen Participation: The Decline of Community Organization* (Beverly Hills, CA: Sage, 1980); and F. M. Wirt and M. W. Kirst, *Schools in Conflict* (Berkeley, CA: McCutchan, 1982).

19. For a more in-depth discussion pertaining to this point of view in the private sector, see Tom Peters, *Thriving on Chaos: Handbook for a Management Revolution* (New York: Knopf, 1987); and Suzanne Estler's article, "Decision Making," cited in note 2, focusing on educational administration. Both works provide novel insights into alternate views of decision making and perspectives on leadership and administration in modern organizations.

20. Estler, "Decision Making," pp. 311–317.

21. Michael D. Cohen, James G. March, and John A. Olson, "A Garbage Can Model of Organization Choice," *Administrative Science Quarterly* (March 1972), pp. 1–25.

22. Estler, "Decision Making," p. 317.

23. James Lipham and Marvin L. Fruth, *The Principal and Individually Guided Education* (Reading, MA: Addison-Wesley, 1976), p. 2.

24. Paula A. White, "An Overview of School-Based Management: What Does the Research Say," *National Association of Secondary School Administrators Bulletin* (September 1989); Jerry J. Herman, "A Vision for the Future: Site-Based Strategic Planning," *National Association of Secondary School Administrators Bulletin* (September 1989); and Sharon C. Conley, "Who's On First? School Reform, Teacher Participation, and the Decision Making Process," *Education and Urban Society* (August 1989), pp. 366–379.

25. Holman, "Should Site-Based Committees Be Involved in the Campus Staffing Process?" p. 65.

26. Daniel F. Griffiths, *Administrative Theory* (New York: Appleton-Century-Crofts, 1959), p. 73.

27. Peter J. Cistone, Joseph A. Fernandez, and Pat L. Tornillo Jr., "School-Based Management/Shared Decision Making in Dade County (Miami)," *Education and Urban Society* (August 1989), pp. 393–402.

28. Duncan, *Great Ideas in Management,* pp. 88–89.

29. Chester Barnard, *The Functions of the Executive* (Cambridge, MA: Harvard University Press, 1938), p. 194.

30. Fraser and Anderson, "Administrative Decision Making."

31. Donovan Peterson and Kathryn Peterson, "Decisiveness—How Important a Quality Is It for School Administrators?" *National Association of Secondary School Administrators Bulletin* (February 1982), pp. 1–9. For more information on decisiveness in decision making, see O. P. Kharbanda and E. A. Stallworthy, "Managerial Decision Making—Part I: Conventional Techniques," *Management Decision* (1990), pp. 4–9.

32. Further discussion of this process may be found in an excellent article by Roger Volkema, "Problem Formulation in Planning and Design," *Management Science* (June 1983), pp. 639–652. Also see Sara Kiesler and Lee Sproull, "Management Response to Changing Environments," *Administrative Science Quarterly* (December 1982), pp. 548–570.

33. Charles A. O'Reilly, "Variations in Decision Makers' Use of Information Sources: The Impact of Quality and Accessibility of Information," *Academy of Management Journal* (December 1982), pp. 756–771.

34. Ray Cross, "A Description of Decision Making Patterns of School Principals," paper presented at the meeting of the American Educational Research Association, New York, February 1971, pp. 14–15.

35. J. Richard Harrison and James G. March, "Decision Making and Postdecision Surprises," *Administrative Science Quarterly* (March 1984), pp. 26–42.

36. Anna Grandori, "A Prescriptive Contingency of Organizational Decision Making," *Administrative Science Quarterly* (June 1984), pp. 192–209. Also see Amitai Etzioni, "Normative-Affective Factors: Toward a New Decision-Making Model," *Journal of Economic Psychology* (June 1988), pp. 125–150.

37. For further discussion of this process and associated problems, see R. H. Beach, "Multiple Alternatives in Decision Making: Implications for Educational Planning and Administration," *Planning and Changing* (Summer 1984), pp. 106–113.

38. James M. Lipham et al., *The Principalship: Concepts, Competencies, and Cases* (New York: Longman, 1985), pp. 86–87.

39. James R. Meindl, "The Abundance of Solutions: Some Thoughts for Theoretical and Practical Solution Seekers," *Administrative Science Quarterly* (December 1982), pp. 670–685.

40. William J. Kritek, "Lessons from the Literature on Implementation," *Educational Administration Quarterly* (Fall 1976), pp. 86–102; and Michael Maccoby, *Why Work: Leading the New Generation* (New York: Simon and Schuster, 1988), Chap. 8.

41. Joseph F. Lagana, "Managing Change and School Improvement Effectively," *National Association of School Administrators Bulletin* (September 1989); and Marc Willinger, "Risk Aversion and the Value of Information," *Journal of Risk and Insurance* (June 1989).

42. Alan J. Rowe and Richard O. Mason, *Managing with Style* (San Francisco: Jossey-Bass, 1987).

43. Luther Gulick and L. Urwick (Eds.), *Papers on the Science of Administration* (New York: Columbia University Institute of Public Administration, 1937), p. 13. Also see L. Urwick, *The Golden Book of Management,* ed. Arthur P. Brief (New York: Garland Publishing, 1987).

44. Kenneth R. Andrews, "Ethics in Practice," *Harvard Business Review* (September-October, 1989).

45. Paul C. Nutt, *Making Tough Decisions* (New York: Jossey-Bass, 1989).

46. John J. Mauriel, *Strategic Leadership for Schools* (San Francisco: Jossey-Bass, 1989). For additional perspectives on strategic planning, see James M. Hardy, *Managing for Impact in Nonprofit Organizations* (Erwin, TN: Essex Press, 1984); and Ben Heirs, *The Professional Decision-Thinker* (New York: Dodd, Mead, 1987).

47. Also see Richard A. Gorton and Gail Thierbach-Schneider, *School Administration and Supervision: Leadership Challenges and Opportunities,* 3rd ed. (Dubuque, IA: Wm. C. Brown, 1991), pp. 102–110, 323.

48. For example, see John Hemphill et al., *Administrative Performance and Personality* (New York: Teachers College Press, 1962). For an empirical study on connections between personality types and biases, see Usha C. V. Haley and Stephen A. Stumpf, "Cognitive Trails in Strategic Decision-Making: Linking Theories of Personalities and Cognitions," *Journal of Management Studies* (September 1989), pp. 477–497.

49. James M. Lipham and James A. Hoeh Jr., *The Principalship: Foundations and Functions* (New York: Harper & Row, 1974), p. 158.

50. Roy Dexheimer, "The Ethics of Chief School Administrators: A Study in Accommodation," paper presented at the meeting of the American Association of School Administrators, Atlantic City, February 1969.

51. Robert Boyden Lamb, *Running American Business* (New York: Basic Books, 1987). The reader is also referred to an excellent review on this subject by Ralph Kimbrough, *Ethics: A Course of Study for Educational Leaders* (Arlington, VA: American Association of School Administrators, 1985), and to statements of ethics for school administrators developed by various national administrator associations. A copy of these may be obtained by writing to any of the national administrator organizations, such as the National Association of Elementary School Principals, 1625 Duke St., Alexandria, VA 22314, or the National Association of Secondary School Principals, 1904 Association Dr., Reston, VA 22091. For examples of business ethics, see William R. Wynd and John Mager, "The Business and Society Course: Does It Change Student Attitudes?" *Journal of Business Ethics*

(June 1989); Barry Castro, "Business Ethics and Business Education: A Report from a Regional State University," *Journal of Business Ethics* (June 1989); and Jeffrey Gandz and Frederick G. Bird, "Designing Ethical Organizations," *Business Quarterly* (August 1989). For a guide on ethical considerations in managerial decision making, see Mary E. Guy, *Ethical Decision Making in Everyday Work Situations* (Westport, CA: Greenwood, 1990).

52. A. Lowin, "Participative Decision Making: A Model, Literature Critique, and Prescriptions for Research," *Organizational Behavior and Human Performance* (February 1968), pp. 68–106; and William R. Kind et al., *Management Science: A Decision-Support Approach* (Reading, MA: Addison-Wesley, 1990).
53. James A. Conway, "The Myth, Mystery, and Mastery of Participative Decision Making in Education," *Educational Administration Quarterly* (Summer 1984), pp. 11–40.
54. John Lindelow et al., "Participative Decision Making," in Stuart C. Smith et al. (Eds.), *School Leadership: Handbook for Survival* (Eugene, OR: Clearinghouse on Educational Management, 1981), pp. 153–155. Also see Ronald L. Cohen, "Procedural Justice and Participation," *Human Relations* (July 1985), pp. 643–663; and James M. Kouzes and Barry Z. Posner, *The Leadership Challenge: How to Get Extraordinary Things Done in Organizations* (San Francisco: Jossey-Bass, 1987), pp. 161–185.
55. D. L. Duke et al., "Teachers and Shared Decision Making: The Costs and Benefits of Involvement," *Educational Administration Quarterly* (Winter 1980), pp. 93–106.
56. C. J. Lammers, "Power and Participation in Decision Making in Formal Organizations," *American Journal of Sociology* (September 1967), pp. 201–216. Also see Fred C. Lunenburg and Allan C. Orstein, *Educational Administration* (Belmont, CA: Wadsworth, 1991), pp. 174–176.
57. Jane L. David, "The Who, What, and Why of Site-Based Management," *Educational Leadership* (December 1995–January 1996), p. 7.
58. F. C. Tunde Palmer, "The Relationship Between Dogmatism, Autonomy, Administrative Style, and Decision Making of Practicing and Aspiring School Principals," PhD dissertation, University of Toronto, 1974, p. 177.
59. Edwin M. Bridges, "A Model for Shared Decision Making in the School Principalship," *Educational Administration Quarterly* (Winter 1967), pp. 49–61. For some additional guidelines for involving others in decision making, see Victor A. Vroom, "A New Look at Managerial Decision Making," *Organizational Dynamics* (Spring 1973), p. 67.
60. J. A. Belasco and J. A. Alluto, "Decision Participation and Teacher Satisfaction," *Educational Administration Quarterly* (Winter 1972), pp. 44–58; and Andrew E. Schwartz and Joy Levin, "Better Group Decision Making," *Supervisory Management* (June 1990), p. 4.
61. David, Jane L. "The Who, What, and Why of Site-Based Management," vol. 53, no. 4, December 1995, 4–9.
62. Ibid.
63. S. R. Hinckley Jr., "A Closer Look at Participation," *Organizational Dynamics* (Winter 1985), pp. 57–67.
64. Bridges, "Shared Decision Making," p. 52.
65. Robert Tannenbaum and Warren H. Schmidt, "How to Choose a Leadership Pattern," *Harvard Business Review,* no. 36 (March–April 1958), pp. 95–101.
66. Richard A. Gorton, "Factors Which Are Associated with the Principal's Behavior in Encouraging Teacher Participation in School Decision Making," *Journal of Educational Research* (March 1971), pp. 325–327. See also Richard P. DuFour, "Help Wanted: Principals Who Can Lead Professional Learning Communities," *NASSP Bulletin* (February 1999), pp. 12–17.
67. To keep up to date on developments with this approach, see *Quality Circle Journal,* found in many university libraries.
68. David Hawley, "The Quality Circle Concept," *Principal* (November 1985), pp. 41–43.
69. Frank Satterfield, *Managing Quality Circles Effectively,* an ERIC report, Ed. 238117.
70. S. A. Zahra et al., "Quality Circles for School Districts," *The Educational Forum* (Spring 1985), pp. 323–330.
71. Robert H. Black, Larry K. Michaelsen, and Warren E. Watson, "A Realistic Test of Individual

versus Group Consensus Decision Making," *Journal of Applied Psychology* (October 1989).

72. D. E. Halverson, *An Effective Time and Management Strategy in Quality Circles,* an ERIC report, Ed. 238113.
73. Mary Bacon, *Team Building in Quality Circles,* an ERIC report, Ed. 238118.
74. Kenneth H. Price, "Problem Solving Strategies: A Comparison by Solving Phases," *Group and Organizational Studies* (September 1985), pp. 278–299.
75. Richard Gorton is indebted to the authors of the following publication for their ideas on the Delphi technique and the nominal group technique: Andre L. Delberg, Andrew H. Van de Ven, and David H. Gustafson, *Group Techniques for Program Planning: A Guide to Nominal Group and Delphi Processes* (Middleton, WI: Greenbriar, 1986).
76. For research on its effectiveness, see Robert E. Erffmeyer and Irving M. Lane, "Quality and Acceptance of an Evaluative Task: The Effects of Four Group Decision Making Formats," *Group and Organizational Studies* (December 1984), pp. 509–529.
77. *ETA Evaluation Briefs,* "Gaining Consensus Among Stakeholders Through the Nominal Group Technique" (November 2006), pp, 1-2. Retrieved from http://www.cdc.gov/HealthyYouth/evaluation/pdf/brief7.pdf
78. Jean M. Bartunsk and J. Kenneth Murningham, "The Nominal Group Technique," *Group and Organizational Studies* (September 1984), pp. 417–432.
79. For further discussion of additional ways of involving others in decision making, see I. Adizes and E. Turban, "An Innovative Approach to Group Decision Making," *Personnel* (April 1985), pp. 45–59; and Richard A. Schmuck and Philip J. Runkel, *The Handbook of Organizational Development in Schools,* 3rd ed. (Prospect Heights, IL: Waveland Publishing, 1988), pp. 240–292.
80. Beverly Geber, "Decisions, Decisions," *Training* (April 1988).
81. For a more detailed discussion of the technique of decision analysis, see David C. Dougherty, *Strategic Organization Planning: Downsizing for Survival* (New York: Quorum Books, 1989); Geoffrey Gregory, *Decision Analysis* (New York: Plenum Press, 1988); and Richard M. Oliver and John A. Smith (Eds.), *Influence Diagrams, Belief Nets, and Decision Analysis* (New York: John Wiley, 1990).
82. Stuart L. Hart, "Toward Quality Criteria for Collective Judgments," *Organizational Behavior and Human Decision Processes* (October 1985), pp. 209–228; and Wayne K. Hoy and Cecil G. Miskel, *Educational Administration: Theory, Research and Practice,* 6th ed. (New York: McGraw-Hill, 2000).
83. 21st Century Decision-Making. Accessed at www.chaosadvantage.com/21st-century-decision-making/, n.d.

CHAPTER

3

Authority, Power, and Influence

APPLICABLE PSEL STANDARDS

- **STANDARD 1:** **Mission, Vision, and Core Values**
  Effective educational leaders develop, advocate, and enact a shared mission, vision, and core values of high-quality education and academic success and well-being of each student.
- **STANDARD 2:** **Ethics and Professional Norms**
  Effective educational leaders act ethically and according to professional norms to promote each student's academic success and well-being.
- **STANDARD 3:** **Equity and Cultural Responsiveness**
  Effective educational leaders strive for equity of educational opportunity and culturally responsive practices to promote each student's academic success and well-being.
- **STANDARD 4:** **Curriculum, Instruction, and Assessment**
  Effective educational leaders develop and support intellectually rigorous and coherent systems of curriculum, instruction, and assessment to promote each student's academic success and well-being.
- **STANDARD 5:** **Community of Care and Support for Students**
  Effective educational leaders cultivate an inclusive, caring, and supportive school community that promotes the academic success and well-being of each student.
- **STANDARD 7:** **Professional Community for Teachers and Staff**
  Effective educational leaders foster a professional community of teachers and other professional staff to promote each student's academic success and well-being.
- **STANDARD 9:** **Operations and Management**
  Effective educational leaders manage school operations and resources to promote each student's academic success and well-being.

National Policy Board for Educational Administration (NPBEA). *Professional Standards for Educational Leaders* (Reston, VA: Author, 2015). Used with Permission.

Any administrator engaged in making decisions, mediating conflict, introducing change, supervising teachers, or any other administrative task or activity should have a reasonable basis for action rather than behaving idiosyncratically or capriciously. In a bureaucratic organization, such as a school district, that basis is typically called authority.[1] *Authority* can be defined as "a right granted to a manager to make decisions within limitations, to assign duties to subordinates, and to require subordinates' conformance to expected behavior."[2] It is the authorization to get things done or accomplished.[3] Authority is, therefore, *power-conferred,* allowing an administrator the right to "decide, direct, or control."[4]

WHAT LEGITIMATES AUTHORITY?

There are several possible, reasonable bases for an administrator's authority in a particular situation.[5] First, authority may come from "higher up." It may be derived from a governing board or a superior within the organization. This type of authority is generally referred to as *legal authority.* Second, authority may come from tradition. An administrator may possess authority in a particular situation simply because administrators have traditionally possessed authority in such situations. Thus people continue to recognize that tradition by accepting the administrator's attempts to exercise authority.[6] According to data from one major study of education, "most teachers do what their principals ask of them because they feel that their principals have a legitimate right to make demands."[7] Third, authority may be earned or perceived as being deserved. In other words, an administrator may be able to exercise authority successfully because people respect the person or the position. Therefore, they are willing to allow their behavior to be directed by a particular person whom they hold in high esteem and consider worthy of their trust, irrespective of how they judge the merits of the directives.[8]

However, because an administrator's authority is usually believed by school boards to be either inherent in the position or associated with the assigned responsibilities, some of the specific elements and scope of that authority may not always be defined.[9] This lack of specificity can sometimes cause problems, especially if the administrator is not supported by superiors or if those under his or her authority resist. As long as superiors back the administrator, however, and as long as the people who respond to the administrator's exercise of authority *believe* it is the administrator's right to exercise it, either because of the position in the organization or for some other reason, no serious problems may occur. This is true, despite the fact that the nature and limits of the authority may have never been fully defined.

TWO COMPETING BASES OF AUTHORITY

Cooper addresses the myths that currently operate in regard to the premises underlying assumptions about where authority for school reform resides.[10] He argues that in educational settings, there are two separate–even competing–bases of authority.

Administrators base their authority on their status in their organizational hierarchy, be it as principals, central office supervisors, or district superintendents. Their expertise is derived from their position in the hierarchy and their specialized knowledge of school system operations and management.

Teachers base their authority on their knowledge of the subject matter and on their expertise in pedagogy as it relates to their students. Superintendents speak generally about curriculum reform measures, whereas teachers can explain how a particular objective worked with a special group of students. Teachers believe that they have authority and control over children and classrooms, whereas administrators believe that all the authority and control emanates from them, that is, top-down control. Unfortunately, these assumptions or beliefs can constrain genuine calls for reform from parents and the community because teachers and school leaders each believe they have proper authority. These myths impair innovations initiated by top leadership because teachers are not part of the process.

Ogawa and Bossert assert that the "medium" and the "currency" of leadership lie in the personal resources of people.[11] This can be true of teachers as well as administrators. The more resources people have and the kinds of resources they possess or have access to can give them greater power. On the basis of their review of studies on power, Fuqua, Payne, and Cangemi conclude that "the currency of leadership, essential to influencing others, involves a wide variety of factors." Eight such factors are listed by these authors: *support systems* (participation in networking opportunities), *information* (knowing where to find information and obtain it quickly, which encourages the practice of good listening), *credibility* (attaining respect and trust through demonstrated abilities and trustworthiness), *visibility* (being noticed as one who takes on difficult tasks and works hard at them), *legitimacy* (being recognized and commended by respected persons in positions of power), *persuasiveness* (effectiveness in winning others over to one's viewpoints through one's confidence, personality, and appeals to reason and emotions), *charisma* (a combination of qualities that add up to a personal dynamism or aura that draws others), and *agenda setting* (in the words of Fuqua et al., "knowing when meetings will be held and accessing the group leader to put items on the agenda at just the right time").[12]

Leadership shapes the systems that produce the patterns of interaction and the meanings that other participants attach to organizational events. As principals fulfill their roles, their ability to influence the organization without dictating their authority affects the productivity of the organization. Whereas authoritarian leaders, intent upon control, undermine the efficiency of an organization, those leaders who work from an inclusion perspective find themselves supported by their personnel. This, consequently, enhances the entire organizational structure. Fuqua and his associates refer to Kanter's studies of corporations and her findings that those leaders who relied more on their personal power than on their job title or credentials were the leaders most able to mobilize resources, instill confidence, motivate those under their authority, and encourage their creativity.[13]

A reorientation and a rethinking of the current paradigm of authority and of who controls what in our schools must occur before any meaningful reform measures can be jointly implemented by teachers and administrators, as well as by the community. This reorientation issue means that an administrator, especially one new to a school or school district, should give high priority to the identification and understanding of sources that grant and limit authority.

SOURCES THAT GRANT AND LIMIT AUTHORITY

As the previous discussion makes clear, the administrator's authority may be derived from more than one source. An important step, then, for any administrator is to ascertain the specific nature and extent of the authority to carry out the responsibilities and to take action when needed. Figure 3.1 identifies a number of possible sources that may, formally or informally, grant an administrator the authority to act and that may also place formal or

FIGURE 3.1
POSSIBLE SOURCES THAT GRANT AND LIMIT ADMINISTRATOR AUTHORITY

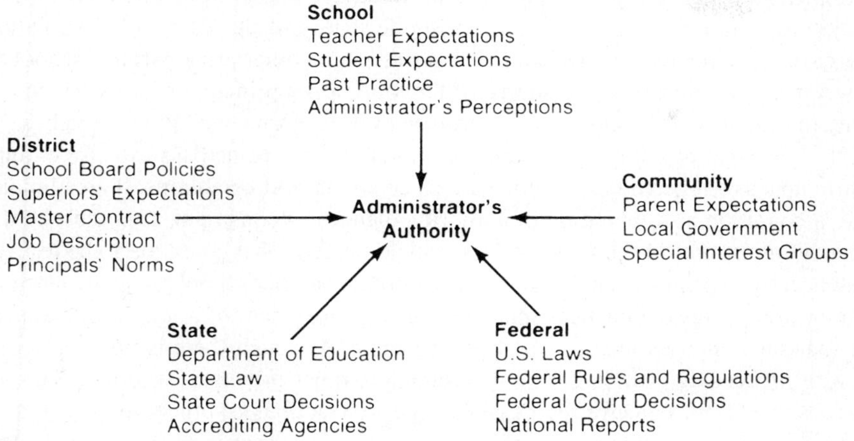

informal limitations on the administrator's prerogatives to exercise authority. In other words, each of the sources identified in Figure 3.1 can potentially serve a dual function, that is, to grant authority and to restrict authority. Authority once granted is not always permanent. Zirkel and Gluckman remind administrators that in a time of downsizing, middle managers' jobs are at risk. In school systems, the middle managers are the principals and assistant principals. Members of both groups can quickly find themselves stripped of authority as they are moved from an administrative role to a teaching reassignment.[14]

A school administrator can usually determine, for the most part, the specific nature and extent of authority by examining the job description, the school board policies, and the district's master contract.[15] The prerogatives to exercise authority may also be broadened or limited, however, by the superior's expectations,[16] state law and regulations, federal court decisions, and a number of other elements that are identified in Figure 3.1. For example, the same superintendent who grants a certain type of authority can also take it away or restrict it in some manner. The same faculty members who, through their expectations, informally grant their principal the authority to take certain actions can change those expectations and remove their support.[17]

Although the number of *potential* sources of limitations presented in Figure 3.1 is large and may seem overwhelming to some readers, an administrator's initial response should be to investigate policies, regulations, expectations, and conditions in the principal's own school situation rather than *assuming* a certain pattern of limitations. (For further discussion of reference group expectations, see Gorton and Thierbach-Schneider.)[18] Some of the potential sources of limitations identified in Figure 3.1 may not be actual constraints in a particular school district.

For example, under "District" in Figure 3.1, "Principals' Norms" are listed as a possible source of limitation to the exercise of authority. Although rarely discussed in the professional literature, a principal's peers in the school district can develop norms that may limit to some extent what a principal can do in school.[19] These peer norms can be especially powerful in influencing the behavior of a new or "outer-directed" principal.[20] It is not inevitable that a new principal will find the norms of peers limiting the exercise of authority in the school. In many school districts the norms of the principals are not well developed, nor is there much evidence that sanctions would be imposed by other principals unless the behavior in question was extreme. Some beginning principals have been assisted in gaining an understanding of peer norms, job expectations, and clarification of subtle signs and signals by implementation of a "buddy system" or mentoring program.[21] The norms of the other principals in a school district do, however, constitute a *potential* source of limitation on a principal who wishes to exercise authority in school, and therefore the importance of these norms needs to be weighed.

Another example of a potential source of limitation on a principal's exercise of authority is the principal's own perception of policies, expectations, and conditions. If an administrator *perceives* a condition as a limitation of authority, then it is a constraint, regardless of whether any other administrator in the same situation would perceive that condition to be restrictive.[22] For instance, some principals who assume a position at another school are reluctant to change any school procedures or practices that have been in existence for a long time because they believe that such changes might upset certain people. Although there is nothing necessarily wrong with proceeding cautiously in a new situation, other principals who face the same circumstances would not perceive the possible negative reactions of others to change as a constraint on their authority. If they were convinced of the need for change, these principals would take whatever steps were necessary to bring about the change. The latter group of principals is not necessarily exercising authority effectively; it is simply that this group does not perceive the same conditions as a constraint to the exercise of authority as does the first group of principals in our example.

A school administrator should not be intimidated or immobilized by the possibility of constraints on existing authority. The wise administrator, however, will make few assumptions about having authority to act, and will carefully and objectively examine the situation to determine the limits and the strengths of the various sources of authority. The administrator will also be constantly aware of a characteristic of formal authority that Blau and Scott have perceptively observed, namely, that formal authority only "promotes compliance with directives and discipline, but does not encourage employees to exert effort, to accept responsibilities, or to exercise initiative."[23]

FACTORS TO CONSIDER IN EXERCISING AUTHORITY

School administrators exercise authority in a variety of ways. For example, they make decisions, promulgate rules and regulations, interpret policies, and issue directives. The purpose of exercising authority should be to bring about some desired response from others. The ideal outcome would be the acceptance of the administrator's right to exercise authority, along with willing cooperation in carrying out the administrator's expectations. Although this ideal is frequently recognized in school administration, it is not always achieved.

Simon has suggested, based on earlier work by Barnard, that subordinates' characterization of the administrator's exercise of authority can range from "clearly unacceptable" to "unquestionably acceptable," with several degrees of variation in between.[24] (Wilkes and Blackbourn have devised a useful instrument for measuring the degree of acceptability of various kinds of administrative directives to teachers.)[25] Whether or not people will find the administrator's directives acceptable would appear to depend on a number of factors, including the personality of the administrator and the way the authority was exercised, as well as the personality and needs of the recipients of the directive.[26] For example, research found that teachers were more likely to accept the directives of the principal when the administrator was perceived as strong in the leadership dimensions of both consideration and initiating structure.[27]

Negative Reactions

Most administrators at one time or another will encounter unavoidable negative reactions when they attempt to exercise authority. In order for administrators to address negative responses effectively, they must first recognize that such responses may take a variety of forms. In Peabody's study of an elementary school faculty, nine different types of negative responses were identified that could result when administrative authority is perceived as unreasonable.[28]

1. The teachers may consciously question the order but accept it as binding.
2. The teachers may inform the administrator of their views and seek to be converted to the administrator's point of view while complying with the order.
3. The teachers may discuss the situation with the administrator and try to work for change while complying with the order.
4. The teachers may attempt to gain support for their contrary views by appealing to coworkers.
5. The teachers may go around their superior and try to gain the support of those above in the hierarchy or people from the outside.
6. The teachers may discuss the order, but ignore, evade, or try to modify it while seeming to comply.
7. The teachers may ignore, evade, or try to modify the order without discussing it.
8. The teachers may openly reject the order.
9. The teachers may transfer or resign.

The type of negative reaction that teachers display toward the exercise of administrative authority would undoubtedly depend on many situational factors. In most circumstances, subordinates are unlikely to reject openly the exercise of administrative authority or resign because of it, unless the authority has been exercised in an extremely arbitrary or capricious manner. Staff members may react to what they perceive as the unreasonable exercise of authority by responding in one or more of the first seven ways identified in Peabody's study.

Responding to Negative Reactions to Authority

When encountering a negative reaction to the exercise of authority, an administrator should first attempt to diagnose the reasons why it is occurring. This approach may not be the initial predisposition of many administrators when they encounter a negative reaction to the exercise of their authority.[29] Instead, they may become upset or defensive and try to *impose* their authority on those reacting negatively. An administrator who attempts the latter may believe the power exists to impose authority, but, as discussion in the next section will make clear, an administrator's power is limited and should always be verified before it is used. Although to some extent these emotions are normal and understandable, the thoughtful administrator will quickly gain control over such tendencies and will try to avoid doing anything that might exacerbate the situation. The administrator should also try to understand the reasons for a negative response to authority in order to be in a more knowledgeable position to take appropriate steps.

Also, it needs to be emphasized that the questioning or challenging of authority is not necessarily bad and can be instructive if its causes are understood. Although organizations (especially large bureaucracies) seldom encourage dissent and frequently do not tolerate it, a negative reaction to the exercise of authority may signal the inappropriate use or understanding of that authority.[30] Teachers, one of the groups that will be a recipient of the administrator's authority, frequently do not consider themselves to be subordinates or employees working for a superior, but as professionals whose expertise and autonomy must be respected.[31]

Diagnosing the Problem through Discussion

The key for an administrator who encounters a negative response to authority is to try to diagnose the causes of the reaction by first conferring with the parties involved. The initial inquiry should be along the line that "perhaps there has been a misunderstanding." An effort should be made to avoid putting the other party on the defensive, and an attempt should be made to understand the other person's frame of reference before explaining the administrator's own position. In this kind of a situation, the use of concepts from "The Administrator as a Recipient of Communication" in Chapter 4, along with concepts from Chapter 5, "Conflict Management," will be very important.

Examining How Authority Is Exercised

If a negative reaction to the exercise of authority persists, the administrator will then need to make a judgment about whether the authority was appropriately exercised. Boucher offers administrators the following suggestions for giving criticism in a way that motivates others to do a better job: (1) See yourself as helping someone improve–you are now a teacher or coach, (2) express sincere concern as you share ways for this individual to be more successful, (3) choose the right moment to offer criticism, (4) drop the word "should" from this conversation ("shoulds" make you appear pedantic and rigid), (5) make a conscious effort to avoid appearing that you are more interested in achieving compliance than in helping the other person improve, (6) discuss how the person will grow and benefit from following the suggestions you are making, (7) be specific–vagueness creates anxiety and doubt, which often makes the situation worse, and (8) be prepared to receive criticism yourself–you'll be perceived as a credible source.[32]

Dealing with Insubordination

Before judging whether authority was aptly exercised, the administrator may want to consult with superiors, as well as examine school board policies, the master contract, and any other sources that are used as a basis for exercising authority. If the basis for the administrator's exercise of authority is sound and if the original objective sought is still desirable *and* attainable, the administrator should insist that the authority of the administrator be obeyed.[33] No administrator should permit the reasonable exercise of legitimate authority to be ignored, evaded, or rejected. Such responses to the exercise of legitimate authority represent possible insubordination and, if permitted, could weaken the authority base of an administrator and could lead to more widespread noncompliance.

The administrator should keep written, dated documentation of the initial negative reaction to the exercise of authority and of all subsequent meetings, contacts, correspondence, and reactions between the administrator and others involved in the situation. An excellent monograph that provides further guidelines to preparing needed documentation has been published by the National Organization on Legal Problems of Education and is entitled *A Documentation System for Teacher Improvement or Termination.*[34]

Insubordination and its variants under applicable state employment laws defy exactitude and uniformity. Nevertheless, the odds tend to favor school districts as long as administrators resist knee-jerk reactions and document repeated efforts to be clear, reasonable, and diligent in their directives and the teacher's intentional noncompliance.[35]

Gaining Compliance from Resisters

The specific steps that an administrator should take to gain compliance from those who are resisting or evading the exercise of authority will undoubtedly vary according to the circumstances. When continued opposition is likely, given the results of an initial conference with the parties involved, the administrator will want to confer with superiors to obtain their ideas and support of certain courses of action. Also, the legality of proposed administrative actions and due process requirements need to be clearly understood and followed.

In most cases, unless the negative response to authority is extreme, it will be better for the administrator to begin insisting on compliance with authority gradually by conferring again with the parties involved. At this second meeting, the administrator should make sure that whoever is resisting or evading the directive fully understands the possible implications of such actions. Before the meeting is over, if the continued reaction of the other party is negative, then the administrator should explicitly state expectations. If the reaction continues to be negative, then the administrator should issue a written warning to the other party that disciplinary action will be taken if compliance is not forthcoming by a certain date. Before writing this letter, the administrator should consult with superiors and obtain legal guidance. At some point, stronger negative sanctions may need to be used, including recommended disciplinary measures or even dismissal of an employee if compliance cannot be obtained. While an administrator should want people to accept the administrator's legitimate authority and carry out the directives cooperatively, in the final analysis, when people are reacting negatively, there must be compliance.

Guidelines for Exercising Authority Successfully

There are no doubt numerous specific reasons why people question, challenge, or resist authority, some of which were discussed in Chapter 2, "Decision Making." Chester Barnard indicated in his analysis of the authority problem in organizations that a person *can* and *will* accept authority when four conditions prevail: when the individual understands the order, when there is the belief that the order is consistent with the perception of the purposes of the organization, when there is the belief that the order is in the individual's own personal interest, and when the individual is mentally and physically able to comply with the order.[36]

Based on Barnard's concept of the prerequisites for compliance with authority, it would appear that administrators should keep in mind the following guidelines in issuing directives or orders:

1. In deciding on the need for a directive and in its formulation, presentation, and execution, administrators should consider how the order will affect the recipients personally, recognizing that people are likely to question or resist directives that they feel are not in their best interest.
2. Administrators should consider the strengths and limitations of those who will be expected to implement a directive. They should avoid issuing orders for which people lack the necessary motivation, skill, or training to carry out.
3. They should explain thoroughly the rationale behind each directive and its relationship to the goals of the organization. They should not assume that people understand the reasons for an order or that people will necessarily see the logic or value of an order.
4. They should leave room for modifying the original order or its method of implementation. Flexibility and a willingness to compromise when appropriate are key factors in exercising administrative authority successfully.
5. They should issue only those directives they are relatively sure either will be obeyed or can be enforced if resisted. Orders that cannot be enforced in one situation weaken the administrator's authority for successfully issuing orders in other circumstances.

Although some administrators and supervisors may be reluctant to exercise authority, particularly in light of the human relations and empowerment emphasis in school administration and challenges by various groups to administrative authority, it should be clear that if the administrator is to perform assigned responsibilities effectively and work with others in the improvement of the organization and the achievement of its goals, it may be necessary to utilize authority. The use of authority is an inescapable aspect of an administrator's job. The important question, then, is not *whether* authority should be exercised, but *how* and *in what circumstances.* The preceding and the following discussion should be helpful to an administrator in answering that question.

ADMINISTRATIVE POWER

Although many administrators and even some theorists use the terms *authority* and *power* interchangeably, these concepts differ in both function and implications. The successful use of administrative authority is based first on the willingness of subordinates to comply with an administrator's expectations and second on the fact that the authority being exercised has been granted by one or more of the sources in Figure 3.1. When these two conditions are adequately met, an administrator does not need power. Power represents the "capacity or potential for effecting desired results in one or more persons that would not have otherwise occurred."[37] According to this definition, administrators possess *legitimate power* if they can get people to do what the administrators want them to do, even when people resist or refuse to accept authority in a certain situation.

Power as Securing Compliance versus Power as Empowerment

The traditional compliance model of power has been replaced with concepts of personal and collective empowerment. In regard to the latter, power is viewed as the ability to predict the consequences of one's actions in complex situations as well as the ability to maintain individual control over one's feelings and behaviors. The administrator or supervisor serves primarily as the catalyst or charismatic leader who prompts individuals to transform themselves at the same time they transform the social environment. Beaven suggests that more attention needs to be focused on those who actually change themselves; on their response to leader control; and on the phenomenon known as charismatic, transformational leadership.[38]

Types of Power

What types of power are available to an administrator? Several theorists have proposed somewhat useful paradigms to answer this question. For example, Etzioni advanced the proposition that there are three general kinds of power: (1) coercive power (e.g., suspending an employee), (2) remunerative power (e.g., control over resources), and (3) normative power (e.g., control over prestige).[39] Parsons has identified four types of power or influence, using the terms interchangeably: (1) persuasion, (2) inducement, (3) activation of commitment (e.g., use of negative sanctions to influence another person's intentions), and (4) deterrence (e.g., negative sanctions to control a situation).[40] Furthermore, French and Raven, in what is probably the most elaborate proposed model of power, have suggested five types of social power, the strengths of which they believe will be determined by certain conditions.[41]

1. *Reward power:* Capacity to provide rewards, such as higher salary or better assignment.

   Conditions

   a. The strength of the reward power of the administrator will increase with the magnitude of the rewards that the other person perceives can be obtained by the administrator.

   b. The strength of the reward power will depend on the actual rewards produced, not on what the administrator hopes or would like to produce.

   c. Unsuccessful attempts by the administrator to exert reward power will tend to decrease the perceived strengths of that power in the future.

2. *Coercive power:* Capacity to provide punishment or negative consequences, such as teacher dismissal.

   Conditions

   a. The strength of the administrator's coercive power will increase with the magnitude of the punishments or costs that the other person perceives the administrator can exercise.

   b. The strength of the coercive power will depend on the *actual* sanctions or costs that the administrator can apply, not just on hopes or possibilities.

   c. Unsuccessful attempts to exert coercive power will tend to decrease the perceived strength of that power in the future.

3. *Legitimate power:* Defined by French and Raven in a way very similar to the definition of *legitimate authority,* discussed earlier.

   Conditions

   a. The successful use of administrative power will depend on the willingness of subordinates to comply with the administrator's expectations.

   b. The power has been granted by one or more of the administrator's authority sources (school, district, state, federal, or community).

4. *Referent power:* The tendency of other individuals to be attracted by and to identify closely with the administrator, for example, the identification of teachers with the administrator.

   Conditions

   a. The greater the perceived attractiveness of the administrator by another person or group, the more likely the identification with the administrator.

   b. The stronger the actual identification with the administrator by another person, the greater the likelihood that reference power can be successfully used by the administrator.

5. *Expert power:* Special knowledge or skill, for example, supervision, scheduling, or group dynamics.

   Conditions

   a. The strength of the expert power of the administrator will vary with the actual knowledge and skill that the administrator possesses and with the perceived expertise of the administrator.

   b. The stronger the perception by others that the administrator possesses expert power, the higher the group's satisfaction and evaluation of the administrator as a leader.

Table 3.1 presents examples of the five types of social power identified by French and Raven.

Paul Hersey and Walter Natemeyer have developed a Power Perception Profile instrument to assess why someone responds to another's attempts to exercise power. They expanded French and Raven's five power types into seven, adding *connection power* based on the perception that the supervisor has relationships with influential people inside or outside the organization and *information* power based upon the leader's possession of or access to information perceived as valuable to others. This latter power base is important to others because they need this information or want to be "in on things."[42]

TABLE 3.1

Categories	*Examples*
Reward power	"I believe that you are interested in. . . . Perhaps we can work something out, but before we do, you need to. . . ."
Coercive power	"I find your behavior unacceptable, and if it doesn't change . . . , I will have no choice except to suspend you."
Legitimate power	"Consistent with my responsibilities as principal, I am assigning you. . . ."
Referent power	"You have believed in me in the past, and I am asking you to trust me now."
Expert power	"This is an area in which I have background and experience, and therefore. . . ."

Also, Buhler stresses the importance of recognizing that power is not unilateral but is generally shared and distributed. Teachers, for example, hold a great deal of potential power in the degree of compliance and in their willingness to comply. Buhler further believes that "most employees throughout the organization have the ability to make their boss look bad." This important political element can often be overlooked by the principal. There is also power in terms of whom teachers are aligned with and the great loyalty they have for these individuals. For example, in business, when a senior executive leaves the company, a whole group generally follows. In school systems, administrators and teachers may not have the flexibility to follow their superior immediately, but the information and communication network of loyal past employees is nevertheless powerful and influential. People tend to group together in order to achieve and sustain power.[43] Particularly in educational settings, power should be used, when possible, as a shared resource.

Power Sharing and Teacher Empowerment

Power sharing encourages teachers, principals, department chairs, counselors, and other staff at all levels of the school to be involved in decision making without feeling coerced or manipulated. A study on empowering teachers at the elementary school level found personal power of the principal who incorporated referent, information, and expert subordinate perception bases highly valued by teachers. Teachers, however, resent principals who falsely see themselves as relying on personal power when, in fact, they use positional power bases such as reward, coercion, connection, and legitimate authority. Connection power, in which the principal has a personal relationship with influential people inside or outside school, could be a source of personal power as well. Yet teachers in this same study tended to "devalue their principals' connections as being part of an old boy's network. They resented the fact that their principals with connections spent a good deal of time away from the schools."[44] Accessibility is an important quality in effective leadership.[45]

"Giving teachers greater power is a major way to make them more professional and to improve their performance."[46] Teachers should have an impact on policy decisions and should work in a collegial relationship, "sharing power" with administrators. Through this relationship, principals become facilitators of school goals, empowering teachers and allowing them to generate their own ideas. This, in turn, gives more dignity to the profession of teaching. As teachers become more empowered, they will have to accept the burden of responsibility. Whereas in the past teachers could "blame the administrators for problems," this blame should decline as teacher empowerment increases. In order to empower teachers and expect them to be successful in carrying out their responsibilities, they must be educated and trained in the skills necessary for appropriate decision making.[47]

Power and Perception

In examining the various conceptualizations of power, a question could be raised about whether, in some cases, the concepts that the theorists are presenting should not more properly be characterized as sources or types of social *influence* rather than power. Types of "power," such as control of prestige, persuasion, and referent and reward power, seem to represent sources of influence rather than sources of, or types of, power (more will be said later about influence). It is difficult to see how these types of power could be used to force someone to comply with authority if the person was determined to resist it.

RESEARCH SPOTLIGHT

Power and Influence: Does Gender Matter?

POWER & INFLUENCE

People decide how competent you are in a fraction of a second. Factors used to determine your competence: 7% words, 38% presentation, and 55% body language.

BODY LANGUAGE OF POWER

Body language can communicate power and status—it sets the stage for who is leading and who is following.
To be perceived as authoritative, act HIGH

- Be expansive, take up maximum space
- Speak in complete sentences
- Hold eye contact when talking
- Don't monitor the responses of others

To be perceived as approachable, act LOW

- Maintain a tight, close body
- Speak cautiously
- Avoid direct eye contact
- Smile and nod in agreement

WOMEN AND POWER

The body language of power are tools to meet dual and competing expectations of women:

- To act authoritative in keeping with the expectations of their organizational roles
- To act approachable in keeping with the expectations of their gender role

If a subordinate is determined to resist an administrator's authority, the only effective type of power may be *coercive power,* defined as "the capacity to force people to do something against their will."[48] It needs to be emphasized, however, that most school administrators are quite limited in their possession of coercive power.[49] By and large, this kind of power is based on the backing of an administrator's superiors; it may also need to be validated by some outside agency—for example, the courts—if the legality of the use of power is challenged. To complicate matters, the basis for the use of coercive power is frequently vague and often not predictable or dependable.[50] For instance, seldom will an administrator find in school board policies or in a job description any discussion of the right to use coercive means to gain compliance from employees. This type of power is rarely made explicit and is usually, at most, implied.

On the other hand, an administrator may be able to achieve initial compliance from others or overcome resistance to the exercise of authority as a result of other people's *perception* of the administrator's coercive power.[51] Three perceptual conditions, however, must be present:

1. Others must perceive the administrator as possessing a certain kind of coercive power.

ACTING WITH POWER

- Modify body language to influence the dynamics of relationships, interactions, and outcomes
- Match your body language to the message or intention

Sangeetha Rajan and Venkat R. Krishnan studied the impact of gender on frequency of use of influence strategies, amount of power, and authoritarianism, using a sample of 109 managers from two organizations in India. Seven downward influence strategies (assertiveness, bargaining, coalition, friendliness, higher authority, reason, and sanctions) and five power bases (reward, referent, legitimate, expert, and coercive) were included in the study. They noted that historically successful managers have been perceived as being identified more with men than with women in terms of emotional stability, aggressiveness, leadership ability, self-reliance, certainty, vigor, desiring responsibility, seriousness, objectivity, knowledge, and straightforwardness.

Analyzing the sources of power that authoritarian men and women tap and the influence strategies they use, the authors found that gender moderates the impact of authoritarianism on influence and power. Authoritarian men are more likely to tap legitimate power but not coercive power. Authoritarian men use assertiveness, bargaining, and friendliness strategies more frequently than authoritarian women. Overall, the findings suggest that gender and personality combine to affect power and influence. Thus ignoring gender and studying the effect of only personality on power and influence may not present an accurate picture.

Source: S. R. Rajan and V. R. Krishnan (2002), "Impact of Gender on Influence, Power, and Authoritarianism." *Women in Managerial Review, 17*(5), pp. 197–206.

2. They must perceive this power as something that they definitely would like to avoid.
3. They must perceive the administrator as ready to use coercive power if compliance is not forthcoming.

If, for example, a teacher believed that a principal could and *would* use punishment in some way for the teacher's failure to monitor the corridor when students are passing between classes, and if the teacher wanted to avoid that punishment, then the teacher would probably comply with the administrator's expectations. In this case, the perception is more important than the reality. If a subordinate *perceives* that an administrator possesses coercive power, then the subordinate will act on that perception, irrespective of whether the administrator possesses that power. As Wheeless and his colleagues point out, "People act not on the basis of the situation but on the basis of their perceptions about the situation. . . . It makes no difference, for example, if the agent [administrator] making a threat has the ability to carry out that threat. If the [individual or group] being threatened perceive[s] such an ability, the agent has power."[52]

WINDOW ON DIVERSITY

Authority, Power, and Influence

Issues of authority, power, and influence are often affected by an individual's own personal experiences. What about the concept of "privilege"? What does it look in your life, both personally and professionally. Take a look at the video "What is Privilege" and then consider how the notion of "privilege" may affect how authority, power, and influence are wielded by a school leader.

Watch the following video, "What is White/Male Privilege?" http://everydayfeminism.com/2014/11/what-is-whitemale-privilege/

Nevertheless, it is important for an administrator to understand that coercive power is most effective when it is not used, but when it is believed that it would be exercised and supported if compliance were not forthcoming. The more an administrator has to resort to the use of coercive power in order to gain compliance, the greater the possibility of exposing its limited or inadequate basis, thereby exacerbating a situation, or resulting in some other unanticipated consequence.[53] Although certain circumstances may warrant the use of coercive power, in most situations the administrator should utilize other means, such as dependence upon personal power, for gaining compliance and, especially, cooperation.

The appropriate exercise of personal power is one of the means of obtaining higher levels of teacher satisfaction and cooperation. Empowerment through the use of personal power gives teachers a sense of ownership, raises their level of self-esteem, and increases participatory decision making and communication. Ross and Webb determined in their study of an elementary school how shared decision making taught administrators and faculty members how to share power and thus provide a better learning environment for their students.[54] Other means that administrators can use for gaining cooperation fall under the category of influence, to be discussed next.

POWER AND INFLUENCE

Most of the kinds of power identified above would seem to represent types of influence rather than power. Power, of course, can be and has been defined broadly by a number of theorists. Kotter aptly notes that inherent in every position in an organization is a certain degree of power, and individuals have the potential either to enhance or to decrease the power of their position by the behavior they display.[55] When power is defined broadly, such a definition (and sometimes the mere use of the term) can inadvertently mislead an administrator into thinking there is more capacity to bring about change than the administrator possesses in certain situations.

Unquestionably, power and influence are closely related on a theoretical basis;[56] however, little research exists about the effects of a leader's influence-seeking behaviors on subordinate perceptions of leader effectiveness in an organizational context. Specific descriptive theory and valid empirical research on possible linkages between perceived leader behavior and attributions of power have been virtually nonexistent.[57] One exception in recent years is the research of Rice and her colleagues, in which the power and leadership practices of school superintendents were studied according to the perceptions of both leaders (principals) and followers (teacher association representatives).[58]

TYPES OF INFLUENCE

Influence, when compared to power, seems to be a more positive concept and more in line with the realities of organizational life for most school administrators. *Influence* can be defined as "the ability of an [administrator] without recourse to force or legitimation, to affect another's behavior."[59] Influence is the shaping of decisions through "informal and nonauthoritative means."[60] It differs from authority in that (1) many people can influence a decision whereas only one person has final authority, (2) influence may be distributed unequally, whereas authority is usually distributed equally, and (3) authority is top-down management, whereas influence is multidirectional.[61] An example of multidirectional influence is described by Bredesen, who was able to use his influence to involve upper elementary and middle school students in a community service project that would have been reserved for high school students.[62] As the principal of a school and a member of the board of directors for a historical society, he was in an ideal position to convince the school board that the habit of community service needed to be established in students before the pressures of their high school years. Working with teachers and the local museum personnel, he was able to implement a successful summer service program for students that reinforced the classroom instruction of local history.

An administrator has influence if other individuals or groups can be persuaded to comply with the administrator's expectations, despite their ambivalence or objections. In light of the limitations of power and considering the periodic challenges to authority that most administrators will experience during their careers, it would appear that the concept of influence offers a positive and constructive alternative basis for many administrative actions.

If the administrator is to exert influence successfully, the administrator's actions must be based on some factor that will persuade people to act in accordance with the administrator's decisions or directives. Successful implementation of directives will, in large measure, be contingent upon the perception of the individual receiving the directive from the administrator.[63]

Furthermore, utilizing (with minor modification,) French and Raven's concepts, it would appear that administrators may be able to exert influence based on other people's identification with them (referent influence), their ability to obtain rewards (reward influence), or their perception of administrators' expertise as educational leaders (expert influence).

Referent Influence

The identification of other individuals or groups with the administrator as a person is the basis for the referent influence of an administrator. An administrator who possesses certain qualities, such as an attractive personality, a strong character, or a charismatic leadership style, may be successful in securing the cooperation of other people as a result of their identification with these characteristics.[64] Even if teachers, parents, or students question the decisions or policies set forth by an administrator, they may oblige, simply because they react positively to the personal qualities the administrator possesses.

There is considerable observational evidence that people will respond favorably to an administrator's attempt to influence them as a result of their identification with the individual. Administrators in business and government, as well as in education, have found it possible to secure the cooperation of others, in spite of objections to a particular policy or action, because of their positive feelings about the administrator. There is little doubt that the identification by others with the administrator can be a powerful basis for influencing them if the administrator possesses the requisite personal characteristics.

One problem with referent influence is that research has not conclusively established the kinds of personal characteristics with which people identify positively. It appears that not all people respond the same way to particular personal characteristics. Qualities that one group may find attractive or charismatic might be perceived by other individuals or groups as undesirable. For example, ingratiation, acting friendly toward another, or flattering another may be enjoyed by some employees but be seen as a sign of weakness by others.[65] Consequently, there is no single pattern of personal attributes that can be recommended without qualification to the administrator for all situations. A study by Hoy and Kupersmith suggests, however, that administrator "authenticity" could be very important.[66] In addition, a study by Johnston and Venable suggests that an administrator's style in administering personnel rules may be significantly related to the degree of loyalty that teachers feel toward the administrator.[67]

Another important limitation of referent influence is the fact that its potential is largely determined by factors over which most administrators have little or no control. By the time a person becomes an administrator, personality and leadership style are usually already developed. Therefore, if the administrator does not currently possess the kinds of personal characteristics with which people identify, the likelihood of developing them is not great. Although an administrator can often improve personal traits, the task is not an easy one, and change is frequently slow. Despite these obstacles, it would be in the best interest of any administrator to improve personal qualities and leadership style so that greater referent influence can be exercised (see Chapter 1, "Leadership").

Reward Influence

A second kind of influence an administrator may be able to utilize in persuading people to adhere to the administrator's wishes is reward influence. This type of influence is based on the administrator's actual or perceived possession of certain rewards that can be distributed to those who comply. Examples of these rewards range from a better work schedule to greater administrative receptivity and accommodation to the recommendations and special needs of certain individuals or groups.

Reward Distribution Issues Unfortunately, it would appear that most administrators do not possess a great deal of influence based on rewards, since they frequently find themselves in a position where they cannot distribute to one individual or group any rewards that do not need to be distributed equally to other individuals or groups. Unlike executives in private enterprise, educational administrators can seldom selectively reward their employees according to merit or increased productivity. They may occasionally be able to offer a reward to one individual or group without having to give similar recognition to other involved individuals or groups, but this possibility does not occur often. In education, preferential treatment seems to be regarded with suspicion, and students, teachers, and parents are alert to situations in which the administrator seems to be favoring one individual or group over another.

Limited Resources There is also the problem that only a limited number of rewards are available to most administrators to utilize in influencing other people. School board policy, bureaucratic regulations, the nature of public control over resources, and teacher, student, and parent militancy are factors that tend to restrict the number and importance of rewards available to an administrator.

Alternative Rewards This does not mean that the administrator possesses no reward influence or that it should not be utilized. There are some administrators who, over the years, have been able to develop a wide variety of rewards. For example, in discussing the behavior of one principal who attempted to use reward influence, Cusick pointed out that "because he administered the schedule, additional assignments, and unallocated resources, he controlled just those things that many teachers wanted in order to fill out their fields. The principal could award a department chairperson with a free period, a favorite class, a double lunch period, an honors section, or support for a new activity."[68] Another practical alternative reward is "modeling." Blase and Kirby found that teachers reported that modeling influences their behavior to be consistent with the principal's expectations. One teacher stated "many of the principals' requests might be viewed as beyond the call of duty, but because of the principal's modeling, they seem to be a part of the job." These teachers reported that this type of influence made them feel "comfortable," "proud," "aware," and "positive."[69] Given this, Henry Griffith, an elementary school principal, demonstrates how a leader's power and influence can be used to enhance school improvement.[70] Under his guidance, the faculty wrote and received a grant for $25,000 a year for five years. The faculty was able to use the grant-writing experience to gain ownership of the ideas Griffith wanted to incorporate, while enjoying not only the benefits of the money but also an enhanced self-respect and collegiality among themselves.

Positive Reinforcement as a Reward In addition to control over resources, a school administrator has available a simple but frequently overlooked source of rewards: positive reinforcement. This can, for example, take the form of oral and/or written appreciation to a person who volunteers for an activity, praise for a job well done, a commendation for a significant effort to improve, or some other type of reward. Although most school administrators may believe that they are already utilizing this potential source of influence sufficiently, there is evidence to the contrary.[71]

To be effective in influencing behavior, positive reinforcement must be directly linked to the specific effort or performance that warrants the reinforcement.[72] For example, the school administrator who gives praise indiscriminately or who does not clearly relate the delivery of praise to the production of a certain type of behavior is not likely to be successful in influencing others with positive reinforcement.[73] In addition, unless the kind of positive reinforcement used by a school administrator is valued by its recipient, the latter's behavior is unlikely to be influenced. Consequently, to be effective in using positive reinforcement, the school administrator needs to become knowledgeable about the reward predisposition of the people to be influenced. Fuqua and colleagues refer to the importance of "rewarding people for their accomplishments, contributions, and ideas," inviting people to participate in decision making, and giving credit where credit is due. Leaders who empower, according to these authors, are leaders who "reward people who generate the greatest impact toward organizational goals, rewarding results rather than processes."[74]

Hierarchical Influence as a Reward An administrator perceived as someone who has influence with superiors may also be able to exert reward influence with teachers. Such influence can be manifested in at least two important ways: by securing additional resources from the district that subordinates need and by being an effective advocate and supporter of subordinates in their interactions with the district office. This type of hierarchical influence has received some research support and represents a frequently overlooked source of rewards that an administrator may be able to generate for subordinates.[75] For two interesting studies of the techniques that people use to try to exert upward influence, see Schmidt and Kipnis[76] and Schilit and Locke.[77]

Although it is important for an administrator to make maximal use of whatever resources or reward influence exists, it should be understood that, in many situations, the administrator's reward influence is not extensive, and there are significant constraints that may make it difficult to take advantage of this type of influence. Therefore, although an administrator should try to develop and use as many sources of rewards as possible, inasmuch as there are limitations to administrative influence based on rewards, other sources of influence will be needed as well. Glinow has written a provocative article on reward strategies that speaks to this issue.[78]

Expertise as a Basis of Influence

Although the foregoing discussion of referent and reward influence has emphasized the personal and situational limitations of these bases for administrative action, there is one source of administrative influence that potentially would seem to offer the administrator a truly viable basis upon which to gain the cooperation of others. That source is expertise, that is, specialized knowledge or skill.

Empirical support for the primacy of this source of administrative influence was furnished in a study by Horstein. He discovered, in an investigation of 325 teachers who worked in 14 different schools in two school districts, that the most important factor associated with teacher satisfaction and high evaluation of principal leadership was the principal's tendency to base attempts to influence teachers on possession of expertise, rather than on other sources of influence.[79] Administrative attempts to influence teachers based on the possession of certain rewards for compliance were not associated with high teacher satisfaction or high evaluation of the administrator's leadership. Referent identification as a source of influence was positively related to teacher satisfaction, but the relationship was not statistically significant. Horstein's research also revealed that in those situations where the administrator based behavior on legitimate authority or coercive power, the faculty was not satisfied with this individual as a principal and did not give the principal a good evaluation as a leader.

While the data from Horstein's investigation seem to suggest that an administrator can successfully influence teachers if the actions are based on expertise as a source of influence, there is other evidence that, regrettably, many administrators seem to lack expertise or are perceived by others as lacking expertise. The ability of administrators to manage a school or school district effectively and humanely has come under attack periodically through the years, and these criticisms have recently escalated with the emphasis on school accountability and on student, teacher, and parent demands for involvement in school decision making. For a further discussion on this problem, see Gorton and Thierbach-Schneider.[80]

On the other hand, research on effective schools has demonstrated that principals with expertise can exert influence in their schools and that their leadership contributions are important to the success of these schools.[81] In the area of instructional supervision, for example, Guditus and Zirkel found that "the influence of principals depends to a considerable degree on their possession of special knowledge and skills which enable them to help teachers achieve their goals."[82] For example, principals could increase their influence on teachers by learning more about teaching and by visiting classrooms. "Managing by walking around may give administrators an opportunity to influence faculty and staff."[83]

The effectiveness of an administrator's influence would also seem to depend on the extent to which attempts to influence others fall within the teachers' zone of acceptance. See Clear and Seager,[84] Kunz and Hoy,[85] and Johnston and Mullins[86] for further discussion of the relationship between the zone of acceptance and administrator influence.

Therefore, it would appear that one of the keys for an administrator's successful exercise of influence is to assist teachers and relevant others to meet their goals and to help them relate those goals to the overall goals of the school and school district. This may require an administrator to develop greater expertise in instructional leadership, program development, student discipline, conflict resolution, working with groups, or some other type of special knowledge or skill that is needed. In many cases, an administrator may need to identify and deploy other people who possess special knowledge and skill that the administrator does not possess and would find difficult to develop. The important consideration is not who possesses the special knowledge or skill but that it be utilized to help the people associated with the school to become more effective.

By empowering teachers, the potential for effecting desired results can be enhanced. Futrell believes that if teachers were empowered to design and create their own professional development, it would improve their performance. For an administrator, improved student, staff, and school performance is the goal, and empowering teachers is a means to that goal.[87]

In Yukl's view of influence, he noted it as the effect, either intended or unintended, of one party (the agent) on another person's (the target's) attitudes, perceptions, behavior, or some combination of these outcomes. He suggests that 11 proactive tactics (Table 3.2) can be used for influence attempts with subordinates, peers, and superiors.

TABLE 3.2
YUKL'S CLASSIFICATION OF PROACTIVE INFLUENCE TACTICS

Rational persuasion	The agent uses logical arguments and factual evidence to show that a proposal or request is feasible, that it is relevant for attaining important task objectives.
Apprising	The agent explains how carrying out a request or supporting a proposal will benefit the target personally or will help to advance the target person's career.
Inspirational appeals	The agent appeals to the target's values and ideals or seeks to arouse the target person's emotions to gain commitment for a request or proposal.
Consultation	The agent asks the target person to express concerns and suggest improvements for a proposed project, activity, or change for which the target person's support is desired.
Collaboration	The agent offers to provide relevant resources and assistance if the target will carry out a request or approve a proposed change.
Ingratiation	The agent uses praise and flattery before or during an attempt to influence the target person to carry out a request or support a proposal.
Personal appeals	The agent asks the target to carry out a request or support a proposal out of friendship or loyalty, or asks for a personal favor before saying what it is.
Exchange	The agent offers an incentive, suggests an exchange of favors, or indicates willingness to reciprocate at a later time if the target will do what the agent requests.
Coalition tactics	The agent seeks the aid of others to persuade the target to do something, or uses the support of others as a reason for the target to agree with a request.
Legitimating tactics	The agent seeks to establish the legitimacy of a request or to verify that he/she has the authority to make it by referring to rules and formal policies or presenting supporting documents.
Pressure	The agent uses demands, threats, frequent checking, or persistent reminders to influence the target to do what he/she wants.

Yukl, Gary A. *Leadership in Organizations,* 7th Edition. Upper Saddle River, NJ: Pearson Education, Inc., 2010, 219.

A FINAL NOTE

By the very nature of their positions in an organization, administrators will be assigned major responsibilities. In order to carry out those responsibilities successfully, authority, influence, and perhaps, in some cases, power must be exercised effectively. Appropriate understanding and use of the concepts presented in this chapter should help the administrator achieve these objectives.

Although most of the case studies, suggested learning activities, and simulations presented in Part II require the appropriate use of the ideas in this chapter on authority, power, and influence, the following exercises should provide the best opportunities for testing understanding and effective use of authority, power, and influence concepts: Cases 20, 27, 28, 30, 37, 38, 49, and 62, and the midyear and end-of-the-year in-basket exercises.

NOTES

1. Max Weber, *The Theory of Social and Economic Organization,* A. M. Henderson and Talcott Parsons, Trans. (New York: Oxford University Press, 1947), pp. 56–57.
2. C. Resser, *Management, Functions, and Modern Concepts* (Chicago: Scott, Foresman, 1973), p. 132.
3. Douglas E. Mitchell and William G. Spady, "Authority, Power, and the Legitimization of Social Control," *Educational Administration Quarterly* (Winter 1983), p. 12.
4. Patrick Houston, "The Power Vacuum: High Anxiety," *Business Month* (June 1990), p. 34.
5. Weber, *Social and Economic Organization,* pp. 56–77.
6. Harvey Bleacher, "Why Teachers Carry Out Orders," *Education* (Spring 1985), pp. 333-336. Also see John Lindelow and James J. Scott, "Managing Conflict" in *School Leadership Handbook for Excellence* (Eugene, OR Clearinghouse on Educational Management, 1989), p. 350.
7. Kenneth A. Tye and Barbara B. Tye, "Teacher Isolation and School Reform," *Phi Delta Kappan* (January 1984), p. 321.
8. Daniel J. Brass, "Being in the Right Place," *Administrative Science Quarterly* (December 1984), pp. 518–539. Also see Herbert A. Simon, *Administrative Behavior* (New York: Macmillan, 1959), p. 22; and Carl D. Glickman, "Directive Control Behaviors," *Supervision of Instruction: A Developmental Approach,* 2nd ed. (Boston, MA: Allyn and Bacon, 1990), pp. 162–174.
9. Joan R. Egner, "Collective Bargaining and Administrative Prerogatives," *Peabody Journal of Education* (November 1968), pp. 142–149. For a more general discussion of this problem, see Robert L. Peabody, *Organizational Authority* (New York: Atherton Press, 1964), pp. 84–89.
10. Bruce S. Cooper, "Bottom-Up Authority in School Organization. Implications for the School Administrator," *Education and Urban Society* (August 1989), pp. 380–391.
11. Rodney T. Ogawa and Steven T. Bossert, "Leadership as an Organizational Quality," *Educational Administration Quarterly* (vol. 31, no. 2, 1995), pp. 224–243.
12. Harold E. Fuqua Jr., Kay E. Payne, and Joseph P. Cangemi, "Leadership and the Effective Use of Power," *National Forum of Educational Administration and Supervision Journal* (vol. 17-E, no. 4, 1999–2000).
13. Ibid. See also Rosabeth Moss Kanter, *Men and Women of the Corporation* (New York: Basic Books, 1977).
14. Perry A. Zirkel and Ivan B. Gluckman, "'Downsizing' School Administrators," *Principal* (March 1996), pp. 60–61.
15. For an interesting analysis of the impact of the master contract, see Donald L. Robson and Marlene E. Davis, "Administrative Authority, Leadership Style, and the Master Contract," *Journal of Educational Administration* (Winter 1983), pp. 5–13.
16. Kent D. Peterson, "Mechanisms of Administrative Control over Managers in Educational Organizations," *Administrative Science Quarterly* (December 1984), pp. 573–597. Also see John Lindelow and James Heynderickx, "School-Based Management" in *School Leadership Handbook for Excellence,* 2nd ed., an ERIC report, Ed. 309–504.
17. For examples, see the cases in this text.
18. Richard A. Gorton and Gail Thierbach-Schneider, *School Based Leadership: Challenges and Opportunities* (Dubuque, IA: Wm. C. Brown, 1991), pp. 93–101.
19. For an insightful discussion of how new administrators are socialized into their role, see William D. Greenfield Jr., "The Moral Socialization of School Administrators," *Educational Administration Quarterly* (Fall 1985), pp. 99–119; also see Mark E. Anderson, "Training and Selecting School Leaders" in *School Leadership: Handbook for Excellence,* 2nd ed., an ERIC report, Ed. 309–504.
20. The concept of outer-directedness was first developed by David Riesman in *Lonely Crowd* (New Haven: Yale University Press, 1973).
21. Anderson, "Training and Selecting School Leaders."

22. For the role of perception, see Lawrence R. Wheeless et al., "Compliance-Gaining and Power in Persuasion," in Robert N. Bostrom (Ed.), *Communication Yearbook 7* (Beverly Hills, CA: Sage, 1983), p. 120.

23. Peter M. Blau and W. Richard Scott, *Formal Organization: A Comparative Approach* (San Francisco, CA: Chandler, 1962), p. 61.

24. Simon, *Administrative Behavior,* p. 133.

25. Sam Wilkes and Jo Blackbourn, *The Design of an Instrument to Measure Zones of Indifference of Teachers to Directives Issued by Administrators,* an ERIC report, Ed. 212-063.

26. Charles B. Handy, *Understanding Organizations* (New York: Pengium, 1981), pp. 119–120. Also see Paul Hersey and Kenneth H. Blanchard, *Management of Organizational Behavior: Utilizing Human Resources,* 5th ed. (Englewood Cliffs, NJ: Prentice Hall, 1988), p. 171; and an empirical study by M. Afzalur Rahim, "Relationships of Leader Power to Compliance and Satisfaction with Supervision: Evidence from a National Sample of Managers," *Journal of Management* (April 1989), pp. 545–556.

27. Daniel W. Kunz and Wayne K. Hoy, "Leadership Style of Principals and the Professional Zone of Acceptance of Teachers," *Educational Administration Quarterly* (Fall 1976), pp. 49–64; see also Ann W. Porter and Donald K. Lemon, "How Teachers Perceive a Principal's Power," *Principal* (January 1988), pp. 30–32.

28. Peabody, Robert L, *Organizational Authority,* New York: Atherton Press, 1964, 107–108.

29. Charles A. O'Reilly III and Barton A. Weitz, "Managing Marginal Employees: The Use of Warnings and Dismissals," *Administrative Science Quarterly* (September 1980), pp. 467–484.

30. John D. Stanley, "Dissent in Organizations," *Academy of Management Review* (January 1981), pp. 13–19. Also see Antoinette A. Kirkwood, "The Role of the Principal as a Manager of Conflict Resolution," an ERIC report, Ed. 321-373.

31. Gorton and Thierbach-Schneider, *School Based Leadership,* pp. 95–98.

32. Jane Boucher, "If You Must Criticize Someone," *Communications Briefings* (vol. 15, no. 1), p. 5.

33. Many of the ideas for the recommended steps in this section come from D. Cameron, "The When, Why and How of Discipline," *Personnel Journal* (July 1984), pp. 37–39; and from O'Reilly and Weitz, "Managing Marginal Employees."

34. Kelly Frels and Timothy Cooper, *A Documentation System for Teacher Improvement or Termination* (Lawrence, KS: National Organization on Legal Problems of Education, 2007).

35. Perry A. Zirkel, "Teacher Insubordination: An Update," *Principal* (January/February 2010), pp. 50–51.

36. Chester Barnard, *The Functions of the Executive* (Cambridge: Harvard University Press, 1948), p. 165.

37. Wheeless et al., "Compliance-Gaining and Power," pp. 105–145.

38. Mary H. Beaven, "Leadership, Charisma, Personality, and Power," paper presented at the annual meeting of the National Women's Studies Association, Towson, MD, June 1989. For further discussion on how constituents gain power, thus developing a sense of personal and collective efficacy and self-control leading to empowerment, see E. J. Langer, *The Psychology of Control* (Beverly Hills, CA: Sage, 1983); A. R. Willner, *The Spellbinders: Charismatic Political Leadership* (New Haven, CT: Yale University Press, 1984); and R. deCharms, *Personal Causation: The Internal Affective Determinants of Behavior* (New York: Academic Press, 1968).

39. A. A. Etzioni, *A Comparative Analysis of Complex Organizations* (New York: Macmillan, 1961), p. 5.

40. T. Parsons, "On the Concept of Influence," *Public Opinion Quarterly* (Spring 1963), pp. 36–62.

41. John R. P. French and Bertram Raven, "The Bases of Social Power," in Darwin Cartwright (Ed.), *Studies of Social Power* (Ann Arbor: University of Michigan Press, 1959), pp. 155–164.

42. Paul Hersey and Walter Natemeyer, *Power Perception Profile* (Escondido, CA: Center for Leadership Studies, 1979).

43. Patricia M. Buhler, "Power and Conflict in the Workplace," *The American Salesman* (September 1988), pp. 3–4.

44. Jerry D. Stimson and Richard P. Appelbaum, "Empowering Teachers: Do Principals Have the Power?" *Phi Delta Kappan* (December 1988), pp. 313–316.

45. T. A. Stewart, "Get with the New Power Game," *Fortune* (January 13, 1997), pp. 58–62.

46. E. I. Maeroff, *The Empowerment of Teachers: Overcoming the Crisis of Confidence* (New York: Teachers College Press, 1989), pp. 4, 82–86.

47. Ibid.

48. Weber, *Social and Economic Organization,* p. 152.

49. For guidelines on how to make the best use of those limitations, see Gary A. Yukl, *Leadership in Organizations,* 7th ed. (Upper Saddle River, NJ: Prentice Hall, 2009), pp. 56–58.

50. Richard D. Arvey, "Use of Discipline in Organization," *Journal of Applied Psychology* (August 1984), pp. 448–460.

51. Wheeless et al., "Compliance-Gaining and Power," p. 127.

52. Ibid.

53. Rodney Muth, "Toward an Integrative Theory of Power and Educational Organizations," *Educational Administration Quarterly* (Spring 1984), pp. 25–42. For more information on the use of coercive power, see Ted J. Foster, "The Nature and Use of Coercion," paper presented at the annual meeting of the Central States Speech Association, April 1988.

54. Dorene D. Ross and Rodman B. Webb, "Implementing Shared Decision Making at Brookville Elementary School," *Building Blocks and Stumbling Blocks* (New York: NCREST, 1994), pp. 39–58.

55. J. P. Kotter, *Power and Influence: Beyond Formal Authority* (New York: Free Press, 1985). Also see Edward R. Lilley, "The Determinants of Organizational Power Styles," *Educational Review* (March 1989), pp. 281–293.

56. Yukl, *Leadership in Organizations;* and John S. Dean, "Principals' Leadership and School Effectiveness: A Descriptive Study of the Principals' Exercise of Authority and Influence in Effective and Ineffective Elementary Schools," PhD dissertation, Pennsylvania State University, 1990.

57. Timothy R. Hinkin and Chester A. Schriesheim, "Relationships between Subordinate Perceptions of Supervisor Influence Tactics and Attributed Bases of Supervisory Power," *Human Relations* (vol. 43, no. 3, 1990), 221–237.

58. Margaret L. Rice, Harold Bishop, Michele Acker-Hocevar, and Barbara Pounders, "Power and Leadership Practices by the Superintendent: What Do They Mean to Leaders and Followers?" *National Forum of Applied Educational Research Journal* (vol 13E, no. 3, 2000). Accessed online, http://www.nationalforum.com/RICEaer10e3.html, December 9, 2000.

59. Muth, "Toward an Integrative Theory," p. 27.

60. Sharon Conley, "School Reform, Teacher Participation, and the Decision-Making Process," *Education and Urban Society* (August 1989), pp. 366–379.

61. Ibid.

62. Tom Bredsen, "Community Service for Middle Graders," *Principal* (March 1996), pp. 44–45.

63. Hinkin and Schriesheim, "Subordinate Perceptions of Supervisor Influence Tactics and Attributed Bases of Supervisory Power," p. 224.

64. For a description of an interesting theory of charismatic leadership, see R. J. House, "A 1976 Theory of Charismatic Leadership," in J. G. Hunt and L. L. Larson (Eds.), *Leadership: The Cutting Edge* (Carbondale, IL: Southern Illinois University Press, 1977). Also see William F. Adams and Gerald D. Bailey, "Managerial Leadership Behaviors: A Model of Choice," *Performance and Instruction* (January 1989), pp. 43–46.

65. Hinkin and Schriescheim, "Subordinate Perceptions of Supervisor Influence Tactics and Attributed Bases of Supervisory Power," p. 226.

66. Wayne K. Hoy and William Kupersmith, "Principal Authenticity and Faculty Trust: Key Elements in Organizational Behavior," *Planning and Changing* (Summer 1984), pp. 80–88.

67. Gladys Styles Johnston and Bernice Proctor Venable, "A Study of Teacher Loyalty to the Principal: Rule Administration and Hierarchical Influence of the Principal," paper presented at the annual meeting of the American

Educational Research Association, Chicago, 1985. Also see J. J. Blase, "Politics of Favoritism: A Qualitative Analysis of the Teacher's Perspective," *Educational Administrative Quarterly* (May 1988), pp. 152–177.

68. Philip A. Cusick, "A Study of Networks among Professional Staff in Secondary Schools," *Educational Administration Quarterly* (Summer 1981), pp. 132–133.

69. Joseph Blase and Peggy C. Kirby, *Bringing Out the Best in Teachers: What Effective Principals Do* (Thousand Oaks, CA: Corwin Press, 2009), p. 112.

70. Henry C. Griffith Sr., "When a Principal Becomes an Entrepreneur," *Principal* (January 1996), pp. 50–54.

71. Gorton and Thierbach-Schneider, *School-Based Leadership: Challenges and Opportunities,* pp. 253–263.

72. Philip M. Podsakoff et al., "Situational Moderation of Leader Reward and Punishment Behavior," *Organizational Behavior and Human Performance* (August 1984), pp. 23–26. Also see James M. Kouzes and Barry Z. Posner, "Recognize Contributions: Linking Rewards with Performance," in J. M. Koocuges and B. Z. Posner (Eds.), *The Leadership Challenge: How to Get Extraordinary Things Done in Organizations* (San Francisco: Jossey-Bass, 1990), pp. 241–258.

73. Podsakoff et al., "Situational Moderation of Leader Reward and Punishment Behavior," pp. 27–28.

74. Harold E. Fuqua Jr., Kay E. Payne, and Joseph P. Cangemi, "Leadership and the Effective Use of Power," *National Forum of Educational Administration and Supervision Journal* (vol. 17-E, no. 4, 1999–2000). Accessed online, http://www.nationalforum.com

75. Johnston and Venable, "Teacher Loyalty to the Principal." *Educational Administration Quarterly* (vol. 22, no. 4, Fall 1986), pp. 4–27.

76. Stuart M. Schmidt and David Kipnis, "Managers' Pursuit of Individual and Organizational Goals," *Human Relations* (October 1985), pp. 781–794. Also see Allan R. Cohen and David L. Bradford, "Influence without Authority: The Use of Alliances, Reciprocity, and Exchange to Accomplish Work," *Organizational Dynamics* (Winter 1989), pp. 5–17.

77. Warren K. Schilit and Edwin A. Locke, "A Study of Upward Influence in Organizations," *Administrative Science Quarterly* (June 1982), pp. 304–316.

78. Mary Ann von Glinow, "Reward Strategies for Attracting, Evaluating and Retaining Professionals," *Human Resources Management* (Summer 1985), pp. 191–206.

79. Harvey Horstein et al., "Influence and Satisfaction in Organizations: A Replication," *Sociology of Education* (Fall 1968), pp. 380–389. For a related study, see Reginald High and Charles M. Archilles, "An Analysis of Influence Gaining Behaviors of Principals in Schools of Varying Levels of Instructional Effectiveness," *Educational Administration Quarterly* (Winter 1986), pp. 111–119.

80. Gorton and Thierbach-Schneider, *School-Based Leadership,* pp. 319–324.

81. For an excellent review of this research, see Jo Ann Mazzarella, "The Effective High School Principal," *R and D Perspectives* (Winter 1985), pp. 1–8. Also see Thomas Biester, *Effects of Administrative Leadership on Student Achievement* (Philadelphia: Research for Better Schools, 1984); and Lawrence F. Rossow, *The Principalship: Dimensions in Instructional Leadership* (Englewood Cliffs, NJ: Prentice Hall, 1990), pp. 34–42. For additional information, see Bill Luche, "The Principal and Supervision," Elementary Principal Series No. 4, Phi Delta Kappan Educational Foundation, 1989, an ERIC report, Ed. 315–914.

82. Charles W. Guditus and Perry A. Zirkel, "Bases of Supervisory Power among Public School Principals," paper presented at the annual meeting of the American Educational Research Association, 1979, p. 16. Also see "The Leadership Needed for Quality Schooling," in T. Sergiovanni and J. H. Moore (Eds.), *Schooling for Tomorrow: Directing Reform to Issues That Count* (Boston, MA: Allyn and Bacon, 1989).

83. Conley, "School Reform, Teacher Participation, and the Decision-Making Process," p. 369.

84. Delbert K. Clear and Roger Seager, "The Legitimacy of Administrative Influence as Perceived by Selected Groups," *Educational Administration Quarterly* (Winter 1971), pp. 46–63.

85. Kunz and Hoy, "Leadership Style of Principals and the Professional Zone of Acceptance of Teachers." *Educational Administration Quarterly* (vol. 12, no. 3, Fall 1976), pp. 49–62.

86. Gladys Styles Johnston and Toni Mullins, "Relationships among Teachers' Perceptions of the Principal's Style, Teachers' Loyalty to the Principal, and Teachers' Zone of Acceptance," paper presented at the annual meeting of the American Educational Research Association, 1985. Also see Wayne K. Hoy and Bonnie Leverette Brown, "Leadership Behavior of Principals and the Zone of Acceptance of Elementary Teachers," *Journal of Educational Administration* (March 1988), pp. 23–28.

87. Mary Harwood Futrell, "Empowering Teachers: Educator-Designed Professional Development Can Turn Teachers Loose," *Virginia Journal of Education* (February 1995), pp. 7–10. See also Joseph Blasé and Jo Blase, *Empowering Teachers: What Successful Principals Do,* 2nd ed. (Thousand Oaks, CA: Corwin Press, 2001); Eithne Kennedy, "Improving Literacy Achievement in a High-Poverty School: Empowering Classroom Teachers through Professional Development," *Reading Research Quarterly* (vol. 45, no. 4, 2010), pp. 384–387; and Teresa M. Petty "Empowering Teachers: They Have Told Us What They Want and Need to Be Successful," *Delta Kappa Gamma Bulletin* (vol. 73, no. 2, Winter 2007), pp. 25–28.

CHAPTER

4

Communication

APPLICABLE PSEL STANDARDS

- **STANDARD 1: Mission, Vision, and Core Values**
  Effective educational leaders develop, advocate, and enact a shared mission, vision, and core values of high-quality education and academic success and well-being of each student.
- **STANDARD 2: Ethics and Professional Norms**
  Effective educational leaders act ethically and according to professional norms to promote each student's academic success and well-being.
- **STANDARD 3: Equity and Cultural Responsiveness**
  Effective educational leaders strive for equity of educational opportunity and culturally responsive practices to promote each student's academic success and well-being.
- **STANDARD 6: Professional Capacity of School Personnel**
  Effective educational leaders develop the professional capacity and practice of school personnel to promote each student's academic success and well-being.
- **STANDARD 7: Professional Community for Teachers and Staff**
  Effective educational leaders foster a professional community of teachers and other professional staff to promote each student's academic success and well-being.
- **STANDARD 8: Meaningful Engagement of Families and Community**
  Effective educational leaders engage families and the community in meaningful, reciprocal, and mutually beneficial ways to promote each student's academic success and well-being.
- **STANDARD 9: Operations and Management**
  Effective educational leaders manage school operations and resources to promote each student's academic success and well-being.

National Policy Board for Educational Administration (NPBEA). *Professional Standards for Educational Leaders* (Reston, VA: Author, 2015). Used with Permission.

The importance of effective communication practices within an organization cannot be overemphasized. As Lysaught has observed, "More frequently than not, failures in communication lie at the heart of problems in organization, goal setting, productivity and evaluation."[1] For this reason, according to St. John, "No one can manage a modern organization who is not knowledgeable in communication principles and techniques and skilled in their use."[2] Guarino considers the ability to communicate the most essential talent in the area of leadership.[3]

Without exception, all the major national school administrator associations in this country stress the importance of effective communication skills. The National Association of Elementary School Principals, for example, identifies communication as an indispensable leadership proficiency for elementary and middle school principals, noting that poor communication skills are a barrier to organization (team) success.[4] When the American Association of School Administrators (AASA) prepared its platform for the beginning of the twenty-first century, effective communication with the public was considered to be crucial. The organization noted that the future of public education is dependent on effective communication and relationship building.[5] Clearly, if any individual aspires to be successful as an administrator or leader, he or she must give high priority to developing effective skills in communication.

COMMUNICATION: THE ADMINISTRATOR'S MULTIPLE ROLES

Many school administrators, when they are asked about the importance of communication, tend to see themselves primarily in the role of *communicator*—a *sender* or *transmitter* of messages that others need to understand. For example, in a study by Morris and his colleagues, using ethnographic methods, principals were observed spending a great deal of time communicating with students, teachers, parents, superiors, and other individuals associated with the school.[6] Although the principal initiated most of this communication, there was no clear indication that the principals in the study had thoughtfully planned their communication or were in control of how much time they spent communicating with various people. Instead, judging from the examples presented in a report of the study, much of the principals' communication seemed unplanned and casual; little effort appeared to have been made by the principals to seek feedback from others or to evaluate what others were telling them.[7] That this problem is not limited to school administrators but is also characteristic of other kinds of managers has been made clear in a study by Luthans and Larsen.[8] Tannen writes that many daily miscommunications in the workplace result from the distinctly unique communication styles of the two genders.[9] With the increasing number of women in managerial positions throughout the work environment, both male and female administrators have the responsibility to examine this aspect of communication and develop strategies to ensure that these differences are addressed. More about this topic will be discussed later in this chapter.

Sending, Receiving, Monitoring, and Seeking

Although not all communication can be planned, nor is it always possible for an administrator to be in control of how much time is spent communicating with different individuals and groups, it would appear that many, if not most, administrators need to improve their communication practices and to adopt additional communication roles.[10] Although the administrator as *communicator* is an important role, it is only one of the many communication roles that are essential to the efficient and effective administration of an organization. School administrators also frequently find themselves in the role of *recipient* of messages from others. If the communication to, from, and within an organization is to be efficient and effective, then a school administrator will need to become a *monitor* and *seeker* of communication. Vail observes that the need for added information and better communication makes technology a powerful ally.[11] In the following sections the different facets of these four communication roles will be discussed, as well as the technology available to assist the administrator in managing these roles.

THE ADMINISTRATOR AS A COMMUNICATOR

The school administrator, whether a superintendent, a principal, or some other type of administrator, occupies a key position in the organizational hierarchy that necessitates communication with a wide variety of people about different situations, problems, and issues. As a communicator, an administrator needs to be aware of six basic aspects of communication:[12]

1. The purpose to be achieved by the message.
2. The person or persons to whom the message is directed.
3. The sender of the message.
4. The content of the message.
5. The alternative channels for communicating the message.
6. The need for feedback or a response to the message.

The Purpose of the Message

The initial task for the administrator who wishes to communicate a message to a particular individual or group is to think carefully about the objectives that the communication is meant to achieve. Is the purpose of the message to inform, to raise questions, to change attitudes, to stimulate action, to inhibit action, to reassure, to solidify support, to clarify, or to achieve some other goal? The administrator may possess a general idea of what the communication is to accomplish, but more time must be spent identifying the specific nature of the objectives the administrator hopes to achieve. As a result of sharpening the focus of the communication goals, the administrator will be in a better position to determine the content of a message and the communication channel to be utilized.

After the specific objectives of the message have been identified and clarified, the administrator should evaluate whether those objectives are attainable. The essential question is whether the goals are reasonable, considering the circumstances. For example, the administrator who has decided to reject a set of demands posed by a militant parent organization may wish to inform the parents about the decision and, at the same time, to dissuade them from taking further action. While the administrator would naturally like to accomplish both goals, is it reasonable to assume that any composed message will effectively do so? The first objective, that of informing the militant parents of the decision, may be achieved without difficulty, but the objective of convincing them that they should take no further action may not be attainable, considering the circumstances. This is not to say that an administrator should restrict communication goals only to those that can be easily achieved. It is suggested, however, that every administrator examine the feasibility of the communication objectives rather than assuming that they will be achieved without difficulty. Such an examination should be conducted after the objectives have been identified–and again after the message has been formulated.

Intended Audience—and Why Some Messages Go Unheard

Every message from the administrator will be interpreted in light of the conditions in which it is received and the characteristics of those who receive it. Depending on the nature of both factors, a message may or may not be successfully communicated. Barriers to effective communication with persons to whom the message is directed may stem from their lack of interest, their inability to understand certain elements of the message, their own personal biases, social barriers, and factors about the situation itself.[13]

Lack of Interest in the Message The administrator may believe that the message planned to be sent is extremely important and that the persons receiving the message should share that attitude. The recipients' interest in the contents of the message, however, will depend on their prior attitude toward the sender, the content, and the implications of the message.

Inadequate Background Knowledge for Understanding Message Content All communications contain particular words and ideas requiring a certain background or degree of knowledge. For example, will the parents who receive a message on "alternative programming" fully and accurately understand what is meant by that term? In the absence of that necessary background or knowledge, the recipients may fail to grasp what the administrator is trying to communicate.

The Bias of the Recipients The administrator needs to recognize that the content of the message will be filtered through the perceptual value screen of the recipients. Certain words in the message may be misinterpreted, or the purpose of the message may be distorted. Research has shown that people tend to seek messages consistent with their own attitudes and values and that they try to avoid disconcerting messages.[14] Although avoidance or misinterpretation of a message cannot always be completely eliminated, the administrator should carefully consider the characteristics of the recipients and the nature of the message to reduce the possibilities of being misunderstood.

Social Barriers that May Hinder the Message Differences in age, gender, position in the hierarchy, and subculture among the recipients or between them and the sender may pose a communication barrier.[15] For example, a message may be interpreted differently by physical education teachers and social studies teachers; women teachers and men teachers; and new teachers and more experienced ones. Particular attention must be paid to the differing rituals that typify the conversational styles of men and women. "Conversational rituals common among men," Tannen states, "often involve using opposition such as banter, joking, teasing and playful put-downs, and expending effort to avoid the one-down position in the interaction. Conversational rituals common among women are often ways of maintaining an appearance of equality, taking into account the effect of the exchange on the other person, and expending effort to downplay the speaker's authority so they can get the job done without flexing their muscles in an obvious way. When everyone present is familiar with these conventions, they work well. But when ways of speaking are not recognized as conventions, they are interpreted literally, with negative results on both sides."[16] Men may appear hostile or arrogant, and women less confident and competent. Any of these social differences may, in a given set of circumstances, pose a communication problem for the administrator.

Sometimes the communication styles associated with women are interpreted as weakness because in business and other aspects of public life, the communication styles most familiar are those associated with men. DiResta suggests that women may sometimes make it harder for themselves to break through the "glass ceiling" due to certain communication traits they use, such as excessive head nodding (which women may use to indicate active listening and understanding, whereas men may see it as agreement). Other traits DiResta cites are such habits as raising the inflection of the voice at the end of a sentence (which makes that sentence seem tentative), using weak language, allowing oneself to be interrupted, being too soft spoken, and not accepting opportunities to speak publicly.[17] On the other hand, as Robin Lakoff, one of the earliest researchers into gender-based linguistic differences, has pointed out, it is important to recognize the part played by female socialization in giving rise to such patterns. According to Lakoff, "If a little girl 'talks rough' like a boy, she will normally be ostracized, scolded or made fun of. . . . If the little girl learns her lesson well, . . . the acquisition of this special style of speech will later be an excuse others use to keep her in a demeaning position, to refuse to take her seriously as a human being. Because of the way she speaks, the little girl–now grown to womanhood–will be accused of being unable to speak precisely or to express herself forcefully."[18]

It must be recognized that differences in tone, inflection, degree of softness or loudness, use of pauses, and many other conversational strategies and habits also differ across cultures, socioeconomic class, and many other demographic variables. Sometimes what may be considered weakness may actually be an effort to be polite.[19] Women are socialized to be empathic and concerned about connecting with others, feeling responsible for their feelings, and desirous of making them feel comfortable–traits that carry over into communication patterns. In that sense, women's conversational style might be said to be well suited in many respects to an increasingly interdependent world where collaboration, inclusiveness, cooperation, and teamwork are viewed as more desirable than competition. At the 2000 Women's Ways of Leading conference sponsored by the American Association of School Administrators, successful educational leaders emphasized the importance of optimism, building alliances and partnerships, and spending much time talking with people–and especially *listening* to them.[20] At the same time, as Tannen points out, "One particular burden of this pattern for a woman in a position of authority is that she must deal with incursions on her time, as others make automatic assumptions that her time is more expendable, although she also may benefit from hearing more information because people find her 'approachable.'"[21]

There are differences in communication styles that exist in culturally diverse communities. Communication differences can have a detrimental effect on the school climate, making some students and their parents feel like unwelcome outsiders. Taylor suggests two major tactics that educational leaders can use to help break down barriers to cross-cultural communication: (1) Remove any expressions that serve to stereotype groups and reinforce bias and (2) become aware of variations in the cultural rules of conversation among different cultures. For example, recognize that cultures vary by degree of physical closeness or distance considered appropriate as people are standing together engaged in a conversation. Cultures also vary in what is considered proper for voice tone, in how pauses and silence are regarded, how softly or loudly a person should speak, or whether or not eye contact is permissible. Certain gestures or words that might seem humorous in one culture may be considered vulgar, sacrilegious, insulting, or taboo in another.[22] A failure to understand students and teachers who come from diverse cultural backgrounds can be a major barrier to effective communication.

The Situation Itself In addition to the factors already mentioned, barriers to communication are sometimes built into the situation itself, including the timing of the message. Distractions, insufficient time to read the message carefully, and overload of the communication channel through which the message is received are all factors that in a specific situation can pose barriers to effective communication. In many circumstances there is little that the administrator can do to overcome these barriers completely. An attempt should be made, however, to consider as much as possible the conditions in which the message will be received. To minimize the effects of the barriers identified previously, the administrator needs to think about the characteristics of the recipients of the message and the nature of the situation in which it will be received. For example, the following questions may need to be asked: What kinds of individuals or groups will be receiving the communication? What is their background or knowledge in relation to the topic or idea being communicated? What is their present interest in and attitude toward the topic or the idea being expressed? What is their attitude toward *me* as a communicator of the idea? What characteristics of the *situation* in which the message is being received may prevent or reduce the possibility that the message will be correctly understood and acted upon by the recipients? What characteristics of the individual or groups may cause the message to be misinterpreted or distorted?

The Sender of the Message

In no small measure, an administrator's success as a sender of messages also depends on the degree of trust that exists between him or her and the recipients of the messages. It also depends on the prestige of the administrator's position in the organization or community, and on the extent to which the individual is perceived as an expert by those who receive the message.[23]

Mutual Trust Trust goes both ways. There must be mutual trust between the communicator and the recipients of the message if effective communication is to occur. According to McGregor, trust is the belief that one party will not take an unfair advantage of the other.[24] If an administrator does not trust the recipients of the communication, then this could affect either how the message is framed or how it is delivered. If the recipients do not trust the administrator, they are unlikely to believe the message or to receive it in a positive manner. Morse stresses that the building of trust can only occur over a period of time and that traditional communication manners often threaten its fragile nature unless open and honest communications are maintained.[25] Mutual trust is a prerequisite to effective communication.

Perception of the Sender's Status Also important to effective communication is the status of the administrator in the organization or the community.[26] If the administrator is not perceived as being very influential in the organizational hierarchy or as possessing requisite competency in the area in which communication is attempted, it is probable that there will be difficulty in getting others to pay attention to the messages. Certainly, the likelihood that the recipients of a message will change their attitude or behavior on the basis of communication will depend greatly on their perception of the administrator's status in the organization and the recipients' evaluation of that person's expert knowledge in the area under consideration.

Setting the Tone The administrator can set the tone for communication throughout the institution. Schools with high trust levels are more likely to be characterized by communication that is honest,[27] and both communication and institutional effectiveness are better in a high-trust setting. Although institutions can be effective in low-trust settings, the environment is likely to have an influence on the process.

Self-Understanding In addition to these factors, it is important that administrators know and understand themselves as communicators. The administrator might ask, "Am I better at communicating in a one-to-one relationship or in a group setting? Am I better at communicating orally or in writing?" (Administrators who would like to improve their ability to give effective speeches and presentations will find helpful suggestions in Ehninger and in Murray and in Bateman and Sigband.)[28,29] The particular circumstances and the objectives an administrator wants to achieve will largely determine the choice of expression. For example, an administrator who wants to establish a secure, mentoring, nurturing climate in the school must know how to communicate successfully with the staff to reach that goal. Staff members use various communication indicators to judge the security of the school climate. Both the actions and the attitude the principal communicates in interacting with the staff will be interpreted as indicators of a secure or an insecure climate.

Understanding Others Knowing preferred personal communication styles is helpful in getting out a message. Pilgrim says that just as people interact with the world by using their senses (visual, auditory, and kinesthetic or tactile), so they interact with each other by communicating in modes related to the senses. She suggests that the verbs people use, along with certain bodily movements and stated preferences, provide clues to the type of communication mode they prefer. *Visually oriented people* think in mental pictures and use expressions such as "I see" or "Looks good." Pilgrim suggests communicating with them through pictures, charts, and other visual aids. *Auditory-oriented people,* on the other hand, like to listen. They tend to make statements such as, "I hear what you're saying."

Pilgrim stresses that it is important to discuss and answer their questions when communicating with people who receive information best in the auditory mode. Pilgrim's third category, *people who operate in a kinesthetic or tactile mode,* are often quite demonstrative and movement oriented. They prefer hands-on activities as a way of grasping new information. They enjoy touching, feeling, and walking through the steps of a new procedure.[30]

Some Pointers for Communicating Effectively Griffin offers the following communication pointers for getting across a message:

> The object is not to convince your audience/customer to buy something from you, but to avail himself [or herself] of your offer to share something good, great, exclusive, and/or beneficial. Sell yourself. Communicate confidence. This means that you should think about your body language. Make frequent eye contact with your audience. This suggests honesty–that you have nothing to hide. In contrast, looking down or aside suggests shiftiness and evasion. Use open gestures. Avoid touching your face; this suggests that you have something to hide. Avoid crossing your arms or putting your hands on your hips; such gestures communicate resistance and defiance. When you speak, open your mouth and take your time. Mumbling suggests evasiveness, and rapid speech is synonymous with the stereotype of the "fast-talking salesman." Both will evoke resistance in your audience/customer.[31]

When nonverbal messages are used without thought and purpose, opportunities to motivate, encourage, and support desired actions may be lost. The resulting negative reaction from the staff may seriously impair the administrator from reaching mutual goals and prevent successful teaching performance.

Communication That Encourages Positive Response from Staff Knoll suggests that the following communicating behaviors foster a secure climate and subsequently encourage staff performance:

1. Be honest by making open statements about your feelings, attitudes, and reactions to situations.
2. Be tactful and sensitive to staff needs, feelings, and problems, and treat people in a nonthreatening manner.
3. Accept people as they are by respecting individual staff differences, opinions, perceptions, and approaches.
4. Have a positive approach when you greet people, smile at them, and inquire about their health, problems, and joys.
5. Finally, be dependable, so that you will be trusted by the staff.[32]

There is also the need to analyze and understand personal strengths and weaknesses as a communicator. In many situations, the administrator will have the opportunity to choose the medium for the message. That choice should be based at least in part on an assessment of the administrator's performance as an individual communicator as well as on an evaluation of the effectiveness of the school's communication system and programs.[33]

Motivating through Effective Communication All administrators are asked to deal with issues or morale and culture in their schools. Often the issues revolve around poorly motivated teachers or teachers who disrupt the climate of the school overall. In order for administrators to surpass these issues, they must learn to communicate on a variety of levels. They may find themselves in the role of motivator, trying to gain the support of those around them. Covey

WINDOW ON DIVERSITY

Communication

TOP 10 TIPS FOR CROSS-CULTURAL COMMUNICATION

JANUARY 27TH, 2016

In today's diverse workplace, communication issues can take on an added dimension of complexity. Every culture has its own set of tacit assumptions and tendencies when it comes to face-to-face interactions, and trying to get your point across effectively can sometimes be difficult. Even when a language barrier doesn't exist, cross-cultural communication can be challenging. Here are our top 10 tips for effective cross-cultural communication:

1. **Maintain etiquette:** Many cultures have specific etiquette around the way they communicate. Before you meet, research the target culture, or if time allows, do some cross-cultural training. For example, many cultures expect a degree of formality at the beginning of communication between individuals. Every culture has its own specific way of indicating this formality: "Herr" and "Frau" in Germany, reversing family and given names in China and the use of "san" in Japan for men and women, etc. Be aware of these familiarity tokens and don't jump straight to first name terms until you receive a cue from the other person to do so.
2. **Avoid slang:** Not even the most educated non-native English speaker will have a comprehensive understanding of English slang, idioms and sayings. They may understand the individual words you have said but not the context or the meaning. As a result you could end up confusing them or at worst, offending them.
3. **Speak slowly:** Even if English is the common language in a cross-cultural situation, it's not a good idea to speak at your normal conversational speed. Modulating your pace will help, as will speaking clearly and pronouncing your words properly. Break your sentences into short, definable sections and give your listener time to translate and digest your words as you go. But don't slow down too much, as it might seem patronizing. If the person you're speaking to is talking too quickly or their accent is making it difficult for you to understand them, don't be afraid to politely ask them to slow down too.

states that to be a successful leader, you must learn to listen within the frame of reference of others.[34] He states that mutual understanding is one of the seven habits required to become an effective leader. Cooper takes a slightly different approach to motivation, stating that recognition of others and their accomplishments is paramount in motivating others to follow your lead.[35] Taking the time to acknowledge each person individually adds to his or her sense of contribution to the organization. This is one way to encourage faculty members to explore new teaching methodologies and take the lead when changes are planned institutionally.

4. **Keep it simple:** In a cross-cultural conversation there's no need to make it harder for both of you by using big words. Just keep it simple. Two-syllable words are much easier to understand than three-syllable words, and one-syllable words are better than two-syllable words. Say "Please do this quickly" rather than "Please do this in an efficacious manner."
5. **Practice active listening:** Active listening is a very effective strategy for improving cross-cultural communication. Restate or summarize what the other person has said to ensure that you have understood them correctly and ask frequent questions. This helps build rapport and ensures that important information doesn't get missed or misunderstood.
6. **Take turns to talk:** Make the conversation flow more freely by taking it in turns to speak. Make a point and then listen to the other person respond. Particularly when people are speaking English as their second language, it's better to talk to them in short exchanges rather than delivering a long monologue that might be difficult for them to follow.
7. **Write things down:** If you're not sure whether the other person has understood you properly, write it down to make sure. This can be particularly helpful when discussing large figures. For example, in the UK we write a billion as 1,000,000,000 but in the United States, it's written as 1,000,000,000,000.
8. **Avoid closed questions:** Don't phrase a question that needs a "yes" or "no" answer. In many cultures it is difficult or embarrassing to answer in the negative, so you will always get a "yes" even if the real answer is "no." Ask open-ended questions that require information as a response instead.
9. **Be careful with humor:** Many cultures take business very seriously and believe in behaving professionally and following protocol at all times. Consequently, they don't appreciate the use of humor and jokes in a business context. If you do decide to use humor make sure it will be understood and appreciated in the other culture and not cause offense. Be aware that British sarcasm usually has a negative effect abroad.
10. **Be supportive:** Effective cross-cultural communication is about all parties feeling comfortable. In any conversation with a non-native English speaker, treat them with respect, do your best to communicate clearly, and give them encouragement when they respond. This will help build their confidence and trust in you.

CHRYSOS: HR Solutions Limited. (2016, Jan. 27). "Top Ten Tips ... for Effective Cross-Cultural Communication." Used with permission.

The Content of the Message

Ideally, all communications from the administrator should be framed and constructed carefully and thoughtfully, although it is recognized that much communication between an administrator and others is spontaneous and casual.[36] Nevertheless, in those situations in which the consequences of the oral or written communication could be significant, the administrator should choose and organize all words with special care. The administrator will want people to regard these messages seriously, for, in many instances, the words will be closely scrutinized and weighed. The administrator should consider the audience for whom words are intended, the specific objectives desired, and the nature of the particular communication channel (e.g., written, oral) to be utilized.

Deal suggests that one memo can generate hours of discussion and set up informal networks at all levels of the organization. Discussion among workers often involves speculation and inference. Administrators can use this informal networking to their advantage by carefully wording all written documents and keeping all employees current regarding institutional choices.[37] A participatory leadership model has been identified as the most effective because it emphasizes open and accurate communication. Goals are set and reached as part of the process of reaching organizational goals.[38]

What Administrators Need to Know in Advance The principal who is trying to persuade teachers of the desirability of introducing a particular innovation should select those ideas, facts, or questions that will be most persuasive to the teachers. In constructing the message, the administrator will want to consider the teachers' current attitude toward the innovation, their present knowledge and understanding of the proposed change, their attitude toward the principal as the communicator, and the extent to which the communication medium chosen may limit or facilitate understanding the content of the message.

To achieve maximum effectiveness in communicating, the administrator should also critically examine the assumptions made in selecting and organizing the content of the message. Some of the questions that may need to be asked when constructing the message include the following: Is the idea clear? Will the words chosen to express the idea achieve the desired goal? How will the receiver perceive the message? Which characteristics of the ideas or words used will be likely to have the intended effect upon the receiver? Which ideas or words could potentially affect the receiver in ways not intended? What assumptions am I making? (For some excellent guidelines on issuing directives and other kinds of messages to subordinates, see St. John, and Himstreet and Baty.)[39]

Constructing the Content of the Message Research on communication would indicate that in constructing the content of the messages, particularly those intended to persuade another individual or group, the administrator should (1) concentrate on arousing desire and concern before suggesting appropriate action; (2) place highly desirable communication to the recipients first, followed by less desirable information; (3) acknowledge opposing arguments before presenting a different line of reasoning, unless the recipients are not aware of contrasting arguments to the course of action being recommended (in which case the administrator can proceed with the position on the issue or problem without mentioning the other side); and (4) recognize that facts alone will not change the opinion or attitude of an individual or group whose emotional predisposition runs contrary to the information being presented.[40]

Communication Channels

In communicating a prepared message, in contrast to a spontaneous response, the administrator can give considerable attention to the communication channels that are available and decide which one would most effectively communicate the message. All too frequently, administrators appear to think of only one or two means for communicating their messages. This is unfortunate because studies such as McCleary's have identified a wide array of possibilities for communication.[41] Figure 4.1 presents a number of these possibilities.

FIGURE 4.1
COMMUNICATION CHANNELS

Writing	Verbal Face-to-Face	Verbal/Electronic/Visual
• Note	• Individual Conference	• Telephone
• Letter	• Small Group Meetings	• P.A. System
• Memorandum	• Large Group Meetings	• Projector
• Community Newspaper	• Social Functions	• LCD Projector Panels
• School Bulletin		• Radio
• Internet/Social Media		• Television
• Whiteboard		• Texts
• Computer		• Internet (including e-mail, Facebook, Twitter, and YouTube)
		• Learning Management System (e.g., BlackBoard)
		• DVD

As Figure 4.1 suggests, a wide variety of communication channels should be considered. Multimedia communication incorporates verbal, writing, visual, and electronic components, such as graphics, sound clips, artwork, and photography. After an administrator has determined which communication channels are available in each situation, the best possible means of communicating the message should be reflected. Although this step may appear obvious, administrators too often fail to analyze the strengths and weaknesses of the various communication media available to them. They habitually write a memo, speak over the public address system, or prepare a staff bulletin instead of carefully and realistically assessing the communication channels that might best serve the needs of each situation. Even in instances where administrators do decide to continue using a familiar communication such as a memo, they should not do so unthinkingly but be very conscious of what they are trying to accomplish. They might want to ask themselves questions such as these: How many people are likely to read this memo before it reaches the target audience? How does the verbiage used in memos from this office affect the climate and culture of the institution? How do staff members, such as administrative support staff, determine compliance with items mentioned in memos? Such questions help administrators become aware of various aspects of their approach to communication, how effective it is, and whether they should examine other communication channels.

Computer-Based Communication An alternative approach might be the use of a computer-controlled voice message system that could ease communication difficulties between parents and schools, teachers, administrators, and staff. Using a computer, a principal can leave messages on the telephone for as many parents and staff as need to be contacted via this electronic mailbox.[42] Huntington discusses several basic Internet resources available to school administrators that can serve as two-way communication devices to other educators, the local community, or a community of peers around the world. These tools are *Internet e-mail, newsgroups* (discussion groups), *electronic bulletin boards* (message boards where specific information related to a topic is posted by various individuals), and *listservs* (electronic mail lists where an individual can send and receive e-mail messages, which go to the e-mail boxes of everyone in a select group simultaneously).[43] A school Web page is another way many schools are using computer-based communication. It is also important to note the use of Facebook, Twitter, LinkedIn, and other social networking sites as valuable forms of electronic communications.

Etiquette for the Electronic Age In using these tools, it is especially important to remember the etiquette of electronic communications. Without the ability to read a facial expression or body language, a recipient can easily misinterpret a message sent electronically. Numerous guidelines may be found on the Internet to aid in creating e-mail messages in a courteous, professional manner, and many institutions now have strict policies regarding the use and wording of such communications.[44] E-mail users need to make every effort to prevent misunderstandings. For example, it is important to avoid such practices as typing certain words or entire messages in all-capital letters (they are harder to read and also suggest shouting) or sending long attachments without the recipient's permission (attachments may be in a format that cannot be opened by the recipient). Where possible, it is often better to copy and paste material into the body of the e-mail rather than sending it as an attachment. Including a subject line identifying the content of the message shows consideration to time-pressed recipients, who can see at a glance what the message is about. When replying to a message, it is helpful to include the original e-mail message (if it is short) or small snippets of it so that the recipient, who may receive hundreds of e-mails, can know that this message is a response to a particular question or comment sent previously. It should be kept in mind that many people have e-mail programs that can only read plain text rather than the *hypertext markup language* (HTML) used on the Internet. Thus it is better to make sure e-mail has been set up to go out as plain text, which works well with all e-mail programs–unless it is known that the recipient's e-mail program can accommodate HTML formatting (which permits colored fonts, italic, boldface, and so on). Additionally, proper etiquette is particularly important for short messages. Twitter, for example, functions more as a real-time communication. As Twitter messages are limited to 140 characters, the following are offered as tips for making your tweets something valuable to followers:

- Beat the 140 character limit by linking to a Web page with more information.
- Don't diminish your effort with misspelled wordz. Typos stand out.
- Add your Twitter address to your e-mail signature and school district letterhead.
- When you issue news releases or parent letters, tweet with a link to your Web site.
- When news media outlets print or air a positive story about your district, tweet it, with a link to the story.
- Limit the personal stuff unless you know followers care where you go or who you meet.
- Do it daily. People value online resources they care about and that are regularly updated.
- Focus on what's ahead with tweets about upcoming events.
- Check your followers occasionally. Some Twitter users follow hoping you will follow back. Block them so you can focus on those followers who really matter.[45]

WINDOW ON DIVERSITY

10 Ways for New School Leaders to Use Twitter

Here are 10 ways new school leaders can use Twitter (without feeling overwhelmed):

1. **Upcoming School Event Details:** The easiest way to start sharing information to your followers on Twitter is to use it as a platform to broadcast upcoming school events and information. Chances are this information is already available on your school's Web site and newsletter, but Twitter is another great place to share this information and interact with the school community. The difference with Twitter is that when you share an upcoming activity, a parent might respond to your Tweet with a question, and then you can answer right back. That's a simple and powerful connection that most Web sites won't allow you to do!
2. **Live Sharing of School Activities:** If you want to get really good at this "Twitter thing" then live-Tweeting an event or activity is the place to get to the next level! The next sporting event you go to, or Reading Olympics, or Spirit Day . . . make sure you have Twitter open and Tweet out what is going on so your followers and community can be included in a real-time feed. If you use a #hashtag while Tweeting you can go back and look at the event through a tool like Storify to see all that happened!
3. **Accomplishments of Students, Teachers, Parents (and Anyone Else in Your School Community):** You probably have a bulletin board up somewhere in your school with Student of the Month and a whole host of other awards and accomplishments. Take those accomplishments and share them on Twitter with your community. Broadcast all of the great things happening in your school and don't be afraid to continue sharing these more than once.
4. **Community Events and Resources:** Sharing school events and activities is just the start. Make sure you are showcasing all of the great things happening outside your school's walls and in the community as well. Follow local organizations, companies, and institutions to Retweet and share what is going on each week. This will keep your followers informed of new opportunities they might not have heard of and provide a new way for you to interact with local companies and organizations that can help your school and students.
5. **Links to Educational Blogs and Resources:** If you are new to Twitter make sure you are following some educators who are blogging and educational sites that are sharing resources. This will allow you to stay current with best and next practices, and share this with your community. A simple Retweet will send it out to all of your followers, and hopefully this will lead to finding other blogs and sites that share the type of educational information you are looking for!

Continued

Continued

WINDOW ON DIVERSITY

10 Ways for New School Leaders to Use Twitter

6. **Quotes:** Quotes are some of the most Retweetable things you can share on Twitter. Share quotes from books you are reading, blog posts you are checking out, or from different places that you have found inspiring.
7. **Pictures:** Who doesn't love pictures? They do say a 1,000 words right? Share pictures of your students, staff, school building, and activities. Allow your followers and community to see what is happening behind those walls and inside the classrooms.
8. **Join a Conversation Using #hashtags:** I believe each school and district needs to have a hashtag that collects all of the Tweets you share and also can be used as an ongoing conversation. To start understanding how hashtags work, begin to join the weekly chats and hashtag conversations already taking place in education. This is another way to show your community the types of conversations that can happen on Twitter to benefit the entire school.
9. **National News/Studies Related to Education/Learning:** Don't be afraid to branch out a bit to national news, especially when stories are tied to education and learning. Your feed can and should be relevant to what is happening in your area, state, country, and world.
10. **Who You Are!:** Last, and probably most important: Be you. Your school community does not want a robot to lead them forward. They want you and your personality needs to shine through your Twitter feed. Just as your personality comes out in conversations with teachers, students, and parents . . . it should also be a part of your Twitter presence. This can be tough to do in the beginning, but look at how some of the other school leaders online are able to be a voice for their school but also be unique . . . that is the real goal here.

Source: Juliani, A. J. "10 Ways New School Leaders Use Twitter." Retrieved at http://ajjuliani.com/10-ways-new-school-leaders-use-twitter/, October 13, 2014.

Nonverbal Messages In becoming aware of different kinds of communication channels, administrators need to recognize that, in a sense, they also represent one type of communication channel. Whether they realize it or not, administrators communicate to people *nonverbally* through facial expressions, gestures, dress, tone of voice, and the physical environment in which they communicate.[46] Through these nonverbal means they can and do (often inadvertently) communicate surprise, fear, anger, disgust, disappointment, sadness, happiness, and other kinds of emotions and reactions. As long as the message communicated through nonverbal means coincides with the message they are communicating in other ways, there is no problem, and, in fact, the nonverbal methods can be helpful. When the verbal and the nonverbal messages contradict each other, problems can definitely result.[47] For example, if an administrator speaking to a parent is asking for cooperation, while inadvertently conveying dislike through facial expression or tone of voice, then there exists a very real possibility of communicating contradictory messages.

It is not always possible, of course, to be aware of how one is communicating nonverbally or to control one's nonverbal messages. An administrator should make an effort to develop a better understanding of this subtle channel of communication, however, and to be aware that an inconsistency between verbal and nonverbal messages could explain certain problems in communication.

Communicating with the Public

In communicating with the public, personal contact is probably the most effective method, but the best way to reach a large number of people in a short time is through the media. Newspaper, radio, or television coverage gives administrators an opportunity to communicate their story to a large group, although the form that story takes is beyond their control. The right of the press to cover news, and the public's right to know it, will frequently dictate the reporting of newsworthy events in schools–both good and bad. Consequently, the school administrator must work with the media to ensure that the communications to the public are as fair and as accurate as possible. A collegial relationship between the reporter and the administrator, based on trust and mutual respect and understanding, can be developed by providing the press with a steady flow of information and frequent communications, not just at budget time. Honesty, credibility, and respect for reporters' deadlines also contribute to a good working relationship. When inevitable mistakes do occur in coverage, the school administrator should make it a practice never to take negative reports or mistakes personally.[48]

Newquist has assembled various tips for administrators in using the media to the best advantage. Drawing upon advice from various public relations specialists, she suggests being alert to possible story angles about various aspects of the school's mission, events, and people. Inviting reporters to special events, informing them about new programs, finding ways that local school news can tie in with a national education story, and spotlighting a special aspect of one of the teacher's or student's lives outside the school are some of Newquist's suggestions.[49] Preparing press releases and even a press kit is a good idea. An excellent example is the National Aeronautics and Space Administration (NASA) guide to aid schools in preparing such materials.[50]

In crisis situations, it is critical that schools be proactive in their communication, including having a plan in place before a disaster or controversial incident takes place.[51] Newquist stresses the importance of a timely response. "No matter how awful or how minor, if an incident has captured the attention of the school, the community, or the world, be prepared to talk about it–publicly and immediately." She stresses that the communication must begin by informing the faculty and staff and, next, the parents. In dealing with the print or broadcast media (if the incident has drawn attention beyond the school), she suggests that one spokesperson be designated to receive all media calls.[52] Newquist points out that not all crisis management is centered on some catastrophic event. It might be related to questions the public has about poor test results, programs that have been eliminated, a change in administration in midyear, or a new policy, to mention only a few.[53] What is important is to anticipate questions and be prepared to answer them in a calm, informative manner.

Public Speaking

Every administrator must develop the skills needed to be an effective public speaker whether making presentations to the school board, addressing students at assemblies, speaking to parents at a PTA program, or training staff at workshops. Robert D. Ramsey, the author of *Lead, Follow or Get Out of the Way,* suggests the following tips for school leaders and public speaking:

- Prepare with both the topic and listeners in mind. Tailor the subject matter and gear the vocabulary to each specific audience.
- Believe in your message. Give your own speech. Use your own words.
- Your goal should be to present a clear message using powerful word choices.
- Always number your note cards. Don't even think about stapling them together.
- When rehearsing, pay attention to timing. Resist the tendency to talk too fast. It's a mistake that many inexperienced speakers make.
- Personally check out the location and setting of each speech in advance.
- Make friends with your nervousness. Use the energy to become more animated in your presentation.

COMMUNICATION HIGHLIGHT
CRISIS COMMUNICATION TACTICS

Crisis communications tactics aren't always necessary for bad news solely—good news can prompt a flood of media attention as well. In either case, instruct those answering the phones to collect complete information—name of person, name of news organization, phone number, and the reporter's deadline—and prioritize phone calls to be returned based on that information.

A few things to keep in mind when talking to the media during a crisis:

- Never tell a reporter anything you are unwilling to see in print. "Off the record" is sometimes misunderstood and misused, so don't rely on it to protect you.
- Listen to yourself speak. This helps you to speak slowly and it helps you monitor your statements for accuracy and clarity.
- If you are asked a question that is off the point, confusing, or inappropriate, answer the question you wish you had been asked. "What's important here is that . . ." Reporters are often satisfied to receive a clear, quotable statement, even if it is not perfectly responsive.
- Stop talking when you are finished—even if a reporter waits in silence for more. Don't feel compelled to fill the silence, or you may say more than you intended.
- If you are angry or upset about an issue, try to postpone the interview until you regain a normal, calm demeanor.
- Plan what to do with your hands. If nothing else, keep them at your side or rest one on the podium.

Source: Newquist, C. (2015) *Public Relations 101: Tips for School Administrators (and Other School Professionals).* Retrieved at http://www.educationworld.com/a_admin/admin/admin123.shtml

- Pay attention to posture. Maintain a professional demeanor. If you look like a leader, you're more likely to sound like one.
- Do whatever it takes to get the audience's attention early in the presentation.
- Stay clear of ethnic stories, risqué humor, and jokes that belittle others.
- Use visual aids, wherever they fit. (Remember that 80 percent of what people remember they pick up visually.)
- Don't be afraid to pause to let your message sink in. An occasional lower and slower tone can also focus the audience's attention.
- Always try to end with a clincher.[54]

THE ADMINISTRATOR AS A RECIPIENT OF COMMUNICATION

Thus far, the emphasis has been placed on the administrator's role as a communicator. In many cases, the administrator is also a recipient of communication. Because administrators occupy an important position in the school organization, they will receive various kinds of written and oral messages from students, teachers, parents, and other individuals with whom they come into contact.[55] These messages need to be evaluated by the administrator as to their *relevance, substance, significance,* and *implications.* The importance of evaluating communication from subordinates to superiors is underscored by findings from several research studies. For example, a laboratory experiment by Kelly found that low-status participants were typically uncritical in their communications to higher-status participants and frequently communicated more irrelevant messages than did the high-status participants.[56] Kelly's findings were supported by Hurwitz, who discovered in a study of communications between various professional participants that lower-status professionals talked less and were less often critical of higher-status professionals.[57] More recent studies confirm this type of communication.[58]

These studies suggest that, due to the administrator's status, subordinates will send few crucial messages. On the other hand, subordinates–particularly those who are aiming to advance their personal interests–will send a number of laudatory messages. The implication is that the administrator may find it difficult to obtain accurate information from subordinates about proposed or executed actions. This poses a significant problem for administrators because they are always in need of valid information. There is probably no perfect solution to this difficulty, but the administrator interested in obtaining complete and honest feedback from subordinates will encourage them to "speak their minds," will avoid reacting negatively to those who do so (even if the message is critical in nature), and will recognize that even under the best circumstances the communication received from subordinates may be less than completely candid.

Examining Messages

As a recipient of communication, both verbal and oral, the administrator should examine all messages by mentally raising the following questions:

1. Why is the message being sent? What is its purpose, either stated or implied? What does the sender hope to accomplish?
2. What is the factual basis for the message? Which statements in the communication rest on fact, which are based on opinion, and which rely on assumption?

3. What necessary information is not included in the message? What questions does the message fail to answer? What additional questions does it raise?
4. What does the message tell the administrator about the sender? What does it reveal about the sender's expectations for the role of the administrator? What does the communication suggest about the sender's perception of or relationship with other people, inside or outside the organization?

The messages that an administrator receives will contain facts, perceptions, opinions, and assumptions. In many, if not most instances, a message will contain few confirmed statements of fact, although it should be noted that the observations or opinions offered in a message may be perceived as factual by the sender.[59] While this perception needs to be considered in responding to a message, the initial task for the administrator is to analyze the communication received, with regard to which aspects of the message appear to be factual and which parts will need to be validated.

In addition, the administrator will want to examine a message for its purpose and the extent to which it provides insight into the sender's personality and the expectations for the behavior of the administrator. All messages are sent for a purpose and are based on an expectation that the administrator will respond in a particular way. It needs to be recognized, however, that the purpose of a message or the sender's expectations and real feelings on a matter may not be stated explicitly.[60] Therefore, the administrator needs to examine each message carefully, trying to "read between the lines" for clues that will offer better information about the true purpose behind the message and the actual behavior expected.

Listening Effectively

Perhaps one of the most important roles an administrator can play as a recipient of communication is that of listener. In an early study Rankin found that the communication day of an administrator was divided into the following activities: writing, 9 percent; speaking, 16 percent; reading, 30 percent; and listening, 45 percent. This study, which has often been replicated, shows that listening is the most frequent communication activity, making up almost half of the efforts spent in communication.[61] Much of the communication that administrators receive is oral; therefore, empathetic, accurate listening is necessary for a valid understanding of what is being communicated.

If an administrator is not a good listener, the very real possibility exists of not fully understanding what is being said. Or, even more seriously, people will avoid expressing themselves because of the administrator's reputation as a "poor listener" or someone who "doesn't care." A recent study found that most people value coworkers and employers who are skilled listeners and who show their interest in others by their focused and genuine empathy.[62] Although most administrators would probably like to believe that they are good listeners, reports from teachers suggest just the opposite.[63] Actually, most people are probably *not* good listeners and tend, all too frequently, rather than listening, to be waiting for the other party to finish talking so their own views can be expressed. One easy way to demonstrate this phenomenon is for a third party to ask the recipient of an oral communication to summarize the communicator's message to the latter's satisfaction.

Effective listening is not a skill that is inherited or automatically acquired; it must be developed and cultivated. In part, it involves an attitude that indicates the administrator is *interested in* and *cares about* what the other party has to communicate.[64] It is an attitude that cannot be easily fabricated without self-betrayal, and, to be effective, it must be sincerely felt and communicated nonverbally as well as verbally. Newton recently wrote that people relate to

FIGURE 4.2
LISTENING HABITS AND RECOMMENDED BEHAVIORS

To Be Avoided

Faking attention (pretending to listen)
Listening for facts without considering the broader meaning
Concentrating on physical appearance and delivery at the expense of verbal content
Yielding to distractions
Dismissing content as uninteresting
Ceasing to listen because the content is difficult to comprehend

To Be Developed

Screening out extraneous distractions
Concentrating mentally *and* physically on what the other person is saying
"Listening with a third ear"—being sensitive to what the person *seems* to be saying . . . or *not* saying
Asking questions to draw the other person out and to clarify ideas
Responding to the other person nonjudgmentally
Summarizing periodically what you think the other person has been saying, and obtaining his or her reaction to whether or not you accurately heard him or her

Recommended Responses	Examples
Showing Attention	"Yes." "Ah, ah." "I understand." Periodic, slight nodding of the head.
Seeking More Information	"That's interesting. Could you tell me more about that?"
Seeking Clarification	"I'm not sure I fully understand. Could you elaborate or give me an example?"
Paraphrasing	"You seem to be saying . . . Is that correct?"
Reflecting Emotion	"You seem upset with me. Is this the way you feel?"
Summarizing	"Let me try to identify the main points you seem to have made, and you let me know if I have missed anything."

us in large part because of our relative effectiveness in communication, and any person who desires to become a better listener must first have a change in attitude. A person must become more resolved to learn from others and to acknowledge that everyone has something to teach.[65]

Effective listening also involves avoiding some bad habits and developing good ones, as indicated in Figure 4.2.[66]

Listening is a skill that must be practiced and continually refined. The administrator who is interested in further developing this skill should examine writings on the subject, including Nostrand and Shelley's *An Educational Leadership Listening Model.*[67]

THE ADMINISTRATOR AS A MONITOR OF COMMUNICATION

It should be obvious that the school administrator is not the only one in the organization who is sending and receiving communications. For example, within a school, students, teachers, support staff, secretaries, and custodians are all communicating to various people and with one another. Staff communications can set the tone and goals of a school. A positive or negative verbal environment is often reflected in the communication skills teachers and administrators choose to use, be they in the elementary, middle, or high school.

Setting a Positive Tone

A positive verbal environment can make children or youth feel good about themselves and see the school as a positive influence in their lives. Adults using words to show affection for children and demonstrating a sincere concern for them by using children's interests as a basis for conversation convey a positive message. Teachers or administrators paying superficial attention to what children have to say, adults speaking discourteously, and staff members actively discouraging students from talking to them create a negative verbal communication environment. The administrator must provide a high level of strong leadership in monitoring the communication climate for learning.[68] Most importantly, administrators need to be aware that those who focus on communicating their own "rightness" become isolated and ineffectual.[69]

Communication Networks Outside the School

In addition, within a school district, communications pass from the people in the district office to the individual schools, and vice versa. There is also the environment external to a school or school district, where special-interest groups, parents, community leaders, and others communicate about and to the school and receive messages from those associated with the school or school district. Complex? Indeed! But it is in the best interest of the school administrator to try to monitor (to the extent feasible) the communication networks, both formal and informal,[70] that operate in the organization and community, and to ascertain message distortions of one kind or another. There are numerous examples of these message distortions that we will describe next.

Monitoring communications means that a school administrator should attempt to stay informed about who is communicating with whom and about what in regard to the school or school district. It will, of course, be impossible for an administrator to always know *all* the different messages that are being sent to, from, and within the school organization. By identifying and then establishing open lines of communication with certain key individuals and groups designated as *key communicators,* however, an administrator should be able to monitor the most important messages emanating from and being sent to the school. The key communicator concept has typically been applied to the school's community setting,[71] but in discussing the administrator's role as a monitor of communication, its application is expanded to communication that occurs within the school organization as well.

School Secretaries as Communicators

One of the key communicator groups consists of the school secretaries, especially those who are in a position either to implement a school administrator's directives or to send messages to and receive them from others in the school organization and community. For example, a principal may have informed the faculty of an "open-door" policy that includes the principal being always receptive to hearing about teachers' problems and concerns. Despite all good intentions, if the principal's secretary is sending a different message to the teachers, either through nonverbal mannerisms or by overzealous behavior–for example, "The principal can't see you now; The principal is too busy!"–then the objectives of the principal's open-door policy are unlikely to be achieved.

School secretaries are also key communicators regarding the messages they send to and transmit from parents and the general public. School secretaries, however, can cause problems through telephone messages transcribed inaccurately or passed along improperly and through any inappropriate demeanor in answering school telephones or greeting people who visit the school.

Training for Secretaries and Other Support Staff An initial question for the school administrator to answer is, Are the school secretaries sending and transmitting accurate and helpful messages to the people within the school and to those persons who contact the school? This will be a difficult question to answer. Nevertheless, by getting out of the office frequently, maintaining a high degree of visibility and accessibility, and actively seeking the perceptions of people who have had contact with the school secretaries, an administrator should be able to monitor the communication behavior of these key communicators. If problems are discovered, the school administrator can either attempt to assist the particular individuals who need improvement or, if the problem is widespread, provide in-service education for all of the secretaries.

The U.S. Department of Labor notes that the numbers of employers utilizing nontraditional workforce members are increasing, as is the amount of technology employers expect those employees to utilize.[72] The most efficient way to create a staff that meets the specific needs of an institution is to train them in-house. How employees are trained will directly reflect the organization they are representing. One of the most important aspects of employee training is communication technique. This includes what is said to employees and how they relay information to others with whom they come in contact. Training must now include many interaction formats–spoken, written, telephone, and electronic.

Research by Kouzes and Posner showed that continual and adequate training significantly reduced employee grievances, absenteeism, and disciplinary problems.[73] They also note that although it may be tempting to reduce the funding required for these in-service training sessions, without employee renewal in place the institution risks falling behind the competition. Part of employee renewal is revision of the team. People become used to communicating with each other and often need to be refreshed in order to ensure they bring the most to the organization as well as get the most satisfaction from their job. They also remind us that work should be fun, and humor can be an effective method of communication when introducing new skills or tasks into the work setting.[74]

Department Chairs and Unit Leaders as Communicators

Department chairpersons or unit leaders in a school represent another key group of communicators. These individuals play what Likert refers to as a "linchpin" role in the school's organizational structure, in that one of the responsibilities of their positions is to transmit messages from the school principal to the teachers in a department or unit, and vice versa.[75] In their roles as transmitters, the department chairpersons or unit leaders may be communicating accurately and completely the intent and content of messages from the principal to teachers in their department or unit. Some of them, however, may be misinterpreting, garbling, or omitting essential details, or may be failing to pass on certain or many aspects of the principal's messages. Of course, the same kinds of problems could be occurring in regard to messages that teachers try to send to the principal through the department chairperson or unit leader. This type of miscommunication may or may not be intentional, but if it occurs, it can negatively influence the operational efficiency and goal achievement of an organization.

To determine whether communication problems are occurring within this group of key communicators, the school administrator should formally and informally survey the teachers in the school to ascertain whether the principal's messages are reaching the teachers as intended, and whether the teachers' messages for the principal are solicited by the department heads and are properly forwarded. Obviously, surveys need to be conducted carefully to avoid upsetting the department chairpersons or unit leaders. The administrator should recognize that one cannot just *assume* that those communicators are doing their jobs; some type of periodic assessment will be needed.[76]

Community Leaders as Communicators

A third group of key communicators is formed by those individuals in the community who are leaders of organizations, such as the PTA, or leaders of special-interest groups, such as the Junior Chamber of Commerce. According to Kindred and his associates, key communicators need not always be leaders of an organization but can be "barbers, beauticians, bartenders, owners of restaurants, gas station operators, doctors, dentists, letter carriers, or people to whom citizens turn and ask, 'What do you think about that?'"[77] The latter group would certainly include individuals who engage in informal discussions at the supermarket or local coffee shop, as well as reporters, who are definitely key communicators in a more formal sense.

The first task for a school administrator who wishes to monitor the communications of the key communicators in the community served by the school or school district is to ascertain their identities. The kinds of persons who might be key communicators in one locality may not be influential in a different community. The leaders of organizations whose primary purpose is to improve education, however, such as the PTA or organizations that have subcommittees devoted to education, are likely to be key communicators in any school community. (For more information on this aspect, see Gorton and Thierbach-Schneider.)[78] These are the individuals with whom the administrator should establish open lines of communication. Frequent and informed contact must be maintained, particularly about whether these key communicators are receiving and sending accurate information about the school or school district. The other types of key communicators referred to by Kindred–for instance, beauticians and barbers–will be more difficult to identify because their communication status and the relevance of their communications about the school may not be obvious. If an administrator lives in the community, over time some insight into who these key communicators are can be developed. In addition, an administrator can try to tap the knowledge of those faculty and staff members who live in the school locality as to the identity of key communicators. Once these key communicators have been identified, it is important for the school administrator to develop and maintain open lines of communication with them. It is typically these kinds of key communicators who tend to hear the rumors and gossip about the school. They can be useful in alerting an administrator to this type of communication.

Monitoring the communication occurring within, to, and from an organization will require an alert, energetic, perceptive administrator. It will also require an administrator who is an active *seeker* of communication, a topic to be addressed in the next section.

THE ADMINISTRATOR AS A SEEKER OF COMMUNICATION

No administrator can afford to limit communication behavior to merely sending, monitoring, and receiving messages. An administrator must also actively *seek* facts, perceptions, and ideas from other people. Administrators who assume that they will be supplied with all the information needed in order to make a decision, or that all the communications transmitted will be accurate, valid, and complete, are not thinking realistically. Important information may sometimes be withheld because it is thought by others to be of little interest to the administrator or because of fear that the nature of the message might adversely affect their rapport. To overcome these barriers to communication, an administrator must make continuous and persistent efforts to learn the attitudes and opinions of coworkers.

For example, after the administrator has initiated messages to others, an attempt must be made to obtain accurate and complete feedback from them on their perceptions of what the intent of the communication *to them* was. It is not enough merely to express decisions, wishes, feelings, instructions, evaluations, or directives for action. The administrator must also ascertain whether the messages have been correctly understood.

In addition, the administrator needs to inquire whether the communications have produced the desired effects. As an illustration, the teachers in a particular situation may have *understood* what the administrator was saying over the public address system, in a memo, or during the faculty meeting, but the crucial question is, Did the message produce the desired results? If the answer is negative, the administrator has not necessarily failed to express the message clearly, but obviously the message was not completely successful. As a seeker of communication, the administrator needs to obtain feedback on two dimensions of any message: (1) Was it correctly understood? and (2) Did it produce the desired effect?

Encouraging Communication at Every Level

The administrator also needs to encourage accurate and full communication throughout the school organization. There is evidence that, in many organizations, communication, particularly formal communication, flows from superior to subordinate; there is frequently little upward or lateral communication.[79] The task for the administrator is to convey to all individuals and groups the need for upward and lateral communication and to develop feasible methods for transmitting this kind of communication. Schmuck and Runkel present several examples of such methods.[80]

In addition, the administrator will need to create a feeling and atmosphere of trust and respect on the part of the people in order to encourage them to communicate more. Unless people feel secure in communicating certain information and feel that what they are communicating will be taken seriously, they are not likely to increase their communication.[81] A principal may need to check out the employees' perceptions of the communication climate within the school and to determine staff perceptions of the communication relationship between the principal and staff, as well as how these are related to the overall communications climate in the school. A communication audit survey designed to measure perceptions about communication sources, messages, channels, and receivers could be administered to obtain quantitative information. Focus group sessions with all staff could provide extremely useful qualitative information on communication patterns, outcomes, relationships, and content within the school. Results may indicate that a school might improve its communications climate by increasing the amount and frequency of internal communication at all levels or that the communication relationship most in need of attention involves the principal. To enhance organizational effectiveness, the principal may discover from such a survey that a need exists to develop strategies to build personal and organizational trust and that all department heads should meet collectively and individually to develop strategies and techniques to improve the school's climate.[82]

EXPANDING INFORMATION SOURCES

If an administrator is to secure the desired kind of feedback to perform all aspects of the job effectively, all sources of information will have to be expanded. Many administrators' sources of information are limited, either because of their position in the organizational hierarchy or because of other people's perception of their availability or receptivity to communication. Although administrators often proclaim an open-door policy, these administrators should realize that the door may not be perceived by everyone as truly open, especially not by people with disturbing or disagreeable messages. Consequently, an administrator's contacts may be restricted to only certain kinds of individuals bearing information that is regarded as nonthreatening.

Administrators, therefore, must be careful to avoid the situation of receiving their information, recommendations, evaluations, and reactions from a select group of people who tend to see things in a similar way, either because they share values or because they do not want to impair their relationship. Since administrators need diversity rather than similarity of opinion, additional sources of information providing perceptions of a problem or situation must be developed. Administrators especially need to identify and secure ideas and opinions from those students, teachers, parents, and other professional or community people who may hold *contrasting* sets of values or objectives. In all respects, in order to serve everyone's best interests, administrators must become active seekers of communication from a wide variety of people, utilizing a wide array of communication resources.

SHARING EXPERIENCES AND NETWORKING

Ackerman offers an innovative technique, the case story, to help break down the isolation of the administrator. It is a combination of the conventional case study and the artistry and imagination of storytelling. Writing and sharing their stories with other educators allows administrators to better understand their own theories of practice and dilemmas, as well as to explore new possibilities with each other. The results are that participants begin to think more critically and less self-centeredly, to assist each other in gaining insight and perspective, and to grow professionally.[83]

In addition, communication with others can be greatly expanded and enhanced by linking computers and developing administrative networks. Through a network, teachers and administrators can communicate about faculty meetings, student progress, and parent conferences. Administrative networks can connect every classroom in the school to the principal's office so as to make regular reporting easy, and can also connect the principal to the superintendent's office or the district's administrative computing system. The computer network streamlines financial management, inventory control, transportation scheduling, word processing, and attendance information for immediate communication to a wide audience. A network communication system also enables principals to communicate with one another, with research organizations, with state departments of education, and with professionals throughout the world, exchanging valuable information on education issues and challenges. Networking is no longer a futuristic concept. Comprehensive networking strategies provide an integrated solution for communicating and sharing information, be it via fiber-optic video delivery or by connecting personal computers, iPods, iPads, and other smartphones.[84]

Most of the case studies, suggested learning activities, and simulations presented in Part II of the text require appropriate use of the ideas in this chapter. The following exercises, however, should provide the best opportunities for testing understanding and effective use of communication concepts: Cases 1, 10, 13, 14, 16, 33, 39, 54, 56, and 60 and the in-basket exercises.

NOTES

1. Jerome P. Lysaught, "Toward a Comprehensive Theory of Communications: A Review of Selected Contributions," *Educational Administration Quarterly* (Summer 1984), p. 101.
2. Water D. St. John, *A Guide to Effective Communication,* Personal and Organizational Communication Series, an ERIC Report, Ed. 057464, p. 1.
3. Sam Guarino, *Communication for Supervisors* (Columbus: Ohio State University, 1974), p. 1.
4. Cathie E. West, "Principals and Superintendents Who Forge a Solid Partnership Will More Effectively Determine What to Do and How to Go about Doing It," *Principal* (January/February 2011), p. 13. Also see statements from the American Association of School Administrators and the National Association of Secondary School Principals pertaining to the importance of communication skills for administrators.
5. http://www.aasa.org; see also E. Joseph Schneider and Lara L. Hollenczer, *Principal's Guide to Managing Communication* (Thousand Oaks, CA: Corwin Press, 2006).
6. Van Cleve Morris et al., *Principals in Action* (Columbus, OH: Charles E. Merrill, 1984), pp. 33-40, 54-56.
7. Ibid., pp. 41-49, 58-65, and chaps. 10, 11.
8. Fred Luthans and Janet K. Larsen, "How Managers Really Communicate," *Human Relations* (February 1986), pp. 161-178. Also see Eugene V. Donaldson, *Predictable Communication Strategies* (Los Angeles: Outcomes Unlimited, 1990).
9. Deborah Tannen, *Talking from 9 to 5: How Women's and Men's Conversational Styles Affect Who Gets Heard, Who Gets Credit, and What Gets Done at Work* (New York: William Morrow, 1994), pp. 22-23. Also see Barbara Arrighi (Ed.), *Understanding Inequality: The Intersection of Race/Ethnicity, Class, and Gender* (Lanham, MD: Rowman & Littlefield Publishers, 2001), pp. 173-181.
10. For suggestions on how administrators can better control the amount of time they spend communicating with individuals and groups, see Stephen Strasser and John Sena, "Why

Managers Can't Disengage," *Business Horizons* (January–February 1986), pp. 26–30. Also see Richard L. Enos (Ed.), *Oral and Written Communication: Historical Approaches* (Newbury Park, CA: Sage, 1990).

11. Kathleen Vail, "Data-Driven Decisions," *Executive Educator* (April 1996), p. 28.
12. William J. Seiler et al., *Communication in Business and Professional Organizations* (Reading, MA: Addition-Wesley, 1982), chap. 1.
13. Richard M. Steers, *Introduction to Organizational Behavior* (Glenview, IL: Scott, Foresman, 1984), pp. 265–267.
14. Mark A. DeTurck, "A Transactional Analysis of Compliance Gaining Behavior: Effects of Noncompliance, Relational Contexts, and Actors' Gender," *Human Communication Research* (Fall 1985), pp. 54–78; also see Peter F. Oliva and George E. Pawlas, *Supervision for Today's School,* 8th ed. (New York: Wiley, 2007).
15. Brent D. Ruben and Lea P. Stewart, *Communication and Human Behavior,* 5th ed. (Boston, MA: Allyn and Bacon, 2005). Also see Raymond A. Dumont and John M. Lannon, *Business Communications,* 3rd ed. (Glenview, IL: Scott, Foresman/Little Brown Higher Education, 1990).
16. Tannen, *Talking from 9 to 5,* p. 23. Also see Arrighi, *Understanding Inequality,* pp. 173–181.
17. D. DiResta, *Ten Ways Women Sabotage Their Communication in the Workplace.* Accessed online, http://www.diresta.com/top10_pu_women.asp, May 9, 2005.
18. Robin Lakoff, *Language and Woman's Place* (New York: Harper & Row, 1975), pp. 5–6.
19. Deborah Tannen, *That's Not What I Meant! How Conversational Style Makes or Breaks Relationships* (New York: Ballantine Books, 1987), pp. 28–30.
20. "'Optimism' Sums Up Women's Ways of Leading," AASA Leadership News (November 6, 2000). Accessed online, http://www.aasa.org, December 28, 2010.
21. Tannen, *Talking from 9 to 5,* p. 117.
22. Orlando L. Taylor, *Cross-Cultural Communication: An Essential Dimension of Effective Education,* rev. ed. (Washington, DC: Mid-Atlantic Equity Center, 1990), chap. 4.
23. Rudi Klauss and Bernard M. Bass, *Interpersonal Communications in Organizations* (Orlando, FL: Academic Press, 1982).
24. Douglas McGregor, *The Professional Manager* (New York: McGraw-Hill, 1967), pp. 163–164.
25. Sheila Morse, Tamara Daniels, and Florence Flieg, "An Early Childhood Professional Development School: Triumphs and Troubles," paper presented at the American Association of Colleges of Teacher Education Annual Conference, Washington, DC, February 13, 1995, p. 8.
26. Robert A. Snyder and James H. Morris, "Organizational Communication and Performance," *Journal of Applied Psychology* (August 1984), pp. 461–465.
27. T. Deal and A. Kennedy, *Corporate Cultures: The Rites and Rituals of Corporate Life* (Cambridge, MA: Perseus Books, 2000).
28. Douglas Ehninger et al., *Principals and Types of Speech Communication* (Glenview, IL: Scott, Foresman, 1986); and Mary Ellen Murray, "Painless Oral Presentations," *Bulletin of the Association for Business Communication* (June 1989), pp. 13–14.
29. David Bateman and Norman B. Sigband, *Communicating in Business* (Glenview, IL: Scott, Foresman, 1989), chaps. 18, 19.
30. Susan Pilgrim, "Identifying Communication Styles for Business Success," Pertinent Information Ltd. Accessed online, http://arif-donk.blogspot.com/2008/03/identifying-communication-styles-for.html, December 28, 2010.
31. Jack Griffin, *How to Say It Best: Choice Words, Phrases & Model Speeches for Every Occasion* (Englewood Cliffs, NJ: Prentice Hall, 1994), p. 201.
32. Marcia K. Knoll, "How to Communicate Successfully: Establishing a Secure Climate," *Supervision for Better Instruction* (Englewood Cliffs, NJ: Prentice Hall, 1987), pp. 191–201.
33. Walter St. John, "Assessing the Communications Effectiveness of Your School," *Practitioner* (Reston, VA: National Association of Secondary School Principals, December 1990), pp. 1–12.

34. S. R. Covey, *The 7 Habits of Highly Effective People* (Philadelphia: Running Press, 2000).

35. R. K. Cooper, "A New Neuroscience of Leadership: Bringing Out More of the Best in People," *Strategy and Leadership,* paper presented at the fifth annual Worldwide Lessons in Leadership Series, Norfolk, VA, October 2000.

36. Peter C. Gronn, "Talk as They Work: The Accomplishment of School Administration," *Administrative Science Quarterly* (March 1983), pp. 1-21; also see Ray Collins and Brian H. Kleiner, "Orders and Instructions," *Industrial Management and Data Systems* (1989), pp. 3-6.

37. T. Deal and A. Kennedy, *Corporate Cultures: The Rites and Rituals of Corporate Rite* (Cambridge, MA: Perseus Publishers, 2000), pp. 98-103.

38. W. Cunningham and P. Cordiero, *Educational Administration: A Problem-Based Approach,* 2nd ed. (Needham Heights, MA: Allyn and Bacon, 2002), pp. 165-173.

39. Walter D. St. John, "Plain Speaking," *Personnel Journal* (June 1985), pp. 83-90; and Carol M. Lehman, William C. Himstreet, and Wayne Murlin Baty, *Business Communications,* 11th ed. (Cincinnati, OH: South-Western College Pub., 1996).

40. Gerald R. Miller (Ed.), *Persuasion: New Directions in Theory and Research* (Berkeley, CA: Sage, 1980). Also see Kenneth J. Tewel, "Improving In-School Communications: A Technique for Principals," *National Association of Secondary School Principals Bulletin* (March 1990), pp. 39-41.

41. Lloyd E. McCleary, "Communications in Large Secondary Schools—A Nationwide Study of Practices and Problems," *National Association of Secondary School Principals Bulletin* (February 1968), pp. 48-61. Also see Anita M. Pankoke, G. Kent Stewart, and Wynona Winn, "Choices for Effective Communication: Which Channels to Use?" *National Association of Secondary School Principals Bulletin* (November 1990), pp. 53-58.

42. Peter West, "Electronic Mailboxes: Novel Phone Links Close Gap between Parents and Schools," *Education Week* (March 1989), p. 1.

43. Fred Huntington, "A Principal's Guide to the Internet," *Principal* (September 1995), pp. 48-51.

44. Adams State College, *Electronic Communications Policy.* Accessed online, http://www.stylewizard.com/apa/apawiz.html, December 28, 2010.

45. Brad Hughes, "Twittering in the Hands of School Leaders," *The School Administrator* (vol. 4, no. 67, April 2010).

46. James M. Lipham and Donald C. Franeke, "Nonverbal Behavior of Administrators," *Educational Administration Quarterly* (Spring 1966), pp. 101-109. Also see James Halleck, "Administrator Nonverbal Communication as Perceived by the Teachers' Ratings of Administrators' Nonverbal Behavior," PhD dissertation, University of Missouri-Columbus, 1984; Robin Chandler, "Moving toward Understanding," *Accountancy* (April 1990), pp. 76-78; and Michael G. Barton, "Manage Words Effectively," *Personnel Journal* (January 1990), pp. 32-40.

47. Joseph A. DeVito, *Human Communication: The Basic Course,* 9th ed. (Boston, MA: Allyn and Bacon, 2003).

48. David Coursen and John Thomas, "Communicating," *School Leadership: Handbook for Excellence,* an ERIC report (1989), Ed. 020964, pp. 252-271.

49. Colleen Newquist, "Best Face Forward: Positive Public Relations through the Media," *Education World* (June 23, 1997). Accessed online, http://www.education-world.com/a_admin/admin003.shtml, May 9, 2005.

50. See Mars Team Online Press Kit. This material was prepared for use with schools involved with the NASA research missions to Mars. It may be adapted by schools interested in publicizing special events or projects. The guidelines are filled with practical advice for obtaining newspaper and television coverage. A sample press release is included. Accessed online, http://quest.arc.nasa.gov/mars/teachers/presskit.html, December 27, 2010.

51. Karen H. Kleinz, "Proactive Communication in a Crisis Driven World," *School Business Affairs* (vol. 65, no. 8, August 1999), pp. 27-31.

52. Colleen Newquist, "Public Relations 101: How-To Tips for School Administrators," *Education World* (August 9, 1999). Accessed online, http://www.educationworld.com/a_admin/admin/admin123.shtml, December 27, 2010.

53. Colleen Newquist, "Best Face Forward." *Education World* (1997). Accessed online, http://www.educationworld.com/a_admin/admin/admin003.shtml, December 27, 2010.

54. Robert D. Ramsey, *Lead, Follow, or Get Out of the Way,* 2nd ed. (Thousand Oaks, CA: Corwin Press, 2005).

55. Morris et al., *Principals in Action,* pp. 31–65.

56. H. H. Kelly, "Communication in Experimentally Created Hierarchies," *Human Relations* (1951), pp. 39–56.

57. J. L. Hurwitz et al., "Some Effects of Power on the Relations between Group Members," in Darwin Cartwright and Alvin Zander (Eds.), *Group Dynamics in Research and Theory* (New York: Harper & Row, 1960), pp. 800–809.

58. Robert A. Giacalone, "On Slipping When You Thought You Had Your Best Foot Forward: Self-Promotion, Self-Destruction, and Entitlements," *Group and Organizational Studies* (March 1985), pp. 61–80; and Fred C. Lunenburg and Allan C. Ornstein, *Educational Administration: Concept and Practice,* 4th ed (Belmont, CA: Wadsworth, 2003), p. 205.

59. Terry Bands, "Toward an Interpersonal Paradigm for Superior Subordinate Communication," PhD dissertation, University of Denver, 1983. For an empirical study on superior-subordinate communication, see Mel E. Schnake, Michael E. Dumber, Daniel S. Cochran, and Timothy R. Barnett, "Effects of Differences in Superior and Subordinate Perceptions of Superiors' Communication Practices," *Journal of Business Communications* (Winter 1990), pp. 36–50; and Thomas D. Gougeon et al., "A Quantitative Phenomenological Study of Leadership: Social Control Theory Applied to Actions of School Principals," paper presented at the annual meeting of the American Educational Research Association, April 1990.

60. See the discussion of masked messages in Andrew W. Halpin, *Theory and Research in Administration* (New York: Macmillan, 1966), pp. 258, 270.

61. P. Rankin, "The Importance of Listening Ability," *English Journal* (1928), pp. 623–630; and A. D. Wolvin and C. D. Coakley, *Listening Instruction,* an ERIC report (1979), Ed. 170827. Wolvin and Coakley conform the earlier Rankin study in their 1983 report to the Virginia Speech Communication Association.

62. C. Brue, "Identifying Effective Listening Behaviors Used by Supervisors Involved in Dyadic Conversations with Subordinates," PhD dissertation, University of Texas-Austin, 1988.

63. Richard A. Schmuck and Philip J. Runkel, *The Handbook of Organizational Development in Schools,* 3rd ed. (Prospects Heights, IL: Waveland Press, 1988), p. 98.

64. Ibid., p. 85.

65. Terry Newton, "Improving Students' Listening Skills," IDEA Paper No. 23, Exchange, Center for Faculty Evaluation and Development, Manhattan, KS, September 1990.

66. Ibid., pp. 99–107; also see Sam Guarino, *Communication for Supervisors* (March 1974), pp. 48–49.

67. Peter Nostrand and Richard Shelley, *An Educational Leadership Listening Model* (Charlottesville, VA: University of Virginia, 1973); Lois W. Johnson and C. Glenn Pearch, "Assess and Improve Your Listening Quotient," *Business Education Forum* (vol. 44, March 1990), pp. 25–27; and Sonya Hamlin, *How to Talk So People Listen: The Real Key to Job Success* (New York: Harper & Row, 1989).

68. Marjorie J. Kostelnik, Laura C. Stein, and Alice P. Whiren, "Children's Self-Esteem, the Verbal Environment," *Childhood Education* (Fall 1988), pp. 29–32.

69. Karen F. Osterman, "Communication Skills: A Key to Caring, Collaboration, and Change," paper presented at the annual conference of the University Council for Educational Administration, October 29–31, 1993.

70. For an extensive review of research on communication networks, see Rebecca Blair et al., "Vertical and Network Communication in Organization," in Robert D. McPhee and Phillip K. Tompkins (Eds.), *Organizational Communication: Traditional Themes and New Directions*

(Beverly Hills, CA: Sage, 1985), chap. 2; and Lawrence F. Frey et al., *Investigating Communication Strategies: An Introduction to Research Methods,* 2nd ed. (Boston, MA: Allyn and Bacon, 2000).

71. Leslie W. Kindred et al., *The School and Community Relations* (Englewood Cliffs, NJ: Prentice Hall, 1984), p. 146. Also see John Thomas, Thomas E. Hart, and Stewart C. Smith, "Building Coalition" in Stuart C. Smith and Philip K. Piele (Eds.), *School Leadership: Handbook for Excellence* (1989), pp. 272–290; and Larry Frase and Robert Hetzel, *School Management by Wandering Around* (Lanham, MD: Scarecrow Press, 2002).
72. Occupational Outlook Quarterly, *Futurework: Trends and Challenges for Work in the 21st Century,* Accessed online, http://stats.bls.gov/opub/ooq/2000/Summer/art04.pdf, December 28, 2010.
73. J. M. Kouzes and B. Z. Posner, *The Leadership Challenge,* 4th ed. (San Francisco, CA: Jossey-Bass, 2007).
74. Ibid.
75. Rensis Likert, *New Patterns of Management* (New York: McGraw Hill, 1961).
76. For guidelines on surveying faculty about communication, see Kenneth J. Tewel, "Improving In-School Communications: A Technique for Principals," *National Association of Secondary School Administrators Bulletin* (March 1990), pp. 39–41.
77. Kindred et al., *School and Community Relations,* p. 146.
78. Richard A. Gorton and Gail Thierbach-Schneider, *School Based Leadership: Challenge and Opportunities,* 3rd ed. (Dubuque, IA: William C. Brown, 1991), pp. 516–517.
79. Michael J. Glauser, "Upward Information Flow in Organizations: Review and Conceptual Analysis," *Human Relations* (August 1984), pp. 613–643; also see Mel E. Schnake et al., "Effects of Differences in Superior Communication Practices," *Journal of Business Communication* (Winter 1990), pp. 37–50.
80. Schmuck and Runkel, *Handbook of Organizational Development in Schools,* pp. 128–129.
81. J. Gaines, "Upward Communications in Industry: An Experiment," *Human Relations* (December 1980), pp. 929–942.
82. Dennis W. Jeffers and Nancy L. Lewis, "A Case Study of Newspaper Employee Perceptions of Communications Variables Related to Organizational Climate, Immediate Superior and Top Management," paper presented at the annual meeting of the newspaper division of the Association for Education in Journalism and Mass Communication, Washington, DC, August 1989.
83. Richard Ackerman, Patricia Maslin-Ostrowski, and Chuck Christensen, "Case Stories: Telling Tales about School," *Educational Leadership* (March 1996), pp. 21–23.
84. *Technological Horizons in Education Journal* (April 1989), pp. 4–5.

CHAPTER

5

Conflict Management

APPLICABLE PSEL STANDARDS

- **STANDARD 2: Ethics and Professional Norms**
  Effective educational leaders act ethically and according to professional norms to promote each student's academic success and well-being.
- **STANDARD 3: Equity and Cultural Responsiveness**
  Effective educational leaders strive for equity of educational opportunity and culturally responsive practices to promote each student's academic success and well-being.
- **STANDARD 8: Meaningful Engagement of Families and Community**
  Effective educational leaders engage families and the community in meaningful, reciprocal, and mutually beneficial ways to promote each student's academic success and well-being.
- **STANDARD 9: Operations and Management**
  Effective educational leaders manage school operations and resources to promote each student's academic success and well-being.

National Policy Board for Educational Administration (NPBEA). *Professional Standards for Educational Leaders* (Reston, VA: Author, 2015). Used with Permission.

It is understandable that an administrator should wish to avoid conflict, especially if a particular conflict could be disruptive. By trying to avoid all conflict, however, an administrator could be ignoring or suppressing significant problems or issues that need to be aired if they are to be ameliorated or resolved. Moreover, as Wexley and Yukl have emphasized, "Interpersonal and intergroup conflict occur to some extent in all organizations and are a natural part of social relationships."[1] The challenge, according to Wynn, "is not to eliminate conflict but to minimize its destructive impact and make it a positive force in the organization."[2]

To meet this challenge, the administrator will need to engage in conflict management. In this chapter, conflict management will be broadly defined to address two aspects of the topic. On one hand, conflict management refers to efforts designed to prevent, ameliorate, or resolve disagreements between and among individuals and groups. On the other hand, conflict management may also include efforts by the administrator to initiate conflict—not for its own sake but because of a need to take an unpopular stand or introduce changes that some will oppose. Although many readers may perceive the concept of initiating conflict as radical, the social science literature supports the proposition that in some cases an administrator may need to take action resulting in possible conflict for an individual or group whose performance has become complacent or stagnant.[3]

Since many of the conflicts arising in an organization are role conflicts, a discussion of the basic concepts of role theory will be presented first, as an introduction to conflict management.

ROLE CONCEPTS

Every administrative position in an effectively managed organization has job descriptions or policy statements, written and emanating from a governing board, that embody the formal expectations of the organization. In addition, every organization usually has implicit, frequently unexpressed expectations for an administrator's behavior that originate with the various individuals or groups with whom the administrator comes into contact. Together, both sets of expectations constitute a behavioral definition of the role different individuals or groups—both formal and informal—believe the administrator *should* perform in a particular situation. As Getzels has observed, "The expectations define for the actor [administrator] . . . what he [or she] should or should not do" while the actor "is the incumbent of the particular role."[4] The expectations, according to Gross and his colleagues, also serve as "evaluative standards applied to an incumbent in a position,"[5] and therefore can represent a powerful source of potential influence on any administrator's behavior.

The behavior of an administrator is also affected by personal needs, however, regarding the role the administrator should play. These needs become the administrator's self-expectations and may be more important than the expectations of others in determining the role to be taken in a given set of circumstances. For example, if an administrator would rather play the role of manager than instructional leader, most energies will be focused on administering an efficiently run school, despite the expectations other individuals and groups have for the administrator to perform the role of instructional leader. Figure 5.1, based on the Getzels model, illustrates major factors that can influence an individual's role behavior.[6] It shows that both the institution and the individual, that is, the administrator, are influenced by the larger culture in the development of their expectations and need dispositions. The model implies that one source of the administrator's self-expectations is underlying personal needs. It further indicates that the administrator's behavior is affected not only by personal needs but also by the role expectations held by other relevant individuals and groups. Finally, the model suggests that the administrator's behavior is a result of *interaction* between personal need dispositions and the role expectations held by others associated with the institution. Based on the Getzels model, it would appear that, as long as the administrator's need dispositions are compatible with the expectations of others, conflict will be minimal. When need dispositions and expectations clash, role conflict is likely.

FIGURE 5.1
MAJOR FUNCTIONS THAT INFLUENCE AN INDIVIDUAL'S BEHAVIOR

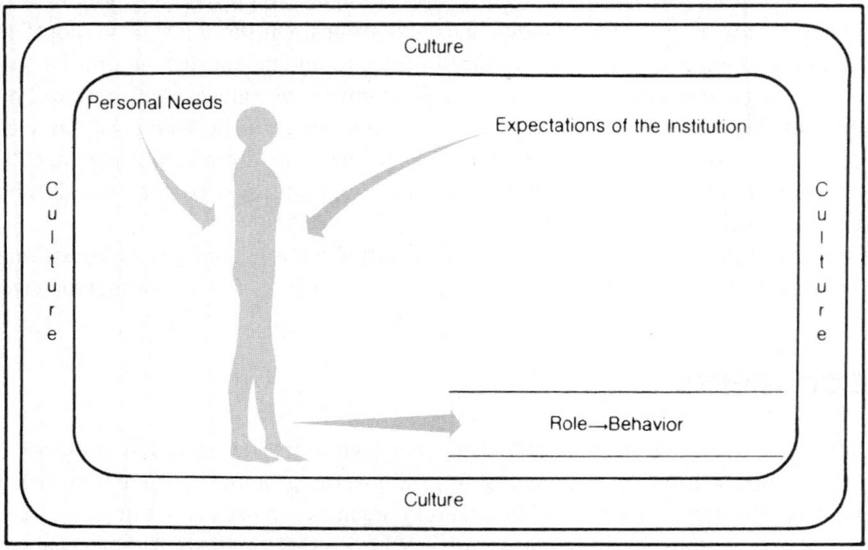

ROLE EXPECTATIONS OF INDIVIDUALS AND GROUPS

The preceding discussion indicates the importance for an administrator of knowing the role expectations of others. No inference should be drawn that an administrator must conform to these expectations. As Campbell has noted, "Only by an understanding of these expectations can the administrator anticipate the reception of specific behavior on his part. Such anticipation seems necessary if the area of acceptance is to be extended and the area of disagreement minimized. Moreover, such understandings are necessary if a program of modifying expectations is to be started."[7]

Figure 5.2 identifies the various individuals and groups whose expectations may generate conflict for the administrator.[8]

The need for the administrator to identify and understand the role expectations of others cannot be overemphasized. Frequently the administrator's problem is deciding which individual or group expectations are the most important to ascertain. It is not inconceivable that all the individuals and groups identified in Figure 5.2 would have an opinion about the way an administrator should behave with respect to a certain issue. It is neither reasonable nor practical, however, for the administrator to attempt to discover and understand the expectations of everyone in the school organization and community. The administrator must, therefore, concentrate on developing an awareness and understanding of the expectations of those individuals or groups who may influence the administrator's effectiveness in some important regard. If expectations, as previously defined, constitute the "evaluative standards applied to an incumbent of a position,"[9] the administrator needs to learn the expectations of those individuals or groups whose evaluation may impair or enhance the administrator's effectiveness. According to Gross, role expectations can vary in three basic ways: *direction, clarity,* and *intensity.*[10]

FIGURE 5.2
REFERENTS HOLDING EXPECTATIONS FOR THE ROLE OF THE ADMINISTRATOR

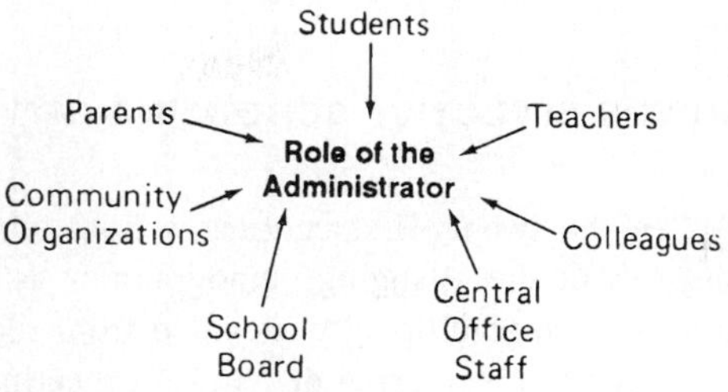

Direction

The direction of the expectations for the administrator's role may range along a continuum, from complete agreement to absolute opposition. The primary factor that seems to determine the direction of an individual's or group's expectations is the nature of the situation that has created the expectations.

For instance, a decision by an administrator not to involve teachers in considering a schedule change may completely agree with the teachers' expectations that it is not necessary for the principal to secure faculty participation on any decision to change the school's schedule. In another situation, concerning a *curricular* change, however, a decision by the administrator not to involve teachers in discussing the change may directly conflict with the expectations of the faculty about the role of the administrator because in the area of curriculum, faculty expects to be involved on all matters. The critical variable, then, that will typically determine the direction of an individual's or group's expectations is the nature of the situation giving rise to the expectations.

Clarity

Another aspect of role expectations that the administrator needs to consider is clarity. Since expectations are frequently unwritten and sometimes unspoken, the administrator may occasionally be unaware that a particular group holds any role expectations. For example, a principal may delegate to one assistant the responsibility for working with various student organizations in the school. In this situation the students of a particular group may expect the principal, rather than the assistant, to help them. Nevertheless, the circumstances may be such that the students are reluctant to express their feelings about the role of the principal. As a result, the principal's behavior may fail inadvertently to meet their expectations, and problems of dissatisfaction may be created.

Intensity

The third dimension of role expectations identified by Gross is intensity.[11] In a given situation, a group may expect that the administrator absolutely *must* act in a certain way or *perhaps*

WINDOW ON DIVERSITY

Conflict Management

BORDER CROSSING FOR EFFECTIVE SCHOOLING IN THE TWENTY-FIRST CENTURY

For effective schooling in the twenty-first century, school administrators must be attuned to the complexities of the changing demographics as well as to the needs of those persons who have been traditionally excluded from the core of educational reform (Capper, 1993). Given the increasing demands of meeting the needs of culturally and linguistically diverse students and the communities they live in, it is imperative that we now effectively "cross borders." These borders include but are not limited to ethnic, cultural, religious, racial, linguistic, ability, and socioeconomic factors. While homogeneity is good for milk (Paley, 1979), it is no longer an appropriate criterion to determine what is effective for teaching or administrative leadership in today's diverse schools. As Ladson-Billings (2001) noted, there is an incredible range of diversity in today's schools. This is further emphatically supported by Hanson and Avery (2000) as they noted the following:

> Making student diversity central to all aspects of the school experience compels adults—administrators, teachers, parents, non-certified staff, and members of the community—to be constantly mindful of the consequences of their actions and decisions especially on categorical groupings of students for historical, political, and social reasons. (p. 119)

Organizations must now become more efficacious to better prepare for cultural diversity. Exemplars from business can be found in the marketability of particular products as demographics (racial and economic) create new customer markets. In this climate opportunities continue to arise for niche marketing to ethnic, economic, and other groups (National Multicultural Institute, 1997). This niche marketing is focused, targeted, monitored, and adaptable. Educational organizations should now be preparing their "market" strategies to better serve these growing diverse populations in an effort to create focused culturally relevant teaching, target and equitable distribution of resources, and adaptability to the ever-increasing school diversity. This diversity is not just relegated to the incoming population of school-age children, but also to those who will teach them and work with them on a daily basis. To that end, educational leaders will be challenged to secure qualified individuals to provide more innovative approaches, solving both culturally induced organizational problems and meeting the workplace learning needs of minority individuals and groups (Saldana, Norwood, and Alston, 2003; Martin and Ross-Gordon, 1990). Conversely, diverse students will be inadequately served by teachers and staff trained in outmoded techniques, led by administrators with mimetic approaches. From this standpoint, it will be imperative for current administrative training to be reformed with cultural and linguistic diversity as indispensable core components, not just as an "add-on" but also as a part of the nucleus for effective schooling training in this new century.

WINDOW ON DIVERSITY

Because we all experience the world through our own eyes, experiences, and perceptions, we, as educators (teachers, counselors, administrators, etc.), must understand that those children who come to our public schools each day also view the world from their unparalleled lived experiences. It is imperative for educators to have some understanding about the larger issues related to diversity—that is, racism, classism, sexism, and other oppressions (Pohan, 1996)—and how families from marginalized groups view education (Weiner, 1993). Expanding on this notion, Sarason (1990) stated:

> First, you must understand and digest the fact that children—all children—come to school motivated to enlarge their worlds. You start with their worlds. You do not look at them, certainly not initially, as organisms to be modified and regulated. You look at them to determine how what they are, seek to know, and have experienced can be used as the fuel to fire the process for enlargement of interest, knowledge, and skills. You do not look at them in terms of deficits.... You enter their world in order to aid them and you try to build bridges between two worlds, not walls. (p. 164)

In studying the multiple worlds of students and the transitions ("border crossing") that they make daily as they attempt to participate in the American public schooling experience, Phelan, Davidson, and Yu (1991) found four patterns for cultural border crossing:

Type I	*Type II*	*Type III*	*Type IV*
Congruent worlds Smooth transitions	Different worlds Border crossings managed	Different worlds Border crossings difficult	Different worlds Borders impenetrable

- *Type I:* Students' worlds in school and out of school are parallel. While circumstances may change daily, students perceive the boundaries to be manageable. Thus movement from one setting to another is uncomplicated. Here, students' worlds are "merged by their common socio-cultural components rather than bounded by conspicuous differences." This is seen, for example, in the experiences of students in a suburban high school where the majority of the students are all upper middle class and the school's values are the same.
- *Type II:* Students' worlds in school and out of school are complete opposites. However, the borders between the two worlds do not prevent students from crossing or adapting to different ways. This is not easy for students; often the result of border crossing in this block is "personal and/or psychological." For example, Lisandra is 15 years old and Latina. She is one of six children living with her extended family whose history of economically fragile subsistence is intergenerational. Lisandra's community is very close knit. Many of the residents

Continued

WINDOW ON DIVERSITY

in her housing complex and neighborhood attend the same church, shop at the same stores, and attend the same schools. Early in her educational trajectory, Lisandra was identified as gifted and soon matriculated to high school. Her neighborhood secondary school does not offer the advanced placement or honors courses, so she is bused to a high school that does. This high school is geographically and culturally different from Lisandra's neighborhood and family. The new high school's demographics are representative of many suburbs, located outside major urban centers, predominately white. The per capita income levels, using census data, would place the family incomes at what we have come to know as upper and middle economic status. Lisandra, however, makes the transition. She maintains a 3.9 grade point average in her honors and AP courses. While this transition was difficult, Lisandra focused on academics and extracurricular activities while maintaining a sense of self. It is as if she has created a bridge that allows passage from her family and home community to school and back. She realized that her success was also the success of her family and community. She is determined to use this opportunity to earn an academic scholarship, be accepted into a well-ranked college program, matriculate successfully to graduation, and begin a successful career. In this way she can help her family economically and make the community proud of her accomplishments.

- *Type III:* Like Type II, students' worlds in school and out of school are complete opposites; however, students in this block find it difficult to cross the borders. Here crossing the borders involves "friction and discomfort" (p. 74). An example of this type is Carl, an 11th-grade African American male who attends a magnet school, whose focus is math, science, and technology. Carl is one of five ethnically diverse students (two African American and three Asian) in a student body of 250 White students. His daily commute consists of approximately 3 hours—80 minutes each way. Carl's neighborhood school's enrollment is 10 percent over capacity and lacks the resources to provide adequate allocation of classroom space or materials such as books. Carl's parents recognized his interest in science and, after placing his name in a lottery and his subsequent selection, agreed to enroll him in this special-focus high school. Although this young man is very bright and excels in his classes, the border crossing for him is difficult. He feels outside of the school culture. Often he does not participate in extracurricular school activities (after-school clubs, sports, field trips that require monetary support) that have contributed to the building of school community because of his long commute and lack of extra financial resources. Carl seldom has time to spend with his neighborhood peer group, many of whom are not supportive of his choice to attend a school "for smart kids." In the school administration and teachers' efforts work to create a school climate that is welcoming for all, they often highlight things in the community directly related to cultural understandings and socioeconomic status,

WINDOW ON DIVERSITY

and are inattentive to the borders that Carl must cross for understanding. His feelings of isolation at school are interpreted by his teachers as a lack of effort, motivation, and ability. For this young African American male, there is a disconnect between the two worlds—the world of school and academic achievement and the world of peers, family, and community. There is no proverbial bridge for Carl; he feels stuck in the dichotomy and tailspins emotionally into depression. After an extended absence from school, he is no longer a part of the magnet program and returns to his former school. Soon, because of the lack of parallel academic challenges, he loses interest and drops out of school—a very capable student unable to successfully cross the border from school to home and back again.

- *Type IV:* "For some students, the values, beliefs, and expectations are so discordant across worlds that border crossing is resisted or impossible . . . it is frequently so painful that, over time, these students develop reasons and rationales to protect themselves against any further distress." Here students will actively or passively resist border crossing. For example, Arzu, a 16-year-old, 10th-grade student, is Islamic. She attends her neighborhood school and walks to school with her peers each day. Arzu wears a hijab (head covering) each day as a part of her Islamic faith, and while students at times have teased her, she rarely feels uncomfortable with her peer group, classmates, or teachers. However, during her regular physical education class, she participated in timed 30-yard sprints, and her clocked time was outstanding. Her physical education teacher soon researched and realized that Arzu was very close to breaking the shortest time recorded by anyone in the state competitions. Her teacher quickly invited her to join the track team. She did. She trained with the team for weeks, and her time improved rapidly. The students, teachers, and administration of the school were all excited about the possibility of state championships. Arzu basked in her newfound fame and popularity at school while also enjoying the team and the sport. As Arzu prepared for the first event, her coach asked her if she had to wear the "scarf." To which she replied yes. The coach told her she could not wear it during a track meet due to existing rules and would have to decide if she would comply with the rule and lead her school to a championship or not. Arzu was distressed; her family and religious community were already not in full support of her participation, especially the attention she received. A young Islamic woman was to be modest while preparing herself to be a good wife and mother. The request to remove her hijab now placed another burden. Would she remove it to run and cross the bridge leaving behind the core of her religious and spiritual belief system? How would she deal with the pressure from the team and the coach to support her team and

Continued

WINDOW ON DIVERSITY

> school? What would her family say when presented with this information? What ostracism would her family suffer in the community if she made this choice not to compromise? Arzu's response to such overwhelming pressure was to ask her parents to allow her to move to another state to live with a relative and attend another school. She told her parents that it was impossible for her to stay at the school due to harassment of her religious beliefs. They wanted to investigate and explore another alternative, but Arzu begged them with many tears not to. They complied; she moved to live with relatives, attending a new school and keeping a very low profile. Arzu felt the pressure of a school pride, the pressure of peers, the pressure of a cultural and religious value system, and the pressure of her own ability to excel. The pain of trying to negotiate the borders of school and family and core values led her to resist crossing borders at all. Instead Arzu surrendered with retreat.

Students cross borders daily as they synthesize home, community, and the world of school. As a part of this border crossing, educators play an integral role with regard to academic and social achievement. Students' engagement with schools and learning is predicated upon the interrelationships of their family, peer, and school worlds (Phelan, Davidson, and Yu, 1991). Through public education, children may have the opportunities to navigate borders related to social, political, personally constructed contexts as "borderlands" (Martinez, 1998). However, far too often, children are found impeded in transcending borders, trapped to be in Types III and IV, particularly now in the twenty-first century when societal technological advancement is incongruent with traditional, "old school" pedagogy. In many cases, students and parents view the school as a foreign land, alienated or at best moving toward assimilation with the organization.

Oftentimes students from economically fragile backgrounds and students of color experience a lower-quality school than their peers in the middle and upper middle class (Marshall, 2002). Thus, a growing need for a cadre of educators to help students cross borders as Type I "borderlanders" with congruence and smooth transitions and to work in and on the behalf of communities of color is emerging in education (Jennings, 1994). Furthermore, leadership preparation programs in colleges and universities across this country are failing to realistically prepare school leaders for a culturally diverse America (Capper, 1993; Maxcy, 1998), thus failing to prepare for truly effective schools. Educational leaders in this new time must address the needs of those traditionally excluded and marginalized voices. Therefore, using multiple theoretical foundations coupled with epistemological specificity in educational

should act in a certain way. It is clearly in the best interest of the administrator to assess accurately the intensity of an individual's or a group's expectations. An expectation that it is absolutely essential for the administrator to play a particular role carries markedly different implications for behavior than one based on the feeling that *perhaps* action on an issue should be taken.

WINDOW ON DIVERSITY

research (Tyson, 1998) and practice, educational leadership preparation programs can be inclusive of these voices and appropriately train the new school leaders to be sensitive and committed to the academic success of new populations. This endeavor will require a vision of effective school leadership and successful border crossing with new techniques and recommendations for twenty-first-century effective schooling.

Sources

Alston, J. A., "The Many Faces of American Schooling: Effective Schools Research and Border Crossing in the 21st Century," *American Secondary Education* (vol. 32, no. 9, 2004), pp. 79-93.

Capper, C. (Ed.)., *Educational Administration in a Pluralistic Society* (New York: SUNY Press, 1993).

Hanson, K., and Avery, M. P., "Valuing Diversity in Schools: Transforming Education through Humanistic Policy, Pedagogy, and Practice," in M. Leicester, C. Modgil, and S. Modgil (Eds.), *Institutional Issues: Pupils, Schools and Teacher Education* (London: Falmer Press, 2000), pp. 119-127.

Jennings, J., "Training Leaders for Multiracial and Multi-ethnic Collaboration." *Trotter Review,* (vol. 8, no. 2, 1994), pp., 4-6.

Ladson-Billings, G., *Crossing Over to Canaan: The Journey of New Teachers in Diverse Classrooms* (San Francisco: Jossey Bass, 2001).

Marshall, P. L., *Cultural Diversity in Our Schools* (Belmont, CA: Wadsworth Thomson Learning, 2002).

Martin, L. G., and Ross-Gordon, J. M. (Eds.), *Serving Culturally Diverse Populations* (San Francisco: Jossey Bass, 1990).

Martinez, O. J., *Border People: Life and Society in the U.S.-Mexico Borderlands* (Tucson, AZ: University of Arizona Press, 1998).

Maxcy, S. J., "Preparing School Principals for Ethno-democratic Leadership." *International Journal of Leadership in Education* (vol. 1, no. 3, 1998), pp., 217-235.

National Multicultural Institute (1997). *Facts about Diversity.* Accessed online, http://www.nmci.org, January 30, 2004.

Paley, V., *White Teacher* (Cambridge, MA: Harvard University Press, 1979).

Phelan, P., Davidson, A. L., and Yu, H. C., "Students' Multiple Worlds: Navigating the Borders of Family, Peer, and School Cultures," in P. Phelan and A. L. Davidson (Eds.), *Renegotiating Cultural Diversity in American Schools* (New York: Teachers College Press, 1991), pp. 52-88.

Pohan, C. A. "Preservice Teachers' Beliefs about Diversity: Uncovering Factors Leading to Multicultural Responsiveness." *Equity and Excellence in Education* (vol. 29, no. 3, 1996), pp., 62-68.

Saldana, D. C., Norwood, P. M., and Alston, J. A., "Investigating Teachers' Unconscious Person Perceptions and Stereotyping of Culturally Diverse Individuals." *Educators for Urban Minorities* (vol. 2, no. 2, 2003), 57-73.

Sarason, S. B., *The Predictable Failure of Educational Reform: Can We Change Course Before it's too Late?* (San Francisco: Jossey-Bass, 1990).

Tyson, C., "A Response to 'Coloring epistemologies': Are Our Qualitative Research Epistemologies Racially Biased?" *Educational Researcher* (vol. 27), pp. 21-23.

Weiner, L., *Preparing Teachers for Urban Schools* (New York: Teachers College Press, 1993).

For example, in regard to an administrator's role in initiating a program to improve student behavior, the expectation by parents that the principal should *perhaps* initiate a program differs in intensity and carries different behavioral implications than an expectation that such a program is *essential* and therefore must be initiated. In the first instance, the administrator will probably feel very little pressure from the parents and may be able to act appropriately, with no repercussions.

If the administrator ignores the expectations of parents when they believe that a program should be started to improve student behavior, however, parents may complain, and the principal's status in the community may suffer. If the principal attempts to ignore parental expectations when parents feel that a program is *essential,* these parents may attempt to impose whatever negative sanctions or pressures they can command in order to make the principal comply.

The problem faced by most administrators in this kind of a situation is that it is usually more difficult to determine the intensity of a group's expectations than the direction of those expectations, since the former characteristic may not be explicit or public. This obstacle points to the need for all administrators to engage in continuous efforts to ascertain the intensity of the expectations of individuals and groups with whom they work.

FOUR SOURCES OF SOCIAL CONFLICT IN SCHOOLS

In another study on managing conflict, Lindelow and Scott outline the types and sources of social conflicts, a prevalent occurrence in schools. They view social conflict as conflict between individuals and conflict between groups common to the school environment. The authors identify four primary sources of social conflict within the school: communication problems, organizational structure, human factors such as personality, and limited resources.

Poor communication is a major cause of conflicts. For example, teachers who do not receive regular feedback about performance may have poor morale and negative attitudes, resulting in an unwillingness to respond to administrative directives.

The type of *organizational structure* also has a direct effect on conflicts. Schools in which the administration encourages empowerment will have more frequent conflicts, although minor. With more people involved in making decisions, more opinions, interests, wants, and needs are likely to be voiced. Major disruptive conflicts lessen, however, as empowerment increases, because the more the staff participates in decision making, the greater the opportunities to express minor conflicts. Such an airing of grievances in the early stages of disagreement can, in turn, prevent minor problems from snowballing into major incidents.

Human factors, specifically personality incompatibilities and different values and goals, are Lindelow and Scott's third category of sources of social conflict; and these cannot be eliminated by an administrator. They must be properly managed, however.

Competition over *limited resources* is the fourth source of conflict, according to Lindelow and Scott. For example, conflict results when teachers fail to get raises they think they deserve or when the science department fails to get desired equipment. The administrator's job is to assure all groups that they have been treated fairly in resource distribution, thus preventing unnecessary conflict of this kind.[12]

CONFLICT INITIATION

No doubt most administrators would like to prevent conflict from occurring. However, in some situations an administrator may not only be unable to prevent conflict but also actually find it necessary to *initiate* action that results in conflict with another individual or group. Usually these circumstances come about because a particular individual or group is not performing as well as expected and does not want to change. The theoretical and research literature on initiating conflict is limited. The ideas in this section are based primarily on an analysis by Robbins and on insights developed from the authors' experiences as administrators.[13]

For example, a principal has observed a teacher who is ineffective in motivating students. In a follow-up conference, the teacher does not perceive a problem and believes a good job of teaching is occurring. To further complicate the matter, suppose that the teacher is tenured, a leader in the union, and an individual with a very strong personality. At this point, the principal could retreat and refrain from discussing the problem that was observed in the teacher's classroom. If the principal is to fulfill the responsibilities of an educational leader, the problem may need to be directly presented, which *could* create a conflict with the teacher. (It should be emphasized that in this context, conflict is not inevitable; much will depend on the principal's approach in working with the teacher.) Nevertheless, the scenario presented thus far suggests that total avoidance of any type of conflict between the principal and teacher may not be easy, and initiating conflict may be necessary to reduce the complacency of the teacher and, ultimately, to bring about improvement.

Administrators must, of course, carefully consider all the possible ramifications before initiating conflict. The administrator will want to be reasonably sure that the problem needing to be addressed is sufficiently serious to warrant intervention and that approaches to solve the problem without arousing conflict are tried first (see Chapter 3, "Authority, Power, and Influence"). Also, it will be important for an administrator to delay initiating conflict with an individual or group, if possible, when the administrator is already involved in other kinds of conflicts that may drain emotions and energies. Too much conflict will impair the administrator's effectiveness. Assuming that the latter is not the case, and that an individual or group does not respond to other approaches the administrator has tried, then conflict may need to be introduced.

In initiating conflict the administrator should begin with the lowest possible profile. Anticipating and preparing for possible negative reactions will be essential. Generally, when individuals or groups are informed of a problem they do not want to address, they will become defensive. When this happens, the administrator should discuss the problem as calmly as possible. This may not be easy, because an individual or group that becomes defensive could grow antagonistic and hostile, thereby stirring the administrator's own emotions. It is a challenging test of self-control to remain calm and rational in the face of a defensive reaction; the administrator should make every effort to do so, and to persist in focusing individual or group attention on the problem and its possible solution.

AN APPROACH TO CONFLICT RESOLUTION

Although research and theory are limited regarding how best to ameliorate or resolve a conflict, Gross has theorized that when an individual is faced with a role conflict, there are four pathways to resolution:

1. The individual conforms to the expectations of Group A.
2. The individual conforms to the expectations of Group B.
3. The individual performs some compromise behavior that represents an attempt to conform, in part, to both sets of expectations.
4. The individual attempts to avoid conforming to either set of expectations.[14]

A fifth alternative identified in a replication of the Gross study is the possibility of the administrator resolving conflict by actively trying to change the direction or intensity of one or both sets of expectations.[15]

If these, then, are the options available to an administrator who is faced with role conflict, which alternative should be chosen? Based on an investigation into the ways superintendents resolve their role conflicts, Gross has theorized that three conditions determine how a role conflict will be resolved:

1. The administrator's feeling about the legitimacy of each of the role expectations that is in disagreement. (*Legitimacy* in this context is defined as the perceived right of an individual or group to expect the administrator to play a certain role.)
2. The administrator's perception of the negative sanctions that the administrator may suffer for nonconformity to one set of expectations, as compared to another.
3. The administrator's primary orientation to either legitimacy or sanctions as a justifiable basis for resolving a role conflict.[16]

Illustrative of the application of Gross's theory of role conflict is the principal who, when faced with a conflict of expectations between teachers and students with regard to the principal's role in student discipline, decides to conform to the teachers' expectations because of a greater concern for their reactions. In this set of circumstances, the administrator resolves this role conflict based on the perception of the sanctions that might result from failure to conform to the expectations of the teachers. The legitimacy of the students' expectations is not a consideration for this principal.

The reader may feel that a principal should try to base resolution of role conflict on the legitimacy of each group's expectations. Conditions can develop, however, that will not allow the sanctions of a group to be ignored. For example, an administrator may feel the members of a group have no "right" to expect the administrator's behavior to conform to their expectations. Yet if the group's power is such that it can disrupt or create problems within the school system, the principal may agree to adhere to its expectations to prevent serious difficulties from arising. While the legitimacy of each group's expectations should be given primary consideration by an administrator in resolving a role conflict, the sanctions a group can bring to bear for failure to fulfill expectations cannot be overlooked. An accurate understanding on the part of the administrator of both the legitimacy of the role expectations *and* the potency of the sanctions associated with noncompliance is essential for the successful resolution of any role conflict.

OTHER APPROACHES TO CONFLICT MANAGEMENT

Gross's model of role conflict resolution identifies some of the basic factors that may influence an administrator in attempting to resolve a role conflict. This model does not, nor was it intended to, indicate the best way to resolve a role conflict.[17] Neither does it address itself to the problem of how an administrator can best resolve conflict arising between two or more individuals or groups who are associated with the school, for example, students versus teachers, teachers versus parents, and students versus parents. Since role and school conflicts seem to be associated with the job of the administrator, it would appear desirable to suggest additional possible techniques that an administrator may consider for managing role or group conflict.

Four Ways of Dealing with Conflict

Barker, Tjosvold, and Andrews, for example, describe four approaches to conflict management: cooperative, confirming, competitive, and avoiding. The *cooperative* approach emphasizes mutual group goals, understanding others' views, and compromising to create a mutually useful solution. The *confirming* approach stresses the importance of communicating mutual respect for group members' competence, whereas the *competitive* approach sees conflict as a win-lose battle in which others must be persuaded or coerced into submission. Finally, *avoidance* occurs when people withdraw from discussing problems or smooth over differences quickly without really resolving them.

Administrative Effectiveness Using the Different Approaches Results of research done by Barker and his colleagues confirm that administrators who use a combination of cooperative and confirming approaches are much more successful in conflict management than are those using a competitive-avoidance approach. Administrators who use a cooperative approach also use a confirming approach. (Neither approach was used exclusively; the two were used always in conjunction with one another.) The authors suggest that perhaps this is because confirmation of competence brings a feeling of security, promoting a cooperative conflict mode by allowing team members to take risks. On the other hand, administrators who use a combination of competitive and avoidance approaches to conflict management are seen as extremely ineffective. "Presumably these managers went back and forth between the two approaches, competing when they thought they could win and avoiding when they were uncertain." The authors recommend that in cases where leaders do not possess the necessary interpersonal skills to use a cooperative and confirming approach, a member of the group who has these skills should be designated to act as a "communication facilitator and group maintenance leader."[18]

How Conflict Management Techniques Are Selected While the theoretical literature on conflict management strongly recommends a contingency approach–that is, the selection of the most appropriate techniques for managing a conflict should depend on the nature of the situation[19]–some evidence suggests administrators may be more influenced by their own personalities in selecting a technique for conflict management than by any other factor.[20] For example, the authoritarian person would appear more likely to select a unilateral, power-based technique for managing a conflict, whereas the cooperative, people-oriented individual would seem more likely to select a joint problem-solving technique. (It should be emphasized that research on the relationship between personality and conflict management is limited, and the findings are only tentative.)

Although an administrator needs to consider individual personal needs in selecting a conflict management technique, the main factor that *should* determine selection is the nature of the conflict situation itself. As Schmuck and Runkel have emphasized, the method an administrator should select for managing a conflict ought to "depend on the type of conflict, the intensity of the disagreement, the persons participating in the conflict, the seriousness of the issues for them, and the authority, resources and knowledge they possess."[21] While this approach, referred to as the *contingency method,* takes into consideration an administrator's personality, it also considers other characteristics and factors in the conflict situation. For example, Utley, Richardson, and Pilkington found in their research that when administrators attempted to resolve interpersonal conflict, personality factors played less of a role than did situational or conflict target factors such as a professor, parent, or friend.[22] Since the kinds of conflict situations that an administrator may encounter are likely to differ, a number of alternate techniques for managing conflict will be presented.

Power Struggle Bargaining

If the administrator is in a situation where conflict is inevitable, agreement or compromise between parties in conflict is impossible, and the achievement of the administrator's objectives in the conflict are extremely important, then the administrator is likely to engage in what is referred to by Blake and his colleagues as *power struggle bargaining.*[23] In other words, the administrator will do everything possible to resolve the conflict in the administrator's favor. This includes refusing to concede the legitimacy of any aspect of the other party's position and downgrading that position. It also involves refusing to compromise any aspect of the administrator's position and rationalizing any shortcomings in that position. This type of conflict resolution is seen all too frequently during the collective bargaining process in public education.

The disadvantages of power struggle bargaining as a method of resolving conflict are that the process used can be destructive to the personal and professional relationships of those involved, and the conflict is often only temporarily and superficially resolved. Conflicts that *appear* to be resolved by power struggle bargaining frequently resurface later, perhaps in a different form, but based on the same old antagonisms that were exacerbated during the previous bargaining sessions.

The main advantage to the administrator of this type of conflict resolution is the possibility of it resulting totally in the administrator's favor. Whether this occurs or not largely depends on the accuracy of the administrator's assessment of possessing more authority, power, or influence than the other party to the conflict so that the conflict can be resolved favorably. At best, this is a tricky assessment for anyone to make, and miscalculations can be disastrous. Power struggle bargaining may be necessary in certain situations, but the administrator should carefully examine the validity of the assumptions about the extent of authority, power, and influence relative to the other party to the conflict, as well as the likelihood of compromise and the long-range effects that power struggle bargaining may exert on interpersonal relationships.

Conflict Avoidance Methods

At the opposite pole from power struggle bargaining is a set of techniques for resolving a conflict that can be characterized as "conflict avoidance" methods. Blake and his colleagues have identified four such methods: (1) withdrawal, (2) indifference, (3) isolation, and (4) "smoothing over."[24] An example of the use of *withdrawal* is the administrator who, in a meeting with a superior, gets involved in an argument over a directive for the school that is felt to be not in the best interest of either students or teachers. Rather than pursuing the matter, however, the administrator withdraws from the conflict and accepts the directive. In the same situation, an administrator employing the use of *indifference* as a method of conflict resolution would not have argued about the matter in the first place but would have acted as though the issue did not really matter. The administrator who utilizes *isolation* as a technique would have tried to avoid any circumstances of conflict with a superior. And, in the case of *smoothing over,* the administrator would have accepted the directive from the superior while emphasizing the elements of agreement on the issue, rather than disagreement, and, in general, would have tried to minimize any discord between the two.

Consensus Seeking consensus, writes Lucas, is another way to minimize fragmentation. With this technique, people have the opportunity to discuss their views and attempt to persuade others. The skills of listening and paraphrasing what was heard promote understanding. Consensus is reached when one viewpoint is preferred over the others by the group as a whole. The essential points are trust that the group is choosing its position for the good of the organization and an understanding that all members' views are listened to and respected. The advantages are enhanced group cohesiveness and increased commitment to decisions made. The largest disadvantage is that this process can be considerably time-consuming. Therefore, leaders must be selective about when to utilize this process.[25]

Avoidance Techniques Evaluated Avoidance techniques do not resolve conflict but rather circumvent it. They may be necessary in situations if the other party clearly possesses the authority, power, or influence to force an opponent's will and/or if negative consequences would result from a more active or aggressive approach. Avoidance methods are typically employed when an individual or group feels somewhat powerless, apathetic, or disillusioned about the likelihood of bringing about change in the other party.

PROBLEM-SOLVING APPROACH

Another method of conflict resolution is the problem-solving approach.[26] It is the approach that seems to be the most effective means of resolving many conflicts.[27] It is based on the assumptions that the parties to the conflict are people of worthy motives and goodwill, that agreement is possible, that each party has something valuable to contribute to the process of resolving the conflict, and that final resolution need not ignore basic interests of all sides.[28] Mattson details seven tips to deal with team/group conflict:

1. Acknowledge the Conflict–Avoid anger buildups by facing the conflict head-on and letting your teammates know you disagree with their course of action. While not always pleasant, getting these small disagreements out in the open can help head off future disputes.
2. Stop and Cool Off–Take a minute to think through the course of action you would like to pursue. Avoid destructive behaviors like:
   - Pointing fingers
   - Insults
   - Ultimatums and rigid demands
   - Defensive attitudes
   - Complaining behind teammates' backs
   - Making assumptions about others behaviors
3. Clarify Positions–Let everyone voice his or her opinions on the conflict and be heard. While people are explaining their viewpoints on the issue in question, practice active listening. Pay attention and refrain from jumping to conclusions.
4. List Facts and Assumptions Based on Each Position–Once each team member has been allowed to explain their stance on the conflict, list out the facts and assumptions that have been made.

5. Break into Smaller Groups and Separate Existing Alliances–Many times, friendships in the workplace can cloud judgments in team projects. By breaking up existing alliances when discussing the final team positions, you often avoid this behavior and allow people to view conflicts free of persuasion.
6. Reconvene the Groups–Resolution becomes much easier once these steps have been followed and the team meets again as a whole.
7. Celebrate the Resolution as a Team–Acknowledge specific contributions from individuals in the group. The "celebration" can be a congratulatory e-mail or an afternoon off as a reward, recognizing the success promotes team bonding.

"Constructive conflict can bring a team closer together if handled properly. Respecting and appreciating your coworker's differences is key to building a strong team. Resolving conflict when it does arise in a quick and proficient fashion helps maintain a strong and healthy team environment. Remaining open to differing beliefs and ideas is vital, and learning to view conflicts from a coworker's perspective will help you become a more effective team member."[*29]

Early Identification

Tjosvold contends that "all organizations try to avoid social conflict,"[30] and there is observational evidence to support his contention. In general, conflict is not viewed as a desirable state of affairs, and consequently people tend to avoid it as long as they can. Although a potential or minor conflict may become worse and eventually develop into a major crisis, the attitude of many administrators seems to be, "Why kick sleeping dogs?"

While it is true that too much attention to a minor conflict may cause it to loom larger in everyone's eyes than it deserves, and a lack of attention may end a problem, the opposite consequences can also occur, and when they do, they are likely to be more significant. By failing to identify and take appropriate action at an early stage of a potential or minor conflict, an administrator risks the very real possibility that the conflict may become worse. By the time the administrator is forced to take action, the conflict may be very difficult to resolve. As Wynn has observed, "The most tragic instances of school conflict are usually those in which the conflict reaches the advanced stages before administrators respond to it."[31] Clearly an important first step in conflict resolution is to identify potential or minor problems at an early stage before they further deteriorate and become unmanageable.

Additional conflict can be prevented by addressing it in its early stages. Kirtman and Minkoff propose following a seven-step systems approach to analyzing and acting upon conflicts that arise from implementing new initiatives.

STEP 1 Examine how the organizational vision is affected by the conflict, and list the steps needed for realignment.

STEP 2 Identify the formal and informal leaders of the initiative, and show how the conflict is affecting them.

STEP 3 Examine the situation and identify the key participants and their roles.

STEP 4 Develop strategies that will modify the affected processes and procedures of the organization into greater alignment with its vision.

---

[*]Mattson, Dave. (2015, Feb. 4). "Ways to Deal with Team Conflict Effectively." Used with permission of Sandler Systems, Inc. All rights reserved.

STEP 5 Determine how the organization's culture and history influence the initiative and their effect on the conflict.

STEP 6 Factor the results of steps 1–5 into an implementation plan.

STEP 7 Establish a monitoring and evaluation process.

The authors caution that any stage of this process contains the possibility for conflict or the breakdown of trust.[32]

Diagnosis and the Importance of Trust

Once an administrator has identified a conflict, the causes need to be diagnosed.[33] In other words, the reason or reasons for the disagreement or dispute must be investigated, for, according to Chanin and Schneer, a conflict may be caused by "incompatible goals, ideas, values, behaviors, or emotions."[34]

Exercising Caution in Diagnosing the Conflict In diagnosing which factors are causing a conflict, it will be important, if the conflict involves the administrator, to try to avoid the natural inclination to assume the other party is wrong. Rather, the administrator's attitude and actions should be based on the assumption that there may be merit in the expectations or positions held by others, and the administrator should try to understand the reasons for these feelings.

Acting as a Mediator Understanding the basis for a conflict is also important for the administrator who hopes to resolve a dispute between two or more other individuals or groups. In this kind of situation, the administrator's role is that of mediator. Before an administrator can effectively mediate between two or more parties, there must be accurate and complete understanding of the way in which each side perceives the other and the way each side perceives the main issue that has created the conflict. Without accurate and complete information on these two variables, the administrator may inadvertently exacerbate a conflict rather than ameliorate it. As Wynn points out, "Perhaps 90% of all human conflict could be satisfactorily resolved if the major parties would take the time to talk and listen."[35]

Building Trust In this early stage of working with the parties to a conflict, it is extremely important for the administrator to develop and maintain an attitude of acceptance and trust on the part of all concerned.[36] If an administrator is to act as a mediator (or in some related role in resolving the conflict), then the participants in the conflict need to accept that role, and to trust that the administrator will act fairly and constructively. It needs to be emphasized that this trust and acceptance will not be easy to earn if the administrator is perceived as favoring one side over another or as possessing a particular vested interest. Objectivity, impartiality, and good human relations skills are essential qualities for anyone attempting to gain the acceptance or trust of others.

Helping Conflicting Parties Respect One Another It is also important that the administrator begin working on developing mutually positive attitudes on the part of the participants in a conflict. This obviously will be challenging. There is evidence that disputants tend to view each other in nonobjective, hostile, and emotional terms.[37] In many situations the mentality of the participants is expressed in the "them versus us" form, and the other side is viewed as the "enemy." The difficulty of changing the attitude of the participants to a conflict in no way negates its importance, however, for until the various parties to a dispute can begin to view each other in a more positive light, compromise and eventual resolution of the conflict will probably not be possible.

Meeting Each Party Separately Because the parties to a conflict are likely to have a negative attitude toward each other, it is recommended that the administrator acting as a mediator attempt, in the early stages of trying to resolve the conflict, to meet with each side *separately* to the extent possible. If the administrator brings together the various parties to a conflict before working with them separately, they may only continue to engage in conflict-provoking behavior that could worsen the situation. The mere presence of conflicting parties together at a meeting may intensify an already emotionally charged situation. By meeting with them separately in the initial stages, the administrator will have a better opportunity to begin persuading each side to think and behave more rationally and to view each other more positively. Crouch and Yetton write that administrators with good conflict management skills should bring subordinates together to solve conflicts. Those with poor conflict management skills, however, should not try to resolve conflict by bringing subordinates together since this will only create reduced employee performance. Further, Crouch and Yetton recommend conflict management training for both managers and subordinates.[38]

Turning Down the Heat In attempting to resolve a conflict, the administrator would do well to ignore the extreme rhetoric used by those involved in a dispute. People who are embroiled in a conflict are usually frustrated and are likely to become angry and immoderate in their speech or writing. Recommendations may be expressed as demands, epithets may be hurled, and ultimatums may be presented. Such extreme behavior may either be a part of a strategy to intimidate others or, as suggested earlier, simply be a result of frustration. Regardless of the reasons for the extreme rhetoric, the administrator should attempt to maintain an objective and professional attitude toward the disputants. This may be a difficult task, particularly if the administrator is the focus of such rhetoric. Administrator reactions that may escalate the conflict are to be avoided.

Fact-Finding

After the administrator has ascertained how the parties to a dispute view each other and the issue in question, the facts need to be validated in the situation. While it is true that the perceptions people hold represent "the facts" from their point of view, those "facts" need to be verified. There is evidence suggesting that people in conflict tend to present their side in a totally favorable light and the other side in a totally negative light.[39] They may not be doing this intentionally, and they may be very sincere in their representations. All too frequently, however, their emotions have distorted their perceptions and memory. Therefore, it is essential that the administrator attempt to validate the information from the various parties to a conflict rather than accepting the information at face value. For example, which statements by the conflicting parties rest on assumptions and which are based on evidence solidly grounded in reality? What are the *additional* facts that, thus far, the parties to the dispute have been unaware of or have failed to take into account?

At this stage the administrator needs to recognize that although people in conflict may ultimately agree on the facts in a situation, they may, nevertheless, fail to reach accord in their *interpretations* of the facts. For instance, agreement may eventually be reached by a group of parents and the superintendent that the attitude of the school board members, rather than that of the superintendent, is currently the main barrier to initiating a proposed program of community involvement. The parents and the superintendent, however, may continue to disagree about their *interpretations* of the problem. The parents may conclude the administrator should play a more active role in trying to change the school board's attitude toward community involvement, while the superintendent, as the school board's representative, may believe the school board to be the one that should try to change the attitude of the parent group. At one level, the parents and the administrator all agree that the school board is the main barrier to achieving community involvement, but they continue to disagree about what should be done in light of this obstacle.

The goal of the administrator in fact-finding should be to clarify and broaden the areas of agreement and to narrow the issues of disagreement. If the administrator is not one of the parties to the dispute, it will be easier to play the role of mediator in reaching this goal. If the administrator is personally involved in the disagreement, an outside resource person may need to be called in for assistance in mediating the conflict.

Developing an Integrative Solution

Long-lasting conflict resolution seldom occurs when one party to a dispute makes all of the gain while the needs of the other party have not been accommodated in some way. The administrator needs to recognize that a conflict between individuals or groups will seldom be permanently resolved if some parties feel they were the only losers in the resolution of the conflict. The administrator should, therefore, try to develop a conflict resolution in which there are no clear-cut winners or losers.

To achieve this result may require compromise on the part of everyone involved in the conflict. Before the administrator attempts to persuade the disputants to compromise, a resolution to the conflict that would meet the needs of all sides should be explored. This type of conflict resolution is referred to in the social science literature as an "integrative solution."[40] It involves ascertaining the needs and objectives of all parties to the conflict and trying to develop a solution in which all the parties could meet their needs and objectives in a way that would not require the others to sacrifice their needs and objectives.

The integrative solution in most conflict situations will not be easy to achieve because it requires considerable creativity and persistence on the part of the conflict mediator, and open-mindedness and flexibility on the part of all those involved in the conflict. It is the ideal solution, however, and the one most likely to result in a permanent resolution of the conflict.

Developing a Basis for Compromise

In many situations the integrative solution will not be possible, and compromise on the part of one or more parties to the conflict will be necessary.

Compromise Is Not Weakness A major obstacle to developing a compromise resolution is that the participants may feel that to compromise is to appear weak and ineffective and that compromising may reduce the chances of achieving their goals.[41] In our society, winning a victory is a more attractive result than compromise. The very term "compromise" has a mixed, or even a negative, connotation to many people. For these reasons, the administrator may encounter resistance to attempts to help both sides see the need for compromise. The approach of the administrator should be to show the participants that without compromise, their conflict is unlikely to be resolved. This won't be easy, but an attempt must be made because the alternatives of a stalemate or heightening of the conflict are likely and undesirable.

True Compromise Is Not One-Sided Assuming the various parties to a dispute can be made to see that compromise is needed to resolve the conflict, an understanding also needs to be reached that it will probably be necessary for *both* sides to compromise. Typically, individuals or groups who are in conflict do not think about the need to modify their own position but assume that the other party is the one who should or must change. It is unlikely that either side to a dispute will change without the assurance that the other side will also agree to compromise. Since in many circumstances each side is convinced it is right and the other side is wrong, the administrator may have difficulty in persuading those who are involved that there must be give and take on both sides before progress can be made in resolving the conflict. Nevertheless, the mediator must attempt to develop this understanding on the part of both sides if resolution of the conflict is to be accomplished.

Implications Must Be Recognized Another important prerequisite to an acceptable solution to a disagreement is an understanding by both sides of the *full implications* of their own point of view, as well as the *full implications* of the other side's position. While both parties may clearly understand their own position, they often fail to recognize the full ramifications of their demands or their stand on a particular issue in relation to the other disputants. Frequently, by showing how one group's demands will affect the other party, the mediator can clarify to all concerned why certain actions are unacceptable or not possible.

Opposing Points of View Must Be Understood Undoubtedly, a major deterrent to the successful resolution of a conflict is a lack of understanding of the opposite point of view on the part of one or more sides to a dispute. Usually the parties in conflict concentrate most of their energies and attention on presenting and arguing the merits of their own position and consequently do not spend sufficient time trying to understand the way the other side looks at the issue. A useful technique that can be employed to reveal this problem is to ask all parties to state the supporting rationale and main components of the opposition's arguments.[42] This step frequently identifies the areas of inadequate understanding and, if periodically employed with appropriate follow-up discussion, can also build the foundation of understanding needed for compromise and ultimate solution of the conflict. If compromise is required to resolve conflict, then certainly a better understanding of the positions and points of view of both parties is needed before that compromise can occur.

The Counterproposal

Conflicts are usually resolved by modifying the original positions taken by one or more parties to a dispute. As stated before, unless there is movement away from the original stand on an issue toward the opposing point of view, there is little likelihood of resolving the conflict. Someone must change, but usually neither party is willing to be the first to modify its position. The perspective that the mediator needs to develop in parties to a conflict is the idea that the alternatives are not restricted to either total rejection or complete capitulation. Instead, each side should be encouraged to offer a counterproposal[43] that at least recognizes the merits of some of the opposing arguments and suggests a compromise representing a better situation possibly for those concerned than would be true if the previous position of the other side were accepted in total.

The development of a counterproposal is a complex task. The proposal must advance sufficiently toward incorporating the main points raised by each party so that it will command attention and study, rather than immediate rejection, and it cannot sacrifice the basic integrity of either point of view. Its presentation must be timed for just the right moment, unless it be rejected because the other side is not yet ready to consider a possible modification of its original position or because the other side is past the point of being willing to consider a change. The key to acceptance of a counterproposal is a recognition on the part of all involved that each side must acknowledge, to some extent, the validity of the other side's arguments if the conflict is to be resolved.

Arbitration

The administrator should recognize that some conflicts cannot always be resolved through the process of mediation and that arbitration may become necessary.[44] Arbitration means that the conflict is submitted to a third party, and both sides to the dispute agree to accept the arbitrator's judgment. The arbitrator may be a superior in the organization or may be an outside party, depending on the nature of the conflict and the surrounding circumstances. When both sides to a dispute agree to submit the issue to an arbitrator, they commit themselves to accepting and implementing the arbitrator's resolution of the conflict.

Arbitration by an outside party is a relatively new phenomenon in education, although the process of internal arbitration by a superior in the organization has existed for many years. The more frequent use of outside arbitration reflects a growing polarization of points of view on the part of many groups in education and a lack of success in utilizing more traditional means of resolving conflict. While arbitration is not acceptable to many because of the freedom that is relinquished in submitting to the judgment of an arbitrator and because it does not guarantee that the conflict will not erupt again, we can probably anticipate its continued use when other methods of resolving conflict fail.

EVALUATION OF CONFLICT MANAGEMENT EFFORTS

Regardless of which conflict management approach is used, the administrator, as well as the other participants, should keep in mind that conflict cannot always be totally resolved, due to its difficult and intractable nature. Figure 5.3 illustrates the variation in possible outcomes of efforts to resolve conflict.

If an administrator cannot achieve a total resolution of a conflict, this does not mean that the administrator has failed. Conflict amelioration represents a worthwhile achievement in many situations and may be the only attainable objective under difficult circumstances.

FIGURE 5.3
CONFLICT RESOLUTION CONTINUUM

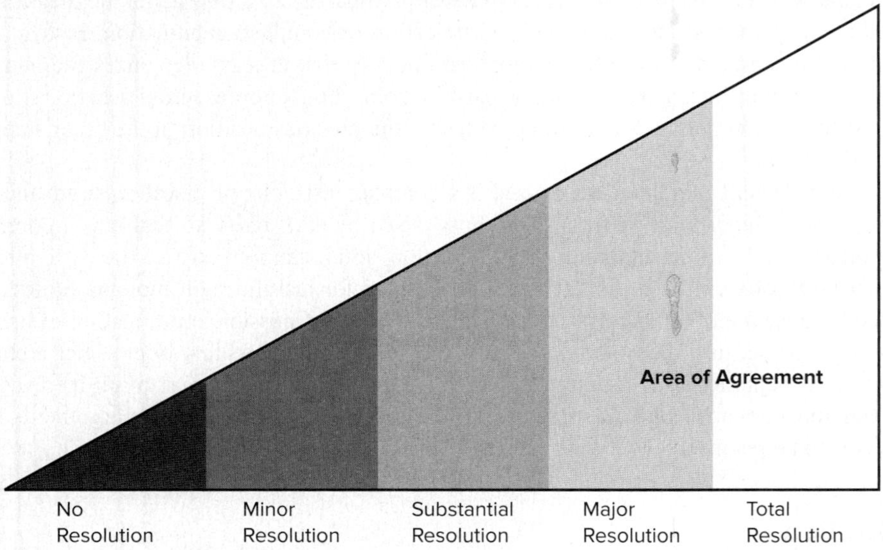

Evaluating whether or not the conflict was totally resolved, however, is not the only aspect of conflict management that should be assessed. In order for an administrator to determine whether the efforts to resolve a conflict have been successful, the following questions should be addressed:

1. To what extent do all parties to the conflict feel that the administrator has acted *fairly*? Evidence?
2. To what degree was the initial problem that produced the conflict ameliorated or resolved? Evidence?
3. How much time, energy, and frustration were spent during efforts to resolve the conflict? Evidence?
4. To what degree do the participants now have a more positive attitude toward each other? Evidence?
5. To what extent have the participants in the conflict developed new skills or approaches to preventing similar conflicts in the future or resolving them more effectively if they were to occur? Evidence?

Obviously, these questions will not be easy for an administrator to answer, nor should there be an attempt to address them without the involvement of the other parties to the conflict. By trying to answer these questions, the administrator will be likely not only to draw accurate conclusions about the success of conflict management efforts but also to learn something during the process of evaluation that could improve future effectiveness.

FURTHER OBSERVATIONS ON CONFLICT RESOLUTION

Although conflict has been studied by many scholars, there still appears to be no single proven method or formula for preventing or resolving discord. Based on experience and the writing of those who have examined the problem, however, the following observations are offered in conclusion:

1. Conflict is often inevitable in an educational organization, and, to some extent, it may indicate that important changes are being proposed, considered, or implemented. A complete absence of conflict over a long period of time may suggest a stagnant organization or educational program.
2. Disruptive, continuous, or pervasive conflict is a sign that all is not well within the organization. This type of conflict is deleterious to the emotional health of those who are associated with the organization and can impede the achievement of organizational objectives if it is not successfully ameliorated or resolved. The administrator must take the initiative in identifying, diagnosing, and mediating this type of conflict.
3. Emotions are as important to consider in dealing with a conflict as are facts. Facts may change emotions, but unless there is a sufficient understanding of the way people *feel* about the issues and about the other parties involved, the conflict will probably not be resolved.
4. The "win or lose" philosophy that characterizes so much of what occurs in our society has no place in conflict resolution. All references to, or impressions of, "winners and losers" or "the good guys and the bad guys" should be avoided. To the greatest extent possible, the final resolution of a conflict should advance the interests of all the parties.
5. The process of conflict resolution should not end at the time of final resolution. Hurt feelings may still exist, and scars incurred during early stages of the conflict may still require the administrator's attention if future problems are to be prevented.
6. A sense of humor, perspective, and a belief in the innate good intentions of most people are important to the resolution of conflict. Disputes are irritating and their resolution can be a frustrating experience. The successful resolution of a conflict may depend in many situations more on the personal characteristics of the participants than on any other factor.

Administrators must be prepared to resolve conflicts. They can gain conflict management skills through internships, case studies, sensitivity training, and simulations, in addition to studying theory and research. For example, Ivarie's article entitled "Strategies for Managing Conflict in the Collaborative Process" contains useful strategies such as "withdrawing, forcing, smoothing, compromising, and confronting."[45]

WHEN CONFLICT TURNS VIOLENT

Increasingly, administrators must solve conflicts of a physical nature that cannot be resolved by consensus or conflict resolution exercises. Schools can no longer be assumed to be the safe havens they were once considered. In recent years, tragic acts of violence have alerted educators, students, parents, and communities that there is no room for complacency. To help prevent violence, schools are employing such various strategies as using metal detectors, controlling access to school property, and having law officers present at schools.

Bullying

Today's headlines are rife with stories of teen suicide due to bullying and, unfortunately, too many stories of teachers and administrators not addressing the situations. According to the recent National Center for Education Statistics (NCES) data report about 22 percent of students ages 12 to 18 reported being bullied at school during the school year. Of students ages 12 to 18, about 14 percent reported that they were made fun of, called names, or insulted; 13 percent reported being the subject of rumors; and 6 percent reported that they were pushed, shoved, tripped, or spit on. Of those students who reported being pushed, shoved, tripped, or spit on at school, about 21 percent reported injury as a result of the incident. Additionally, about 4 percent of all students reported being excluded from activities on purpose, 4 percent reported being threatened with harm, 2 percent reported that others tried to make them do things they did not want to do, and 2 percent reported that their property was destroyed by others on purpose.[46]

Research compiled from various sources by the National Bullying Prevention Center (NBPC) notes following statistics regarding bullying:

- Rates of bullying vary across studies (from 9 to 98 percent). A meta-analysis of 80 studies analyzing bullying involvement rates (for both bullying others and being bullied) for 12- to 18- year-old students reported a mean prevalence rate of 35 percent for traditional bullying involvement and 15 percent for cyberbullying involvement (Modecki, Minchin, Harbaugh, Guerra, & Runions, 2014).
- 64 percent of children who were bullied did not report it; only 36 percent reported the bullying (Petrosina, Guckenburg, DeVoe, & Hanson, 2010).
- More than half of bullying situations (57 percent) stop when a peer intervenes on behalf of the student being bullied (Hawkins, Pepler, & Craig, 2001).
- School-based bullying prevention programs decrease bullying by up to 25 percent (McCallion & Feder, 2013).
- The reasons for being bullied reported most often by students were looks (55 percent), body shape (37 percent), and race (16 percent) (Davis & Nixon, 2010).[47]

NBPC also reported other research regarding bullying incidents:

- Among high school students, 15.5 percent are cyberbullied and 20.2 percent are bullied on school property (Center for Disease Control, 2015).
- Among middle school students, 24 percent are cyberbullied and 45 percent are bullied on school property (Center for Disease Control, 2015).
- Students with disabilities or special education needs are twice as likely to be identified as bullied targets and as bullies when compared to peers without disabilities (Rose, Monda-Amaya, & Espelage, 2011).
- 24.7 percent of African American students, 17.2 percent of Hispanic students, and 9 percent of Asian students report being bullied at school (National Center for Educational Statistics, 2015).

- 4.1 percent of Lesbian, Gay, Bisexual, and Transgender (LGBT) students were verbally bullied (e.g., called names, threatened) in the past year because of their sexual orientation and 55.2 percent because of their gender expression (National School Climate Survey, 2013).
- 36.2 percent of LGBT students were physically bullied (e.g., pushed, shoved) in the past year because of their sexual orientation and 22.7 percent because of their gender expression (National School Climate Survey, 2013).
- 49 percent of LGBT students experienced cyberbullying in the past year (National School Climate Survey, 2013).[48]

The latest 2015 Youth Risk Behavior Survey (YRBS) showed that 20 percent of high school students reported being bullied on school property in the 12 months before the survey.[49]

Bullying is a very serious issue that must be addressed. "Being bullied is not just an unpleasant rite of passage through childhood," said Duane Alexander, M.D., director of the National Institute of Child Health & Development (NICHD). "It's a public health problem that merits attention. People who were bullied as children are more likely to suffer from depression and low self-esteem, well into adulthood, and the bullies themselves are more likely to engage in criminal behavior later in life."[50] School administrators must be attuned and prepared to deal with any incidents of bullying. The U.S. Department of Health and Human Services, Health Resources and Services Administration (HRSA) suggests that school administrators assess bullying at your school and your staff's commitment to address bullying and learn about good bullying prevention programs.[51]

Zero Tolerance

Many schools and school districts have taken the precaution of establishing *zero-tolerance* policies. Such policies establish in advance what the consequences of particular offenses will be and impress upon students that certain actions absolutely will not be tolerated. Zero means zero. The National Center for Education Statistics (NCES) reports that most schools have such policies for at least some types of behavior. The center's researchers found that more than 9 out of 10 schools reported zero tolerance for weapons of any kind. Similarly, nearly 9 out of 10 schools reported policies of zero tolerance for drugs (88 percent) and alcohol (87 percent). Zero tolerance was also found to apply to tobacco products and to physical fighting or other types of violence on school property.[52]

At the same time, such policies have their critics. "Critics say these policies lead to overreaction, pointing to such cases as suspending a child for bringing a toy gun to school," writes Rasicot, "but many school officials stand by the policies."[53] In her overview of attitudes toward such policies, Rasicot cites the worries of some civil rights advocates who fear that "students' rights might be trampled by efforts to ensure a safe school." She also mentions the concerns of mental health authorities who would prefer that a student's *motives* be explored before penalties are meted out and that penalties be meted out on a case-by-case basis suited to the particular offender.

In an article entitled, "Does Zero Mean Zero?" Martin points out the frustration school administrators often feel over the enforcement of zero-tolerance policies because there is a constant weighing of two sets of students' rights–the rights of the individual student accused of violating a zero-tolerance policy and the rights of the entire student body to learn in a safe environment. No matter how the administrator handles a given situation, including turning the matter over to the school board if that is district policy, there are still circumstances, Martin says, when "parents of the disciplined student–and sometimes, other interested parties–might question the judgment used by school administrators and disagree with their decisions."[54]

Martin urges school boards, superintendents, and building-level administrators to acknowledge the apprehension of parents and the community and thus to make every effort to publicize the weapons policy of the school or district. Such publicizing would include "highlighting the consequences for noncompliance and defining the weapons that are considered deadly and dangerous, for which possession would result in mandatory expulsion." He goes on to say that "the district also should acknowledge that only special circumstances may be taken into account when determining the appropriate consequence." Examples of such circumstance might include the offender's age, ability to understand the policy's requirements, intent, past disciplinary record, and how the presence of the weapon (or item defined as a weapon) affected others. Martin has put together a list of suggestions designed to help principals avoid "communication pitfalls" in carrying out zero tolerance. He concludes:

> Trying to balance strict policy enforcement with practical procedural implementation is the greatest public relations challenge facing today's school administrators. But remember: Any school would rather gain a reputation for zealously enforcing a strict weapons policy than receive notoriety for a shooting incident. And communities will support their schools' effort to increase safety and decrease violence–as long as schools don't lose sight of common sense.[55]

Other Strategies for Preventing School Violence

Many schools are attempting to find additional ways to address the issue of potential violence. "Security measures such as metal detectors can stop students from bringing weapons to school but do little to address the anger, meanness, and fistfights that are the much larger, although less newsworthy, part of the problem," Shapiro observes. He expresses concern over the way anger, fear, and fighting harm students both academically and emotionally, and distract them from the learning experience. "When arguments and threats escalate into violence," he writes, "the result is disruption of school activities, agitation of other students, disciplinary incidents, and sometimes, suspensions and expulsions which cause further loss of learning."[56]

School Violence Prevention Programs Shapiro's suggested remedy is the institution of school violence prevention programs such as the Peacemakers Program for grades 4 to 8. He points out that the program helps students develop specific skills for handling conflict. These skills are essentially built around three basic strategies: "proactively avoiding conflicts, responding effectively to conflicts once they have begun, and removing oneself from conflict situations in which the other person's maladaptive behavior makes resolution impossible." Particularly important, Shapiro stresses, is the need to recognize that some young people look upon violence as "the most honorable and admirable response to conflict." Such students are not motivated to learn skills for dealing with conflict by nonviolent means. Therefore, special attention must be given to addressing the proviolence values such students hold.[57]

Mediation Mediation, including peer mediation, is another way that schools are working to deal with dispute resolution and violence prevention. Trevaskis points out benefits that both disputants and mediators gain through such programs and describes the important life skills both parties learn when the mediation approach is applied. In his *ERIC Digest* summary of mediation practices in schools, Trevaskis has included a "checklist for mediation," outlining how the mediation process works.[58] As Beyer points out in a discussion of the legal rights of students with regard to school safety, "Certainly, violence prevention training, as opposed to criminal enforcement techniques, is the course most consistent with a recognition of children's human rights."[59]

Resources to Help in Violence Prevention

The Internet provides many resources that may help school leaders deal with the problem of school violence and concerns about school safety. Figure 5.4 provides an overview of some of the best material from reliable sources that is available online from the Internet.

FIGURE 5.4
ONLINE RESOURCES TO AID EDUCATIONAL LEADERS IN KEEPING SCHOOLS SAFE

Description	Web Page URL
Safe from Harm: An Online Anthology on School Security. This collection of articles on school safety, security, and violence prevention has been compiled from articles in various publications of the National School Boards Association (NSBA).	http://www.asbj.com/TopicsArchive/SafeFromHarm.aspx
NEA Safe Schools Now. The National Education Association's effort to "fortify families, communities, and schools with information and tools to promote school safety and keep children from harm." Includes links to many useful resources.	http://www.nea.org/home/16364.htm
Safe and Drug-Free Schools Program. "The Federal government's primary vehicle for reducing drug, alcohol and tobacco use, and violence, through education and prevention activities in our nation's schools."	https://www2.ed.gov/admins/lead/safety/edpicks.jhtml
How to Protect Students from Sexual Harassment: A Primer for Schools. This fact sheet is part of a series of tools designed by the National Women's Law Center to help schools address the dropout crisis, in particular those students who dropout due to sexual harassment and bullying.	http://www.nwlc.org/sites/default/files/pdfs/Final SH Fact Sheet-Schools.pdf
A Dozen Things Principals Can Do to Stop School Violence. A succinct summary provided by the National Crime Prevention Council.	http://www.ncpc.org/resources/files/pdf/school-safety/principals12.pdf
Indicators of School Crime and Safety, 2015. A report from the National Center for Education Statistics and the Bureau of Justice Statistics.	https://www.bjs.gov/content/pub/pdf/iscs15.pdf
Early Warning, Timely Response: A Guide to Safe Schools. This detailed guide was published by the U.S. Department of Education in response to a presidential directive after a tragic school shooting in 1998. It is filled with practical help to enable "adults to reach out to troubled children quickly and effectively."	http://www2.ed.gov/about/offices/list/osers/osep/gtss.html
Consortium for Appropriate Dispute Resolution in Special Education. CADRE, the National Center on Dispute Resolution, encourages the use of mediation and other collaborative strategies to resolve disagreements about special education and early intervention programs.	http://www.directionservice.org/cadre/index.cfm

ACLU Youth & Schools. The Youth & Schools program strives to make public schools safe and bias-free, defending free expression in public schools.	https://www.aclu.org/issues/lgbt-rights/lgbt-youth
LGBTQ YOUTH OF COLOR: Discipline Disparities, School Push-Out, and the School-to-Prison Pipeline	https://gsanetwork.org/files/aboutus/LGBTQ_brief_FINAL-web.pdf
Best Practices: Creating an LGBT-Inclusive School Climate. List of resources.	http://www.tolerance.org/lgbt-best-practices
National Youth Violence Prevention Resource Center. Information on youth violence, youth at risk, youth suicide, gangs, and firearm violence. Good source for statistics.	www.safeyouth.org
Stop the Hate. Dedicated to helping students, educators, police and the community to stop hate crimes and violence. Also a good connection to other communities about activities in these areas.	www.stopthehate.org
Bullying.org. An excellent resource to see, read, and hear the impact that bullying has had on people's lives. Read personal testimonials, hear songs, watch videos, or read poems.	www.bullying.org
ERIC (Educational Resource Information Center). Information for parents and teachers about many educational issues.	www.eric.ed.gov
Take Action Against Bullying. Information about bullying from recent articles. www.bullybeware.com	www.bullybeware.com
Stop Bullying Now. Does not believe that bullying is a part of growing up. View letters from students.	www.stopbullyingnow.com
Teasing Victims. Provides an online "Revolutionary Manual for Handling Kids' Aggression" and "Columbine Made Simple." Includes areas for parents and teachers.	www.Bullies2Buddies.com
Gay, Lesbian and Straight Education Network (GLSEN). Antibullying resources and support for schools to implement effective and age-appropriate antibullying programs to improve school climate for all students.	https://www.glsen.org/article/bullying-prevention-resources
GLSEN 2015 National School Climate Survey, Gay, Lesbian and Straight Education Network (GLSEN). Nearly 9 of 10 LGBT Students Experience Harassment in School.	https://www.glsen.org/article/2015-national-school-climate-survey

The U.S. Department of Education has in recent years placed great emphasis on understanding what leads to school violence and what is most effective in preventing it. Its 1998 publication, *Early Warning, Timely Response,* was written as a guide for school leaders and all others interested in school safety. Summing up research on violence prevention and intervention, the publication includes early warning signs (but with a caveat about not misinterpreting or misusing them), principles for helping troubled children, information on how to develop a prevention and response plan, and how to respond to crisis in the event that a tragic act of violence does occur.[60]

A companion publication for principals, teachers, mental health professionals, and families was issued by the Department of Education in 2000 after the positive reception of its *Early Warning, Timely Response* guide resulted in requests for a follow-up resource. *Safeguarding Our Children: An Action Guide* was developed to help schools utilize a three-stage comprehensive school safety model built around "schoolwide prevention, early intervention, and intensive services for students with significant emotional or behavioral needs, including those with disruptive, destructive, or violent behaviors."[61]

Effective leadership requires a knowledge of conflict management that is applicable to a wide variety of situations, including situations that could escalate into violence. Materials that can assist in gaining this knowledge are readily available, and research is showing which strategies are most effective.

Although most of the case studies, suggested learning activities, and simulations presented in Part II of the text require the appropriate use of this chapter's material on managing and resolving conflict, the following exercises should provide the best opportunities for specifically testing understanding and effective use of these concepts: Cases 13, 20, 24, 25, 28, 31, 32, 33, 41, 56, and 60; the midyear in-basket exercises; and the end-of-the-year in-basket exercises.

NOTES

1. Kenneth N. Wexley and Gary A. Yukl, *Organizational Behavior and Personnel* Psychology (Homewood, IL: Richard D. Irvin, 1984), p. 192.
2. Richard Wynn, *Communication: The Key to Conflict Management* (Reston, VA: National Association of Secondary School Principals, 1985), p. 1. Also see D. W. Johnson and R. T. Johnson, *Joining Together* (Englewood Cliffs, NJ: Prentice Hall, 1987).
3. Stephen P. Robbins, "'Conflict Management' and 'Conflict Resolution' Are Not Synonymous Terms," *California Management Review* (Winter 1978), pp. 69–70; Richard A. Cosier and Charles R. Schwenk, "Agreement and Thinking Alike: Ingredients for Poor Decisions," *Academy of Management Excellence* (February 1990), pp. 69–74; and *Group Theory and Group Skills,* 3rd ed. (Englewood Cliffs, NJ: Prentice Hall, 1987).
4. Jacob W. Getzels, "Administration as a Social Process," in Andrew Halpin (Ed.), *Administrative Theory in Education* (Chicago: University of Chicago Midwest Administration Center, 1958), p. 153. Also see Andrew W. Halpin (Ed.), *Administrative Theory in Education* (London: Macmillan, 1958).
5. Neal Gross et al., *Explorations in Role Analysis: Studies of the School Superintendency Role* (New York: John Wiley, 1958), p. 58. For additional information on role expectations, see James M. Kouzes and Barry Z. Posner, *The Leadership Challenge,* 4th ed. (San Francisco: Jossey-Bass, 2007).
6. Numerous studies have been conducted supporting the validity of the Getzels model. These are described in detail in Jacob W. Getzels, James M. Lipham, and Roald Campbell, *Educational Administration as a Social Process: Theory Research and Practice* (New York: Harper & Row, 1968). Also see Wilburn R. Clouse, "A Review of Educational Role Theory: A Teaching Guide for Administrative Theory," *Clearinghouse Educational Management* (1989), an ERIC report, Ed. 314824.
7. Roald F. Campbell, "Situational Factors in Educational Administration," in Roald Campbell and Russell Gregg (Eds.), *Administrative Behavior in Education* (New York: Harper & Row, 1968), p. 264. Also see Lynne L. Adduci et al., "The Department Chair: Role Ambiguity and Role Strain" (Philadelphia: Research for Better Schools, Inc., 1990), an ERIC report, Ed. 321398.
8. Larry W. Hughes and Thomas A. Robertson, "Principals and the Management of Conflict," *Planning and Changing* (Spring 1980), pp. 3–16. Also see Robert J. Bies, Debra L. Shapiro, and Larry L. Cummings, "Causal Accounts and Managing Organizational Conflict: Is It Enough to It's Not My Fault," *Communication Research* (August 1988), pp. 381–399.
9. Gross et al., *Explorations in Role Analysis,* p. 58.
10. Ibid., pp. 59–60.
11. Ibid.

12. John Lindelow and James Scott, "Managing Conflict," in *School Leadership: Handbook for Excellence* (Eugene, OR: Clearinghouse on Educational Management, 1989), an ERIC report, Ed. 309519, pp. 339–355.
13. Robbins, "'Conflict Management' and 'Conflict Resolution,'" pp. 67–75.
14. Gross et al., *Explorations in Role Analysis,* p. 284. Also see Kenneth A. Shaw, "Making Conflict Work for You," *New Directions for Higher Education* (Spring 1988), pp. 53–58.
15. Donald L. Sayan and W. W. Charters Jr., "A Replication among School Principals of the Gross Study of Role Conflict Resolution," *Educational Administration Quarterly* (Spring 1970), pp. 36–45; Walter F. Daves and C. L. Holland, "The Structure of Conflict Behavior of Managers Assessed with Self and Subordinate Ratings" (January 1990), pp. 741–756; and Patricia B. Link, "How to Cope with Conflict between the People Who Work with You," *Supervision* (January 1990), pp. 7–9.
16. Gross et al., *Explorations in Role Analysis,* pp. 285–318.
17. For identification of some additional ways of resolving role conflict, see Mary van Sell et al., "Role Conflict and Role Ambiguity," *Human Relations* (vol. 34, no. 1, January 1981), pp. 63–64; and Lindelow and Scott, *School Leadership,* chap. 15.
18. Jeffrey Barker, Dean Tjosvold, and Robert Anderson, "Conflict Approaches of Effective and Ineffective Project Managers: A Field Study in a Matrix Organization," *Journal of Management Studies* (March 1988), pp. 167–178.
19. For related research on this point, see Ann Case, "The Role of Power in Conflict Resolution among School Administrators," PhD dissertation, Boston University, 1984.
20. Michael N. Chanin and Joy A. Schneer, "A Study of the Relationship between Jungian Personality Dimensions and Conflict-Handling Behavior," *Human Relations* (vol. 37, no. 10, October 1984), pp. 863–879; and Robert E. Jones and Charles S. White, "Relationships among Personality, Conflict Resolution Styles, and Task Effectiveness," *Group and Organizational Studies* (June 1985), pp. 152–167. Also see Walter F. Daves and C. L. Holland, "The Structure of Conflict Behavior of Managers Assessed with Self and Subordinate Ratings," *Human Relations* (August 1989), pp. 741–756.
21. Richard A. Schmuck and Philip J. Runkel, *The Handbook of Organizational Development in Schools,* 3rd ed. (Palo Alto, CA: Mayfield, 1985), p. 295.
22. Mary Utley, Deborah Richardson, and Constance J. Pilkington, "Personality and Interpersonal Conflict Management," *Personality and Individual Differences* (October 1989), pp. 287, 293.
23. Robert R. Blake, Herbert A. Shepard, and Jane S. Mouton, *Managing Intergroup Conflict in Industry* (Houston, TX: Gulf, 1964), pp. 18–49. For a more recent discussion of these techniques, as well as the conflict avoidance and problem-solving approaches, see Wexley and Yukl, *Organizational Behavior and Personnel Psychology,* pp. 198–205; and Phillip B. DuBose and Charles D. Pringle, "Choosing a Conflict Management Technique," *Supervision* (June 1989), pp. 10–12.
24. Blake et al., *Managing Intergroup Conflict in Industry,* p. 18.
25. Ann F. Lucas, *Strengthening Departmental Leadership: A Team-Building Guide for Chairs in Colleges and Universities* (San Francisco: Jossey-Bass, 1994), p. 196.
26. Dean Tjosvold and Don W. Johnson (Eds.), *Productive Conflict Management: Perspectives for Organizations* (New York: Irvington, 1983).
27. C. James Riggs, "Dimensions of Organizational Conflict," in Robert N. Bostrom (Ed.), *Communication Yearbook,* vol. 7 (Beverly Hills, CA: Sage, 1983), pp. 517–531. Also see Hughes and Robertson, "Principals and the Management of Conflict," p. 5.
28. Dean Tjosvold, "Making Conflict Productive," *Personnel Administrator* (June 1984), pp. 121–130.
29. Dave Mattson, "Ways to Deal with Team Conflict Effectively." Accessed online, www.sandler.com/blog/ways-to-deal-with-team-conflict-effectively, February 4, 2015.

30. Tjosvold, "Making Conflict Productive," pp. 121–130.

31. Richard Wynn, "Administrative Response to Conflict," *Today's Education* (February 1972), p. 32.

32. Lyle J. Kirtman and Maxine Minkoff, "A Systems Approach to Conflict Management," *School Administrator* (March 1996), p. 17.

33. M. Afzalur Rahim, "A Strategy for Managing Conflict in Complex Organizations," *Human Relations* (January 1985), pp. 81–89.

34. Chanin and Scheer, "A Study of the Relationship between Jungian Personality Dimensions and Conflict-Handling Behavior," p. 864.

35. Richard Wynn, "Communication: The Key to Conflict Management," *Practitioner* (May 1985), p. 3.

36. Robert A. Rothberg, "Trust Development: The Forgotten Leadership Skill," *National Association of Secondary School Principals Bulletin* (December 1984), pp. 18–22. Also see Kouzes and Posner, *Leadership Challenge,* pp. 146–160; and C. John Tarter, James R. Bliss, and Wayne K. Hoy, "School Characteristics and Faculty Trust in Secondary School," *Educational Administration Quarterly* (August 1989), pp. 294–308.

37. Wynn de Bevoise, "Conference Explores Effects of Collective Bargaining on Schools and Administrators," *R and D Perspectives* (Summer 1982), p. 5.

38. Andrew Crouch and Phillip Yetton, "Manager Behavior, Leadership Style, and Subordinate Performance: An Empirical Extension of the Vroom-Yetton Conflict Rule," *Organizational Behavior and Human Decision Process* (June 1987), pp. 282–286.

39. Rensis Likert and Jane G. Likert, *New Ways of Managing Conflict* (New York: McGraw-Hill, 1976), pp. 61–62. Also see Michael Maccoby, *Why Work: Leading the New Generation* (New York: Simon and Schuster, 1988), pp. 226–227.

40. A. C. Filley, "Some Normative Issues in Conflict Management," *California Management Review* (vol. 21, no. 2, Winter 1978), pp. 61–65. Also see Robert R. Blake and Jane S. Mouton, *Solving Costly Organizational Conflicts* (San Francisco: Jossey-Bass, 1984); John Gray and Angela Pfeiffer, "Skills for Leaders," National Association of Secondary School Principals, an ERIC report, Ed. 279964, 1987, p. 62; and Kouzes and Posner, *Leadership Challenge,* pp. 142–145.

41. Dean Tjosvold, "Control Orientation, Nonnegotiable Demands, and Race in Conflict between Unequal Power Persons," paper presented at the annual meeting of the American Educational Research Association, April 1976. For more recent information on the political advantage of compromise, see Joseph L. Badaracco Jr. and Richard R. Ellsworth, *Leadership and the Quest for Integrity* (Boston: Harvard Business School Press, 1989), pp. 29–31; and for a discussion on confrontation versus compromise, see chap. 7 in Badaracco and Ellsworth, *Leadership and the Quest for Integrity.*

42. Malcom E. Shaw et al., *Role Playing: A Practical Manual for Group Facilitators* (San Diego: University Associates, 1980), pp. 57–58; and William M. Fox, *Effective Group Problem Solving: How to Broaden Participation, Improve Decision Making, and Increase Commitment to Action* (San Francisco: Jossey-Bass, 1987), pp. 157–164.

43. Donald Livingston, "Rules of the Road: Doing Something Simple about Conflict in the Organization," *Personnel* (January–February 1977), pp. 23–29. Also see Dan DeStephen, "Personnel," *Management Solutions* (March 1988), pp. 5–10.

44. William W. Notz et al., "The Manager as Arbitrator: Conflicts over Scarce Resources," in Max H. Bazerman and Roy J. Lewicki (Eds.), *Negotiating in Organizations* (Beverly Hills, CA: Sage, 1983), pp. 143–164. The reader is encouraged to examine other articles in the same book in order to develop additional background in the utilization of techniques of negotiating in situations that are outside the management-labor bargaining setting. More information can also be found in Loraliegh Keashly, "A Comparative Analysis of Third Party Interventions in Intergroup Conflict," PhD dissertation, University of Saskatchewan (Canada), 1988.

45. Judith J. Ivarie, "Strategies for Managing Conflict in the Collaborative Process," an ERIC report, Ed. 385064.
46. Indicators of school crime and safety: 2010. Accessed online, http://nces.ed.gov/programs/crimeindicators/crimeindicators2010/tables/table_11_1.asp, December 28, 2010.
47. Bullying statistics 2009. Accessed online, http://www.bullyingstatistics.org/content/bullying-statistics-2009.html, December 28, 2010.
48. Ibid.
49. Ibid.
50. Duane Alexander, "Bullying statistics: Effects of bullying." Accessed online, http://bullyingstatistics.blogspot.com/, December 28, 2010.
51. U.S. Department of Health and Human Services, Health Resources and Services Administration (HRSA), "Stop bullying now. Steps to address bullying at your school: Tips for school administrators," Accessed online, http://www.stopbullyingnow.hrsa.gov/HHS_PSA/pdfs/SBN_Tip_15.pdf. For more information on bullying, see also http://www.education.com/topic/school-bullying-teasing/ and http://www.aasa.org/content.aspx?id=218, December 28, 2010.
52. Phillip Kaufman, et al., *Indicators of School Crime and Safety, 2000* (Washington, DC: U.S. Department of Education, National Center for Education Statistics, and the U.S. Department of Justice, Bureau of Justice Statistics, 2000), App. A.
53. Julie Rasicot, "The Threat of Harm," *American School Board Journal* (March, 1999). Accessed online, http://www.asbj.com/199903/0399coverstory.html, January 21, 2001.
54. W. Michael Martin, "Does Zero Mean Zero?" *American School Board Journal* (March 2000). Available as part of "Safe from Harm: An Online Anthology on School Security." Accessed online, http://www.asbj.com/security/contents/0300martin.html, January 20, 2001.
55. Ibid.
56. Jeremy P. Shapiro, "The Peacemakers Program: Effective Violence Prevention for Early Adolescent Youth," *National Association of School Psychologists (NASP) Communiqué* (vol. 27, March 1999). Accessed online, http://www.naspweb.org/publications/cq276peace.html, December 28, 2000.
57. Ibid.
58. David Keller Trevaskis, "Mediation in the Schools," *ERIC Digest* (1994), Ed. 378108. Accessed online, http://202.198.141.77/upload/soft/0-article/+020/20078.pdf, December 28, 2010.
59. Dorianne Beyer, "School Violence and the Legal Rights of Students," an *ERIC Digest* based on Beyer's longer monograph. The digest is published by the ERIC Clearinghouse on Urban Education (May, 1997) and is available on the Internet. Accessed online, http://www.ericdigests. org/1998-2/safety.htm, December 28, 2010.
60. K. Dwyer, D. Osher, and C. Warger, *Early Warning, Timely Response: A Guide to Safe Schools* (Washington, DC: U.S. Department of Education, 1998). Accessed online, http://www2.ed.gov/about/offices/list/osers/osep/gtss.html
61. K. Dwyer and D. Osher, *Safeguarding Our Children: An Action Guide* (Washington, DC: U.S. Department of Education, U.S. Department of Justice, and American Institutes for Research, 2000). Accessed online, http://www2.ed.gov/admins/lead/safety/actguide/action_guide.pdf, December 28, 2010.

C H A P T E R

6

Organizational Culture

APPLICABLE PSEL STANDARDS

- **STANDARD 1:** **Mission, Vision, and Core Values**
  Effective educational leaders develop, advocate, and enact a shared mission, vision, and core values of high-quality education and academic success and well-being of each student.
- **STANDARD 3:** **Equity and Cultural Responsiveness**
  Effective educational leaders strive for equity of educational opportunity and culturally responsive practices to promote each student's academic success and well-being.
- **STANDARD 7:** **Professional Community for Teachers and Staff**
  Effective educational leaders foster a professional community of teachers and other professional staff to promote each student's academic success and well-being.
- **STANDARD 9:** **Operations and Management**
  Effective educational leaders manage school operations and resources to promote each student's academic success and well-being.

National Policy Board for Educational Administration (NPBEA). *Professional Standards for Educational Leaders* (Reston, VA: Author, 2015).

Scholars have long been interested in the social factors that seem to influence individual or group behavior in an organization.[1] A classic example of this focus was the Western Electric studies in the 1930s that found employees develop a set of implicit group norms that influence, and in some cases restrict, the levels of performance for an individual in a group.[2] Another example is provided in Anderson and Poe's more recent description of the entrepreneurial society created in certain companies in which employees work together with nothing less than a zeal to perform.[3] Since the 1930s, there have been several studies of the types of social and professional norms that develop in a school,[4] and research on effective schools has identified the culture of a school as an important effectiveness variable.[5] The Education Commission of the States has found that quality learning experiences start with an organizational culture that values high expectations and respects diversity of talents and learning styles.[6] Therefore, if school leaders desire to improve the morale and productivity of those they lead, it is imperative that they strive to understand and enhance the organizational culture of their school or school district.

In the following sections the theory of organizational culture will be examined, especially as it relates to effective schools.

MAJOR ELEMENTS OF ORGANIZATIONAL CULTURE

What is the organizational culture of a school, and how would an administrator recognize it? Any organization operates according to a set of values, goals, principles, procedures, and practices that help define what it is all about. Another word for these combined operating characteristics is "culture." According to Smircich, who synthesized a number of ideas from other theorists, "Culture is usually defined as social or normative glue that holds an organization together. It expresses the values or social ideas and beliefs that organization members come to share."[7] Brighton and Sayeed describe culture as "the social energy that drives (or fails to drive) organizations" and that enables organizations "to survive the external environment and manage the internal environment."[8] For Peterson and Deal, "Culture is the underground stream of norms, values, beliefs, traditions, and rituals that has built up over time as people work together, solve problems, and confront challenges." They emphasize that "this set of informal expectations and values shapes how people think, feel, and act in schools" and serves as a "highly enduring web of influence [that] binds the school together and makes it special."[9] Cunningham writes that effective school cultures are characterized by people "who have learned to trust and to share as well as to accept other's needs to trust and share."[10]

Halpin's research has shown that schools differ in their cultures and that those cultures have an impact on students. To illustrate, he writes:

> In one school the teachers and the principal are zestful and exude confidence in what they are doing. They find pleasure in working with each other; this pleasure is transmitted to students. . . . In a second school the brooding discontentment of teachers is palpable; the principal tries to hide his incompetence and lack of direction behind a cloak of authority. . . . And the psychological sickness of such a faculty spills over on the students who, in their own frustration, feed back to teachers a mood of despair. A third school is marked by neither joy nor despair, but by hollow ritual. . . . In a strange way the show doesn't seem "for real."[11]

Whether or not schools differ in their organizational cultures, conceptually every organizational culture seems to be composed of several elements, depicted in Figure 6.1.[12]

Values and Ideals

As Figure 6.1 indicates, an administrator's analysis of a school's organizational culture should begin with developing a good understanding of the values and ideals that the school represents.[13] The basic question to be asked is, "What kinds of behavior are valued in this school, and what does the school aspire to become?" (It will be important for an administrator to distinguish between those values and ideals given only lip service by the people who are associated with the school and those on which their behavior is based.)

FIGURE 6.1
MAJOR ELEMENTS OF ORGANIZATIONAL CULTURE

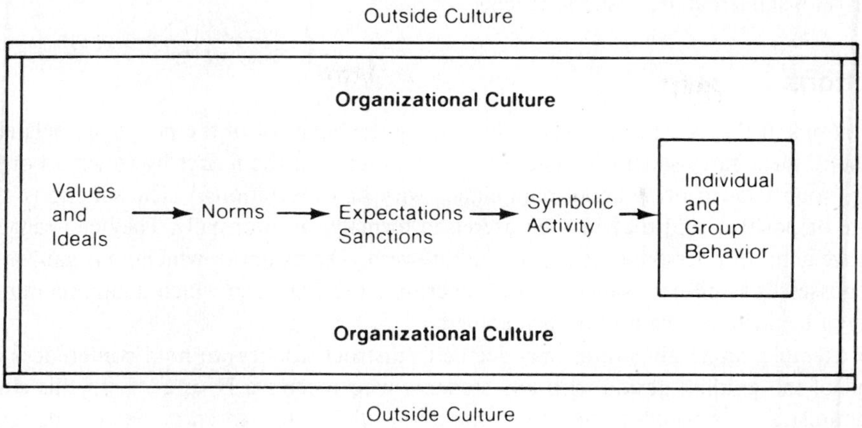

Norms

The values and ideals of a school may be difficult to ascertain, but they usually will be reflected in its *norms.* Norms, according to Josefowitz, are "the unwritten rules stating what people should and should not do."[14] They serve the purpose of regulating and controlling behavior. An example of a desirable faculty norm would be, "Teachers should share ideas about how to improve instruction."

Norms, it should be emphasized, are not values that an administrator can *impose* on a group. For example, faculty and staff come to school with personal value systems. Organizational values are then communicated to the individual through rules and processes. Shockley-Zalabak and Morley's research demonstrates that when organizational rules and personal values are congruent, an individual is more satisfied with the job and projects high estimations of organizational quality and success.[15] Consequently, as Miller points out, "Any lasting change of a school will occur only because the staff itself changes norms of expectations, appropriate role definitions, standards of accountability, and patterns of behavior."[16]

Expectations

The *expectations* of an organizational culture are the norms applied to a specific situation.[17] For example, "Bob Elliott, an experienced sixth-grade teacher, should be willing to share his expertise with Julie Adams, a new sixth-grade teacher" is a specific expression of the faculty norm presented previously. In another situation, "Dr. Brown, the principal, should support Mr. Armstrong's attempts to discipline a student" represents an expectation based on a faculty norm that maintains, "The principal should always support the teachers, right or wrong." Although it is important for an administrator to become *aware* of the expectations of others as part of understanding the culture of the school, an administrator must also evaluate the merits of those expectations before deciding to meet them. For example, for a school to become more effective, it may require that teachers expend effort and time beyond the normal workday, and improvement may require a focus on teaching reasoning and analytical skills, with a reduced emphasis on skills that are easier to teach.[18]

Sanctions

Expectations, if they are to be effective in shaping the behavior of the people associated with the school, must carry sanctions. These sanctions represent the *means* by which an organization or group tries to bring about compliance with its expectations.[19] The sanctions may be negative or positive, and they may be exercised formally or informally. They can range from a punitive action to personal recognition and reward. The extent to which an organization or group possesses significant sanctions will determine the degree to which it can maintain conformity of behavior on the part of its members.

For example, an administrator may decide to instruct teachers to hold conferences before the end of the grading period with any students who receive a D or an F. In this situation the administrator is counting on the cooperation of the staff to carry out the directive. A majority of the faculty may feel that holding these conferences will take too much time, however, so they decide to ignore the administrator's directive. Unless the administrator possesses adequate monitoring procedures for detecting a lack of follow-through on the part of the faculty, the principal may never discover that the policy on teacher–student conferences is not being carried out. If the failure to comply with the instruction is discovered, the principal may not be able to do anything about it unless the administrator can persuade the teachers of the desirability of these conferences or possesses adequate sanctions to force them to adhere to the directive, despite their lack of voluntary cooperation.

The noncompliance of an individual or group ordinarily does not take the form of a direct challenge to the administrator. Instead, resistance is usually expressed by underachievement or lack of implementation in response to the administrator's expectations. As U.S. President Harry Truman observed in recalling the problems of the presidency, the executive may say, "Do this! Do that!" and yet find, to his chagrin, that "nothing will happen."[20] Often the reason for the lack of follow-through is that the subordinates in the hierarchy have concluded that the action desired by the administrator is either not in their best interest or not in the best interest of the institution–so they have ignored the instructions. As a result, the implementation of administrative policy is completely delayed or thwarted.

Communication through Symbolism

The expectations and sanctions of a school or a group associated with a school may be communicated directly, or they may be expressed indirectly through *symbolic activity.* As Morgan and his colleagues note, "Many organizations consciously attempt to create complex symbol systems which are intended to signify the desirability of engaging in rigorous patterns of rational, instrumental, and pragmatic action. Symbols [reinforce] the pursuit of excellence, achievement, aggressiveness, competitiveness, and intense commitment to organizational ends."[21] An organization's symbolic activity, according to Smircich, may take different forms, including storytelling about important events, such as how an organization faced up to a particular challenge; group rituals, such as the annual banquet at which awards of recognition are presented; or organizational slogans,[22] such as "excellence is our goal."

Symbolic Activity through Behavioral Example

Symbolic activity can also be found in the behavior of an administrator. For example, the principal who would like to show support of a "reading break" program and encourage teachers to support the program can certainly communicate these feelings and expectations at a faculty meeting. If the administrator does so, and yet is never seen reading a book during the reading break and does not use negative sanctions against teachers who fail to participate in the program, this constitutes a stronger message to the faculty about the principal's attitude than any comments made at a faculty meeting. On the other hand, if the principal is regularly observed reading a book in classrooms, this nonverbal behavior is likely to send a symbolic message to teachers that will be more effective than anything that might be said at the meeting. The main impact of symbolic activity is not so much what is said as what can be inferred from the behavior of the people who are formal and informal leaders in an organization.

CULTURAL ELEMENTS OF AN EFFECTIVE SCHOOL

"Organizational culture and the symbols which are a part of this culture are not politically neutral but represent levels of power and control," write Reilly and DiAngelo.[23] Blanch studied culture as a control mechanism. Her research indicates that four core values define school culture: (1) cooperative community-parent relationships, (2) cooperative teacher relationships, (3) student needs, and (4) principals as cultural transmitters. Her research further demonstrates that strong congruence of "group sensemaking" with school values indicates culture is a strong control mechanism. She suggests that schools should attempt to foster consensus and that principals should act as consensus builders in the early stages of culture development dominated by indirect strategies. Direct strategies are diluted to minimize divisiveness, and "principal/teacher sensemaking acts as a gauge of cultural controls," according to the author. Her research implies that strong cultural control impedes change, neglects instruction, and ultimately affects achievement.[24]

A Positive Organizational Culture

Earlier studies tended to focus on the negative influence that the culture of an organization could exert on the achievement and behavior of the individuals or groups associated with the organization. Researchers have recently emphasized the importance of developing and maintaining a positive organizational culture, however, if a school is to be effective. For example, Purkey and Smith have concluded that "an academically effective school is distinguished by its culture: a structure, process, and climate of values and norms that channel staff and students in the direction of successful teaching and learning."[25]

But what kind of an organizational culture best promotes successful teaching and learning? While scholars continue to pursue this question, research has produced some tentative findings that suggest a number of major elements of the culture of an effective school, as shown in Figure 6.2.[26] Snyder and Snyder indicate that changing organizational culture through a systems thinking approach is based on "organizational planning, developing staff, developing a program, and assessing school productivity."[27] With this model, schools will more easily effect change and improve the instructional environment.

FIGURE 6.2
MAJOR ELEMENTS OF THE CULTURE OF AN EFFECTIVE SCHOOL

1. A clear set of schoolwide norms that emphasize the values of academic effort and achievement.
2. A *consistently* applied set of expectations that stress the importance of staff members striving for excellence and students performing up to their potential.
3. A system of symbolic activity and sanctions that encourages and rewards effort, improvement, and accomplishment, while discouraging disorder and complacency.

Emphasis on Academic Effort and Achievement

An examination of Figure 6.2 shows that the organizational culture of an academically effective school includes a set of schoolwide norms stressing academic effort and accomplishment. Although other kinds of effort and achievement, such as developing ethical behavior, may also be important to parents and students, the research on effective schools stresses that the norms of an academically effective school will give the highest priority to academic effort and achievement.[28] These norms may be reflected in an organization's mission statement, educational goals, or other documents.[29] Regardless of how the norms manifest themselves, Saphier and King underscore the point that norms should represent "a clear, articulated vision of what the school stands for, a vision that embodies core values and purposes."[30]

Since organizational norms are usually expressed in the form of expectations for the members of the organizations, what are the expectations for those associated with effective schools? In general, these expectations emphasize academic effort, improvement, and accomplishment. For example, "striving for excellence" would be one important expectation in an effective school. Saphier and King illustrate this emphasis by quoting a staff member, "In this school the teachers and administrators are held accountable for high performance. . . . While we [teachers and administrators] often feel under pressure to excel, we thrive on being part of a dynamic organization."[31]

Belief That All Students Can Achieve

A second important expectation for teachers in an effective school is adopting the attitude that all students are capable of achieving, and therefore that teachers should behave accordingly. In a study of effective inner-city elementary schools, Larkin found that "staff members verbally and behaviorally expressed the belief that all of their students could achieve, regardless of socioeconomic status or past academic performance."[32]

Ongoing Faculty Development and Innovation

A third expectation characteristic of an effective school culture is that the faculty members should strive to improve themselves, in part by helping each other and in part through experimenting with different approaches. An example of this expectation, presented by Saphier and King, is, "In this school the professional staff help each other. . . . Around here we are encouraged by administrators and colleagues to experiment with new ideas and techniques because that is how teachers and schools improve. . . . We are always looking for more effective ways of teaching."[33]

A Safe and Orderly Learning Environment

A fourth major expectation associated with the culture of an effective school is that students and teachers will behave in ways contributing to a safe and orderly school environment.[34] As Purkey and Smith point out, "Common sense alone suggests that students cannot learn in an environment that is noisy, distracting, or unsafe."[35] Edmonds found that in effective schools, a safe and orderly environment was established when "all teachers take responsibility for all students, all the time, everywhere in the school."[36] Moreover, in a study of several hundred schools, Wayson and Lasley discovered the following:

> Schools with well-disciplined students have developed a sense of community, marked by mutually agreed upon behavioral norms; these norms surround students with examples of subtle rewards and sanctions that encourage students to behave appropriately.[37]

How an Effective School Culture Benefits Students

Yale's Child Study Center, through its Comer School Development Program, found that students improve in many areas, such as "self-efficacy, relationships with peers and adults, general mental health, achievement on standardized tests, and classroom grades." Squires and Kranyik attribute this success to two reasons: The program supports change in the culture of the school and focuses on the child's total development–social, moral, physical, and psychological. The Comer School program involves three teams–a parents' program, the mental health team, and the school planning and management team–all working to bring key stakeholders together to coordinate school activities. All three teams are committed to the primary principles of no-fault problem solving, consensus decision making, and collaboration.[38]

Although there may be other expectations associated with the culture of an effective school, it would appear that the ones described are the most important. Of course, these expectations will need to be communicated and reinforced, activities that usually occur in an effective school as a result of symbolic actions and sanctions.[39] Such symbolic activity may, for example, take the form of a school slogan on the importance of learning, a school policy that students who fail a subject will not be allowed to participate in extracurricular activities, or a procedure requiring all students to make up their work, irrespective of the reason for their absence. In these examples a certain symbolic message is being communicated: "Academics are important!"

Both positive and negative sanctions will also be necessary to encourage the achievement of school expectations. Some administrators may be reluctant to use negative sanctions, such as those discussed in Chapter 3, "Authority, Power, and Influence," but individuals or groups whose behavior conflicts with the ideals and values the administrator is trying to promote should not be ignored. Of course, use of positive sanctions is preferable in encouraging adherence to organizational expectations. Several researchers have found that schools recognizing student accomplishment tend to have higher levels of achievement.[40] In addition, the recognition and support of teachers are also characteristic of the culture of an effective school. For example, in another illustration presented by Saphier and King, it was observed, "Good teaching is honored in this school and community," and, "Despite financial constraints, we have sabbaticals, summer curriculum workshops, and funds to attend professional conferences."[41]

THE ADMINISTRATOR'S ROLE IN SCHOOL CULTURE

"The only thing of real importance that leaders do is to create and manage culture," asserts Schein.[42] The administrator's role in regard to the organizational culture of a school is multifaceted. First, the administrator needs to develop and maintain an adequate understanding of the various elements of the school culture. Few new administrators are likely to assume they know the organizational culture of the school, but many experienced administrators may falsely assume that they already know their school culture because they have held a position in the school for several years. An organization's culture is not a static entity, however, but is constantly changing and evolving.[43] Figure 6.3 shows a number of major factors that can affect the nature of the organizational culture existing in a school.[44]

By analyzing the factors identified in Figure 6.3, an administrator can take an important step toward better understanding how the present organizational culture has developed into what it is today and how it may be changing. To help achieve this understanding, the administrator should consider using one or more of the instruments that have been designed for assessing the organizational culture of a school. Although most of these instruments have been developed for the purpose of measuring the *climate* of a school (a broader concept), the data from such an assessment would also be valuable in understanding the organizational culture. Instruments that would be useful for this objective include the Organizational Climate Description Questionnaire,[45] the Elementary School Environment Survey,[46] the Quality of School Life Questionnaire,[47] and the Effective Schools Battery Survey.[48] In addition, the National

FIGURE 6.3
MAJOR FACTORS AFFECTING ORGANIZATIONAL CULTURE

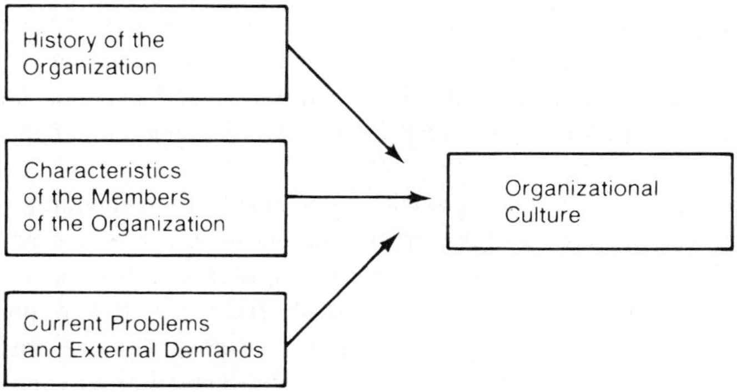

Association of Secondary School Principals has developed the Comprehensive Assessment and School Improvement, a climate instrument that appears to hold promise.[49] These standardized instruments measure factors common to schools and typically have a high degree of validity and reliability. These instruments may not address the specific areas of interest of a particular administration, however. Rojewiski and his colleagues outline steps that may be used to develop an individualized school-climate survey.[50]

Enhancing School Culture

Once an administrator has attained a good understanding of the organizational culture of the school, the administrator will then, and only then, be in a position to try to enhance that culture if changes are needed. While most, if not all, administrators would probably like to develop an organizational culture that is characteristic of effective schools, trying to change an organizational culture, especially a school culture, will not be easy. Krajewski offers the following principles for modeling creative teaching and leadership behaviors that enhance school culture: (1) Envision a future direction of collaboration, (2) clearly establish the connection between mission and practice by being an enthusiastic facilitator, meeting the needs of teachers and students, understanding the motivations of each employee, and promoting growth in all school personnel, (3) view problems as opportunities and focus on solutions, (4) be creative in stimulating good teaching practices, (5) think of others, (6) foster staff development, (7) create networks that decrease teacher isolation and promote professional sharing, and (8) stay focused on the most important outcome, student performance.[51]

One problem is that schools, particularly secondary schools, are often referred to as "loosely coupled" organizations;[52] that is, the authority and other bureaucratic linkages between the principal and the staff are often indirect. For example, an administrator may want teachers to emphasize more time on tasks in their classrooms and may, in fact, direct them to do so. But once the classroom doors are closed, a school administrator frequently has no adequate mechanism to enforce these wishes.

Subcultures and Countercultures

Moreover, although the discussion in this chapter, for the purpose of simplification, has referred to the organizational culture of a school as though it were a homogeneous entity, it is, in reality, more complicated than that. As Smircich has observed, "Much of the literature refers to an organizational culture, appearing to lose sight of the great likelihood that there are multiple organization subcultures, or even countercultures, competing to define the nature of situations within organizational boundaries."[53] This type of condition is particularly characteristic of secondary schools with their different departments, orientations, and needs. It is conceivable that in a secondary school, each of the departments may have its own subculture, and, more important, many of the subcultures may not be compatible–and may be in conflict–with what the administrator would like to see as the overall organizational culture. Considering that students may also have their own subculture (or several of them),[54] which may be in conflict with the other subcultures of the school, then the complexity and the difficulty of trying to change the organizational culture of the school become apparent.[55] As Conway points out, "We are asking schools to restructure themselves and their culture, to go through an organizational learning of the most difficult type."[56]

Promoting Values, Respecting Diversity

Rothstein states that issues involving class, culture, and race have influenced students for centuries and are gaining in importance with the increasing diversity of today's society.[57] Darling-Hammond cautions that more than ever before, the ability of America to survive as a democracy is dependent on public education preparing citizens to think independently and forge out common ground among many diverse experiences and ideas.[58] Dietrich and Bailey note that facilitating students in discussion and expression of their points of view, as well as working in cooperative groups, is important to their social development and enforces a sense of community by fostering a cohesive environment in which to learn.[59] Boyer believes that schools have the obligation not only to guide students into becoming literate and well informed but also to "help them develop the capacity to live responsibly and to judge wisely in matters of life and conduct." He sees the crucial problem as deciding which values should be taught within the diversity of today's society. He concludes that the following core of virtues might be agreed upon: honesty, respect, responsibility, compassion, self-discipline, perseverance, and giving.[60]

"A school's greatest impact occurs not in the formal lessons taught, but in creating a climate in which virtues are learned by example," according to Boyer. For example, the character education program in Boston is centered around books that have been chosen for their treatment of specific character traits and values. In grades K–5 the values emphasized are trust, self-love, self-esteem, compassion, self-awareness, and justice. The skills taught are expressing one's point of view, expressing and managing feelings, and resolving conflicts. In grade 6, the values emphasized are sharing, hope, and courage, and the skills taught are expressing someone else's point of view, empathy, and compromise.[61]

Kohn, on the other hand, voices concern about current character education programs and advocates that teachers facilitate student thinking about the way the students want themselves and others to be: "Students and teachers should decide together what they want their communities to be like, so students will understand values 'from the inside out.'"[62] The topic of character development in schools is a controversial issue that future administrators will need to address.

Challenges in Shaping School Culture

In spite of these complexities and difficulties, an administrator may be able, to a limited extent, to shape the organizational culture of the school or school district. Principals should remember, however, that combining "professional management with inspirational leadership and a collectivist culture" may lead to role conflicts and confusion.[63] Based on an analysis of the social science and educational literature on organizational cultures,[64] the following suggestions are offered.

Clarity about Values and Ideals First, an administrator needs to be clear about which values and ideals the school should be promoting. An administrator who has no notion of what an ideal school would look like will not be able to create policies for moving in a positive direction.[65] Research by Hallinger indicates, "Principals can influence student learning by developing a clear mission that provides an instructional focus for teachers throughout the school."[66] Unfortunately, many administrators become bogged down in the everyday duties of managing a school and have not thought through what it is that their school should aspire toward. A basic question that needs to be answered is, "What should be the primary mission and goals of this school?"[67] Obviously, the administrator should not be the only one who attempts to answer this question; teachers, students, and parents, among others, also need to be involved in order to gain deeper insights and commitment. The principal appears to play the major role, however, beyond that of parent, in developing a school climate of high expectations.[68] If an administrator is not clear about what the school should stand for and should be aspiring toward, the administrator will be in a poor position to shape the organizational culture in a different direction. As Firestone and Wilson have emphasized, "The principal's task and challenge is to develop a clear vision of the purposes of the school that give primacy to instruction and to carry it through consistently during those countless interactions with [important others]."[69]

Shaping the Culture through Choice of Staff Once an administrator has developed a clear vision of the "purpose" of the school, particular attention must be paid to the kinds of individuals recommended as future members of the faculty and to the people appointed to important leadership positions within the school. For example, every time an administrator has an opportunity to replace a member of the faculty, the potential exists for shaping the culture.[70] Since the principal's greatest influence may well be in the power "to recruit, select, promote, and demote staff members," it may take years of this process for a principal to reshape the school's culture. Hiring and retaining teachers who especially value experimentation, for example, will certainly make innovation or change easier to facilitate for principals.[71] It is true that, in the instance of a single vacancy, there is little chance of hiring someone whose values and ideals are exactly what the administrator wants the organizational culture to reflect. The *cumulative* effect of selective hiring over a number of years, however, could potentially change the culture of a school in important ways.[72] In the final analysis, the people associated with an organization are the major contributors to its culture. Their values and ideals are the building blocks of the group norms that greatly influence individual and group behavior. By emphasizing certain values and ideals in the hiring process, an administrator can shape the culture of an organization over a period of time.

Shaping the Culture through Formal Leadership Appointments An administrator will also have an opportunity to shape the culture of the organization when making appointments of people to leadership positions within the organization.[73] Periodically, an administrator will need to appoint a chairperson of a committee or select someone for an important position, for example, department head. In these situations an administrator should take care to select or appoint people who will best represent the organizational values and ideals that the administrator is trying to promote. By selecting such individuals, the administrator will not only obtain people who share a commitment to certain organizational priorities but, perhaps more important, be communicating symbolically to others in the school those values and ideals the administrator thinks are important for people to possess. The administrative act of selection or appointment can potentially carry great symbolic influence, especially if the administrator emphasizes publicly the reasons for these selections. According to Hallinger, however, these appointments also lessen the opportunity for the administrator to personally communicate key values and place greater reliance on instructional leaders to aid in fostering a positive school climate.[74]

Working with the Informal Leaders In addition to selecting with care those individuals who will occupy important leadership positions in the school, an administrator who wishes to shape the organizational culture will need to identify and develop an appropriate relationship with the *informal leaders* of the school.[75] This is particularly true for a new principal because the formal and informal leaders who are already in place form a large portion of the school's power structure. Developing a commitment from the school leaders will be crucial to the achievement of the principal's goals.[76]

An informal leader generally operates in every group. The informal leader may be the same person as the formal leader; however, whether or not that is true depends on the formal leader's personal influence with other members of the group rather than on any formal appointment by the principal. An informal leader can best be identified by examining a group's interaction patterns: the individual with whom there is the greatest interaction and communication within the group and whose opinion and judgment are most respected by the other members is the informal leader.

Obviously, in most situations it would be best for an administrator if the informal leader and the formal leader were the same person. That may not be the case, especially if an administrator has not exercised good judgment in selecting the formal leaders within the organization, or if there has been very limited opportunity to appoint new formal leaders, or if the informal leader's values are not consistent with those that the administrator would like to see adopted by the organization.

Handling Conflict between Formal and Informal Leaders When the informal leader of a group is a different person from the formal leader, a potential for conflict may exist. For example, the administrator and a department chairperson may be trying to promote a certain work ethic on the part of members of a particular department. If the informal leader of that department is opposed to the new work ethic, then the other members of the department may develop a group norm that will influence the members to resist the proposed work ethic. This type of conflict can be detrimental to developing a cohesive organizational culture.

Unfortunately, there are no easy answers to resolving this type of conflict between formal and informal leaders, although the concepts that are presented in Chapters 3 and 5 should be helpful. The administrator could, of course, attempt to influence the informal leader by using persuasion to convey the desirability of what the organization is trying to accomplish. In addition, the administrator could attempt to develop a rival informal leader within the group who could possibly lead the group in a direction that would be more compatible with the overall purposes of the organization. The social science literature provides few clues as to how the administrator might accomplish this, but it would appear that the key to a solution lies in identifying and nurturing some individual in the group whose personal qualities are liked and respected by colleagues but whose values and ideals are more congruent with the administrator's. By encouraging the administrator-approved informal leader to exert leadership within the group and then rewarding such efforts, an administrator may be able to change the group norms of a subculture to make them more consistent with the overall purposes of the organizational culture.

Keeping the School's Mission in the Public Eye

In attempting to shape the culture of an organization, it will be important for the administrator to articulate at every opportunity those values and ideas being promoted.[77] This needs to be done in such documents as student and teacher handbooks and at meetings with faculty,

WINDOW ON DIVERSITY

Organizational Culture

For issues of diversity in relation to shaping organizational culture, consider the following:

- "Making student diversity central to all aspects of the school experience compels adults–administrators, teachers, parents, non-certified staff, and members of the community–to be constantly mindful of the consequences of their actions and decisions especially on categorical groupings of students for historical, political, and social reasons are denied the opportunities and benefits of this society." (p. 119)
- "Schools are open systems, permeable institutions: beliefs about race and gender, about class and language, about intelligence, ability, and achievement emerge in the classroom" (Source; M. Rose, *Possible Lives: The Promise of Public Education in America* [Boston: Houghton Mifflin Company, 1995]). (p. 120)
- "Valuing diversity is a way in which individuals and groups within education and beyond could stand in solidarity with one another, challenge one another and empower themselves in ways that did not diminish others." (p. 121)
- "Individuals are both immersed in and impacted by culture, but individuals also impact and change the larger culture. . . . This idea of a living, changing culture is important to understanding how critical schools are to changing our stereotypes, biases, and negative paradigms." (p. 121)

Source (unless otherwise indicated): K. Hanson and M. P. Avery, "Valuing Diversity in Schools: Transforming Education through Humanistic Policy, Pedagogy, and Practice," in M. Leicester, C. Modgil, and S. Modgil (Eds.), *Institutional Issues: Pupils, Schools and Teacher Education* (London: Falmer Press, 2000), pp. 119–127.

students, and parents. For example, Brookover and his colleagues suggest that in an effective school the administrator and faculty should develop a statement of purpose and beliefs that would include the following:[78]

1. The purpose of the school is to educate all students to high levels of academic performance.
2. To fulfill this purpose, the members of this school staff believe that
   a. All students should have a challenging academic program.
   b. All students should master their grade level objectives.
   c. Teachers are obligated to prepare all students to perform at mastery level on the objectives for the course.

Whether a school administrator and faculty should adopt this particular statement of purpose and beliefs, or some other, is not the issue. The important concept is that if the administrator is to shape the organizational culture of the school, a clear statement of purpose and beliefs must be formulated and communicated.

Communication: A Tool for Shaping Culture

Formal communication will be essential, but an administrator needs to use informal and symbolic communication as well to shape the future of the organization. Some researchers have discovered that informal and symbolic communication, which takes the form of stories, rituals, and slogans, can influence the culture of an organization.[79] For example, the slogan, "Academic excellence–no sweat, no gain," communicates symbolically the value that a school places on hard work. Anecdotes retold to new personnel about how students and teachers have invested extra efforts to improve themselves and to help achieve certain organizational goals symbolically emphasize the types of values and ideals that a school promotes. What a principal talks about, pays attention to, and reinforces while walking around the building or conducting school activities will greatly influence teachers' behavior, and thus the organization's culture, according to Peterson.[80]

In addition, rituals or ceremonies that an administrator initiates and supports provide an opportunity to stress the values and ideals the administrator is trying to emphasize while providing an occasion for rewarding behavior exemplifying these values and ideals. For example, one high school that is attempting to promote academic excellence has established a comprehensive program of rituals and rewards for students and teachers.[81] Examples of this program include the following:

1. *Academic superstar recognition:* Each week the school honors a student for outstanding performance in a particular academic area by displaying on the office bulletin board a picture of the student at work.
2. *Homework recognition:* The school honors students who have completed all their homework assignments in all their classes with a grade of B or better, providing them with special certificates and rewards–for example, tickets to a movie.
3. *Average-raisers recognition:* The school honors students who raise their grade point averages from the previous term by 0.5 on a 4.0 scale by presenting them with special certificates and rewards.
4. *Teacher of the month recognition:* One teacher is selected monthly by a PTA committee to receive a special certificate and a night's dinner and entertainment for the teacher and a guest.

Although the total program of this school is much more comprehensive than is revealed in the examples, the four illustrations are intended to give a sense of communicating symbolically the values and ideals that are important to an organization. As Iannaccone and Jamgochian point out, "When symbol and ceremony fit student perception that teachers care about their achievement and the perception of teachers that administrators place improved student performance foremost in their orientation in their jobs, then a strong and consistent school cultural consensus [will emerge]."[82]

"School leaders from every level are key to shaping school culture," write Peterson and Deal, summing up their point in the following description of the part leaders play:

> Their words, their nonverbal messages, their actions, and their accomplishments all shape culture. They are models, potters, poets, actors, and healers. They are historians and anthropologists. They are visionaries and dreamers. Without the attention of leaders, school cultures can become toxic and unproductive. By paying fervent attention to the symbolic side of their schools, leaders can help develop the foundation for change and success.[83]

SCHOOL CLIMATE

When asked to distinguish between school *culture* and school *climate*, Christine Emmons, coordinator of program evaluation at the Comer School Development Program, replied that climate may be viewed as a "subset of culture." Whereas school culture consists of "the belief systems that undergird the patterns of activities that characterize the functioning of the school," school climate relates to human interactions. "School climate," explained Emmons, "is the quality and frequency of interactions between staff members in the school and students, among the students, among the staff members themselves, and between staff at the school and parents and the community." Whether a school climate is positive or negative can be ascertained by the atmosphere set up through such interactions.[84]

Haynes, another author concerned about school climate, suggests that "school climate is the sum total of, and dynamic interactions among, the psychosocial, academic, and physical dimensions of the school's environment." The academic and psychosocial dimensions cannot be separated, according to Haynes. "They must be addressed together consistently."[85]

Measuring School Climate

The question arises, "How can school climate be effectively measured?" *Perceptions* provide an important gauge. "Perceptions held by stakeholder groups (e.g., students, parents, teachers) about the physical, social, and learning environments of a school may influence both the processes and outcomes that occur," say researchers at Western Michigan University's Evaluation Center. Because of the impact of perceptions on processes and outcomes, it is important for educational leaders to know what those perceptions are. One way of finding out is to conduct a survey asking people *not* how they personally feel about a school, but their opinions about what "most people" perceive to be true about the school in its various aspects. For this purpose the National Association of Secondary School Principals (NASSP) School Climate Survey was developed. The survey questionnaire is designed to find out what each stakeholder group perceives most people to believe about 10 areas: teacher–student relationships, security and maintenance, the effectiveness of the administration, student academic orientation, student behavioral values, academic and career guidance and counseling services, student–peer relationships, relationships between the school and parents/community, instructional management, and student activities.[86] The value of these data is summed up by the Western Michigan evaluators:

> The shared perceptions of climate represent what most people believe, not the individual's personal reaction to the environment. These shared perceptions tend to be persistent over time. Just as meteorological climate is largely unaffected by daily shifts in temperature, the climate of the school is a relatively stable phenomenon.[87]

They go on to point out that by comparing the perceptions of the various stakeholder groups, school leaders can become aware of areas that need appropriate interventions to improve the school's environment.

> One educator who has devoted much attention to school climate is H. Jerome Freiberg. He points out many different ways that school climate can be raised, such as student concerns surveys, entrance and exit interviews, and even "ambient noise checklists" that pinpoint areas where

excessive noise levels cause stress and distraction and where changes need to be made. "School climate can be a positive influence on the health of the learning environment or a significant barrier to learning," writes Freiberg.[88]

Figure 6.4 shows another example of climate measurement questions that are part of a larger questionnaire for entry-level educational leaders and human resources staff. It was designed to ascertain work experiences within their school or district and perceived career and promotional opportunities. The portion of the questionnaire reprinted in Figure 6.4 was designed specifically to serve as a "culture/climate audit" of *diversity* attitudes and practices within the school or school district. It provides a means of obtaining information on respondents' observations of the organizational culture and climate. Diversity, as used here, means recognizing, accepting, and appreciating human differences (or demographic variables). Basic tenets in this definition are these: (1) Respect is to be shown to all persons without regard to such differences as national origin, race, color, ethnicity, religion, gender, age, sexual orientation, or ability/disability and (2) members of any one of these categories are not to be regarded as superior to members of any other category or group.

The information gained through this questionnaire can aid in (1) identifying any problems, (2) ascertaining needs for changes and improvements in the organizational climate, and (3) formulating action plans to ensure a recognition of the contributions of each person. The findings can then be used to generate programs and policies that will provide each person with equal opportunities for developing his or her potential to the full. This culture audit is intended as a first step toward eliminating artificially imposed barriers (based on such characteristics as

FIGURE 6.4

CULTURE OR CLIMATE AUDIT: DIVERSITY QUESTIONNAIRE FOR ENTRY-LEVEL EDUCATIONAL LEADERS AND HUMAN RESOURCES STAFF

I. Opportunities for Women

1. Do you think that the female population is well represented in administrative positions in your school or district?
   Please explain your answer.
2. Do you feel that women who are otherwise qualified for administrative positions are leaving your school/school district?
   Yes ______ No ______
   (If you answered yes, go to question 3. If you answered no, go to question 4.)
3. If you believe your school or district is not retaining qualified women, why do you think these women are leaving?
4. Is the school/school district successful in promoting career advancement for women beyond entry level administrative positions?
5. How far up the administrative ladder do you think women can go in your school or district?
   Please explain your answer.
6. Is there within your school/school district a shortage or surplus of qualified women candidates for administrative positions? (Please check the answer you believe best applies.)
   a. shortage ______
   b. surplus ______
   c. There is neither a shortage nor a surplus. ______
7. What do you see as your school/school district's commitment to women in administrative positions?
8. What opportunities does your school/school district provide for women in administrative positions?
9. What factors facilitate the advancement of women in your school/school district?

FIGURE 6.4 *Concluded*

10. What factors hinder the advancement of women in your school/school district?
11. What is your perception of your school/school district's commitment to equal opportunities for women as compared to that of other organizations?

II. Opportunities for Minorities

1. Do you think your school or district exercises equal opportunity in:
   a. the recruitment of minorities?
   b. the selection of minorities?
   c. the hiring of minorities?
   d. the retention of minorities?
   Please explain your answers.
2. Do your think persons from minority populations are well represented in administrative positions in your school or district? Please explain your answer.
3. Do you feel that members of minority populations who are otherwise qualified for administrative positions are leaving your school/school district? Yes ______ No ______
   (If you answered yes, go to question 4. If you answered no, go to question 5.)
4. If you believe your school or district is not retaining qualified members of minority populations, why do you think these persons are leaving?
5. Is the school/school district successful in promoting career advancement for minorities beyond entry level administrative positions?
6. How far up the administrative ladder do you think minorities can go in your school/school district? Please explain your answer.
7. Is there within your school district a shortage or surplus of qualified minority candidates for administrative positions? (Please check the answer you believe best applies.)
   a. shortage ______
   b. surplus ______
   c. There is neither a shortage nor a surplus. ______
8. What do you see as your school district's commitment to minorities in administrative positions?
9. What opportunities does your school/school district provide for minorities in administrative positions?
10. What factors facilitate the advancement of minorities at your school/school district?
11. What factors hinder the advancement of minorities at your school/school district?
12. What is your perception of your school district's commitment to equal opportunities for minorities as compared to that of other organizations?

III. Diversity

1. How would you describe your school's commitment, if any, to diversity?
2. Do you believe a diverse cultural climate is beneficial to a school or district? Please explain your answer.
3. What do you see as your role in building a climate that fosters diversity?
4. What do you need to be a more effective manager of a diverse workforce?
5. Are there any unique aspects in working with a diverse workforce?
   With women?
   With racial minorities?
   With ethnic minorities?
   With persons with disabilities?
   With persons who are considerably younger or older?
   With persons who are gay or lesbian?
   With persons of a different religion?
6. What advice would you give entry level persons from the above categories who are interested in attaining promotion to an administrative position in your school/school district?
7. What advice would you give entry-level persons in general who are interested in attaining a promotion to an administrative position at your school/school district?

Source: Adapted from a longer form developed by Petra E. Snowden.

gender, race, color, ethnicity, national origin, religion, age, ability/disability, or sexual orientation) that sometimes hinder recruitment, hiring, selection, retention, and advancement.

Why Climate Is Important

In the physical world, climate can determine whether plants thrive or fail to grow. The climate of a school can similarly have a major influence on morale, learning, and productivity. A welcoming, safe, and supportive environment can help students believe in their potential and provide motivation for success—particularly if they feel they are respected in all their diversity, including differing types of talents and learning styles. Establishing such a climate also requires dealing with school safety issues, as discussed in Chapter 5, including protecting students from intimidating tactics such as bullying and harassment. Banks has written that many students frequently stay home because of bullying. "Victims often fear school and consider school to be an unsafe and unhappy place."[89] Such an assessment of the school environment is completely opposite the positive climate that fosters academic achievement and social development.

A FINAL NOTE

An organizational culture is a complex entity, one that is constantly evolving. Unless there is a positive organizational climate and culture, it is unlikely that the necessary technical improvements that benefit students in teaching and curriculum will be implemented.[90] For example, the rapidly increasing cultural diversity of students in our schools can create serious misunderstandings among students, teachers, parents, and administrators and further diminish or erode a positive climate. Principals and staff must be able to recognize and resolve culturally based school and community problems.[91] A guide from the U.S. Department of Education Office for Civil Rights and the Bias Crimes Task Force of the National Association of Attorneys General urges educational leaders to examine the school environment regularly for any evidence of harassment:

> Regular, focused observation of school activities and environments, especially less structured settings like school hallways and school buses, will identify harassment that staff may neglect to report. It is possible that, in some instances, harassment may be so widespread that no one actually reports it. Periodically examine the school site and furniture for racially and sexually derogatory graffiti. Monitor possible trouble spots in the school for incidents of hostility and harassment. For example, ensure that students of racial and national origin minority groups and both sexes who drop out of courses and activities in which they are under-represented have not been subjected to harassment.[92]

Sellers and Hall have explored the role that school counselors can have in assisting administrators and teachers "in creating a school culture that empowers all individuals to succeed and reach their fullest potential." Counselors can help (1) provide training in multicultural competencies, (2) encourage sensitivity to individual differences and understanding of oneself and others, and (3) provide knowledge and skills necessary to work with special populations. These authors go on to say that school counselors can "respond proactively to pre-judicial attitudes and values that influence assessment and treatment with multicultural students."[93]

An administrator should not be intimidated by the challenges of creating an effective school culture and climate. Instead, the focus should be on maintaining an accurate understanding of the school's culture and direction and on those factors influencing its development. Educators are advised to place less attention on reform initiatives and more on creating a clear vision and mission to provide direction for the school. The administrator can then try, with the assistance of others, to shape the culture toward desirable ends.[94] Fullan recognizes that the keys to effective change involve reshaping the school culture and also providing time for teachers to develop professionally.[95] In the process of pursuing positive results, the administrator will be involved in school change, the subject of the next chapter.

Although many of the case studies, suggested learning activities, and simulations presented in Part II of the text require the appropriate use of the ideas in this chapter on organizational culture, the following exercises should provide the best opportunities for testing understanding and effective use of the concepts about organizational culture: Cases 22, 26, 29, 45, 52, 56, 57, and 65; and the midyear and end-of-the-year in-basket exercises.

NOTES

1. Some theorists refer to these social factors as the "climate" of an organization, e.g., Carolyn S. Anderson, "The Search for School Climate: A Review of the Research," *Review of Educational Research* (Fall 1982), pp. 368–420; others refer to the "culture" of an organization, e.g., Edgar H. Schein, "Coming to a New Awareness of Organizational Culture," *Sloan Management Review* (Winter 1984), pp. 3–16; and some writers use the two terms interchangeably. The two concepts will be discussed separately in this chapter.
2. F. J. Roethlisberger and W. J. Dickson, *Management and the Worker: An Account of a Research Program Conducted by the Western Electric Company, Hawthorne Works, Chicago* (Cambridge, MA: Harvard University Press, 1939).
3. Duncan Maxwell Anderson and Richard Poe, "A Culture of Achievement–Creating the Entrepreneurial Society," *Success* (June 1992), p. 31.
4. For example, see Donald Willower, *The Teacher Subculture and Curriculum Change* (May 1968), an ERIC report. Also see Mark S. Rosenbaum, "The Organizational Cultures of Two Academically Dissimilar Elementary Schools," EdD dissertation, Hofstra University, 1988.
5. Stewart C. Purkey and Marshall Smith, "Too Soon to Cheer? Synthesis of Research on Effective Schools," *Educational Leadership* (December 1982), pp. 64–69. Also see Daniel U. Levine, "Creating Effective Schools: Findings and Implications from Research and Practice," *Phi Delta Kappan* (January 1991), pp. 389–393.
6. Education Commission of the States, "Better Higher Education: What Research Says," *Making Quality Count in Undergraduate Education* (February 1996), p. 48. For more information go to http://www.ccsse.org/publications/resources.cfm, May 16, 2005.
7. Linda Smircich, "Concepts of Culture and Organizational Analysis," *Administrative Science Quarterly* (September 1983), pp. 64–69.
8. Harvey J. Brighton and Lutfus Sayeed, "The Pervasiveness of Senior Management's View of the Cultural Gaps within a Division," *Group and Organization Studies* (September 1990), pp. 266–278.
9. Kent D. Peterson and Terrence E. Deal, "How Leaders Influence the Culture of Schools," *Educational Leadership* (vol. 56, September 1998), pp. 28–30.
10. William G. Cunningham and Donn W. Gresso, *Cultural Leadership–The Culture of Excellence in Education* (Boston: Allyn and Bacon, 1993), p. 143.
11. Andrew W. Halpin, *Theory and Research in Administration* (New York: Macmillan, 1966), p. 131.
12. This figure is based on conclusions drawn from Peter J. Frost et al., *Organizational Culture* (Beverly Hills, CA: Sage, 1985); and

Meryl R. Louis, "Organizations in Culture Bearing Milieux" in Louis R. Pondy et al. (Eds.), *Organizational Symbolism* (Greenwich, CT: JAI Press, 1983), pp. 39–54.

13. Edgar H. Schein, "Coming to a New Awareness of Organizational Culture," *Sloan Management Review* (Winter 1984), pp. 3–16.
14. Natasha Josefowitz, *Paths to Power: A Woman's Guide from First Job to Top Executive* (Reading, MA: Addison-Wesley, 1980), p. 56.
15. Pamela Shockley-Zalabak and Donald Dean Morley, "Adhering to Organizational Culture: What Does It Mean? Why Does It Matter?" *Group and Organization Studies* (December 1989), pp. 483–500.
16. Stephen K. Miller, "Significant Achievement Gains Using the Effective Schools Model," *Educational Leadership* (March 1985), pp. 38–43. Also see Cynthia Cherrey, "Understanding and Shaping Organizational Culture," *Campus Activities Programming* (April 1990), pp. 60–64; and Michael Paul Kirsch, "Organizational Culture as a Third Order Control System: A Cognitive Approach" (vols. 1 and 2) PhD dissertation, Michigan State University, 1988.
17. Wilbur Brookover et al., *Creating Effective Schools: An In-Service Program for Enhancing School Learning Climate and Achievement* (Holmes Beach, FL: Learning Publications, 1982), pp. 55–58. Also see Lawrence C. Stedman, "The Effective Schools Formula Still Needs Changing: A Reply to Brookover," *Phi Delta Kappan* (February 1988), pp. 439–442.
18. Barbara O. Taylor and Daniel U. Levine, "Effective Schools Projects and School-Based Management," *Phi Delta Kappan* (January 1991), pp. 394–397.
19. Richard C. Wallace and Wendy D. Wallace, *Sociology,* 2nd ed. (Boston, MA: Allyn and Bacon, 1989), p. 49.
20. Richard E. Neustadt, *Presidential Power: The Politics of Leadership* (New York: New American Library, 1964, 1980).
21. Also see Barry Kampol, "Empowerment: The Institutional and Cultural Aspects for Teachers and Principals," *National Association of Secondary School Principals Bulletin* (October 1990), pp. 104–107.
22. Gareth Morgan, *Beyond Method: Strategies for Social Research* (Beverly Hills, CA: Sage Publications, 1983), p. 13. Also see Louis R. Pondy et al. (Eds.), *Organizational Symbolism* (Greenwich, CT: JAI Press, 1983).
23. Linda Smircich, "Organizations as Shared Meanings," in Louis R. Pondy et al. (Eds.), *Organizational Symbolism* (Greenwich, CT: JAI Press, 1983), pp. 55–65.
24. Bernard J. Reilly and Joseph A. DiAngelo Jr., "Communication: A Cultural System of Meaning and Value," *Human Relations* (February 1990), pp. 129–140.
25. Mary Cristine Blanch, "Culture as a Control Mechanism in Schools," PhD dissertation, University of Utah, 1989.
26. Purkey and Smith, "Too Soon to Cheer? Synthesis of Research on Effective Schools," p. 68.
27. This figure is based on an analysis of a large number of reports on effective schools, especially those by Brookover et al., *Creating Effective Schools,* pp. 23–74; Jon Saphier and Matthew King, "Good Seeds in Strong Cultures," *Educational Leadership* (March 1985), pp. 67–74; and Carolyn S. Anderson, "The Search for School Climate: A Review of the Research," *Educational Leadership* (Fall 1982), pp. 368–420.
28. Kristen M. Snyder and Karolyn J. Snyder, "Developing Integrated Work Cultures: Findings from a Study on School Change," *NASSA Bulletin* (January 1996), p. 67.
29. For an excellent discussion of other important school outcomes, see Stewart C. Purkey and Susan Degen, "Beyond Effective Schools to Good Schools: Some First Steps," *R and D Perspectives* (Spring 1985), pp. 1–6.

30. Brookover et al., *Creating Effective Schools,* p. 46.

31. Saphier and King, "Good Seeds in Strong Cultures," p. 67.

32. Ibid., p. 68. Also see Carolyn Carter and Jack Klotz, "What Principals Must Know before Assuming the Role of Instructional Leader," *National Association of Secondary School Principals Bulletin* (April 1990), pp. 36–41.

33. Maureen McCormack Larkin, "Ingredients of a Successful School Effectiveness Project," *Educational Leadership* (March 1985), pp. 31-37. Also see Jeannie Oakes and Martin Lipton, *Making the Best of Schools: A Handbook for Parents, Teachers, and Policymakers* (New Haven, CT: Yale University Press, 1990); Diane S. Pollard, "Against the Odds: A Profile of Academic Achievers from the Urban Underclass," *Journal of Negro Education* (Summer 1989), pp. 297-308; and Ellen C. Baylor and Petra E. Snowden, "Expanding the School's Role as Care Provider," *Principal* (January 1992), pp. 8-9.

34. Saphier and King, "Good Seeds in Strong Cultures," p. 68. For additional information on professional development, see Mary Louise Holly and Cavens McLoughlin, *Perspectives on Teacher Professional Development* (New York: Falmer, 1989); and Daniel L. Duke, "Setting Goals for Professional Development," *Educational Leadership* (May 1990), pp. 71-75. For a comparison of professional development and staff development, see D. Duke, "Setting Goals for Professional Development," *Educational Leadership* (May 1990), pp. 71–75.

35. Ronald R. Edmonds, "Programs of School Improvement: An Overview," *Educational Leadership* (December 1982), pp. 4–11. Also see California State Department of Education, *Safe Schools: A Planning Guide for Action,* an ERIC report, Ed. 313815, 1989.

36. Stewart C. Purkey and Marshall S. Smith, "Effective Schools—A Review," paper presented at a conference sponsored by the National Institute on Education, June 1982, p. 41.

37. Edmonds, "Programs of School Improvement: An Overview."

38. William W. Wayson and Thomas J. Lasley, "Climates for Excellence: Schools that Foster Self Discipline," *Phi Delta Kappan* (February 1984), p. 419. Also see Helen Bain et al., "A Study of First Project STAR Class-Size Research: A Study of Fifty Effective Teachers Whose Class Average Gain Scores Ranked in the Top 15% of Each of Four School Types in Project STAR," paper presented at the Annual Meeting of the American Educational Research Association, March 1989.

39. David A. Squires and Robert D. Kranyik, "The Comer Program: Changing School Culture," *Educational Leadership* (December 1995–January 1996), pp. 29–32.

40. William A. Firestone and Bruce L. Wilson, "Using Bureaucratic and Cultural Linkages to Improve Instruction: The Principal's Contribution," sponsored by National Institute of Education (November 1983), pp. 7–30.

41. Michael Rutter et al., *Fifteen Thousand Hours: Secondary Schools and Their Effects on Children* (Cambridge, MA: Harvard University Press, 1979). Also see E. A. Wayne Edward Winne, *Looking at Schools: Good, Bad, and Indifferent* (Lexington, MA: Lexington Books, 1980); and James M. Dowdle, "Keeping Kids in School," *North Central Association Quarterly* (Winter 1990), pp. 470–472.

42. Saphier and King, "Good Seeds in Strong Cultures," p. 68.

43. E. H. Schein, *Organizational Culture and Leadership* (San Francisco, CA: Jossey-Bass, 1992), as quoted in Richard McAdams and Richard Zinck, "The Power of the Superintendent's Leadership in Shaping School District Culture: Three Case Studies," *Educational Research Service Spectrum* (Fall 1998). Accessed online,

http://eric.uoregon.edu/trends_issues/rolelead/selected_abstracts/profiles.html, May 16, 2005.

44. See also Purkey and Smith, "Effective Schools—A Review," p. 43. Also see Sofia Zamanou, "Managing Organizational Culture," PhD dissertation, University of Oregon, 1988; and Terry Michael Dearstone, "Using a Cultural Change Intervention to Improve Organizational Effectiveness: An Evaluative Case Study," EdD dissertation, University of San Diego, 1989.

45. This figure is based on conclusions reached after analyzing several of the sources previously identified. The major sources of insight were *Creating Excellence* by Craig R. Hickman and Michael A. Silva (New York: New American Library, 1986), pp. 72–78; and an article by Alan L. Wilkins and William G. Ouchi, "Efficient Cultures: Exploring the Relationship between Culture and Organizational Performance," *Administrative Science Quarterly* (September 1983), pp. 468–481.

46. Andrew W. Halpin and Donald B. Croft, *The Organizational Climate of Schools* (Chicago: University of Chicago, 1963). For a recent attempt to update OCDQ, see Wayne K. Hoy and Sharon I. R. Clover, "Elementary School Climate: A Revision of the OCDQ," *Educational Administration Quarterly* (Winter 1986), pp. 93–110. Also see C. Halderson, E. A. Kelley, J. W. Keefe, and P. S. Berge, *Technical Manual: School Climate Survey, Student Satisfaction Survey, Teacher Satisfaction Survey, Parent Satisfaction Survey* (Reston, VA: National Association of Secondary School Principals, 1989); and Betty Ann Topalosky, "Culture and Innovation in Higher Education: A Semiotic Study," PhD dissertation, Ohio University, 1989.

47. Robert L. Sinclair, "Elementary School Educational Environments: Toward Schools That Are Responsive to Students," *National Elementary Principal* (April 1970), pp. 53–58.

48. Joyce L. Epstein and James M. McPartland, "The Concept and Measurement of the Quality of School Life," *American Educational Research Journal* (Winter 1976), pp. 15–30.

49. Gary Gottfredson, *Assessing School Climate in Prevention Program Planning, Development and Evaluation* (August 1984), an ERIC report, Ed. 250804.

50. James W. Keefe et al., "School Climate: Clear Definitions and a Model for a Larger Setting," *National Association of Secondary School Principals Bulletin* (November 1985), pp. 70–77. Also see James W. Keefe and Edgar A. Kelley, "Comprehensive Assessment and School Improvement," *National Association of Secondary School Principals Bulletin* (December 1990), pp. 54–63. For an instrument to measure a principal's attitude about organizational culture, see Beverly Jean Weldon Ihinger, "Development of an Attitude Scale for Elementary Principals about Organizational Culture and the Role of Cultural Leader," EdD dissertation, Texas Tech University, 1988.

51. Jay W. Rojewski, Frederick C. Wendal, Sara McInerny, DeAnn Currin, and Elizabeth Smith, "Individualizing School-Climate Surveys," *Clearing House* (January 1990), pp. 202–206.

52. Bob Krajewski, "Enculturating the School: The Principal's Principles," *NASSP Bulletin* (January 1996), pp. 3–9.

53. Arthur Blumberg, *Supervision in Weakly Normed Systems: The Case of the Schools* (April 1983), an ERIC report, Ed. 239381. Also see Earl E. Weick, "Educational Organizations as Loosely Coupled Systems," *Administrative Science Quarterly* (March 1976), pp. 1–19; David Gomez and Richard Jamgochian, "The Kinds of Behaviors Teachers Value," *Thrust for Educational Leadership* (September 1989), pp. 40–44; and Michael Elmer and David Wilemon, "Organizational Culture and Project Leader Effectiveness," *Project Management Journal* (September 1988), pp. 54–63.

54. Smircich, "Concepts of Culture and Organizational Analysis," p. 346.

55. James S. Coleman, *The Adolescent Society: The Social Life of the Teenager and Its Impact on Education* (New York: Free Press of Glencoe, 1961).

56. For further discussion of the problems of subcultures, see Frost et al., *Organizational Culture,* chaps. 2, 8.

57. James A. Conway, "A Perspective on Organizational Cultures and Organizational Belief Structures," *Educational Administration Quarterly* (Fall 1985), pp. 7-25.

58. Stanley William Rothstein, *Class, Culture, and Race in American Schools: A Handbook* (Westport, CT: Greenwood Press, 1995), an ERIC report, Ed. 382750.

59. Linda Darling-Hammond, "The Right to Learn: Education as Democracy," *Clinical Schools Update* (Spring 1996), p. 3.

60. Amy P. Dietrich and Elsie L. Bailey, "School Climate: Common Sense Solutions to Complicated Problems," *NASSP Bulletin* (January 1996), p. 20.

61. Ernest L. Boyer, "Making a Commitment to Character," *Principal* (September 1995), p. 29.

62. Arthur W. Steller and Walter K. Lambert, "Teach the Children Well," *Executive Educator* (June 1996), pp. 25-26.

63. Alfie Kohn, "What's Wrong with Character Education," *ASCD Education Update* (May 1996), p. 5.

64. Edward Vaughan, "The Leadership Obsession: An Addendum to Mangham's 'In Search of Competence,'" *Journal of General Management* (Spring 1989), pp. 26-34.

65. Sources especially helpful, either for specific suggestions or for stimulating insights, were Edgar H. Schein, *Organizational Culture and Leadership*, 3rd ed. (San Francisco, CA: Jossey-Bass, 2002); Brookover et al., *Creating Effective Schools*; and Edgar A. Kelly, *Improving School Climate* (Reston, VA: National Association of Secondary School Principals, 1980). Also see Kery D. Kafka, "Organizational Culture in Four High School Effectiveness Programs," PhD dissertation, Marquette University, 1988.

66. Richard P. DuFour, "Clear Vision for Successful Leadership," *National Association of Secondary School Principals Bulletin* (April 1990).

67. Phillip Hallinger et al., "What Makes a Difference? School Context, Principal Leadership, and Student Achievement," paper presented at the annual meeting of the American Educational Research Association, March 1989.

68. Hickman and Silva, *Creating Excellence,* p. 64. Also see William E. Webster, *The High Performing Educational Manager: Fastback No. 273,* an ERIC report, Ed. 296470.

69. Hallinger et al., "What Makes a Difference?"

70. William A. Firestone and Bruce L. Wilson, "Using Bureaucratic and Cultural Linkages to Improve Instruction: The Principal's Contribution," *Educational Administration Quarterly* (Spring 1985), p. 22. Also see Gomez and Jamgochian, "The Kinds of Behaviors Teachers Value," pp. 40-44.

71. Gareth R. Jones, "Psychological Orientation and the Process of Organizational Socialization," *Academy of Management Review* (July 1983), pp. 464-474. Also see Mark S. Rosenbaum, "The Organizational Cultures of Two Academically Dissimilar Elementary Schools," EdD dissertation, Hofstra University, 1988; and Thomas F. Casey, "Making the Most of a Selection Interview," *Personnel* (September 1990), pp. 41-43.

72. Kent D. Peterson, "Mechanisms of Culture Building and Principals' Work," *Education and Urban Society* (May 1988), pp. 250-261.

73. For an interesting example of how this happens in the business world, see Tom Peters and Nancy Austin, *A Passion for Excellence: The Leadership Difference* (New York: Random House, 1985), pp. 268-269.

74. Ibid., part 4.

75. Phillip Hallinger, "Developing Instructional Leadership Teams in Secondary Schools: A Framework," *National Association of Secondary School Principals* (May 1989), pp. 84–92.

76. Elbert W. Stewart, *Sociology: The Human Science* (New York: McGraw-Hill, 1981), pp. 146–147. Also see S. J. Brown et al., "Teachers' Powerlessness: Peer Assessments and Own Perceptions," *Planning and Changing* (Spring 1985), pp. 22–34; and Katherine I. Miller, "Cultural and Role-Based Predictors of Organizational Participation and Allocation Preferences," *Communication Research* (December 1988), pp. 699–725.

77. Michael A. Morehead and Lawrence Lyman, "Three Strategies for New Principals," *National Association of Elementary School Principals* (January 1990).

78. Maryan S. Schall, "A Communication-Rules Approach to Organizational Culture," *Administrative Science Quarterly* (December 1983), pp. 557–577. Also see Jack Blendinger and Linda T. Jones, "Start with Culture to Improve Your Schools," *School Administrator* (May 1989), pp. 22–25.

79. Brookover et al., *Creating Effective Schools,* p. 46. For a good discussion of how to develop a mission statement, see John Farley, *How to Build a Mission Statement for School Improvement* (Reston, VA: National Association of Secondary School Principals, 1986); and Joseph F. Rogus, "Developing a Vision Statement—Some Considerations for Principals," *National Association of Secondary Schools Bulletin* (February 1990), pp. 6–12.

80. Peters and Austin, *A Passion for Excellence: The Leadership Difference,* pp. 274–283. Also see William A. Firestone and Bruce L. Wilson, "Culture of School Is a Key to More Effective Instruction," *National Association of Secondary Schools Bulletin* (December 1984), pp. 7–11.

81. Peterson, "Mechanisms of Culture Building and Principals' Work."

82. John Childs and Jim McCoy, "A Positive Approach to Academic Excellence," *National Association of Secondary School Principals Bulletin* (May 1985), pp. 64–67; Elaine Phillips, "Developing a District-wide Academic Awards Program," *Gifted Child Today* (November–December 1989), pp. 6–10; and Barry S. Raebeck, "Transformation of a Middle School," *Educational Leadership* (April 1990), pp. 18–21.

83. Laurence Iannaccone and Richard Jamgochian, "High Performing Curriculum and Instructional Leadership in the Climate of Excellence," *National Association of Secondary School Principals Bulletin* (May 1985), pp. 28–35. Also see J. Thomas Mitchell, "In Search of Organizational Culture: A Case Study of an Excellent High School (Effective Schools)," PhD dissertation, Pennsylvania State University, 1989.

84. Kent D. Peterson and Terrence E. Deal, "How Leaders Influence the Culture of Schools," *Educational Leadership* (vol. 56, September 1998), pp. 28–30.

85. Cynthia Savo, "An Interview with Christine Emmons on School Climate," *School Development Program Newsline* (Spring 1996). Accessed online, http://info.med.yale.edu/comer/emmons.html, January 25, 2001.

86. Norris M. Haynes, "Positive School Climate Is More than 'Feel Good,'" *School Development Program Newsline* (Spring 1996). Accessed online, http://info.med.yale.edu/comer/feelgood.html, January 25, 2001.

87. Western Michigan University Evaluation Center, "The NASSP School Climate Survey: Description of the Instrument." Accessed online, http://www.wmich.edu/evalctr/charter/pacharter/climate.html, May 17, 2005.

88. Ibid.

89. H. Jerome Freiberg, "Measuring School Climate: Let Me Count the Ways," *Educational Leadership* (vol. 56, September 1998), p. 22.

90. Ron Banks, "Bullying in Schools," *ERIC Digest,* EDO-PS-97-17 (April 1997). Accessed online, http://www.uncg/edu/ericcass/bullying/DOC/banks.htm, January 19, 2001.

91. Gerald Grant, *The World We Created at Hamilton High* (Cambridge, MA: Harvard University Press, 1988).

92. Sheldon S. Varney and Kenneth Cushner, "Understanding Cultural Diversity Can Improve Inter-cultural Interactions," *National Association of Secondary School Principals Bulletin* (October 1990), pp. 89–94.

93. U.S. Department of Education and the National Association of Attorneys General, "Creating a Supportive School Climate That Appreciates Racial, Cultural, and Other Forms of Diversity," *Protecting Students from Harassment and Hate Crime: A Guide for Schools* (Washington, DC: U.S. Department of Education, 1999). Accessed online, http://www.ed.gov/offices/OCR/archives/Harassment/climate1.html, July 10, 2005.

94. Darlene Sellers and Tonya Hall, "What a School Administrator Needs to Know about the School Counselor's Role with Multicultural Student Populations," from *Maximizing School Guidance Program Effectiveness* (published by ERIC Counseling and Student Services). Accessed online, http://ericcass.uncg.edu/virtuallib/diversity/1066.html, January 19, 2001. Site closed by U.S. government in 2003.

95. Cerylle Moffett, "Inventing New Cultures for Continuous Learning," *ASCD Professional Development Newsletter* (Spring 1996), p. 5, an article review of Michael Fullan, "The School as a Learning Organization: Distant Dreams," *Theory into Practice* (vol. 34, no. 4), pp. 230–235.

CHAPTER

7

Change

APPLICABLE PSEL STANDARDS

- **STANDARD 1:** **Mission, Vision, and Core Values**
  Effective educational leaders develop, advocate, and enact a shared mission, vision, and core values of high-quality education and academic success and well-being of each student.

- **STANDARD 2:** **Ethics and Professional Norms**
  Effective educational leaders act ethically and according to professional norms to promote each student's academic success and well-being.

- **STANDARD 3:** **Equity and Cultural Responsiveness**
  Effective educational leaders strive for equity of educational opportunity and culturally responsive practices to promote each student's academic success and well-being.

- **STANDARD 4:** **Curriculum, Instruction, and Assessment**
  Effective educational leaders develop and support intellectually rigorous and coherent systems of curriculum, instruction, and assessment to promote each student's academic success and well-being.

- **STANDARD 7:** **Professional Community for Teachers and Staff**
  Effective educational leaders foster a professional community of teachers and other professional staff to promote each student's academic success and well-being.

National Policy Board for Educational Administration (NPBEA). *Professional Standards for Educational Leaders* (Reston, VA: Author, 2015). Used with Permission.

Change is the one persistent phenomenon in life and in organizations; thus schools experience change often. For school leaders, implementing and managing change and improvement in school leadership is a difficult and daunting task. As Michael Fullan and others note, school leaders need to understand the change process in order to lead and manage change and improvement efforts effectively. Furthermore, they must learn to overcome barriers and cope with the chaos that naturally exists during the complex process of change.

In the recent 2016 the Phi Delta Kappa/Gallup Poll stated that "despite the recent emphasis on academic achievement (with state standardized test scores serving as the measure), less than half (45%) of poll respondents believe that preparing students academically is the main goal of a public school education. The remainder split between saying that public education should prepare students either for work or good citizenship."[1] Surveys have consistently shown over the years that, the majority of Americans believe that the best way to improve education is to reform the existing system.

Much is expected of schools today. Words such as *accountability, standards-based education, high-stakes testing,* and *effectiveness* have become buzzwords in the U.S. Congress, state legislatures, gatherings of business leaders, and other circles beyond the walls of higher education and local schools.[2]

Key findings from the 2016 Phi Delta Kappa/Gallup Poll revealed:

- Parents who give As and Bs to their local schools report that the schools communicate more effectively with them, give them frequent opportunities to visit and offer input, and are interested in what they have to say.
- By the most lopsided result in the survey, the public by 84 percent to 14 percent says that when a public school has been failing for several years, the best response is to keep the school open and to try to improve it rather than closing the school. But if a failing school is kept open, then, by a 2-to-1 margin, Americans say replacing administrators and teachers is preferable to giving the school more resources and support staff.
- A majority of Americans opposes (59 to 37 percent) allowing public school parents to excuse their children from taking standardized tests.
- Most public school parents (56 percent) say that new standards are changing what's being taught in their child's school, although one-third says there has been no change.
- For the fifteenth consecutive year, Americans say that lack of funding is the No. 1 problem confronting local schools.
- More Americans support (53 percent) than oppose (45 percent) raising property taxes to improve public schools, but there is broad skepticism (47 percent) that higher spending would result in school improvements. If taxes are raised, there's little consensus on how the money should best be spent. A plurality (34 percent) says it should go to teachers but divides on whether that means more teachers or higher pay for teachers.

While there is still concern about the increase in standardized testing, most Americans oppose allowing students to opt out of standardized state tests (59 to 37 percent). That includes public school parents, though in this group the division is closer (55 to 43 percent).[3] Furthermore, there is increased support for offering more career-technical or skills-based classes (68 percent), which far exceeds a preference for more honors or advanced academic classes (21 percent), including 51 percent who strongly prefer more vocational classes.[4]

Schools are dynamic, reflecting the constantly changing world around us. However, schools are also expected to conserve our values while meeting higher achievement standards. Schools cannot afford to stand still; they must develop processes and techniques to facilitate effective change. That said, Americans overwhelmingly prefer trying to improve failing public schools than closing them; the 70-point margin on this question is the largest of any in the survey.[5]

PREMISES GUIDING THE CHANGE RATIONALE

The rationale for change in education seems to be based on the following premises: (1) Even if the status quo is not necessarily bad, there is usually room for improvement; (2) while all change does not necessarily lead to improvement, improvement is not likely to occur without change; (3) unless we attempt change, we are not likely to know whether a proposed innovation is better than the status quo; and (4) participation in the change process can result in greater understanding and appreciation of the desirable features of the status quo and can lead to a better understanding and appreciation of, and skill in, the change process itself. Although it is clear that proposed change holds the potential for improvement in education, an administrator would be well advised to be skeptical of those who say, "This is *new* and therefore good," or, conversely, "This is *old* and therefore better." Periodic assessment of traditional practices and careful evaluation of proposed innovations are essential first steps in validating the need for improvement in education.

PRESSURES FOR CHANGE

In recent years schools have been bombarded with proposals, research findings, and mandates for change. For example, schools have been told that they need to increase student time on tasks, provide career ladders for teachers, introduce computer study into the curriculum, enhance their organizational culture, improve students' basic skills, increase parental involvement, improve personnel evaluation, tighten curriculum standards, develop partnerships with business, and so on. Many of these pressures for change emanate from various national reports and pressure to implement national standards at the state and local levels, as well as pressure to change principal preparation programs.

Why Change Efforts Fail and What Can Be Done

Although national reports and research findings can be helpful in identifying possible areas in need of change in the schools, evaluations of change efforts that were made during the 1960s through the 1980s raise grave doubts as to whether national prescriptions, state mandates, and school district directives can be successful in bringing about significant *and lasting* school improvements.[6] Sergiovanni has said that educational change itself must be changed.[7] In general, studies show that past attempts to impose certain changes on the schools have not been successful, for the most part. State regulations frequently usurped the authority of teachers, principals, parents, and local communities. The regulations sought to make the curriculum "teacher-proof" when, in fact, they served to make schools "learning-proof."[8] Many of the proposed changes either were not implemented at all or were modified in such a way to fit local needs that the value of the change was questionable.[9]

Schwahn and Spady have highlighted "five interdependent reasons why productive change doesn't happen," and from these reasons, they have extrapolated five change "rules" or principles: (1) "People don't change unless they share a compelling reason to change," (2) "People don't change unless they have ownership in the change," (3) "People don't change unless their leaders model that they are serious about the change," (4) "People are unlikely to change unless they have a concrete picture of what the change will look like for them personally," and

(5) "People can't make a change—or make it last—unless they receive organizational support for the change."[10]

Federal and State Mandates Are Not Enough

Although the federal and state governments can make an important contribution to school reform by publicizing the need for improvement and by providing financial and technical assistance to schools that would like to change, the history in this country of attempts to change the schools suggests that significant and lasting school improvement can seldom be prescribed, mandated, or directed by agencies or individuals outside of the school. Part of the difficulty is that, as mentioned in Chapter 6, schools are "loosely coupled organizations";[11] that is, there are seldom explicit and direct connections or linkages between the external agents pressuring the schools to change and the people (in most cases, teachers) who will have to implement the changes. This makes it hard to direct and monitor adequately what is going on in the schools. Another difficulty is that many teachers and building administrators have become accustomed to pressures for change—after all, there has been a lot of change over the years—and educators realize that much proposed change is faddish in nature and that the pressure for change will likely diminish when the change agent leaves or funds are cut back.[12]

A basic implication of research on change efforts over several decades is that the primary leadership for bringing about school improvement must come from the organizational level of education where the change is to take effect. In most situations, that will be at the school site level, even though important contributions can be made at all levels.

NEEDED LEADERSHIP FOR CHANGE

There is little doubt that the involvement and cooperation of many people will be necessary for the successful implementation of school improvement. An administrator cannot and should not attempt to introduce and implement a proposed change single-handedly. As Joyce and his colleagues have pointed out, "Charismatic superintendents and principals can change schools, sometimes quite rapidly, by developing ad hoc executive structures; but the institutionalization of change is very difficult."[13] In order for change to occur, one "highly-motivated, goal-oriented individual must serve as the initial change agent. However, lasting change requires more than the efforts of a single individual."[14] Consequently, introducing lasting change will require the cooperation and support of a variety of people.[15] The administrator should recognize that the leadership for introducing school improvement can come from many sources and thus should try to encourage ideas and support for change throughout the school or school system.

School Improvement Committees

One specific way in which an administrator can attempt to facilitate school change is to establish a school improvement committee.[16] Such a committee should be established at the district level to provide overall direction and coordination of school improvement efforts, and each school should also establish a school improvement committee to focus on improvement at the school site level. At the latter level, the committee should be headed by the principal and should comprise representative assistant administrators, teachers, parents, and students who are interested in school improvement and possess skills and/or insights that would be helpful in bringing about needed and successful change. For an excellent example of how students can be involved in the change process, the reader is referred to Furtwengler.[17] The school improvement committee should be charged with the responsibility for assessing the need for change, encouraging efforts to improve the school, coordinating and providing assistance to those efforts, and monitoring and evaluating progress and achievements.

Importance of a Collaborative Approach In order for this type of committee to be successful, its membership should be voluntary rather than required, and each member should have something useful to offer. Once established, the committee will need adequate resources, assistance, and periodic recognition from the administrator. In some cases, in-service training for committee members may even be needed. It will also be important for the committee to be supported by the rest of the school. Every effort needs to be made to avoid a perception that the committee is a behind-the-scenes, elitist group. Open meetings and frequent communications will help eliminate or reduce this possible problem.

Principals and Implementation of Innovation

While the establishment of a school improvement committee represents an important organizational step toward successfully bringing about school improvement, it also needs to be recognized that the administrator, particularly the principal (if the proposed change is to be introduced at the building level), is a key figure in the implementation of an innovation. Seldom can a proposed change be successfully implemented without the understanding, support, and, frequently, the leadership of the building administrator. As Demeter observed in his study of innovation in local schools, "Building principals are key figures in the innovation process. Where they are both aware of and sympathetic to an innovation, it tends to prosper. Where they are ignorant of its existence, or apathetic, if not hostile, it tends to remain outside the bloodstream of the school."[18]

Reinforcing the importance of the principal to the successful implementation of any proposed change, Sarason emphasized, "The principal is the crucial implementor of change. That is to say, any proposal for change that intends to alter the quality of life in the school depends primarily on the principal."[19] Nickols has said that managing change requires numerous skills—especially political skills, analytical skills, people skills, system skills, and business skills.[20] According to Nickols, four basic questions can help direct change. Each is built around a particular concept as expressed in the verbs "achieve, preserve, avoid," and "eliminate." The questions are (1) "What do you want that you don't have?" (achievement goals), (2) "What do you want that you already have?" (preservation goals), (3) "What don't you have that you don't want?" (avoidance goals), and (4) "What do you have now that you don't want?" (elimination goals).[21]

Characteristics of Principals Who Implement Change The nature of the situation should determine the specific role an administrator should play in regard to introducing and implementing a particular change.[22] One study of principals who had successfully implemented new programs in their schools found that:

> [The principal] *was a believer,* feeling a genuine commitment to the project; an *advocate* who promoted and defended the project before a variety of audiences; a *linker* who connected the project with other parts of the system; a *resource acquirer* who obtained and allocated tangible and

intangible resources for the project; an *employer* who hired project staff or assigned teachers to it; a *leader* who supplied initiative, energy, and direction; a *manager* who provided problem-solving assistance and support; a *delegator* who "moved backstage" when teachers assumed leadership; a *supporter* who provided words of encouragement and acts of assistance; and an *information source* who gave feedback to teachers and project staff.[23]

Another study finds six common characteristics of principals who were successful when implementing educational change: being visionary, believing that schools are for learning, valuing human resources, communicating and listening effectively, being proactive, and taking risks.[24]

Leadership Styles of Principals Hall found that the principal's leadership style determines the successful implementation of change. Principals in his study had three main styles: (1) the initiator, (2) the manager, and (3) the responder. The initiator's style was most successful, followed by the manager's; the responder's style was least successful. The specific styles are described as follows:

1. *Initiators:* Have clear goals that include implementation of innovation. They place high expectations upon the students, their staff, and themselves.
2. *Managers:* Fall between initiators and responders. They may initiate action in support of change but also demonstrate responsive behavior.
3. *Responders:* Rely on teachers and others to act as change agents while they proceed with administrative tasks.[25]

Hitt identifies the following 10 characteristics of managers who are effective change agents:

1. They view change as a friend–see it as a challenge and an opportunity.
2. They have "power tools" and know how to use them. These "power tools" include the following:
   a. Information (knowledge and expertise).
   b. Resources (people, funds, materials, space, and time).
   c. Support (from influential people at many levels).
3. They are able to deal with both the logical planning aspect of change and the psychological aspect, that is, the ability to handle the people problems associated with change.
4. They establish a climate for change through exemplary, day-to-day actions.
5. They start the change process within themselves rather than within others.
6. They do not force change but facilitate it.
7. They create their own enthusiasm.
8. They are able to let go of an old idea and experiment with alternative concepts. They are open-minded.
9. They seek out and accept criticism of their ideas.
10. They are able to get others to buy into their ideas for change.[26]

The multifaceted role of these principals may seem a little overwhelming to many readers, especially prospective administrators. The Institute for Educational Leadership identified perhaps the most important qualities needed in school improvement efforts when it concluded, "There is no magic. All it takes is the commitment, the time, and the guts to stay with it."[27]

THE PROCESS OF CHANGE

Although it seems clear that the administrator is a pivotal figure in the change process and, in many cases, may need to be the primary change agent in introducing and implementing a proposed innovation, the administrator's effectiveness and the innovation's success are not automatic or inevitable. Although many factors can influence the likelihood of successful school improvement, it is not likely to occur in a school or school district without the administrator and the school improvement committee developing an understanding of, and skill in, the process of introducing and implementing change. Kilmann identifies the following four critical stages in planning a "completely integrated program for improving organizations":

1. Ascertaining whether the organization is ready for a successful improvement.
2. Diagnosing problems—using a questionnaire.
   a. Designating the barriers (problems).
   b. Designating the channels for success (opportunities).
3. Scheduling planning tracks.
   a. Culture.
   b. Management skills.
   c. Team building.
   d. Strategy structure.
   e. Reward system.
4. Implementing planning tracks.
   a. Encouraging flexibility as change is implemented in each track.
   b. Making sure employees take responsibility for the change.[28]

Although theorists on change may differ somewhat in their terminology and emphasis, most social scientists and innovators would agree that the process of introducing change should include the stages and steps listed in Figure 7.1.[29] The administrator and school improvement committee who adopt the process outlined in Figure 7.1 should greatly increase the likelihood of successfully introducing and institutionalizing a proposed change in a school and school district. The process recommended is a rational one, although it is recognized that what actually occurs does not always follow rational lines. It begins with the identification of the need for change and ends with the integration of the proposed innovation into the routine of the school. Throughout the process, there is an emphasis on decision making, planning, organizing, diagnosing, and evaluating—the very skills that are central to administration.

In the remaining sections of this chapter, each stage in the change process found in Figure 7.1 will be further analyzed and discussed.

Initial Considerations

Assessing the Need for Change The first stage in the process of change may well be the most important one. If the administrator, with the cooperation of relevant others, does not periodically evaluate the current program, activities, and practices in the school and school district, the administrator is unlikely to be aware of, or be sensitive to, the need for change.

FIGURE 7.1
IMPORTANT STAGES AND STEPS IN THE CHANGE PROCESS

Stage I
Conduct a Needs Assessment

A. Identify the need for change. Examine the present system to ascertain which aspects need to be improved.
B. Develop or evaluate and select a new approach or system that will replace the former method.

Stage II
Orient the Target Group to the Proposed Change

A. Create an awareness of and interest in the proposed innovation on the part of the target group, e.g., teachers.
B. Institute with the target group an examination of the strengths and weaknesses of the proposed change. Pilot-test and refine the new system prior to its introduction.
C. Identify, with the help of the target group, the commitments that will need to be made in terms of additional resources, in-service training programs, and/or building modifications.

Stage III
Decide Whether to Introduce the Proposed Change

A. Identify those who should participate in the decision.
B. Decide on the process by which the decision will be made.
C. Decide whether to proceed with the implementation of the proposed change.

Stage IV
Plan a Program of Implementation

A. Plan and carry out a program of in-service education for those involved in the proposed change.
B. Provide the resources and facilities necessary for successfully introducing the change.
C. Anticipate and attempt to resolve in advance the operational problems that may be encountered in implementing the proposed innovation.

Stage V
Implement the Proposed Innovation

Stage VI
Conduct In-Process Evaluation

A. Design and institute a system that will provide feedback on the extent to which the proposed change is accomplishing its objectives.
B. Diagnose those aspects of the program or its implementation that need improvement.

Stage VII
Refine and Institutionalize the Innovation

A. Modify the innovation and, if necessary, provide additional orientation, training, resources, facilities, etc.
B. Gain the acceptance of the innovation (if it is successful) as a regular and permanent part of the total educational program in the school or school district.

Worse yet, the administrator may react defensively to external pressures for change and attempt to defend a status quo that has not been examined carefully. Therefore, an effective administrator will have in operation a needs assessment plan providing objective information about the strengths and weaknesses of the various educational programs and activities. Such an assessment plan will be essential for identifying and validating the need for change, and it will also be helpful to others in developing an understanding of the need for change. An excellent description of how to develop such a plan is presented by Kaufman and Stone.

Determining the New Direction Once the need for change has been established, the administrator, in cooperation with relevant others, should attempt to develop, or evaluate and select from various alternatives, a new approach or system to replace or modify the current program or practice. This will be a challenging task. Administrators are faced with what must seem at times to be a virtual barrage of proposals for changing the school program. The challenge for the school practitioner is to select those innovations that show potential for significantly improving education in the school. Unfortunately, this is easier said than done. The main problem is finding an innovation that has been systematically developed on the basis of theory and research, with subsequent experimental testing and refinement before dissemination to the schools. Research and development centers and regional laboratories are a source for information on innovations. Also, the local school district may need to establish contact with its state department of public instruction to ascertain its participation in the U.S. Office of Education's National Diffusion Network. Since many of the innovations to be considered are not "proven" products in any sense of the term, the administrator will need to evaluate carefully the strengths and limitations of each proposed change before seeking its adoption in the school or school district.

Evaluating a Proposed Innovation In conducting an evaluation of a *proposed* innovation, the administrator and the school improvement committee should attempt to seek answers to the following basic questions:

1. What are the objectives of the proposed change or innovation? What is it supposed to accomplish?
2. Are the objectives of the proposed innovation sufficiently relevant to the particular need for improvement in the local school or school district? How do we know this?
3. How will the proposed innovation accomplish its objectives? What is the evidence that the proposed innovation will accomplish its objectives, and how adequate is that evidence?
4. How difficult will it be for people to understand and accept the proposed innovation?
5. To what extent do people have the skills to implement the proposed innovation? If skills are lacking, how easily can these skills be acquired?
6. What are the financial costs of implementing the proposed innovation? Are there sufficient resources for implementing the proposed change?
7. How will we know, if we implement the proposed innovation, that it has accomplished its objectives?
8. In general, what are the advantages and disadvantages of implementing the proposed change?

As mentioned earlier, evaluating a proposed innovation is seldom an easy task. It is an essential activity, however, for the administrator who wishes to avoid introducing an innovation that may not only be inappropriate for the needs of the school or school district but, if not successful, also result in disillusionment and cynicism about future efforts to innovate.

Important Reference Groups

For most proposed changes, it will be important for the change agent to develop understanding, commitment, and possibly new skills on the part of those individuals or groups who will be affected by a school innovation. Generally, the groups who will be most affected will include the faculty, the students, the parents, the school board, the administrator's superiors, and the state department of public instruction.

Gaining Support, Reducing Resistance In most circumstances, the six groups just mentioned represent the greatest sources of potential support for—or resistance to—a proposed change.[30] The administrator who wishes to play the role of the change agent needs to recognize that the acceptance and effectiveness of the proposed innovation may also be enhanced or impeded by the attitudes and actions of other individuals and groups associated with the school district: the personnel of other schools in the district; social and civic organizations within the community; visitors to the school; and the news media.[31] Because each group is part of the informal communication network within a school district or community, the change agent must identify the potential of these groups for support or resistance and must consider these factors in introducing an innovation. As Baldridge and Deal have perceptively noted in regard to the external environment of the school (which includes not only local community but also the state and national scenes), "The environment is a major impetus for change, for new environmental demands are an initial source of new ideas, new procedures and new activities. Not only is change promoted by the environment, but changes made internally must also be supported by environmental connections."[32]

Involving the Faculty Perhaps the most important group to consider in establishing the need for change, and in selecting and introducing a proposed innovation, is the faculty. If the faculty of a school or school district does not understand a proposed innovation, or lacks the skill for participating effectively in its implementation, the likelihood of the innovation's successful implementation is slight. This is particularly true of an innovation that is to be implemented in the classroom. Therefore, the administrator should make every effort to be sure that the faculty or its representatives are involved in each step of the change process, that they understand thoroughly the different facets of the proposed innovation, and that they are provided with adequate opportunity to acquire the skills necessary to implement the change.

Adoption of the Innovation

According to Havelock and his colleagues, an individual (or group) in the process of adopting an innovation goes through the following six stages:

1. *Awareness stage:* The individual is exposed to an innovation and becomes aware of it, although not necessarily knowledgeable about it or possessing a strong interest in finding out more about it.
2. *Interest stage:* The individual is developing an interest in finding out more about the innovation and is beginning to develop some possible negative and positive attitudes toward it.
3. *Mental stage:* The individual is now actively evaluating the innovation as to how it might be implemented and is also seeking the assessment of the innovation from respected people.
4. *Trial stage:* The individual actually attempts to implement the innovation on a pilot basis to see if it will work.

5. *Adoption stage:* The individual adopts the innovation and implements it fully.
6. *Integration stage:* The individual internalizes the innovation in such a way that it becomes a routine part of the person's behavior or situation.[33]

The Complexity of Instituting Change An individual or group will not always, of course, go through all six stages. Possibly at the end of the mental or trial stage the proposed innovation will be rejected. Clearly, Havelock's concept of stages indicates that adoption is a more complicated process than perhaps is realized. For example, the implementation of an innovation from a leadership perspective occurs in four different stages, according to Sergiovanni. In the first stage, *initiation,* the leader and the follower have independent, but organizationally related, objectives. Sergiovanni refers to this stage in leadership as "bartering." Stage two, *uncertainty,* is a time to muddle through. The leadership is "building." In the third stage, *transformation,* there is a breakthrough as the goals of leaders and followers are shared. The leaders and followers are bonded together in a moral commitment. In the fourth stage, *routinization,* improvements are turned into routines so that they become second nature. Leadership is "banking."[34]

Hall and Hord have divided change facilitator behaviors into several clusters: (1) a "concern for people" cluster that is composed of social/informal and formal/meaningful interactions, (2) an "organizational efficiency" cluster in which the focus is on the degree of trust in others to carry out responsibilities and the establishment of procedures that keep the system running smoothly and permit teachers to do their jobs better, and (3) a "strategic sense" cluster that focuses on the dimensions of day-to-day activities in the context of a long-range vision and the planning that accompanies it.[35]

What Teachers Worry About Adequate orientation to the innovation is a key factor to successfully proceeding through Havelock's first three stages of adoption. In attempting to orient the faculty to the proposed innovation, the administrator needs to be aware of the typical concerns teachers have about innovations. According to a model developed at the Research and Development (R&D) Center at the University of Texas, teachers go through several stages of concern.[36] Initially, their concerns seem to focus on how the proposed innovation, if it is implemented, will affect them *personally.* If these self-concerns can be ameliorated or eliminated, then the teachers' questions are likely to reflect concern about how to perform the tasks associated with the innovation. Finally, if the task-related concerns can be resolved, then the teachers' concerns will center on how the innovation will affect students.

Research at the R&D Center at the University of Texas subsequently supported the validity of the concept of stages of concern.[37] This research found that it was possible, using an instrument based on the concept of stages of concern, to predict with better than 90 percent accuracy those teachers who eventually used an innovation and those who did not. Although the concept and instrument have not been validated with other groups that might also have concerns about an innovation, for example, students and parents, it does appear logical that the administrator consider adapting the instrument for use with these groups as well.

Creating an Atmosphere of Trust "Trust is a key to system change that appears to be in short supply," write Hall and Hord. "Currently it seems as if everyone at each point across the system not only does not trust and respect persons at other points along the continuum, but also is cynical about the intents of those other people."[38] During the process of addressing concerns, the administrator's role should not be one of "selling" or "advocating" an innovation. Such an approach will impair the administrator's objectivity and sensitivity to people's concerns. Instead, the administrator should be trying to develop an understanding of the innovation and people's concerns about it. To accomplish these objectives, the administrator needs to create a climate or atmosphere conducive to objectivity, trust, and confidence. Research by a number of individuals and groups suggests that to create this type of atmosphere, the change agent will need to be perceived by the teachers as someone who:

1. Is not trying to "foist" a change on them or manipulate them into making a change.
2. Is a good communicator who not only understands a particular innovation but also knows how to explain it clearly.
3. Respects teachers and encourages them to voice their concerns.
4. Listens carefully when concerns or objections surface and takes action to try to ameliorate those concerns and objectives.
5. Practices the perspective that successful change requires the cooperation and contribution of everyone.
6. Has skills for helping to facilitate the proposed change.[39]

RESISTANCE TO CHANGE

Resistance to change exists in all organizations, be they public or private. Bowsher classified seven types of resisters to change in the following manner:

1. *"Positive" resister:* The person who agrees with all the new programs but never does anything about them.
2. *"Unique" resister:* Although the changes may be good for other areas of the organization, they are never right for this individual's department.
3. *"Let me be last" resister:* Will not say change is wrong, but uses the strategy of trying to be last to implement change, hoping all new ideas will die out before his or her department must institute a new program.
4. *"We need more time to study" resister.*
5. *"States rights" resister:* Resists any new program from headquarters, stressing that only local programs will be effective.
6. *"Cost justifier" resister:* Prior to any changes, everything must be cost-justified.
7. *"Incremental change" resister:* The most difficult to win over to a new system. New approaches are tried only if they have everything the old system had.[40]

Two Kinds of Forces: Facilitating and Restraining

In every situation involving change, there will operate certain restraining, as well as facilitating, forces.[41] The facilitating forces—those conditions that make it easier to introduce a particular innovation—will probably be obvious to the administrator. They include such factors as outside pressures for change and the administrator's own convictions about the need for change. On the other hand, the restraining forces—those conditions that will make it difficult to introduce the innovation—may not be so obvious. Their symptoms are usually manifested, however, in people's concerns or expressions of resistance to a proposed change. One should assume that change will often be resisted; experience and research both indicate that resistance to change is not unusual.[42] Sample verbal reactions to proposed change that suggest resistance include the following.

"Everything is going all right, so why change?"

"People aren't ready for change."

"Has anyone else tried this?"

"It won't work in this school."

"We've never done it before."

"We're not ready for that."

"We're doing all right without it."

"It's too radical a change."

"We don't have enough time to do it."

"It's too complicated."

Factors behind Resistance

These comments suggest concern as well as possible resistance to proposed change and should not be dismissed lightly. The worst thing the administrator can do is to dismiss resistance without examining its merits or to react defensively when opposition to change is expressed. Instead, the administrator should view the expression of resistance or concern as a warning sign that needs to be taken seriously, and should attempt to better understand and diagnose the motivation and reasoning behind such expressions. In so doing, the administrator needs to be aware that resistance to change may be based on one or more of the following restraining factors:

Habit. Habit is the tendency of people to behave in the same way that they have always behaved, and the familiar becomes a form of security. Proposed change challenges this security, and the challenge is frequently met with resistance.[43]

The Bureaucratic Structure of the School District. The school district as a bureaucratic institution emphasizes the maintenance of order, rationality, and continuity. Uniformity of educational programs and procedures among the schools of the district seems to be valued, whereas diversity does not. Attempts by individual schools to introduce new programs or procedures are sometimes viewed with suspicion. Because of these attitudes and the hierarchical structure of the district, proposed change may be diluted before it is finally approved, or it may be rejected because it threatens the stability of the institution.[44] Recent research suggests, however, that the bureaucratic structure of a school district can, depending on its nature and on how it is used, facilitate the process of change rather than restrict it.[45]

The Lack of Incentive. Change can be a difficult and frustrating experience for the individuals or groups involved. Although the administrator may be personally convinced of the benefits that will accrue if a proposed change is adopted, the administrator can seldom guarantee those benefits or offer incentives (monetary or otherwise) to persuade others to adopt the innovation.[46] As a result, the administrator is dependent upon the ability to influence others to adopt a proposed change that may have high personal costs in terms of time and frustration and no immediate gain.

The Nature of the Proposed Change. Innovations can vary according to complexity, financial cost, compatibility with the other phases of the school's operation, ease of communicability, and time and energy needed to make the change.[47] Some innovations, because of these factors, are more difficult to introduce into a school system than are other proposed changes. As Baldridge and Deal note, "Many plans fail because they simply are not viable in terms of what the organization can afford."[48] Therefore, the characteristics of the innovation itself may constitute a major obstacle or problem in securing its adoption.

Teacher and Community Norms. Teacher and community norms can act as significant barriers to innovating in the schools. For example, there is evidence that teacher norms support autonomy and do not encourage interaction and exchange of new ideas among colleagues.[49] As a result, efforts by the administrator to bring about change in a teacher's role or methods may be viewed as a challenge to that teacher's professional autonomy. Research has further revealed that community groups may feel threatened by change because of its implications for upsetting the stability of the power relations within the community.[50] Both sets of norms—teacher and community—can act as powerful sources of resistance to the administrator who is trying to introduce a particular innovation.

Lack of Understanding. People may resist a proposed change because they don't possess an adequate or accurate understanding of it. Their deficiency may be caused by a failure to pay close attention when the proposed change was explained, or, on the other hand, information about the change may have been poorly or inaccurately communicated. In any respect, a lack of understanding of a proposed change can act as a significant deterrent in its successful implementation.[51]

A Difference of Opinion. A proposed change may be resisted because of an honest difference of opinion about whether it is needed or whether it will accomplish all that its proponents claim. The difference in opinion may be based on conflicting philosophies and values of education in regard to teaching and learning, or it may result from variant assessments of how much improvement would actually occur if the proposed change were implemented.

A Lack of Skill. A proposed change may be resisted by an individual or group who will be required to perform new skills and roles. The change from traditional roles and skills to new ones is viewed as an unsettling experience by many people. Therefore, any innovation requiring new skills or roles from the participants should be accompanied by an in-service program enabling these people to develop the new skills or roles.[52]

Resistance to change is a complex phenomenon, and the administrator should spend a considerable amount of time in diagnosing its source or sources before drawing any conclusions about how it might best be reduced. Many situations manifest more than one reason for resistance to change, and the administrator should assess the validity of each of the possible factors identified previously. By accurately diagnosing the reasons for resistance, the administrator will be in a better position to ameliorate it and smooth the way for successful implementation of a proposed improvement. A useful approach to diagnosing whether or not a school is ready for change has been developed by McCalley.[53]

One recommended means for dealing with the possibility of resistance to change is to introduce an innovation in such a manner as to avoid or minimize the likelihood of resistance. The following generalizations, which Goodwin Watson developed from a review of the research and theoretical literature on resistance to change, may be useful to the school administrator.[54] Resistance will be:

1. Less if administrators and other participants feel that the project is their own—not one devised and operated by outsiders.
2. Less if the project innovation clearly has wholehearted support from top officials of the system.
3. Less if the participants see the change as reducing, rather than increasing, their present burdens.
4. Less if the project is in accord with values already acknowledged by participants.
5. Less if the program offers the kind of new experience that interests participants.
6. Less if participants feel their autonomy and security are not threatened.
7. Less if participants have joined in diagnostic efforts leading them to agree on what the basic problem is and its importance.
8. Less if the project is adopted by consensual group decision.
9. Reduced if proponents are able to empathize with opponents, to recognize valid objections, and to take steps to relieve unnecessary fears.
10. Reduced if it is recognized that innovations are likely to be misunderstood and misinterpreted, and if provision is made for feedback of perceptions of the project and for further clarification of need.
11. Reduced if participants experience acceptance, support, trust, and confidence in their relations with one another.
12. Reduced if the project is kept open to revision and reconsideration—if experience indicates that changes will be desirable.

Although it may be difficult, if not impossible, to meet all these conditions in every situation, the administrator and the school improvement committee should consider Watson's guidelines in planning a school improvement.

FACILITATING THE INTRODUCTION OF CHANGE

Although many administrators have felt that the crucial, if not the sole, problem in successfully introducing an innovation was to overcome the initial resistance of the individuals and/or groups whose behavior and attitude were going to be affected by a change, this belief has now been challenged. Gross and his associates, for example, found that despite an initially favorable predisposition by those who were going to be especially affected by a certain change in a school, the proposed innovation ultimately met with failure.[55]

Reasons for Unsuccessful Innovations

Based on teacher interviews, questionnaires, and daily field observations, Gross and his colleagues identified four factors that seemed to account for the innovation's lack of success, all possessing implications for the educator who is concerned about the successful implementation of a proposed change.

1. Although the faculty had received orientation about the innovation prior to its introduction, six months after the innovation had finally been initiated, most teachers still did not seem to understand what was involved in their new role.

   Implication. The administrator should not assume that one or two explanations of an innovation will be adequate. Rather, the administrator must continuously secure feedback and provide clarification to those who will be affected by the change.

2. The teachers seemed to lack the knowledge and skills necessary for performing their new role. When they encountered problems as a result of these inadequacies, teacher resistance to the innovation developed.

   Implication. Behavioral and attitudinal change is complex and difficult to achieve. The job of the administrator is to identify clearly and precisely those skills and understandings needed by the people affected by the innovation and to provide the training necessary to acquire them. Teachers, for example, need continual assistance in adopting a new role.

3. The teachers' role in the new program was designed on the assumption that much of the student learning would result from contact among the students, who were using highly motivating, self-instructional materials. Unfortunately, the materials were in short supply and apparently not sufficiently motivating and self-instructing.

   Implication. If the success of an innovation depends on materials possessing special characteristics, (for example, highly motivating, self-instructing), the administrator must see that such materials are available in sufficient quantity.

4. Other aspects of the school program, such as grading and developing the school schedule, were not changed to facilitate the adoption of the new teacher role.

   Implication. A change in one aspect of the school program may affect and be affected by other aspects of the program and may necessitate further change.

The research conducted by Gross would appear to suggest two conclusions about proposed change: (1) that it will not always be initially resisted and (2) that an innovation may ultimately fail, despite its preliminary acceptance, if the people involved have not been provided with adequate role orientation, training, materials, and other prerequisites.[56]

More Reasons for Failure in Attempts at Innovation

In a related review of the literature on the implementation of change, Kritek found that, in addition to the factors identified by Gross, attempts to innovate failed because of goals that were too vague and ambitious, minimal planning to operationalize the innovation and to integrate it into the school, resources that were too limited, and failure to anticipate adequately and address constructively the developments that occurred after the innovation was implemented.[57]

What Administrators Can Learn from Failed Attempts at Change

Several implications are suggested by Kritek's review. The administrator who is thinking about introducing change must define the objectives of the innovation clearly and realistically. Full and accurate communication to those who could be affected by the proposed change is essential.

Pilot Projects to Introduce Change To avoid the problem of excessively ambitious goals, it may be necessary to consider introducing the innovation on a pilot project basis rather than to the entire school or school district.[58] A pilot project represents a scaled-down version of the originally proposed change. The proposed innovation might be reduced in terms of size, length of operation, or number of participants involved. For example, rather than introducing a new, schoolwide language arts curriculum, the change could be implemented on a pilot basis at only one grade level; or perhaps rather than implementing a curricular change at one grade level, several *units* of the curriculum could be introduced by all the teachers in the school during the first semester of the school year; and, of course, other variations of the pilot project approach are also possible.

The pilot project approach to introducing change has several distinct advantages. It can be conducted with a smaller number of participants and can involve those who would be more willing to try out new ideas. If the pilot project is successful, its results may favorably influence other people who initially resisted the proposed change. It can also be useful in identifying and addressing defects or weaknesses in the originally proposed innovation that may not have been obvious before implementation. Finally, a pilot project may prove useful in demonstrating that a proposed change will not work, either because of a defect in the concept of the proposed change or because local conditions make it impossible to implement fully.

The pilot project is no panacea for introducing change, but it may avoid the problem of overly ambitious objectives for an innovation and, for that reason alone, should be considered by the administrator.

Making Sure a Realistic Plan Is in Place After planning for the introduction of an innovation, the administrator should attempt to ascertain whether or not it was planned carefully enough and in sufficient detail. Many innovations seem to fail because there was not a well-conceived *plan* for implementing the innovation. Planning is concerned primarily with the question of how an objective is to be achieved or a decision implemented.[59] In a situation involving the planned implementation of an innovation, the following types of questions need to be answered:

1. What kinds of activities or actions must occur in order to introduce the innovation?
2. What kinds of resources—personnel, facilities, supplies—must be obtained to introduce the innovation?
3. What kinds of problems and possible consequences might the introduction of the innovation generate? How should these problems and consequences be addressed?
4. How should activities be sequenced to the best advantage and resources most efficiently coordinated in order to introduce the innovation?
5. What kind of time schedule should be followed in implementing the plan of action?

In an oversimplified sense, the administrator who engages in the planning process is attempting to answer the question, "Who does what, with whom, and over what period of time in order to implement the innovation?"

Another important question that faces administrators in a time of budget constraints is the availability of funding. Many schools have turned to grant writing to obtain the needed dollars to implement change. To write successful grants requires additional expertise that administrators and leaders may acquire by following Orlich's three suggested steps: (1) begin with a good idea, (2) search out a source that has funded similar ideas, and (3) craft a well-written proposal. Novice grant writers should realize that the basic elements of any grant, no matter what the dollar amount, are similar. These are (1) a carefully worded introduction, (2) an identification of the problem to be solved or the need to be addressed, (3) a list of goals and objectives, (4) a work plan or procedures, (5) the evaluation plan to measure the program's success, and (6) an expenditure plan with budget justifications.[60]

In summary, a well-conceived plan for implementing an innovation will go far toward avoiding the problems referred to by Gross and Kritek and will increase the possibility that the innovation will be successfully implemented.

POSTIMPLEMENTATION PROBLEMS

Although somewhat mixed, considerable evidence indicates that many implemented innovations are later abandoned or drastically modified. There are many possible reasons for the failure of an innovation, most of which have been discussed in the previous two sections of this chapter. Certainly any innovation attempt in which the objectives and operational activities are not well understood, the implementation is not well planned, and implementation is attempted despite the opposition of significant members of relevant reference groups carries with it the seeds of self-destruction. Even if these negative factors can be avoided, however, some innovations still encounter problems after they are implemented, problems that can lead to their demise.[61]

Burnout

One of these problems is that the individuals who are responsible for implementing the innovation may eventually become "burned out." Implementing change frequently requires a high level of energy expenditure. There may be new roles to be learned and long hours to be invested; furthermore, anxiety and frustration often are associated with the implementation of an innovation. Introducing change is usually hard work, and, typically, there are few external rewards for the participants. The morale in a school implementing an innovation frequently vacillates from high to low, without much stability.

If not ameliorated, over a period of time these conditions will negatively influence the attitude of the participants toward the innovation and will impair their effectiveness. The administrator who is sensitive to conditions in the school will provide timely assistance and rewards to those individuals who need them, and the problem of the participants becoming burned out can be prevented or reduced.

Coping with problems is very important for successful change. According to Miles and Louis, "Good problem coping (dealing with problems, actively and with some depth) is the single biggest determinant of program success." The authors suggest that problems should be solved structurally.

For example, if teachers complain about being overloaded, a proper solution would be to allow shared planning or to give added technical assistance rather than just asking teachers to persevere or to be more dedicated. Problems should be located and seen as "natural, even helpful occurrences, without blaming anyone, arousing defensiveness, or implying a predetermined solution."[62]

Negative Media Coverage

Two frequently unanticipated problems that can occur after an innovation has been implemented are a "bad press" and the reduction of resources and support by the district administration or external agency funding the innovation. Negative newspaper or television reports on an innovation can immeasurably damage the image of the innovation and can significantly affect the spirit of the participants and the attitudes of those who are judging the merits of the innovation. It matters little whether the press or television reports are accurate or not—media coverage usually has the appearance of validity.

A major problem with press coverage is that generally the press will want to report on the innovation soon after it has been implemented, even though at that stage the school is still discovering and trying to iron out the "bugs." Consequently, the media spotlight is on the innovation early and tends to focus on the problems it is encountering, resulting in a "bad press." There is no easy answer to this problem, given the nature of the press and the process of introducing change. The media are generally more interested in problems because they are newsworthy, and the period just after the innovation has been implemented is frequently the time when many problems arise. The administrator can, however, attempt to develop a positive relationship with the news reporters in the community and try to develop an understanding on their part (*before* the innovation is introduced) about types of problems likely to occur because of the innovation's novelty as well as the school's contingency plans for addressing those problems.

Funding Reduction or Loss of Other Resources

Another possible postimplementation problem is the gradual reduction in resources and moral support provided by the central office of the district or an outside funding agency. A school attempting to innovate will frequently need a higher level of resources and support than one that is not. Over a period of time, the central office may encounter budgeting pressures, as well as criticism from the other schools in the district about the better treatment of the innovative school; or, if the innovative school is funded by an external agency, that source of funding may be gradually reduced or terminated and the school district may not make up the difference. If the innovative school has received any bad press and/or has encountered some problems after the innovation has been implemented, the principal may find that the moral support of the central administration may be lacking when it is most needed.

Coping with Problems

Fortunately, most of the circumstances described in this section can be avoided, or at least reduced, if the administrator anticipates them and takes corrective action before the problems become major. The difficulties essentially are a result of events going less smoothly after the innovation has been implemented than had been anticipated. In these situations some of the famous Murphy's laws are operating: "Most things are more complicated than they initially appear to be," and "Most things take longer than originally anticipated."

WINDOW ON DIVERSITY

Diversity in the Workplace: Benefits, Challenges and Solutions

by Josh Greenberg

Workplace diversity refers to the variety of differences between people in an organization. That sounds simple, but diversity encompasses race, gender, ethnic group, age, personality, cognitive style, tenure, organizational function, education, background and more.

Diversity not only involves how people perceive themselves, but how they perceive others. Those perceptions affect their interactions. For a wide assortment of employees to function effectively as an organization, human resource professionals need to deal effectively with issues such as communication, adaptability and change. Diversity will increase significantly in the coming years. Successful organizations recognize the need for immediate action and are ready and willing to spend resources on managing diversity in the workplace now.

Benefits of Workplace Diversity

An organization's success and competitiveness depends upon its ability to embrace diversity and realize the benefits. When organizations actively assess their handling of workplace diversity issues, develop and implement diversity plans, multiple benefits are reported such as:

Increased adaptability

Organizations employing a diverse workforce can supply a greater variety of solutions to problems in service, sourcing, and allocation of resources. Employees from diverse backgrounds bring individual talents and experiences in suggesting ideas that are flexible in adapting to fluctuating markets and customer demands.

Broader service range

A diverse collection of skills and experiences (e.g., languages, cultural understanding) allows a company to provide service to customers on a global basis.

Variety of viewpoints

A diverse workforce that feels comfortable communicating varying points of view provides a larger pool of ideas and experiences. The organization can draw from that pool to meet business strategy needs and the needs of customers more effectively.

More effective execution

Companies that encourage diversity in the workplace inspire all of their employees to perform to their highest ability. Company-wide strategies can then be executed; resulting in higher productivity, profit, and return on investment.

Continued

Continued

WINDOW ON DIVERSITY

Challenges of Diversity in the Workplace

Taking full advantage of the benefits of diversity in the workplace is not without its challenges. Some of those challenges are:

Communication—Perceptual, cultural and language barriers need to be overcome for diversity programs to succeed. Ineffective communication of key objectives results in confusion, lack of teamwork, and low morale.

Resistance to change—There are always employees who will refuse to accept the fact that the social and cultural makeup of their workplace is changing. The "we've always done it this way" mentality silences new ideas and inhibits progress.

Implementation of diversity in the workplace policies—This can be the overriding challenge to all diversity advocates. Armed with the results of employee assessments and research data, they must build and implement a customized strategy to maximize the effects of diversity in the workplace for their particular organization.

Successful management of diversity in the workplace—Diversity training alone is not sufficient for your organization's diversity management plan. A strategy must be created and implemented to create a culture of diversity that permeates every department and function of the organization.

Recommended steps that have been proven successful in world-class organizations are:

Assessment of diversity in the workplace—Top companies make assessing and evaluating their diversity process an integral part of their management system. A customizable employee satisfaction survey can accomplish this assessment for your company efficiently and conveniently. It can help your management team determine which challenges and obstacles to diversity are present in your workplace and which policies need to be added or eliminated. Reassessment can then determine the success of you diversity in the workplace plan implementation.

Development of diversity in the workplace plan—Choosing a survey provider that provides comprehensive reporting is a key decision. That report will be the beginning structure of your diversity in the workplace plan. The plan must be comprehensive, attainable and measurable. An organization must decide what changes need to be made and a timeline for that change to be attained.

Implementation of diversity in the workplace plan—The personal commitment of executive and managerial teams is a must. Leaders and managers within organizations must incorporate diversity policies into every aspect of the organization's function and purpose. Attitudes toward diversity originate at the top and filter downward. Management cooperation and participation is required to create a culture conducive to the success of your organization's plan.

WINDOW ON DIVERSITY

Recommended diversity in the workplace solutions include:

Ward off change resistance with inclusion–Involve every employee possible in formulating and executing diversity initiatives in your workplace.

Foster an attitude of openness in your organization–Encourage employees to express their ideas and opinions and attribute a sense of equal value to all.

Promote diversity in leadership positions–This practice provides visibility and realizes the benefits of diversity in the workplace.

Utilize diversity training–Use it as a tool to shape your diversity policy.

Launch a customizable employee satisfaction survey that provides comprehensive reporting–Use the results to build and implement successful diversity in the workplace policies.

As the economy becomes increasingly global, our workforce becomes increasingly diverse. Organizational success and competitiveness will depend on the ability to manage diversity in the workplace effectively. Evaluate your organization's diversity policies and plan for the future, starting today.

Greenberg, Josh. (2004). "Diversity in the Workplace: Benefits, Challenges and Solutions. *The Multicultural Advantage.*" Retrieved from http://www.multiculturaladvantage.com/recruit/diversity/diversity-in-the-workplace-benefits-challenges-solutions.asp. Used with permission of AlphaMeasure Inc.

Problems are a normal occurrence because the planning process–even under the best of conditions–always involves assumptions, some of which may turn out to be untenable. Problems need not significantly influence the fate of an innovation, however, if the administrator becomes aware of them at an early stage before they develop into a crisis and if the administrator takes quick action to remedy the situation. Catching problems early requires the initiation of a formative evaluation system that will alert the administrator to incipient problems, and good leadership skills on the part of the administrator are necessary for quick action in a crisis.

FORMATIVE AND SUMMATIVE EVALUATION

Formative Evaluation

If the administrator is to be aware of problems associated with the implementation of an innovation before these problems become major crises, arrangements need to be made for the initiation of some type of formative evaluation. A *formative* evaluation represents an assessment of both an innovation's strengths and its areas in need of improvement before a conclusion or decision is reached on its success.[63] Formative evaluation is diagnostic in nature because it is searching for aspects of the innovation, or the implementation plan, that are in need of improvement.

■ **FIGURE 7.2**
FORMATIVE EVALUATION SURVEY

Feedback on the Implementation of the Computer Literacy Program

Instructions: Please make an X below to indicate whether you are a teacher or a student, add your grade level, and then give your reactions on the remainder of the form. You need not sign your name on this form unless you so desire.

Teacher ______________________ Grade Level ______________________

Student ______________________ Grade Level ______________________

1. What do you see as the main problems that need immediate action? Please be as specific as possible, and if you have ideas about resolving these problems, so indicate.
   Main problems ____
   Possible solutions ____
2. What do you see as the main advantage or advantages of the computer literacy program so far? ______________________________
3. Is there any special help or assistance that you need? ______________
   ____

____
Signature (optional)

This type of evaluation is very important in the early stages of implementing an innovation because it is during this period that unanticipated problems are likely to arise and immediate corrective action may be needed to avoid exacerbating the problems. For ease of understanding, an example of a relatively simple formative evaluation survey used by one school is presented in Figure 7.2.

A formative evaluation can range from simple to complex in the nature of its data gathering format and analysis, but the important consideration is that it provides the administrator with useful information on the progress and problems of the innovation and/or the plan for implementation. This type of evaluation should not, however, be used by the administrator, or anyone else for that matter, for making decisions about whether or not the innovation is a success and should be continued or discontinued. *After* the innovation has been given a reasonable amount of time to prove itself, then a decision should be considered with regard to continuing or discontinuing the innovation, and, at that point, the administrator will need to make arrangements for the initiation of what is referred to as *summative* evaluation.

Summative Evaluation

Summative evaluation, as applied to the assessment of an innovation, represents an attempt to ascertain whether or not the innovation is adequately meeting school or school district objectives and whether or not the advantages of the innovation sufficiently outweigh the disadvantages.[64] Summative evaluation usually necessitates the collection of data, but it also frequently involves subjective judgments on what the data mean. Examples of some different kinds of summative evaluations include the following:[65]

1. Comparison of *student behavior* before and after the innovation has been implemented.
2. Comparison of *student achievement* before and after the innovation has been implemented.
3. Comparison of *student attitudes* before and after the innovation has been implemented.
4. Comparison of *teacher attitudes* toward the innovation before and after the change.
5. Comparison of *parent attitudes* toward the innovation before and after the change.
6. *Effectiveness of the plan* for introducing the innovation.
7. Extent of *disruption* of other activities because of the change.
8. Amount of *additional costs* as a result of implementing and operating the innovation.

Methods of Summative Evaluation The methods one uses to conduct summative evaluation should depend on three factors: (1) what is to be evaluated, (2) what information is needed, and (3) what method is most appropriate and most accessible to provide the desired information. Possible evaluation methods range from questionnaires and interviews to content analysis and standardized tests.[66] There is no perfect method! All too frequently administrators reject or criticize an evaluation method without offering a better alternative; as a result, no evaluation is ever performed. Instead, administrators should select the best possible alternative from the evaluation methods that are available and appropriate for assessing the innovation.

Ultimately, administrators cannot avoid evaluating an innovation. If arrangements are not made to see that a sound assessment is carried out, then other people, including parents and members of the community, will make their own evaluation, using their own criteria and methods.

A FINAL NOTE

In most situations, change is inevitable.[67] An administrator can watch it occur, can resist it, or can help guide and direct it. By utilizing the concepts presented in this chapter, the administrator should be able to make an effective contribution by responding constructively to the need for improvement in education.

Although many of the case studies, suggested learning activities, and simulations presented in Part II require the appropriate use of the ideas in this chapter on school improvement, Cases 62–71 in Chapter 15 should provide the best opportunities for testing understanding and effective use of the concepts concerning the change process.

NOTES

1. Phi Delta Kappan. "The 48th Annual Phi Delta Kappa/Gallup Poll of the Public's Attitudes toward the Public Schools," *Phi Delta Kappan* (vol. 98, no. 1, September 2016), p. K3.
2. Ibid., pp. K4–K6.
3. Ibid., pp. K17–K18.
4. Ibid.

5. Ibid.
6. John De Santis and David Cohen, "The Lawn Party," in J. Victor Baldridge and Terrence Deal (Eds.), *The Dynamics of Organizational Change in Education* (Berkeley, CA: McCutchan, 1983), pp. 114–126. Also see the chapter by Terrence Deal and Samuel Nutt, "Planned Change in Rural School District" in the same book; and E. Deal, "Reframing Reform," *Educational Leadership* (vol. 47, no. 8, May 1990), pp. 6–12.
7. Thomas J. Sergiovanni, "Changing Educational Change," *Education Week* (vol. 19, no. 23), p. 27. Accessed online, http://www.edweek.org/ew/ewstory.cfm?slug523sergiovanni19, February 21, 2000.
8. Mary Hartwood Futrell, "Mission Not Accomplished: Education Reform in Retrospect," *Phi Delta Kappan* (vol. 71, no. 1, September 1989), pp. 10–14. Also see Mark. E. Goldberg, "The Ability to Persuade People to Change; An Interview with Mary Hartwood Futrell," *Phi Delta Kappan* (vol. 82, no. 6, February 2001), pp. 465–467.
9. De Santis and Cohen, "The Lawn Party," p. 114. Also see John I. Goodlad and M. Francis Klein, *Looking behind the Classroom Door* (Worthington, OH: Charles E. Jones, 1974).
10. Charles Schwahn and William Spady, "Why Change Doesn't Happen and How to Make Sure It Does," *Educational Leadership* (vol. 55, no. 7, April 1998), pp. 45–47.
11. Karl Weick, "Educational Organizations as Loosely Coupled Systems," in J. Victor Baldridge and Terrence Deal (Eds.), *The Dynamics of Organizational Change in Education* (Berkeley, CA: McCutchan, 1983), pp. 35–37. Also see Larry Cuban, "Reforming Again, Again, and Again," *Educational Researcher* (vol. 19, January–February 1990), pp. 3–13.
12. Frances C. Fowler, "Why Reforms Go Awry," *Education Week* (November 1985), pp. 17, 24.
13. Bruce R. Joyce et al., *The Structure of School Improvement* (New York: Longman, 1983), p. 71.
14. Bruce Bowers, "Initiating Change in Schools," *Research Roundup* (vol. 6, no. 3, April 1990), p. 1.
15. Michael Fullan, *Implementing Educational Change,* an ERIC report, April 1990, Ed. 221540; and Michael Fullan, "Staff Development, Innovation, and Institutional Development," in *Changing School Culture through Staff Development* (Alexandria, VA: ASCD, 1990), pp. 3–25. Also see Pat L. Cox, "Complementary Roles in Successful Change," *Educational Leadership* (vol. 41, no. 2, November 1983), pp. 10–13; and David F. Salisbury, *Major Issues in the Design of New Educational Systems,* an ERIC report, April 1990, Ed. 321403, pp. 1–9.
16. Joyce et al., *Structure of School Improvement,* an ERIC report, 1983, Ed. 228-233, chap. 6. Also see Herbert Klausmier, *A Process Guide for School Improvement* (Lanham, MD: University Press of America, 1985).
17. Willis J. Furtwengler, "Implementation Strategies for a School Effectiveness Program," *Phi Delta Kappan* (vol. 67, December 1985), pp. 262–265; and Murry H. Dalziel and Stephen C. Schoonover, *Changing Ways: A Practical Tool for Implementing Change within Organizations* (New York: Amacom, 1988), pp. 21, 58–63, 146.
18. Lee Demeter, "Accelerating the Local Use of Improved Educational Practices in School Systems," PhD dissertation, Columbia University, Teacher College, 1951. Also see Gene F. Hall, "The Principal as Leader of the Change Facilitating Team," *Journal of Research and Development in Education* (vol. 22, Fall 1988), pp. 49–59; and William D. Hitt, *The Leader-Manager* (Columbus, OH: Battelle Press, 1988), pp. 17–38.
19. Seymour B. Sarason, *Revisiting the Culture of the School and the Problem of Change,* 2nd ed. (New York: Teachers College Press, 1996), p. 148; Grant W. Simpson, "Keeping Alive: Elements of School Culture That Sustain Innovation," *Educational Leadership* (vol. 47, no. 8, May 1990), pp. 34–37; and Connie Golman and Cindy O'Shea, "A Culture for Change," *Educational Leadership* (vol. 47, May 1990), pp. 41–43.
20. Fred Nickols, "Change Management 101: A Primer." Accessed online, http://home.att.net/~nickols/change.htm, April 2, 2000.

21. Fred Nickols, "The Goals Grid: A Tool for Clarifying Goals and Objectives." Accessed online, http://home.att.net/~nickols/goals_grid.htm, April 29, 2000.

22. Gene Hall et al., "Effects of Three Principal Styles on School Improvement," *Educational Leadership* (vol. 41, February 1984), pp. 22–29; and Dalziel and Schoonover, *Changing Ways,* p. 59. Also see France R. Westley, "The Eye of the Needle: Cultural and Personal Transformation in a Traditional Organization," *Human Relations* (vol. 43, no. 3, March 1990), p. 273.

23. Spencer H. Wyant, *Of Projects and Principals* (Reston, VA: Association of Teacher Education, 1980). For additional discussion of the administrator's role or style, see Hall et al., "Effects of Three Principal Styles on School Improvement," *Educational Leadership* (vol. 41, February 1984); and Richard I. Arends, "The Meaning of Administrative Support," *Educational Administration Quarterly* (Fall 1982), pp. 79–92. Also see Jane M. Howell and Christopher A. Higgins, "Champions of Change: Identifying, Understanding, and Supporting Champions of Technological Innovations," *Organizational Dynamics* (vol. 19, no. 1, Summer 1990), pp. 40–46; and Kent D. Peterson, "Mechanisms of Culture Building and Principal's Work," *Educational and Urban Society* (vol. 20, May 1988), pp. 250–261.

24. SEDL, "Leadership Characteristics that Facilitate School Change," Accessed from http://www.sedl.org/change/leadership/character.html, December 29, 2010.

25. Gene F. Hall, "The Principal as Leader of the Change Facilitating Team," *Journal of Research and Development in Education* (Fall 1988), pp. 49–59.

26. Hitt, *The Leader-Manager,* p. 22.

27. Institute for Educational Leadership, *What Makes for an Effective School?* (Washington, DC: George Washington University, 1980), p. 102.

28. Ralph H. Kilmann, "A Completely Integrated Program for Creating and Maintaining Organizational Success," *Organizational Dynamics* (vol. 18, no. 1, 1989), pp. 5–19.

29. The recommended process of introducing change is not based on any particular source, but instead represents the conclusions of the authors after analyzing various research reports on change.

30. David Crandall and Susan Loucks, *A Roadmap for School Improvement: Executive Summary of the Study of Dissemination Efforts Supporting School Improvement,* an ERIC report, 1983, Ed. 240722.

31. Leslie W. Kindred et al., *The School and Community Relations,* 7th ed. (Boston, MA: Allyn and Bacon, 2001). Also see Tom R. Vickery, "ODDM: A Workable Model for Total School Improvement," *Educational Leadership* (April 1990), pp. 67–70.

32. J. Victor Baldridge and Terrence E. Deal, *Managing Change in Educational Organizations* (Berkeley, CA: McCutchan, 1975), p. 16; Sharon Conley, "'Who's On First?' School Reform Teacher Participation, and the Decision-Making Process," *Education and Urban Society* (vol. 21, August 1989), pp. 366–379; and Richard F. Elmore, "Early Experience in Restructuring Schools, Voices from the Field," an ERIC report, Ed. 306634, 1988, pp. 5–6.

33. Ronald G. Havelock, Janet C. Huber, and Shaindel Zimmerman, *A Guide to Innovation in Education* (Ann Arbor, University of Michigan Center for Research on the Utilization of Scientific Knowledge, 1970).

34. Thomas J. Sergiovanni, "Adding Value to Leadership Gets Extraordinary Results," *Educational Leadership* (vol. 47, no. 8, May 1990), pp. 23–27.

35. Gene E. Hall and Shirley M. Hord, *Implementing Change: Patterns, Principles, and Potholes* (Boston, MA: Allyn and Bacon, 2001).

36. William L. Rutherford, "An Investigation of How Teachers' Concerns Influence Innovation Adoption," paper presented at the annual meeting of the American Educational Research Association, 1977, p. 4. Also see David Salisbury, "Major Issues in the Design of New Educational Systems," an ERIC report, 1990, Ed. 321403, pp. 1–9.

37. Rutherford, "How Teachers' Concerns Influence Innovation Adoption," p. 26.

38. Hall and Hord, *Implementing Change,* p. 11.

39. For example, see Susan S. McCoy and Geralyn Shreve, "Principals—Why Are Some More Successful Than Others in Implementing Change?" *National Association of Secondary School Principals Bulletin* (vol. 67, September 1983), pp. 96–103; and Sauita Kumari and Kamah Dwivedo, "Effect of Organizational Climate in Attitude toward Change—A Comparative Study," *Social Science International* (June–July 1988), pp. 9–14.

40. Jack E. Bowsher, *Educating America, Lessons Learned in the Nation's Corporations* (New York: John Wiley, 1989), pp. 144–146, 170.

41. Kurt Lewin, "Group Decision and Social Change," in G. E. Swanson et al. (Eds.), *Readings in Social Psychology* (New York: Holt, Rinehart, & Winston, 1952), pp. 463–473; and Kilmann, "Completely Integrated Program," p. 9.

42. Stuart M. Klein and R. Richard Ritti, *Understanding Organizational Behavior* (Boston: Kent, 1984), pp. 569–572.

43. "Why Reform Was 'Dead on Arrival,'" *Education Week* (January 29, 1986), p. 20; and Michael Beer and Elise Walton, "Developing the Competitive Organization," *American Psychologist* (February 1990), pp. 40–46, 157–158.

44. Max G. Abbott, "Hierarchical Impediments to Innovation in Educational Organizations," in Max G. Abbott and John T. Lovell (Eds.), *Change Perspectives in Educational Administration* (Auburn, AL: Auburn University School of Education, 1965), pp. 40–53. Also see Joseph Raiche et al., *School Improvement: Research-Based Components and Processes for Effective Schools,* an ERIC report, Ed. 239396; and Thomas W. Rhoades and Phyllis H. Sunshine, *History and Politics in State Accountability Reform*, 1990, an ERIC report, Ed. 321347, pp. 1–23.

45. M. Fullan, *The Meaning of Educational Change* (New York: Teachers College Press, 2001).

46. Robert E. Blum, "Pitfalls in Implementing Secondary School Improvements," paper presented at a conference sponsored by the Center for Educational Policy and Management, University of Oregon, October 1983. For an example of the use of incentives to facilitate change, see Dale Mann, "The Impact of Impact II," *Phi Delta Kappan* (May 1982), pp. 612–614.

47. David L. Clark et al., "Effective Schools and School Improvement: A Comparative Analysis of Two Lines of Inquiry," *Educational Administration Quarterly* (vol. 20, Summer 1984), pp. 56–58.

48. Baldridge and Deal, *Managing Change,* p. 18.

49. J. E. Deal and L. D. Cellotti, "How Much Influence Do (and Can) Educational Administrators Have on Classrooms?" *Phi Delta Kappan* (March 1980), pp. 471–473. For ideas on how to address the problem of teacher norms, see H. Dickson Corbett, "To Make an Omelet, You've Got to Break the Egg Crate," *Educational Leadership* (vol. 40, no. 2, November 1982), pp. 34–35; and Mary E. Dietz, "On the Road to Change," *Instructor* (April 1990), p. 36.

50. Fullan, *The Meaning of Educational Change,* p. 194. For ways of addressing community norms, see Thomas Popkewitz, *The Myth of Educational Reform* (Madison, WI: University of Wisconsin Press, 1983).

51. J. Stanislao and B. C. Stanislao, "Dealing with Resistance to Change," *Business Horizons* (vol. 26, no. 4, July-August 1983), pp. 74–78. Also see Mathew B. Miles and Karen Seashore Louis, "Mustering the Will and Skill for Change," *Educational Leadership* (vol. 47, no. 8, May 1990), pp. 37–61.

52. For further guidelines on this topic, see Joyce et al., *Structure of School Improvement* (New York: Longman, 1983), chaps. 9, 10; and Leonard Allen, "A Model for Creating Effective Change," *Directions* (February 1990), pp. 1–2.

53. Warren Bell, "Diagnosing a School's Readiness for Change: What to Look for When Starting an Innovation," an ERIC report, 1990, Ed. 188310. Also see Yoram Zeira and Joyce Avedisian, "Organizational Planned Change: Assessing the Chances for Success," *Organizational Dynamics* (vol. 17, no. 4, Spring 1989), pp. 31–45.

54. Goodwin Watson, "Resistance to Change," in Goodwin Watson (Ed.), *Concepts for Social Change* (Washington, DC: NTL Institute for Applied Behavioral Science, NEA, 1969), pp. 22–23; and Kenneth K. Tewel, "Restructuring

Urban High Schools," *The Clearing House* (October 1989), pp. 73–77.

55. Neal Gross et al., "An Attempt to Implement a Major Educational Innovation: A Sociological Inquiry," paper presented at the Center for Research and Development in Educational Differences, Harvard University, 1968; and Robert E. Herriott and Neal Gross (Eds.), *The Dynamics of Planned Educational Change* (Berkeley, CA: McCutchan, 1979).
56. Also see Ralph Parish and Richard Arends, "Why Innovative Programs Are Discontinued," *Educational Leadership* (vol. 40, no. 4, January 1983), pp. 62–65.
57. William J. Kritek, "Lesson from the Literature on Implementation," *Educational Administration Quarterly* (Fall 1976), pp. 86–102; and see Jack P. Krueger and Ralph Parish, "We're Making the Same Mistakes," *Planning and Changing* (Fall 1982), pp. 131–138.
58. Richard A. Gorton and Gail Thierbach-Schneider, *School-Based Leadership: Challenges and Opportunities,* 3rd ed. (Dubuque, IA: William C. Brown, 1991), pp. 376–378.
59. W. E. Webster, "Operating the Planning Process in Schools," *Planning and Changing* (Summer 1985), pp. 82–87.
60. Donald C. Orlich, *Designing Successful Grant Proposals* (Alexandria, VA: Association for Supervision and Curriculum Development, 2002), pp. 1, 3–4.
61. The discussion in this section is based on the authors' experience and observation, coupled with an analysis of a number of studies already mentioned, and by John Daresh, *Factors Supporting or Inhibiting Innovative Practice in Senior High Schools,* an ERIC report, 1981, Ed. 206285.
62. Mathew B. Miles and Karen Seashore Louis, "Mustering the Will and Skill for Change," *Educational Leadership* (vol. 47, no. 8, May 1990), pp. 37–61.
63. Harriet Talmage, "Evaluation of Programs," in Harold E. Mitzel (Ed.), *Encyclopedia of Educational Research* (New York: Free Press, 1982), p. 603. Also see Roland Kimball, "Program Evaluation for School Improvement: Cultivating Excellence–A Curriculum for Excellence in School Administration" (New Hampshire School Administrators Association, June 1989), p. 7.
64. Talmage, "Evaluation of Programs," p. 603.
65. Adaptation and extension of factors identified by Joseph A. Kreskey, "A Critical Review of Procedures and Organizing for Curriculum Improvement in High Schools," EdD dissertation, New York University, 1967, p. 635. An excellent discussion of additional variables and designs for evaluating a variety of programs can be found in Bruce Joyce and Beverly Shower, "Evaluating Staff Development Programs," *Student Achievement through Staff Development* (New York: Longman, 1988), pp. 111–129.
66. Gerald R. Adams and Jay Schvaneveldt, *Understanding Research Methods* (New York: Longman, 1985), section 4; and Blaine R. Worthen and James R. Sanders, *Educational Evaluation: Theory and Practice* (New York: Longman, 1987).
67. See "Leaders for the 21st Century," a theme issue of *Phi Delta Kappan* (vol. 82, no. 6, February 2001).

PART

II

Case Studies and Simulations

Clinical Materials and Learning Experiences for School Administrators and Supervisors

CHAPTER

8

Introduction to Clinical Materials and Learning Experiences

Part II of the book presents a large number of representative case studies, suggested learning activities, and in-basket exercises designed to help the reader become more skilled in using the various concepts discussed in Part I. Because many readers may not be familiar with case study analysis, in-basket experiences, role-playing, or other kinds of clinical experiences, the following sections will discuss these approaches, identifying possible problems and offering strategies for preventing and resolving problems that may develop.

THE NATURE OF CASE STUDIES

Case studies and simulations have been used in training programs for a long time and in many fields of endeavor, including the military, medicine, social work, business management, and education. These approaches have shown wide variation in their content and formats.[1] Although it is hoped that the case studies in this text will provide interesting reading, their primary purpose is to stimulate individual and group involvement in "real-life" situations requiring the application of the concepts in Part I.

The majority of the cases emphasize critical problems in educational administration and supervision. They are organized around particular themes: problems encountered by new administrators; student problems; administrator–staff relationships; school–community relations; administrative role and organizational problems; and problem solving as applied to current issues, such as drugs, violence, disability, ethics, racial and ethnic diversity, and problems related to change.[2] Although most of the problems focus on the principalship, certain cases are devoted to problems associated with other administrative and instructional leadership positions, as in higher education administration, military, and agency training units.

In most of the cases, the characters depicted are either creating problems through their own actions or being confronted with problems resulting from the behavior of others. This emphasis on school problems reflects the primary orientation of the text. The reader should not conclude that administrators and others associated with the schools are *always* creating or facing problems. Nor should the reader assume that the individuals described in the cases are typical of all administrators, supervisors, teachers, parents, or students. Although it should be obvious, it perhaps needs to be pointed out that not all teachers cause problems, not all students are troublesome, and not all administrators behave the way the administrators act in these cases. It is the *problem* dimension of human behavior in school administration, however, rather than the routine duties, that should be studied; and it is this aspect toward which preparation and in-service training programs need to direct most of their attention if prospective and experienced administrators and supervisors are to be equipped with the skills required for the twenty-first century.

Professional licensure societies and state departments of education are increasingly recommending demonstration of professional standards via case study problem solving, vignettes, or decision-making scenarios to either supplement or replace internship experiences in principal preparation programs as part of a licensure test. The 2015 Professional Standards for Educational Leaders (PSEL), formally known as ISLLC standards, identify 10 administrative standards upon which student solutions to the problems must be based.[3] The licensure test is designed to determine the extent to which, for example, a student in a principal preparation program possesses occupation-related knowledge and skills at the time of entry into the principalship. This book can serve as an ideal practice vehicle for an assessment test like PSEL or any other assessment activity requiring hands-on problem solving because the case studies, simulations, and in-basket exercises in Part II are complemented with the requisite theoretical knowledge base presented in Part I. The theoretical knowledge base enables students to appropriate skill applications in solving the many problems and issues confronted in the licensure exam and in the actual administrative positions to which they aspire.

An examination of the cases will reveal that most of them have limited contextual information. For example, the nature of the community and school district, as well as other details that the reader might desire for the resolution of a problem, may be missing. This approach of limiting the available information has been taken for two reasons: (1) It allows for a much larger number of cases to be presented in the text and (2) it provides the instructor or group leader with an excellent opportunity to tailor a case to specific local circumstances by supplementing the case with pertinent situational or demographic details, such as urban versus suburban setting or elementary student body versus secondary.

It should also be noted that the cases in the text are open-ended. While the attempted resolution of subsidiary problems is sometimes described and the application of theoretical concepts from Part I encouraged, the administrator in each case is generally left with the need to resolve a major conflict or dilemma. Some individuals may have mixed feelings about case studies of this type, and there is little doubt that an unresolved problem or conflict will demand more thought and effort from the student and the instructor. However, the cases were constructed on the premise that students would derive greater benefit from cases requiring a resolution to the problems identified than from cases presenting readymade solutions.

ANTICIPATED PROBLEMS IN CASE STUDIES

The case study approach requires a great deal of hard work and effort, and it may at times prove to be frustrating. The purpose of the remainder of this section is to present possible problems that students may experience in responding to a case and to offer suggestions for ameliorating these problems or, at least, placing them in proper perspective.

"There Isn't Enough Information." After perusing a case, the student may complain that insufficient information has been provided about the situation or problem.

Since no case can ever provide more than a partial representation of reality, a certain amount of ambiguity is inevitable and frequently is intentional. Each case has been constructed loosely enough to be adapted to different learning environments.

Because real-life problems are seldom clearly defined or neatly packaged, the student of administration should recognize that in an actual crisis or conflict, rarely will there be readily available all facts and information that could possibly shed light on a matter and facilitate decision making. In the class situation, the individual who is bothered by insufficient information for analysis and resolution can choose either to work with the facts provided or to request the instructor "complete" the case by introducing additional facts and information as new variables.

"This Couldn't Ever Happen to Me." More experienced students sometimes take the position that a problem, issue, or conflict described in a case would never have arisen in their school or school system because things are done differently there. It is entirely possible that the particular circumstances presented in the cases would be unlikely to take place in some schools or districts. It is easier, of course, to reach this conclusion when one is evaluating a situation that has already taken place and has resulted from someone else's error. Almost all administrators make errors in judgment that in retrospect may seem very obvious. Nevertheless, they are faced with the unhappy consequences of that judgment and must proceed to deal with the problem at hand. Perceptive administrators also recognize that problems occasionally develop as a result of action that at the time seemed rather innocuous. It is unlikely that students of administration will improve their problem-solving skills by saying, "This couldn't ever happen to me," so it is incumbent upon these students to assume that such a situation could, indeed, have occurred and to continue the task of solving the resultant problem described in the case.

"I'm Not Sure That I Like This Type of Learning." Case analysis and subsequent role-playing activities place weighty and frequently unfamiliar responsibilities on the shoulders of the learner. Many students are accustomed to attending classes or meetings and doing little more than listening or taking notes on someone else's ideas. Because they are not often required to participate actively in the process of learning, students may initially react with ambivalence or apprehension to requests for their active participation. Consequently, they may withdraw and fail to take part in group discussion or to volunteer for the role-playing activities because they would prefer that the instructor or group leader assume the primary responsibility for what transpires.

If students are to progress in the development of their problem-solving skills, however, it is essential that they become involved in the suggested activities. Their participation in case analysis, group discussion, and role-playing is fundamental to improving their problem-solving abilities and receiving the most benefit from this book. The information in this chapter can assist in the development of sample criteria for assessing these skills.

"I Am Reluctant to Question or Challenge Others." Group discussion of a case requires relatively free interaction among all members of the group. Unfortunately, a few barriers must be surmounted before this goal can be achieved.

Occasionally a group may encounter an initial barrier represented by a dominating instructor or group leader who restricts group discussions to the degree that most of the interaction is between the instructor and one or two students. When the case study approach is utilized, the main obstacle is more typically the reluctance of the participants in the group to challenge each other's points of view. For example, when one member of a group presents an idea, the other members may react in only a limited way, or not at all. This occurs either because they are concentrating on what *they* are going to say next to the group leader or because they are reluctant to react to the comments expressed previously.

The lack of response from the other members of the discussion group to an individual's contribution is obviously a major barrier to the group's reaching the best possible solution to the problem or conflict under consideration. It is only through interaction among the members of the group that such a goal can be accomplished. Students who simply sit quietly without reacting are not contributing to their own growth or to that of the group as a whole. Therefore, each student needs to respond to the other members of the group by raising questions or reacting to ideas or proposals that have been expressed. A free exchange of ideas and thoughts among all members of a group is required in order for each individual and the total group to progress and to determine the best solution to a problem.

"What Did He (or She) Say?" Too frequently the participants in a discussion pay insufficient attention to what others have said and then inadvertently repeat or ignore preceding comments or observations. Sometimes they aren't listening to the speaker at all because they are concentrating on what they are going to say next, or they are thinking about something else.

Paying attention involves listening carefully to what the speaker has to say. Furthermore, it requires *thinking* about what has been said. It is entirely possible for a person to *hear* what has been said without the message registering. Parents accuse their children of letting conversation "go in one ear and out the other," but often adults may be inattentive.

The person who is really paying attention must not only listen to what the speaker is saying but also evaluate the content and implications of the comments. Such a process involves mentally asking, "What is the speaker really saying? Is it true? What assumptions have been made? Does the speaker have all the facts? Does it make sense? What implications should be considered if what was said is true?"

"What about This Solution?" Students will occasionally attempt to ignore or distort the nature of the information presented in the case or will fabricate additional "facts" that will allow the problem to be resolved more easily. Most thoughtful administrators recognize that problem solving is seldom an easy task. Therefore, the person who wants to gain experience and further develop skill in dealing with problems will avoid the easy way out and will concentrate on working with the realities presented in the case.

"There Doesn't Seem to Be Any Solution to This One!" Individuals and groups whose experience with the case study approach and with problem solving in general is rather limited may initially feel, after reading a case, that the problem described is irresolvable. It is true that most of the cases in this book represent difficult and complex problems calling for skills and attitudes that are not immediately or easily acquired. At the same time, however, it should be stated that many of the problems described are no more involved or frustrating than those that today's school administrators face on a regular basis.

Although easier problems could have been selected, it is questionable whether the student of administration would profit greatly from being spoon-fed more simplistic problems or situations. It should also be recognized that few problems in real life have a single, easy, or perfect solution. Fortunately, most issues or problems can be eventually resolved if the student is willing to exert sufficient initiative, imagination, perseverance, and hard thinking.

THE NATURE OF IN-BASKET EXERCISES AND PRIORITY SETTING

Each of the case studies, as discussed previously, provides an opportunity for the reader to focus on a particular situation. Usually only one problem is initially apparent, although complications may be discerned by further analysis.

How In-Basket Exercises Differ from Case Studies

The in-basket exercises provide a different kind of learning opportunity in which the reader can analyze problem situations in school administration and supervision, applying the concepts presented in Chapters 1–7. Rather than offering only one task to accomplish or one problem to address, as in the case studies, the in-basket exercises present a large number of representative problems and situations.[4] Although the typical administrator or supervisor may not *often* be confronted with a large number of problems within a short time frame, such circumstances do arise in actuality, so prospective administrators and supervisors need to gain experience in responding effectively to myriad problems of varying complexity in a time-critical setting.

The scope of the problems presented and the limited time frame within which to address them stress the importance of setting priorities. Few administrators have the luxury of dealing with a single problem at a time or taking as much time as they would like to resolve a situation. Problems and assigned tasks frequently arrive in bunches, and an administrator must decide what should be addressed first, second, and so forth. Therefore, it is essential for a prospective administrator to develop skills in establishing priorities.

At this point the reader may be asking, "But *how* do I establish priorities?" Although there is probably no best way to establish priorities that will be effective for every situation, the following guidelines extracted from a review of the literature and interviews with successful administrators have been designed to help the readers of this text to improve their priority-setting skills.

Guidelines for Priority Setting

For effective priority setting, the reader needs to examine a number of factors that may influence the level of a priority to be assigned to any particular problem or task (within a larger set of problems or tasks to be addressed or accomplished). Those factors are identified in Figure 8.1, which presents an overview of the *process* of priority designation.

How Many Problems or Tasks Require a Response? The first factor to consider in priority setting is the *number* of problems and tasks for which priorities must be established. In other words, how many problems and/or assigned tasks require an administrative response? If only two or three problems or assigned tasks must be addressed, then priority setting may not be as important, and the administrator may be able to take more time in the process than if many problems and tasks call for a response.

In general, a fairly useful guideline is this: *The more problems and/or assigned tasks that call for an administrative response, the more decisive the administrator needs to be in evaluating the other factors identified in* Figure 8.1 *and in deciding the priority of each problem and assigned task.* Effective participation in the in-basket exercises presented in this book will require the reader's *decisiveness* because of the large number of problems and assigned tasks represented.

■ **FIGURE 8.1**
PRIORITY DESIGNATION

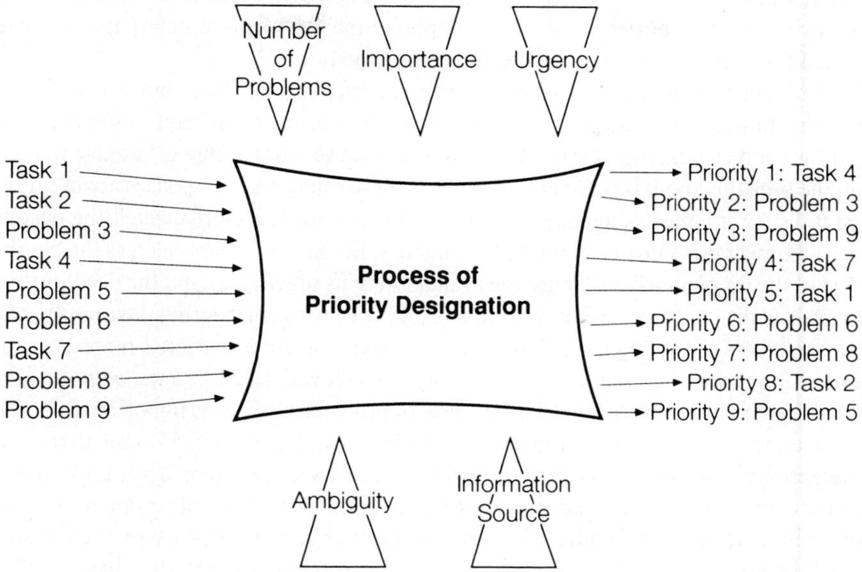

How Important Is Each Problem or Task? Considering the number of problems and assigned tasks to be prioritized is not the only factor in effective priority setting. The reader also needs to consider the *importance* of each problem or assigned task. But the reader may wonder, "How does one *determine* importance?" Although some people may equate *importance* with *urgency*–another factor, to be discussed in the next section–the authors offer a different perspective on *importance.* We evaluate the importance of a problem or assigned task in terms of the possible consequences of an incorrect or ineffective decision on a particular problem or assigned task.

Those problems or assigned tasks that are most likely to result in *significant negative* consequences if an incorrect decision is made regarding their solution or implementation should be assigned a higher priority than those problems or tasks that are most likely to result in few, if any, negative consequences for the administrator (in the event that an incorrect decision is made in trying to address them). The more serious the potential consequences of an incorrect administrative action on a problem or assigned task, the higher the priority that should be given to that problem or task. Giving a problem or task a higher priority generally means that it will receive *more attention sooner* than a lower-priority problem or task. Obviously, those problems or tasks with the greatest potentially negative consequences in the aftermath of an incorrect decision demand more immediate and more extensive attention than other kinds of problems and tasks that carry fewer potentially damaging consequences.

How Urgent Is a Response to Each Problem or Task? The *urgency* of each problem and assigned task is, perhaps, the factor with which most readers are more familiar in priority setting. Urgency is defined in this discussion as the explicit or implicit deadline by which a problem or assigned task must be addressed.

Many assigned tasks or problems are presented with specific deadlines. For example, the superintendent may request a particular report from all principals by a certain date. A parent's letter about a certain problem that a son is experiencing with a teacher may request a response from the principal by a particular date. A telephone message from a newspaper reporter may request that the principal respond to the call within the hour.

Other problems or assigned tasks may not carry explicit deadlines, but a deadline may be *implicit* in the message to the administrator. For example, a teacher may request some action by the principal "as soon as possible." Or the principal may receive a bomb threat message that does not mention the time the bomb is set to go off. Each of these examples of messages about problems or assigned tasks communicates an explicit or implicit deadline. The more explicit the deadline, the easier the administrator's task of evaluating its urgency. But in some cases, such as the bomb threat, the *nature* of the problem will influence the evaluation of its urgency, even if the deadline for action is unstated. The difficulty many administrators experience with considering the urgency of a problem or assigned task is failing to recognize that the deadline communicated represents someone else's expectation. Whether that expectation should be met will depend on the *administrator's* consideration of other factors associated with the task or problem, such as its importance or ambiguity.

For instance, suppose the administrator receives a message at 8:55 A.M. that requests a return telephone call to a tennis partner by 9 A.M. The message seems urgent, given the deadline for returning the call. The administrator may know that it is not an *important* deadline, however, based on the personality of the tennis partner and the history of their association. Suppose, further, the administrator has been given other messages that have later or less explicit deadlines but that are potentially more important, such as a bomb threat. Clearly, the urgency of a message needs to be compared with the pressing needs of other messages to be addressed; furthermore, urgency should not be the *sole* factor considered in determining the priority of a particular problem or assigned task.

How Clear or Ambiguous Is the Problem or Task Requiring a Response? The *ambiguity* of a problem or task is another factor that a prospective administrator should learn to consider in establishing priorities. Two types of ambiguities may characterize a problem: (1) the content of a message and (2) the nature of a problem or task to be addressed.

Some messages will be more ambiguous than others. The individual communicating the message may deliberately have chosen to be cryptic in expressing a problem, or the communication may be unintentionally vague or lacking in the detail needed to evaluate its priority. On the other hand, even if the description of a problem or assigned task is clear, the characteristics of the problem or assigned task may be highly complex, making it difficult for an administrator to determine how best to proceed.

As an example, the superintendent may want each principal to prepare a report on how the school could raise its student test scores by 10 percent. The message seems clear enough, and if the superintendent stated that she wanted the report in a month, then the urgency of the matter could also be evaluated. Certainly the fact that the request is coming from the superintendent suggests the *importance* of addressing the request successfully. A major question remaining is, What would be involved in the preparation of such a report that would meet the superintendent's expectation and goal? In this case, the nature and scope of the superintendent's requests are ambiguous because the extent and time commitment of the activity are not readily discernible.

Administrators frequently must deal with problems and tasks that differ in their ambiguity. In general, the more ambiguous a problem or assigned task, the higher the priority that should be assigned. As with any other factor, ambiguity should never be the only consideration. All the factors in Figure 8.1 should be evaluated for every problem and assigned task before determining each one's priority. Obviously, the judgment that will be reached during this process will weigh certain factors more heavily than others. The reader should avoid any tendency to focus on only one, or even two factors, however, while ignoring the others.

How Knowledgeable or Trustworthy Is the Information Source? The last factor shown in Figure 8.1 on the lower right is one rarely, if ever, mentioned in the professional literature. Nevertheless, in priority setting it is important to ascertain the potential "information value" of the person communicating a message about a certain problem or task. Is that individual likely to be as knowledgeable as an *information source* concerning that issue? A certain messenger may be familiar with various aspects about only one particular problem or task but know little or nothing about other pertinent factors that must be weighed. On the other hand, if the messenger is also likely to be aware of some other problem facing the administrator, or about some of the individuals involved in other problem situations, then the problem or task that this messenger has presented should be given a higher priority than would otherwise be true. By giving that problem a higher priority, the administrator will likely contact this particular message sender before giving attention to the concerns of other messengers. By so doing, he or she will not only be working toward a resolution of that particular problem but may also be gaining potentially valuable information about some other significant problems or individuals.

Key information sources in the school are likely to be such people as assistant principals, secretaries, department chairs, and custodians, as well as informal leaders (see Chapter 6). Therefore, even when these information sources present problems that do not intrinsically warrant a high priority, the administrator may increase the priority ranking because of the messenger's potential for offering additional information that could contribute to a better understanding of *other* problems.

Although it may seem to the reader that setting priorities is a very complex and time-consuming process, additional experience with the process will increase proficiency and reveal shortcuts. Learning the skill of priority setting is hardly different from learning any other skill, such as learning how to drive. Given an effective procedure for developing the skill, all that remains are practice and experience, and before long, the application of the skill becomes automatic, and the time required is reduced significantly. One of the purposes of the in-basket exercises in this book is to give prospective administrators an opportunity to practice and gain experience with setting priorities.

Keeping Track of Priorities with a Priority Worksheet As readers prioritize the various problems and tasks included in each in-basket exercise, they are advised to assign each of these problems or tasks one of three levels of priority: high, moderate, or low. The sample worksheet in Table 8.1 has been designed to facilitate the assignment of priorities. To provide the reader with a better idea of how the form is to be used, the form has been completed, based on a hypothetical set of problems and tasks.

In examining an in-basket exercise, the reader will note that each of the items has been numbered to make it easier in a class situation to direct attention to a particular problem. The assigned numbers also facilitate the use of a priority worksheet, obviating any need to write out a description or title for each in-basket item.

It should also be emphasized that the number of items that should be assigned high, moderate, or low priority in any given in-basket exercise will depend on many factors, including the

TABLE 8.1
PRIORITY WORKSHEET

High-Priority Items	*Moderate-Priority Items*	*Low-Priority Items*
1	5	2
3	7	6
4	8	10
9	11	13
18	12	15
14	16	20
	17	
	19	

time of year and the kind of school being administered. The profile in Table 8.1 is, therefore, only a hypothetical one, and it is not intended to be illustrative of any typical set of circumstances.

In-Basket Problem Solving

The problems presented in these exercises differ from the case studies not so much in their nature or severity as in the amount of information provided. The paucity of information available in the messages underscores the importance of the first step in decision making—namely, attempting to define more precisely the nature of the problem or situation. (It should be emphasized that the reader will also need to utilize other relevant concepts presented in Chapters 1–7 in solving the problems described in the in-basket material, but the nature of the in-basket items makes *essential* the reader's attention to problem definition, the all-important first step in any decision making.)

The crucial questions that the reader needs to be asking while first addressing an in-basket problem are, What do I know and what *don't* I know about this situation? and How, or from whom, could I obtain more information in order to define more accurately the nature of this problem? Figure 8.2 illustrates the process involved in defining more precisely the nature of a problem and shows how this process leads to the next step of problem solving: the generation of *alternatives.*

Once the reader becomes proficient in applying the concepts in Part I, it will not usually be necessary to *write* out the analysis and describe the steps to be taken. In fact, in a crisis situation (such as a student's threatening a teacher with a knife) the administrator obviously wouldn't be able to take time to write it up even though it might be desirable. In those circumstances that do not involve an immediate crisis, but do possess potentially long-range, serious consequences, the administrator should attempt to write out the analysis of the problem and a proposed plan of action, time permitting. Frequently the act of putting ideas on paper helps to clarify them and to assess considerations that may have initially only *appeared* to be sound in the conceptual process. (Further consideration of one's own written thoughts often may reveal gaps in logic or errors or lead to additional insights.)

Although the overall discussion of ways to respond effectively to the in-basket exercises has been designed to be helpful to the readers, the authors recognize that, initially at least, the

FIGURE 8.2
PROBLEM DEFINITION PROCESS

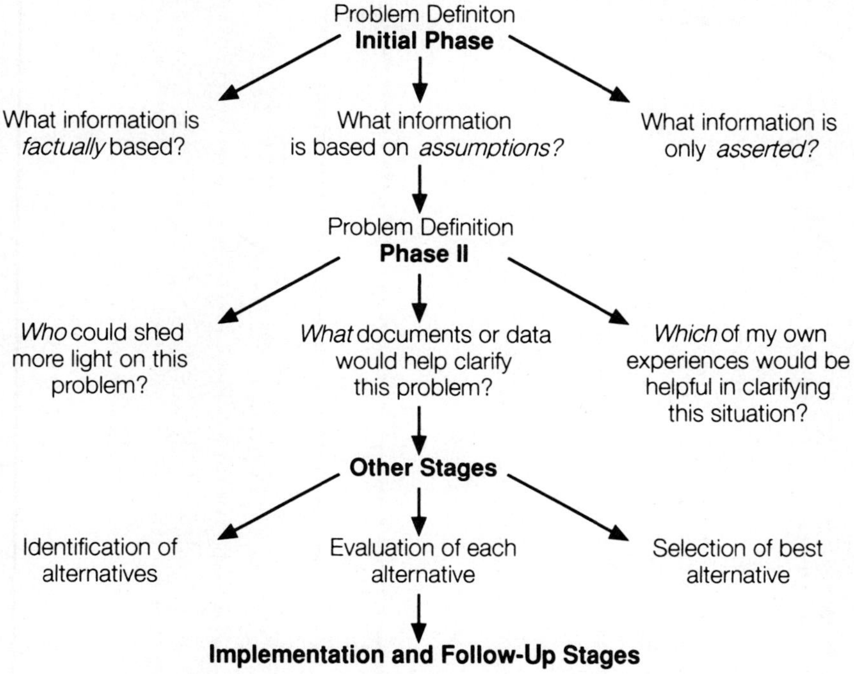

process and analysis of problem solving may be somewhat overwhelming and may even temporarily complicate matters. Pilot testing of the guidelines on priority setting and the suggestions on problem solving, however, has shown that after readers gain some practical experience in applying them, these recommendations prove to be very helpful. The key for the reader is to be persistent and patient in applying the process. As in developing most other skills, the initial stages may be difficult, but with continued practice, things get easier.

A FINAL NOTE

In the following chapters a large number of case studies, suggested learning activities, and in-basket exercises are presented. Although there are more materials and activities than any reader or group is likely to complete, the variety represented should provide a sufficient opportunity to gain experience in applying the concepts presented in Part I and, more specifically, this chapter. The cases, simulations, and in-basket activities offer additional insight into the reality of school administration and supervision and the essential role of school leaders and effective leadership based on knowledge and skills–in other words, *standards*–to promote student success.

Readers should note that at the end of each concept chapter in Part I of this text, specific case studies and in-basket exercises are identified that can be used to the best advantage for applying the ideas in that chapter. Additionally, a matrix of cases is presented on pages 226–229 for professors wishing to focus on specific leadership skills or concepts.

#	*Case*	*Leadership*	*Decision Making*	*Authority, Power, and Influence*	*Communication*	*Conflict Management*	*Organizational Culture*	*Change*
1	Preparing for the Job Search				X			
2	From Teacher to Administrator	X						
3	The New Principal (In-Basket Activities)	X	X	X	X	X	X	X
4	The New Assistant Principal (In-Basket Activities)	X	X	X	X	X	X	X
5	Resentment over Appointment	X						
6	Do I Need to Act Like a Man to Be a Leader?	X						
7	Dragging and Sagging: Is It Fashion, Expression, or a Violation?	X						
8	Is Being Busy Necessarily Productive?	X						
9	Changing Demographics and Teacher Attitudes							
10	Matter of What?							
11	School Yard Dangers	X						
12	What Should Be the Role of the Student Newspaper?	X						
13	A Complex Discipline Problem	X						
14	The Dropout Problem (Simulation Exercise)				X	X		
15	Student Can't Take Pressure Any Longer				X			
16	"Zero Tolerance" for Weapons in Schools				X			
17	Student Drug Problem at Washington School	X						

#	Case	*Leadership*	*Decision Making*	*Authority, Power, and Influence*	*Communication*	*Conflict Management*	*Organizational Culture*	*Change*
18	What to Do about the "Morning After"?		X					
19	Working with Students with Disabilities and IDEA							
20	Student-Formed Gay–Straight Alliance							
21	Teacher Selection		X	X		X		
22	Problems of a Beginning Teacher		X					
23	Faculty Teamwork	X					X	
24	Who Needs Lesson Plans?							
25	Teacher Rights: Public vs. Private Citizenship		X			X		
26	Faculty Dissatisfaction and Low Morale					X		
27	Teacher Files a Grievance						X	
28	Teacher Reacts Negatively to Personnel Evaluation			X				
29	Faculty Slowdown			X		X		
30	Do Women Have Power?						X	
31	Collaboration Woes	X		X				
32	Curriculum Unit Upsets Parents	X				X		
33	Communication and Constructed Reality					X		
34	Parental Apathy	X	X					
35	Wanted: A Plan for Improving Parental and Community Involvement		X					

#	Case	Leadership	Decision Making	Authority, Power, and Influence	Communication	Conflict Management	Organizational Culture	Change
36	The School–Community Web	X						
37	Developing Student Talent	X						
38	A New Role for the Parents' Organization				X			
39	How Much Should Parents Be Told?			X				
40	Administrator–Press Relations				X			
41	Public Relations: What's Really Important?	X						
42	Censorship or Parents' Rights?					X		
43	Financial Crisis!			X				
44	Integration: An Old/New Problem							
45	Parents Challenge Racial Disparity							
46	Principal's Midyear Problems and Priorities (In-Basket Activities)	X	X	X	X	X	X	X
47	Principal's End-of-the-Year Problems and Priorities (In-Basket Activities)	X	X	X	X	X	X	X
48	Principal's Dilemma						X	
49	Principal's Personal Conduct Results in Possible Suspension	X						
50	Supervisor–Principal Relationship							
51	The Superintendent and the New School Board Members	X						

#	Case	*Leadership*	*Decision Making*	*Authority, Power, and Influence*	*Communication*	*Conflict Management*	*Organizational Culture*	*Change*
52	Administrator Evaluation	X						
53	Teacher Tries to Individualize Instruction			X				X
54	Effective Schools: How Do We Get There from Here? (A Group Activity)							X
55	Planning for Improvement		X					X
56	School-Based Management						X	X
57	Restructuring Staff Evaluation and Supervision		X					X
58	Changing the Role of the Building Principal	X	X					X
59	In-Service or Disservice Education? Part I							X
60	In-Service or Disservice Education? Part II	X						X
61	School Choice	X						X
62	School District Chips Away at Student Technology Literacy Problems							X
63	When NCLB Meets You at Your School Door	X	X		X			
64	Do Extreme Times Call for Radical Action? (A Leaderless Group Activity)	X						
65	Teacher Difficulty in a Multicultural Climate							

NOTES

1. For additional sources of clinical materials and learning experiences, see Carl R. Asbaugh and Katherine L. Kasten, *Educational Leadership: Case Studies for Reflective Practice* (New York: Longman, 1991), and *Simulations and Games,* an ERIC bibliography, Ed. 288877; Sanford F. Borins, "Simulation: The Case Method and Case Studies: Their Role in Public Management Teaching and Research," *Canadian Public Administration* (Summer 1990), pp. 214-228; George Thornton and Jeannette N. Cleveland, "Developing Management Talent through Simulation," *American Psychologist* (February 1990), pp. 51-58; and Gwendoline Williams, *The Case Method: An Approach to Teaching and Learning in Educational Administration,* an ERIC report, Ed. 270136. See also Edwin M. Bridges and Philip Hallinger, *Problem-Based Learning in Leadership Development,* an ERIC book, 1995; Reginald L. Green, *Practicing the Art of Leadership: A Problem-Based Approach to Implementing the ISLLC Standards* (Upper Saddle River, NJ: Prentice Hall, 2001); and Williman Sharp, James K. Walter, and Helen M. Sharp, *Case Studies for School Leaders: Implementing the ISLLC Standards* (Lanham, MD: Scarecrow/Technomic, 1998).
2. Periodic surveys, interviews, and observations of beginning and experienced administrators and supervisors by Richard A. Gorton provide strong support for the kinds of cases presented in Part II of the text.
3. National Policy Board for Educational Administration, *Professional Standards for Educational Leaders 2015* (Reston, VA: Author, 2015).
4. For an early use of the in-basket approach in assessing school administrators' performance, see John K. Hemphill et al., *Administrative Performance and Personality* (New York: Columbia University, Bureau of Publication, 1962). Later uses of in-basket exercises by NASSP Assessment Centers throughout the United States and ETS School Leaders' Licensure Assessment are well documented.

CHAPTER

9

Beginning Challenges

Beginning a new job can be a challenging experience. Whether you are a neophyte starting your first year as an administrator or an experienced administrator who has obtained a different position in another school or school district, there are certain adjustments to be made and problems to be faced that may be caused or complicated by your unfamiliarity with the new circumstances.

The case studies and related exercises presented in this chapter represent the kinds of problems and issues that can surface when you seek, and then assume, an administrative position in a new situation. The first case presents some of the challenges involved in seeking and preparing for a first job interview in school administration. The next case describes some of the frustrations and considerations involved in obtaining an entry position in school administration, moving to a different city, planning for the beginning of a new school year, and starting to develop relationships with other people at the school. Following this case are two in-basket exercises, one involving a new principal, the other a new assistant principal. Both in-basket exercises place the reader in a new administrator's position at the beginning of the school year and include a large number of representative problems and issues that could confront any school administrator who takes a new position in different circumstances. (Chapter 13 presents two additional in-basket exercises involving the same new principal, with midyear problems and end-of-the-year problems.)

After the in-basket exercises, the reader will find a case involving a teacher promoted to assistant principal. This case presents possible effects on relationships with former peers. The following two case studies focus on female administrators, including an assistant principal. For most individuals who obtain an entry position in school administration, that position will be an assistant principalship, especially if it is in a secondary school. In addition, in recent years, the number of women entering the field of school administration has increased significantly—although the number of female administrators is still not proportional to the number of women in the field of education. Perceptions and practices of administrators and their colleagues are often affected by societal attitudes toward gender. Therefore, a major emphasis on both the assistant principalship and on female administrators seems appropriate in a chapter entitled "Beginning Challenges." (It should be noted, however, that the problems experienced in these two case studies could, for the most part, be faced by any beginning administrator.)

The final case study describes a common problem for many administrators, experienced as well as novice: time management. By analyzing the behavior of the administrator in this case study, discussing the larger issues, addressing the problems identified in "Be a Problem Solver," testing the solutions that are reached, and further investigating related matters, the reader should gain insights on how to become a more perceptive and more competent manager of time.

It should be emphasized that most, if not all, of the problems and issues presented in the case studies and in-basket exercises require considerable analysis, discussion, and problem solving. Therefore, appropriate utilization of the ideas contained in Part I (and in Chapter 8) and participation in the suggested learning activities at the end of each case study will be important.

1
PREPARING FOR THE JOB SEARCH

It was now February, and Wes Johnson was in the final semester of his administrator preparation program. He wouldn't be certified as an administrator until after the present semester, but he wanted to get started with his plans for seeking employment.

It had been seven years since Wes had last sought a new job, so he was a little fuzzy about all the elements in the process. He knew that he probably needed to begin a new placement file, and should get some recommendations for it. He didn't know whether he should also prepare a résumé, but he decided that he probably should.

Other ideas he had been exploring in his own mind were whether to direct that his placement file be sent only to those school districts where the university placement office informed him that vacancies existed or whether to send a copy of his résumé to other school districts where he wanted to work, but where there were no current vacancies. (That way, he thought, he would be in on the ground floor with the latter group of school districts if an administrative vacancy did occur.)

Tomorrow, Wes decided, he would begin his work on the résumé and then initiate steps to develop his placement file.

Sarah Santee was disappointed with the way her job search for an administrator vacancy was progressing. It was already June and, thus far, she had not obtained any job interviews. She couldn't figure out why no one had contacted her.

Sarah had been a teacher for six years, had completed her administrator preparation program last December with excellent grades, and had also received very good recommendations for her placement file regarding her potential as a future administrator. (She had established an open file with the placement office, so she knew the content of the recommendations.)

What was going on, she wondered? She had been tempted to call or write some of the school districts that had sent her letters of rejection to ask them why she hadn't even been given an interview. (Typically, the rejection letters were very general and not especially instructive.) But she decided not to follow up, for fear that the school districts might think she was being too aggressive.

On Tuesday of the next week, however, Sarah received a letter from the people in one of the school districts where she had recently applied, inviting her to contact them to schedule a job interview. Sarah was elated, although the school district was located in another part of the state with which she was not too familiar.

Sarah called the school district immediately and set up an interview for the following week. She had about 10 days to get ready for the interview. The question now was what she should be doing during those 10 days to prepare herself.

Suggested Learning Activities

Analyze the Case

1. What is your evaluation of Wes Johnson's decision making and planning? What assumptions does he seem to be making?
2. What might be some possible reasons Sarah Santee has not been getting any job interviews until now? Is there anything she may be doing or not doing that has hampered her in securing interviews?
3. What are the advantages and disadvantages of Sarah Santee's attitude toward seeking more informative responses from school districts regarding the reasons for her rejection?

Discuss the Larger Issues

1. To what extent does a university department or college have the responsibility for helping the students prepare a placement file and prepare for job interviews?
2. What should be the role of an individual university adviser in helping the advisees to find a job?
3. What are the advantages and disadvantages of open file recommendations?
4. What is the responsibility of school districts to help applicants to better understand why they were not selected for interviews and/or the job itself?
5. To what degree are there ethical considerations that should be observed in the preparation of placement files? A résumé? Conducting a job interview?

Be a Problem Solver Assume that you are, first, Wes Johnson and, second, Sarah Santee. What decisions need to be made and steps taken in order for you to be successful? (For Wes, the initial objective is to obtain job interviews; for Sarah, it is getting the job.) Utilize relevant concepts from Part I of the text.

Test Your Solution To test your thinking about the problems just presented, you and the class should create and role-play one of the following situations:

1. Prepare a résumé, and have the class and/or instructor critique it.
2. Discuss the kinds of people you should contact to ask for recommendations, and have the class and/or instructor critique your choices.
3. Simulate a job interview. Videotape it, and have the class and the instructor critique it.

Investigate Further

1. Investigate the extent of services offered by your university placement office regarding the preparation of a placement file and résumé and approaches to interviewing.
2. Consult with your university adviser about possible steps you need to take to secure an administrative position in education.

3. Interview your administrative superior or superiors in your present school district to ascertain what advice they might offer you in seeking an administrative vacancy.
4. Ascertain what books your library might have available on preparing résumés and job interviewing.

2
FROM TEACHER TO ADMINISTRATOR

This was his first job as a principal. He had been a teacher for several years and had obtained his master's degree in educational administration the preceding summer. Last spring he had looked around for a position in administration, but nothing seemed to be available for someone with no previous administrative experience.

During the summer he had gradually accepted the idea of another year of teaching, but in mid-August he had received a call from the superintendent of a small school district that was looking for a building principal. The former principal had just resigned to take a job in a larger school system, and since classes were scheduled to begin in two weeks, the superintendent was anxious to hire someone to fill the vacancy. Within a few days, after several telephone conversations and a personal interview, the superintendent had offered him the job.

Although the offer had been rather flattering, he had experienced mixed emotions about accepting it. It had bothered him a little to think about requesting a release from his own school district so late in the year, although he had been fairly sure that there would be no problem in obtaining it. He had also had reservations about working in such a small school system and community. Still, he had realized that a person had to start somewhere, and this job would at least provide him with experience. So with that thought in mind, he had accepted the position.

His decision had precipitated the need for numerous other decisions within the next week and a half. Such matters as putting his home up for sale and locating suitable housing for his family in the new community had to be taken care of, and before he knew it, the time that he had hoped to spend learning about the educational program of the district and planning for the opening of school had almost dwindled away.

Now, with only two days left before the faculty was to return for its annual fall workshop, the principal began to panic a little. He still hadn't come to a decision about which items should be covered during the two-day teacher workshop, and he was beginning to become concerned about how the teachers would react to him as their new principal. Several of them had stopped by the previous day, but it was difficult to tell how they felt about him. He suspected that he was younger than many of the faculty members, and he had misgivings about how the older and more experienced teachers might perceive him. He had also started to experience some uncertainty about how well the students and their parents were going to accept him. Although he had always gotten along all right with both groups while he was a teacher, he wasn't sure that they would respond to him the same way now that he was a principal.

He wondered whether he was ready for all the responsibilities that a principal had to handle. He recalled that in the past he had never been especially awed by the principal's duties, but, from this new perspective, things seemed to look a lot different.

Suggested Learning Activities

Analyze the Case

1. What additional questions or reservations might the new principal have raised about resigning from his teaching position in mid-August? What is your evaluation of the thought process that the principal went through prior to accepting the new position?
2. If the principal had taken sufficient time, what specific aspects of the educational program of the district should he have investigated, and what plans should he have made for the teacher workshop and the opening of school?
3. Assess the validity of the concerns expressed by the principal with respect to gaining the acceptance of the faculty, the students, and the parents.

Discuss the Larger Issues

1. What are the ethical considerations with regard to requesting a release from a present contract to accept a better position somewhere else?
2. How important is it for an administrator to be accepted by the faculty, student body, and the parents? What are the advantages and disadvantages of such acceptance?

Be a Problem Solver The principal of the school has no administrative experience and is concerned about the fast-approaching teachers' in-service workshop and about establishing good relationships with teachers, students, and parents. If you were the principal, what would you do? What assumptions would you make? Utilize ISLLC standards and administrative and social science concepts from Part I of the text in planning and implementing your approach.

Test Your Solution To test your proposed plan of action, you and the class should create and role-play one or more of the following situations:

1. The principal as he begins the first day of the two-day workshop.
2. The principal in his first formal meeting with the student body.
3. The principal at the first Parent Teacher Association (PTA) meeting.

Investigate Further

1. What does research suggest are the expectations that teachers hold for the behavior of the principal?
2. What do new principals believe to be the most difficult aspects of the first year as an administrator?

3
THE NEW PRINCIPAL (IN-BASKET ACTIVITIES)

Background

You are Dr. Brown. You were approved by the school board on August 11 to succeed Mr. Sanders as principal of Kennedy School. Due to a death in your family, however, you were unable to report to Kennedy School until the weekend of August 22–23. You have arrived at the school on Saturday morning to look at your mail and start organizing things.

Specific information about the context of this situation, including a description of the school, the district, and the community, has not been provided in order that these details might be varied, depending on the composition of the class or group and the objectives of the instructor. Information of this nature may be provided by the instructor, to the extent needed and at an appropriate time.

Instructions

1. You will be given 90 minutes to read and take action on all the in-basket items presented following the instructions. You are not expected merely to *describe* what you would do, but to *do* it. For example, if you decide to write a letter, then compose the letter. If you decide to telephone a person or see someone for a conference, then outline your objectives, as well as the main points or questions that you would present. (Utilize relevant concepts from Part I of the text in your responses.)
2. Each in-basket item requires a separate action that you should present on another sheet of paper, adding the identification number in the upper-left-hand corner of the in-basket item. Although the in-basket items are numbered, you may deal with them in whatever sequence you prefer; however, you should indicate on your response sheet the priority number that you have assigned to each item: 1 for high priority, 2 for moderate priority, and 3 for low priority.
3. Proceed to address the in-basket items.

IN-BASKET ITEM #1

August 19

Dear Dr. Brown:

I am writing you to request a meeting to establish a Parent Council for the school. I was a member of the PTA that folded a couple of years ago because of a lack of leadership from the principal. What we need now is a new parent group with more responsibility and more enlightened leadership from the principal than we have received in the past. As someone with an advanced degree, I am sure you support parent involvement in education.

I look forward to working with you.

Sincerely,
Peggy Kim
Parent

IN-BASKET ITEM #2

Telephone Message

FOR: Dr. Brown
FROM: Tom Roberts (*State Journal*)
TIME: August 14 9:30 A.M.

Please call back. The newspaper would like to do a feature on you as the new principal, and I need to set up a time for interviewing you and some of the teachers and students.

IN-BASKET ITEM #3

Dr. Brown,

I hope that things are going to be better this year on the first day of school than they were last year. Last year I had to begin classes without enough textbooks, and some important supplies, like chalk, didn't arrive until Friday of the first week. I know you are new and you have a lot on your mind, but teachers think it is important that classes run smoothly on the first day of school. With your help, I hope we can get off to a better beginning.

Pattie Quinn

IN-BASKET ITEM #4

Dear Dr. Brown:

First of all, welcome to Kennedy School. From all I have heard, you should bring some much needed leadership to the school.

The reason I am writing you (I tried to get in to see you but your secretary said you weren't seeing anyone for a while) is that I would like you to emphasize at the first meeting with the teachers the importance of consistently enforcing the discipline rules, especially the rules on students being on time to class with appropriate materials to work with (you know, like pencils and paper–that kind of stuff) and the gum-chewing rule. The last two years things have been deteriorating, and last spring was a mess–too much teacher inconsistency. I don't like to complain about my colleagues, but something has got to be done before the kids take over the school. What this school needs is a real crackdown. I have heard that you're the type that is prepared to "bite the bullet," and in my judgment that time has definitely arrived.

Sincerely,
Bill Stone

IN-BASKET ITEM #5

August 17

Dear Dr. Brown:

The purpose of this letter is to request your approval to conduct a study on the impact of new leadership at the school site level. The study would employ ethnographic methods–essentially, shadowing and interviews—of your first six months on the job. I am trying to ascertain the kind of impact a new principal can have on a school. Having a doctorate yourself, you value research, I am sure, and can appreciate the need for someone like myself—a doctoral student—to complete my dissertation.

Thank you in advance for your interest and cooperation. I look forward to hearing from you.

Sincerely,
Bob Turtle
Doctoral Student

IN-BASKET ITEM #6

July 17

MEMO

TO: Principals
FROM: Assistant Superintendent

All principals should remind teachers at the first faculty meeting before school begins this year that *all* teachers will be evaluated, using the new Teacher Accountability Evaluation form that the school board approved last year. Also, principals should emphasize at this first meeting that teachers need to be more careful in using their sick leave days, as there were apparent abuses last year.

IN-BASKET ITEM #7

Dear Dr. Brown:

I would like to have a *confidential* conference with you to discuss an urgent matter in regard to another staff member. I have been reluctant to say anything until now, but I feel this is something you would want to know. I must, however, have your written commitment that you will keep all of this *strictly confidential,* including the fact that I would be telling you this. I really don't want to be involved or implicated in any way.

Hazel Smith

IN-BASKET ITEM #8

August 20

Dear Dr. Brown:

You don't know me, but I have been a substitute teacher in this school from time to time for the last several years. I don't like to complain because I am really not that kind of person, and, besides, I really like the school. But I feel there are a few things that you should know about, and maybe some improvements will result. They didn't with Mr. Sanders, but I have heard that you are a real "take-charge" person, and certainly there are some things about this school that need to be improved. I don't think this is the time and place to go into all of the various problems, but there is one thing that I would hope could be changed immediately, and that is the lack of lesson plans that substitute teachers encounter when they come to school. Rarely have I found (and I am not alone in this regard) an up-to-date lesson plan from a teacher who is absent for that day. And frequently I can't find any lesson plan at all. A substitute teacher's job is tough enough, but without a decent lesson plan, it is terrible.

As a parent with children in this district, I certainly have to wonder about the quality of planning by teachers, and since Mr. Sanders didn't take any action, one also wonders whether administrators really care or are willing to take a tough stand with teachers. I hope that with new leadership at the school something can be done about this deplorable situation.

Sincerely,
(Mrs.) Ruth White

IN-BASKET ITEM #9

Dr. Brown–

We may have to shut off the water for a short time during the first week of school to repair the main boiler. I know this is a bad time to be shutting off the water, and we hope it won't be necessary. Sam and I are trying to get the thing fixed ourselves, but we have to call upstate to see if we can get it done. They can't get here until the week after the Labor Day weekend and even that is uncertain. I am trying to get them to come at night. I'll get back to you if anything changes.

Al
Head Custodian

IN-BASKET ITEM #10

Dear Dr. Brown:

I hope this year is going to be different. At least with a new principal there is hope. I live near the school, and for several years now, I have had trouble with students vandalizing my flowers. I have complained to the principal before, but Mr. Sanders only said he "would look into it," but nothing was ever done. I hope this year SOMETHING will be done. Maybe you could say something to the students at the first assembly program or maybe over the PA system. I know something has got to be done this year, or I am going to the school board. It's not right. I am a taxpayer who pays for these schools, and I don't even have any kids. I want something done!

Alice Snap

IN-BASKET ITEM #11

August 1

MEMO

TO: All Principals
FROM: The Superintendent

Please clear your calendars for Monday afternoon of the second week of school for a meeting in my conference room to discuss how we can improve student achievement test scores for each of your schools. Bring your ideas!

IN-BASKET ITEM #12

July 20

Dear Mr. Sanders:

I am president of the Council on Children's Problems, and we would like to present an assembly program to your students this fall on child abuse. As you know, child abuse is a very pervasive problem, and all of us must do everything that we can to prevent this kind of problem from happening to any child, regardless of age and regardless of who the abuser is. Our assembly program is very stimulating with many activities and experiences available.

I look forward to hearing from you as to when it would be possible to present our program.

Sincerely,
Ted Allen, President
Council on Children's Problems

IN-BASKET ITEM #13

Dr. Brown–

You might want to give some thought to what you are going to do with the teachers during the preschool in-service day. Mr. Sanders sort of "played it by ear," but maybe you have something specific in mind. I know the faculty will be interested in hearing your views at the first meeting. (Also, do you want to send any message to parents?)

Peg Albright
[principal's secretary]

IN-BASKET ITEM #14

Mr. Sanders:

I will need to leave school a little early each Monday this fall (10 minutes after dismissal) to get to my university class. I know you will understand since you are working on your advanced degree too. Plus, I always stay late on other nights anyway, and other teachers have left early in the past.

Mary Eager
Teacher

IN-BASKET ITEM #15

August 17

Dear Dr. Brown,

We tried to get an appointment to see you, but your secretary said you were going to be too busy to see people until you got your feet on the ground.

Anyway, we would like to use this letter to formally recommend that you eliminate hall passes for this coming school year. Hall passes are demeaning to students and reflect a lack of trust on the part of the faculty and administration toward students.

We recognize that there are a few students who can't be trusted, and they probably do need hall passes. But why should the rest of us be penalized for the few?

We have been told that you graduated with a doctor's degree from one of the leading universities. We would hope that you would bring a more enlightened view of students to this school. Let's all start out fresh this year by trusting one another. Are you willing to take the first step? We have!

Sincerely,
Jack Staker
Camilla Black
Bill Elliot
Student Council Representatives

IN-BASKET ITEM #16

Dr. Brown,

I hope that you can do something this coming year about the litter in the hallways and in the cafeteria during lunch. Maybe you could say something to the teachers during your first meeting with them. The last few years, things have really gotten out of hand. We need to crack down and take responsibility for ourselves.

Sam Clean
Custodian

IN-BASKET ITEM #17

July 15

Dear Mr. Sanders:

Jim and Alice won't be in school for the opening day because our family will not be returning to town from our cottage until September 5. I am sure you will understand.

Sincerely,
(Mrs.) Patricia Rosehips

IN-BASKET ITEM #18

August 18

Dear Dr. Brown:

I am writing this letter to request permission for my children to be absent from school next March 15 to April 15 in order to be with me while I am attending an international law conference in Durban, South Africa.

I am sure you recognize the cultural and educational benefits of such a trip. In addition, since I am a single parent and there is no one with whom I could leave my children, there is a practical aspect of my request. Furthermore, the trip will provide a nice change of pace for them, since they tend to get easily bored around that time of the year.

Sincerely,
Thomas Steele
Attorney at Law

IN-BASKET ITEM #19

August 12

MEMO

TO: Dr. Brown
FROM: Tim Parker, Assistant Principal

Just a short note to congratulate you on being chosen as new principal of our school. As you can probably imagine, I would have been happier if the school board had chosen me, but I guess those are the breaks. After twelve years as assistant principal, they must figure that's all I'm good for. Anyway, good luck.

4
THE NEW ASSISTANT PRINCIPAL (IN-BASKET ACTIVITIES)

Background

You are Dr. Chris Allen. You were previously a teacher for a number of years, and during that time you obtained a doctorate in curriculum and instruction. You intended to be a central office supervisor. But when Mr. Reeves, assistant principal in another school in the district, suddenly resigned in the third week of school, you were asked to take over and you agreed to take the assistant principalship post. After only four days on the job, you had to be away from school on Friday, October 1, because of illness in your family. It is now Saturday morning, October 2, and you have returned to school to check on your mail and telephone messages.

Instructions

1. You will be given 90 minutes to read and take action on *all* of the items presented following the instructions. You are not expected merely to *describe* what you would do, but to *do* it. For example, if you decide to telephone a person or see someone for a conference, then outline your objectives, as well as the main points or questions that you would present. (Utilize relevant concepts from Part I of the text in your responses.)
2. You may respond to the in-basket items in whatever sequence you prefer. You should, however, first read *all* of them, *quickly*. As you do so, indicate on a separate piece of paper in one of three columns whether a particular in-basket item represents (1) a high-priority, (2) a moderate-priority, or (3) a low-priority situation.
3. Each in-basket item requires a separate action, which you should present on another sheet of paper, adding the identification number in the upper-left-hand corner of the in-basket item. If you understand all the instructions up to this point, you may begin now or when your instructor so indicates.

IN-BASKET ITEM #1

September 26

Dear Dr. Allen:

I know this is short notice but your predecessor, Mr. Reeves, had promised to give a talk to the PTA at its meeting on October 12, and I am hoping that you are willing to take his place. The topic is "The Parent's Role in Helping Students to Stop Bullying in Schools," but if you don't feel comfortable with that, maybe some related topic could be selected. I know the parents will all be eager to meet you and hear your ideas. Please let me know as soon as possible.

Mrs. Trudy Spellman
PTA President

IN-BASKET ITEM #2

Dr. Allen,

I don't normally complain about *anything,* but I am getting sick and tired of putting up with the noise and fooling around that goes on in Janet Webster's class. As you know, her classroom is next door to mine, and she had discipline problems last year. But because she was new, I didn't say anything to her or to anyone else. This year–even with different students–it is all starting in again, and I have concluded that she just doesn't know how to handle kids. I have mentioned the noise to her a couple of times already this year, but it doesn't seem to have any lasting effect. I request that you stop in and get this situation squared away before something major erupts. It has already had a negative effect on my own class.

Rocky Bell

IN-BASKET ITEM #3

September 29

MEMO

TO: All Assistant and Vice Principals
FROM: Assistant Superintendent

Since you are the ones who administratively deal most directly with dropouts and children at risk, I am inviting you to a meeting at the Central Office, Room 1131, on October 5, to discuss this problem. Please bring ideas about how we might deal more effectively with the students.

IN-BASKET ITEM #4

Telephone Message

FROM: Mr. Yaeger
TIME: Friday, 9:00 A.M.

Yesterday after school two students kicked a soccer ball into his yard and smashed right through his roses getting the ball. Please return his call as soon as possible.

IN-BASKET ITEM #5

MEMO

TO: Chris Allen
FROM: Dave

Late last spring the superintendent directed all of us principals to come up with criteria and a process for evaluating their assistant/vice principals. I got really busy with a number of things at school during this last summer and didn't get to this task. Now the superintendent wants us to submit something by October 5. Chris, I know this is short notice, but could you give me your ideas on possible criteria and the process by October 3? I would like to involve you in this since it will be your evaluation, and I will definitely appreciate your ideas about the evaluation criteria and process. One of my ideas is that we would provide for some teacher participation in the process, but I would like your own ideas.

IN-BASKET ITEM #6

Dr. Allen:
Friday was a relatively quiet day, fortunately. But we did get some referrals from a few teachers, and they will need some action on Monday. I've stapled them to this memo.

Nan Wing
Secretary

Eastside School Referral Form

Date: Oct. 1
Student's Name: Stanley Bauer
Teacher: Maria Gomez
Problem: Stanley was wearing a button on his shirt that said "Question Authority." I told him to take it off, but he refused, so I'm sending him to your office to be disciplined.

Eastside School Referral Form

Date: Oct. 1
Student's Name: John Chang and Kevin Dortch
Teacher: Brad Lee
Problem: John and Kevin got into a fight during the noon hour. John got his nose broken (at least I think it was broken) and had to be sent to the doctor. I told them both that you would be wanting to speak to them first thing Monday morning.

Eastside School Referral Form

Date: Oct. 1
Student's Name: Betty Burmeister
Teacher: Kay Seritoma
Problem: Betty was fooling around in the classroom and refused to settle down. I didn't know what to do with her, and she was disrupting the class. So I thought maybe you could perform some kind of miracle with her. (This kid is a loser.)

Eastside School Referral Form

Date: Oct. 1
Student's Name: George Edgar
Teacher's Name: Mary Wynn, Librarian
Problem: Last May George Edgar was supposed to pay his library fine of $35.00 before taking his final exams. (He ruined an art book.) He said that he would take care of it but never did, and the teachers felt sorry for him and let him take his exams anyway. This year I have excluded him from the library, but he still hasn't paid me. I think he should be suspended until he pays what he owes.

IN-BASKET ITEM #7

Dear Dr. Allen:

This Thursday my teacher Mr. Bell made me stand for 45 minutes in class because I didn't get my homework done on time and because he said I talked back to him. I thought about talking to you Thursday after school, but my foot hurt so much (I have flat feet and have trouble with my feet) that I had to go see the doctor. Then I told my mother Thursday night, and she said I should tell you, but when I went to your office on Friday, they said you were gone. Anyway, I don't think what Mr. Bell did was right, and besides making my foot worse, it embarrassed me in front of all the other people in the class. I don't know what you can do, but something ought to be done.

Marilyn Pick

IN-BASKET ITEM #8

Telephone Message

TO: Dr. Allen
FROM: Detective Stevens

He says the police heard a rumor that a group of your students is planning a big party on Saturday, when the parents of one of the students are gone. Please call him as soon as possible at 392-9782.

IN-BASKET ITEM #9

Dear Mr. Reeves:

This is probably none of my business since I don't have any kids at school anymore, but I thought you ought to know that one of your students is being sexually abused by her stepfather. Don't ask me how I know because I won't tell you, since I really don't want to get involved. The only thing I will tell you is that the student lives in my neighborhood, and I think the situation has gotten pretty bad. Somebody has to help this girl, but I can't.

Mrs. Rachel Sprechter

IN-BASKET ITEM #10

Telephone Message

FOR: Chris Allen
FROM: Scoop Jackson, *Herald Express*
TIME: Friday, 3 P.M.

Please call him as soon as possible. He has been assigned a feature on the drug problem in our schools, and he'd like to interview you on Monday.

IN-BASKET ITEM #11

Telephone Message

TO: Dr. Allen
FROM: Mrs. Stuart
TIME: Friday, 9:14 A.M.

Mrs. Stuart's son was kept after school for detention on Thursday by his math teacher, Mary Colbert, causing him to miss his ophthalmologist appointment. Please call her Monday morning as early as possible at 354-2298. She says it takes nearly four weeks to get in to see this doctor, and she may have to pay for the missed appointment.

IN-BASKET ITEM #12

Dear Dr. Allen:

I don't know whether I should be telling you this or not—probably not—but I can't handle it by myself anymore. One of my friends (I wish I could tell you her name, but she made me promise not to breathe a word of any of this to anyone!) is being sexually harassed by her teacher, Mr. Wiley. She was too ashamed to give me many details, but she is very upset, and I am afraid that she will commit suicide or something. Please talk to him but don't use my name!

Betsy Meadows

IN-BASKET ITEM #13

Dear Dr. Allen:

Congratulations on your new appointment. By way of introducing myself and several of my staff, I would like to invite you and your spouse to a small gathering at my home on October 5 for hors d'oeuvres, and so on, followed by a special event treat I am sure all will enjoy and remember forever. Please rest assured that no business conversations will be permitted, and the emphasis will be on getting acquainted and enjoying ourselves. Directions to my home can be secured when you RSVP at 377-4040.

Nick Strokely,
Representative
Banner Yearbooks

P.S. I wonder if you've had an opportunity to meet my daughter, Joy, who is a student at your school.

IN-BASKET ITEM #14

Dr. Allen,

I wanted to let you know that when I substituted for Ken Clark on Friday, he didn't leave any lesson plans. Also, he didn't answer his phone when I tried to reach him. Needless to say, this made teaching his class very difficult. An inexperienced sub would have faced an impossible situation! It would be unfortunate if this would occur again.

Toni Wolff

IN-BASKET ITEM #15

Dear Mr. Reeves:

I hope you can help my son. He is being harassed by some other boys on the school bus when he rides to and from school. Apparently, they don't like the fact that he is reading his Bible, and they make remarks about him and about our religion.

I have already tried contacting the boys' parents. While only one of them was completely uncooperative (she told me my son shouldn't even be reading the Bible on a school bus), the other parents don't seem to have much control over their children.

My son doesn't bother anyone, and I would like you to intervene and get this harassing to stop. We're supposed to have freedom of religion in this country.

Mrs. Marilyn Smith

IN-BASKET ITEM #16

Dr. Allen:

It looks like we got a problem already this year with drugs. I found some drug paraphernalia on the floor in the boys locker room which somebody dropped by mistake. I haven't told anybody else about this, except my wife, which may have been a mistake. I don't know how you want to handle it. I don't have any idea about who may have had the stuff.

Lew Armstrong, Custodian

IN-BASKET ITEM #17

Telephone Message

FOR: Dr. Allen
FROM: Mrs. Alice Pick
TIME: Friday, 11:30 A.M.

Please call her early Monday morning.

IN-BASKET ITEM #18

Dr. Allen,

I don't think you know me (no reason you should know all students), but I and several of my friends want to establish a club called Christians for New World Order, and we want to meet every Wednesday after school. I don't know whether we need a sponsor or not, but Mrs. Webster, our English teacher, said she would do it. We would like to meet this coming Wednesday, so if there is no problem, would you please assign us a room. You are welcome (in fact encouraged) to attend our meetings.

Sue Clemens

5
RESENTMENT OVER APPOINTMENT

Shasha New has recently been appointed assistant principal of a middle school. After teaching in the system for 15 years, she feels that she has earned her way to the position and that her hard work and advanced degrees in leadership and supervision have made this opportunity possible. Knowing that her thorough training, her staff development activities, and her facilitation of school improvement plans have prepared her for her new challenges, she is eager to advance education within the district even further. At her first districtwide Parent Teacher Association orientation meeting as an assistant principal, Ms. New quickly scans the audience. There, sitting together, are board members and prominent local politicians. They are not smiling. Ms. New has heard rumors that many of them are not pleased with her appointment, and she now begins to worry about the facial expressions and rigid posture being displayed by these influential citizens. Could the rumors be true?

Ms. New and the principal proceed with the meeting as planned. Following the meeting, she volunteers to lock the building so that the principal can get home in time to attend his daughter's dance recital. After turning off all the lights and securing the building, Ms. New exits the building and walks toward the parking lot. There she notices several prominent community members clustered together talking. One member of the group, whose car is parked near Ms. New's car, approaches and begins talking to her. He makes it clear that the group is not pleased with her having been chosen assistant principal. The political leaders had intended that Ms. Jones, who had worked as a campaign assistant and who currently teaches in the building, would be appointed to the position instead. Uncertain how to react, Ms. New smiles politely and assures the politician that she will do the best job possible.

As the school year begins, Ms. New eagerly greets the challenges awaiting her. One of the assignments that her principal had delegated to her upon her appointment as assistant principal was the task of scheduling students and classes. She has carefully scheduled the workday for faculty members and places students in each of the appropriate classes. However, Ms. New changes one aspect of scheduling from the way it had been done in the building previously. Having knowledge of current research on the topic, she elects to distribute advanced math classes evenly among all math teachers at each grade level. One hour after class assignments are announced and class rolls are disseminated, Ms. Jones, the campaign assistant favored by the politicians, approaches Ms. New sternly. She immediately voices her complaints about the schedule. Having expected to have been appointed to the assistant principal position herself, she does not appreciate Ms. New's decision. Arguing that she has taught every advanced math class on her grade level for the past five years, Ms. Jones says her colleagues have never complained and she sees no reason for change. Ms. Jones has been powerful in the school community over the years and has used her informal power to convince the other math teachers that she should be the one to instruct the advanced classes, citing her experience, accumulated teaching resources, and university course work in gifted education.

Ms. New is aware that Ms. Jones possesses these qualities, but many other math faculty members also possess these attributes. As the conversation continues, Ms. Jones informs Ms. New that the grade-level math teachers have had a meeting since the assignments were announced and that they agree that one teacher should instruct all the advanced classes. Ms. Jones then reminds the new assistant principal that she is the most experienced candidate and the one logical choice for the staffing of that position. She also reemphasizes her credentials and reminds Ms. New of her political pull within the school and the community.

Her voice becomes louder as she announces, "You just wait until the superintendent hears about this!" She hurries out of the room, slamming the door behind her, giving Ms. New no chance to reply. Stunned and shaken by the angry exchange, Ms. New sits down and wonders, *What just happened?*

Suggested Learning Activities

Analyze the Case

1. Should Ms. New have offered any further explanation to the group in the parking lot? Should she inform anyone of the parking lot confrontation?
2. What aspects of class scheduling might Ms. New have neglected to consider? Should the scheduling be changed this close to school opening?
3. Should Ms. New attempt to earn Ms. Jones's respect? If not, why not and what repercussions might Ms. New experience by having Ms. Jones oppose her? If yes, why and how could Ms. New accomplish this task?

Discuss the Larger Issues

1. How should advanced and remedial classes be scheduled and staffed within a school building?
2. What effects might political power, or lack thereof, have upon a candidate's ability to obtain and succeed in an administrative role?
3. When should a principal support the decisions of the assistant principals, and when should decisions be reversed in order to maintain a favorable staff climate?

Be a Problem Solver Ms. New told the principal about the disagreement with Ms. Jones regarding the scheduling of mathematics classes. He suggests that he meet with Ms. Jones and Ms. New in his office that afternoon. What background information, if any, might Ms. New want to accumulate before the meeting? Should she discuss the matter with other math teachers? Utilize appropriate social science and administrative concepts from Part I in your approach to the problem or problems.

Test Your Solution To test your proposed approach to the problems described in this case study, your group should role-play the following aspects of the afternoon meeting:

1. *The principal,* as he begins the meeting with Ms. New and Ms. Jones. What tone does he want to set with each of the participants and how will he set it?
2. *Ms. New and Ms. Jones,* when asked to justify their positions on the scheduling of advanced math classes.
3. *The principal,* as he makes a final scheduling decision, imparts the decision, and closes the meeting. What effects will his decision have on school climate, power structure, student achievement, and community relations?

Investigate Further

1. Interview middle school principals to learn and compare their approaches to scheduling.
2. Investigate the advantages of automated versus manual scheduling.

6
DO I NEED TO ACT LIKE A MAN TO BE A LEADER?

She was beginning the second semester of her first year in the principalship at Doolittle School. Her predecessor had apparently been a strong disciplinarian and was well respected by the faculty. He had left for a job as assistant superintendent in a different state. She had been hired, according to the superintendent, because the school board wanted someone at Doolittle School who was the change agent type with excellent interpersonal skills, and her recommendations indicated that she would fit the bill. She had a specialist's degree in school administration and supervision from a major university. She had developed a strong concentration in curriculum and instruction within her degree program and had achieved high grades. She was a small person, but possessed a lot of drive and energy. She was considered to have a warm and accepting personality and to believe in the basic goodness of people.

Although she had approached the beginning of the school year with great enthusiasm, things had not gone particularly well during the first semester. The faculty was an older group who, for the most part, placed a high priority on strict student discipline and the absolute backing of the principal. She wasn't opposed to student discipline, but she felt that the school needed to develop some alternatives to simply punishing students. She also felt that the teachers needed to spend more time with those students who were misbehaving in class to try to diagnose why the students were acting out, instead of simply referring the students to the assistant principal. Most teachers, however, had resisted this approach, and she had heard rumors that they felt she wasn't "tough enough."

Al Kicker ("Big Al," as he was called by the teachers), the assistant principal, was another problem. He had applied for the principal's vacancy at Doolittle School and had been passed over. She knew he was unhappy about that, although he had never talked to her about his disappointment; but the main problem was that he just couldn't seem to accept her as the principal of the school. True, he was polite and respectful of her, with his

"Yes, ma'am" and "No, ma'am" and "If that's what you really want, ma'am," but he never opened up with her. He treated her more like a woman on a pedestal than a capable professional who was his superior. Also, he was himself a very strict disciplinarian who encouraged teachers to send misbehaving students to him ("to get straightened out") rather than trying to get the teachers to first work with problem students on their own. She sensed that the teachers liked Al better than her and that they looked to him for leadership more than to her.

Although she wasn't sure what to do about her assistant principal, she was most troubled by her lack of acceptance by the other principals in the school district. The male principals were older, much more experienced, and, apparently with only one exception, quite conservative in their philosophy of education and their attitudes toward teachers and students. They had sort of a "them versus us" mentality, and they espoused a strict, rigid approach toward student discipline. As a group, they seemed aloof and appeared to her to have a "you still need to prove yourself to us" attitude toward her.

She had initially thought that her lack of acceptance by the male principals was due to the fact that she was a woman (and she continued to believe that many of them, if not most, were sexist). But since the other female principals seemed to get along with the male principals all right, she had concluded that her lack of acceptance was because she was new and really did need to prove herself. She wasn't sure how to do this or even whether she should need to prove herself to the male principals. Thus far, she hadn't figured out how to handle this problem.

Complicating the matter was the fact that the other female principals seemed to be acting differently toward her. Initially they had appeared friendly to her, but during the first semester they had gradually become more reserved. As she reflected more about this development, it seemed to her that the other female principals were more like the male principals in their attitudes and behavior than they were like her. Whereas she was a warm, open, trusting kind of person, the other women seemed to be more abrasive and circumspect. It was almost as though the other female principals felt that they had to be tough and to "out-macho" the male principals. She wondered whether that was the kind of personality and approach they had had when they joined the school district, or whether they had changed in response to conditions and expectations that existed within the district.

She wasn't sure what she was going to do about her numerous problems, but she felt herself being pulled in various directions. Maybe she would have to become tougher in order to survive. But if that was required, would she be willing to pay the price? She still believed that it should be possible for a woman who is warm, open, and trusting, and who holds progressive ideas, to succeed, but she certainly hadn't figured out what her strategy should be for the second semester. One thing she did know was that she still believed in herself. She wouldn't give up easily.

Suggested Learning Activities

Analyze the Case

1. Should the new principal have taken steps during and after the hiring process to become better informed about some of the conditions she experienced later? If so, what might those steps have been?

2. If you were the new principal in the case study, what additional information would you want to know before attempting to solve the problems identified, and how would you go about obtaining that information? Explain why the additional information you seek is necessary in order to ameliorate the problems.
3. To what degree do you think the new principal has brought on some of her own problems, and to what extent do you think she is overreacting to some of the problems?

Discuss the Larger Issues

1. Is there a certain kind of personality or set of attributes that a school administrator is expected to possess in order to be successful?
2. Are women administrators expected to meet an essentially masculine set of expectations, that is, "Be strong, be tough"? To what extent are expectations for female or, for that matter, male administrators related to research on administrator or leadership effectiveness?
3. To what extent should an individual administrator attempt to resist, modify, or even reject expectations of others when they are not compatible with the administrator's own administrative style or educational vision?

Be a Problem Solver Assume that you are the new principal at Doolittle School. Outline the steps you would try to take to resolve each of the problems identified in the case study. Utilize administrative and social science concepts from Part I of the text in planning and implementing your problem-solving approach.

Test Your Solution To test your proposed plan of action for dealing with the circumstances described in the case study, you and your colleagues should create and role-play one or more of the following situations:

1. A faculty meeting to discuss philosophy and procedures for handling student discipline.
2. A conference between the new principal and the assistant principal.
3. A meeting or conference between the new principal and one or more of the male or female principals.

Investigate Further

1. Investigate the literature on problems that administrators face in becoming socialized into a new situation.
2. Interview one or more female administrators to determine the extent to which they encountered an acceptance problem because of their gender.
3. Investigate the extent to which there exists within your school or district any support groups to help new administrators with initial problems adjusting to a new job setting.

7
DRAGGING AND SAGGING: IS IT FASHION, EXPRESSION, OR A VIOLATION?

Shirley Nolan had been appointed vice principal only a week before classes were to begin in the fall. She had been certified as a school administrator for the last two years, but had been unable to find a job, so she had continued teaching.

Her opportunity to become a vice principal had occurred when the previous vice principal had left education at the last moment to become a salesman for an insurance company. The school district hadn't had much time to fill the vacancy, so they had called Shirley, interviewed her, and then informed her that she had the job if she wanted it–all on the same day. She wasn't prepared for events to move that fast, but despite some misgivings about facing the challenge of becoming a new administrator (in addition to relocating to a different school), she had accepted the district's offer. She felt that she had a certain advantage in her new position, inasmuch as she would still be working for the same school district.

Her first two days on the job consisted of attending the various district and building meetings that occur just before fall classes begin. She had, of course, spent some time with the principal, who seemed nice but whose philosophy of discipline was much different from her own. She had first recognized this during the job interview but had decided to "tell them what they wanted" in order to get the job. The principal believed in strict discipline and strong punitive consequences for misbehavior, while her own approach was more one of trying to understand what was causing the misbehavior and attempting to counsel the student in order to improve the behavior. She had been successful with this approach as a classroom teacher, and she knew of no reason why it wouldn't work in her new role as vice principal. Still, she didn't argue with the principal about their differences when they had met, in the hope that maybe over time he would "soften up" a little and, if she were effective with her approach, might gradually change his mind.

Unfortunately, most of the faculty members she met also seemed to be from the old school of student discipline and appeared to subscribe fully to the principal's views. Shirley was pleased that some of the younger teachers were more attuned to her approach to student discipline, but one of her problems was that the school had the following very rigid set of discipline rules. Additionally, this is the first year of the new dress code, which now included uniforms for these high school students. There has been a trend in recent years to institute school dress code policies or the requirement of wearing uniforms in order to achieve a variety of goals including better classroom management and overall student improvement:

FOLSUM SCHOOL'S STUDENT DISCIPLINE CODE

Introduction

Everyone needs discipline: Athletes need discipline, executives need discipline, soldiers need discipline.

Rules are developed and promulgated in order to facilitate and promote discipline. Without rules, there would be no discipline.

The following rules have been developed in order to achieve the discipline necessary for the orderly environment that is required for effective teaching and learning. By following these rules, you will become a good school citizen, develop better self-discipline, and become a more effective learner. You will also help us create a positive atmosphere needed for a quality educational program. Although the rules may seem to you to be a little strict, they are really for your own good and for the best welfare of the greatest number of students in the school.

Obey the rules. Be a good citizen. Be a positive example for others.

Behavioral Guidelines

1. All students will come to school prepared for class, appropriately dressed, and with necessary materials and equipment.
2. Students will be on time for school and for class. Punctuality is very important at Folsum School.
3. Student fighting or fooling around will not be tolerated anywhere in the school, on the school grounds, or coming to or going from school.
4. Smoking or use of drugs will not be tolerated and will result in immediate suspension or recommendation for expulsion, depending on the nature of the offense.
5. Acts of vandalism will be punished by suspension or expulsion, depending on the seriousness of the offense.
6. Students are not allowed to chew gum in class or to eat candy or other food in or out of class, except during the lunch period in the cafeteria.
7. The use of profanity will not be tolerated in this school and may subject a student to suspension or other appropriate action.
8. Disrespect for teachers will not be permitted, and appropriate action will be taken if it occurs.
9. Students are not allowed to run or fool around in the hallways.
10. Any student action that interferes with teaching, learning, the rights of others, or the smooth operation of the school will receive disciplinary punishment.

Specific Uniform Code

Shirts: Shirts will be Black, Red, or White Polo style or buttoned dress shirt, long or short sleeve. Shirts shall be tucked into the waistband of the pants or skirt. Exceptions will be allowed in individual cases based upon the discretion of the principal or designee.

Pants and Skirts: Pants and Skirts will be Black or Tan. Pants with belt loops shall be worn with a belt that is properly fastened. Pants shall be worn so that the waistband is worn at the waist and not below the waist. The hem of girls' skirts or dresses shall be no shorter than mid-thigh as determined by the principal or designee in the exercise of his or her judgment.

Appropriate Sizes: Students shall wear clothing of appropriate size as determined by the principal or designee exercising his or her judgment. The size of shirts and pants shall be appropriate to the student's body size and shall not be unduly oversized or undersized.

Students are not allowed to wear clothing, jewelry (including body piercing jewelry and "grills"), buttons, haircuts, tattoos, or other attire or markings which are offensive, suggestive, disruptive, or indecent such as:

- Clothing associated with gangs,
- Clothing encouraging the use of tobacco, drugs, alcohol, or violence,
- Clothing associated with discrimination on the basis of age, color, handicap, national origin, sexual orientation, marital status, race, religion, or sex.

- Clothing exposing the torso or upper thighs such as see-through garments, mini-skirts or mini-dresses, halters, backless dresses, tube tops or tank tops without over shirts, spaghetti strap garments without over shirts, bare midriff outfits, or shirts tied at the midriff.
- Clothing not properly fastened or with tears.
- Clothing or outer garments traditionally designed as undergarments such as boxer shorts, bloomers, tights, hosiery, sleepwear.
- Clothing or footwear that is construed by the principal or designee as hazardous or dangerous to the health of the student or others.
- Hats, headgear, or any head covering, except when approved by the Principal.

After looking over the student discipline and dress codes again, Shirley considered what, if anything, she could or should do to try and change the rules. She had been told by one of the older teachers that the present code had been in existence for about seven years and, as far as that teacher was concerned, had worked very well. For Shirley, however, the code was at odds with her philosophy and approach to student discipline. The question was, What could or should she do in light of all the various circumstances in this school?

Suggested Learning Activities

Analyze the Case

1. Given the circumstances that the new vice principal had faced at the time she was offered the job at Folsum, should she have taken it? Why or why not?
2. If you had been Shirley Nolan, would you have acted any differently in your meetings with the principal?
3. Analyze and evaluate the Folsum School student discipline code, using concepts from communication theory and recommendations from authorities on school discipline.

Discuss the Larger Issues

1. To what extent should a person seeking a position "tell them what they want" in order to get a job? What ethical problems might be involved? Is this approach to getting a job ever justified and, if so, under what sort of circumstances?
2. What is the ultimate objective of a student discipline/uniform code, and what type of a code is likely to achieve that objective?
3. What should be the role of punishment in disciplining students? What does research say about its effectiveness?
4. To what degree should students and parents be involved in the development or revision of a student discipline/uniform code?

Be a Problem Solver Assume that you are the vice principal in this case study. Outline objectives and plans for responding to the various circumstances that the vice principal faces. Utilize appropriate administrative or social science concepts from Part I of the text in planning and implementing your approach.

Test Your Solution To test your proposed plans for dealing with the circumstances described in the case study, you and the class should create and role-play one or more of the following interactions:

1. A follow-up conference between you and the principal to discuss the student discipline/uniform code.
2. A teacher referral to the vice principal about a student who persists in sucking on lozenges in class.
3. The first meeting of a special committee composed of representative students, teachers, parents, and the vice principal, whose charge is to make recommendations on what changes, if any, are needed in the student discipline/uniform code.

Investigate Further

1. Determine what criteria and methods are used to evaluate your school's student discipline/uniform code and how often evaluation occurs.
2. Ascertain the extent to which your school's discipline code is understood and accepted by teachers, parents, and students.
3. Evaluate the student discipline code in your own school, using concepts from communication theory and recommendations from authorities on student discipline.

8
IS BEING BUSY NECESSARILY PRODUCTIVE?

Driving to school, Steve Fuller slowed reluctantly for a traffic light. As he waited for the signal to change, the new principal of Franklin School speculated idly about what the day might bring. It seemed that he was always busy, regardless of how a day started out.

Today, for example, he didn't have any conferences or meetings scheduled until later in the afternoon, to the best of his memory. He was certain, however, that something would come along to dominate the morning. He had hoped to get into some classrooms and do some supervision, but he hadn't mentioned anything to the teachers yet in case something were to come up to prevent him from accomplishing that task.

Finally, the green light appeared, and Steve accelerated the car to compensate for lost moments. By 7:55 he pulled into the school parking lot at his usual time, parked the car, and entered the school. His secretary had arrived some time earlier, and after five minutes of chitchat with her, the principal was interrupted by a teacher who wanted to talk about the faculty party that was to occur in about two weeks. The conversation lasted until 8:25, at which time the teacher had to leave for a class that began at 8:30.

At 8:40 Steve Fuller was sitting in his office thinking about what he should do next, when he remembered that he had hoped to do some classroom supervision that morning. As he started to leave, his secretary intercepted him, asking whether they could talk now about revising some of the office procedures. Since there was a lull in her work schedule, it seemed to her like a good time to discuss the matter. The principal momentarily experienced some mixed feelings, but he didn't reveal them to his secretary. Instead, he smiled and said that he would be happy to discuss those matters with her.

At 9:20 the principal and his secretary were still talking (although they had been interrupted by two telephone calls to the principal), when the secretary brought to the attention of the principal his scheduled conference with a parent, Mrs. Channing, at 9:30. The principal was mildly surprised, as he had anticipated that the parent conference was to be held in the afternoon. He thought to himself that the classroom observation would have to wait until after the parent conference.

At 9:45 Mrs. Channing finally appeared for her conference with the principal. Mr. Fuller was a little frustrated because he had expected her to arrive at 9:30, and he hadn't been able to get much done except to talk with a student who had dropped by the office. He concealed his frustration and tried to be as friendly and helpful to Mrs. Channing as possible. The parent wanted to talk with him about her son's discipline difficulties in school, but it quickly became clear that she should have talked to the assistant principal or the counselor instead, each of whom could have been more helpful to her. Unfortunately, when he asked his secretary to contact one of them, neither was free at that time.

As the conference with the parent dragged on and on, the principal became more and more frustrated. Finally, at 10:40, the parent concluded her conference with the principal and thanked him for his help. The principal thought to himself that he really hadn't been very helpful, but he was happy that he was finally rid of the parent.

Since it was now 10:45, the principal decided that he needed a coffee break, and he left his office to go down to the faculty room. After he had poured his coffee, he decided to sit in the back of the faculty room where he hoped to be somewhat alone, and perhaps clear his head from the parent conference. Almost immediately, however, a couple of teachers came over and initiated a discussion about last Sunday's pro football game. The principal had hoped for some privacy, but he was reluctant to turn away the two teachers and besides, he really liked football. So the conversation continued, and before he knew it, it was 11:15.

Excusing himself, the principal left the faculty room and returned to his office. While he was sorting through some papers on his desk, a teacher stopped by and asked if he was busy. The principal thought to himself that he really wasn't busy yet, but there were some things that he knew should be done. On the other hand, at this point, he hadn't started anything specific, and since he had told his faculty that he had an open-door policy and they could see him anytime he wasn't busy, he indicated to the teacher that he would be happy to see her.

The principal's conference with the teacher was about the possibility of the school's or the district's purchase of a television set for her classroom so that she could begin to teach students to become more critical consumers of television. The conference lasted until 11:45, when the principal had to excuse himself to go to lunch with the PTA president.

After returning from lunch, Mr. Fuller answered several telephone messages on his desk, and attempted to open and process his mail. This took about 40 minutes, until nearly 1:45 P.M. At that point, his secretary came in to remind him of the meeting that he had to attend at the district office at 2:30. The principal had forgotten about the meeting, although he knew that there was some type of meeting that he was supposed to attend later in the afternoon. He thanked his secretary for reminding him and decided that he'd better prepare to leave, as it would take about 30 minutes to drive downtown to the district office.

At 4:00 the district office meeting concluded. Mr. Fuller decided against returning to the school and instead proceeded home. It had been a boring meeting and, in general, a frustrating day. He felt he had been busy all day but wondered what he had really accomplished. He knew there was something important that he meant to do that he hadn't accomplished, but he couldn't remember anymore what it had been. He thought to himself that he needed to relax, and that perhaps tomorrow would bring a more satisfying and productive day.

Suggested Learning Activities

Analyze the Case

1. What planning steps might the principal have taken before he arrived at work that would have improved his productivity?
2. Analyze the different activities in which the principal engaged during the day, and suggest how he might have handled things more efficiently.

Discuss the Larger Issues

1. To what extent should an administrator be concerned about how efficiently he uses his time?
2. What costs are there to not being well organized or efficient?
3. What costs are there to being too organized and efficient?
4. Why are some administrators more productive than others? Do they have more time, or is it due to other factors?

Be a Problem Solver Assume that you are the supervisor of the principal in this case. How would you approach the principal to help him use his time more productively? Utilize administrative and social science concepts from Part I of the text in planning and implementing your approach.

Test Your Solution To test your proposed approach to dealing with the circumstances presented in this case, you and your colleagues should create and role-play one or more of the following situations:

1. A conference between the principal and his supervisor.
2. The development of a plan for implementing the supervisor's suggestions.

Investigate Further

1. To what extent are the problems experienced by the principal in the case similar to the problems experienced by the administrators in your district? What seems to be causing the problems?
2. What kinds of assistance are being given to the administrators in your district to deal with these problems?

9
CHANGING DEMOGRAPHICS AND TEACHER ATTITUDES

Dr. Riccardo Mendozza was in his first year in Capital City and his first position as a principal. The former principal had left to complete work on his doctorate, but during the last two years of his administration, the school's student body demographics had changed and the student body was currently composed of about 25 percent White and 75 percent non-White. At one time the faculty had been predominantly White, but several "minority" teachers had been hired. Several White teachers had transferred or moved to other districts because they felt that the changes were lowering the standards in the school, a culture that has pervaded the school.

Dr. Mendozza has been very busy during the first few weeks of the school year. He had been learning the schedule; becoming acquainted with students, teachers, and other people in the district; familiarizing himself with the program of studies; and dealing with the day-to-day routine and minor crises that are a part of the job of the building principal.

Although he was reasonably well satisfied with his new situation, two aspects troubled him. In spite of the fact that the school, including the faculty, had been integrated, there was very little social interaction between White and non-White teachers. As a rule, they did not mingle in the faculty room, and they sat together at faculty meetings or during the noon hour. Although Dr. Mendozza had not detected any actual antagonism or hostility, it was apparent that the two groups of teachers were not associating with each other.

He had talked to his assistant principal about the matter, but his assistant didn't believe that any significant problem existed and took the position that even if it did, there wasn't much that could be done about it; people couldn't be *forced* to associate with each other. Dr. Mendozza wasn't ready to accept his assistant principal's assessment of the situation, but at the moment he didn't have any ideas on how to improve relations between the White and non-White teachers. Besides, there was another problem that was possibly even more fundamental to quality education in an integrated school.

Dr. Mendozza had noticed, in the process of becoming familiar with the program of studies in the school, that the curriculum seemed to give inadequate attention and emphasis to non-White history and culture. Although the former principal had apparently tried to stimulate some interest in offering a course focusing on the culture and history of minority groups in the United States, no one on the faculty had been willing to develop an outline of study. As a result, the present social studies program was still very traditional.

The same type of situation existed in the language arts curriculum, which devoted little attention to non-White literature. Although the principal was in favor of students learning about recognized White U.S. and European writers, he believed that there should be a better balance in the curriculum and that there was a great deal of worthwhile non-White literature to which all students should be exposed. Certainly the minority students needed this type of relevant education to develop a better self-identity and a deeper understanding of their culture and history. Perhaps even more important, the White students needed a multiracial education if they were ever going to learn to appreciate the non-White culture and develop a more positive attitude toward relating and interacting with non-White people.

Dr. Mendozza realized that there would be problems in trying to achieve a truly integrated faculty and multicultural curriculum. There would no doubt be resistance from teachers of both backgrounds who did not want to associate with each other and who questioned the need for a multicultural curriculum or doubted the school district's commitment to this approach. There was also likely to be the feeling on the part of many White parents that minority group studies were either not necessary or not desirable. Dr. Mendozza was deeply committed to the ideal of an integrated society, however, and believed that it was the school's responsibility to play a major role in contributing to that end. It was true that he was new and a little uncertain about how to proceed, but he had been taught that the principalship was a leadership position, and he intended to face up to the challenges in his school.

Suggested Learning Activities

Analyze the Case

1. What might be some of the more subtle reasons the White and non-White teachers were not associating with each other? How could you ascertain the actual reasons for their lack of interaction?
2. What is your evaluation of the assistant principal's assessment of the racial situation in the school? What might be some of the reasons he doesn't view things the same way the principal does?
3. From what sources is there likely to be opposition to the goals of the principal in the case? What might be some of the possibly less obvious reasons people may oppose the principal?

Discuss the Larger Issues

1. What should be the school's objective in regard to the nature of interracial relations within the faculty? What role should the principal play in attempting to achieve that objective? What role should the superintendent or other central office personnel play?
2. What type of a curriculum should a school offer or develop for an integrated student body? A desegregated student body? Should there be any differences, and if so, why?

Be a Problem Solver If you were the principal in the situation described in this case, what would you do? What are the alternatives? Utilize appropriate administrative and social science concepts from Part I of the text in planning and implementing your approach.

Test Your Solution To test your proposed plan of action for dealing with the problems presented at the end of this case, create and role-play one or more of the following situations in class:

1. A meeting between the principal and the faculty.
2. A meeting between the principal and the non-White or the White teachers.

Investigate Further

1. Regardless of the racial composition of your student body, to what extent does the curriculum in your school promote a positive attitude toward the different racial and ethnic groups in our country?

2. What is the attitude of your superintendent, principal, department heads, and faculty toward investigating ways in which the curriculum in your school and school district can do an even better job of fostering and promoting a positive attitude among the different races and ethnic groups?
3. What barriers and obstacles would have to be overcome in your district before a more multiracial faculty and curriculum could be achieved?

10
MATTER OF WHAT?

Sheila Mason, the new first year principal, was supervising the last lunch shift at Mariner North Middle School when a student came running up to her. It had been a quiet day, so she was taken by surprise when Vicki started yelling, "Ms. Mason, Ms. Mason, there's a fight up the hall!" By now students were pouring out of the cafeteria in response to the commotion. It was several minutes before Ms. Mason could push through the crowd. By then the fight had stopped, and several students were being escorted up the hall. At that point several students began shouting at Mr. McGowan, one of the teachers. He was standing in a daze, just staring down the hall. Ms. Mason took charge of the situation and ordered the students back to class. Several students kept shouting, "Did you see Mr. McGowan!? Did you hear what he said!?"

Ms. Mason directed Mr. McGowan into his classroom and closed the door. He was one of the new teachers, a young White man from the suburbs. This was his first experience in an inner-city middle school where the student population was predominately African American and Hispanic. So far, he had done a good job. The students appeared to like him, and he had established a rapport with many of the more difficult students.

"What happened?"

"I was just coming back to my room when Robert, you know Robert Hedges, started a fight with James, ah, James Simmons. I was right there when it started, so I stepped in right away. I thought they were going to stop when James hit Robert; I tried to stop James from hitting him again. That's when Mr. Sommes stepped in and pulled Robert up the hall. I guess, I guess I sort of lost my temper because I grabbed James and was shaking him around. I mean, he had stopped at that point, but I was angry that he hit Robert. Then James told me to let go of him. I guess I threatened him or something, and he pushed me. That's when I punched him. I, I wasn't thinking. Then we just started to fight and I guess I must have called him a couple of strong names; I don't know. Then Ms. Davis stepped in and pulled James up the hall. I just, I just have a real headache today, and I didn't feel like dealing with it."

Ms. Mason's first reaction was one of sympathy and then anger. Mr. McGowan had put her in a very difficult situation. Not only had the only White teacher been involved in the fight but also Robert was one of the few White kids in the school. The racist overtones were hard to ignore, although in her heart Ms. Mason was positive Dan McGowan was not racist. "I'll have to see you in my office. We'll need to go up and work this thing out."

As they walked up the hall, several students made comments regarding Mr. McGowan and the fight. It was a tense situation. Ms. Mason was glad when they reached her office, but her relief was short lived. "You racist pig!" James shouted as they entered the office. Ms. Mason had James taken to an inner office. Then Mr. Sommes and Ms. Davis both confirmed the situation as described, including the racial overtones of the fight. Both were concerned that Dan McGowan had reacted against James because Robert was White. Ms. Mason was the first African American principal at the high school. This was the first situation involving a teacher fighting a student. She liked Dan, and she knew that neither James nor Robert was a real discipline problem. She also knew that the entire school was polarized as a result of this fight. She tried to think through the problem. She wanted to consider every avenue before she called Bob Willis, the assistant superintendent, at the central office.

Suggested Learning Activities

Analyze the Case

1. Evaluate Sheila Mason's handling of the fight. What could she have done differently, if anything? Why?
2. Analyze the position of each major player in this incident. What are some possible outcomes? How would you, as principal, handle the situation?
3. What part, if any, should race play in the principal's solution? Where should she seek advice? What values will play a part in her final decision?
4. How would you discipline the following:
   a. Mr. McGowan?
   b. James Simmons?
   c. Robert Hedges?
5. In disciplining each person listed in question 4, explain what you would hope to accomplish and why you would hope to accomplish it.

Discuss the Larger Issues

1. To what extent are the school and its program responsible for student discipline problems?
2. What should be the role of the following individuals and groups in regard to preventing and dealing constructively with student discipline problems?
   a. The vice principal
   b. The principal
   c. The teachers
   d. The student body
   e. The parents
3. To what degree are current practices for preventing and dealing with student discipline problems effective? How could improvement be best achieved?

Be a Problem Solver The principal is facing an incident that, if not handled correctly, could create a serious problem with the climate of the school. Review Chapter 3 and, considering the concepts discussed there, decide how you would handle this situation. Remember, you have two students waiting to be seen. One is openly hostile. You also have a teacher in your office who faces possible suspension. Test your solution. Create your own role-play for this case.

Investigate Further

1. What innovative approaches to preventing and dealing constructively with student discipline problems have been developed during the last several years?
2. What is the school board policy in your district for preventing and dealing constructively with student discipline problems?
3. What is the role of the following individuals or groups in your school or school district with regard to student discipline problems?
   a. The assistant principal
   b. The principal
   c. The teachers
   d. The student body
   e. The parents

BACKGROUND READING

For the reader who would like to develop further background and understanding of the problems and issues presented in this chapter, the following list is provided:

Bailey, Susan McGee, "Shortchanging Girls and Boys," *Educational Leadership* (May 1996), pp. 75–79.

Boutte, Gloria Swindler, "Beyond the Illusion of Diversity: How Early Childhood Teachers Can Promote Social Justice," *Social Studies* (vol. 99, no. 4, July 2008), pp. 165–173.

Burton, Laura J., and Jennie M. Weiner, "'They Were Really Looking for a Male Leader for the Building': Gender, Identity and Leadership Development in a Principal Preparation Program," *Frontiers in Psychology* (vol. 7, 2016), p. 141. https://www.ncbi.nlm.nih.gov/pmc/articles/PMC4754431/.

Carnes, William J., "Unleashing the Kraken: The Perils of Ignoring Community Values," *Educational Leadership* (November 1995), pp. 84–86.

Checkley, Kathy, "The Contemporary Principal," *Education Update* (vol. 42, no. 3, May 2000). https://www.edweek.org/ew/articles/2000/05/03/34prins.h19.html?qs=building+on+experience+inmeta:Volume 3D19+inmeta:Issue 3D34.

Colwell, Christopher, *Impact: How Assistant Principals Can Be High Performing Leaders* (Lanham, MD: Rowman & Littlefield, 2015).

Crow, Gary M. "Complexity and the Beginning Principal in the United States: Perspectives on Socialization," *Journal of Educational Administration* (vol. 44, no. 4, 2006), pp. 310–325.

Fullan, Michael, *The Principal: Three Keys to Maximizing Impact* (San Francisco, CA: Jossey-Bass, 2014).

Gorton, Richard A., and Gail Thierbach-Schneider, "Part VI, Career Considerations," in *School-Based Leadership: Challenges and Opportunities,* 3rd ed. (Dubuque, IA: William C. Brown, 1991), pp. 573–629.

Hackman, Donald G., "Ten Guides for Implementing Block Scheduling," *Educational Leadership* (November 1995), pp. 24–27.

Hicks, Anna T., *Speak Softly & Carry Your Own Gym Key* (Thousand Oaks, CA: NASSP and Corwin Press, 1996).

Keller, Bess, "Building on Experience," *Education Week* (vol. 19, no. 34, May 3, 2000). https://www.edweek.org/ew/articles/2000/05/03/34prins.h19.html?qs=building+on+experience+inmeta:Volume 3D19+inmeta:Issue 3D34.

Knight, Jim, *Strategic Planning for School Managers* (Bristol, PA: Kogan Page, 1996).

Landry, Tracey K., "Block Scheduling for The 21st Century High School: A Change Leadership Plan,"

Dissertations, 2016, p. 199, http://digitalcommons.nl.edu/diss/19.

Legters, Nettie, and Leigh Parise, "A Community of Practice Approach to Support for Ninth-Graders in Urban High Schools, Policy Brief," *MDRC* (2016), https://eric.ed.gov/?id=ED565716.

Marshall, C., and R. M. Hooley, *The Assistant Principal: Leadership Choices and Challenges* (Thousand Oaks, CA: Corwin Press, 2006).

Mattox, Kim, Hancock, R. Dawson, and J. Allen Queen, "The Effect of Block Scheduling on Middle School Students' Mathematics Achievement," *NASSP Bulletin* (vol. 89, no. 642), pp. 3–13.

McCown, Claire H. et al., "Developing Urban School Leaders," *Journal of Staff Development* (vol. 18, no. 3, Summer 1997), pp. 16–19.

Pijanowski, John C., Paul M. Hewitt, and Kevin P. Brady, "Superintendents' Perceptions of the Principal Shortage," *NASSP Bulletin* (vol. 93, no. 2, 2009), pp. 85–95.

Pollard, Diane S., "Perspectives on Gender and Race," *Educational Leadership* (May 1996), pp. 72–74.

Queen, J. Alan, *The Block Scheduling Handbook* (Thousand Oaks, CA: Corwin, 2008).

Quong, T., "Asking the Hard Questions: Being a Beginning Principal in Australia," *Journal of Educational Administration* (vol. 44, no. 4, 2006), pp. 376–388.

Rebore, Ronald W. Jr., "Placement and Induction," in *Personnel Administration in Education,* 5th ed. (Boston: Allyn and Bacon, 1998), pp. 135–158.

Rusch, Edith A., "Gender and Race in Leadership Preparation: A Constrained Discourse," *Educational Administration Quarterly* (vol. 40, no. 1, February 2004), pp. 16–48.

Sergiovanni, Thomas J., "Refocusing Leadership to Build Community," *High School Magazine* (vol. 17, no. 1, September 1999).

Seyfarth, James T., *The Principal: New Leadership for New Challenges* (Upper Saddle River, NJ: Merrill, 1999).

Shields, Thomas, and Kate Cassada, "Examination of Access and Equity by Gender, Race, and Ethnicity in a Non-traditional Leadership Development Programme in the United States," *School Leadership & Management* (vol. 36, no. 5, 2016), pp. 1–20.

Temes, Peter S., *Teaching Leadership* (New York: Peter Lang, 1996).

Tonnsen, Sandra, "Achieving Equity in the Training of School Leaders: An Essay," *Connections* (vol. 1, no. 1, May 1998), pp. 28–30.

Tucker, M. S., and J. B. Codding, *The Principal Challenge: Leading and Managing Schools in an Era of Accountability* (San Francisco, CA: John Wiley & Sons, 2002).

Walker, A., and H. Qian, "Beginning Principals: Balancing at the Top of the Greasy Pole," *Journal of Educational Administration* (vol. 44, no. 4, 2006), pp. 297–309.

Webb, L. Dean, and M. Scott Norton, "Placement and Induction," in *Human Resources Administration*, 6th ed. (Boston: Pearson, 2013), pp. 110–129.

Weiner, Jennie Miles, and Laura J. Burton, "The Double Bind for Women: Exploring the Gendered Nature of Turnaround Leadership in a Principal Preparation Program," *Harvard Educational Review* (vol. 86, no. 3, 2016), pp. 339–365.

Young, Phillip, Don Reimer, and Karen Holsey Young, "Effects of Organizational Characteristics and Human Capital Endowments on Pay of Female and Male Middle School Principals," *Educational Administration Quarterly* (vol. 46, no. 4, October 2010), pp. 590–616.

WEB EXPLORATIONS

American Association of School Administrators. http://www.aasa.org/

National Association of Elementary School Principals. http://www.naesp.org/

National Association of Secondary School Administrators. http://www.nassp.org/

Top 27 School Administration Resources. http://blog.capterra.com/top-27-school-administration-resources/

"Block Scheduling: A Solution or A Problem." http://www.educationworld.com/a_admin/admin/admin029.shtml

CHAPTER

10

Student Problems

Many student problems are as old as formal schooling itself. Student truancy, vandalism, cheating, smoking, profanity, talking back to teachers, and other similar kinds of problems have confronted most administrators at one time or another over the years. Although student strikes, assaults on teachers, and other more extreme behavior may seem to be of recent origin, one historical record reported that in 1837 over 300 schools in Massachusetts alone were broken up by rebellious students. Still, the limited data available suggest that student misbehavior has become a more serious problem in recent years. Increasingly, administrators are confronted with issues concerning school safety, weapons, and sexual assault. Student discipline has become a topic of growing concern to the public.

Disruptive student behavior certainly merits the attention of administrators and the general public, but other kinds of student problems that may not be so obvious to the school and the public because they cause little, if any, immediate difficulty are nevertheless worthy of consideration. Examples would be the student who is apathetic, underachieving, or overachieving, or who is not meeting personal or academic goals. These kinds of students may have problems that, if not addressed by someone at the school, could result in extreme behavior, such as suicide or drug abuse. There are also those students who don't react in such a life-threatening manner but simply drop out of school. The point is that administrators should not limit their attention to only the more obvious student misbehavior; early diagnosis of more subtle symptoms of student problems is also necessary.

Why students experience problems or cause the school difficulty is, of course, a complex question that must be approached on an individual basis, as well as at a class or school level. Certainly, there are a number of theories, and these may be pursued in the list of readings provided at the end of this chapter. Also, the reader will need to examine and utilize the administrative and social science concepts presented in Part I of the text. There are no easy, ready-made answers to student problems, but an accurate understanding and an appropriate utilization of these concepts are prerequisite to effective action.

Finally, it needs to be emphasized that not all students experience problems or cause the school difficulty, and what may be a problem for one student or school may not be a problem for another student or school. Administrators must not underestimate the advantages of recognizing the positive behaviors of the many well-behaved students and the effects of that recognition on the few students who exhibit poor behaviors. It seems clear that dealing with student problems will continue to be a major aspect of the school administrator's responsibilities. For that reason, representative case studies are presented in this chapter for study and analysis.

11
SCHOOL YARD DANGERS

The dark skies were just beginning to lighten as the principal drove into the school's parking lot. He had decided to arrive at work early so he could catch up on some paperwork that had piled up on his desk, and he was looking forward to a quiet time of concentration without teacher or student interruptions. Approaching the back door of the school, he was surprised to see seven or eight students standing around. Having made a special effort to arrive early himself, he wondered briefly how early these students must have left home that morning, and why.

He greeted the students and unlocked the door, aware that they were watching him, hopeful that he might allow them into the building. "Sorry," he said, with a regretful smile. "No students are allowed inside until the bell rings at 8:15." As an afterthought, he asked, "What are you kids doing here so early in the morning, anyway?"

There was little response from the students. One of the girls gave him a half-smile, and others turned away. Not wanting to put them on the defensive, he didn't persist, but commented, "You really shouldn't get here so early. Get a little more sleep tomorrow morning, and try not to show up until 8:15."

The door closed behind him, locking automatically, and he groped his way down the dark corridor to flip the light switch on the wall and headed toward his office. Inside, he checked the answering machine and then settled himself at his desk to sort through the paperwork.

An hour later he heard his office door open, and his secretary's voice called out, "Are you here already, Mr. Lasky?" She poked her head around the corner and gave him a smile. "What an early bird today! Trying to catch up after yesterday's busy schedule?"

He made an affirmative noise, finishing one of the forms he was completing for the state, and turned to her. "Martha, I noticed there were a number of students out behind the school when I arrived. Is today a special day or something that they couldn't wait to get here?"

Martha snorted. "Special? Hardly! Those are just kids whose parents drop them off on the way to work in the morning, and they hang around the doors, waiting to get into the school. I don't know what time you arrived, but there are usually 20 or more by the time I get here at 7:45. By the time we unlock the doors at 8:15, 40 or 50 kids will come streaming in. And every year the number seems to grow. I guess it's because there are a lot of families in which both parents work, and the parents don't like to leave the kids at home alone. They must think it's safer at school."

Phil Lasky was a little uncomfortable at the thought. "But it was just getting light when I drove in this morning. Those kids must have been dropped off pretty early."

"I expect so," Martha agreed, hanging up her coat and turning on the computers.

Off and on during the day Phil Lasky would be reminded of the little group of students who had been outside the school that morning, and he marveled at how things had changed since he went to school. He remembered sleeping as late as possible until his mother called him. Then he'd smell the aroma of eggs and bacon, and sleepily stumble down the stairs, plunking himself in front of the table to be served. At the time it had seemed like the natural order of things, but obviously times had changed.

In the interoffice mail that arrived in the afternoon, he pulled out an envelope from the superintendent, to give it immediate attention. As he read the memo, the timeliness of the message hit home.

TO: All Principals
FROM: Harvey Richards, Superintendent

It has been brought to my attention that we need to take purposeful steps to deal with a problem of student safety. Many students are arriving at school in the early morning while it is still dark, dropped off by parents on their way to work. While we can appreciate the motivation and reasoning behind this practice, it is not in students' best interest to be left unattended at a deserted school an hour or more before adults arrive. Parents apparently have the mistaken idea that their students will be supervised, no matter how early they arrive at school.

Obviously, the school is incurring undesirable liability in this situation. We need to develop a policy that addresses not only the school's liability for students before and after the formal school day, but preferably a program to deal with the need for student supervision, which is evident at almost all schools.

Within the next week I would like you to (1) assess the situation at your own school, documenting the time at which students first arrive, and a general time-graph of the numbers involved and (2) develop some ideas to deal with the problem. It goes without saying that the alternatives you identify cannot further strain our already tight budget, nor do I think it realistic to look at parents as a source of volunteers, inasmuch as the ones who are employed will not be available, and the ones who aren't will want to stay home to supervise their own children. Also, remember anything involving teacher supervision would have to go to the bargaining table.

This is a sticky issue, but we need to address it as expeditiously as possible.

That evening at the dinner table Phil mentioned the problem to his wife. "I was really appalled to see those kids at school this morning while it was still *dark,*" he commented. Then he noticed a strained expression on her face. "What's wrong? Is there something I should know?"

She rose from the table, and he watched questioningly as she went to the kitchen counter and returned with the newspaper. "Apparently, you haven't seen the evening headlines yet," she said, thrusting the paper into his hands.

A headline read, "Middle School Student Sexually Assaulted," and the story related how a girl had been accosted in the early morning as she approached the playground of a city school.

Phil's first thought was that the incident described could easily have occurred at *his* school. His next thought was that he was living on borrowed time. Things were going to heat up–fast.

Suggested Learning Activities

Analyze the Case

1. Which concepts from Part I of this text would have been helpful in preventing or ameliorating the problem of student safety before and after regular school hours?
2. Why was Phil Lasky caught off guard by this problem?
3. How might Phil Lasky best assess the *extent* of need for supervisory activities and/or personnel before and after school?

4. How do you think Phil Lasky would have responded to learning about students arriving early in the morning if he had not received the letter from the superintendent?

Discuss the Larger Issues

1. The problem of unsupervised children appears to be one consequence of changing demographic and economic patterns in this country. What should be the role of the school, if any, in responding to this problem? What should be the role of the community?
2. Evaluate the role of the news media in identifying areas for improvement in education. Is the influence basically positive or negative?
3. To what extent should funding for extended hours of student supervision at school come from parent fees or from local taxes? Should state funds be provided?

Be a Problem Solver Assume that you are Phil Lasky. In light of potential danger to unattended children at school in the early morning hours, how would you:

1. Address the immediate problem at your school?
2. Respond to the superintendent's request for recommendations for a long-term resolution of the problem?

Test Your Solution To test your proposed plan of action for dealing with the problem presented in the case, you and the class should create and role-play one or more of the following interactions:

1. A telephone call from a local television reporter who plans to do some videotaping at your school one day this week, early in the morning, and wants to interview you briefly regarding student safety before and after the school day.
2. A telephone call from the Parent Teacher Association (PTA) president, communicating concerns expressed to her by neighbors and friends after seeing the newspaper article on the student's assault.
3. A meeting of the district administrative team with the superintendent to review recommendations and select a course of action for ensuring student safety before and after normal school hours.

Investigate Further

1. How does your school ensure student safety for students who may arrive early in the morning?
2. What is your district's *written* policy regarding students who come to school early or who are not picked up by parents until 5 or 6 P.M.?
3. Does your district sponsor an after-school program for students who have no home supervision?
4. What is the school's legal liability for students who arrive on the premises before school hours and/or stay late in the afternoon?

12
WHAT SHOULD BE THE ROLE OF THE STUDENT NEWSPAPER?

It had been two weeks since the school year's first issue of the Riverside student newspaper, *The Sword,* had been published. Although the tempers in the guidance department had now cooled, the principal sensed that the emotional vibrations generated by the paper's attack on the counselors had still not completely subsided.

The principal himself had been rather upset about the article–a strong indictment of the guidance department for its alleged lack of interest and concern with the non-college-bound students. The principal felt the facts and observations made in the news story were essentially true, so he didn't think he should censor or criticize the student editors–in spite of strong pressure from the counselors that he do so. When they came to him complaining about the newspaper article, he conceded that the students should have used more tact and diplomacy, but the counselors were not easily mollified, and it was clear they were going to be unhappy for some time.

Although the school newspaper had become more and more outspoken in recent times, it had never before attacked any department or made editorial comments about educational or professional matters. In the past, *The Sword* had primarily confined itself to reporting on social activities, athletics, student personalities, clubs, or specific subjects in the curriculum. It had occasionally included articles on abortion, militarism in America, and other social issues, but in general, the principal had been pleased with the content. He felt fortunate that *The Sword* was not like some of those school papers–particularly of the underground variety–that spent all their time on either social issues or attacks on the school itself. In fact, the principal could recall only one other article that might have been considered critical, and in that instance, the criticism had been directed toward the school prom. At the time he hadn't been very happy about it, but he had overlooked the article, hoping that there would not be a recurrence.

This year, it appeared that the principal might face a troublesome situation if the first issue of the student newspaper was any harbinger of things to come. The editorial board was now composed of students who were bright and very independent, and they would not be easy to deal with. The principal had already decided–contrary to the recommendations of his assistant principal and the guidance department–that he would ignore the tenor of the first edition. He preferred to avoid a conflict with the student editors and the journalism adviser, all of whom had strong feelings about adult interference. He also hoped that things would settle down and the paper would become more occupied with student-oriented activities. Now, as he thought about that decision, the principal hoped fervently that it had been the right one.

On Friday the second issue of *The Sword* was distributed in classes during the last five minutes of the school day. Normally the teachers looked over the paper before passing it out to the students, but this Friday there was no such opportunity because the paper arrived late. Immediately after the papers were handed out, the dismissal bell rang and the students flocked out of the classrooms, reading and chattering on the way to their lockers. With few exceptions, the teachers headed down to the faculty room for their after-school cup of coffee.

As several of the teachers in the faculty room began to read *The Sword,* one of them swore and directed the attention of the others in the room to the student editorial on the paper's second page.

As the teacher finished reading the editorial aloud, there was considerable muttering and complaining from the other people in the room. Everyone was upset about the paper's criticism, although a few teachers silently conceded to themselves that its main thrust was accurate.

Someone suggested that the administration should immediately take disciplinary action against the student editor and the newspaper staff, and most of those in the room seemed to agree that such a step would be the least that should be done. A counselor proposed that in the future all editorials and newspaper articles should be screened by a faculty committee prior to publication. The counselor's suggestion was viewed by a few faculty members as representing censorship and an extra burden on the faculty, but many of the teachers felt that the administration, or someone else with authority, should pass judgment on the contents of the newspaper before it was approved for publication. Obviously no one had carefully examined the current issue in advance.

Finally the guidance director volunteered to go see the principal and apprise him of how most of the faculty felt about the student newspaper. No one could predict how the principal would respond to the editorial, but the teachers were hopeful that he would be as concerned as they were. As one of them put it, "First the guidance department and now the teachers. The next attack could easily be on the administration!"

Suggested Learning Activities

Analyze the Case

1. What is your assessment of the concept held by the principal about the role of the student newspaper in this school?
2. If you had been the principal in this situation, how would you have responded differently, if at all, from the way the principal in this case did to the counselor's complaint about the article in the student newspaper criticizing the guidance department?
3. At what point would you have taken action either to change the role of the student newspaper or to prepare the other members of the school community for a more critical paper? What is the specific nature of the action that you think should have been taken?
4. Assume that the editorial on page 2 of the second issue of *The Sword* contained charges that were accurate.
   a. Do you think the student paper has a right to print this kind of editorial?
   b. What action, if any, do you think the principal should take in regard to the conditions described in the editorial?

Discuss the Larger Issues

1. What should be the role of the student newspaper in the school? Should it be permitted to criticize and expose groups and/or individuals associated with the school? What might be the ramifications of such criticism? Where should the line be drawn on what may be printed in the student newspaper?
2. Who should determine what is published in the student newspaper? What role, if any, should the administration play? The faculty adviser to the newspaper? The faculty as a group? The students?
3. What is the best way to ensure that the policies and procedures established for the operation of the newspaper, whatever they may be, are followed by all concerned?

Be a Problem Solver In this case the criticism of the student newspaper has offended the faculty. They have decided to send a representative to the principal to inform him of their feelings and persuade him to take action to prevent future articles of this nature from being printed. If you were the principal, how would you handle this situation?

Test Your Solution To assess the strengths or weaknesses of your proposed solution, create and role-play one or more of the following situations in class:

1. A conference between the guidance director and the principal.
2. A conference between the principal and the newspaper adviser.
3. A meeting between the principal and the student editorial board.
4. Any other situation that would provide feedback on the strengths or weaknesses of your proposed solution.

Investigate Further

1. What are the *legal* rights and obligations of the student newspaper in your school?
2. What is the school board and administration policy in your district on what the student newspaper can or cannot print?
3. If the editorial presented in this case appeared in the student newspaper at your school, and the observations of the student editor or editors were true, how would the following groups react?
   a. Teachers
   b. Administrators
   c. Central office
   d. Parents

13
A COMPLEX DISCIPLINE PROBLEM

After the assistant principal concluded his telephone conversation with Mrs. Richardson about her daughter Cindy's attendance problems, he started to leave his office to go down to the faculty room for coffee. As he went out the door, he felt a surge of irritation as he confronted Mike Cunningham, no stranger to the assistant principal's premises. The boy explained that Mrs. Blackman had kicked him out of class. Should he wait in the outer office?

The assistant principal had really been looking forward to a few moments of relaxation in the faculty lounge and didn't feel in the mood for talking with Mike Cunningham, but as he weighed the alternatives, he decided that he might as well take care of the boy now.

Frowning, the assistant principal directed Mike toward the inner office and sighed as he remembered his earlier contacts with the student. Mike had been sent to the assistant principal's office a number of times in the past and on at least two other occasions this semester, usually for attendance and disciplinary reasons. The boy was frequently absent or tardy, and he had been sent to the office previously by Mrs. Blackman for talking back to her.

Mike did poorly in school, and his grades were usually low. His family had limited education and both of his parents worked. They had been called to the school for conferences several times, and although they seemed interested in their son's welfare, they were apparently unable to exercise any control over him.

The assistant principal knew that he hadn't been very successful in working with Mike in the past, and he wondered what kind of luck he would have this time. Obviously, it wasn't going to be easy to square this kid away.

In response to the assistant principal's questioning, Mike explained with a shrug that Mrs. Blackman had always "had it in" for him. Today, when he was trying to find out an assignment from someone, she had chewed him out for fooling around in class. He had tried to establish his innocence, but the teacher became angry, accused him of back talk, and told him to get out.

The assistant principal listened carefully to the student's explanation and tried to pin down or expose inconsistencies, but Mike stuck to his story. Recognizing that it would be necessary to talk with Mrs. Blackman, the assistant principal told Mike to wait in the outer office for a few minutes while he went to see the teacher.

When the assistant principal knocked on the door to Mrs. Blackman's classroom, she responded as though she had been expecting him. They discussed the incident in the hallway, and Mrs. Blackman related that Mike had been persistently inattentive and was distracting other students. When she had directed him to quit bothering the people sitting around him and to start paying attention to what was going on in class, he started to argue with her, claiming that he hadn't done anything wrong and that she was always picking on him. She had told Mike that she would be glad to discuss it with him later, but he had continued to argue, so she finally just sent him to the office.

The assistant principal was momentarily stymied. The two stories were obviously in conflict. He decided not to mention the discrepancies to the teacher, but told her that he would talk to Mike.

Walking back down the corridor to the office, he tried to evaluate what he had heard. Although he leaned toward accepting Mrs. Blackman's version of what had happened, he couldn't be sure. The assistant principal had occasionally heard parents complain that Mrs. Blackman was too strict and rigid in her expectations for student behavior. It was possible that Mike, annoying as he might be, was simply unfortunate in drawing the teacher's ire without actually being responsible for disrupting the class. In light of the student's previous record, however, the assistant principal was hesitant to reject the teacher's explanation of what had happened in the classroom.

Even if the teacher were right, the assistant principal knew that he would have trouble improving Mike's behavior. The assistant principal had not experienced much success in the past in working with Mike, and he certainly didn't have any ideas now about how to proceed with the boy.

Suggested Learning Activities

Analyze the Case

1. What personal and situational factors may be responsible for Mike's performance in school?
2. In what way, if any, would you have handled the conference with Mike Cunningham differently?

3. What aspects of the assistant principal's attitude toward the student and toward the teacher may unconsciously influence his resolution of the discrepancies between the two stories and his final action in regard to either the student or the teacher?

Discuss the Larger Issues

1. To what extent are the school and its program responsible for student discipline problems?
2. What should be the roles of the following individuals and groups in preventing and dealing constructively with student discipline problems?
   a. The assistant principal
   b. The principal
   c. The teachers
   d. The student body
   e. Parents
3. To what degree are current practices for preventing and dealing with student discipline problems effective? How could improvement be best achieved?

Be a Problem Solver The assistant principal is faced with the fact that the story the student related to him and the story that the teacher told him are in conflict. He also still has Mike Cunningham in his office. If you were the assistant principal in this situation, what would you do? What assumptions are you making? Utilize appropriate administrative and social science concepts from Part I of the text in planning and implementing your approach.

Test Your Solution To test your proposed plan of action for dealing with the problem presented at the end of the case, create and role-play one or more of the following interactions in class:

1. A conference between the assistant principal and Mike Cunningham.
2. A conference between the assistant principal, Mike Cunningham, and Mrs. Blackman.

Investigate Further

1. What innovative approaches to preventing and dealing constructively with student discipline problems have been developed during the last several years?
2. What is the school board policy in your district for preventing and dealing constructively with student discipline problems?
3. What are the roles of the following individuals or groups in your school or school district with regard to student discipline problems?
   a. The assistant principal
   b. The principal
   c. The teachers
   d. The student body
   e. Parents

14
THE BULLYING PROBLEM (SIMULATION EXERCISE)

Background and Instructions

The coordinator of research in your district has completed a study showing that the school district has a significant rise in bullying at all of the school levels. The school board has directed the building administrators and supervisors (of which you are one) to address the problem. To accomplish this objective, you (and the rest of the class) need to:

1. Ask those questions of the coordinator of research (the instructor or group leader will play this role) that will elicit information on the nature of the problem.
2. Develop a set of recommendations for ameliorating the bullying problem.
3. Present those recommendations in a simulation in which several class members play the role of the superintendent's cabinet receiving your report.

Note to instructor or group leader: One of the main purposes of this exercise is to provide students with practice in asking relevant, incisive questions, so no information is provided in the text about this district's bullying problem, other than that it is a significant one. The instructor may assume whatever characteristics of the problem he or she believes would be likely, given the background of students in the class.

15
STUDENT CAN'T TAKE PRESSURE ANY LONGER

Miss Edwards looked up from the paper she was correcting, scanning the room for what seemed like the umpteenth time, carefully looking for any unusual behavior as her students worked on their test. She supposed that she was being unnecessarily vigilant, but she knew that this test was very important to the students, and she felt that with so much riding on it, there might be efforts by some students to cheat.

The examination the students were laboring over was an end-of-the-year competency test to ascertain whether they had mastered certain skills deemed appropriate for that grade level. The school district had moved to competency testing recently because of a belief shared by most administrators and teachers, as well as a large segment of the community, that students were not achieving as well as they should and that there needed to be a tightening of standards. The district policy now required that students who did not achieve a certain level on the end-of-the-year competency test be retained in the same grade for another year, unless they could pass the exam during summer school.

Most students had little reaction to the testing program, perhaps resigned to its inevitability, but a small group of students had vigorously protested the policy of keeping students back for a year. Their protests, however, were to no avail. The school board and administration had decided that something had to be done to improve academic standards.

As Miss Edwards tried to concentrate again on correcting her papers, she remembered how quiet the classroom had grown on the day she had announced the date of the examination and the subject matter that the test would cover. She had asked whether anyone had any questions about the examination, but no one had said anything. At the time, she was puzzled by their lack of responsiveness, but she knew today from the students' expressions that they were nervous about the test. She supposed that she would be worried too, if she were in a similar situation, and thanked her lucky stars that she wasn't.

Miss Edwards looked up from her papers and again scanned the room, checking on her students. As she looked around, she suddenly noticed that Tim Brown appeared to be looking at the answer sheet of the student to his left. She couldn't be certain, but it seemed as though Tim Brown was cheating. She knew that if she got up from her desk and walked around, her students would be alerted that she was looking for something unusual, so she remained at her desk and pretended to continue correcting papers. As she worked on her papers, she continued to view Tim. There seemed to be little question that the boy was cheating.

At the end of the examination period Miss Edwards asked Tim Brown to remain in the room, and she proceeded to compare his answers with those of the boy seated to his left. There could be no doubt: with only two exceptions, the answer sheets were identical. Obviously, Tim had copied most of his answers. When she confronted him with the evidence, he refused to admit his guilt.

Sensing that she would not be able to extract a confession, Miss Edwards told Tim that he would have to see the principal.

A short time later, Miss Edwards and Tim entered the principal's office, where Miss Edwards proceeded to explain to Mr. Matthews what had transpired. When Tim maintained only silence in response to the teacher's report, Mr. Matthews decided to interrogate the boy.

"Well, Tim, it appears as though you were caught in the act, weren't you?"

"No, I didn't do it."

"Then why were your answers almost exactly the same as the ones on the other answer sheet?"

"I don't know."

"You realize that if you don't tell us the truth, something very serious will happen to you. We already know that you cheated. You were observed copying someone else's answers, and we have evidence that you were cheating. If you lie to me, then you're committing another serious offense. Perhaps we need to give your parents a call about this matter."

Tim didn't say anything for a few moments, but then a tear escaped from one of his downcast eyes. In a shaky voice he finally conceded that he may have cheated, but only because a number of the other students in the class were also cheating. Several students had managed to obtain copies of the answer key and had been using it during the test. He also mentioned that there were discussions on a Facebook private group page where the answer key was shared as well.

The principal had heard a rumor just that morning that a teacher's answer key had been stolen, but the rumor had seemed far-fetched, and no one on the staff had reported such a loss. Now he tried to press Tim Brown for more information.

"Who are these other students?"

Silence.

"You'd better tell me, because you know I'm going to find out sooner or later."

Silence.

Since Tim did not appear inclined to be cooperative, and it was nearly the end of the day, the principal told the boy that over the weekend he had better decide to come up with the names of the other students who had been cheating. Tim was also instructed to bring his parents to the principal's office when he returned to school on Monday. Mr. Matthews concluded the conference by saying that, as things stood now, Tim would probably be given a failing grade on the end-of-the-year competency test, although that decision *might* be changed if Tim would agree to identify the students who had the answer key.

Tim's expression was strained as he left the principal's office, and Miss Edwards could tell that he was shaken. She felt sorry for him because she knew from a previous conference with his parents that he would be in deep trouble when they found out about the matter. They were achievement-oriented people who set high standards for Tim. He generally worked very hard to meet those expectations, but because his ability was only average, his efforts frequently disappointed his parents. Tim's latest behavior would surely contribute further to their frustration.

After Tim had left, the principal questioned Miss Edwards a little about her perception of the other students who were taking the examination, but she couldn't give much help. Mr. Matthews instructed her to meet with him the first thing on Monday morning so they could map out a strategy for resolving the problem. Perhaps, before then, Tim would reveal the names of other students who had been cheating.

Miss Edwards left the principal's office and went to the faculty room for a cup of coffee. There she discussed with a colleague, Mrs. Bailey, what had happened. Mrs. Bailey was not particularly surprised by the behavior of Tim or the other students and even contended that it was perfectly understandable, given the importance placed on passing the competency test. She felt that students were subjected to too much pressure by the testing program and by the policy of retaining students in the grade if they did not do well on the end-of-the-year examination.

"Besides," she observed, "a lot of people in our society cheat. I'm not condoning what Tim did, but look at the people who cheat on their income tax, pad their expense accounts, exceed posted speed limits, or cheat in other ways. For that matter, think about how many teachers 'cheat' on their daily school arrival and departure times, or take 'sick days' when they're just tired of coming to school. I wonder what kind of models we adults are providing for kids like Tim."

Miss Edwards disagreed with Mrs. Bailey, told her so, and then walked out of the faculty room feeling distressed. She was not looking forward to the weekend or the following Monday morning.

On Sunday the following brief item was in the city newspaper.

> Tim Brown, son of Dr. and Mrs. Lester Brown, 8415 Newcastle Road, was found unconscious in the basement of his home on Saturday. Nearby was found an empty bottle of amphetamines. He was rushed to City Hospital where his stomach was pumped, and he is now in satisfactory condition. A handwritten note found in the basement suggested a possible suicide attempt.

Suggested Learning Activities

Analyze the Case

1. What, if anything, should the teacher have done differently when she observed Tim Brown cheating?
2. Evaluate the principal's approach to Tim Brown. What administrative and/or social science concepts does he appear to be employing? Not employing?
3. What is your assessment of the arguments advanced by Mrs. Bailey?

Discuss the Larger Issues

1. Why do some students cheat and other students not cheat?
2. What can the school do about preventing student cheating? What should it do when it apprehends student cheaters?
3. What kinds of factors contribute to student suicides? What can the school do about these factors?
4. What is the impact of social networking such as Facebook and Twitter on cheating? What can administrators do?

Be a Problem Solver Assume that you are the principal in this case and you have just finished reading the newspaper article about Tim Brown. What would be your approach to dealing with this situation and the other problems mentioned in the case study? Utilize administrative and social science concepts from Part I of the text in planning and implementing your approach.

Test Your Solution To test your proposed plan for dealing with the problems presented in this case, you and your colleagues should create and role-play one or more of the following situations:

1. A meeting between the principal and Tim Brown's parents.
2. A conference between the principal and Miss Edwards.
3. A conference between the principal, Miss Edwards, and Tim Brown.

Investigate Further

1. What is the attitude of students, teachers, administrators, and parents at your school toward student cheating?
2. How widespread is student cheating at your school? How reliable and valid are the data about the extent of cheating?
3. Ascertain your school's or district's policy toward student cheating.
4. How significant a problem is student suicide in your school? How reliable and valid are the data about this problem? What, if anything, is the school doing about the possibility of student suicides?

16
"ZERO TOLERANCE" FOR WEAPONS IN SCHOOLS

Green banks is a suburban middle school located in a state that has a law forbidding students to carry any item that resembles a weapon on school property. The penalty for noncompliance is a minimum of one-year suspension from school for the student and a year in jail or a $3,500 fine for the parents. The local school division enforces this law, which was designed to undercut a serious problem of violence on school grounds. The school principal can deviate very little from the code. When a student is recommended for a long-term suspension, a hearing is held with a police officer who may accept the recommendation, reduce the time, or refer the student to an alternative school environment. The weapons policy is in the *Student Code of Conduct,* the guidebook students receive each year and that parents must sign and return to confirm that they understand the policies.

Edward Hangly is a 13-year-old honor roll student with no disciplinary record during his seven years of schooling. Recently, Edward was helping clean out his dad's car, a vehicle used in the family's body-shop business. He picked up several items, including a Swiss army knife, which he placed in his backpack and carried into the house. Edward failed to empty his backpack the next day before he left for school. Another student spotted the knife in Edward's backpack. Bound by the school's honor code, the student reported Edward to the gym teacher who took the knife from Edward, asked no questions, refused to hear Edward's explanation, and delivered the knife to the assistant principal. The assistant principal had the secretary fax a letter to Edward's parents, asking them to pick Edward up at school immediately and informing them that he would be recommended for a one-year suspension.

In less than one hour Mr. and Mrs. Hangly arrived at school with an attorney to explain the situation resulting in Edward's having a closed Swiss army knife in his backpack and asking for a more tolerant approach. The assistant principal read the school policy and dismissed the parents and the attorney, who informed the assistant principal they would see him in court.

A local television channel showed a happy Hangly family on the evening news with mom's arm around Edward and dad's hand on his shoulder as they spoke. The parents' message indicated they would continue their efforts to fight the suspension.

Suggested Learning Activities

Analyze the Case

1. Is a closed Swiss army knife with a 2-inch blade a weapon?
2. What, if anything, could the gym teacher have done differently when she received the student's report concerning the knife?
3. Evaluate the manner in which the assistant principal handled the situation. What administrative concepts does he appear to apply? What other concepts could he have used?
4. What is your assessment of the arrival of the parents with an attorney?
5. If the item collected from the father's car had been a plastic toy knife, would it have been handled the same way?

Discuss the Larger Issues

1. Evaluate the procedure used to teach students school policies.
2. When is there a need to search for alternative disciplinary approaches and when should a principal recommend maximum punishment?
3. What public relations effect could this issue create?
4. Could this become a major political issue and result in legislative action to alter the state law? If so, how?

Be a Problem Solver Assume you are the assistant principal and have just viewed the evening news to learn this issue is on the way to court. How would you prepare for the court hearing? Consider administrative and public relations concepts in planning and implementing your approach.

Test Your Solution To test your proposed action plan for this case, you could do the following:

1. Research other similar cases.
2. Role-play a court hearing.

Investigate Further

1. What is the attitude of students, teachers, administrators, and parents at your school toward zero-tolerance punishment?
2. How significant a problem are items that could be considered weapons in schools?
3. Does the political climate demand zero tolerance for student cellular phones on school property?

17
STUDENT DRUG PROBLEM AT WASHINGTON SCHOOL

The faculty members congregating in the teachers' lounge before school were upset about last night's newspaper article on the rise of heroin sales, distribution, and usage at Washington School. Rumors had previously been circulating for some time about drugs sold in the school restrooms and cafeteria, but until now no one seemed to have any actual evidence that this was indeed taking place—although one couldn't be sure from the newspaper story.

> DRUG PROBLEM AT WASHINGTON SCHOOL
>
> Rumors continue to fly at Washington School about a recurring heroin problem. While facts are difficult to ascertain, the problem seems to have started again on a very limited basis last spring and has grown, until now drug use is said to be rampant among students at the school. It has been alleged that along with the heroin problem, a variety of drugs, including crack, marijuana, and amphetamines, is being sold in the cafeteria during the noon hour. They are also reportedly being sold and used in school restrooms.
>
> Although some differences of opinion have been expressed by students, faculty, and parents on the extent of the problem, the general feeling is that steps must be taken immediately to curb this dangerous situation.

The administration of the school has voiced concern and has the matter under surveillance but has indicated that there is "no evidence that a serious problem does, in fact, exist."

As school started that morning, classes buzzed with conversation about the newspaper article, and teachers experienced difficulty in beginning the day's lesson. When several of them finally decided to allow discussion about the issue, students spent an entire class period talking about the article and the purported problem.

In the meantime, the principal and his assistants were meeting to discuss the situation, as they had done on numerous other occasions. When rumors of drug use on school premises had first started to circulate again last spring, the administration had tried to track down each story, but to no avail. No one would volunteer any information about the actual sale or use of drugs, and the administration had not been successful in catching anyone in the act.

After school had opened in the fall, the administration had tried to increase the surveillance of restrooms and the cafeteria but encountered certain difficulties. Girls' restrooms, in particular, had always constituted a problem, even in trying to catch cigarette smokers. The custodial matron had been told to check the restrooms periodically as she moved from area to area in her work, but this had not proved to be very effective. Either the matron did not check often enough or she wasn't sharp enough to outwit the girls. There was also some indication that she didn't relish this additional task.

The major hindrance in surveillance, of course, was the practical impossibility for the administration to be everywhere; there were too many restrooms and too many other administrative responsibilities to carry out. Still, it was obvious that *something* had to be done. The central office had indicated concern, and several members of the school board had expressed displeasure about the unfavorable publicity. There had been some mention of assigning faculty members to cafeteria and restroom patrol duty, but the principal had rejected this idea because of the continuing lack of clear-cut evidence that drugs were indeed being sold. He was also aware that the faculty might resist or reject such an assignment. But what should be done? None of the alternatives seemed very desirable.

The following week the local newspaper printed an editorial aimed at the drug problem. It was somewhat critical of the school administration because of its unsuccessful efforts to identify and cope with the situation, and it highlighted the growing concern of parents in the community.

Not unexpectedly, the principal received a telephone call the next morning from his immediate superior conveying the central office staff's feeling that the situation was getting out of hand and that corrective measures must be taken. No concrete suggestions were offered, however, other than assigning teachers to patrol the halls and restrooms.

At 10:00 A.M. the principal called another meeting with his assistants. There was unanimous recognition that the situation demanded action but few ideas on how to proceed. An assistant principal finally suggested that students might be able to help with the problem. Perhaps representatives from the student government or some other student group could help in the cafeteria during the noon hour and could check restrooms during their free periods.

Was it a good idea? The principal wasn't sure. Perhaps students would be willing to help, but in an actual situation, would they inform on their peers? More important, was this a proper use of students? What if someone was hurt?

After weighing the potential advantages and disadvantages, the use of students was rejected and the possibility of assigning teachers was again brought up for discussion. The principal was still concerned about assigning the faculty to patrol duty, yet he was conscious of the fact that his present program of surveillance was being criticized by the community because no one had been caught selling or using drugs at the school. The principal had an uneasy feeling about whether patrol duty represented an appropriate use of professional personnel and whether it would be accepted by the faculty. Unfortunately, no other alternatives were presented, so the principal reluctantly decided to utilize faculty assistance to cope with the problem.

At 2:00 P.M. that day a memo was placed in the faculty mailboxes announcing a meeting after school, and at 4:00 P.M. the teachers filed into the room. The principal began immediately to explain the situation thoroughly and, after 20 minutes, concluded by pointing out the limited alternatives available to the administration. Then he distributed the faculty assignments to cafeteria and restroom patrol duty, which were set up on a rotating basis so that everyone would be participating for the same length of time, not more than twice a week or a total of 60 minutes.

Although no one said anything directly or asked any questions during the principal's presentation, there were many side glances and low murmurs between faculty members. When he invited the teachers to ask questions after they had received their assignments, there was a dead silence. Uncertain about the meaning of the faculty's reaction, the principal tried to elaborate on his earlier remarks about the need to deal with the drug problem but found himself only repeating much of what he had already said. He therefore concluded the meeting by offering to meet later in his office with anyone who wished to ask questions or to discuss the matter further. No one ever showed up.

There was considerable discussion in teachers' offices, in the faculty room, and on the way home from school that day. Some teachers perceived the duty with distaste but felt that the administration had no choice other than assigning the faculty to help out with the problem. Others felt that the problem was strictly administrative in nature and that teachers should not be involved.

The discussion continued the next morning in the faculty room and elsewhere in the school over the merits of assigning teachers to cafeteria and restroom duty. Although there were some who felt that this extra duty might violate a provision of their contract dealing with the assignment of teachers, particularly during the noon hour, the assignments thus far had been made in such a way that no one lost out on a lunch period.

The major issue finally seemed to boil down to whether this was something that a professional teacher should do (although there were a few faculty members who simply didn't want to be bothered with an extra responsibility). *Should* a teacher be required to participate in, or become involved with, this type of activity? Wasn't surveillance an area that the administration should handle or, perhaps, even the police?

Counselors, who also had been placed on the duty roster, were particularly concerned. What would this do to their rapport with the students? How could they expect students who might be bothered about drugs or even be users of drugs to come to counselors to discuss their problems if counselors were viewed as arms of the administration? Wouldn't their effectiveness be impaired?

The following Monday the schedule of faculty patrols began. After a week and a half, the administration began to hear via the grapevine that some teachers and counselors were less than thorough in "making the rounds," and that others were not carrying out their duties at all. It was not known how widespread this was, but if it was at all prevalent, some action would be called for by the administration or the situation would soon deteriorate.

The principal was in a quandary. Since the faculty patrol had been initiated, parental and community complaints had died down, and the central office and school board seemed generally pleased with the improvement. Still, no one had been caught selling or using drugs, and now it appeared that an incipient faculty–administration confrontation might be brewing. What should he do? What *could* he do? Sometimes he wondered why he had gone into administration.

Suggested Learning Activities

Analyze the Case

1. What is your reaction to the newspaper story? To what extent do you believe that it is a good article? What would you do if you disagreed with the article or with an editorial that followed later in the case?
2. From the information presented in this case, do you feel that there is a drug problem at Washington School? What is the basis for your opinion? Would you take no further action if you believed that drugs were not being used or sold at the school itself?

3. What alternatives for coping with the alleged drug problem were available to the administration? What pressures and constraints were operating in the situation that made decision making difficult for the principal? Do you think that the administration should have tried the idea of using students to help with solving the drug problem? What assumptions are you making?
4. What are your feelings about the way the faculty meeting was handled? How would you have conducted this meeting differently?

Discuss the Larger Issues

1. Should a teacher take class time to discuss something like the school's alleged drug problem, even though the topic may be controversial and the discussion could be embarrassing to the administration? If so, under what set of circumstances would such action be clearly *inappropriate*? What kind of a school policy should be developed to cover this type of situation?
2. To what extent is coping with a drug problem the responsibility of everyone in the school or only the administration? What is the professional responsibility of a teacher or counselor in regard to coping with a possible drug problem in the school?

Be a Problem Solver At the end of this case, the principal is faced with an incipient faculty revolt and the possibility that the drug problem still has not been solved. If you were the principal, how would you handle the situation? What factors may limit your flexibility in arriving at a solution?

Test Your Solution To test your proposed plan of action for dealing with the problems presented in this case, create and role-play one or more of the following situations in class:

1. A conference between the principal and those faculty members who are not carrying out their patrol duties.
2. A meeting between the principal and the faculty.
3. A telephone call to the principal from the superintendent.
4. A meeting with the student council, which is protesting the faculty's patrolling of the restrooms.
5. A telephone call to the principal from the newspaper.

Investigate Further

1. What is the possibility that drugs are being sold or used in your school? How would you ascertain that a problem exists?
2. What is your school board's policy on drugs in the school? To what extent are there problems in enforcing the policy?
3. What program does your school have for detecting student use or selling of drugs on school premises?

18
WHAT TO DO ABOUT THE "MORNING AFTER"?

School had been in session for approximately two months, and it appeared that Madison School was off to a good beginning. It was true that for the last several years there had been a drug problem at the school, but that was now almost under control. During that period of time, however, the school had undergone considerable turmoil. Parents had been upset, the administration had had difficulty in coping with the situation, and the school had received a great deal of unfavorable publicity. Therefore, everyone was relieved that the drug problem had been successfully dealt with and pleased that no other issues had yet developed this school year.

At the weekly meeting of the school counselors, a problem was discussed that appeared to possess grave implications. Steve Williams, one of the counselors, reported that a rather popular student had come to see him about a personal problem that upset her greatly. She said that she had been going steady for some time, and her boyfriend had begun to make sexual advances. She had rejected his advances thus far, on moral grounds and from a fear of possible pregnancy, but now she was weakening. She further confided that her boyfriend had offered to provide her with the new "morning-after" pill, which he said he could secure from a source in the school. But she wanted the counselor's advice. Should she take the pill? Was it wrong for her to have sexual relations with someone she loved?

The questions posed by the girl had created several dilemmas for the counselor. At the time he had wondered what his position should be on the matter. Does a counselor have the right to influence a student about what the counselor believes is morally wrong?

Unable to resolve this inner conflict, the counselor had encouraged the girl to talk about her problem. When she had asked him point-blank what she should do, however, he had tried to hedge and finally had suggested that perhaps she should discuss the problem with her minister or her parents. At that point, the girl had walked out.

Now as Steve related the incident to his colleagues, he expressed concern about his own behavior. Had he acted appropriately during the conference? Should he have informed the principal of the possibility that someone was selling the pill in the school?

The discussion at the meeting quickly warmed up as the counselors argued about Steve's actions and whether the administration should be informed about the possibility that the pill was being sold on school premises. Most of those at the meeting seemed to agree that it was not really the role of the counselor to respond to the moral question presented by the girl, but others felt that a position of neutrality offered her no assistance at a time when a word from a trusted adult might have guided her in the right direction. On the issue of whether the administration should be advised that the pill was being sold in the school, the counselors were almost equally divided, although the guidance director felt very strongly that the principal should be alerted.

After the meeting, the counselor, Steve Williams, took time to sort out his feelings. In some respects he was sorry that he had brought the problem to the attention of his colleagues. He had received no real help or ideas from them on how he might have better handled the situation, and he didn't know what he would do if the problem arose again. He was glad of one thing, though, and that was that he had not revealed to the other counselors the name of the girl or any other names she had mentioned in connection with the pill. He had now decided not to inform the administration about what the girl had confided in him.

Two days later, Steve Williams was called into the principal's office. The principal had been informed by the guidance director of the possibility that the morning-after pill was being sold in school and that Steve might have some information that could shed light on the situation. Rumors were circulating in the school that this pill was being peddled, and the principal had received several calls from concerned parents. What did Steve know about the circumstances surrounding the problem?

This was a difficult situation for both the counselor and the principal. Steve respected the principal and enjoyed working at the school but felt a loyalty to the girl who had placed her trust in him. He was not going to tell the principal what she had related to him.

The principal, on the other hand, wanted to "nip this thing in the bud" before the situation grew out of hand. He liked Steve and was aware of the confidentiality issue but felt that the general welfare of the school transcended that issue. He was determined to get to the bottom of things!

Suggested Learning Activities

Analyze the Case

1. What do you think the counselor should have done in the conference with the student who was seeking advice? What assumptions are you making?
2. What are the advantages and disadvantages of the counselor trying to obtain help from the guidance department? To whom would you have gone for assistance if you had been the counselor?
3. What are some of the social and personal factors that are influencing the principal and the counselor as they face each other in the situation at the end of the case?

Discuss the Larger Issues

1. Should a school counselor discuss with a student personal problems like the one identified in this case? Why or why not?
2. To what extent should a counselor working in a school setting have the right to classify information obtained from a client as confidential? Are there limits to this right? If so, what are they?

Be a Problem Solver In the situation described at the end of the case, both the principal and the counselor have stated their views. If you were either the counselor or the principal, what would be your next step? What would be your course of action if the other person didn't change his position?

Test Your Solution To test your proposed plan of action for dealing with the problem presented at the end of the case, create and role-play one or more of the following situations in class:

1. The conference between the principal and the counselor.
2. A meeting between the principal, the counselor, and the teachers' association representative.
3. A meeting between the principal and the guidance department.
4. A call to the principal, inquiring about a rumor of the morning-after pill being sold at the school.

Investigate Further

1. How do the counselors in your school feel about the situation described in this case? What might be the reactions of the principal?
2. What is the school board policy in your district on what the school counselor should do if students tell him or her that they (or others) are using or selling drugs in school?
3. What is the law in your state on the confidentiality issue in this case?

19
WORKING WITH STUDENTS WITH DISABILITIES AND IDEA

Arthur Lowe, the principal of Midtown High School, was sorting paperwork when two faculty members entered his office. Although he already had an idea of why they were there, he invited them to tell him what was on their minds. Judy League was a special education teacher who had taught students with emotional disturbance at Midtown High for 10 years. She chaired the Child Study Team and was extremely dedicated to student progress. Sarah Bird, the other teacher, taught ninth-grade English. She was also a highly respected teacher and had been nominated for the Teacher of the Year award last year. Mr. Lowe knew that if these two teachers had a concern, it was one he needed to know about.

Throughout this school year, the two teachers had spent a great deal of time focusing on student Billy Bass. Mr. Lowe was aware of many of the interventions the two had made in Billy's educational program. Billy and his behaviors were well known throughout the high school. As an incoming ninth-grader, he had quickly made an impact throughout the building.

A note in the teacher records indicates that Billy's mother, a single parent with two jobs, has been unavailable for conferences and in a phone conversation said that she is baffled by Billy's behaviors. She said she is often unable to supervise Billy at home and has had little time to focus on changing his actions. Billy was mainstreamed from Ms. League's classroom for students with emotional disturbances to Ms. Bird's English class. The teachers had been coordinating efforts to assist Billy to be successful. For example, they had made efforts to modify his instructional and environmental triggers, provided opportunities for positive social exchanges and emotional support, offered praise and appropriate academic pacing, avoided power struggles, and completed a behavioral improvement plan and daily performance contracts. Billy also had weekly meetings with the school guidance counselor.

The teachers' efforts had resulted in some improvements lately, and Billy had begun to trust their intentions. Incidences of behavioral difficulties at school and at home had decreased over the past two months. Ms. League, Ms. Bird, and Mr. Lowe were extremely pleased with the success.

However, Mr. Lowe could tell by the looks on the teachers' faces that something was wrong today. Their concern was clearly evident. Ms. Bird had witnessed a heated discussion between Billy and another child in the hallway after her class, and Ms. League confirmed that Billy was extremely agitated when he entered her second-bell class.

While the teachers were voicing their concerns to the principal, Billy was in third-period physical education class. As they discussed the hallway altercation, Ms. Pennington, the school secretary, burst into the office nearly out of breath. "Mr. Lowe, you need to get to the gym right away!" she said. "Please hurry!" She had already sent for the school nurse.

When Mr. Lowe arrived in the gymnasium, three physical education teachers were moving students from the gym to the locker room. One teacher was restraining Billy by the gym wall as the nurse hovered over another student, Jason Miller, on the floor. The school security guard had removed a third child, Tom Thompson, from the scene already. Jason was bleeding and had just regained consciousness. The nurse sent Ms. Pennington to summon an ambulance and call Jason's parents.

By the time Mr. Lowe removed Billy from the gym, watched the paramedics place Jason in the ambulance, sent the other third-bell physical education students to the auditorium to wait for fourth bell, and ensured the safe cleanup of bodily fluids from the gym floor, Jason's father was waiting in his office. Mr. Miller was irate. "How can you let this happen in a public school? I thought this was a 'safe school'!"

Mr. Miller's voice quivered as he demanded answers. "What are you going to do to those children who beat my son?" The principal was shaken. Mr. Lowe had not had time to gather all the facts leading up to the incident. How could he offer any answers? He was, however, aware that Billy had previously been identified as a student with emotional disturbances, and he knew that under new Individuals with Disabilities Education Act (IDEA) mandates, Billy's consequences might be limited.

The principal was not familiar with the other child involved, Tom Thompson, although he had heard one of the physical education teachers speaking derogatorily about his previous behaviors. All that Mr. Lowe could tell Mr. Miller was that he needed more time to investigate what had happened. He promised to call Mr. Miller with any new information as it unfolded and suggested that he join his wife and Jason at the hospital while the investigation proceeded.

Mr. Miller was dissatisfied with this response. What was there to investigate? His child was in the hospital–and these two boys had put him there.

Suggested Learning Activities

Analyze the Case

1. Is there anything else that Ms. League or Ms. Bird could have done to prevent this incident?
2. How should Mr. Lowe investigate the event? Offer sequential steps and a rationale for each step.
3. How might this incident and its consequences be expected to affect Billy's behavioral improvement?
4. How might resolution of this incident affect expectations for student behavior in the rest of the school?

Discuss the Larger Issues

1. What role should the school or school system play in preparing teachers and administrators for serious incidents of violence in school?
2. Investigate the discipline regulations of the Individuals with Disabilities Education Act and the effects they have on administrative decisions.
3. At what point do the parents' right to information concerning their child intersect with another student's right to confidentiality?

Be a Problem Solver Mr. Lowe has completed his investigation of the matter and found that Jason had called Billy "stupid" in the hallway after first period because Billy had provided an incorrect response to a question asked in English class. Billy was extremely upset by this and enlisted the help of his friend Tom to "jump" Jason during gym class. All accounts by teachers and students indicate that Billy and Tom beat up Jason without any resistance from Jason or any other classmates. Billy's mother, a single parent insisted that the event had been a manifestation of his emotional disabilities and that his consequences must be minimal. Tom's mother requested testing for her son. She stated that she believes her child also has emotional disabilities and that he should receive minimal consequences. Mr. Miller has called the school, central office, and school board daily to check on the progress of the investigation. He is adamant that the students be expelled in order to maintain a safe public school environment. If you were Mr. Lowe, how would you handle the situation? Utilize social science and administrative concepts from Part I in your approach to the problem.

Test Your Solution Develop a plan of action for dealing with incidents of violence at Midtown High School. Then test your proposed plan by role-playing one or more of the following situations:

1. A conference in which Mr. Lowe explained the results of the investigation to Mr. Miller.
2. The screening process for determining Tom's eligibility for special education services and thus possibly limited consequences for the violent act.
3. Mr. Lowe as he addresses the issue at the next PTA meeting.

Investigate Further

1. What percentage of the students at your school have emotional disturbances? Does each of them have a written individual education plan (IEP) and behavioral intervention plan (BIP)?
2. Are the teachers in your building aware of their mainstreamed students' IEPs and BIPs? Do they adhere to them in their daily classroom practices?
3. What percentage of the acts of violence in your school are committed by students in special education programs?
4. What interim alternative educational settings (IAES) are utilized by your school district? How do they provide for the general curriculum requirements?

20
STUDENT-FORMED GAY–STRAIGHT ALLIANCE

The principal of Equalville High School was walking down the hall of this 780-student high school. She routinely checked the bulletin boards that were in the entrance to the cafeteria for improper notices, either those that reached their expiration date or those not having prior permission. She stopped as her eye caught a bright neon pink flyer:

> COME ON OUT! GLBTQ STUDENT CLUB TUESDAY AFTER SCHOOL IN THE LIBRARY! FOR MORE INFORMATION E-MAIL TINA (tina_is_out@loa.com) OR MATT (luvaqueen@loa.com).

The flyer did not have the proper stamp of approval for posting, so she removed it. On her way back to her office, she noticed several other flyers posted in various places and removed each one. A teacher approached her and stated he was glad that someone was going to do something to stop that nonsense. The principal replied that she had removed the flyers only because they were in violation of school policy: They lacked the "stamp of approval" for posting.

The principal used her two-way radio to call her assistant principal. She told the assistant that he was to find out who these students were and get them to her office as soon as possible. The assistant principal e-mailed both addresses to find out who had posted the flyers. He wrote: "Dear Students,

The principal and I would like to meet with you to find out more about your student club. If we could meet before school tomorrow, please e-mail me. We will meet in principal's office at 7:30 A.M.

Sincerely, Assistant Principal"

Later that evening, the assistant principal received an e-mail answer from both students. Tina was a junior honors student and Matt was a sophomore. They both were excited to hear from the administration of the school and were looking forward to telling them more about the new student organization.

The next morning Tina and Matt arrived early for the meeting. The assistant principal greeted them. He knew Tina well–she was the vice president of student council. Matt was a new transfer student.

The principal commended Tina and Matt for their initiative to create a new student organization to meet the needs of a segment of the school community. She handed them all the flyers from around the school and stated that they were not permitted to post any bill around the school without going through the proper channels. Tina and Matt apologized for bypassing the proper channels and agreed to adhere to the proper procedures immediately.

Because Tina and Matt didn't know the procedure for starting a new student club, the principal gave them the packet of information. A week later, Tina and Matt were back in the principal's office. They had a teacher who had agreed to be the academic adviser, and all the forms had been completed. The principal looked over the information and sent the students to the guidance counselor for the "stamp of approval" for the leaflets. The guidance counselor looked over the information and told Tina and Matt that this was a noncurricular club and would need further investigation. She promised to get back to them after she had a conversation with the principal. The guidance counselor met with the principal and expressed concern that to support a gay-straight school club would be impossible given the climate in the community. She suggested they not support this as a school-sanctioned club to avoid community backlash. The principal agreed.

Later that day Tina and Matt went to the guidance counselor's office for the flyers so that they could post them right away. Both of their requests were met with a resounding no: The club would not be approved, and the flyers could not be posted. Both students were stunned and asked whether the forms were not correct or whether they needed to petition for the club's approval. The guidance counselor told the students to take the matter up with the principal if they had further questions. After a week of trying to schedule an appointment with no success, Tina and Matt told their parents. Tina's mother and father called for an appointment. It was quickly granted. The principal told them that the club could not be allowed because of the potential for school and community discord. Tina's father disagreed and stated that the students should be allowed to meet. After a long unproductive meeting, Tina's father told the principal that he would contact the superintendent and the school board.

The next morning the principal called for an emergency meeting of all faculty and staff to present the matter. She shared the request of Tina and Matt for a new student organization and the denial in the process due to concern about student and community uproar. This was an information-only meeting and therefore was not open for questions or comments.

Later that day the superintendent called the principal to discuss the issue. He agreed that this was a good move on the part of the principal, and troubleshooting before trouble started was the best way to go. Tina's father had tried with no success to meet with the superintendent. After two weeks of attempting a meeting, Tina's and Matt's parents signed up to speak during the public comments and concerns section during the bimonthly school board meeting. Each person was given 3 minutes to speak, and the school might or might not respond. It was an opportunity for community members to have a voice. Both parents contended that the gay, lesbian, bisexual, questioning/straight student club was the same as any other noncurricular club and should be give the rights and privileges per district policy as all other school system–sponsored student organizations. Matt's mother stated that the group would provide a place to feel safe and get support, and give students, teachers, and administrators a place to figure out a way to change the school environment–to stop harassment before it began.

The school board president responded that a subcommittee, with the superintendent as chair, would be formed to examine and make recommendations about the application of that policy governing the formation of student groups. At the next public forum, over 50 parents, religious leaders, teachers, and students signed up to speak: some in support, others pledging to stop this "immorality" in our public schools. Three weeks later, the school board subcommittee recommended dropping all clubs in the school district. The subcommittee further suggested that all extracurricular clubs be replaced with a system of clubs sponsored and led by local adults. Local and national news outlets profiled the story. In the wake of all the negative publicity and the violation of its own district policy, the school board agreed to allow the students to start the club.

The principal, however, eliminated all noncurricular clubs at Equalville High School. At the time, the superintendent said the policy change had been in the works for months. "Clubs have not lived up to what they are supposed to be doing, and the legislature is requiring that we submit additional paperwork and things of that sort. In addition, we want to focus on academics this coming school year."

Prompted by the Equalville High drama club, parent groups pushed the state board of education to back a proposal that would require students to get permission from their parents to join high school clubs. The proposal, which was defeated in a 10–3 vote, would have required students to get a signed notice from their parents to join any of the 100 or more clubs that some schools offered.

Suggested Learning Activities

Analyze the Case

1. What should be the principal's first plan of action?
2. What alternative measure could she have chosen to deal with the issue?

Discuss the Larger Issues

1. How can principals enforce district policies that support students in the face of controversial community issues?

2. In what ways were the students' and parents' right to due process violated? How can principals ensure that underage students and their parents are given the opportunity to exercise their right to appeal school-level decisions?

Be a Problem Solver If you were the principal in this high school, what would you do? Utilize appropriate administrative and social science concepts from Part I of this text in planning and implementing your approach.

Test Your Solution Test your proposed plan for dealing with the circumstances in this case. You and your colleagues should create and role-play one or both of the following situations:

1. A meeting between the principal and students.
2. A press conference that is televised on the evening news.

Investigate Further Research your school district policies related to the formation and support of noncurricular student organizations. Review cases that have received local, state, and national attention. Be sure to research nonmainstream media outlets for multiple perspectives.

BACKGROUND READING

For the reader who would like to develop further background and understanding of the problems and issues presented in this chapter, the following list of readings is provided:

"28 Students Suspended for Cyber Bullying," *Curriculum Review* (vol. 49, no. 7, March 2010), p. 3.

Adair, Jan, "Tackling Teens' No. 1 Problem," *Educational Leadership* (vol. 57, no. 6, March 2000), pp. 44–47.

Baumgartner, Susanne E., Patti M. Valkenburg, and Jochen Peter, "Unwanted Online Sexual Solicitation and Risky Sexual Online Behavior across the Lifespan," *Journal of Applied Developmental Psychology* (vol. 31, no. 6, November 2010), pp. 439–447.

Campbell, Linda, and Bruce Campbell, *Multiple Intelligences and Student Achievement: Success Stories from Six Schools* (Alexandria, VA: Association for Supervisor and Curriculum Development, 1999).

Cavazos-Rehg, Patricia A. et al., "Type of Contraception Method Used at Last Intercourse and Associations with Health Risk Behaviors among U.S. Adolescents," *Contraception* (vol. 82, no. 6, December 2010), pp. 549–555.

Cole, Robert W., *Educating Everybody's Children: Diverse Teaching Strategies for Diverse Learners* (Alexandria, VA: ASCD, 2000).

Conroy, Maureen, Denise Clark, Robert A. Gable, and James J. Fox, "A Look at IDEA 1997 Discipline Provisions: Implications for Change in the Roles and Responsibilities of School Personnel," *Preventing School Failure* (Winter 1999), pp. 64–70.

Cooper, Robert, "Urban School Reform from a Student-of-Color Perspective," *Urban Education* (vol. 34, no. 5, March 2000), pp. 597–622.

Drame, Elizabeth R., and Elise Frattura, "A Charter School's Journey toward Serving All Learners: A Case Study," *Urban Education* (vol. 46, no. 1, January 2011), pp. 55–75.

Duncan, Garrett Albert, "Theorizing Race, Gender, and Violence in Urban Ethnographic Research," *Urban Education* (vol. 34, no. 5, January 2000), pp. 623–644.

Dupper, David R., "Does the Punishment Fit the Crime? The Impact of Zero Tolerance Discipline on At-Risk Youths," *Children & Schools* (April 2010), pp. 67–69.

Feldhusen, John F., "How to Identify and Develop Special Talents," *Educational Leadership* (February 1996), pp. 66–69.

Frymier, Jack, *Values on Which We Agree* (Bloomington, IN: Phi Delta Kappa, 1995).

Giangreco, Michael F., "What Do I Do Now? A Teacher's Guide to Including Students with Disabilities," *Educational Leadership* (February 1996), pp. 56–59.

Goddard, Connie, "Cyber World Bullying," *Education Digest* (vol. 73, no. 7, March 2008), pp. 4–9.

Graybill, Emily C., Kris Varjas, Joel Meyers, and Laurel B. Watson, "Content-Specific Strategies to Advocate for Lesbian, Gay, Bisexual, and Transgender Youth: An Exploratory Study," *School Psychology Review* (vol. 38, no. 4, December 2009), pp. 570–584.

Guerra, Daniel S., "Integrate Violence Prevention into Schools," *New Jersey Education Association Review* (December 1995), pp. 14–19.

Hoff, David J., "Testing Foes Hope to Stoke Middle-Class Ire," *Education Week* (vol. 19, March 22, 2000), pp. 24, 31.

Hyman, Irwin A., and Pamela A. Snook, "Dangerous Schools and What You Can Do about Them," *Phi Delta Kappan* (March 2000), pp. 489–495.

Johns Holder, Beverley, "What the New Individuals with Disabilities Act (IDEA) Means for Students Who Exhibit Aggressive or Violent Behaviors," *Preventing School Failure* (Spring 1998), pp. 102–105.

Johnson, David W., and Roger T. Johnson, *Reducing School Violence through Conflict Resolution* (Alexandria, VA: ASCD, 1995).

Johnston, Robert C., and Debra Viadero, "Unmet Promise: Raising Minority Achievement," *Education Week* (vol. 19, March 15, 2000), pp. 1, 18–21.

Kersey, Katherine C., *Don't Take It Out on Your Kids!: A Parent's Guide to Positive Discipline,* rev. ed. (New York: Berkley Books, 1994).

Khadaroo, Stacy Teicher, "School Bans Facebook for a Week: Five Lessons Students Learned," *Christian Science Monitor* (December 29, 2010).

Landau, Barbara McEwan, and Paul Gathercoal, "Creating Peaceful Classrooms," *Phi Delta Kappan* (February 2000), pp. 450–454.

Lantieri, Linda, "Waging Peace in Our Schools: Beginning with Children," *Phi Delta Kappan* (January 1995), pp. 386–392.

McCown, Clarie H., et al., "Developing Urban School Leaders," *Journal of Staff Development* (vol. 18, no. 3, Summer 1997), pp. 16–19.

McGiboney, Garry W., "Keeping Guns Out of School," *Executive Educator* (November 1995), pp. 31-32.

Mercier, Matthew T., "Fighting to Fit in: Gay-Straight Alliances in Schools under United States Jurisprudence," *International Journal of Human Rights* (vol. 13, no. 2/3, April 2009), pp. 177-191.

Perlstein, Daniel, "Failing at Kindness: Why Fear of Violence Endangers Children," *Educational Leadership* (vol. 57, no. 6, March 2000), pp. 76–79.

Pool, Harbison, and Jane A. Page, *Beyond Tracking: Finding Success in Inclusion Schools* (Bloomington, IN: Phi Delta Kappa, 1995).

Raack, Lenaya, "How Poor Kids Really Are at Risk," *Cityschools* (Fall 1995), pp. 22–26.

Raywid, Mary Anne, and Libby Oshiyama, "Musings in the Wake of Columbine: What Can Schools Do?" *Phi Delta Kappan* (February 2000), pp. 444–449.

Rettig, Michael, and Janice Crawford, "School Phobias," *Streamlined Seminar* (vol. 18, no. 3, March 2000).

Rogalski, Anne, and Rebecca Jacoby, "Giving Failing Students Extra Help: An Alternative to Social Promotion or Retention," *NASSP* (March 2000).

Rousell, Michael A., "Helping Kids Believe in Themselves," *Educational Leadership* (May 1996), pp. 86–87.

"Safe, Disciplined, Drug-Free Schools," *Journal of Virginia Education* (October 1995), pp. 9–14.

Schiffbauer, Pam, "A Checklist for Safe Schools," *Educational Leadership* (vol. 57, no. 6, March 2000), pp. 72–74.

Slavin, Robert E., "Neverstreaming: Preventing Learning Disabilities," *Educational Leadership* (February 1996), pp. 4–7.

Teske, Steven C., and Brian Huff, "The Paradox of Education in America: Integrating Systems for Children with Disabilities," *Children's Rights Litigation* (vol. 12, no. 3, March 2010), pp. 1–15.

Viadero, Debra, "Lags in Minority Achievement Defy Traditional Explanations," *Education Week* (vol. 19, March 2000), pp. 1, 18–19, 21–22.

Wagner, Jennifer Y., and Antonis Katsiyannis, "Special Education Litigation Update Implications for School Administrators," *NASSP Bulletin* (vol. 94, no. 1, March 2010), pp. 40–52.

Walling, Donovan R. (ed.), *Open Lives, Safe Schools* (Bloomington, IN: Phi Delta Kappa, 1996).

Walls, N. Eugene, Sarah B. Kane, and Hope Wisneski, "Gay-Straight Alliances and School Experiences of Sexual Minority Youth," *Youth & Society* (vol. 41, no. 3, March 2010), pp. 307–332.

Watson, Laurel B., Kris Varjas, Joel Meyers, and Emily C. Graybill, "Gay-Straight Alliance Advisors: Negotiating Multiple Ecological Systems When Advocating for LGBTQ Youth," *Journal of LGBT Youth* (vol. 7, no. 2, April 2010), pp. 100–128.

Whittaker, Keola R. "Gay-Straight Alliances and Free Speech: Are Parental Consent Laws Constitutional?" *Berkeley Journal of Gender, Law & Justice* (vol. 24, May 2009), pp. 48–67.

Williams, Debra, "Security Efforts Cut Chicago-School Violence," *Catalyst: Voices of Chicago School Reform* (November 1994), pp. 18–21.

Wisniewski, L., and S. Alper, "Including Students with Severe Disabilities in General Education Settings," *Remedial and Special Education* (vol. 15, no. 1, January 1994), pp. 4–13, 15.

Zehr, Mary Ann, "Poorer Schools Still Lagging Behind on Internet Access, Study Finds," *Education Week* (vol. 19, no. 24, February 2000), p. 5.

WEB EXPLORATIONS

The Web links below contain useful material related to Chapter 10.

School Climate & Discipline. "Rethinking Discipline." https://ed.gov/policy/gen/guid/school-discipline/index.html

Center for the Prevention of School Violence. http://test.ncdjjdp.org/cpsv/

"Council for Exceptional Children: Policy & Advocacy." http://www.cec.sped.org/Policy-and-Advocacy/

"IDEA–Individuals with Disabilities Education Act." http://idea.ed.gov/

"You Can Help Them All." http://www.disciplinehelp.com/

"School Survey on Crime and Safety." https://nces.ed.gov/surveys/ssocs/index.asp

"School Violence." http://www.nsscl.org/

CHAPTER

11

Administrator–Staff Relationships

Although the overall relationship between school administrators and their staffs has historically passed through periods of tranquility and crisis, the advent of collective bargaining and teacher militancy in the 1960s complicated that relationship and made it increasingly difficult. Prior to collective bargaining, the relationship between many school administrators and their staffs was often paternalistic. In most situations the administrator had a choice of whether or not to consider teachers' grievances, consult with them about work assignments, or involve them in school decision making, and all too often—at least, according to teachers' perceptions—the administrator chose not to do so.

The advent of collective bargaining and teacher militancy markedly changed the nature of the relationship between the administrator and the staff. The introduction of collective bargaining and the resultant master contract have meant that in most situations, an administrator must consider teacher grievances and must consult with teachers regarding working conditions and other matters affecting their welfare.

It should be emphasized that collective bargaining and the master contract have neither eliminated the authority of the administrator nor removed the person in that position as head of the school or school district. Administrators need to recognize, however, that they can no longer act unilaterally on decisions that may affect teachers' welfare without encountering difficulty; they will now, in most situations, need to administer the school with the assistance of faculty input and consultation. It should be noted that recent research shows that multiple input into decision making is beneficial to progress. In most cases, while those on the "front lines" know better what is needed than administrators in the office, the administrative staff has the power to obtain needed resources.

Although in recent years most school administrators have adapted to the new realities of working with a professional staff, even those administrators with good intentions and a collaborative leadership style may occasionally run into difficulty with a teacher or staff member who, for whatever the reason, sees things differently from the administrator.

The cases presented on the following pages do not represent typical teachers, faculties, or administrators. The vast majority of school personnel are friendly, dedicated, hardworking, and competent people. Such individuals are not the ones likely to cause problems; they don't provide the kind of case study material that gives the reader the best opportunity to use the concepts in Part I of the text and become an effective problem solver. Consequently, the case studies presented in this chapter are problem-oriented. Although the problems may not be "typical," they do represent realistic situations that could confront any administrator. With regard to the first case on teacher selection, most administrators will need to carry out this task at one time or another in their careers.

21
TEACHER SELECTION

It was late spring, and the principal was reviewing with a central office supervisor the applications received for a teaching position to be available at Silver Spring School in the fall. The position had opened after Brent Thomas, a teacher who had been at the school for three years, had decided to move out of the state and had returned unsigned the contract that had been offered to him for the following year.

Silver Spring School served a rather heterogeneous student clientele, characterized by a wide range of student backgrounds, interests, and ability and achievement levels. The school was experimenting with team teaching, and since Mr. Thomas was a member of one of the teams, the principal was particularly sorry to see him leave. He felt that it was very important that a good replacement be secured.

After looking over a number of applicants' placement papers, the principal and the central office supervisor had narrowed their choice to two candidates: Mr. James Timm and Ms. Sylvia Goldstein. Each candidate's folder contained an application form providing general background information and a set of recommendations.

After the principal of Silver Spring School and the central office supervisor had reexamined all the data on Mr. Timm and Ms. Goldstein, a number of issues about each candidate still needed to be clarified. Before that could be accomplished, the two candidates would need to be interviewed. The immediate question was, "Which of the two should be interviewed first?" Once that was decided, the administrators would have to give some thought to the areas that were most important to explore further with each candidate, as well as some thought to the interview techniques and questions that should be employed to secure the kinds of information necessary for reaching a final decision with respect to filling the vacancy.

With those points in mind, the principal and the central office supervisor continued their discussion and scrutiny of the candidates' papers.

Background Information on Mr. Timm

Mr. James Timm was 28 years old, married, and the father of two children. He had attended a state university and had graduated with a BA. He had completed six hours of course work beyond his bachelor's degree. There was no transcript, but his grade point average was listed at 3.0. His application form stated that his hobbies were hunting, fishing, golfing, and his family. He had taught for five years in another school district. Two rating forms were in Mr. Timm's folder, one completed by his principal and the other one by a colleague.

Background Information on Ms. Goldstein

Ms. Sylvia Goldstein's application stated that she was 25 years old and single. She had attended a private college and had graduated with a BA. She had taught for two years and had nearly completed all the requirements for a master's degree in her subject field. Her undergraduate grade point average had been 3.7, and her graduate grade point average was 3.6. Reading was the only hobby that she had listed.

Two rating forms were also in Ms. Goldstein's folder, one completed by her principal and the other by an assistant superintendent.

Suggested Learning Activities

The nature of the vacancy in this case is intentionally left for the reader to specify, for example, grade level and subject.

Analyze the Case

1. On the basis of the information provided in the case, what do you see as the main strengths and limitations of each candidate?
2. Why might the principal and the central office supervisor disagree in their evaluations of the candidates or on the criteria that should be applied in the selection of a teacher to fill the vacancy?
3. What are the areas that you think should be explored further with Mr. Timm and Ms. Goldstein in an interview?

Discuss the Larger Issues

1. What are the strengths and limitations of the kinds of information (e.g., rating scales and application forms) that are typically included in the papers of applicants for a vacancy?
2. What are the main elements of the criteria that an administrator should use in selecting a teacher? What should these criteria be based on? Which aspects of the criteria should receive top priority?
3. Why is it difficult to be completely objective in the process of selecting a teacher? What factors may interfere with the objectivity of the process?
4. Who should be involved in the recruitment, selection, and assignment of teachers, and what role should each individual or group play?

Be a Problem Solver A vacancy exists at Silver Spring School, and the field of applicants has been narrowed to two candidates. If you were the principal or the central office supervisor, which candidate would you invite for the first interview and which interview techniques and questions would you employ with each candidate to secure the kinds of information needed to make a good decision with regard to selecting one of the applicants?

Test Your Solution To test your proposed plan of action for dealing with the problem described previously, create and role-play one or more of the following situations in class:

1. Continue the discussion between the principal and the central office supervisor, focusing on the identification of interview techniques and questions that will be used in the interviews with both candidates.
2. Carry out interviews between the principal, the central office supervisor, and each candidate.

Investigate Further

1. What are the procedures utilized by your school district in the recruitment, selection, and assignment of teachers?
2. What criteria are used by your district in the selection of teachers? What are the criteria based on?
3. How does your district ascertain whether its current program of teacher recruitment, selection, and assignment is effective?

22
PROBLEMS OF A BEGINNING TEACHER

As he walked from the parking lot to the school building, the principal of Mitchell School noticed Mrs. Carter, the nurse, who was heading in the same direction. She smiled and waited for him, and they discussed the weather as they entered the building. As the principal started to enter his office, Mrs. Carter followed him, asking whether he might have time after school to talk with her about a problem. He nodded and suggested that they could take a few minutes to talk before school started, but Mrs. Carter declined, saying that she would rather wait until after school when there would be more time.

After the nurse left the principal's office, he wondered what the nature of her problem might be. She had been serving as school nurse at Mitchell School for six or seven years, and usually spent two or three days each week in the building, checking on absences, screening the students for visual and hearing defects, and so forth. Whatever her difficulty was, he hoped that it wasn't too serious.

At 3:30 that afternoon, Mrs. Carter entered the principal's office. He greeted her and tried to put her at ease, but when he asked how he could help her, she hesitated. Finally, she explained that she would like to talk with him in confidence about Miss Hiller, the new math teacher who had just graduated last spring from college and had begun teaching at Mitchell School this fall.

From a recent conversation with Miss Hiller, Mrs. Carter had learned that the new teacher was becoming very discouraged and disillusioned. For example, she had admitted that she didn't seem to know how to motivate her students, and said that they didn't appear to be very interested in what she was teaching. They were often inattentive, and Miss Hiller was worried not only about their failure to learn what she was presenting but also about her own inability to develop a good, positive relationship with them. She was rather shy and quiet by nature, but it bothered her that the students didn't seem to like her.

Mrs. Carter went on to say that Miss Hiller had confided that she was also experiencing problems with discipline. The students didn't seem to respond to her attempts to keep order in the classroom. The noise level was usually high, and there were two boys, in particular, who were about ready to drive her "up the wall."

Finally, and perhaps most shattering to the new teacher's morale, was Miss Hiller's feeling that the other teachers on the staff did not accept her. Most of the teachers had taught at the school in previous years and had already established relationships with one another. The faculty was divided into cliques, and Mrs. Carter knew for a fact that it was difficult for any newcomer to gain acceptance. She had personally experienced trouble along that line, but she was older and more self-possessed, so she hadn't let their reactions bother her. Besides, she was only at Mitchell School part-time anyway. She could see how the situation would be difficult for a shy, sensitive girl like Miss Hiller, who didn't have much self-confidence.

The principal was troubled to hear about the new teacher's problems and inwardly blamed himself for not being more perceptive about her difficulties. Still, she had always seemed rather aloof to him, and he had assumed that she was quite self-sufficient. He asked Mrs. Carter whether Miss Hiller had asked anyone for help. Why hadn't the teacher herself come to him with her problems?

Mrs. Carter believed that Miss Hiller's reluctance to seek help could be attributed to her shyness and to the fact that the teacher probably didn't want to admit that she was having difficulties. It was only by chance that Mrs. Carter had found out anything. She had gone into Miss Hiller's classroom to discuss a student's health problem and had discovered the teacher sitting at her desk, crying. The nurse had encouraged her to talk about her problems; otherwise the teacher would never have opened up to her. In fact, Mrs. Carter was sure that Miss Hiller would be horrified to know that the principal had even been told about the situation.

The only reason Mrs. Carter had finally decided to relate the incident to the principal was her conviction that Miss Hiller desperately needed help. Since Mrs. Carter was just a nurse and not really a member of the faculty, she didn't feel adequate to provide advice or assistance. But surely there must be something that the principal could do before that poor young girl completely lost hope in her future as a teacher!

Suggested Learning Activities

Analyze the Case

1. What circumstances and psychological factors will make it particularly difficult for the principal to discuss Miss Hiller's problems with her?
2. What situational barriers will need to be overcome before Miss Hiller can feel more accepted in the school?
3. Why will the nurse's friendship with Miss Hiller probably be of little help in integrating the teacher into the social structure of the school?
4. How can the principal best ascertain to a greater extent the teacher's classroom problems without upsetting her?

Discuss the Larger Issues

1. What should be the role of the principal in helping the beginning teacher to become accepted in the school and in the community?
2. What type of in-service procedures should be designed to help the inexperienced teacher resolve classroom problems successfully?

Be a Problem Solver The school nurse has just related to the principal, in confidence, the difficulties being experienced by a new, inexperienced teacher. Recognizing that Miss Hiller is an extremely shy, sensitive person, what would you do, if you were principal, to help resolve her problem? Utilize appropriate administrative and social science concepts in planning and implementing your approach.

Test Your Solution To test your proposed plan of action for dealing with the problem presented at the end of the case, create and role-play one or more of the following situations in class:

1. A continuation of the conference between the principal and the nurse.
2. A conference between the principal and Miss Hiller.
3. A faculty meeting.

Investigate Further

1. What procedures, formal or informal, does your school have that facilitate the acceptance of new teachers by students and other teachers?
2. What do the new teachers in your school believe to be the most difficult aspects of being in a first-year teaching situation?

23
FACULTY TEAMWORK

Cohesive Middle School is a school most people would like to attend—or have their children attend. In the eight years since Kathryn Goode has been principal, real estate values in the attendance zone area have increased dramatically, as well as increased property taxes.

The school's strength and desirability lie in its teaming. Ms. Goode is a firm believer in the philosophy of teamwork for middle schools and has staffed, budgeted, managed, and led her building accordingly. All students and staff are placed on teams at the beginning of the school year, and each team acts as a minischool within its grade level. She ensures that each teacher is granted one period per day for personal planning and one period to plan team activities and interventions. Cohesive Middle School's reputation has gone beyond its local area. The school has even been recognized at the National Middle School Conference as being extremely effective.

Team Wonder is an eighth-grade team and is staffed with science, social studies, math, and language teachers. The teachers, with the exception of the language teacher, have worked together for five years. The team dynamics have been spectacular. Team Wonder, like many of the other teams in the building, has established its own practices and traditions that enhance the education, pride, and sense of belonging experienced by students.

This year, a change in the makeup of Team Wonder has introduced some serious problems, and its smooth-working, cooperative spirit is being tested. The problem stems from differences in philosophy that could affect one of Team Wonder's most cherished traditions—Frontier Day. Each fall on Frontier Day the students rotate among various outdoor activities. A storyteller from the local library dressed in traditional western attire tells the dramatic story of a band of gypsies forging through the frontier. A farrier demonstrates making horseshoes and proper horseback riding technique. A local artist demonstrates candle making and allows the students to make their own candles. The science teacher has students panning for gold-painted rocks in a kiddy pool and measuring the mass of their treasures. The math teacher helps students to calculate the value of their findings as though they were living at different times throughout history and then graph the inflation trends. Parents assist in the preparation of many crock-pots of beanie weenies for lunch on the frontier.

Each year Frontier Day has been an overwhelming success and has served as a rite of passage for those eighth graders fortunate enough to be placed on Team Wonder. This year, there is a rift as the planning gets under way.

Ms. Prior, the language teacher, is new to Team Wonder. She has worked on another eighth-grade team at Cohesive for three years. Her previous team also had traditions, and she is unwilling to give them up. "I have lots of experience with this," she insists. "I know how to work on a team and what we need to do!" She would like Team Wonder to replace Frontier Day with the more traditional, classroom-based Westward Ho activity that her team did last year. Ms. Prior believes that the best learning takes place in a structured classroom setting. She guards her classroom instructional time carefully. She even expressed distaste for the student orientation assembly presented to the grade level earlier in the year. "Such things waste valuable instructional time," she argued.

The other teachers on Team Wonder are concerned. Every new suggestion they make is blocked by Ms. Prior's objections. The other teachers have worked together so well for so long, and they find the resistance frustrating. They have pooled their ideas, and all of them feel that the structured approach that Ms. Prior wants will block student creativity and dampen student enthusiasm. The team members have talked about their differences of opinion, but they cannot come to an agreement about what to do—although they all agree that an activity of some sort is needed.

As the daily debates about the unit on the American West become more and more heated, Ms. Goode is invited to the team meeting to offer advice. She does not relish her role as the arbiter because she strongly believes in letting the team come to a consensus on the plans for Frontier Day.

Suggested Learning Activities

Analyze the Case

1. How could Ms. Goode have prevented this problem from occurring? Considering her support for the team concept, why do you think she did not take this course of action?
2. How can the principal defuse the emotions of the teachers as she enters the team meeting?
3. What can Ms. Goode do to ensure that the team does not have further decision-making difficulties of this magnitude?

Discuss the Larger Issues

1. Is team teaching the most effective organization for increasing student achievement? At what grade levels?
2. Does the most effective instruction occur in a seated, classroom situation or in a project such as Frontier Day?
3. As an administrator, how and to what extent do teacher personality and instructional style affect your staffing decisions?

Be a Problem Solver If you were the principal in this kind of situation, how would you plan your meeting with the team? What role would you play during the meeting? Utilize the social science and administrative concepts from Part I in approaching this situation.

Test Your Solution To test your proposed solution to this staff agreement problem, you and your group should role-play one or more of the following situations:

1. The team meeting with all Team Wonder teachers and Ms. Goode as each expresses opinions about Frontier Day.
2. Ms. Goode as she offers her solution to the problem and the teachers as they respond.
3. Ms. Goode and her associates at the staffing meeting where teaming decisions for the following year are being discussed.

Investigate Further

1. How is the staff organized (departmentally, by grade level, in teams) at each building level in your district? What do administrators view as pros and cons of this type of organization?
2. Interview administrators in your district to determine how staff confrontations are minimized through optimal staffing and staff placement.
3. How does your principal cope with staff disagreements such as the one presented in this case study? When should the principal stay out of the conflict and at what point should there be intervention? Offer one example of a situation that should not involve the principal and one that necessitates administrative intervention.

24
WHO NEEDS LESSON PLANS?

The principal had just finished his third and final observation of the day. He was rather pleased. All three observations had proved productive. The classes were well behaved and on task, and were obviously well organized. He returned to his office and finalized his written reviews before attending to other duties.

The following day he met with all three teachers. The last two were night and day. Ms. Green was a veteran teacher with 14 years of experience. She had established a routine that varied only to adjust to the needs in each class. In the principal's mind, Ms. Green was the ideal teacher. She had perfect control and inspired her students to learn. She rarely if ever had a discipline problem. As the principal completed his meeting with Ms. Green, he did note that he failed to see her lesson plans for the week, or even for the day. Ms. Green informed him that she kept her daily plans in an old logbook and very rarely consulted the book since she had her plans securely ingrained in her head. The principal noted this and gave Ms. Green an excellent review and a letter of commendation. His last meeting was with Ms. Louis. She was a second-year teacher. For the most part, her classes were well-behaved and stayed on task. As the principal reviewed his notes, however, he expressed concern that Ms. Louis's class was not quite as organized as he would like to see. He noticed that she had a sketchy set of lesson plans that did not follow the prescribed method set forth in the teacher handbook. He finished by suggesting Ms. Louis write up next week's lesson plans in the correct method and submit them in advance for review. He noted this on the evaluation and gave her an average review.

Later in the day, Ms. Louis returned to the principal's office. She was visibly upset. The principal had noticed that she was somewhat of a perfectionist and sensed that she was less than happy with her evaluation. Ms. Louis presented him with copies of both her and Ms. Green's evaluations. Her argument was that the principal had obviously not been totally objective in his review. She knew for a fact that Ms. Green did not keep lesson plans or consult them and hadn't for several years. Furthermore, Ms. Green, who was her mentor, had actually told her that the lesson plans were only necessary for first-year teachers. Ms. Green had also said that the principal rarely, if ever, considered them important. The principal was perplexed. First, how did Ms. Louis get a copy of Ms. Green's evaluation? Second, why would Ms. Green make such obviously incorrect statements? Finally, was she right? He hesitated to reply.

Suggested Learning Activities

Analyze the Case

1. What is your opinion of the steps taken by the principal to evaluate Ms. Green and Ms. Louis? How would you have acted differently?
2. What is your assessment of Ms. Louis's objections to her evaluation? What factors may be influencing the principal's objectivity in assessing Ms. Green's and Ms. Louis's evaluations?
3. What is your evaluation of the arguments Ms. Green sets forth for lesson planning? What is your opinion of Ms. Louis's objections to her evaluation?

Discuss the Larger Issues

1. Should written lesson plans be required? Should they be daily, weekly, monthly?
2. How should lesson plans be used?
3. What responsibilities do administrators and supervisors have for improving the effectiveness and value of teacher-prepared lesson plans?

Be a Problem Solver The principal has scheduled a meeting with Ms. Green after school to discuss her conversation with Ms. Louis regarding lesson planning and the recent evaluations. How would you—if you were the principal—handle the teachers?

Test Your Solution To test your proposed plan of action for dealing with the problem presented at the end of the case, create and role-play one or more of the following situations in class:

1. A conference between the principal and Ms. Green.
2. A faculty meeting requested by the teachers to discuss lesson planning and evaluation procedures.
3. Any other situation that might provide feedback on strengths and weaknesses of your proposed situation.

Investigate Further

1. What is the lesson plan format and policy in your district?
2. What use is made of lesson plans in your district?

3. How do the following groups in your district feel about required lesson plans?
   a. Building principals
   b. Department heads
   c. Teachers
   d. Central office administration

25
TEACHER RIGHTS: PUBLIC VS. PRIVATE CITIZENSHIP

As the telephone rang at 6 A.M., interrupting his sleep, the superintendent groped for the receiver, longing for the luxury of an unlisted number. Still half-asleep, he answered the phone, only to be startled by a barrage of questions from a reporter calling for a local television station. What did the superintendent think about the disturbance over the welfare budget cuts that had broken up the county supervisors' meeting last night at the courthouse? Was he personally opposed to the action that had been taken by the supervisors?

Rather irritably, the superintendent pointed out that the welfare department did not fall within the jurisdiction of the superintendent of schools and suggested that the reporter direct his questions to the head of the welfare department. The reporter persisted. Didn't the superintendent have anything to say about Sara Conklin, the teacher at Lincoln School who had participated in the demonstration and had to be forcibly removed from the meeting?

"Not at this time," the superintendent replied curtly, hanging up the phone. A teacher involved in a violent demonstration? Well, he could expect a lot of telephone calls this morning at the office.

By the time he arrived at his office an hour later, the morning newspaper had been delivered. As he read the lengthy front-page account of the disturbance, he wondered how long it would take before he would begin to hear from the conservative element of the community, demanding that Ms. Conklin be fired. He decided that he'd better call her principal.

The principal at Lincoln School had already heard the news on the radio about the courthouse disruption involving Sara Conklin, and he agreed with the superintendent that it would be a good idea to relieve her of all teaching responsibilities until further notice. If Ms. Conklin returned to her classroom that morning and her classes proceeded smoothly, the school might have a more difficult time taking further action, should it prove necessary to do so because of community complaints about her out-of-school activities. The superintendent also suggested that the principal talk with Ms. Conklin if she came to school and, on the basis of that discussion, prepare a recommendation that could be considered by the superintendent and several of the school board members when they conferred informally the next day.

When Ms. Conklin arrived at Lincoln School shortly before classes began that morning, the principal immediately called her into his office. He informed her that she had been identified on several radio and television news reports as one of the protestors who had participated in the disturbance at the courthouse the preceding evening. He further mentioned that she had been described as a teacher at Lincoln School, which would cause many parents to wonder about the example she was setting for her students. He indicated that he seriously questioned whether participation in a demonstration or protest–particularly one in which the participants had to be forcibly removed from the meeting—was an appropriate activity for a professional teacher. Was there any rational explanation that she could offer for her behavior last night?

The teacher appeared tired, but sparks blazed in her eyes as she exclaimed, "Why in the world should I have to give *you* any explanation about my personal out-of-school activities? As long as I carry out my responsibilities here at school, you have absolutely no basis for criticizing me! Whatever I do during the rest of my time is *my* business and nobody else's."

The principal started to reply, but Ms. Conklin plunged on in a sudden torrent of emotion. "You talk about setting an example for kids. Well, I happen to believe that a teacher has the responsibility to set an example in ways other than showing the traditional virtues of promptness and neatness. I happen to think that it's important to try to teach more than just what's written between the covers of a book. I want to show these kids that there are certain things in life that are important enough to go all out for, to lay your job on the line for. Or maybe even your career! But it seems to me that all *you* can think about is how this minor episode might reflect unfavorably on the school or on you, personally. Are you afraid that people might think you don't have your teachers completely under control? If I had my way, *more* teachers in this school would be taking a hard look at the significant issues facing society and doing something about them. Didn't you ever hear that all that is needed for evil to flourish is for good men to do nothing?"

The principal waited until the teacher paused to take a breath, and then he countered with his own views. "I'm not questioning your motivation, Sara, but there are certainly more proper channels for changing society: legal action, persuasion, political power. Other teachers in this district have equally strong convictions about improving conditions for the poor, but they don't go around getting themselves forcibly ejected from meetings! Instead, they write letters to their representatives and to the communications media, trying to peacefully influence public opinion. They participate in voluntary programs to try to clean up the city and to help kids read. Surely, you can't believe that protests and demonstrations are the only means of ameliorating society's problems!"

The principal concluded by saying that he did not believe teachers should engage in any activity that might reflect adversely on the school where they taught or on their image as professional educators. Further, he told Ms. Conklin that, although he had not yet determined what his final recommendation to the superintendent would be, he had decided she was to be relieved temporarily of her teaching responsibilities until further notice.

Ms. Conklin was obviously trying to control herself, but when she spoke, her voice quivered with anger as she expressed her total disagreement with the principal's position. It seemed to her that teachers still had certain rights as private citizens, including the right to engage in public demonstrations. She wasn't going to spend the rest of her life writing letters to public employees while people lived in poverty!

Finally, beginning to cry from frustration, the teacher started for the door but turned back to say, "This isn't the last you've heard from me on this issue! I haven't broken any laws, and no charges have been filed against me. The only thing I may be guilty of is being thrown out of a public meeting." Before the principal could respond, Sara Conklin hurried out of his office, slamming the door angrily behind her.

After she left, the principal found that he was experiencing difficulty regaining his emotional stability. He had been upset by the teacher's reaction, but now he had to think carefully. What should he recommend to the superintendent? If she were disciplined, there would probably be an outcry from many of the students or their parents and from some of the faculty members who approved her motives and identified with what they perceived as her courage.

Ms. Conklin was not yet tenured, but the teaching association might back her in her stand, and it was possible that the local civil liberties union would defend her also.

On the other hand, if she were to resume her teaching responsibilities without any further action taken by the administration, there would surely be complaints from several important sectors of the community. It was hard to know what to do about Sara Conklin.

Suggested Learning Activities

Analyze the Case

1. If you had been the superintendent, how might you have responded differently to the reporter calling from a local television station? Why do you suppose the superintendent did not want to talk to the reporter at that time about the teacher who had participated in the demonstration?
2. What factors appear to be significant in influencing the decision by the administration to relieve Ms. Conklin of her teaching responsibilities? What options, other than relieving her of her teaching duties, should have been explored?
3. What is your assessment of the position taken by Sara Conklin during her conference with the principal? What is your evaluation of the position taken by the principal during the conference?
4. In what way, if any, would you have proceeded differently during the conference if you were the principal?

Discuss the Larger Issues

1. In relation to the issue presented in this case, what rights should a teacher be able to exercise as a private citizen? Are there any rights that teachers should voluntarily relinquish, in view of their status in the community and their relationship with young people?
2. At what point would a teacher's out-of-school activities impair effectiveness as a teacher? What criteria should be used in making this judgment? What evidence should be used in determining whether the criteria have been met? Who should be involved in making such a decision?
3. What procedures of due process should be followed by the administration regarding problems similar to the one presented in this case?

Be a Problem Solver The superintendent has requested that the principal submit a recommendation on the disposition of the problem involving Sara Conklin. Ms. Conklin told the principal, "This isn't the last you've heard from me on this issue!" If you were the principal in this set of circumstances, what would you do?

Test Your Solution To test your proposed action for dealing with the problem presented at the end of the case, create and role-play one or more of the following situations in class:

1. A meeting between the principal and the superintendent to go over the principal's recommendation.
2. A telephone call from the president of a local group of conservatives.

3. A telephone call from the president of the civil liberties union, who indicates that he is representing Ms. Conklin in her protest against being relieved of her teaching duties.

Investigate Further

1. What is the policy (written or unwritten) in your school district regarding the out-of-school activities of teachers?
2. What laws or court decisions in your state would have a bearing on the main issues in this case?
3. What would be the attitude of the following groups in your district toward the out-of-school activities of the teacher and the response of the administration?
   a. The school board
   b. The teacher association
   c. The executive committee of the parent organization
   d. The administrators

26
FACULTY DISSATISFACTION AND LOW MORALE

Entering the faculty workroom, Mary Beth Williams crossed the room to a table where Alice Spencer was correcting papers, spread out before her in organized confusion.

"At it again, I see," Mary Beth greeted the other teacher.

"It never ends, does it?" Alice responded. "And I have a meeting right after school, besides. I hope I can finish these, because there's another stack on my desk that I have to take home tonight."

"You're on that lesson plan committee, aren't you?" Mary Beth said, sitting down across the table. "How's that going?"

"About as well as you might expect. I mean, what good is this committee going to do anyway? It's the *principal's* committee—he's the one who thinks there needs to be a change in the lesson plan format. As far as I can make out, none of the teachers see any need to change it at all, except maybe Bill Challenge, who wants to eliminate lesson plans altogether. You should have seen the principal's face when Bill brought up that idea! Mr. Hizway has previously been making this big statement about how the teachers on this committee need to participate more and get involved, and how receptive he was to hearing our ideas on the subject when Bill Challenge brings up this suggestion to eliminate lesson plans completely—although I don't think he meant to eliminate planning. I thought Mr. Hizway was going to have a stroke. He got very red in the face and then quickly said that Bill's ideas weren't worth discussing and immediately changed the subject."

"You mean," Mary Beth asked incredulously, "he just cut Bill off and didn't even permit discussion of the idea?"

"Exactly. Cut him off *cold,*" Alice replied, sorting through the papers to find her gradebook.

"How did Bill react?"

"He wasn't happy about it, but when the principal cuts you off that way, it doesn't do much good to object."

"I bet that didn't help his problems any," Mary Beth observed.

"What problems?"

"Well, I don't know if I should say anything, Alice. . . ."

Alice turned back to her gradebook, entering the scores from the papers. "It's okay. I understand."

"I don't think it's really confidential. . . . Bill's wife and I are pretty good friends, and I know she's worried about him. Apparently he's been under a lot of pressure this year. He has that different teaching assignment that he was given, and it's always hard to do one new preparation, let alone your whole teaching load. And then he has more problem students assigned to him this year. Bill has never had discipline problems before, but he really does this year, and it bothers him a lot. His wife is concerned that he may also be going through a midlife crisis, both personally and professionally. She didn't elaborate on the personal bit, but she has said that he's expressed uncertainty as to whether he is even the same teacher he once was and whether he has the same capabilities he once possessed."

"Bill Challenge? Mary Beth, you can't be serious. He's always seemed to me to be an excellent teacher, always so confident."

"I guess he's not feeling so confident these days."

"Really!" Alice sat back, reflecting on Mary Beth's disclosures. "You'd never know it from his behavior on the lesson plan committee. He's *very* outspoken at the meetings."

"That may just be the pressure building up and then exploding," Mary Beth speculated. "Lord knows, there's enough going on in this school to upset anybody! And Bill has always been such a perfectionist."

"I suppose that's true. Serving on this committee for lesson plan revision has to be as frustrating for him as it is for me. I mean, this committee is going *nowhere.* I've been here eight years, and this is just like so many committees that I've served on at the district level: the administrator already has his mind made up when he establishes the committee, so all he really wants—at least this is how it seems—is for us to endorse his thinking, and then he can say that he provided teacher involvement and input. Sometimes I feel like saying, 'Just tell us what you want, and we'll say it, and then everybody can go home.' What difference does it make, anyway, what the teachers do on this lesson plan committee? The principal never even does anything with the lesson plans. I can't tell that substitute teachers use them very much, and I don't follow them all that strictly myself—not that I'm against planning, of course."

"I know what you mean," Mary Beth agreed. "Even if a committee comes up with some good ideas, the administrator rejects them on the spot if they don't agree with what he wants to do. Or else we don't ever hear any more about them. Doesn't it seem sort of dumb for Mr. Hizway to always be asking us for our ideas if his mind is already made up? Or if he's going to ignore our recommendations?"

Alice nodded. "Definitely. A lot of these committees and meetings, particularly faculty meetings, are a waste of time. They hardly ever deal with teachers' needs."

"That's for sure. You want more coffee, Alice?"

She shook her head, now engrossed with their discussion. "Mary Beth, I don't know how you feel about this, but I think a lot of teachers are getting fed up with their situation at this school. Here we are, getting larger classes, being assigned to more committees, and always being asked to do more with less. And yet, what appreciation do we get? Look at our salaries!

Compared with my expenses, I tell you, I'm going backward! And I don't think most parents really *care* any more about their kids or about teachers. I don't see much appreciation from the administration for the job we're doing. It seems to me that, at best, we're taken for granted and, at worst, we're being exploited!"

"Absolutely. The administration is more concerned with public relations and raising students' achievement test scores. I think a lot of teachers are just plain burned out. I know I am."

"Well, Mary Beth, burned out or not, I've got to get back to my room and put some things on the board before next period begins. I've been working on these papers like mad, and I still haven't finished recording all the grades."

"I've got to get back to my room too. I have a student coming in for some extra help before class begins."

Later that month the lesson plan committee presented its report to the faculty at an after-school meeting. The principal explained the report, which proposed a more elaborate lesson plan format, requiring more details of teacher planning. When he asked for reactions to the proposed plan, no one responded. Waiting a moment or two for comments, the principal finally indicated that the changes would go into effect the next fall.

During the summer, the principal of the school left for an administrative position in another district. The new principal who was hired for the school had not previously worked in the district, so she didn't know too much about the students and faculty. She felt optimistic about her new assignment and looked forward to the challenges and opportunities for leadership in the school. She would be starting the next day, and she was to begin the morning with a meeting with two of her teachers who had requested to see her: Mary Beth Williams and Alice Spencer. With only three weeks before classes began, the principal was delighted to have an opportunity to meet with some of her faculty.

Suggested Learning Activities

Analyze the Case

1. Analyze the conversation between Mary Beth Williams and Alice Spencer, using concepts from Chapter 4, "Communication."
2. Analyze the conversation between Mary Beth Williams and Alice Spencer in regard to its implications for faculty morale.
3. What is your assessment of the possible reasons for the lack of faculty reactions to the proposed lesson plan format changes? If you had been the principal, what would you have done at this point in the meeting?

Discuss the Larger Issues

1. What responsibility, if any, does an administrator have for becoming aware of the personal problems that members of the faculty are experiencing? If he or she has such responsibility, what would be the best approach to becoming more aware of personal problems?
2. If an administrator becomes aware of certain personal problems that a member of the faculty is experiencing, what steps, if any, should be taken?
3. Why are teachers frequently frustrated by committee work? What can an administrator do to prevent or ameliorate that *frustration*?

Be a Problem Solver Assume that you are the new principal of this school and that Mary Beth Williams and Alice Spencer have filled you in on the status of faculty morale in the school. How will you approach this situation? What assumptions are you making? Utilize social science and administrative concepts from Part I of the text in planning and implementing your approach.

Test Your Solution To test your proposed approach to the problems described in this case study, you and the class or group should create and role-play one or more of the following situations:

1. A conference between the new principal, Mary Beth Williams, and Alice Spencer. Assume that they are initially a little reluctant to talk about the problems of the school and that you will need to draw them out.
2. Preparation of a response to a memorandum from the superintendent asking all principals to make a strong statement to their teachers about the importance of not abusing sick leave and about the importance of volunteering for district committees.
3. A faculty meeting.
4. A conference between the new principal and Bill Challenge.

Investigate Further

1. What is your school district's policy *and* practice with regard to developing high faculty morale and satisfaction?
2. What does the educational literature suggest about programs and/or approaches for developing and sustaining high faculty morale?

27
TEACHER FILES A GRIEVANCE

Eileen Turner was looking forward to taking some guidance courses during the coming summer. She felt that the courses would help her in her teaching and would prepare her for the day when she might decide to get out of teaching and become a school counselor.

She had decided that she was going to make a determined effort that morning to see the principal. The school's master contract stipulated that a teacher must submit a form the principal was to use to indicate to the teacher his approval of courses that could be applied toward meeting the district's professional development requirement and the salary schedule. Eileen had submitted the appropriate form a month earlier, but she had as yet received no response from the principal. She had already tried several times last week to see him, but his secretary always said that he was busy. Today Eileen was going to see him—one way or another.

Later in the morning, as Eileen was on her way to the principal's office, she encountered him in the hallway. She asked if she could see him for just a few minutes in his office.

The principal responded that he wouldn't be able to return to his office, because he was on his way to see the assistant principal. Unfortunately, he wouldn't have time to see her in the afternoon, either, because he had to leave the building to attend some meetings. He would take a moment to talk with her in the hallway, however, if it was something that could be taken care of easily.

Feeling that she had better capitalize on whatever opportunity was available, the teacher proceeded to explain that she wanted to take some guidance courses during the summer and had requested earlier that he approve them for professional development and salary schedule purposes. When the principal seemed puzzled and hesitant, the teacher reviewed for him her reasons for wanting to take the courses, namely, that they would help her improve as a teacher and would also prepare her for a counseling job, should a vacancy ever develop at the school.

As the principal listened to the teacher explain the reasons for her request, he suddenly remembered having come across the form that she had submitted and recalled his ambivalence about the matter. He didn't really like the idea of discussing the situation in the hallway, and he was already late for his conference with the assistant principal. In fact, he would be busy all afternoon. He supposed that he could tell Mrs. Turner that he would see her tomorrow to discuss the matter, but he wasn't sure he wanted to see her then. He had reservations about whether the guidance courses would help the teacher that much, and, even if they would, he wasn't certain that he wanted her as a counselor on the staff. Still, he didn't know whether he felt strongly enough to reject her request, and at this moment he hadn't figured out what to tell the teacher. Also, he remembered that he had approved related courses for other teachers in the past. He needed more time to think.

The principal told Mrs. Turner that he needed more time to consider her request before he could approve it. She pressed the principal further, however, for some kind of an indication of his feelings about the request. "Can you tell me whether you have any particular or strong objections to my taking these courses?"

"Well, I . . . I guess that . . . I don't . . . have any ah ah ah. . . ."

"Is it all right to take these courses, then, this summer?"

"Well, I suppose that . . . that it . . . might not hurt . . . but . . . but I would really like to talk to you again about this matter. I just don't have the time right now. I'm late for my meeting with the assistant principal." Already edging away from Mrs. Turner as he was speaking, the principal turned and hurried down the corridor.

As the teacher watched the principal walk away, she felt rather pleased with what she had accomplished. True, the principal had not been enthusiastic about her request, but he seemed to have given it his tentative approval.

By the end of the week, Eileen Turner still had not heard from the principal. Since she needed to send in her summer school registration by the Tuesday of the following week, she decided to write the principal a brief reminder.

Dear Mr. Peters:

As I am sure you remember, we discussed my request to take some guidance courses this summer in order to meet the district's professional development and salary schedule requirements. Tuesday of next week is the last day that I can send in my registration for summer school. Unless I hear from you by then to the contrary, I will assume that—on the basis of our earlier conversation—it is all right to send in my registration materials for the guidance courses.

Sincerely,
Eileen Turner

The following Tuesday passed without any response from the principal, so the teacher sent in her summer school registration materials to the university. Nothing was mentioned by either the principal or the teacher about the matter during the rest of the school year.

In the summer the teacher attended classes at the university and took nine credit hours of guidance courses.

In September, Eileen Turner attempted to apply the summer school credits toward meeting the district's professional development requirement and the salary schedule. Her application was rejected by the district office because she had not obtained prior approval of her summer school plans by the principal of the school. When she went to her principal to secure help in appealing the rejection, he refused to help her and took the position that he had never given her his approval.

Later in the day, the teacher filed a grievance against the principal. Her position was that although the principal had not formally approved her request, he had never formally rejected it either, despite the fact that he had had an opportunity to do so for over a month. In addition, the teacher felt that since the principal had given her request oral approval in the hallway and had never responded to her follow-up letter, she was more than justified in believing that she had his approval, particularly since he had approved such courses for other teachers in the past.

The following day a grievance conference was scheduled for the principal, the teacher, and the union representative to take place on Friday at 3:30 P.M.

Suggested Learning Activities

Analyze the Case

1. What alternatives should the principal have considered in deciding whether or not to talk with Eileen Turner in the corridor? How feasible are those alternatives?
2. Evaluate the conversation held between the principal and Mrs. Turner, utilizing concepts of communication and school administration. In your judgment, did the principal agree to the teacher's request during the conversation?
3. What should the principal have done upon receiving the letter from the teacher? Why did he appear to take no action?

Discuss the Larger Issues

1. What sorts of conditions or circumstances can lead to teacher grievances?
2. How can an administrator's behavior sometimes contribute to a teacher grievance?
3. What can and should an administrator do to *prevent* the conditions that lead to teacher grievances?

Be a Problem Solver Assume that you are the principal of the school. How will you handle the grievance conference? Or assume that you are the principal's central office supervisor, and the principal's attempted resolution of the grievance is being appealed by the teacher. How will you handle the appeal? Utilize administrative and social science concepts from Part I of the text in planning and implementing your problem-solving approach for these situations.

Test Your Solution To test your proposed approach to dealing with the circumstances described in the case, you and your colleagues should create and role-play one or more of the following situations:

1. A grievance conference between the principal, the teacher, and the building representative for the teachers' union.
2. A conference between the principal, the principal's superior, the teacher, and a representative for the teachers' union.

Investigate Further

1. What circumstances might call for a grievance in your district?
2. What are the grievance procedures in your school district?
3. What is the attitude of teachers in your school toward the principal's handling of teacher grievances?

28
TEACHER REACTS NEGATIVELY TO PERSONNEL EVALUATION

The deadline for submitting teacher evaluations was nearing, and the principal had stayed after school to write up the results of class visitations made that day. He was pleased that he had hired a fairly good group of teachers. There was one notable exception, however: Mrs. Stevens. He had visited her classroom several times, and it was evident that she was having difficulty. The students didn't appear to be sufficiently involved in learning, most seemed disinterested in the classroom proceedings, and many of them hardly bothered going through the motions of responding when the teacher called on them. There was no doubt that Mrs. Stevens was intelligent and had an excellent background in her subject matter, but she didn't seem to know how to motivate her students. Perhaps as a result, she was also experiencing difficulty with pupil control.

The principal had noticed each time before entering the teacher's classroom that there was an unusual amount of noise coming from inside. Students were apparently talking at will, and there seemed to be considerable movement. Of course, as soon as he entered the room, things would settle down; but even then the principal observed that the students showed little respect for their teacher. Not that they openly defied her–it was just that she seemed to exert little influence on them.

On Thursday of that week he held a postvisitation conference with Mrs. Stevens. He found her to be irritable, hostile to suggestions, and difficult to communicate with. When he tried to subtly suggest that she might try to involve her students more, as there seemed to be a problem in motivating her students, the teacher reacted very defensively.

She countered that she did try to motivate the students by involving them in informal discussion and said it wasn't her fault if the students clammed up every time the principal came into the room! Besides, she retorted, there was no conclusive research that would prove classroom achievement depended on student involvement. The principal was discouraged by the teacher's intractability and finally brought the meeting to an end with no progress having been made in eliciting from Mrs. Stevens any admission of inadequacy in her teaching. As he later reflected on the conference, he wondered whether it would really be worth the effort to continue working with her. Finally he decided he had better visit her classroom once more before submitting his evaluation to his superior and the recommendation about whether she should be rehired.

The following Monday he again visited Mrs. Stevens's class. There was little noticeable improvement in the class situation, and Mrs. Stevens seemed to be encountering her usual problems in carrying on class discussion. There was too much teacher lecturing, and student participation was limited to rote recitation.

The principal knew he ought to say something to the teacher at the end of the period, but since he couldn't think of anything positive, he left without comment. He had decided that he would recommend Mrs. Stevens's contract not be renewed for the following year. There would, no doubt, be some unpleasantness in informing her of this decision, but a favorable recommendation from him at this time would grant tenure to the teacher. Once that happened, the principal would be stuck with her, and he was determined to avoid that kind of catastrophe.

TEACHER EVALUATION FORM

	Below Average	*Average*	*Above Average*
Personality	X		
Relationship with Others			
Students		X	
Parents		X	
Fellow Teachers		X	
Administrators		X	
Professional Interest and Attitudes	X (not responsive to supervision)		
Teaching Ability	X (great difficulty in motivating students)		
Discipline		X (some problems in class management)	

The teacher's contract for next year is to be _____ renewed

__X__ not renewed

That afternoon he painstakingly completed the teacher evaluation form, noting Mrs. Stevens's inadequacies and concluding with a recommendation that her contract not be renewed. Then he put a note in the teacher's mailbox indicating that he would like to see her after school the following day to review his evaluation of her before forwarding it to the superintendent's office.

At the scheduled time the following afternoon, the teacher and the principal met for the conference. She pointedly ignored his attempts to put her at ease, so he handed her the rating form and asked her to look it over.

The teacher looked at the rating form briefly and threw it back on the principal's desk, denouncing the evaluation as inaccurate and unfair. She exclaimed that she did not deserve the low ratings and that she was a much better teacher than the principal had indicated. Perhaps she had not done her best when he was in her classroom, but this was as much his fault as hers. The presence of anyone in the back of the room always upset her and also affected the behavior of her students.

"Besides," the teacher went on, "what basis do you have for telling me what's wrong with my teaching! You've never taught my classes. You say that I need to motivate my students by involving them to a greater degree, but they are already involved as much as they can be. It's easy to say 'involve them more,' but you haven't ever offered any practical ideas on how to do it and neither has my supervisor. As far as I'm concerned, the supervision I've received has not been helpful. How can you say that I haven't been responsive to supervision? I haven't received any real supervision yet!"

At that point the teacher stood up and walked to the door. "What you decide to do with this form is up to you. But I want you to know that I don't intend to take this kind of rating without a fight. It's not a fair evaluation, and if I do have problems, I certainly haven't received any help from you. It's the supervision in this school that has failed, not me. I'll take that issue to court, if necessary!"

Suggested Learning Activities

Analyze the Case

1. What factors may be influencing the behavior of Mrs. Stevens and her class while the principal is conducting his classroom observations?
2. What factors seem to be influencing the conclusions drawn by the principal, based on his classroom observations of Mrs. Stevens? What other kinds of conclusions could be drawn?
3. Why did the principal's first conference with Mrs. Stevens seem to go poorly? How would you have handled the situation differently? What assumptions are you making?
4. What are the strengths and weaknesses of the particular teacher evaluation form used in this case?
5. What is your evaluation of the principal's rationale for not recommending renewal of Mrs. Stevens's contract? Considering the circumstances, what would you have done?
6. In what way would you have approached the second conference with Mrs. Stevens differently?

Discuss the Larger Issues

1. What do you think is the likelihood that a teacher will be unaffected by a supervisor's presence in the classroom and that the supervisor will observe her as she typically behaves?
2. What, if anything, can be done by a supervisor to obtain an accurate impression of how a teacher usually acts in a classroom situation?

3. What teacher characteristics and behaviors, if any, are *known* to be associated with teacher effectiveness and should be observable to a supervisor during class observation?
4. What are the responsibilities of a principal for helping a teacher to become more effective?

Be a Problem Solver The teacher has accused the principal in this case of failing to provide her with adequate supervision, and she has threatened to take the issue to court if the district fails to rehire her. As the principal in the situation, what would be your response to the accusation and the threat?

Test Your Solution To test your proposed plan of action for dealing with the problem presented at the end of the case, create and role-play one or more of the following situations in class:

1. Continue the conference between the principal and the teacher.
2. Conduct a meeting between the building representative for the teachers and the principal.
3. Have the teacher's attorney call the principal on the telephone.
4. Have the superintendent call the principal.
5. Role-play any other situation that would provide feedback on the strengths and weaknesses of your proposed solution.

Investigate Further

1. What are the characteristics and format of the teacher evaluation form used in your district?
2. What is the school board and administrative policy in your district in regard to classroom visitation and to teacher supervision and evaluation?
3. Determine whether there are state laws or court decisions that would have a bearing on whether the teacher in this case could be legally dismissed in your district.

29
FACULTY SLOWDOWN

CITY COUNCIL CUTS SCHOOL DISTRICT'S BUDGET

Class Sizes Will Have to Go Up, Says Superintendent

The headlines in the local paper highlighted the problem for Skyline School District. The superintendent and the school board had tried valiantly to keep the budget down this year, recognizing that the city was determined to hold the line against any tax increase. The attempt to economize had failed to overcome the costs of inflation, building modifications, and higher salaries negotiated by teachers earlier in the year.

Ultimately there had been no alternative for the school district except to submit an increased school budget, but, in the face of a threatened taxpayers' revolt, the city council had felt that it had no choice except to cut the budget. After the council meeting, the superintendent was quoted in the newspaper as saying that because of the budget cuts, the district would probably have to lay off teachers and, as a result, class sizes would be larger in the fall.

The following Monday, acting on the recommendation of the superintendent, the school board voted to eliminate several major items in the budget, including salaries for several teachers who were to be notified that they were no longer needed.

Several days later the newspaper printed an open letter from the local teachers' association to the superintendent of schools:

> We, the teachers, are appalled by the recent action taken by the city council and share your concern about its effects on the educational program of our school district. We deplore your recommendation and the school board's action to cut the budget and to lay off teachers.
>
> As you have publicly admitted, the result will be increased class sizes. We recognize that the city, in effect, forced you into this untenable position. But the teachers of this district want to make it perfectly clear that we may have no alternative other than to cut back on professional services. We feel that the teacher-pupil ratio is already too high, and, if it is increased, teachers will find it impossible to carry out many of the activities that contribute to quality education.
>
> The teachers of this district should not and cannot be expected to provide the same level of professional services in the future that would be possible if class sizes were lower. It is impossible to say at this time exactly which services may be affected, but unwieldy class sizes will inevitably curtail the teachers' ability to conduct courses as they would like.

Surprisingly, the public's reaction to the teachers' letter was minimal.

During the next month the superintendent made several attempts to ascertain the precise nature of the implications in the letter. The representatives of the teachers' association refused to elaborate, indicating only that several possibilities were being considered.

The following September, school opened smoothly, in spite of the increased number of students. Classes were larger and teacher complaints were heard, but there was no evidence of a cutback in teacher services. By the end of the second week, classes were proceeding as usual, and the central administration and school board began to relax, unaware that a problem was starting to develop at Jefferson School.

On Tuesday a parent called the principal to report that her son's teacher was not correcting all the written work that the students had been assigned. The parent had previously complained to the teacher but had received no satisfaction. The teacher had said that, as a result of the heavier workload created by larger classes, it would be impossible to correct all the written work, and that less would be assigned during the year. The parent had not wanted to become involved in an argument with the teacher, but now wanted to know what the school was going to do about the problem. The principal replied that he would talk to the teacher and "try to straighten things out." After school he met with the teacher, Mr. Sullivan, and related the parent's complaint to him. When the principal asked whether the allegation was true, the teacher admitted it at once. He took the position that his heavier workload had made it impossible for him to do the job that he wanted to, and added that he was not alone in this regard. All the teachers had decided that their larger classes prevented them from maintaining their usual professional standards. The administration should understand that this was not a condition for which the teachers were responsible, and they deplored its effects. But correcting homework was a tremendously time-consuming task, and, with the additional students, there was really no other choice than to assign less written work and to spot-check the completed assignments.

The principal thought to himself that at one time he would have been flabbergasted by such an attitude. Now he merely wondered wearily whatever had happened to the dedicated teacher who placed the education of his or her students and their needs before his or her own. The principal recognized the additional burden that larger classes placed on a teacher's workload, but what could a principal—or, for that matter, the superintendent—do about that now? The city council had already established the amount to be spent by the schools, and everyone would simply have to work a little harder. It was unfortunate, but the problem wouldn't be solved by people refusing to meet the challenge!

The principal decided that in his present frame of mind, it would be better not to say anything at the moment to the teacher. Moreover, he wasn't sure about the extent of his own authority in the event that Mr. Sullivan should adamantly refuse to correct any additional papers. So he told the teacher that he was disappointed with his attitude and that the issue would have to be referred to the central office.

After Mr. Sullivan left, the principal called the superintendent and informed him of the recent developments. The superintendent seemed upset and was quite critical of the teachers. He pointed out that if they had not been so insistent on higher salaries this year, the district probably could have afforded to hire more teachers, and class size would not have become a problem. He was not sure what the principal should do—particularly if the teachers should refuse to carry out aspects of their normal teaching assignment. He would have to return a call to the principal later.

By the end of the week the principal had not heard from the superintendent. In Friday's afternoon mail, however, a letter arrived from the superintendent.

I am sorry to be so long in responding, but the problem at your school has caused us a great deal of concern. Your situation has been discussed informally with members of the school board, and we at the central office have concluded that the teachers in your school are engaged in an unprofessional and unethical slowdown that can in no way be justified by the current class sizes.

To be quite frank, we are uncertain about the legal remedies available to the school district if your teachers do not desist from their present course of action. Nevertheless, we would encourage you to exercise whatever influence and leadership you can exert on these teachers to make them "see the light." It should be emphasized that your efforts in this regard are particularly important. We have heard that if the teachers at your school are successful, the practice of cutting back on assigning and correcting student work may spread to other schools. All of us must do everything we can to prevent that from happening.

In closing, may I suggest that you exercise great care not to stir up the teachers. They are very unhappy about the higher class sizes as well as some of the other effects of necessary budget cuts. If the situation becomes greatly exacerbated, they could stage a walkout. Obviously, we don't want that to happen!

Do the best you can and keep us posted on developments.

Sincerely,
Malcom Lewis
Superintendent of Schools

Suggested Learning Activities

Analyze the Case

1. What action, if any, should have been taken by the school administration when the local teachers' association publicly criticized the administration and the school board?
2. What is your evaluation of the position taken by Mr. Sullivan in his conference with the principal? In what way would you have acted differently, if you had been the principal, during the conference with Mr. Sullivan? What assumptions are you making?
3. What might be some of the reasons the superintendent responded in the way he did to the principal's request for assistance?

Discuss the Larger Issues

1. Should a teachers' association—or an individual teacher, counselor, or administrator—take a public stand that may be critical of certain actions by the administration and the school board?
2. Under what set of circumstances, if any, is a work slowdown a legitimate tactic by an individual school employee or a teachers' organization?
3. Administratively, who should have the primary responsibility for solving the main problem described in this case? Why?

Be a Problem Solver The superintendent has encouraged the principal to exercise his influence on the teachers to make them "see the light" but not to "stir them up." If *you* were the principal, how would you handle this situation? Outline the steps you would take and the people you would involve. Utilize appropriate administrative and social science concepts from Part I of the text in planning and implementing your approach.

Test Your Solution To test your proposed plan of action for dealing with the problem presented at the end of this case, create and role-play one or more of the following interactions in class:

1. A telephone call between the principal and the parent who had previously called.
2. Another meeting between the principal and Mr. Sullivan.
3. A telephone call to the principal from a newspaper reporter.

Investigate Further

1. What is the school board policy in your district in regard to how much written work a teacher *must* assign and correct?
2. What is the policy of your local teachers' association and that of the state and national teachers' associations on how much written work a teacher must assign and correct?
3. What written statements and documents could you produce that could be used in court to support the position of the teachers or that of the administration on the issue of homework practices?

30
DO WOMEN HAVE POWER?

Mrs. Gazzlois is in her fourth year as assistant principal of instruction at Baytown High School. Three males act as assistants to the male principal. Their duties are discipline and school management. Prior to arriving at Baytown, Mrs. Gazzlois served as director for employee training with a regional utility company. Her business experience provided an abundance of opportunities to implement changes that improved human resources for a more efficient management style.

Baytown High School is restructuring its management plan to empower teachers to participate in shared decision making. The superintendent recognized Mrs. Gazzlois's abilities and desire to contribute to a quality school. Her business experience plus her interpersonal skills had made Mrs. Gazzlois the most desirable individual for transformational change at Baytown.

During her employment at Baytown, Mrs. Gazzlois had maintained a positive attitude through difficult change implementations. She had diplomatically implemented business management procedures while instructing teachers in strategies to shift their paradigms toward connecting the classroom and workplace. Additionally, much of her attention was directed toward creating a cooperative administrative team with a twenty-first-century vision for educating students. This effort met with resistance as each of the male administrators practiced authoritative management. Mrs. Gazzlois was increasingly isolated from administrative decisions, causing numerous difficulties for her as the teachers began to exhibit a lack of trust and respect for her authority.

The other administrators placed heavy emphasis on athletics and would very often pass many of their duties to Mrs. Gazzlois, claiming urgent needs elsewhere. Her attempts to confront those administrators concerning the situation were only ignored. She believed this situation to be one in which female administrators were looked upon by male colleagues as "no-power-allowed" employees.

A recent incident occurred when the Baytown soccer team participated in the state tournament held two hours away. According to school board policy, the coach, players, and bus driver must return home following any defeat. Coach Waterman's team lost the semifinal game. After boarding the bus, the coach was adamant about seeing the final game, which would require an overnight stay. Coach Waterman's statement shocked the bus driver, Mr. Patrick, and the coach's assistant, who reminded Mr. Waterman of the school policy.

After the final match, the team enjoyed dinner in a nearby restaurant. When all were boarded to depart, the bus would not start. Student cheers filled the air with shouts "overnight, overnight!"

Mrs. Gazzlois, principal on duty at Baytown that night, received Mr. Patrick's call regarding bus motor difficulty. She instructed him to have a mechanic check the bus, repair it, and return as soon as possible while she phoned the superintendent, principal, and parents. She requested that Mr. Patrick phone again with their expected time of arrival.

The mechanical bus check revealed sugar in the gas tank. Again the team cheered "overnight, overnight!" Mr. Patrick was assured the repair could be completed and the team would be on the road in a couple of hours.

Coach Waterman phoned for a rental van for the evening, made overnight lodging arrangements, and took his players to the final tournament game.

The next day Mrs. Gazzlois requested an administrative team meeting to discuss the incident. No meeting was held. A principal memorandum was placed in her mailbox stating the matter had been effectively managed and closed.

Suggested Learning Activities

Analyze the Case

1. What was the principal's role in building an effective team to utilize Mrs. Gazzlois's strengths?
2. Could the faculty have been involved in an effort to improve the situation of administrative division?

Discuss the Larger Issues

1. Were there legal factors involved in Coach Waterman's decision?
2. How could parents influence a coach's decision in future situations?
3. How should the principal have acted in this situation?

Be a Problem Solver Assuming you were the bus driver, what would you have done? What is your position as to the legality involved in the situation?

Test Your Solution To test your action plan, do the following:

1. Role-play with your classmates the entire series of events. Develop a consensus for action.
2. Conduct a meeting with the principals and superintendent.

Investigate Further

1. Review educational and business literature on team building.
2. Determine rationale for decision making in these circumstances.

31
COLLABORATION WOES

Longsworth Elementary School was widely recognized for its successful collaborative leadership program. The School Leadership Team (SLT) was selected as a model for other schools in the district, encouraging them to develop improved communication, time management, and shared decision making. "High test scores are just one of the many positive outcomes schools can expect to see by using this approach," said the principal, Dr. Jewel Botts, whose collaborative leadership style was well known and highly praised. She explained that the role of the representative SLT committee was to provide consistent information and innovative ideas while ensuring that the entire staff was involved in making academic and financial decisions. In addition, staff needs and staff feedback were regularly brought to the committee's meetings.

Serving on the School Leadership Team was understandably a time-consuming task. Teachers were divided into grade level teams, and each team had an SLT representative. Wednesdays, at 7:50 A.M., the committee met in the principal's conference room. It was the team's job to follow up on previous ideas and plans while considering all new issues carefully and thoroughly. The tool of choice in seeking effective answers to school and academic issues was *brainstorming*. After extensive problem-solving discussion in the weekly meeting, each team member was to share the information with the group he or she represented.

These grade level groups were to meet every Thursday at 7:50 A.M. When there were decisions to be made concerning the school and programming, each staff member had a vote and was encouraged to bring up other ideas and concerns. The members of SLT brought back to the committee all information, votes, problems, requests, and new issues. Exact note taking and follow-through were critical for the success of this collaborative approach. Additionally, the SLT members were to report all problems that had occurred within the group they represented. Most of the time, when the problems were small (like tardiness), the SLT leader handled it privately with that particular teacher.

Because of this collaborative leadership style, faculty meetings were rare. Even some of the in-services were provided only to the SLT and then spiraled down to the grade level teams of teachers. Also, any teacher could request to attend an SLT meeting and present needs, requests, and information, which could assist the leaders and other staff members in reaching a popular and beneficial decision. All budget decisions were handled through SLT, along with implementing instructional and motivational plans. Material distribution and discipline policy, clubs, enrichment activities, remediation programs, and academic unit planning all fell to these designated team leaders.

Sometimes attendance at the SLT meetings was not at 100 percent, so every team had a substitute representative who could step in as the communicator. The only compensation for the vast amount of work required was a sense of pride, responsibility, and school leadership. If the member's attendance was consistent and prompt and if she or he contributed insightful feedback and ideas, this leadership role was stated positively in the end-of-year evaluation.

The principal had no idea of the dissatisfaction, frustration, and negative attitudes that were brewing among the SLT members until the day that Shirley Rodgers, one of the teachers, came to her office to tell her how the SLT members were feeling. The complaints documented by Mrs. Rodgers included the following:

- Some teams left voting entirely up to the representative.
- Several teams rarely met because the representative's notes were passed around.
- The SLT leaders felt that more tasks were delegated to them as time passed.
- A few representatives, including Principal Botts, dominated the decision-making process.
- Many teachers considered the leaders to be pawns of the principal because the leaders were rarely switched year after year.
- The SLT members were handpicked by the principal rather than selected by each team.
- Teachers requesting admittance to the Wednesday meetings felt hesitant and intimidated.
- Those teachers who were more adamant and convincing often received more money out of the school budget for supplies and programs.

Dr. Botts was flabbergasted as she listened to the complaints. As principal, she had always envisioned her role during the team meetings to be that of a facilitator, cheerleader, or mediator. She also knew that her responsibility was to make the team aware of the school and district policies and to make sure that the team stayed within those guidelines.

Dr. Botts pondered the situation. She had never expected to hear these complaints. She found herself wondering whether Mrs. Rodgers was really in her office as a spokesperson for leaders and teachers or she simply wanted to be relieved of her own extra work, even though the collaborative leadership might be working well for most of the staff. In either case, it was clear that some genuine concerns needed to be addressed. It was time to evaluate and modify the widely recognized collaborative leadership model at Longsworth Elementary.

Suggested Learning Activities

Analyze the Case

1. Prioritize the list of complaints given to the principal.
2. What should be the role of each team leader? How can this role be consistent for every team?
3. What concepts should Principal Botts use in resolving the negative feelings and making the situation fair to all staff members?
4. What steps can an administrator take to ward off collaboration problems?
5. What are alternatives for improving the function of SLT?

Discuss the Larger Issues

1. What steps should be taken to evaluate the effectiveness of a collaborative leadership program? Who should be included in conducting the evaluation? How should the results be distributed?
2. What are the positive and negative points in using a committee to communicate and make decisions?
3. When leadership is shared, what role does the principal take in making sure the choices are effective and inspirational to both teachers and students?

Be a Problem Solver Step into the shoes of Dr. Botts and write a description of how you would introduce to the staff the need for an evaluation of the School Leadership Team. Assuming that the complaints in this case study turn out to be true, make plans for effective changes in utilizing the collaborative leadership team. You may wish to consider each complaint separately or restructure the entire leadership system. Utilize social science and administrative concepts from Part I in designing your approach to the problem.

Test Your Solution To test some of your ideas for modification of the School Leadership Team, role-play one or more of the following situations in class:

1. A meeting between the SLT members and Dr. Botts to discuss the needed changes, along with the fairest way to vote on the modifications and implement them.
2. A conference between Dr. Botts and Mrs. Rodgers to clarify the documented complaints.
3. A meeting between the superintendent and Dr. Botts concerning future improvements of Longsworth Elementary's collaborative leadership model program.

Investigate Further

1. Describe an example of a collaborative leadership program utilized in your school district.
2. How are shared leadership responsibilities evaluated in your district? How can staff dissatisfaction and complaints be monitored?
3. Determine the criteria and process used to evaluate collaborative leadership in your school district.

BACKGROUND READING

For the reader who would like to develop further background and understanding of the problems and issues presented in this chapter, the following list of readings is provided:

Aldridge, Jill M., and Barry J. Fraser, "Teachers' Views of Their School Climate and Its Relationship with Teacher Self-Efficacy and Job Satisfaction," *Learning Environments Research* (vol. 19, no. 2, July 2016), pp. 291–307.

Alston, Judy A., and Patrice A. McClellan, *Herstories: Leading with the Lessons of the Lives of Black Women Activists* (New York: Peter Lang Publishers, 2010).

Barnett, Bruce G., and Howard Stevenson, "Leading High Poverty Urban Schools," in Simon Clarke and Tom O'Donoghue (eds.), *School Leadership in Diverse Contexts* (New York: Routledge, 2016), pp. 23–42.

Bettini, Elizabeth, Amber Benedict, Rachel Thomas, Jenna Kimerling, Nari Choi, and James McLeskey, "Cultivating a Community of Effective Special Education Teachers Local Special Education Administrators' Roles," *Remedial and Special Education* (vol. 38, no. 2, March-April 2017), pp. 111–126.

Byrd-Blake, M., et al., "Morale of Teachers in High Poverty Schools: A Post-NCLB Mixed Methods Analysis," *Education & Urban Society* (vol. 42, no. 4, May 2010), pp. 450–472.

Christianson, Carley L., and Robin D. Everall, "Breaking the Silence: School Counsellors' Experiences of Client Suicide," *British Journal of Guidance & Counselling* (vol. 37, no. 2, May 2009), pp. 157–168.

Cleaver, Samantha, "We Love It Here," *Instructor* (vol. 120, no. 3, November 2010), pp. 41–43.

Davignon, Michelle Marie, *New Teachers' Perceptions of Teacher Leaders: Trust in the Educational Setting*, PhD diss., Southern New Hampshire University, 2016.

"Evaluations That Help Teachers Learn," *Educational Leadership* (vol. 68, no. 4, December 2010), pp. 35–39.

Grissom, Jason A., Luis A. Rodriguez, and Emily C. Kern, "Teacher and Principal Diversity and the Representation of Students of Color in Gifted Programs: Evidence from National Data," *The Elementary School Journal* (vol. 117, no. 3, March 2017), 396–422. DOI: 10.1086/690274.

Hanselman, Paul, Jeffrey Grigg, Sarah K. Bruch, and Adam Gamoran, "The Consequences of Principal and Teacher Turnover for School Social Resources," in Grace Kao and Hyunjoon Park (eds.), *Family Environments, School Resources, and Educational Outcomes (Research in the Sociology of Education, Volume 19)* (West Yorkshire, UK: Emerald Group Publishing Limited, 2016), pp. 49–89.

Hicks, Anna, *Speak Softly and Carry Your Own Gym Key: A Female High School Principal's Guide to Survival* (Thousand Oaks, CA: Corwin Press, 1995).

Huling, Leslie, Virginia Resta, Tom Manderville, and Penny Miller, "Factors in the Selection of Secondary School Teachers," *Teachers for the 21st Century Bulletin* (May 1996), pp. 57–63.

Jellinek, Michael, Jeff Q. Bostic, and Steven C. Schlozman, "When a Student Dies," *Educational Leadership* (vol. 65, no. 3, November 2007), pp. 78–82.

Klassen, Robert M., Ellen L. Usher, and Mimi Bong, "Teachers' Collective Efficacy, Job Satisfaction, and Job Stress in Cross-Cultural Context," *Journal of Experimental Education* (vol. 78, no. 4, Summer 2010), pp. 464–486.

Koehler, Michael, "Showing New Teachers the Instructional Ropes," *ASCD Professional Development Newsletter* (Winter 2000), p. 2.

Lamis, Dorian A., Maureen Underwood, and Nicole D'Amore, "Outcomes of a Suicide Prevention Gatekeeper Training Program among School Personnel," *Crisis* (vol. 38, no. 2, March 2017), pp. 89–99. DOI: http://dx.doi.org/10.1027/0227-5910/a000414.

Oner, Diler, and Emine Adadan, "Are Integrated Portfolio Systems the Answer? An Evaluation of a Web-based Portfolio System to Improve Preservice Teachers' Reflective Thinking Skills," *Journal of Computing in Higher Education* (vol. 28, no. 2, August 2016), pp. 236–260.

Peterson, Kenneth D., and Catherine A. Peterson, *Effective Teacher Evaluation: A Guide for Principals* (Thousand Oaks, CA: Corwin Press, 2005).

Sawchuk, Stephen, "Teacher Evaluations," *Education Week* (vol. 30, no. 13, December 2010), p. 5.

Seymour, Clancy, and Mark Garrison, "What They Think about How They Are Evaluated: Perspectives of New York State Physical Educators on Teacher Evaluation Policy," *International Journal of Education Policy and Leadership* [Online] (vol. 11, no. 6, December 13, 2016).

Steinberg, Matthew P., and Morgaen L. Donaldson, "The New Educational Accountability: Understanding the Landscape of Teacher Evaluation in the Post-NCLB Era," *Education Finance and Policy* (vol. 11, no. 3, Summer 2016), pp. 340–359.

Vaught, Clair Cole, "A Letter for Helping Middle-School Counselors," *National Association of Secondary School Principals Bulletin* (April 1995), pp. 20–23.

Waintroob, Andrea R., "Don't Fool with Incompetent Teachers," *School Administrator* (May 1995), pp. 20–24.

Wise, Arthur E., and Jane Leibbrand, "Standards and Teacher Quality," *Phi Delta Kappan* (April 2000), pp. 612–616, 621.

Wolf, Kenneth, "Developing an Effective Portfolio," *Educational Leadership* (March 1996), pp. 34–37.

WEB EXPLORATIONS

The Web links below contain more useful material related to Chapter 11.

On women in leadership:

Glass, Thomas E., "Where Are All the Women Superintendents?" AASA Online (May 29, 2000). http://aasa.org/SchoolAdministratorArticle.aspx?id=14492

Gewertz, Catherine, "Race, Gender, and the Superintendency." http://www.edweek.org/ew/articles/2006/02/17/24supes.h25.html

On teacher morale:

"On Teacher Development and Care." http://www.vtaide.com/png/teacher.htm

Research on Teacher Morale. https://relwest.wested.org/system/documents/pdfs/476/original/REL_West_Memo_Teacher_Morale.pdf?1465942871

"Teacher Morale." https://teacherscount.wordpress.com/2010/01/09/teacher-morale/

On collaborative leadership:

10 Collaborative Leadership Characteristics. http://yscouts.com/10-collaborative-leadership-characteristics/

On evaluation:

Teacher Evaluations: New Directions and Practices. www.teacherevaluation.net

On the changing role of the principal:

Alvoid, Lee, and Watt Lesley Black Jr., "The Changing Role of the Principal." https://www.americanprogress.org/issues/education/reports/2014/07/01/93015/the-changing-role-of-the-principal/

Kantor, Hope, "Role of the Assistant Principal in Leadership Transitions." http://www.nais.org/Magazines-Newsletters/ISMagazine/Pages/The-Role-of-the-Assistant-Principal-in-Leadership-Transitions.aspx

"The Role of the Principal." http://www.scholastic.com/administrator/red/principal.htm

CHAPTER

12

School-Community Relations

The primary purpose of education in most societies is twofold: It perpetuates the culture and prepares students for productive adult roles. In the United States, the control over these aspects of acculturation has historically been vested by the state in local boards of education that are usually elected by their respective communities.

Although the dominant orientation of many communities seems to be toward maintaining the status quo, some educators have introduced new ideas, materials, and approaches to learning that they feel will make the school more relevant to the needs of students and the larger society. These educators–teachers and administrators–believe that the primary purpose of the school is to stimulate students to become more independent, to think for themselves, and to assess their own values as well as those of the community. In the process of introducing change, they have, in many instances, challenged the norms of the local community or groups within the community, and conflict between the community and the school has frequently resulted.

Although professional challenges to community norms represent one major source of potential school-community conflict, community challenges to professional norms have also tended to lead to friction between the school and its constituencies. In recent years many parents and community groups have grown increasingly dissatisfied with the effectiveness of school programs, achievements, and personnel. These individuals and groups reject the concept that the school board should have sole responsibility for the development of school policy and that other professionals in the school should be accountable only to each other and to the board of education. Such parents and community groups desire more meaningful involvement in the establishment and modification of school policies and in the evaluation of the extent to which the school and its personnel are meeting their responsibilities. These expectations represent a direct challenge to the professional norms of many educators and constitute a major source of school-community conflict.

It should be noted that, paradoxically, in spite of the emphasis in the educational literature on the desire of citizens to become more involved in school affairs, administrators may encounter considerable apathy as well as interest when they try to increase community involvement in the schools. An inescapable conclusion is that the task of maintaining and improving school-community relations is challenging and sometimes frustrating. Educators must be careful not to underestimate the importance of community relations in publicly funded institutions. Newspapers, videos, local and national television, the Internet, and other information technologies create new opportunities for instant response to coverage of cataclysmic–and even embarrassing–events. Most of the cases presented in this chapter illustrate the two main factors responsible for school-community conflict: professional challenges to the norms of the community and community challenges to the professional norms of the school. In addition, cases are included that focus on parental apathy, school public relations, and the recurring financial crisis in the schools. All the cases represent serious problems that, if not constructively addressed, could result in the deterioration of school-community relations.

32
CURRICULUM UNIT UPSETS PARENTS

Placards and shouts greeted visitors to the city council meeting: "Clean up Morgan River!" "Vote funds for antipollution and beautification!" For the past two hours, students had been picketing near the entrance to City Hall, and now they moved inside the building as the meeting of the city council began.

The students, about two dozen of them, were from Morgan Falls School. They had come to protest the council's recent deletion of funds from the budget, funds that had earlier been tentatively allotted for a cleanup and beautification project for the river that flowed near the city.

The young people had carried on a local campaign for several months, stressing the potential of the river for recreation and scenic enjoyment. The local newspaper had supported their idea and had even printed pictures, which were found in the files, showing families swimming and boating in Morgan River 40 years ago.

Although the students had managed to raise $975, the cost of the project to clean up the river far exceeded that sum. When they took the idea to the city council, the aldermen had initially responded favorably to their plans and included a large allocation in the proposed budget. Recently, however, a tight financial situation had developed, and at their last meeting the members of the city council had eliminated the item.

As the mayor called for order, the student chants grew louder. Furious with what he felt was a deliberate disruption of the meeting, the mayor directed the guards to clear the building of all students. In the next moments bedlam broke out. Placards were thrown, there was much screaming and yelling, and finally several of the students had to be literally dragged from the building.

That night the late television news carried a filmed report of the disruption at City Hall, followed by an editorial that was quite critical of the students' tactics.

The next morning the school buzzed about the incident. Were the students justified in their use of such tactics? Should the school punish those who had actually been involved? There was considerable difference of opinion on these issues, and tempers flared more than once during the many informal discussions that took place in various parts of the building.

At 1:00 P.M. the principal received a call from someone identifying herself as Mrs. Thompson. Was the principal aware that her son's teacher was actually *instructing* students in approaches to overthrowing the government and that most of the students involved in the previous night's disruption were in that teacher's class?

The principal assured Mrs. Thompson that he was quite certain no one at his school was advocating that students overthrow anything. Yes, it was possible that some of the students at last night's meeting were from the same class, but he doubted whether that teacher could be held responsible for the students' actions. Well, he would check into the matter and call her back if there appeared to be a problem.

After school that day, the principal called to his office the teacher whom Mrs. Thompson had identified. The principal informed the teacher that a call had been received from a parent who complained that her son and others were being taught radical methods of changing society. Was this true?

The teacher responded by explaining that the whole question of how to achieve social change was a major issue with young people because there were many pressing problems needing solutions. It seemed to the teacher that the topic of how to deal with those problems and how to overcome resistance to change was important for students to learn about, so this year he had introduced a special unit on strategies for bringing about change. Obviously, many methods had been discussed with students, including tactics of confrontation and disruption. At no time had violent or extreme approaches been recommended as superior to peaceful means. Students had been told, though, that in some situations when everything else had failed, radical methods might represent their only viable recourse. Nevertheless, he had tried to emphasize to his class that his personal philosophy was that the critical point in a situation was a question of judgment and the individual's conscience. Each person would have to make that determination for him- or herself and live with the consequences.

After the teacher finished his explanation, the principal didn't comment for a few moments. Then he said that he would have to talk with the teacher's subject matter supervisor before he could make a decision on what should be done about the situation.

The following morning the principal didn't have a chance to see the district supervisor, but he continued to receive telephone calls from parents complaining about the students. Evidently, the news was out that a unit including the study of both violent and nonviolent means of bringing about change was being presented at Morgan Falls School, and that some of the young people who had been involved in the disruption at City Hall were from the class where the unit was being taught. The parents were very upset, and the principal was a little at a loss as to what to say to them.

At 10:15 A.M. the superintendent also called to inquire about the situation, and although he appeared concerned about the lack of a decision from the principal on the problem, he refrained from giving any directive that the unit be abandoned. He did say his wife had mentioned that the whole matter was a primary topic of conversation where she worked. People generally seemed to be attributing the incident at the city council meeting to the school's unit on bringing about change. It appeared that a major controversy might be shaping up.

The superintendent concluded the conversation by saying that he could appreciate the students' and teacher's convictions about the role of the school, but they might have to reconsider their position on the issue if the community strongly objected. Until that time, the superintendent wanted the principal to know that he would support the school 100 percent.

After the principal put down the phone, he thought about what the superintendent had told him. It was clear that at least a certain segment of the public (how large, he couldn't be sure) was quite disturbed. In addition, there was now a measure of doubt in his own mind about whether the superintendent would support him and the teacher if the community outcry should reach the school board in the form of an organized protest against the school's curriculum. There was little question that it was imperative to get together with the department head.

Just then the phone rang again. It was the president of the school's parent group, who had been deluged with calls all day from parents wanting a special meeting to air their complaints about the school's unit on change processes. The president suspected it might be a rather heated meeting, and there was a good possibility the press would attend, and perhaps several school board members. Should he go ahead and schedule the meeting?

The principal didn't say anything immediately. He was thinking. The opposition had organized itself more rapidly than he had anticipated, and a strategy for dealing with the problem was badly needed.

He informed the president of the parents' group that he would call him back in an hour.

As the principal put down the phone, he thought to himself that regardless of what he did, he was going to make somebody very unhappy.

Suggested Learning Activities

Analyze the Case

1. What, if anything, should or could the principal have done to prevent the student demonstration from ever taking place?
2. What action do you feel the principal should have taken in regard to the particular students who had disrupted the city council meeting?
3. What assumptions is the principal making in his response to the comments of:
   a. Mrs. Thompson?
   b. The teacher?

   How tenable are those assumptions?
4. What is your evaluation of the superintendent's comments? What are their implications?

Discuss the Larger Issues

1. What is the responsibility of the school for preparing students to adjust to and/or change society and its institutions?
2. What should be the attitude of the school toward students who go into society to carry out techniques of change they have learned in school?
3. Do teachers have a right to discuss issues in class that may violate the customs or mores of the community? Or does the community have the right to determine the content of their children's education?

Be a Problem Solver A large number of people are urging that an open meeting be held to discuss a recent community disturbance and its relationship to what has been taught by a social studies teacher. How should the situation be handled?

Test Your Solution To test your proposed plan of action for dealing with the problem presented at the end of this case, create and role-play one or more of the following situations in class:

1. A conference between the principal and the department head.
2. A conference between the social studies teacher, his supervisor, and the principal.

3. The telephone call between the principal and the president of the school's parents' group.
4. A general meeting among the principal, the supervisor, and the parents.
5. Another phone call to the principal from the superintendent.

Investigate Further

1. What is the extent to which a teacher is legally liable for acts carried out by students in his or her class, that they have previously discussed in that teacher's class? What is the principal's or department head's liability for what their teachers teach?
2. What is the policy in your district in regard to teaching controversial issues?
3. May a teacher in your state be legally dismissed for teaching content that is strongly opposed by the community?

33
COMMUNICATION AND CONSTRUCTED REALITY

Greenvalley is a high school with an enrollment of 2,700 students and a faculty of 250. Located in an exclusive suburb of a high-tech urban area, Greenvalley is capable of providing a variety of specialty courses to its students. The area is rich in cultural activities, with heavy emphasis on communications and media productions. Funding from the entertainment industry is extremely generous, thereby providing numerous opportunities for students to obtain school-to-work learning and training.

Mr. Avery is an accomplished instructor of film production at Greenvalley. He has been on staff for seven years, during which time he has established rapport within the school and community as well as having entrenched himself in the film production industry. Many of his former students as well as present ones are employed in the film production industry in the area.

Mr. Avery assigns his students the task of photographing and producing a video each semester. Topics are assigned, but students are encouraged to be creative in their work. Recently, two students, Sam and Mary, opted to produce a video cooperatively. Their video, *Preparing for a Day at School,* presented footage of Mary brushing her teeth clad only in a bra and panties of matching black lace. Immediately Mr. Avery stopped the presentation and addressed the issue of appropriate footage. The students' reactions were mixed, with many stating it was creative while others stated it was risqué and should not be aired.

The class was dismissed with Mr. Avery retaining the video. The conversations were lively as the students departed for other classes and to assigned duties as assistants to the nurse and guidance counselors. Mr. Avery assumed that the issue was closed, but when he later checked his office in-basket for messages, he found a note from Mr. Blake, the department chairperson, stating he would like to view the video with him. During planning time, the two viewed the video when Mrs. Ellis, a retired English teacher, entered the viewing studio and recognized the students on the film. Immediately she reported to the principal that Mr. Avery and Mr. Blake were viewing pornographic films they had made of their students. Mrs. Leers, the young principal, was scheduled to board a flight in less than one hour. Mrs. Ellis was assured by

Mrs. Leers that this matter would be addressed when she returned in three days; and given the reputation of Mr. Avery and Mr. Blake, she was confident that there would be a satisfactory explanation for the film.

As school closed, a local news reporter was in the student parking lot interviewing students concerning the video and Mr. Avery's type of assignments. Many students, some of whom did not study film production, reported that Mr. Avery often encouraged them to use sexually stimulating material in their photos. The reporter talked with Mr. Avery, who assured the news reporter that he did not promote child pornography and that the students were clearly instructed concerning the type of work he deemed appropriate. The next day's edition of the local newspaper featured this headline: "Greenvalley High Teacher Assigns Pornography Filming to Students."

Immediately the chairman of the school board called for Mr. Avery's release from duty and the superintendent placed him on leave without pay. Three days later Mr. Avery's body was discovered in a local motel with the cause of death determined as suicide. His suicide note declared his innocence with an apology to his students and peers.

Suggested Learning Activities

Analyze the Case

1. What details could Mr. Avery have addressed in making the students' filming assignment?
2. As principal, how would you have handled the video of the girl brushing her teeth?
3. Should the principal have managed Mrs. Ellis's message differently? If so, how?

Discuss the Larger Issues

1. How much freedom should the media have in talking directly with students on school property concerning teacher evaluation of student materials?
2. What role should other colleagues assume in such incidences as described in this case?

Be a Problem Solver If you were principal in this situation, what would you do? What role could the guidance counselor and/or nurse have carried out assuming the student assistants had shared the video incident with them? Utilize appropriate administrative and social science strategies to implement your approach.

Test Your Solution To test your proposed plan of action dealing with Mr. Avery, interview practicing administrators for their strategy to manage this incident and develop a consensus for an action plan.

Investigate Further

1. What is the board policy in your school division for dealing with sexually oriented (either intentional or unintentional) assignments given by a teacher?
2. What is the crisis-management approach for teacher suicide offered by your system?
3. What are the legal responsibilities for a job-related suicide?

34
PARENTAL APATHY

Mrs. Rose was a new assistant principal at John F. Kennedy School. She had just finished her final course work during the summer and had been looking forward to her new job. Now, four months after being on the job, she wasn't sure about some aspects of the situation.

In summer school she had taken a course on school-community relations and had come away from the course convinced of the need for a comprehensive program of school-community relations, and with some ideas and considerable enthusiasm for getting something started. Certainly, it appeared, after only two months on the job, that her own school had a very limited program of contact or involvement with the parents and the larger community. For example, there was no Parent Teacher Association (PTA) or parents' organization, and there was no parent newsletter sent home on a regular basis. There were also no advisory committees operating, although apparently there had been some parents' groups at one time or another.

She had talked to her principal about her concerns and ideas, but she hadn't received much encouragement from him. The principal had taken the position that everything was going fine at the school and that the parents were better off left alone. He had informed her that he had felt differently when he first started in administration, but he had encountered a lot of parental apathy. Not many parents showed up for meetings, and when he had tried to solicit parent volunteers to work in the cafeteria, he had received a very poor response. The principal wasn't sure that parents really wanted to get involved, and if the school tried too hard to get them involved, that effort might just get them stirred up about something and they might be harder to handle.

The principal had also asserted that he was in direct contact with the community and he felt, on the basis of the telephone calls he received and the parents he saw who came in for conferences, that he could sense the pulse of the community. His sense of the community was that people didn't want to be involved and they expected the educators to do the work.

Mrs. Rose had been dismayed by the principal's comments, but while she didn't agree with his assessment of the situation, she had decided at that moment not to say anything.

Later in another conference with the principal, she had again brought up the need for *some* type of parent involvement. To her surprise, the principal agreed, although with some ambivalence, to schedule a meeting to find out whether parents would even be interested in getting involved. He had made it clear, however, that he wasn't going to approve of any type of PTA. He might go along with the idea of a parents' advisory group, but nothing more.

On Friday, an announcement was distributed to the students in their classrooms at the end of the day, and they were asked to give the following announcement to their parents:

> AN INVITATION TO PARENTS
>
> There will be a special meeting at the school a week from this coming Monday at 7:30 P.M., on parent involvement. If you are interested and can attend, please come to the auditorium by 7:30.

The night of the meeting, eight parents showed up. In the back of the auditorium the principal and Mrs. Rose were discussing whether to go ahead with the meeting, in light of the low attendance. The principal was not in favor of proceeding with the meeting, given the poor turnout and the probable nonrepresentativeness of those who were present.

Suggested Learning Activities

Analyze the Case

1. What is your assessment of the attitude initially expressed by the principal about school-community relations? How typical is that attitude?
2. What, if anything, would you have done differently in the first conference with the principal if you had been the vice principal? How might the amount of your experience in the position and your gender influence the response you received?
3. Evaluate the parents' invitation presented at the end of the case utilizing concepts of communication and school-community relations. Hypothesize as to why only eight parents attended the meeting.

Discuss the Larger Issues

1. What should be the main objective of school-community relations? What should be the role of the school, and what should be the role of the community?
2. What are the implications of a limited program of parental involvement?
3. What factors contribute to parents' apathy? What factors contribute to parental and community involvement, confidence, trust, and support of the school?

Be a Problem Solver Assume that you are the vice principal of this school. Considering the circumstances described in this case, how do you propose to handle the situation? Utilize appropriate administrative and social science concepts from Part I of the text in planning and implementing your approach.

Test Your Solution To test your proposed plan for dealing with the problems described in the case, create and role-play one or more of the following situations in class:

1. The meeting on parental involvement attended by the eight parents, the principal, and vice principal.
2. A conference between the principal and the vice principal.
3. A new communication from the school to the parents.

Investigate Further

1. Ascertain the nature and scope of your school's community relations program.
2. What is the evidence of the effectiveness of your school's community relations program? What are the attitudes of faculty, parents, and administrators toward the program?
3. What are the roles of the administration, faculty, and parents in your school or district in developing and maintaining good school-community relations?

35
WANTED: A PLAN FOR IMPROVING PARENTAL AND COMMUNITY INVOLVEMENT

Tim Faust was leaving the central office where he had been meeting with Fred Thomas, the assistant superintendent. He was anxious to get back to his office and get some paperwork done before tonight's big game. As the principal of Tech High, one of his greatest accomplishments had been to expand the sports program. The baseball team was playing in the division title game tonight, and he couldn't wait to see it. Suddenly, Mrs. Emma Sterret, superintendent, called to him from her office doorway. "Timothy, come in here a minute, I have something I want you to see."

Oh no, thought Tim, the superintendent was always thinking up new schemes to get herself in the paper or just to get recognized. She really seemed to be out of touch with the schools, in her own world. Most everyone knew that Fred Thomas ran the show. The board just wanted Emma because her late husband, Bill, had worked for the state department of education. It seemed that Emma was always trying to outdo her husband's memory.

Tim shuffled into Emma's office.

"Oh, do sit down, Tim. I've got a real winner here!"

"What's that Mrs. Sterret?"

"Well, you know how the board has been pushing for more partnerships between the school and community, ever since that article in last month's paper about how Tech High parents want more say in the curriculum. Well, I've got the perfect plan. I just developed it yesterday. It's called CSP, community school partnerships. The idea is to partner teachers and staff with families within the community and arrange activities in which they can share. Of course, it would be mandatory for the teachers to . . ."

"Wait, wait just a minute. Mrs. Sterret, that article you are referring to was an editorial by Jean Garvey. She is a past president of the PTA and was concerned that the present PTA has been spending too much time in its meetings on fund-raisers and not more important issues like this one. Plus, Mrs. Sterret, don't you think the recent successes of our athletic teams at Tech have brought the community and school closer? I mean the turnout for games has tripled and recognition has been statewide."

"Yes, Tim, but you know how the board is. Education first! They want something on paper, Tim. Something that can be published and shared. We're not just a jock school, Tim. You have to remember that we need the association of all sorts of people, not just the parents who attend those games. We're trying to appeal to the right people."

"But Mrs. Sterret, what does that mean, 'right people'? Parents have never been more involved or prouder of their school than they were last semester when our football team won the regional title. Remember the old-timers who chartered a bus just to go see the team? You know as well as I do that people balk at almost everything else we try when it comes to getting parents or anyone involved in school activities."

"Now, Tim, that's not true. My last program, CPWS, community partnerships with schools, would have worked had you and Frederick gotten behind it."

"Mrs. Sterret, we really tried . . ."

"Tim, I mean to have this program implemented. So I suggest you look it over and suggest any modifications you feel will be of benefit."

Tim picked up the packet and stormed out of Emma's office. He had to see Fred right away.

After a brief consultation with Fred, Tim decided to bite the bullet. He poured over the program while the game was playing. He watered it down as best he could and decided to hold it for a week, at least. Maybe by that time Emma Sterret would have forgotten or changed her mind about it.

Suggested Learning Activities

Analyze the Case

1. Assess the relationship between the superintendent and the principal using the concepts from Chapter 3, "Authority, Power, and Influence."
2. Evaluate the arguments of both individuals using the concepts from Chapter 5, "Conflict Management."
3. What do you think took place during the consultation between the principal and the assistant superintendent after the meeting with the superintendent?

Discuss the Larger Issues

1. Should the principal continue to patronize the superintendent? What other possibilities should be sought?
2. What criteria and methods should be used to ascertain whether there is a need to improve school-community relations? What criteria and methods should be employed to evaluate the adequacy of a proposed improvement plan and its eventual implementation?
3. What role should teachers, parents, and other members of the community play in developing and implementing a plan for improving school-community relations?

Be a Problem Solver Assume that you are the principal and a week has gone by since your initial conference with the superintendent. She contacts you and instructs you to be in her office that afternoon with your suggestions. Review the program overview presented in the case and, utilizing the concepts in Chapter 7, "Change," modify her plan to reflect what you feel would be a successful program to increase parental involvement at your school.

Test Your Solution To test your proposed plan for improving school-community relations for your school, create and role-play one or more of the following situations in class:

1. An initial meeting between the principal and a committee appointed by the principal to help develop the plan.
2. A meeting at which the principal and the planning committee decide on the adequacy of a plan that a subcommittee has developed.
3. A meeting of the superintendent's cabinet at which you, as principal, present your school's plan.

Investigate Further

1. Examine the educational literature on school-community relations to identify elements that should be included in a comprehensive, effective program of school-community relations. What is the role of the principal and the superintendent in developing these elements?
2. Ascertain what criteria and methods are used in your school and school district to monitor the effectiveness of school and district programs of school-community relations.
3. Determine which schools in your district have effective programs of school-community relations. What factors contribute to their effectiveness?

36
THE SCHOOL–COMMUNITY WEB

Ms. Cromwell, the principal of Progressive Middle School, was fortunate in her administrative placement. For the last 10 years, Progressive had been characterized by extremely active parents and a vast array of community support. The school had effectively utilized over 100 volunteers each year. Many local businesses offered support through guest speakers, facilities, resources, and finances. Two local businesses participated at the "adopt-a-school" level. They provided academic assemblies, receptions, and monthly student birthday parties. School improvement surveys indicated that staff and parents were pleased with the level of open two-way communication between the school and the community.

The school district was also aware of the educational benefits of strong school-community relations and had prioritized this in the strategic plan adopted in September, listing enhanced school-community relations as one of the system's seven strategic goals. Principals were asked to submit plans to the central office by November, explaining how their schools intended to strive toward each of the seven goals.

The community relations goal presented a challenge for Ms. Cromwell and the faculty of Progressive Middle School. There were already so many positive practices in place that it was hard to develop new ideas for improvement in that area. They analyzed aspects of their current practices: written and verbal communication, community meetings, PTA activities, invitations to school activities, participation in school events and programs, community outreach to the school, school outreach to the community, and student and staff participation in community events. Each of these efforts appeared optimal. Yet a plan for improvement still had to be submitted.

Ms. Cromwell announced an open meeting of the advisory council, made up of parents, staff, administrators, and community leaders. She wanted to hear their suggestions. After much discussion the group came up with an idea that had not previously been explored. Perhaps a school Web site, accessible by the community 24 hours a day, would enhance the already strong school-community relations. Furthermore, if the Web site offered an opportunity for visitor comments, more people could communicate with the school on their own schedule without having to leave their homes or call during work hours. The school secretary could read the comments and suggestions daily and respond to those that requested response. In some cases, the secretary might need to consult a staff member, but the council felt the idea feasible and desirable. The committee was quite pleased with their suggestion. They saw it as a way to enhance school-community relations as outlined in the strategic plan while also addressing an additional area of concern: the implementation of technology in school programs.

When the idea was presented by the committee chair at the following faculty meeting, the staff and administration agreed that this was a good plan for increased communication and awareness of school events. Some staff members immediately expressed enthusiasm over the opportunity it would provide for publicizing classroom activities.

The Web site was developed and online within one month, and it provided an additional benefit that the committee did not foresee. The students enjoyed visiting the site and were excited to check it each week to see whether their class was mentioned. It became so popular that the computer resource teacher suggested that selected students begin to take part in modifying the site each month. This relieved the workload of the technology faculty, encouraged computer exploration relative to the workforce, and excited students. Soon after this suggestion a Web site team was formed. Membership was contingent upon teacher recommendation, and a number limit was set. The team collected information from throughout the building all week and worked after school each Wednesday to update the Web site. Parents, staff, and community members appreciated the creativity, knowledge, and ability of the students. When the students provided the Web site content, it covered more activities more effectively. No longer did the information have to come from teachers who might forget to submit activities. In addition, the Web site now focused on activities that the students, not the teachers, found beneficial.

Ms. Cromwell had received various positive comments about the Web site and about publicized events taking place at Progressive Middle. She was quite pleased with the reception. One particular Monday morning she received four telephone messages referencing the Web site. This was more response than typical for one morning. She guessed that there was an impressive display this week and completed her scheduled teacher observations before reading the messages. Upon returning to her desk before lunch, she found three additional messages. This mandated a look at the site. At the site, Ms. Cromwell found photos of sexually inappropriate acts; worse yet, the faces of the participants had been digitally altered to depict faculty members.

Suggested Learning Activities

Analyze the Case

1. Was the principal's decision to hold an open advisory meeting an appropriate measure for developing a plan to comply with the division strategic plan?
2. Was the Web site suggestion an appropriate tool for accomplishing the objective of enhanced school-community relations? What are some other solutions that the committee (or principal) might have considered?
3. To what extent should the principal have been more careful in monitoring the content of the Web site?

Discuss the Larger Issues

1. To what extent should students be involved in the creation of publications concerning the school and school system? What role should students play in selecting the content of these publications? What role should faculty play in selecting the content of these publications? What role should the administration play?
2. Should a school system be allowed to mandate areas for improvement in its individual schools? Should each school's centrally mandated goals be standard or individual? Is it professionally or morally satisfactory to have different standards in different attendance zones?
3. Does parent–community communication via the computer disregard important socioeconomic factors such as families who cannot afford or choose not to purchase a home computer? Should this be of concern? If so, how might the issue be remedied? What limitations are placed on this type of information when dissemnated in this manner?

Be a Problem Solver After discovering the contents of the Web site, Ms. Cromwell is distraught. She must notify central office, return the telephone calls of the seven parents, and change the contents of the Web page. Ms. Cromwell knows her community well enough to realize that she will have to address the issue at an open meeting and create a plan for finding out who uploaded the inappropriate content and issuing consequences. In addition, Ms. Cromwell is concerned that her faculty members may be disgusted enough at some of the photos containing their faces that there could be legal issues to resolve. How can she accomplish these tasks in such a way that damage to the positive relationship between the school and community will be minimal? Please use social science and administrative concepts from Part I in your approach to these problems.

Test Your Solution To test your proposed plan of action for this case study, role-play one or more of the following situations in class:

1. The phone call to the central office explaining the situation. Include the response from the central office.
2. A phone call to one of the seven community members who called about the Web site.
3. The open community meeting in which the principal discusses the problem and her proposed solution.
4. A meeting with pupil personnel staff who will recommend the consequences for the student or students who uploaded the material.
5. The design meeting for the next Web site. Who is present? In what capacities?

Investigate Further

1. Does your school district mandate strategic objectives? If so, what are they?
2. Does your school or district have a Web site? How often is it updated? Who updates it? What type of information does it provide?

3. Do parents in your community have access to computer communication with your building? If not, are any other means in place for after-hours communication?
4. What efforts does your school put forth in the realm of parent–community relations? Is this out of educational need or mandate? Do parents and staff feel that these means are sufficient?
5. What are your school district's policies on screening student publications?

37
DEVELOPING STUDENT TALENT

Like most school districts, the Midtown School District serves students with varying abilities. Its goal of meeting the needs of all the students is known throughout the community and has been internalized by administration, staff, and parents. However, it is expensive to individualize instruction and add programs as a response to addressing individual needs. Midtown's tax base is sufficient to continue current programs into the near future, but the limits of that tax base will be reached at some point.

The school system is a fiscally dependent district, with the budget having to be approved by the school board and the city council. As the time for planning the school district's budget draws closer, parents and community leaders convene to discuss what items should be included. A central office staff member is present at each of the formal meetings to inform the community of policies, practices, or legislation relevant to the discussions.

The parents begin with a speech on how to discover and enhance various talents in the youth of Midtown. Some of the parents were aware of recent literature that pointed out the difference in traditional "gifted" programs and those that identify and encourage talents. They felt that the current gifted program offered limited domains for enrichment. The community leaders likewise expressed concern about the current level of service the schools were providing in areas beyond academics. Employers had found that many recent graduates demonstrated academic knowledge but were lacking in other abilities and skills necessary in the workforce, especially creativity and problem solving. The parents felt that opening new areas of talent enhancement was the only way to provide "free and appropriate" education to students who possessed the motivation, interest, ability, and commitment to discover their talents and develop their potential. It was the school's responsibility, these parents argued, to provide the identification, teaching, and enrichment experiences needed. The parents promised to do their part by providing a supportive home environment.

Impressed by the level of research and preparation the core parent group had demonstrated, the central office staff member agreed with their thinking and acknowledged the need for such programs in the district. But his job was to insert financial reality into their thinking. Exactly what types of programs were they talking about? Were the facilities adequate to provide these services? How would these programs be staffed? Where was the line between public necessity and educational luxury? How could the district finance these programs when so much money was earmarked for government-mandated individualized education programs for other students with special needs? He assured the parent–citizen group that he would share their ideas with the superintendent's staff and arrive at their next meeting with comments and data.

When the superintendent's staff heard about the citizen group's idea of further enhancing student lives and talents, they conceded the idea's merit. In fact, they found it exciting. Unfortunately, the staff members did not foresee having the money or facilities to accomplish such a task. The school district had run into these budgetary concerns before.

The superintendent recalled her last battle, which was to seek funding to hire more teachers and reduce class size. She had presented her proposal and expected positive outcomes. But as soon as she had finished stating her proposal, a request for increased funding came from another source. The refuse collection department proposed an additional garbage collection each week. Representatives of the sanitation department had come well prepared to present their arguments, and they backed them up with photographs showing trash piling up in the streets. The proposed additional trash pickup carried the same price tag as reducing class sizes throughout the city, but the benefits would be immediately noticeable.

"Needless to say," the superintendent reminded the staff, "our schools were cleaner, yet more crowded, the following year." She was aware that developing multiple talents would require multiple programs with specially trained staff. She had no hope of receiving the funding needed for such an extremely expensive proposal. The staff member from budgeting would have to share these constraints with the community group.

At the next community meeting, the members of the parent–citizen group were clearly aware that their idea, however worthy, was being disregarded by the central office. Consequently, they decided to organize further. At the next school board meeting, the parents and community members arrived en masse with proposals for year-round after-school, weekend, and summer programs to help students develop their talents to the full. They urged that the services they deemed necessary be provided. Community members are willing to make concessions, such as restructuring scheduling, in order to realize their goal, but they will not be pushed aside with a simple, "We can't afford it."

Suggested Learning Activities

Analyze the Case

1. What should or could the central office staff member have done at the initial meeting to guide the discussion?
2. If the superintendent backs the beliefs and assumptions of the proposal to develop programs for students with varying talents, how might she acquire funding?
3. At what point are the needs of the students and the curriculum *secondary* to budgetary concerns? What are the principal's, superintendent's, and community members' roles in establishing budgetary limits?

Discuss the Larger Issues

1. What is the responsibility of the schools in providing enrichment instruction and activities in areas beyond the academic domain? For which students, if any, should these activities be offered?
2. Are gifted and/or talented students entitled to the same additional funding for individual instruction as students with academic disabilities?

3. What avenues should be explored for providing and/or funding additional programs in a school system?
4. What problems does the school district face in getting its budget approved by the city council?

Be a Problem Solver After the presentations and various editorials in the local paper, the school board realizes that the community is adamant about the need for talent enrichment programs throughout the division. In view of the community members' determination to have such programs, their willingness to cooperate with schedule changes to make such programs work, and their strong feelings about not being "pushed aside" because of budget considerations, how could the situation be resolved? Utilize the social science and administrative concepts from Part I in approaching the problem.

Test Your Solution To test your proposed plan of action for this program and funding issue, you and your colleagues should role-play the following situations:

1. The superintendent as she writes a response to the parent editorials in the local newspaper.
2. The school board and superintendent in their meeting on how to resolve the issue.
3. The parents as they present their public proposal to the superintendent and school board.
4. The city council and the superintendent presenting the proposal for programs to develop student talent.

Investigate Further

1. What funding sources are utilized in your school district? What percentage of the funding is acquired from each source?
2. What percentage of your district's budget is used to fund special education programs, resources, and staff? How much of this is spent on gifted and talented programs?
3. What resources and programs are available in your district for students with special talents? Are they available at the elementary and secondary level? How are students identified for these programs?

38
A NEW ROLE FOR THE PARENTS' ORGANIZATION

The principal was concerned about the newly formed parents' organization. He had experienced mixed feelings about the group ever since last spring when the group members had decided to discontinue their affiliation with the national PTA and to function as an independent organization. He personally felt that the PTA had been a positive force in education, and he had always known he could count on its support. He wasn't sure about the new organization. When the newly formed parents' group had elected officers the previous spring, there had been considerable discussion about "parent participation" and "community involvement."

The principal had had difficulty in assessing the rhetoric he had heard at the meeting because there didn't seem to be anything specific that parents were unhappy about other than their own alleged lack of involvement. Their attitude had puzzled him since he had always tried diligently to give his PTA an important role in the school program. For example, under his administration, the PTA had taken a greater part in the planning of the annual parents–staff picnic, had initiated parent–teacher conferences, and had helped in promoting a bond referendum for an addition to the building.

Although the principal didn't feel that the PTA should actually be involved in school decision making or the development of instructional or curricular policies, he did believe that they had an important role to play in supporting the school program: He only hoped that he could get the new group to accept this role.

On Thursday the principal met in his office with the representatives of the new parents' organization. He had scheduled the meeting to discuss the annual back-to-school night program that he had planned.

After the usual exchange of amenities, the principal proceeded to review the way in which the back-to-school night had been presented in the past and finally concluded by asking for the parents' reactions. He didn't have to wait long.

The president of the parents' group, a young attorney, responded that the officers, having already discussed the traditional program, had decided that a change was needed. Back-to-school nights in the past had done little more than familiarize parents with their children's schedules and, in many instances, had confused parents rather than helped them to understand the educational process.

This year, he said, the parents wanted to find out what was really going on in the classrooms. Specifically, they wanted the school to sponsor a series of back-to-school meetings focusing on one or two subjects each evening of the week and also teacher–parent conferences during American Education Week. Parents would be free to participate in any or all of the meetings, and the teachers would be responsible for making individual presentations on their respective evenings, as well as being available on the remaining evenings for parent–teacher conferences.

At that point the principal attempted to raise a question, but the president ignored him and continued speaking. Beyond a new back-to-school night program, he stressed, the parents' organization wanted to become more involved in the decision- and policymaking processes of the school. Parents had an important stake in the quality of education offered to the students and felt that they had something to contribute. In fact, parents believed that they should become equal partners with the school in deciding what was best for the children. He and the other parents recognized that the school board set the broad policies for the district, but they were convinced that the local parents' organization needed to play a greater role in developing and deciding on policies affecting their particular school.

The president went on to explain that the officers had met the preceding week and had established parents' committees on discipline, teacher performance, curriculum, and total school evaluation, which would meet regularly during the school year. The committees planned to observe conditions in the school; collect data from students, parents, and teachers; and issue policy statements on the need for change. All the parents were hopeful that they could work cooperatively with the administration of the school and that they could count on the principal's support.

The parents' proposal for greater involvement took the principal by surprise. He wondered why he hadn't been informed about the meeting the parents had held to establish those committees. Wouldn't the new committees end up interfering with the normal operations of the school? Surely the parents must recognize that he was in favor of appropriate parental involvement and participation in school affairs. As principal, however, he was the one who would be held accountable if anything went wrong, and therefore, he must be the one to decide policy. Why couldn't these parents understand that and be satisfied with the role they had played in the past?

Regardless of his personal feelings about the situation, the principal recognized he needed to respond to the parents in a way that would meet their concerns. The problem was how to accomplish this without upsetting the educational program of the school.

Suggested Learning Activities

Analyze the Case

1. Why do you suppose that the principal in this case feels the way he does about what the role of a parent organization should be?
2. How do you evaluate the leadership of the parents' organization?
3. What questions do you feel the parents' recommendations raise? What are the merits of their recommendations? What personal and situational factors may be influencing your evaluation of the proposal?
4. What barriers would have to be overcome before the parents' recommendations could be implemented by the school?

Discuss the Larger Issues

1. What do you feel should be the role of the PTA or other parent groups in helping to improve education in the school?
2. What might be the reason or reasons PTAs or other parent organizations are unwilling to play the limited role proposed by some administrators?
3. What should be the role of the principal in regard to the PTA or parent organization? What should be the role of the faculty in relation to the PTA or parent organization?

Be a Problem Solver The officers of a new parent organization have presented to the principal a rather extensive proposal for a different back-to-school night and for increased involvement in school affairs. As the principal in that situation, what would you do? What are the available alternatives? Utilize appropriate administrative and social science concepts in planning and implementing your approach.

Test Your Solution To test your plan of action for dealing with the problem presented at the end of the case, create and role-play one or more of the following situations in class:

1. Continuation of the meeting between the officers and the principal.
2. A faculty meeting during which the principal explains the parents' proposals.
3. A conference between the principal and the building representative for the teachers.

Investigate Further

1. What is the role of the PTA or parent organization at your school?
2. How do the principal, teachers, and parents at your school feel about the current role of the PTA?
3. To what extent would certain school board policies restrict increased involvement by parents (or a parent organization) in your district?
4. Are there any legal constraints on the role that can be played by a PTA or parent organization in your state?

39
HOW MUCH SHOULD PARENTS BE TOLD?

There was no longer any doubt. This was going to be a sticky issue! For some time, the superintendent had heard rumors that the South Side Parent Advisory Council was organizing a protest against the district's policy of denying public access to IQ and achievement test results. This morning he had received a letter from the group that revealed the nature of their concern. The communication was addressed "An Open Letter to the Superintendent of Schools and Members of the Board of Education from the South Side Parent Council." He read the letter again, slowly:

> We believe that the purpose of the school system should be to educate our children. At the present time we have no *satisfactory* way of knowing whether that goal is being effectively accomplished. Our contacts with the school and with other parents raise grave doubts about whether the needs of our children are being met.
>
> At present we lack the kind of information that would either confirm or alleviate our concern. We have asked our principal to provide us with the school's IQ and achievement test scores, but he has rejected our request because of "Board Policy." We therefore seek to have that policy changed so that our parent council can be provided with student IQ and achievement test scores that show:
>
> 1. How our school compares with the other schools in the district, in terms of potential for learning (IQ) and actual accomplishment (achievement test scores).
> 2. How teachers in the same subject area and grade level in our school compare with one another in terms of capitalizing on the potential learning ability of our children.
>
> There is much talk in education today about accountability. We believe that the school, in general, and each teacher, in particular, should be held accountable to the *parents* for making the most effective utilization of every child's potential for learning and growth. In order to evaluate and ascertain whether that objective is being met, the Parent Council, which represents the South Side community, needs student IQ and achievement test results for every class and for the total school.
>
> In conclusion, we would like to point out that the information we seek is in the public domain. The schools are public institutions and, therefore, have no right to maintain secret records. We do not ask for the identification of individual student names but rather the individual and class scores and averages for *each* teacher and for the total school, with data on how these scores compare with results in other situations. No teacher or administrator who is doing a good job need fear

> public disclosure of this information. It is time for everyone in our community—including the policymakers—to become more concerned about whether the children of our school and of this school district are receiving the kind of quality education that they need and deserve.

The superintendent sighed and put the letter down on his desk. It had been less than two years since he had urged the school board to establish parent advisory councils as a means of promoting greater community participation and involvement in the schools, particularly at the building level. The councils were designed to play strictly an advisory role to the principal and staff. But several of the groups had not been satisfied with limiting their role to that function, and many of the principals had mixed feelings about the whole idea of parent involvement in the school. It was interesting to note that the South Side parents' group had changed its title, removing the word "advisory" altogether; the parents now referred to themselves as the "Parent Council." Judging from their letter, they planned to do more than just render advice!

The superintendent decided that this was an issue that needed to be dealt with carefully. He knew that the president of the school board would probably be calling him later in the day for his tentative reactions to the letter. The superintendent wanted to be prepared. Whatever was decided in regard to the South Side group's request would not only carry implications for the other schools' treatment of test results but also might set a precedent for the future exercise of power by other parents' advisory councils. This would be an important decision, one that should be thoroughly discussed by all concerned.

He called his secretary into the office and asked her to arrange a meeting at 1:30 that afternoon with his administrative council and all the building principals. She was not to inform them of the nature of the meeting.

At 1:30 P.M. the superintendent began the meeting promptly by reading the letter from the South Side Parent Council. Then he asked for reactions to the group's request for test information, indicating that he wanted to hear the other administrators' ideas before he made any comments of his own. No one said anything at first, but finally the assistant superintendent spoke up. It seemed to him that the South Side parents had overstepped their bounds. They were not a school board, but only an advisory group, and were not authorized to receive test information. Beyond that, the school district had a long-standing policy of denying public access to test results.

At that point the superintendent emphasized that the South Side Parent Council was recommending a *change* in board policy and that its request for test information could not be turned down simply because it violated current policy. The issue was, what *should* the policy be?

For the next two hours the different aspects of the issue were discussed, and tempers grew short as the arguments became heated. Most of the principals opposed the release of test information that would permit comparison among schools. They felt the test scores could be misinterpreted, were not always reliable or valid, and could not possibly reflect the many intangible outcomes of education the school promoted and fostered. Several principals took the position that the tests, while not perfect, were perhaps the best available method for evaluating the schools' performance. If a particular test was not reliable or valid for a school, then another test should be secured. Although it was true that the achievement tests did not measure all the schools' outcome, that limitation should not be used as an argument against allowing the public to evaluate the measurable aspects of the program.

"How about the parents' request that test information be released about classes of the individual teachers?" the assistant superintendent asked.

On this point there was general agreement. Almost no one felt that it would be a good idea to release either IQ or achievement test scores for individual teachers' classes, particularly if that procedure would allow parents to make comparisons among teachers. The consensus was that parents would use this information to try to evaluate their children's teachers, and this could stir up trouble. Besides, parents were not qualified to evaluate teachers. This was the responsibility of the school system.

"Then how can parents assure themselves that an individual teacher is doing a good job?" the guidance director inquired.

"They can ask us!" one of the principals immediately responded, and the rest nodded in agreement. "The principal is accountable for what goes on in the building, and if a teacher isn't doing a good job, then it's the responsibility of the building administrator to take action. Of course, this can't be done on the basis of some emotional complaint or personal animosity–there has to be *evidence* that the teacher is not doing a good job. The teacher associations and the courts can make it tough to get rid of teachers these days, particularly if they're on tenure."

It was growing late and the superintendent thought it was time to end the meeting. He indicated it was his impression that, with perhaps a few exceptions, the administrators were opposed to any change of board policy in regard to disclosing test results. He personally agreed with that opinion and felt the school board was the only group that represented the public and that should have access to IQ and achievement test information. Test scores could easily be misinterpreted if they fell into the wrong hands, and they should not be used for comparing individual schools anyway–certainly not for evaluating the teachers within a school! In essence then, this would be his recommendation to the school board.

That evening Mr. Wilcox, the president of the school board, called the superintendent. Mr. Wilcox was concerned about the letter from the South Side parent group and wanted to know how the superintendent felt about the request.

The superintendent described his meeting with the administrative cabinet and the building principals, and said that the administration's recommendation would be to leave the board policy unchanged. A full report detailing the reasons for this position, as well as a proposal for a more structured role for the parental advisory councils, would be sent to all board members before the next meeting.

Mr. Wilcox sounded relieved and agreed that this was probably the best way to handle the situation. He was not, however, looking forward to the next board meeting.

The remainder of that week passed without incident. First-semester grades had been distributed, and the schools were closed for the semester break. The city paper carried a brief news item on the parents' request for a change in board policy, but the letter to the superintendent and board members was not printed, nor did the paper take an editorial stand on the issue.

The following Monday evening the school board held its regular meeting. It was customary for the board to allocate the first 15 minutes for receiving communications and questions from the floor. The superintendent had anticipated that a representative from the South Side Parent Council might be present and had advised Mr. Wilcox to expect some type of a statement.

As the meeting was opened for questions and comments, a man jumped to his feet and requested recognition. He said he knew the school board had received a letter from the South

Side Parent Council and that the board would be interested in some additional information that had recently come to light. Would the board permit him to read a brief statement?

Mr. Wilcox looked at the superintendent, but receiving no clear sign as to how to proceed, he indicated that the man should go ahead with his statement.

The gentleman in the audience cleared his throat and then began to read from a rather crumpled piece of paper. "Last week the South Side Parent Council sent a letter to the superintendent and the school board requesting a change in board policy in releasing IQ and achievement test results to the public. This weekend the council surveyed the South Side parents to ascertain the distribution of grades given by teachers for the first semester. Two facts were revealed as a result of our investigation: First, a large number of the students at South Side School, over 40 percent, received Ds or Fs; second, two teachers in particular failed about one-third of their students. These facts have dramatized the need for and have strengthened our determination to secure IQ and achievement test results for each teacher's classes and for the total school. What is needed is an accounting of who is failing–our kids or the school. We will not be satisfied with anything less!"

As the speaker sat down, the superintendent looked over at the president of the school board and then out into the audience where the executive secretary of the teacher association sat. The secretary's face was livid; the school board president seemed worried. There was a murmur of voices from the audience.

All eyes were now looking expectantly at the superintendent.

Suggested Learning Activities

Analyze the Case

1. What action, if any, do you think the superintendent should have taken when he *first* began to hear "rumblings" about and from the South Side Parent Council? What should he have done after receiving the letter from the parents?
2. What is your assessment of the different arguments advanced for and against the parents' proposal during the superintendent's meeting with the administrators? What are some of the less obvious factors that may (even unconsciously) be affecting the thinking of the administrators about this proposal?
3. In what ways would you have behaved differently than the superintendent did during the administrators' meeting or during the week prior to the school board meeting?

Discuss the Larger Issues

1. What do you think should be the role of parent advisory groups–for example, the Parent Council or the PTA–in the school system? Under what set of circumstances can parent advisory groups become quite powerful? How much power should they have? What aspects of the school's program should legitimately come under their review?
2. Should each school or "cluster" of schools have its own school board, in addition to the city school board? What are the advantages and disadvantages of decentralized school boards?

3. Should the results from standardized tests be used to evaluate a school's program? An individual teacher? Can or should test results remain confidential within the school system? What are the advantages and disadvantages?
4. How can parents and the larger community be assured that the school is doing a good job? Why are some people unwilling to accept the district's or the principal's word that the school is meeting the needs of their children? How can this situation be corrected?

Be a Problem Solver It would appear at the end of this case that everyone is waiting for the superintendent to make the next move. If *you* were the superintendent, what would you do to solve the immediate problem? The long-range problem?

Test Your Solution To test your plan of action for dealing with the problem presented at the end of the case, create and role-play one or more of the following situations in class:

1. The continuation of the school board meeting.
2. A meeting between the superintendent, the principal, and the South Side Parent Council.
3. Any other situation that would provide feedback on the strengths and weaknesses of your proposed solution.

Investigate Further

1. Are there any legal constructs in your state that would restrict the public disclosure of IQ and achievement test information?
2. What is your school board's policy on public disclosure of IQ and achievement test results?
3. What would be the opinion of your superintendent, school principal, parents, and teachers on public disclosure of IQ and achievement test results?

40 ADMINISTRATOR–PRESS RELATIONS

Bill Image, principal of Roseview School, was feeling frustrated. He had been trying to get in touch with a reporter, Miss Hardin, at the local newspaper, but after several weeks had not been successful. He had first written the reporter a letter inviting her and a photographer to attend and write a story on next month's school assembly program honoring the students who had achieved perfect attendance during the first semester, 10 percent of the student body. Since the reporter had not responded, he telephoned her several times, but she always seemed to be out of the office on assignment and never returned his phone messages.

The principal was initially surprised by Miss Hardin's lack of responsiveness and later became annoyed by it. He could perhaps understand her behavior if he were frequently calling her to cover school news and had worn out his welcome. But in the two years he had been principal of Roseview School, he had phoned her only once before, on some minor matter, and even then she hadn't called back. In fact, he had never actually met the woman, although he had seen her a number of times at school board meetings he had attended. He had thought at the time that Miss Hardin seemed young, rather aggressive, and brash. Pretty, he conceded, but in a hard sort of way. Still, the reporter appeared to be bright, and the thought had occurred to him that he would need to be on his toes in dealing with her, or she might draw something out of him that would be better kept out of the newspapers. He felt that the papers tended to exaggerate and sensationalize things. Why couldn't they concentrate on reporting more of the good things happening in the schools, like this upcoming assembly program?

The principal decided to try one more time to reach the reporter, and to his amazement, after only one ring of the phone, she was on the line.

"Hello, Sylvia Hardin speaking. What can I do for you?"

The principal cleared his throat. "Uh, this is Bill Image, Miss Hardin. As you probably know, I'm the principal at Roseview School, and—"

"Who?"

"It's Mr. Image," he repeated, "Principal at Roseview School."

"Oh, yes. And what is it that I can help you with?"

"Well, as you probably remember, I wrote to you two weeks ago and invited you to an assembly program we're holding to honor 10 percent of the students with perfect attendance for the first semester of the year."

Hearing no response at the other end, he moved on quickly. "I know you've been busy, since you didn't answer my letter or phone calls, but could you find the time to cover this assembly program?"

"Yes, I have been very busy, but I apologize for not returning your calls," the reporter acknowledged. "I guess I've been avoiding the need to respond to your invitation, but now that we're talking about the matter, I must tell you, quite honestly, that I don't think your assembly program is very newsworthy."

The principal was taken aback. "Why not?"

"Because it just isn't that unusual," Miss Hardin explained. "Oh, I know that it's nice to recognize the kids who have had perfect attendance. In fact, if you would send me their names, I'd try to get them mentioned in a future issue of the paper. However . . ."

The principal interrupted. "But here is an opportunity for the press to show the community some of the *good* things that are happening in the schools, and I personally feel that there are a lot of good things happening at Roseview School that deserve publicity and that would improve people's perceptions of the school."

Miss Hardin sighed audibly. "Really, Mr. Image, I don't care much about 'people's perceptions' of the school, but for the sake of discussion, what *are* these so-called good things?"

Put on the spot, the principal hesitated, trying to think of some activities that this reporter would be impressed with. "Well, just recently we had our first semester's honor roll, and . . . and . . . well, there's some fantastic stuff being done in our art classes. This teacher has so much enthusiasm, she just keeps all the kids going. And . . . and . . ."

The reporter interrupted. "That all sounds very worthwhile, but I'm not sure that it's *newsworthy.* I am sorry, but I have an appointment I need to keep. Perhaps we could talk more later, if you would like. But for now, I must be on my way. It's been nice talking with you."

After the reporter had hung up the phone, the principal slammed down his receiver, frustrated and somewhat angered by his conversation with the reporter. Why hadn't she answered his call when he initially telephoned her? And what did she mean, expressing skepticism about whether the school's assembly program and the art program were newsworthy. If perfect attendance for these kids wasn't newsworthy, then what *was?* He decided that it was futile to continue to get Miss Hardin to cover next month's assembly program. In fact, it was probably useless to talk with her anymore, since they obviously had such different points of view on what was newsworthy. His only hope was that maybe she would get transferred, or married, or *something.*

For the next eight weeks Bill Image was busy with various aspects of developing the next year's class schedule and proposed budget, as well as a variety of tasks and problems that occupy a principal's time during the late winter–early spring months. In March the students took their competency tests, and by mid-May the results for Roseview School were returned to the principal.

As Bill Image sat in his office, looking at the competency test results, he was initially surprised and then worried about the large number of students who had not passed the examination. At least it seemed to the principal that a larger number of students had failed than in previous years. It looked as if there was going to be a sizable number of students who would have to attend summer school this year, and if they still couldn't pass the competency test, they would have to be retained in the same grade for another year.

The principal decided that he would present the overall results to the faculty before giving the bad news to individual students and parents so that the teachers could help cushion the blow for the failing students. Next Monday's regularly scheduled faculty meeting seemed to the principal like a good time to present the test results to the teachers.

On the Tuesday following Monday's faculty meeting, the principal came back to his office after going out for lunch. On his desk he discovered a phone message from Miss Hardin, the local reporter. He asked his secretary whether she knew the nature of the call, but she indicated that the reporter had declined to comment, saying only that it was urgent.

The principal thought to himself that he wasn't aware of anything that was urgent—at least from his vantage point—and he had some other activities that he needed to pursue that afternoon. Besides, he wasn't sure that he *wanted* to talk with Miss Hardin, considering his last experience with her. He acknowledged to himself that he would probably have to talk with her sooner or later, but it would have to be later, when he might feel more like talking to a reporter.

Pushing the phone message into his coat pocket, the principal informed his secretary that he was going to be working on the final details of next year's class schedule in a small unused room in a different part of the building, and he didn't want to be disturbed for *any* reason.

The rest of the afternoon the principal worked on the next year's class schedule. When he returned to his office, he found several additional phone messages from Miss Hardin (all marked "urgent") and one telephone message from a gym equipment salesman who was responding to a letter from the principal. He knew that he should call Miss Hardin, but instead he added her recent phone messages to the one already in his pocket and then telephoned the gym equipment salesman instead. After a very pleasant conversation, which lasted longer than the principal had anticipated and resulted in a scheduled conference at the school with the salesman on Friday, the principal went home.

That night, about seven o'clock, the principal answered his phone. It was the reporter.

"Hello, this is Sylvia Hardin. Why haven't you answered my phone messages? I told your secretary that it was urgent that I talk with you."

The principal immediately felt a surge of irritation, which turned to apprehension after hearing the reporter speak. "Well, I . . . uh . . . well, I . . . uh . . . was really *busy* this afternoon and uh . . . I, ah, planned to call you right away when I got to school tomorrow."

"I can't wait until tomorrow," the reporter responded angrily. "I need some information *now.* I have heard from a reliable source that a large number of students at Roseview School flunked their competency tests. Is that true?"

The principal hesitated. "Well, I, ah, I wouldn't necessarily say it was real large . . . but . . . anyway, I can't really discuss those test results because the test results of those students are, ah, *confidential* information."

"What is confidential about them?" persisted the reporter.

"They are confidential," the principal explained, "because . . . that is . . . ah . . . ah . . . *personal* information about a student that would be violating his or her privacy to discuss."

"But I'm not asking you to tell me the test scores of *individual* students," the reporter shouted in an exasperated voice, "but only how many of them failed."

The principal thought for a moment and then replied, "Well, ah, I don't see where that information will do anybody any good." His voice became stronger and more authoritative. "Besides, these test scores are a very complex matter, and I believe that unless someone has a really good understanding of all the complexities involved, he or she wouldn't know how to put them to proper use."

"What complexities?" queried the reporter.

"Well, ah . . ." the principal's voice began to falter, "ah, that's something that is a little hard to talk about on the phone. Ah, I really don't appreciate," the principal's voice picked up strength again, "receiving a call like this at my home. Please call me tomorrow at school if you *really* need to talk to me further." The principal hung up the phone.

The rest of the evening the principal fretted as he wondered whether he had handled the call from the reporter in the right way, and he worried about what he would do if she called him the next morning. *What* was he going to do?

Early Wednesday morning the local newspaper was distributed to the community. In the second section was an article by Sylvia Hardin about the competency testing program. The article followed a heading that announced, "Principal Refuses to Answer Questions about Test Scores; Doesn't Think Information Would 'Do Anybody Any Good.' "

When Mr. Image arrived at school, his secretary gave him two telephone messages about calls that had already come in. One was from the superintendent of schools; the other came from a reporter for a local television station who wanted to visit the school that morning to interview the principal. Both callers had asked that the principal return their calls as soon as possible.

Suggested Learning Activities

Analyze the Case

1. Are there any steps that the principal should have taken to become acquainted with the reporter *before* calling her about school news?
2. Evaluate the telephone dialogue between the principal and the reporter when he first talks with her. How would you have handled this conversation if you had been the principal? What should have been your goal or goals during this telephone conversation?

3. Assess the principal's decision-making behavior in regard to the way he handled the competency test results and the phone messages he received on Tuesday, following the faculty meeting on Monday.
4. Evaluate the Tuesday evening telephone dialogue between the principal and the reporter. How would you have handled this conversation if you had been the principal? What should have been your goal or goals during the conversation?

Discuss the Larger Issues

1. What type of relationship should an administrator (principal or superintendent) try to develop with the press? How should an administrator go about developing that relationship? *Be specific.*
2. What should be the role of teachers and other adults working at the school in school-press relations?
3. What should be a school's or a district's policy on disseminating and releasing information to the press? On providing access by the press to the school building and its occupants?
4. What are the responsibilities of a school district and of a news organization to provide in-service education to their personnel on how to function more effectively with each other?

Be a Problem Solver Assume that you are the principal of this school (it is recognized that you probably would not have gotten into this much trouble). How would you respond to the circumstances that have developed, especially those at the end of the case study? Utilize appropriate administrative and social science concepts from Part I of the text in planning and implementing your approach.

Test Your Solution To test your proposed plan for resolving the problems described in the case study, create and role-play one or more of the following situations in class:

1. You as a principal make a telephone call to a reporter for the purpose of asking the latter to cover some aspect of the school program.
2. You as a principal receive a call from a reporter who wants to ask you some questions about your school's competency test results. Set up another simulation in which a reporter leaves a telephone message at the school that he wants to talk to you about a "possible *teacher* drug problem" at the school.
3. Handle a television reporter's request to come to the school during the noon hour to interview students on what they think about the competency testing program.

Investigate Further

1. Examine the educational literature to identify elements that should be included in a *policy* on school–press relations and on the role of the administrator in dealing with the press.
2. Ascertain and evaluate the nature of your school district's or school's policy on school–press relations.

3. Identify the role of the principal in your school district in regard to press relations.
4. Determine what in-service education is provided to administrators in your school district to help them with their role in school–press relations. Evaluate the adequacy of that in-service education and propose improvements.

41
PUBLIC RELATIONS: WHAT'S REALLY IMPORTANT?

As the principal had anticipated, the first month of school had been hectic. In October he decided to send a letter home to parents and offer his impressions of the beginning weeks of the school year.

He believed that school communication to the home was an essential public relations technique, and it was important for community support that parents be kept informed of all the good things happening. He further felt the news media tended to be too critical of education and that he had a responsibility to see that the parents received the true story about what was happening at school.

For the next 20 minutes he thought about and wrote the letter that he wanted to send home to the parents. The message read as follows:

Dear Parents:

As you know, we are now in the second month of the school year and we are off to a tremendously fine beginning. Although there were a few minor problems the first day—which, of course, could be expected—everything has been proceeding smoothly, and we expect a truly excellent year. We have an outstanding staff and, we believe, a truly exciting curriculum representing a wide diversity of enriching experiences for students with varying interests and aspirations. This year we have initiated several new educational thrusts that should offer a more multifaceted, individualized program for your children. I hope to have more to report to you later on these new educational ventures. I know that this coming year will be filled with countless new challenges for your children, and we are gratified to offer them so many learning opportunities. We have had your continuing support and trust in the past, and we hope that we can continue to receive it in the future.

In closing, I would like to emphasize that my door is always open to you if you have a question or concern. I believe that this is a school about which you can truly be proud, and I would welcome the opportunity to talk with you at any time.

Sincerely,
Dr. William Kendall

The letter to the parents looked fine to the principal. He instructed his secretary to have it typed and to make sufficient copies for distribution to the students at the end of the school day so that they could take it home.

During the time the principal had been working on his letter to the parents, a visitor had come to the school. The visitor, who supervised student teachers from the university, had not been to the school previously and mistakenly entered through the back of the building. Since he was early for his appointment with the student teacher, he decided to wait in the principal's office. Because it was not immediately clear how to get to the principal's office, he asked a couple of students, who merely giggled and shrugged their shoulders. Fortunately, the very next person he asked was a teacher who directed him to the principal's office on the other side of the building.

As he proceeded toward the office, the supervisor couldn't help noticing how littered and messy the corridors appeared. He also noticed that the people in the halls—both students and teachers—didn't seem to pay much attention to him. They weren't exactly unfriendly, but they just seemed to ignore him.

When the supervisor reached the principal's office, he took a seat in what appeared to be a general administrative office and reception area. He was going to tell anyone who asked that he was just waiting for his appointment with the student teacher, but no one asked.

As the supervisor sat in the reception area, he observed the school secretaries at work. One of them answered the phone: "Lakeview School. What is it you want? No, he isn't here now. I don't know where he is. He probably will be back before very long." The supervisor watched the same secretary take another telephone call: "Lakeview School. What is it you want? No, he is in conference right now. I'm not sure when he will be done; can I have him call you? You will call some other time? All right."

During the last telephone conversation, the supervisor noticed that a student had approached the counter and was waiting for someone to acknowledge him. At the end of the telephone conversation, the vice principal walked into the reception area and stood beside the student at the counter. When the secretary greeted the vice principal and asked if she could help him, the vice principal responded that the student had been there first. But before the student could say anything, the secretary said sharply, "Administrators always come first—students can be taken care of later," and she proceeded to wait on the vice principal, who apparently agreed. The supervisor looked at the student for some reaction but the student seemed resigned to the matter.

For the next 10 minutes, the supervisor continued to observe the secretaries at work and was struck by their casual, almost indifferent attitude toward the people who came into the reception area, particularly students. The supervisor wondered whether or not he should say anything to the principal, but decided not to pursue the matter. He remembered from talking previously to the student teacher at the university that she had felt the principal was very ego-involved with his school and seemed to have the attitude that everything was perfect at Lakeview. It didn't appear that it would do any good to talk to the principal. Still, it seemed that *something* should be done.

Shortly after the first of the year, the principal, Dr. Kendall, suffered a heart attack and had to take a medical leave for the remainder of the school year. The vice principal of the school was appointed by the school district to be acting principal, and one of the teachers who had completed a master's degree in school administration was appointed acting assistant principal.

In the latter part of January, the university supervisor who had visited the school earlier in the year was meeting for a conference with one of his student teachers at Lakeview. As long as he was at the school, he decided that he might as well drop in on the acting principal and share some of his observations about the school. Perhaps the acting principal would be more interested in improving conditions.

Suggested Learning Activities

Analyze the Case

1. What is your assessment of the principal's conception of public relations?
2. Evaluate the principal's letter to the parents, utilizing concepts and principles of communication and public relations.
3. What factors may be negatively affecting the public relations of this school? How likely is it that the principal is aware of the factors? Why or why not?

Discuss the Larger Issues

1. What should be the main purpose and emphasis in a school's public relations program?
2. How can the administration, faculty, students, and parents best contribute to these purposes?
3. When does public relations become public manipulation? And by what criteria and methods should the public relations program of a school or district be evaluated?

Be a Problem Solver Assume that you became the principal of this school in the middle of the year, and circumstances described in the case came to your attention. What would be your approach to dealing with this matter? Utilize appropriate administrative and social science concepts from Part I of the text in planning and implementing your approach.

Test Your Solution To test your proposed plan for dealing with the problems described in the case, you and your colleagues should create and role-play one or more of the following situations.

1. A faculty meeting
2. A meeting with the secretaries
3. A letter to parents

Investigate Further

1. What concept of public relations and its purpose do the administration, teachers, students, and parents in your school or school district hold?
2. Describe the public relations program, including the role of the administrator and faculty, in your school or school district. How is this program evaluated?
3. How effective is the public relations program in your school or school district? How reliable and valid are the data upon which judgments of effectiveness are made?

42
CENSORSHIP OR PARENTS' RIGHTS?

Something was obviously wrong with Barb Smith, a student in the fifth-period class at White-cliff School. The teacher had noticed that the usually talkative girl was very quiet this week and had hardly participated in group discussion. The class had been studying Stephen Chbosky's *The Perks of Being a Wallflower,* and the teacher wondered momentarily whether Barb's reticence might be related to the book they were reading. He dismissed the possibility as he remembered the girl's initial enthusiasm when the class had chosen the book from several alternatives presented. Nevertheless, he decided that he should schedule a conference to see what was bothering her.

After school he discovered that his first premonition had been correct. Barb informed him that she personally liked the book and agreed with what the teacher had said about the need to better understand adolescence. But when her father examined the novel, he had exploded and had refused to let her finish it. He had further forbidden her to participate in any class discussions or to complete any assignments. Her father planned to get in touch with the school, but meanwhile he wanted her to be assigned another book.

The teacher tried to explore with Barb her father's objections, but the girl seemed too embarrassed to discuss the matter further. She would say only that her father felt it was a "dirty book" and not something a girl should be allowed to read. The teacher wanted to question Barb further, but he could see that she was becoming upset. So he told her not to worry about the situation and indicated he would try to work something out.

Early the next morning the teacher met with the principal and presented the problem. The principal's initial reaction was one of concern, but he admitted he was unfamiliar with the book and could not recall why it had been originally selected.

The teacher explained that this particular novel was being used because it depicted problems of adolescent children everywhere. The teacher had requested and received approval from Mr. Collins, his department head, to teach on an experimental basis a book on being on the brink of adulthood to one section of students. The teacher hoped that through class discussion and study of *The Perks of Being a Wallflower* students would develop better coping skills for some of the problems of growing up.

At that point the principal brought up the main objection by Barb's father. Was it a dirty book? The teacher vehemently rejected such a characterization and went on to strongly defend Brown's work as being exceptionally worthwhile.

Finally the principal broke in on the teacher's somewhat lengthy and emotional defense of the book, pointing out that no one was questioning its literary merits. The issue was whether a school should—or even could—force a student to read a book that her parents strongly opposed. Besides, the principal went on to say, there was no reason another book couldn't be provided since only one student was involved.

The teacher could hardly believe what he had heard and inwardly felt that the principal was taking the father's side, but, not wishing to antagonize his superior, he reluctantly agreed to provide the student with an alternate assignment.

That evening the principal received two calls from parents who wanted him to know that an undesirable book had been made required reading for their children. Both callers were very outspoken in demanding different assignments for their children and were critical of the principal for approving *The Perks of Being a Wallflower* for school use. They warned him that many other parents were also upset. The principal tried to discover the basis for their concern, but only one of the parents would comment, and she alluded to the presence of several sexual scenes in the book. She indicated that a number of parents were calling each other and that the matter had become an important issue in the community, even among parents whose children were not in that class.

The principal felt very uncomfortable during both telephone conversations because he still had not read the book. Although quite reluctant to permit different student assignments without first talking to the teacher, he finally conceded that the school would provide alternatives to the selection currently being studied. After finishing the telephone conversations, he made a mental note to talk to the teacher in the morning and to definitely get his hands on that book! Could it be as bad as those parents were suggesting?

First thing the next day, the principal secured a copy of the book. As he read the novel, he did not feel that it was a dirty book, but he could see why some parents might be bothered. He decided he'd better send a note to the teacher describing the complaints he had received last night and the decision he had made to provide alternate assignments for two more students. He would be sure to emphasize that although future consideration might result in withdrawing the book from class study, its use for present class purposes was still approved.

The teacher received the principal's message that afternoon and read it with mixed feelings. He, too, had received calls from parents outraged about the book who had demanded its elimination from the curriculum, but he had responded negatively to their demands and was irritated that the principal had approved alternate assignments without first consulting him. He was concerned about what the principal might do if the objections grew or if a formal protest was made to the school board. He doubted whether the principal could stand up under that kind of pressure.

On the other hand, the teacher was glad that the book would not be immediately withdrawn from his course. It was entirely possible that if the school held its ground, the book would ultimately gain greater acceptance. Just this morning several students had mentioned in class that their parents approved the book as a relevant and timely choice for student discussion. One boy said his father felt that it was about time the school began to deal with the vital issues facing the nation.

In the meantime, though, the teacher was faced with the problem of making different class assignments for two additional students. What should he do about them? He decided that he would seek the advice of Mr. Collins, his department head.

At that moment the principal was reading a copy of a letter that had been delivered to his office, although it was addressed to the superintendent and the school board. Apparently a copy had also been sent to the newspaper. The letter, signed by 33 individuals, read as follows:

> We, the undersigned, take extreme exception to the teaching of Stephen Chbosky's *The Perks of Being a Wallflower* at Whitecliff School. The book presents some of the worst aspects of growing up and does nothing to show students the more positive choices.
>
> It is clear from only a cursory reading of the novel that its author is a troublemaker who is trying to promote feelings of anxiety and guilt on the part of the white people about the blacks' problems.

> In addition, we strongly object to the school's approval of a book that uses such foul language and that depicts sexual activities in detail. We demand that this book be immediately eliminated from the school curriculum and from the required reading of any student at the school. It is time for someone in a position of authority to take a strong stand in support of those parents who want the school to become more responsible to the moral climate of our community.

The principal slammed the letter on top of his desk. It was obvious that the problem was getting out of hand. *No* book was worth this much conflict or unfavorable publicity. He would simply withdraw the book. After all, the class had been studying it on an experimental basis, and clearly the experiment had failed; the community was not ready for this type of material. He decided to inform Mr. Collins, the department head, about his decision, and together they would explain to the teacher why it was not possible at this time to continue the study of the book.

Just then the principal's secretary said that Mr. Collins wanted to talk with him for a few minutes. After Mr. Collins came into the office, the principal began to fill him in on the situation. While the principal was speaking, the department head waited quietly with a very serious and determined expression on his face. When the principal finished explaining his position, Mr. Collins indicated that he had previously spoken with the teacher, and they had both decided against providing alternatives for the three students whose parents had objected to the original selection.

The department head further informed the principal that the entire department believed that the school, and particularly the administration, should take a very strong stand in support of the study of *The Perks of Being a Wallflower.* The department felt that the school should not allow a minority of parents to dictate to the teachers the books that could or could not be read in class. It seemed inevitable that once the minority had succeeded in imposing their will on the school, no teacher would be immune from their attacks. To withdraw the book now would be tantamount to surrendering to the minority, and his department had no intention of capitulating. "The real question," Mr. Collins said, "is, Who is running the school?" With that parting shot, the department head walked out.

The principal sat down slowly. It looked as if he had a real school-community conflict on his hands.

Suggested Learning Activities

Analyze the Case

1. What might account for the fact that the principal had not previously read the book in question and could not recall why it had been originally selected?
2. What is your reaction to the reasons given by the teacher for studying *The Perks of Being a Wallflower*?
3. What is your evaluation of the principal's actions in the following situations?
    a. His conference with the teacher.
    b. His telephone conversations with the two parents.

c. His memo to the teacher.

d. His decision to withdraw the book.

4. What is your assessment of the position taken by the English Department on the issue of using *The Perks of Being a Wallflower*?
5. What are some of the factors that add to the complexity and difficulty of resolving the problems in this case?

Discuss the Larger Issues

1. To what extent should a teacher be influenced in the selection of class materials by the fact that they may conceivably disturb a number of parents? Under what set of circumstances (if any) should a school concede to parent or community objections?
2. What role should parents and the larger community play in book selection or approval? What role should the faculty play? The principal? The central office? What criteria should determine the nature and extent of the responsibilities of each of these groups or individuals in book selection or approval? Who should have the final responsibility for approving a book for classroom or library use if there is objection to the selection?
3. What should be included in a school policy statement covering the circumstances described in this case? Who should be involved in developing the statement? What difficulties might be encountered in applying such a policy to problems of the nature described in this case?

Be a Problem Solver Assume that you are the principal and you are facing a situation entailing apparently growing parental objection to a book and potential faculty-community and faculty-administration conflict. What should be done to resolve these problems? What alternatives are available to you, and what factors will you need to take into consideration in solving the problems? Utilize appropriate administrative and social science concepts from Part I of the text in planning and implementing your approach.

Test Your Solution To test your proposed plan of action for dealing with the problems presented at the end of the case, create and role-play one or more of the following situations in class:

1. A telephone call to the principal from the superintendent, who reports that board members have received complaints about the book and would like to know what the principal is going to do about it.
2. Another meeting between the principal and the teacher involved.
3. A telephone call from a reporter for a national press dispatch who has gotten wind of the controversy and wants to know the details.
4. A telephone call from an officer of the state civil liberties union who has been contacted by a parent who fears that censorship may take place.

Investigate Further

1. What is your school's or district's written policy on teaching controversial literature?
2. What legal precedents have been set in cases in which a parent has sought to remove a book from the curriculum or the library?
3. How do administrators and teachers in your district feel about the right of parents to decide whether or not their children should be taught controversial material?

43
FINANCIAL CRISIS!

The superintendent shuddered as he looked again at the sheets of figures spread across his desk. This was going to be a tough year financially for the school district. The mayor and several city council members had already publicly made a stand to hold the line on taxes. Flying in the face of that commitment were the cold facts: Proposed building operating costs were up, reflecting previously delayed expenditures, and the state legislature had reduced state aid.

He thought back to previous years. The costs of education had been rising for some time, but in the past the PTA and other community groups had always campaigned for the budget while putting pressure on city hall for more money toward education. Now everyone seemed concerned about rising taxes, and there was not much outward support for the school.

It seemed to the superintendent that people these days were more critical and demanding of education yet were unwilling to provide the necessary funds. He realized that part of the problem was the way in which education was financed, but what could *he* do about that?

During the development of the budget the superintendent had instructed his staff and all the principals to cut proposed expenditures wherever possible and to recommend only items that a school absolutely needed. He had told them that the goal was to achieve a bare-bones budget. He knew that anything not absolutely essential for next year would eventually be cut by either the school board or the city council.

The superintendent remembered that the principals had complained about his instructions. He could understand their feelings, since there was only so much that a principal could cut from the teachers' requests. He had been disappointed to hear through the grapevine that they felt he was sacrificing quality in education for economy. Well, maybe they were right. But what do you do when you face a fiscal crisis and an adamant city council? Do you fight? Do you compromise? Do you work for fiscal independence? Although the latter was a potentially viable alternative, it would certainly not solve the immediate problem. It was easy for the principals to talk–they didn't have the responsibility. Still, the superintendent knew that the principals had their troubles too, and they had to contend with their faculties when budget items were cut. There didn't seem to be any easy way out. He only hoped that next week's board meeting wouldn't go too badly.

The following Monday the school board met to consider the budget. Represented at the special meeting were several taxpayers' groups and others who opposed raising the mill rate. There didn't seem to be anyone in the audience who in the past had been a "friend of the schools."

As the meeting began, the questions started to flow. Why were teachers' salaries so high? Why not increase class sizes in order to save money? Why was so much money spent on athletics? Why should items for teachers' professional improvement be paid by the public? Why couldn't a citizens' committee be established to examine more closely the rationale behind each budget item?

These were difficult questions for the superintendent and his staff to answer. For example, they were unable to *prove* that increasing class sizes would impair teacher effectiveness, although a logical case could be presented in that regard. But this year people simply were not satisfied with "explanations"–they wanted *evidence.* It wasn't so much that they were against education. Rather, they were determined to hold the line against any tax increase; a reduced school budget was necessary to achieve that end. Although the superintendent and the school board were sympathetic, they felt that to cut the budget further would result in significant damage to the overall school program.

As the last speaker finally finished at 11:30 P.M., the president of the board asked for a formal motion on the budget. It had been a long evening, full of heated and sometimes hostile discussion. The superintendent was hopeful, however, that the school board would pass the budget as proposed. He had involved the members of the board in the budget process from the beginning, and they had considered every item.

The board approved the budget, five to two, and the superintendent felt a momentary relief until he remembered the city council meeting scheduled to be held in two weeks. The budget would have to be sent to the council immediately for their consideration.

During the next week the newspaper and the radio carried several editorials criticizing the school budget, particularly class sizes and the number of classes teachers taught. Letters to the editor also reflected concern about the tax money spent on athletics and other extracurricular activities. The major problem seemed to be that people were tired of raising taxes; they were not going to stand for another hike. Taxes were already at an all-time high, and the proposed school budget would raise the rate by 2.34 mills.

Worried by the widespread community opposition to the budget, the superintendent arranged to speak to various PTAs and civic organizations. In these talks he repeatedly emphasized that the proposed budget represented essential items for the education of the children in the community and that further cuts would mean a curtailment in services. Although the audiences seemed to understand the rationale behind the budget, they continued to return to the point that property owners could not afford higher taxes.

By the time the city council met on Monday, it was clear that a confrontation was inevitable. Long-suffering taxpayers, eager to express themselves, filled the council chambers. Speaker after speaker elaborated on the tax squeeze and denounced the "frills" of education. Throughout the evening, there were only sparsely sprinkled statements from citizens who favored meeting the schools' needs.

Finally at 10:30 P.M. a formal motion was introduced to cut the school budget by 10 percent. After an hour of discussion, the president of the council called for a vote on the motion. The superintendent held his breath as the results were announced: The motion carried, nine to five; the school budget was cut 10 percent. The school board was to determine where the specific cuts would be made.

Afterward, completely disheartened by the action of the city council, the superintendent and his staff met for a brief time with the members of the school board. There would be a number of difficult decisions to be made. Educational priorities would have to be reexamined, and undoubtedly some services would have to be curtailed. Where should the cuts take place? What was essential to keep in the budget? The future of education in the district was at stake.

Suggested Learning Activities

Analyze the Case

1. Why do the superintendent and the building principals look at the budget in different ways? How can this difference in perception be narrowed?
2. How would you assess the superintendent's preparation for the school board meeting on the budget? Were the questions asked at the meeting inquiries for which the superintendent should have possessed definitive answers? Why or why not?
3. What additional steps could the superintendent have taken before the city council meeting to cope with the growing resistance of the community to the budget?

Discuss the Larger Issues

1. In what ways is the school at least partially responsible for the deterioration or reduction of support by groups that have traditionally supported it? What can schools do to maintain the support of important community groups in the face of rising school costs?
2. What do you feel is the "answer" to the financial problems faced by the schools? What problems or barriers would have to be overcome before any solution to the schools' financial problems could be successfully implemented?
3. What can administrators, teachers, and parents do individually or collectively to bring about change in the way education is presently financed?

Be a Problem Solver Assume that you are the superintendent and you must decide with your board how to cut the school budget by 10 percent. You have already eliminated every possible item that was not basic to the students' education. Now something essential will have to be curtailed or eliminated. How do you propose to solve this problem? Utilize appropriate administrative and social science concepts from Part I of the text in planning and implementing your approach.

Test Your Solution To test your proposed plan of action for dealing with the problem presented at the end of the case, create and role-play one or more of the following situations in class:

1. A call to the superintendent from a local reporter.
2. A call from the representative of the local teachers' organization.
3. A call from a parent who has heard that you may eliminate a program in which her daughter is enrolled for the following year.
4. A meeting between the superintendent and the principals to cut the budget further.

Investigate Further

1. What types of public relations procedures have proved effective in averting community resistance to greater school expenditures?
2. What steps would be necessary in your state for a school board to obtain fiscal autonomy? What would be the advantages and disadvantages of such a move? From what individuals or groups would you be likely to obtain support? Resistance?
3. What legal changes can be made to reduce the burden of school taxes on local property owners?

44
INTEGRATION: AN OLD/NEW PROBLEM

The state legislature, finally acting in response to the resegregation of the state's city schools, had enacted a law requiring metropolitan integration between large city school districts and the adjacent suburban school districts. The statute required busing some of the minority students to the suburbs for their education and busing some of the White students to the large city school systems. The exact number of students to be bused and the procedure for selection were defined in a rather complicated formula that had a number of factors. The statute's main purpose was to integrate suburban schools to a much greater extent and to increase the number of White students attending city schools. The integration program, mandated by the legislature in February, was to begin in September, now only two months away.

Bob Edwards, assistant principal at Pleasant View School in a suburban district, felt ambivalent about the metropolitan integration. He really didn't think that busing was the answer to racial problems, and he wasn't looking forward to dealing with some of the discipline problems from the city school system. On the other hand, he felt that the White students in his school probably needed more exposure to minority students, and since metropolitan integration was now the law, he thought that it was important to do as good a job with the integration program as possible.

Edwards was concerned about his school's lack of planning and in-service preparation for the minority students. With the beginning of classes only two months away, nothing much had been done yet to get ready for the minority students, but he had tried to discuss his concerns with the principal who had minimized them. The principal's philosophy was that "students were students," and to make any special provisions for the minority transfer students would serve only to single them out and put the spotlight on them. The principal believed that it was better not to make any big deal about the transfer students, and then they would be more likely to fit in, just like any other students.

The assistant principal was still concerned because of the negative attitudes of a number of students, teachers, and parents at Pleasant View and because of the very real adjustment problems that the minority transfer students were likely to encounter due to differences in the cultural background and lifestyle; but in light of the principal's stated philosophy, Edwards felt that his hands were tied.

Suggested Learning Activities

Analyze the Case

1. What is your assessment of the assistant principal's thoughts regarding metropolitan integration? Are there any factors that may be important that he is not considering?
2. Assume for the moment that the assistant principal's perception of the principal's position on the minority transfer students is accurate. What is your assessment of the principal's position? What assumptions is he making?

Discuss the Larger Issues

1. What are the pros and cons of metropolitan integration?
2. To what extent should educators attempt to promote metropolitan integration as a remedy to racial problems as contrasted with waiting for a court or a state legislature to require it?

3. What is the role of the school and, in particular, the school administration in planning for and implementing a program of metropolitan integration? What specific activities should be carried out?

Be a Problem Solver Assume that you are the assistant principal in the case. How could you respond constructively to the problems presented? Utilize administrative and social science concepts and principles in planning and implementing your problem-solving approach.

Test Your Solution To test your proposed plan of action for dealing with the circumstances described in the case, create and role-play one or more of the following situations in class:

1. A second conference between Mr. Edwards and his principal regarding the minority transfer students.
2. A faculty meeting at which the principal has asked you to plan and present an ikn-service for the faculty in reference to the new minority transfer students.

Investigate Further

1. Is there any metropolitan integration in your area? If so, what is its extent?
2. What is the attitude of administrators, teachers, parents, and students toward metropolitan integration?
3. Where metropolitan integration exists, what problems appear to be associated with it, and what approaches seem to be effective in dealing with these problems?

45
PARENTS CHALLENGE RACIAL DISPARITY

Waterview is a metropolitan area with a population of over 200,000. The tourist industry is sizable, thereby stimulating the local government to market the city's tourist industry globally. Military installations and population heavily influence the area. The city's educational system is recognized nationally and often featured as a model. The local funding for schools is sizable because education is a high priority. The school population is made up of 15 percent African Americans, 5 percent other multicultural groups, and 80 percent Caucasians.

A group of African American parents have formed the Forward Action Committee to challenge what they believe to be a disparity in the acknowledgment of African American students in the school district. Several of these parents filed complaints with the U.S. Department of Education's Office for Civil Rights. Committee members want the local school board to address their concerns. These parents express strong concern regarding the quality of education their children receive; many believe that the educators do not embrace diversity and very often view African American children as monolithic.

The committee would like the school district to address some of the following issues related to African American students: (1) the number suspended, (2) the number attending at-risk programs, (3) available opportunities for them at the magnet school, (4) the need for staff development on ethnic groups, and (5) the need to increase the multicultural population in administration and education. Furthermore, the committee believes that much of the information required to address these issues is not computerized or recorded in a manner easily attainable. Hence the database is less than valid.

Although parents from several schools are members of the Forward Action Committee, a large majority has students in Viewside Middle School. One parent, Mrs. Timmes, became involved as a result of the manner in which her seventh-grade son was perceived. Sam Timmes was transferred to Viewside Middle School in November, at which time his grades began to decline. Mrs. Timmes stated that she had requested meetings with staff members in January because of her concerns that Sam was not doing well academically. She had realized that the more she interacted with the school staff, the more resistance she encountered. One teacher worked with her, but others contacted her for disciplinary reasons only. Finally, an administrator had questioned whether Sam was respectful at home; Mrs. Timmes thought that the administrator had seen this as a way Viewside School could refer Sam to an alternative program for students with behavioral problems. Mrs. Timmes had told the administrator that she believes Sam is only an immature 12-year-old and that African American parents are stereotyped as not being interested in their children. This motivated her to join the action group.

Sally L. Thompson, the young African American female principal at Viewside, says the problems at the school involve a very small number of parents among the large majority of African Americans enrolled at this particular middle school. She acknowledges the many activities at the school, which include an African American culture club, after-school tutoring, and multicultural field studies, show its commitment to diversity. She has met with the Forward Action Committee and expressed her feeling that "these students have been treated fairly and to make a federal case out of it goes beyond the bounds of reason."

The school district is told that more parents plan to file complaints with the Office of Civil Rights and that they plan to hand out information pamphlets at several predominantly African American churches over the weekend. The local newspapers and television channels have covered the committee's work several times.

Suggested Learning Activities

Analyze the Case

1. What do you think could be an appropriate strategy to handle the parents' initial complaints?
2. Is there a data collection method that would enable you, as principal, to readily access the needed information to determine racial disparity of the type discussed in this case?
3. Will the reactions of the Viewside Middle School principal establish positive negotiating strategies? If so, explain.
4. Given the lengthy investigation process of complaints filed with the U.S. Department of Education Civil Rights Office, do you recognize methods that may be used to settle racial disparity on the local level? Describe.
5. How could the principal and staff assist the superintendent and school board in the investigation of this case?

Discuss the Larger Issues

1. Is this a matter to be taken to the church population?
2. Should this issue be viewed as an impact on the city's global image? What might be some of the perceptions by other states and countries? Describe them.
3. What positive impact could this issue have on the local school district?

Be a Problem Solver Evidently, this issue is going to be presented to the local school board and is already on the national agenda. As the principal, what steps would you take to prepare for the expected developments?

Test Your Solution To test your action plan for addressing this issue, create and role-play one or more of the following situations in class:

1. A meeting with the superintendent and all the principals in the district to determine a plan of action.
2. A work session with the faculty to develop consensus on the issue of racial disparity in the school.

Investigate Further

1. How can faculty address this parental concern over racial disparity?
2. How can local organizations such as the Chamber of Commerce and Tourist Bureau assist the schools in demonstrating the recognition of diverse cultures in the community?

BACKGROUND READINGS

For the reader who would like to develop further background and understanding of the problems and issues presented in this chapter, the following list of readings is provided.

Bauml, Michelle, Antonio J. Castro, Sherry L. Field, and Deborah L. Morowski, "Learning from Preservice Teachers' Thoughts about Teaching in Urban Schools: Implications for Teacher Educators," *Education and Urban Society* (vol. 48, no. 1, 2016), pp. 4–29.

Bracey, Gerald W., *Setting the Record Straight: Responses to Misconceptions about Public Education in the United States* (Alexandria, VA: ASCD, 1997).

Day, Christopher, and Ji Hong, "Influences on the Capacities for Emotional Resilience of Teachers in Schools Serving Disadvantaged Urban Communities: Challenges of Living on the Edge," *Teaching and Teacher Education* (vol. 59, 2016), pp. 115–125.

Fiore, Douglas, *School-Community Relations,* 4th ed. (Larchmont, NY: Eye on Education, 2016).

Gaikhorst, Lisa, Jos Beishuizen, Bart Roosenboom, and Monique Volman, "The Challenges of Beginning Teachers in Urban Primary Schools," *European Journal of Teacher Education* (vol. 40, no. 1, 2017), pp. 46–61.

Gardner, Ralph, and Carolyn Talbert-Johnson, "School Reform and Desegregation: The Real Deal or More of the Same?" *Education and Urban Society* (vol. 33, no. 1, November 2000), pp. 74–87.

Gestwicki, Carol, *Home, School, and Community Relations* (Boston, MA: Cengage Learning, 2015).

Green, Terrance L., "From Positivism to Critical Theory: School-Community Relations Toward Community Equity Literacy," *International Journal of Qualitative Studies in Education* (vol. 30, no. 4, 2017), pp. 370–387.

Green, Terrance L., and Mark A. Gooden, "The Shaping of Policy: Exploring the Context, Contradictions, and Contours of Privilege in Milliken v. Bradley, over 40 Years Later," *Teachers College Record* (vol. 118, no. 3, 2016), n3.

Horsford, Sonya Douglass, "Social Justice for the Advantaged: Freedom from Racial Equality Post-'Milliken,'" *Teachers College Record* (vol. 118, no. 3, 2016), n3.

Kaimal, Girija, and Will J. Jordan, "Do Incentive-Based Programs Improve Teacher Quality and Student Achievement? An Analysis of Implementation in 12 Urban Charter Schools," *Teachers College Record* (vol. 118, no. 7, 2016), n7.

Kerr, Kirstin, Alan Dyson, and Frances Gallannaugh, "Conceptualising School-Community Relations in Disadvantaged Neighbourhoods: Mapping the Literature," *Educational Research* (vol. 58, no. 3, 2016), pp. 265–282.

Kunen, James S., "The End of Integration," *Time* (April 29, 1996), pp. 39–45.

Madsen, Jean Ann, and Etta R. Hollins, "African American Teachers' Role in School Desegregation at the Dawn of a New Millennium," *Urban Education* (vol. 35, no. 1, March 2000), pp. 5–30.

Monzó, Lilia D., "Latino Parents' 'Choice' for Bilingual Education in an Urban California School: Language Politics in the Aftermath of Proposition 227," *Bilingual Research Journal* (vol. 29, no. 2, Summer 2005), pp. 365–386.

Olson, Jennifer D., and Arthi B. Rao, "Becoming a Culturally Responsive Teacher: The Impact of Clinical Experiences in Urban Schools," *Journal of Urban Learning, Teaching, and Research* (vol. 12, 2016), pp. 133–141.

Pawlas, George E., *The Administrator's Guide to School-Community Relations*, 2nd ed. (Larchmont, NY: Eye on Education, 2005).

———, "Vision and School Culture," *NASSP Bulletin* (vol. 81, March 1997), pp. 118–120.

Peavy, Liz, "I Can See Clearly Now: The Kukona Process," *Urban Education* (vol. 35, no. 1, March, 2000), pp. 57–78.

Rothstein, Stanley William, *Class, Culture, and Race in American Schools* (Westport, CT: Greenwood Press, 1995).

Schmaus, Luann, "Parents Share in School Decision-Making," *Excellence* (Fall 1995), pp. 4–7.

Sergiovanni, Thomas J., "Refocusing Leadership to Build Community," *High School Magazine* (vol. 77, no. 1, September 1999), pp. 10–15.

Siegel-Hawley, Genevieve, *When the Fences Come Down: Twenty-first-century Lessons from Metropolitan School Desegregation* (Chapel Hill, NC: UNC Press Books, 2016).

Shujaa, Mwalimu J., *Beyond Desegregation* (Thousand Oaks, CA: Corwin Press, 1996).

Tatum, Bervely Daniel, "Examining Racial and Cultural Thinking," *Educational Leadership* (May 2000), pp. 54–57.

Tatum, Beverly Daniel, *"Why Are All the Black Kids Sitting Together in the Cafeteria?": A Psychologist Explains the Development of Racial Identity* (New York: Basic Books, 2003).

Yantis, John, "Get Staff Involved in Community Relations," *Journal of Educational Relations* (July 1995), pp. 2–6, 26.

WEB EXPLORATIONS

The Web links below contain more useful material related to Chapter 12.

"Steps to Developing a School Communications Plan." https://www.campussuite.com/3-steps-creating-school-communications-plan/

National Network of Partnership Schools. http://www.buffaloschools.org/family.cfm?subpage=93742

"Community and Family Engagement: Principals Share What Works." http://www.communityschools.org/assets/1/AssetManager/CommunityAndFamilyEngagement.pdf

Cultivating Community Relations. http://www.nais.org/Magazines-Newsletters/ISMagazine/Pages/Cultivating-Community-Relations.aspx

Improving School-Community Relations. http://www.edulink.org/parcomm.htm

Resources for Parents and Communities. http://www.schoolcommunitynetwork.org/RFP.aspx

CHAPTER

13

Role and Organizational Problems

Whether a school district is large or small, role and organizational problems arise. In some cases, the problems are due to personality or individual behavior. In other cases, the problems stem from lack of clarity in defining roles and responsibilities. Regardless of the root of a problem, administrators are almost certain to be involved.

This chapter begins with in-basket exercises entitled "Principal's Midyear Problems and Priorities" and "Principal's End-of-the-Year Problems and Priorities." In these exercises the reader is asked to play the role of principal and assume the same characteristics of the school, school district, and community that were assumed for "The New Principal" in-basket exercise from Chapter 9. This second set of in-basket items arises during the middle of the year and the last month of the school year, and the principal is presented with a wide variety of problems and issues in the form of memos, telephone messages, notes, and so forth. Addressing these problems and issues effectively will require the appropriate use of many of the concepts presented in the first eight chapters of the book.

Also included in this chapter are a number of case studies that focus on problems of role and organizational conflict. Because there are, of course, many different problems associated with role and organizational conflict, only a sampling of such problems is possible in this chapter. The case studies that are presented, however, should give the reader exposure to a number of representative problem situations that could develop during the career of an administrator or supervisor. By responding to the situations described in the case studies on the basis of careful analysis and appropriate utilization of the concepts in Part I of the book, the reader should develop increased effectiveness in preventing, dealing with, and resolving problems of this nature.

46
PRINCIPAL'S MIDYEAR PROBLEMS AND PRIORITIES (IN-BASKET ACTIVITIES)

Background

You are Dr. Brown and are in your first year as principal of Kennedy School.

It is the first week in December, and you have gone to the school on Saturday morning to check your mail and telephone messages, having been out of town since Wednesday evening participating in an accreditation evaluation of another school.

You are to assume the same characteristics of the social context of this situation, including the nature of the school, the district, and the community, as assumed in responding to the in-basket items in Chapter 9. Any other additional information will be provided by the instructor or group leader, as appropriate.

Instructions

1. You will be given 90 minutes to read and take action on *all* the items presented following the instructions. You are not expected merely to *describe* what you would do but to *do* it. For example, if you decide to telephone a person or see someone for a conference, then outline your objectives as well as the main points or questions that you would present. (Utilize relevant concepts from Part I of the text in your responses.)
2. You may respond to the in-basket items in whatever sequence you prefer. You should first read *all* of them *quickly.* As you do so, indicate on a separate piece of paper in one of three columns whether a particular in-basket item represents (1) a high-priority, (2) a moderate-priority, or (3) a low-priority situation.
3. Each in-basket item requires a separate action, which you should present on another sheet of paper, adding the identification number in the upper-left-hand corner of the in-basket item. If you understand all the instructions up to this point, you may begin now or when your instructor so indicates.

IN-BASKET ITEM #1

Confidential Note

Dr. Brown:

You were busy, and I have tried unsuccessfully several times to get in to see you, so I am writing you this note. As you know, I'm a conscientious member of this faculty, and I believe in change and innovation and all that "good stuff." I'm getting tired, however, of Bob Love's kids coming into my classroom all excited, some of them holding hands and others hugging each other. It takes me an extra 5-10 minutes just to get them settled down again whenever he has those kids doing certain exercises. I know Bob has introduced this unit on human relations and nonverbal communication, and I suppose it is a good unit, but he gets the kids all worked up.

Is there anything you can do about this problem? Please don't use my name because I don't want to get in trouble with Bob. Also, as you know, he is very popular with the students and most of the faculty.

Kay Stern

IN-BASKET ITEM #2

MEMO

TO: Dr. Brown
FROM: Tim Parker, Assistant Principal

I have been thinking for some time about this idea and finally decided that I would propose it to you. As you know, we are presently developing an individualized education program (IEP) for students with disabilities of one kind or another. What I would like to propose is that the teachers develop an IEP for each nondisabled student who is a chronic or serious discipline problem.

These students are just as much in need of an IEP as the students with disabilities, and it would probably do more to improve their discipline behavior than anything that I could do out of my office. I know this would require the cooperation of the teachers, but I believe that with your leadership the idea can be sold to the faculty. Let me know what you think.

IN-BASKET ITEM #3

November 29

Dear Dr. Brown:

My purpose in writing this letter is to register a formal complaint about the fact that I am being left out of my daughter Valerie's education. As you may or may not know, I am divorced from Valerie's mother who, in a travesty of justice, was given custody of our daughter. At the present time the decision about custodianship is being appealed. In the meantime, I am also challenging the visitation access to my daughter provided by her mother.

All of the preceding is by way of background. My specific complaints with the school are that I am not being informed by the school of my daughter's grades, nor am I being invited to parent-teacher conferences when they are held. Dr. Brown, I want you to know that I love my daughter dearly, and I know she loves me. I continue to be very interested in her education, and I would like you to rectify the present situation regarding communication about Valerie's grades and providing for participation in parent-teacher conferences.

I look forward to your positive action at the earliest possible date.

Sincerely,
Anthony Springfield

IN-BASKET ITEM #4

MEMO

TO: Dr. Brown
FROM: Pat Concern, Counselor

Dr. Brown, I have been giving a lot of thought to this, and I feel we need some sort of a *faculty* in-service on AIDS and other sexually transmitted diseases, and ways of preventing them. I know in the health classes we try to address these problems for students, but we have never done anything for faculty. I don't know for sure that there is any specific need, but I have heard rumors, which of course I would never repeat. Anyway, I think we should do something in this area, and I know someone who would do a good job in presenting the in-service. May I contact him?

IN-BASKET ITEM #5

Dr. Brown,

While you were gone, something happened that I thought you should know about. On Friday Mary Eager wore a button on her dress that says, "Sexism is a social disease." I didn't say anything to her but I did overhear some students talking about it. What do you think we ought to do?

Tim Parker, Assistant Principal

IN-BASKET ITEM #6

MEMO

TO: Dr. Brown
FROM: Cathy Collins

As president of the Teachers' Association, I tend to be in close contact with the various concerns expressed by the faculty, not only in our building but also in the district at large. The latest issue to surface is administrator evaluation. What many (if not most) of the teachers seem to want is the opportunity to evaluate or offer feedback to the administrators on their performance. At this stage I don't believe there is any consensus on what form the evaluation of administrators would take, but it seems there is agreement that something should be done.

Therefore, I have been asked to request that you add to the agenda for the next faculty meeting the topic of faculty evaluation of the administrators.

IN-BASKET ITEM #7

Telephone Message

For: Dr. Brown
From: Al Wood, Channel 12
Time: Friday, 12:15 P.M.

Please call as soon as possible, at 332-8562. I want to do a feature on at-risk students, and I have already obtained their parents' permission.

IN-BASKET ITEM #8

November 28

Dear Dr. Brown:

This is not an easy note to send you, and I wish I didn't have to, but I think you should know that one of your teachers, Mr. King, has AIDS. The reason I know this is that I have dated Mr. King and I recently was tested and found to have been infected with AIDS. I have confronted Mr. King about this situation, but he doesn't want to talk about it. I am concerned that he may infect someone else at the school. I am writing this anonymously because I don't want any trouble. But I thought you should know about Mr. King.

A Concerned Parent

IN-BASKET ITEM #9

Dr. Brown, I am afraid that we are going to have a problem on Monday. While you were gone, the clocks and the bell system got screwed up. The clocks aren't all on the same time, and the bells aren't ringing at the right time. This all happened Friday afternoon, and Sam and I tried to get it fixed but nothing seemed to work. So I called the company late Friday to ask them to come in and fix it, but they said they couldn't send anyone until sometime Monday. I guess we will have to make the best of it until then.

Al, Head Custodian

IN-BASKET ITEM #10

Dr. Brown–

You may or may not know of me, but I teach a course on the principalship at the University. I have heard many positive things about you and your school, and I would like you to talk to my class next semester sometime on the topic of Instructional Leadership.

Please let me know as soon as possible which week might be most convenient for you. My class meets on Wednesday evenings from 6:30 to 9:30 P.M.

Sincerely,
Thomas Sloan, Ph.D.
Professor, Educational Leadership

IN-BASKET ITEM #11

Dr. Brown, something happened on Friday that I thought you should know about. Candy Williams fainted in the faculty lounge, and Mr. Parker gave her mouth-to-mouth resuscitation to revive her. I don't know much about it because I wasn't there. But I heard via the grapevine that Candy was embarrassed by the incident and that Wendy Stack tried to pull Mr. Parker away from Candy before he had finished reviving her. This is all probably very innocent. I thought you ought to know about the situation, just in case.

Peg Albright
Secretary

IN-BASKET ITEM #12

TO: All Principals
FROM: Superintendent Ramirez

I have just come from a conference with a group of parents who are concerned about improving school–home communications. One of their recommendations, which I strongly endorse and am directing you to implement beginning with a faculty meeting, is that teachers take the initiative to schedule a conference with any parents whose child is in danger of failing a course during any particular marking period.

The conference should be held in sufficient time before grades are given so that the student would have a reasonable amount of time to improve the grade. I believe this procedure will greatly alleviate the concern of a number of parents who presently don't find out if their children are failing until grades are sent home.

IN-BASKET ITEM #13

Dr. Brown, while you were away on Friday, three kids showed up (two boys and a girl, who said they weren't related) who wanted to enroll here. I questioned them a bit because they looked really pathetic, with ratty-looking clothes and were generally unkempt. I found out that they are homeless, although they all apparently live in two old cars that are located within our school boundaries. I didn't know what to do, so I told them to come back before school begins on Monday, and you would meet with them.

Peg Albright

IN-BASKET ITEM #14

Dr. Brown:

I don't know whether I should tell you this or not, and Al wasn't sure either. But I talked to my wife, and she says that I should, before something gets very messy. Anyway, late Wednesday after the students and faculty had long left the building, I found a used condom in the faculty lounge. I didn't know what to do with it for sure, but I saved it in case you wanted it for evidence or something. Al thinks it's two faculty members, but he really doesn't know anything. Please let me know as soon as possible what to do because I would like to get rid of it.

Sam Clean, Custodian

IN-BASKET ITEM #15

November 30

MEMO

TO: Principals

FROM: Assistant Superintendent Fong

In the last meeting of the superintendent's cabinet, it was decided that this year the guidance counselors should be evaluated more formally and consistently. Because the district does not currently utilize a standard counselor evaluation instrument, we need to develop something defensible and useful. Please submit your ideas within two weeks on what should be included in such an evaluation instrument, the steps that should be followed in the evaluation process, who should be involved in the process, and so on. Once I have all your ideas, I will try to put together a model evaluation instrument and process for counselors and get your reactions to it before formal adoption by the district.

IN-BASKET ITEM #16

November 26

Dear Dr. Brown:

As you know, there is considerable discussion these days about abortion and use of contraceptives. Students are exposed almost daily to these ideas, and I know in the district's own health classes these topics are explored.

What my group would like to do is to present the pro-life point of view. Specifically, we would like to present a program at a future PTA meeting and at a future student assembly this year. Parents and students alike need to receive positive information about the wonderful miracle that God has bestowed upon us all.

Dr. Brown, our group is offering some excellent films that can be shown, and we have an array of outstanding speakers for this purpose. We would like to schedule something in January. Please let me know as soon as possible what specific dates might be available.

Alice Darling, President
Council for the Beauty of Life

IN-BASKET ITEM #17

Dear Dr. Brown:

The Student Council members have been discussing informally two ideas that we would like you to react to. First, although we are sure that the cafeteria staff works hard, the food is terrible. Therefore, we would like you to see if McDonald's couldn't be used as either a substitute or as some additional choice we could have for our lunch.

Second, we would like to be able to listen to some of our own music during the noon hour while we are eating. We did a little poll, and almost everyone likes rap music. And because you really have to listen to the words to get the most out of it, the cafeteria would be a lot quieter. Please let us know what you think of our ideas.

Sincerely,
Jack Staker
Sandy Elliot
Student Council Reps

IN-BASKET ITEM #18

Telephone Message

From: Betty Spokes
Time: Friday, 3 P.M.

Betty Spokes called about her daughter Valerie. Her ex-husband has been picking up Valerie after school, and she wants Valerie to take the bus instead.

IN-BASKET ITEM #19

November 26

Dear Mr. Brown:

I would like to know what is going on in Mr. Love's classroom. My son comes home from school and complains because in Mr. Love's class the students are supposed to hug each other and to do other things with their faces. My son says that this is some sort of a human relations unit, but he doesn't like it, and from what I have heard about it, I don't like it either.

It seems to me that the school has enough to do with just teaching the basics without getting into all of this other stuff. Mr. Clark and I feel that we do just fine in teaching our son all the human relations he needs, and we definitely don't like the idea of the school requiring him to hug someone from a different background if he doesn't want to.

I expect some sort of action on this matter and look forward to a response from you—*soon.*

Bea Clark

47
PRINCIPAL'S END-OF-THE-YEAR PROBLEMS AND PRIORITIES (IN-BASKET ACTIVITIES)

Background

You are Dr. Brown, and it is your first year as principal of Kennedy School.

It is May 10, and you have gone to the school on a Saturday morning to check over your mail and telephone messages, having been out of town since Wednesday evening, attending a conference on instructional leadership.

You are to assume the same characteristics of the social context of this situation, including the nature of the school, the district, and the community, as were assumed in responding to the in-basket items in Chapter 9. Any other additional information will be provided by the instructor or group leader, as appropriate.

Instructions

1. You will be given 90 minutes to read and take action on *all* the in-basket items presented following the instructions. You are not expected merely to *describe* what you would do, but to *do* it. For example, if you decide to write a letter, then compose the letter. If you decide to telephone a person or see someone for a conference, then outline your objectives, as well as the main points or questions that you would present. (Utilize relevant concepts from Part I of the text in your responses.)
2. Each of the in-basket items requires a separate action, which you should present on another sheet of paper, adding the identification number in the upper-left-hand corner of the in-basket item. You may deal with the in-basket items in whatever sequence you prefer; however, you should indicate on your response sheet the priority: 1 for high, 2 for moderate, and 3 for low priority.
3. Proceed to the in-basket items.

IN-BASKET ITEM #1

May 9

MEMO

TO: Dr. Brown
FROM: Mary Eager

Dr. Brown, I have applied for summer school curriculum work, and although I haven't been turned down yet, I feel that the district is dragging its feet.

As you know, my proposal is to work on developing a peace studies component in our curriculum. I would appreciate it if you would write a letter or do something to get them moving in the district office. I don't know what their problem is!

IN-BASKET ITEM #2

May 6

MEMO

TO: All Principals and Supervisors
FROM: Superintendent

The school board has expressed interest again in the concepts of career ladders and merit pay. What I would like each of you to do is to develop some recommendations for establishing an effective and feasible merit pay program and a career ladders program for teachers. I know these ideas are controversial, but put your ideas in memorandum form and send them to me as soon as possible. Consult with whomever you would like. The school board would like to get some initial input on this before the end of the school year.

IN-BASKET ITEM #3

Telephone Message

For: Dr. Brown
From: Tom Roberts (*State Journal*)
Time: Thursday, 12:05 P.M.

Please call him back today. He wants to set up an "in-depth interview" with you about your experiences during this first year.

IN-BASKET ITEM #4

May 5

Dear Dr. Brown:

As you may know, my son Randy has not been achieving up to his potential this year. We think we know now that the reason is he has an unusual reading problem. We are considering having someone at the school work with him this summer, or sending him to a private learning center that has recently opened in the community. What do you think? Do you have anyone on your staff that you could recommend? What do you think of this private learning center? I think it is called Horizons Unlimited.

Sincerely,
Mrs. Eddie Grover

IN-BASKET ITEM #5

Dr. Brown, you may not be aware of this, but Mr. Sanders, the previous principal, always put out a memo toward the end of the year, identifying for teachers the various things they needed to do before they left school on the final day. Also, he usually made a little speech at the last faculty meeting of the year, commenting about the type of year it was and projecting some goals for the school for the following year. I don't know whether you want to continue these practices, but I thought you should be aware of them.

Peg Albright
Secretary

IN-BASKET ITEM #6

May 4

Dear Dr. Brown:

I tried to call you several times last week, but your secretary always said you were busy. Therefore, I decided to write you. I'm a single, working parent with a child in your school. It has seemed to me that the faculty in this school need to be made more sensitive to the fact that there are a lot of us, and that because of our circumstances, it is not as easy for us to become involved in school as when there are two parents and one of the parents is not working. I'm not sure what the answer is to this, but I would like your help in setting up a single-parent school organization or support group. I also think the school needs to set up some type of a program for "latchkey" students, of which my son is one. Would you be willing to help me? I know there are a lot of people like me out here.

Sincerely,
Nancy Drive

IN-BASKET ITEM #7

May 9

Dr. Brown, I just received a call from my husband, and he is being transferred to another location out of state. He will have to leave in two weeks, and, of course, he wants me to go with him. I really hate to leave my job, and I would like to stay at least until the end of the school year, but when I mentioned this to him, he didn't seem too receptive. I don't know what to do. Do you have any advice?

Peg Albright
Secretary

IN-BASKET ITEM #8

Dr. Brown, I don't know what you want to do about it, but a student told me that Mary Eager is distributing the enclosed leaflet. I would think that a union rep would know better than this. I thought you would want to handle this.

Tim Parker
Assistant Principal

A MESSAGE TO THE CHILDREN AND YOUNG PEOPLE OF THE WORLD

All of you know the name Hiroshima, and you remember what it means . . . nuclear holocaust. Today we are drawing ever closer to an even greater holocaust because of the actions or inactions of political "leaders." If the world is to be saved, then young people need to show leadership. Join the Crusade to Stop Nuclear Warfare. Send your ideas and contributions to Young People for a Peaceful America, Colgate Building, Suite 317, Washington, DC 20036.

IN-BASKET ITEM #9

Dr. Brown, do you have any problem with my taking my classes outside if the weather is nice? The kids begin to get restless this time of the year.

Hazel Smith
Language Arts Teacher

IN-BASKET ITEM #10

May 9

MEMO

TO: Dr. Brown
FROM: Wendy Stack, Teacher

The purpose of this memorandum is to register a formal complaint against Mr. Parker, our assistant principal. This man has sexually harassed me on various occasions, and I want it to stop. He has made remarks about my bust, and he has placed his hands on my buttocks numerous times. He has also propositioned me, twice. I know I am a new teacher, but I don't think I should have to take this kind of abuse! I have also heard that he has done similar things with some of the other young female teachers. Please help me.

IN-BASKET ITEM #11

Dr. Brown, it's probably none of my business but I think faculty morale is pretty low right now. I don't know why exactly, but many of the teachers seem to lack spirit. I'm not sure what can be done about the situation, but I thought you ought to know about it.

Pat
Concerned Counselor

IN-BASKET ITEM #12

Dr. Brown,

I know you are busy, but I think we have a problem on our hands. Some of these kids are starting to use smokeless tobacco in school, and it is staining the floors and some of the fixtures where they spit. I heard that even Bill Stone is using the stuff. I mean if teachers can use it, what can we expect of the kids? Anyway I think something's got to be done about it before it spreads.

Sam Clean

IN-BASKET ITEM #13

May 5

Dear Dr. Brown:

Our organization, The Pro-Nuclear Energy Group, would like to make a presentation at one of your assembly programs. Our organization is made up of power companies in the area that attempt to provide safe and economically efficient energy for the people. We feel that, as a result of various television programs and newspaper reports, the young people are receiving an inaccurate impression about nuclear energy and its advantages. What is needed is a more balanced report, and we would intend to do that in our presentation at your school.

Please consider our request, since we are taxpayers too, and we want to work cooperatively with the school.

We look forward to hearing from you at your earliest convenience.

Sincerely,
(Signed) Bud Strong
President

IN-BASKET ITEM #14

Dr. Brown–

I am not sure what I should do about this referral. As you probably know, Bill Morris (the student) is the son of one of the school board members. I have never gotten along with the old man too well (we were on rival teams when we were in high school) so I would appreciate it if you would handle this one.

Tim Parker

Kennedy School

Student Discipline Referral Form

Date: Thursday

Student's Name: Bill Morris

Teacher: Jack Armstrong

Problem: Kid keeps fooling around and is disrespectful to me. I am sick and tired of this kid and I don't want him back in class until he shapes up.

IN-BASKET ITEM #15

May 6

Dear Dr. Brown:

For some time now, I have been wanting to bring something to your attention, but my daughter has not wanted me to contact you about the matter. I feel now that I must say something, whether my daughter wants me to or not.

You are probably not aware of this, but one of your teachers, a Miss Spencer, is dating a high school student, and from what I hear, things have progressed pretty far if you know what I mean. I think this situation sets a poor example for students, and it makes it difficult for those of us parents who are trying to set a moral tone in our own families. I know you will want to take a strong stand on this. The talk around town is that this boy already has Miss Spencer in trouble if you know what I mean and that she is considering an abortion.

Obviously, Miss Spencer should not be allowed to continue in her position.

Sincerely,
(Mrs.) Roberta Little

IN-BASKET ITEM #16

Telephone Message

For: Dr. Brown
From: Mr. Morris
Time: Friday, 9:00 A.M.

Please call as soon as possible.
332-9698

IN-BASKET ITEM #17

May 5

Dear Dr. Brown,

I would like to register formally my objection to the way my daughter has been abused in physical education classes. Because she was supposedly "fooling around in class" (whatever that means), she has been required several times by Mr. Jack Armstrong to do push-ups. Now, my daughter tells me she wasn't fooling around, and even if she was, it seems to me that there must be a more educationally sound way of dealing with this matter than requiring students to do push-ups!

My daughter is not a physically strong person, and when she can't do the push-ups, everyone in the class–including the teacher–laughs at her. This causes her to cry, and it embarrasses her in front of the entire class.

I want something done about this matter immediately, or I am going to pursue it with the proper authorities.

Sincerely,
Priscilla Block

cc: President of the School Board
Superintendent of Schools

48
PRINCIPAL'S DILEMMA

Scowling, the supervisor turned the pages of the report on her desk. It was her first opportunity this week to examine the departmental summary of teacher grades for the quarter, and she was appalled by the large number of Ds and Fs that had been assigned. She had tried to persuade the teachers before school opened in the fall that grading standards would have to become more flexible due to the different nature of the student body, now composed of a large proportion of minority and economically disadvantaged students. Apparently she had convinced very few of them.

It seemed unlikely that additional attempts to persuade the teachers would prove to be any more productive, but it was obvious to the supervisor that she could not sit by and allow the current grading practices to continue.

After lengthy consideration, she decided that the solution to the grading problem might lie in a new program of increased teacher–student conferences. If each teacher in the department were required to hold at least one conference during the first six weeks of every quarter with each potential D or F student, it seemed probable that grading practices would improve. Teachers would develop a better understanding of the special learning problems of their students, and the students would receive remedial assistance that should enable them to improve their classroom performance. The supervisor was confident that a program of teacher–student conferences would improve the grading situation in the department immensely.

The following Monday she met after school with the members of her department and distributed a statement to them. It read as follows:

NEW DEPARTMENT POLICY ON TEACHER–STUDENT CONFERENCES

1. Beginning with this nine-week session and continuing thereafter, each teacher will confer some time during the first six weeks of the quarter with every student who might conceivably receive a D or F grade at the end of the quarter.
2. The teacher should schedule at least one conference with potential D students and at least two conferences with potential F students.
3. The teacher should encourage D and F students to schedule the conferences themselves. If a particular student has not scheduled a conference by the beginning of the fifth week, however, it is the responsibility of the teacher to take the initiative in scheduling the conference. If the student refuses to come to the scheduled conferences, the teacher is not required to schedule additional meetings but should continue to be receptive to helping the student.
4. Teachers are encouraged to go beyond the minimum number of conferences indicated above. Also, it is assumed that teachers will continue to hold conferences *after* the first six weeks of each quarter, and that conferences with A, B, and C students will be scheduled whenever appropriate throughout the quarter.

After distributing the policy statement to the teachers, the supervisor explained her belief that students should not be assigned a D or F until after the teacher had attempted to work with them individually to improve their performance. The supervisor went on to say that she realized individual conferences would be time-consuming and probably would have to take place during the teachers' free periods, or before or after school. If the student failed to respond to the teacher's efforts, then the student would be held accountable. The initial responsibility, however, would be the teacher's.

After the supervisor finished, she invited teacher reactions. One of them asked whether the conferences were recommended or required. The supervisor responded that teacher–student conferences were in the teachers' best interest as well as the students'. She added that she hoped the teachers would agree, and that it would not be necessary to formally require the conferences.

Although the supervisor continued to encourage the teachers to express their feelings, no other questions or comments came forth. Recognizing that it was useless to persist, she terminated the meeting, emphasizing her expectations that the new program of student–teacher conferences would begin that week.

The next morning, before school began, a delegation of teachers from the department appeared at the principal's office. They were disturbed about the new policy on teacher-student conferences, and it was obvious to the principal that they had met previously as a group to discuss the situation at length. Now they wanted the principal to tell them whether their supervisor could actually require them to hold student conferences and, if so, where they were going to get the time.

They informed the principal that the entire department opposed the new policy and did not plan to carry it out. They indicated that they did not object to the teacher–student conferences, but they felt that it was the students' business, not the teachers' responsibility, to schedule conferences. If the individual teacher found time to schedule conferences and there were not too many of them, fine. But the matter should be left to the professional judgment of each teacher.

The principal was faced with a dilemma. He believed that, in theory, it was the teachers' responsibility to confer with the D and F students on an individual basis before assigning nine-week grades. He wasn't sure, however, that teachers should be *required* to hold such conferences. He didn't want to undermine the position of the supervisor, and he realized that if the conferences were not required, some teachers would fail to hold them. He tried to quickly weigh the consequences of a decision either way, realizing that the teachers were waiting for his response.

Suggested Learning Activities

Analyze the Case

1. What alternatives, in addition to the program of teacher–student conferences, should have been considered by the supervisor in response to the apparent grading problems in the department?
2. What is your assessment of the supervisor's strategy for introducing change? How would you have proceeded differently? What assumptions are you making?
3. What is your evaluation of the teachers' position on the issue of teacher–student conferences?

Discuss the Larger Issues

1. What steps do you think a school should take in order to adapt its total educational program to the type of student population described in the case?
2. What is the role of the principal in bringing about the changes identified in response to question 1? The role of the supervisor? What are the roles of other individuals or groups within or outside the school?
3. What should be the nature and scope of a supervisor's authority over the teachers in the department?
4. What position should the principal take in a conflict between a supervisor and the teachers in the department? What should be the role of the principal in resolving the conflict?

Be a Problem Solver As principal, you have been approached by a delegation of teachers who are asking, essentially, that you overrule the decision of their supervisor. What should you do? What preliminary steps might be necessary?

Test Your Solution To test your proposed plan of action for dealing with the problem presented at the end of the case, create and role-play one or more of the following situations in class:

1. A conference between the supervisor and the principal.
2. A meeting of the entire department that you have been asked to attend by the supervisor.
3. A telephone call from the representative of a delegation of parents who wants to schedule a meeting with you, the principal, to discuss the consistently low grades that their sons and daughters received at the end of the last quarter.

Investigate Further

1. How does your district define the role of supervisor in terms of actual authority? Your school? How specifically is the policy spelled out?
2. How would the majority of teachers in your department react to the idea of requiring teachers to hold conferences with students who may receive low grades?

49
PRINCIPAL'S PERSONAL CONDUCT RESULTS IN POSSIBLE SUSPENSION

Superintendent Yolanda Mims had been in her office for only a few minutes when she was buzzed by her secretary. Shelly Foeman, Principal Yusef Blilecki's personal secretary, wished to see her immediately. The matter seemed urgent, so Yolanda told her to come in. She greeted her warmly at the door, but Shelly was visibly nervous and upset. It took Shelly a few minutes to collect her thoughts and open up to Yolanda once they were seated in her office. "I really like Mr. Blilecki, but this has gone on too long," Shelly stammered. Then she proceeded to accuse, in detail, Mr. Blilecki of sexual harassment. Most of what Shelly related was somewhat offensive, but Yolanda was not sure whether it constituted harassment or not. Yolanda knew Yusef fairly well. He was a very strict man in his midforties. This kind of behavior was not at all characteristic of him. What's more, he had a wife and four children to whom he was closely attached. He always talked about his family. This was Dr. Mims's first year as superintendent, and the first time she had been confronted with such an issue. She knew that Shelly, a 20-year-old who had a somewhat troubled past, really needed this job, so she could not imagine her making up accusations like this. She decided to see Yusef right away.

When Yolanda arrived at the high school, she went directly to Yusef's office where she found him working on the master schedule. She closed the door and confronted him with the accusations made by Shelly. Yusef was very quiet for a few minutes. Then he opened up. "Listen, I could deny that anything happened at all, but this has to end. It is true I have taken Shelly to lunch, and some of our conversations may have been, well, colorful. But this was not at school or on school time. It was totally harmless. Besides, she is the one who opens up and is so frank. I just responded."

"But Yusef, she says that you approached her in this office only yesterday."

There was a brief silence. "I cannot deny it. She came in, and I guess a little harmless joking got carried away. But, ah, this doesn't have to go any further than this office, does it?"

"Yusef, I am shocked by your behavior. You are 20 years this girl's senior, and you have jeopardized your career. I have no other choice but to act upon the information I have received. Your secretary is claiming sexual harassment and you have not denied it. Yusef, how could you?"

As Yolanda left Yusef's office, she tried to determine the next step she should take.

Suggested Learning Activities

Analyze the Case

1. Did the superintendent handle the conference with Shelly in the correct manner? Was her reaction appropriate? If not, what would you have done differently?
2. Is the superintendent's reaction to the principal's response justified? What about the principal's suggestion to forget the whole matter? Would you?
3. What additional steps should the superintendent take before she determines what to do about the principal? What about the secretary? Should she be disciplined for her part?

Discuss the Larger Issues

1. What guidelines should personnel working together follow when spending time together away from the job? What should the employer's concerns be?
2. What rights does the accused have in situations like the one in this case, and what should be the role of the employer in protecting those rights?
3. To what degree should the attitude of students and parents toward an administrator's alleged or real misdeeds be considered by an employer in deciding what to do about the administrator?
4. What action should an employer take if it has been validated that an administrator has committed an indiscreet act or has broken the law?

Be a Problem Solver Assume that you are the superintendent in this case. What would be your approach to dealing with the circumstances that have developed? Utilize administrative and social science concepts in planning and implementing your approach.

Test Your Solution To test your proposed plan of action, you and your colleagues should create and role-play one or more of the following situations:

1. A conference between the superintendent and several board members.
2. A telephone call from a parent, who has heard rumors, to the superintendent.
3. A telephone call from a local newspaper reporter who has talked to Shelly.

Investigate Further

1. Ascertain whether or not your district has a policy on procedures to be followed when an administrator breaks certain ethical codes of conduct.
2. Has a situation similar to the one described in the case ever happened in your school or school district? If so, how was it handled?

50
SUPERVISOR–PRINCIPAL RELATIONSHIP

The central office supervisor was supposed to visit Hillcrest School in the afternoon in response to a teacher's request for assistance with a classroom problem. Sitting in his office an hour before he was scheduled to arrive at the school, he was torn between the knowledge that a definite appointment had been established and his feelings of ambivalence about the school.

With respect to the faculty at Hillcrest, he felt that he had developed rather good rapport with the teachers he supervised, and they had called on him frequently for assistance with their instructional plans or difficulties. The problem was that Mr. Sawyer, the principal of the school, seemed to regard him with suspicion. Last fall the supervisor had visited Hillcrest, and Mr. Sawyer had stopped him in the hall and had asked him to check in at the principal's office in the future so that the principal would know when the supervisor was in the building. Reluctantly, the supervisor had complied with the principal's request.

Several months later, during one of the supervisor's subsequent visits to the school, Mr. Sawyer had implied that it would be a good idea for the supervisor to make a full report on whom he had seen each time he was in the building, what he had accomplished, and so on. Since the principal had not specifically required such a report, the supervisor had chosen to ignore the suggestion—not because he minded writing the report, although he didn't relish additional bureaucratic requirements, but because he was afraid that the teachers would no longer feel free to seek his assistance if they knew that he was relating to the administration the substance of their conferences with him.

The supervisor was aware that he had considerably reduced the number of visits he typically made to Hillcrest, primarily because he wanted to avoid any conflict with the principal. This compromise was unpleasant to the supervisor because he felt that he was letting the teachers down by being available less frequently; but certain kinds of instructional assistance necessitated a classroom visitation, and that was the reason he had agreed to visit the school today.

The supervisor knew that the principal regarded himself as the instructional leader of the school and that he probably felt threatened by the strong relationship the supervisor had been able to build with the teachers at Hillcrest. Although the principal's attitude was perhaps understandable, his defensiveness had made it very difficult for the supervisor to work openly and freely with the teachers. The supervisor was troubled by the principal's reaction to him, but at this stage he was at a loss about how matters could be improved.

Suggested Learning Activities

Analyze the Case

1. Assess the appropriateness of the principal's requests or suggestions to the supervisor and the supervisor's attitude toward and response to the principal.
2. What might be some of the less obvious reasons for the behavior of the principal and the central office supervisor?

Discuss the Larger Issues

1. What should be the responsibility of a principal and central office supervisors with respect to working with teachers and improving instruction? What should be the relationship between the two levels of supervision?
2. Whose responsibility is it to specify the appropriate relationship between central office supervision and the principal? Whose responsibility is it to resolve conflicts between the two levels of supervision?

Be a Problem Solver The supervisor in the case is concerned about his strained relationship with the principal of Hillcrest School. He does not want to alienate the principal, but he does not believe that the request to report his activities in the school is in the best interest of his own relationships with the teachers. If you were the supervisor, what would you do? Utilize appropriate administrative and social science concepts from Part I of the text in planning and implementing your approach.

Test Your Solution To test your proposed plan of action, you and the class should create and role-play one or more of the following situations:

1. A confrontation between the supervisor and the principal.
2. A conference between the principal, the supervisor, and the superintendent.

Investigate Further

1. What is the school board policy in your school district regarding the working relationship between the principal and the central office supervisors?
2. What administrative policy or guidelines have been formulated in your district to prevent or to handle the kind of problem presented in this case?
3. What is the attitude of your building principal and the majority of the supervisors in the central office about the current relationship that exists in your district between principals and central office supervisors?

51
THE SUPERINTENDENT AND THE NEW SCHOOL BOARD MEMBERS

It was late in the spring, and as the superintendent thought about the recent school board election, he felt uneasy. The two incumbents had been unseated, and the composition of the school board would be changed significantly. The superintendent had given little thought to the school board election prior to the day that the voters had cast their ballots. He had assumed that since both incumbents had been excellent board members, they would be reelected with little or no difficulty. It had been quite a shock when he had learned that neither of them had won, but had been replaced by candidates with little background or contact with the schools.

One of the newly elected board members was a man named George Thompson, an accountant, whose election flyers had described him as "a taxpayer determined to hold the line on school spending." The superintendent had heard Thompson present his views at a pre-election candidates' forum and had not been very favorably impressed by the man's abrasive manner and suspicious attitude toward the schools. Apparently it was going to be difficult to develop good rapport with Mr. Thompson.

Complicating the matter was Mr. Thompson's relationship with one of the building principals in the district. During the recent candidates' forum, Mr. Thompson had made comments and had drawn conclusions about an alleged surplus in the school budget, citing a building principal as the source for his information. In response to Mr. Thompson's statements, the superintendent had been forced to concede that, in a sense, there was a surplus in the budget but that it had already been earmarked for other purposes, so a surplus no longer existed.

It bothered the superintendent that Mr. Thompson and the building principal, who were next-door neighbors, had apparently been discussing school business with regard to a matter that the superintendent felt should have remained within the school "family." The superintendent was concerned about the behavior of the principal, as well as Mr. Thompson, and could foresee major problems if they continued to carry on the same relationship after Mr. Thompson assumed his new role as a board member. At the moment, the superintendent wasn't sure how to proceed with either of the two men.

The second newly elected member of the school board was Harvey Sutton, who managed a gas station. Mr. Sutton hadn't said much during the campaign, but his few public statements suggested that the new board member didn't know very much about schools. He seemed friendly enough, but the superintendent was doubtful whether Mr. Sutton was going to make a very strong contribution to the school board without considerable orientation. The problem was how best to orient him to his role as a school board member and to education in general.

The superintendent was deeply concerned about the possible implications of the election of the two new school board members in terms of the board's continued support of his plans for the school district. He had already initiated a number of changes in the educational program of the school district during the past two years, and thus far the board had always supported him, although some of the votes had been rather close. He had plans for instituting a new sex education program and for remodeling some of the older buildings in the district. He hoped that steps could be taken to gain the cooperation of the two new members of the board as he attempted to move ahead with his plans.

Suggested Learning Activities

Analyze the Case

1. Based on the information presented in the case, what can you infer about the superintendent's values? What aspects of the superintendent's personality may make it difficult for him to develop a good relationship with each of the new board members?
2. How would you evaluate the superintendent's attitude toward Mr. Thompson, particularly with regard to the latter's relationship with the building principal?
3. What factors may the superintendent be failing to consider in his assessment of Mr. Thompson and Mr. Sutton?

Discuss the Larger Issues

1. What role, if any, should a superintendent take with reference to the election of school board candidates?
2. What methods and prerequisites should be established for the election of school board members?
3. What should be the position of any administrator or teacher in the school system with respect to discussing school affairs with school board members or candidates?

Be a Problem Solver The superintendent is bothered about the relationship between one of his newly elected board members and one of his building principals. He is also concerned about his own future relationship with the new board members and about orienting them to their role on the board and to education in general. If you were the superintendent, what would you do in this situation? Utilize appropriate administrative and social science concepts from Part I of the text in planning and implementing your approach.

Test Your Solution To test your proposed plan of action for dealing with the problems presented at the end of the case, create and role-play one or more of the following interactions in class:

1. A conference between the superintendent and the principal identified in the case.
2. A conference between the superintendent and either of the new board members or both.

Investigate Further

1. What guidelines or established procedures exist in your school district for the campaigning and election of school board members?
2. What problems do the following individuals or groups in your school district see in the election of school board members?
   a. The superintendent
   b. The teachers
   c. Your building principal
   d. A sample of parents

52
ADMINISTRATOR EVALUATION

Francine Gorday was halfway through her first year at the high school. This was her first experience as principal. She had taught at the middle school for 17 years and was well respected there. When the principal left the high school for another job, Francine had applied only after Mike Carlton, the assistant superintendent, had called and encouraged her to apply. He felt that, even though she had no experience in an administrative position, she was more than qualified for the job. She reluctantly applied, figuring someone more qualified would impress the superintendent and the board. She was shocked when she was offered the position.

Once at the high school, Francine began a thorough review of the programs and policies. She spent all summer reworking the master schedule and planning for her first year. The first semester started off smoothly, but several weeks into it, Francine noticed that some teachers were beginning to appear frustrated under her leadership. She was tough, that's true, but she knew what teachers could be like, and she was determined to bring out the best in her staff.

When spring came, Mike Carlton visited the school. He seemed somewhat pleased. He stopped to see Francine for a few minutes. Their conversation was rather general. The following day Francine received a note from Mike. It was attached to a formal review form. The note told Francine to fill out the form according to how she felt she rated herself in each area. Mike Carlton had already signed the bottom. Francine felt very uneasy about this, so she put the form aside. The following week, Mike called her at her office.

"Francine, I need that evaluation form ASAP."

"Oh, OK. But are you sure this will be OK? I mean aren't you supposed to fill this out?"

"Well Francine, I trust your judgment. Besides, I already have an idea in my mind as to how I will rate you in each category. I determine that by talking with the faculty and observing the school. I'd just like to match what I feel with what you have on paper."

"Well, could I get a copy of your sheet? I mean, I would really like to know how you rate me on these things."

"I'll give you a copy later. But I'll need yours first. OK?"

Francine reluctantly filled out the sheet and sent it to central office. Another week passed and no formal evaluation came. Mike continued to put Francine off. She began to worry a little about the entire issue. Finally she called the superintendent's office to invite the superintendent to the school. After a tour of the school, Francine asked the superintendent to evaluate her. Francine handed her a blank form. The superintendent talked with Francine at length about the school and her expectations for Francine; however, she did not fill out the form. She referred Francine to Mike, whose job it was to do the formal evaluations. In fact, the superintendent was a little concerned because Mike had not yet submitted a formal evaluation on Francine. She promised to look into it.

The next day Francine received a call from Mike Carlton in her office.

"Francine, what's the idea? The superintendent was all over me yesterday. I thought we had an understanding. Why did you have her get down there? Well, let me tell you, I just finished filling out your evaluation, and I'm afraid you're going to be disappointed. I've been getting a lot of complaints from teachers down there that you are just too hard on them. Now I see what they mean. I'm sending copies of my evaluation to you, the superintendent, and one is going in your file. If you have any complaints or comments, call my office and we can set up an appointment."

He hung up abruptly. Francine was at a loss for words. She had not really been sure about taking this job at first, but she had worked hard to make this a good school and she felt her efforts had made a difference. She wanted this job, liked the new challenges, but felt she had jeopardized her position. She felt she didn't deserve a negative evaluation, particularly one done out of spite. All she wanted was a real evaluation that would help her improve.

Suggested Learning Activities

Analyze the Case

1. Evaluate the relationship between the new principal and the assistant superintendent. What potential problems existed before Francine started her new job?

2. What are some things the new principal might have considered doing differently in planning for the new year? How could she have involved her faculty?
3. What is your assessment of Mike Carlton's evaluation procedures? How can Francine get a valid evaluation at this time? Discuss her options.

Discuss the Larger Issues

1. Should administrators, especially new ones, be provided a formal evaluation of their performance each year?
2. What criteria and procedures should be utilized in the administrators' evaluations?
3. To what extent should the individuals being evaluated be involved in the development of criteria and procedures to be used in evaluating their performance?

Be a Problem Solver Assume that you are the principal in this case. What should you do to respond to the circumstances confronting you? Utilize administrative and social science concepts from Part I of the text in planning and implementing your approach.

Test Your Solution To test your proposed plan for dealing with the circumstances described in the case, you and your colleagues should create and role-play one or more of the following situations:

1. A conference between Francine and Mike Carlton.
2. A conference involving Francine, Mike Carlton, and the superintendent.
3. A conference between Francine and the superintendent.

Investigate Further

1. What evaluation criteria and procedures for evaluating administrators does your district employ?
2. To what extent do the administrators being evaluated in your district have a role in the development of the evaluation criteria and procedures?
3. What is the attitude of the individuals being evaluated toward the fairness and usefulness of the evaluation criteria and procedures?

BACKGROUND READINGS

For the reader who would like to develop further background and understanding of the problems and issues presented in this chapter, the following list of readings is suggested:

Alston, J. A., "Climbing Hills and Mountains: Black Females Making It to the Superintendency," in C. C. Brunner (Ed.), *Sacred Dreams: Women and the Superintendency* (New York: State University of New York Press, 1999).

Barker, Cherri Sue, "School Board Members and the Underrepresentation of Women in the Superintendency: A Case Study," PhD diss., Liberty University, 2012.

Biddle, Bruce J., Role Theory: *Expectations, Identities, and Behaviors* (Cambridge, MA: Academic Press, 2013).

Bjork, L. G., and T. J. Kowalski (Eds.), *The Contemporary Superintendent: Preparation, Practice, and Development* (Thousand Oaks, CA: Corwin Press, 2005).

Black, Susan, "Redefining the Teacher's Role," *Executive Educator* (March 1996), pp. 23-26.

Brunner, C. Cryss (Ed.), *Saved Dreams: Women and the Superintendency* (Albany: State University of New York, 1999).

Brunner, C. C. "Ethnic Minority Superintendents," in T. C. Glass, L. Bjork, and C. C. Brunner, (Eds.), *The Study of the American School Superintendent* (Arlington, VA: American Association of School Administrators, 2000).

Brunner, C. C., "Female Superintendents," in T. C. Glass, L. Bjork, and C. C. Brunner, (Eds.), *The Study of the American School Superintendent* (Arlington, VA: American Association of School Administrators, 2000).

Brunner, C. C., and M. Grogan, *Women Leading School Systems* (Lanham, MD: Rowman and Littlefield, 2007).

Bynum, Yvette P., and Clara Young, "Female Superintendents and the Effects of Mentoring Relationships," *International Journal for Innovation Education and Research* (vol. 3, no. 10, 2015).

Dana, J. A., and D. M. Bourisaw, *Women in the Superintendency* (Lanham, MD: Rowman and Littlefield, 2006).

Farmer, Barbara Wilson, and Edgar I. Farmer, "Organizational Structures of Teachers in Traditional and Magnet Schools in a Large Urban School District," *Education and Urban Society* (vol. 33, no. 1, November 2000), pp. 60–73.

Fernandez, Rick, Rebecca M. Bustamante, Julie P. Combs, and Cynthia Martinez-Garcia, "Career Experiences of Latino/a Secondary Principals in Suburban School Districts," *International Journal of Educational Leadership Preparation* (vol. 10, no. 1, 2015), pp. 60–76.

Gorton, Richard A., and Gail Thierbach-Schneider, "The School Administrator's Role, Expectations, and Social Factors," in *School-Based Leadership: Challenges and Opportunities,* 3rd ed. (Dubuque, IA: William C. Brown publishers, 1991), pp. 84–117.

Grogan, M., "Women Leading Systems. What the Latest Facts and Figures Say about Women in the Superintendency," *School Administrator* (February 1, 2005). Accessed online, http://www.aasa.org/publications/saarticledatail.cfm?ItemNuber=1020&1020YsnItemNumber=950&inItemNumber-1995, December 20, 2010.

Guskey, T. R., and K. D. Peterson, "The Road to Classroom Change," *Educational Leadership* (December 1995), pp. 10–17.

Jackson, B. L., "Getting Inside History–Against All Odds: African-American Women School Superintendents," in C. C. Brunner (Ed.), *Sacred Dreams: Women and the Superintendency* (New York: State University of New York Press, 1999).

Jackson, J., "Breaking the Hiring Barrier," *American School Board Journal* (June 2006), pp. 24–26.

Kelsey, Cheryl, Kathy Allen, Kelly Coke, and Glenda Ballard, "Lean in and Lift up: Female Superintendents Share Their Career Path Choices," *Journal of Case Studies in Education* (vol. 6, 2014).

Nave, Bill, Edward Miech, and Frederick Mosteller, "A Lapse in Standards: Linking Standards-Based Reform with Student Achievement," *Phi Delta Kappan* (October 2000), pp. 128–132.

Northouse, Peter G., "Gender and Leadership" in *Leadership: Theory and Practice*, 4th ed. (Thousand Oaks, CA: Sage Publications, 2016), pp. 397–420.

Paven, B. N., "The First Years: What Should a Female Superintendent Know Beforehand," in C. C. Brunner (Ed.), *Sacred Dreams: Women and the Superintendency* (New York: State University of New York Press, 1999).

Price, Hugh, "Committed to High Quality Education for All Children," *Phi Delta Kappan* (April 2000), pp. 604–606.

Rhode, D. L., *The Difference "Difference" Makes: Women and Leadership* (Stanford, CA: Stanford University Press, 2001).

Rodríguez, Cristóbal, Melissa A. Martinez, and Fernando Valle, "Latino Educational Leadership across the Pipeline: For Latino Communities and Latina/o Leaders," *Journal of Hispanic Higher Education* (vol. 15, no. 2, 2016), pp. 136–153.

Simmons, J. C., "Superintendents of Color: Perspectives on Racial and Ethnic Diversity and Implications for Professional Preparation and Practice," in L. G. Bjork and T. J. Kowalski (Eds.), *The Contemporary Superintendent: Preparation, Practice, and Development* (Thousand Oaks, CA: Corwin Press, 2007).

Spillane, James P., and Linda C. Lee, "Novice School Principals' Sense of Ultimate Responsibility Problems of Practice in Transitioning to the Principal's Office," *Educational Administration Quarterly* (vol. 50, no. 3, 2014), pp. 431–465.

Tallerico, M. *Accessing the Superintendency: The Unwritten Rules* (Thousand Oaks, CA: Corwin Press, 2000).

Treffinger, Donald, J., "From Gifted Education to Programming for Talent Development," *Phi Delta Kappan* (June 1998), pp. 752–755.

Van den Berg, Rudolf, and Anje Ros, "The Permanent Importance of the Subjective Reality of Teachers during Educational Innovation: A Concerns-Based Approach," *American Educational Research Journal* (vol. 36, no. 4, Winter 1999), pp. 879–906.

Van Tassel-Baska, Joyce, "The Development of Academic Talent: A Mandate for Educational Best Practice," *Phi Delta Kappan* (June 1998), pp. 760–763.

Walter, James K., and William L. Sharp, "Moving On," *Executive Educator* (February 1996), pp. 21–23, 36.

Webb, L. Dean, and M. Scott Norton, *Human Resources Administration,* 6th ed. (Columbus, OH: Pearson, 2013), pp. 337–371.

Williams, Karla A., "The African American Female Superintendent: Barriers and Facilitators to Success," PhD diss., Capella University, 2016.

WEB EXPLORATIONS

The Web links below contain more useful material related to Chapter 13.

National Association of Elementary School Principals, Statement of Mission, History, and Ethics. Accessed online https://www.naesp.org/sites/default/files/docs/NAESP-Manual-as-of-8-29-16.pdf

National Association of Secondary School Principals. Accessed online http://www.nassp.org/

National Institute for Urban School Improvement. Accessed online http://www.urbanschools.org

State Affiliates' Membership Links. Accessed online http://www.naesp.org/naesps-state-affiliates

CHAPTER

14

Problems of Change

In recent years, educators have been bombarded with various proposals for improving education, most of which would require major changes in the schools. Although the topic of introducing change has generally been written about in glowing terms focused on the end results, it needs to be recognized that various problems and issues are frequently associated with the process. A proposed change, however positive the results might be, challenges the status quo and tends to be threatening to a number of people. An attempt to implement a certain change can also be disruptive to school routine and debilitating to the people adversely affected by it. The extent to which each or all of these negative consequences occur will depend in large part on the effectiveness of the administrator in assessing the need for change, facilitating effective proposals to satisfy that need, and then planning for and implementing a particular innovation. Therefore, readers are encouraged to examine carefully the ideas in Part I of this book before addressing any of the cases in this chapter.

By focusing on various problems and issues that an educator may encounter in trying to bring about change, the case studies provide an opportunity to apply the concepts learned in Chapters 1–8. Although most of the cases center on difficulties that can occur in the process of introducing a change, attention is also given to problems of institutionalizing a change. The innovations described could be proposed at either the elementary or secondary level, and an attempt has been made to identify different levels and types of administrators and supervisors in the role of change agent.

53
TEACHER TRIES TO INDIVIDUALIZE INSTRUCTION

The teacher was excited about trying some of the new techniques for individualizing instruction that he had learned during the summer. He had waited until things had settled down in the fall, but it was now the third week of school, and he was ready to begin experimenting with his classes.

Basically, he wanted to redesign and reschedule his classes so that he could spend more time working with individual students and small groups. He also hoped to release students from class to work on independent study projects of their own choosing. He had given considerable thought to the means by which all this might be accomplished and, with the help of his summer school professor, had come up with a plan of action.

He would separate each of his classes into two groups and would send half the students to the library where they would be free to work on independent study projects while he met with the remaining students for small-group discussion or individual conferences. The following day he would reverse the procedure, so the students who had previously been engaged in class discussion would go to the library for independent study while those who had previously been in the library would meet with him.

On the third day in the cycle, he would bring the two small groups of students together for a regular class meeting that would be designed to discuss and synthesize what had been learned independently. By varying the sizes of the groups and the nature of the teaching and learning activities, he hoped to individualize his own program to a much greater extent and, perhaps, set an example that might stimulate other teachers to diversify their methods of instruction.

The following morning he initiated the new program by explaining its rationale to the students and discussing with them their responsibilities, in and out of class. An out-of-class permit was written for the group going to the library, explaining for the benefit of anyone who might stop them in the hallway or in the library that the students had been excused from the teacher's class in order to work on independent study projects. The teacher had not felt it necessary to contact the librarian in advance since there were usually few students in the library, and the students' out-of-class permit made it clear that their activity had the approval of their teacher.

After half the students left for the library, the teacher rearranged the chairs in the room with the help of the remaining students and introduced the discussion topic. Almost immediately he sensed that the creation of a small group had brought about a change in atmosphere. Student discussion became livelier and more spontaneous, and there was greater participation from those students who, in the past, had seemed reluctant to take part in class activities. The teacher was delighted.

Suddenly, the classroom door opened and in walked the students who were supposed to be studying in the library. They claimed that the librarian had refused them admittance because her approval for the project had not been secured in advance. She had also informed them that the library was not a place for students who did not know specifically what they wanted to do and that, before coming to the library again, each student should identify in advance the area he or she wanted to investigate and obtain the teacher's approval.

The students reported that the librarian seemed annoyed by the prospect of other groups from the teacher's classroom coming to the library during that day—and on succeeding days.

The teacher tried to calm the students, many of whom seemed irritated and upset. He told them that he would attempt to straighten out matters with the librarian, but in the meantime the entire class would have to proceed as they had in the past.

At the end of the afternoon, he sought out the assistant principal for advice. It was only the second year at the school for the teacher, and he certainly didn't want to get into a conflict with the librarian. All he wanted was to try something different in an effort to improve his classroom instruction.

Unfortunately, his conference with the assistant principal was not very reassuring. The assistant principal did not think that the librarian would ever be very cooperative or receptive to the idea of students using the library on a regular basis during class time—occasionally, perhaps, but not regularly. He doubted whether it would do much good to talk to the librarian, but he encouraged the teacher to continue experimenting with new approaches to teaching, whenever possible, and not to give up hope. It was apparent to the teacher that the assistant principal had little inclination to become involved in helping to bring about the desired changes.

Nevertheless, the teacher was determined not to give up. He wasn't sure at the moment what his next step should be, but he certainly wasn't going to scuttle the idea of individualizing instruction in his classroom. Perhaps he should see the principal for assistance.

At that moment, the principal was in his office talking on the telephone to a parent who had called to ask how the school expected his son to get a good education if one of the boy's teachers was going to allow him to spend half his time out of class, working on whatever he chose.

It was the second time that day that the teacher's name had been mentioned to the principal. Earlier, several members of the faculty had complained about the noise in the halls caused by students going to and from the teacher's classroom after passing time. The principal decided he would have to find out what was causing all the trouble.

Suggested Learning Activities

Analyze the Case

1. Why did the teacher run into difficulty in this school in trying to introduce new techniques for individualizing instruction? What might be some of the reasons the teacher incorrectly made certain assumptions and, in other instances, did not pursue other sources of help in trying to implement his new approach?
2. What is your evaluation of the role played by the librarian? By the assistant principal? What might be some of the reasons each of them responded the way he or she did? What implications do their responses have for how the principal would handle the overall problem in the case?
3. Considering the type of innovation the teacher wanted to initiate, how might he have proceeded differently? What assumptions are you making?

Discuss the Larger Issues

1. What should be the role of the teacher in initiating change?
2. What institutional conditions act as a deterrent to teacher-initiated change?
3. Should there be a school policy on teacher innovations? If so, what should constitute the main elements of the policy?
4. What should be the role of the principal or other administrators in regard to teacher-initiated innovation?

Be a Problem Solver Several teachers and one parent have complained to the principal about the teacher and his innovations. If you were the principal in that situation, what would be your reactions? What action, if any, would you take to deal with the situation?

Test Your Solution To test your proposed plan of action for dealing with the problem presented at the end of the case, create and role-play one or more of the following situations in class:

1. A conference between the principal and the teacher.
2. A conference among the principal, the teacher, the librarian, and the assistant principal.
3. A telephone call to the principal from another parent complaining about the teacher and his innovation.

Investigate Further

1. What is the written policy in your school on teacher-initiated innovations? What is the feeling of your principal, your central office supervisor, and your assistant principal about teacher-initiated innovations?
2. To what extent are funds available in your district and school for implementing teacher-initiated innovations?
3. In your district and school, what barriers or obstacles would a teacher or principal have to overcome in order to initiate any program of individualized instruction?

54
EFFECTIVE SCHOOLS: HOW DO WE GET THERE FROM HERE? (A GROUP ACTIVITY)

Background

A new superintendent, Maria Rodriguez, has been selected by Ambition School District. A recent PhD graduate from a major research university in a different state, she is a nationally recognized educational leader. The school board has informed her that her most important assignment is to bring about significant educational reform by creating effective schools for all students, not only for the academically oriented ones.

Dr. Rodriguez believes that if she is to be successful in meeting the school board's expectations, she first needs to ascertain the leadership capabilities of the school principals. To make that determination, she asks each principal in the district to propose, in a three- to five-page report, a plan outlining how the principal would develop an effective school. The superintendent indicates in her request that although it will be impossible for the school district to fund all the plans the first year, she wants each principal to develop a proposal, and those plans that cannot be funded initially will receive consideration in the future. To help the superintendent select the most deserving proposals, she will ask a committee of principals to review them and recommend to the central office the top three in rank order.

Instructions

1. Members of the class are to assume that they are the principal of the school in which they are currently employed, and that their school is a part of Ambition School District.
2. Each member of the class should prepare the proposal requested by the superintendent, identifying the name of the school and his or her own name at the beginning and conclusion of the proposal, respectively. The proposal should utilize the concepts in Chapters 6 and 7. Anyone who is not already knowledgeable about the research on effective schools should review this research because the superintendent is knowledgeable and expects her principals to be so.
3. Copies of each proposal should be supplied for each member of the class and distributed when requested.

4. Each class member should assume appointment by the superintendent to the committee that has responsibility for reviewing the various proposals and selecting the top three. Once the copies of the proposals have been disseminated and read, the members of the committee should attempt in group discussion to persuade the others of the merits of their own proposal for creating an effective school. The final goal of the group, however, should be to reach consensus regarding the three best proposals. The decisions of the committee should be prepared in writing, with reasons for the final selections.
5. The role of the instructor during the group activity should be that of a resource person and observer during the initial stages and should be that of an evaluator during the critique of the activity. The time allocated for the activity may range from 45 to 90 minutes, depending on the size of the group and the objectives of the instructor. Evaluation of student performance during group discussion should be based on the use of concepts in Chapters 4, 6, and 7.

55
PLANNING FOR IMPROVEMENT

Sameway School District has a long-standing reputation for maintaining the status quo and upholding tradition. For the last 20 years, schools in Sameway have generally used unchanging teaching techniques and managerial strategies with the exception of a concession to the limited use of computer technology. The community takes comfort in knowing that its children will have virtually the same educational experiences that the parents had. Most of the graduates of the Sameway district remain in the area as adults, and the community is pleased with the education provided to its citizens.

Sameway's superintendent has been in office for 15 years. He grew up in Sameway and understands the community's comfort with the status quo. At the same time, his studies in educational leadership and his awareness of what is happening in education throughout the country have made him aware of the skills students will need if they are to be prepared for an increasingly global society. He does not want Sameway to be left behind, yet he does not want to shake up community norms more than necessary. He realizes that no plan will succeed if it is not accepted by the faculty and the community.

For the past five years, in keeping with educational trends in the rest of the state, he has mandated the creation and submission of test improvement plans and school safety plans for each building. By allowing for a very gradual implementation of these mandates, and because of his own familiarity with the community, the superintendent was able to secure the community's acceptance of these few changes. The superintendent did, however, notice that the bulk of these plans were recommending only slight revisions of what was already being done in the school. He was pleased, nonetheless, to see gradual increases in programs and academic improvement efforts, knowing that progress comes in small increments.

When the superintendent's wife became terminally ill, he decided to retire and devote his time to the care of his family. A new superintendent was hired from a neighboring state. Although the members of the community understood the superintendent's need to leave office, they were wary of the "outsider" who was going to take over.

The new superintendent was extremely experienced in the field of strategic planning. He had worked in three school systems during the last 10 years. In each system, he had created and implemented a districtwide strategic plan and facilitated the development of site plans that complemented the district goals. He immediately began outlining a similar strategy for the Sameway School District. He spent the first two months in office getting to know the community and assessing current practices and readiness for change. The community appears to respect the fact that he is taking the time to get to know them. During his third month in office, he plans to introduce his idea of creating and implementing a districtwide strategic plan.

Suggested Learning Activities

Analyze the Case

1. Do you agree with the original superintendent's reluctance to create change? Why or why not? What would you have done differently?
2. If the community, the school board, local employers, parents, and students are satisfied with the current instruction and curriculum, is there a need for change? Support your answer.
3. What is your assessment of likelihood of the new superintendent's success in the Sameway district? What measures might he take to increase his chances?

Discuss the Larger Issues

1. In determining the need for change within a school district, what role should be played by each of the following: The superintendent? Principals? Faculty? Community? Parents? Students?
2. Is pencil-and-paper planning the most effective way to implement change?
3. Who is responsible for determining the direction of progress in a district?

Be a Problem Solver The new superintendent has taken over the Sameway School District. He has devoted the first two months to becoming acquainted with the community and assessing its readiness for change. Now he is prepared for the next step in which he will introduce his ideas about a districtwide strategic plan. What is the best way for him to begin the process? Utilize social science and administrative concepts from Part I in approaching this situation.

Test Your Solution To determine the feasibility of your plan for creating and implementing strategic planning in Sameway School District, role-play the following situations with your group:

1. The superintendent's announcement to the community of his intention to create and implement a strategic plan. Include the community's reaction.
2. The creation of the committee that will develop the plan. Who will be involved? To what extent?
3. The superintendent as he divulges to the principals the contents of the plan and distributes the forms for documenting the implementation. How will he ensure a positive reception? What advice or direction should he give the principals to assist in inducing the cooperation of the faculty? Is it the principal's responsibility to enforce the plan?

Investigate Further

1. Does your district have a strategic plan? How was it created? How is implementation ensured?
2. Does each site in your district have a site improvement plan? Are the plans congruent with the district plan?
3. How many "plans" is your principal responsible for implementing? (Examples are a school improvement plan, accreditation plan, test improvement plan, student achievement plan, school safety plan, grounds maintenance plan, and the like.) Are these efforts coordinated? Are they mandated by the federal, state, or local governments, by the school district, or are they voluntarily created?

56
SCHOOL-BASED MANAGEMENT

Elmtree School District had been experimenting with school-based management for several years. Most of the schools in the district had implemented school-based management in varying degrees, and overall the evidence seemed to indicate that this was an innovation worth continuing.

On Friday, May 10, the following memorandum reached Steve Works, principal of 64th Street School:

MEMO

TO: Steve Works
FROM: Adrian Han, Superintendent
SUBJECT: School-Based Management

Steve, I know that this has not been an easy year for you as a new principal with a faculty that has not been especially receptive to change. However, because 64th Street School is one of the few schools that hasn't volunteered to participate in school-based management (this is certainly not a criticism of you, as you are new to the school), I would like to see your school move forward in that direction next year.

Therefore, please attempt to develop a school-based management plan that your school could implement next fall, and submit your plan to me in three weeks so that we will have time to discuss it and get it approved by the end of this school year.

Steve read the superintendent's memo a second time, placed it on his desk, and stared out the window of his office for a few moments. His first thought was that this would not be an easy assignment. He had talked informally with most of his faculty during the year to assess their attitudes toward school-based management, and they seemed to be divided among three different viewpoints. About a third of them were adamantly opposed to the idea on the basis that it sounded like more work than they could handle, another third seemed interested in the prospect, and the remainder were apathetic.

As Steve thought more about his situation, he grew a little depressed. Finally, he decided that, like it or not, he was obviously going to need to develop some plan of action. The initial questions were how he should get started and whom he should involve.

In another school in Elmtree School District, Shirley Verano, principal of Advanced School, was reading a memorandum she had received from the superintendent of schools.

MEMO

TO: Shirley Verano
FROM: Adrian Han, Superintendent
SUBJECT: The Next Stage in School-Based Management

Shirley, I have been pleased with your school's efforts in experimenting with school-based management during the past several years. So far, your school's efforts to involve teachers, parents, and even students, on some occasions, in decision making about budget questions, school discipline policy, and scheduling problems have paid dividends, from all indications.

In my judgment your school should be ready to move into some new areas using school-based management. Specifically, what I would like you to do is to prepare a plan for expanding school-based management at Advanced School to include the following additional areas: staff and administrator evaluation and curriculum planning. Of course, I recognize that these are potentially controversial matters, but I would like to see at least one school in our district tackle these problems, and I have assessed Advanced School as most likely to succeed in this endeavor. Please submit your plan to me in three weeks.

Suggested Learning Activities

Analyze the Case

1. Evaluate each of the memoranda using concepts from Chapter 4, especially regarding the administrator as a recipient of communication.
2. What concepts from Chapter 7 should each of the principals choose in preparing a response? How should these concepts be utilized?
3. How do the assignments from the superintendent and the situation of each principal differ as to expectations and possible problems?

Discuss the Larger Issues

1. What are the advantages and disadvantages of school-based management?
2. What individuals and/or groups are likely to be affected by the introduction or expansion of school-based management? Which individuals and/or groups are likely to oppose school-based management, and why?
3. What criteria and methods should be used to evaluate the effectiveness of school-based management?

Be a Problem Solver Assume first that you are in Steve Works's situation; later, assume that you are in Shirley Verano's circumstances. Prepare an outline of a proposed school-based management plan, including a description of *how* you would go about introducing, instituting, and evaluating the change. Utilize appropriate concepts from Part I of the text in preparing your responses.

Test Your Solution To test the adequacy of your response to the superintendent, create and role-play one or more of the following situations in class:

1. A faculty meeting during which you, as principal, present your ideas and plans for change. (Other members of the class should simulate different reactions to the principal's presentation.)
2. A meeting between you, as principal, and the superintendent's cabinet, during which you present your ideas and plans for change. (Other members of the class should simulate various reactions to the principal's presentation.)

Investigate Further

1. Examine the educational literature on school-based management.
2. Ascertain what plans, if any, your school district is considering for the introduction or expansion of school-based management.
3. Talk with people associated with schools that have experimented with school-based management. Visit these schools, if possible.

57
RESTRUCTURING STAFF EVALUATION AND SUPERVISION

For the first time in several years the superintendent was looking forward to teacher negotiations. The teachers in the district generally seemed content with their welfare, and there currently appeared to be no major problem or crisis for their association to use as a bargaining lever. Of course, there were always a few who would never be completely satisfied, and the superintendent anticipated that there would continue to be demands for higher salaries and other fringe benefits, but the superintendent felt on top of things for a change and was confident that he and the board could handle whatever the teachers would come up with.

The following Monday he and the negotiating team that represented the school board met with the bargaining team from the teacher association. After the initial exchange of pleasantries, the teachers presented their demands for the coming year. As the superintendent listened to the list of items being read, he was pleased with the accuracy of his predictions–until the chairman of the teachers' negotiating team started reading the last demand:

"Teachers will no longer be observed, supervised, or evaluated by administrators. All supervision, including classroom visitation and working with teachers to improve their instruction and the curriculum, will be carried out at the secondary level by the department heads and at the elementary level by master teachers released for that purpose. All teacher evaluation will be conducted by a special committee of teachers elected by and from the faculty in each building. This committee will evaluate only those nontenured teachers about whom there is some question in regard to whether their contracts should be renewed for the following year or whether they should receive tenure. No other teachers will be formally evaluated.

"The administration and the school board may decide to review and reverse a decision by the Teacher Evaluation Committee that a teacher's contract not be renewed. In such a situation, the administration and the school board will assume full responsibility for the future actions of the teacher. Under no circumstances, however, may the administration dismiss a teacher whom the Teacher Evaluation Committee has determined to be professionally competent. Such a dismissal would constitute a violation of the master teacher contract and would be subject to further action by the association."

The superintendent barely managed to retain his composure. He had never encountered such a blatant demand before. What were the teachers thinking? Could they be serious?

He decided not to make any comment until he had an opportunity to talk privately with the chairman of the teachers' bargaining committee. Instead, he presented a number of other items about which the administration and the school board were concerned. There was no immediate reaction from the teachers, so he suggested that both groups take some time to study each other's proposals and meet again in two weeks. That recommendation seemed agreeable to everyone, so a date was set for the next meeting.

As the various participants moved out of the room, the superintendent asked the head of the teachers' committee to stay a few minutes longer to talk informally about one of the teachers' demands. The superintendent explained that he was puzzled by the association's proposal that all administrators be removed from teacher supervision and evaluation. What was the basis for this recommendation? Were the teachers serious about pushing it?

The teacher representative responded that the association was indeed serious about the supervision proposal. The teachers did not believe that most administrators were competent to supervise or to evaluate them. Perhaps in the past, when teachers were not as well trained and when teaching methods and curriculum were rather standard, administrators could effectively supervise and evaluate teachers, but now teaching methods and curriculum were becoming diverse and very specialized. Today's teachers were better educated in their subject fields and simply did not think that administrators had the background or the training to help them to improve. In fact, teachers found administrators' suggestions to be neither relevant nor helpful. Furthermore, the teachers think that they should not be evaluated by people who were no longer involved with the act of teaching as their primary function in the school.

The representative went on to say that the teachers believe personnel evaluation to be a professional task. In the other professions, evaluation was conducted by one's peers. For example, in medicine, the hospital administrator didn't evaluate doctors–they were evaluated by each other. In education, teachers' own colleagues were the people most qualified to supervise and evaluate them (not nonteaching administrators), and the association was prepared to battle all the way for that principle.

The superintendent didn't know what to think about the position that the association had taken, but it was clear that the teachers were dead serious about their newest demand. He told the teacher representative that he appreciated knowing more about the teachers' feelings but that he couldn't comment at the present time on the merits of their proposal. He assured the representative that all the teachers' recommendations would receive careful study and consideration, and that the board's negotiating team would be ready with some reactions of their own at the next meeting.

After the teacher representative left, the superintendent sat in his office and reflected on the situation. He had mixed feelings about the association's proposal on supervision and evaluation. In a way he agreed with many of the points that the teacher representative had made.

Perhaps there did need to be a change toward giving teachers more responsibility in this area. He wondered how the other administrators and the school board would react to this rather extreme proposal. It was certain that many of the principals would reject the idea, and he doubted whether the school board would be in favor of acceding to the demand.

The superintendent had two weeks before the next meeting with the teachers. What position should he take on the matter? What strategy should he employ with the teachers' negotiation team? With the other administrators in the district? The school board? He had his work cut out for him, but the first task was to come to a decision in his own mind about what was best for education in the district.

Suggested Learning Activities

Analyze the Case

1. What factors prevented the superintendent from anticipating the nature of the new teacher demands?
2. What is your assessment of the strengths and weaknesses of the proposal on teacher supervision and evaluation?
3. What assumptions is the teacher representative making in his explanation of why the teachers want a new system of supervision and evaluation?
4. What is your evaluation of the superintendent's reaction and follow-up actions to the proposal advanced by the chairman of the teachers' negotiating team? If you were the superintendent in that situation, how would you have behaved differently?

Discuss the Larger Issues

1. What are some of the reasons teachers may be dissatisfied with the present system of teacher supervision and evaluation?
2. How can the current system of teacher supervision and evaluation be improved so that it will be perceived more positively by teachers?
3. What should be the role of the following individuals or groups in the process of teacher supervision and evaluation?
   a. Central office supervisors
   b. The principal
   c. Department heads or special learning coordinators
   d. The faculty
   e. Students
   f. Parents

Be a Problem Solver The superintendent agrees with many of the points that the teacher representative has made but doubts whether the other administrators and the school board would be in favor of the teachers' position. He will be meeting with the teachers again in two weeks. If *you* were the superintendent, how would you proceed and with whom would you talk during the weeks before the next meeting with the teachers?

Test Your Solution To test your proposed plan of action for dealing with the problem presented at the end of this case, create and role-play one or more of the following situations in class:

1. A meeting between the superintendent and the building principals.
2. An informal closed-door session between the superintendent and the school board.
3. The next meeting between the teacher bargaining committee and the school board bargaining committee.
4. Any other situation that might provide feedback on the strengths and weaknesses of your proposed plan of action.

Investigate Further

1. What is the school board and administrative policy in your district on *who* is responsible for supervision and *how* the supervision will be conducted?
2. To what extent are teachers dissatisfied with their supervision and evaluation?
3. How would the following groups react to the teacher association demands as presented in this case if the same demands were made in your district?
   a. School principals
   b. Central office supervisors
   c. Department heads
   d. Superintendent
   e. Elementary teachers, junior high teachers, high school teachers
   f. School board
   g. Parents

58
CHANGING THE ROLE OF THE BUILDING PRINCIPAL

The assistant superintendent was convinced of the need for administrative reorganization at the building level. He had concluded, based on his previous experience as a principal, recent professional reading, and a review of the current status of the instructional and curricular program in the schools, that the role of the building principal should be changed.

In the opinion of the assistant superintendent, the building principal was no longer the instructional and curricular leader of his or her school–if such had ever been the case. These days teachers were better trained and were specialists in their subject fields. The principal, on the other hand, was a generalist with intensive preparation on the undergraduate college level in only one subject field. In graduate school, principals had specialized in administration but, as a rule, had taken only one course in supervision and curriculum. Consequently, they were not really knowledgeable about the content and methodologies of the various disciplines, nor did they have the time to keep up with the many changes that were taking place. As a result, many teachers, particularly experienced ones, did not recognize or accept the principal's judgments in matters of instruction and curriculum, and most principals seemed reluctant to approach experienced teachers with suggestions for improvement. Therefore, there was a decided lack of instructional and curricular leadership in the schools, and the assistant superintendent believed that it was his job to correct the situation.

That afternoon he met with the superintendent and proposed that the emphasis in the role of the principal be changed from instructional leader to professional manager, formally recognizing the role that most principals were performing anyway. Although their job descriptions still assumed that they were educational leaders in their schools, in reality the principals were generally more concerned and occupied with maintaining the ongoing program in their buildings.

What was needed, the assistant superintendent suggested, was a realization on the part of the principals that they could no longer function effectively as instructional leaders and that it was necessary for them to concentrate on improving their managerial skills. Principals should recognize that they were middle management. In many ways, their position was similar to that of hospital administrators who worked with professionals, for example, doctors, who were more specialized in their knowledge and skills than the administrator.

At that point the superintendent indicated that he agreed, but he wanted to know who would provide the instructional and curricular leadership in the schools if the principal's role was changed.

The assistant superintendent had anticipated that such a question would be raised and showed the superintendent a proposal he had worked out.

RECOMMENDED ADMINISTRATIVE REORGANIZATION

1. The role of the principal would become that of professional manager; instructional and curricular supervision and leadership would be delegated to other individuals within the school. In-service programs would be planned and instituted to assist the principals in becoming better acquainted with and more skilled in the use of techniques and procedures of middle management, for example, PERT and PPBS.
2. At the secondary level the department heads would provide the instructional and curricular leadership for the teachers within their departments, coordinated by the assistant principal for instructional services. Each department head would be granted two additional periods of released time to carry out his or her responsibilities.
3. At the elementary level each school would be staffed with grade-level coordinators who would teach part-time and work with teachers the remainder of the time to improve instruction and curriculum.
4. Central office supervisors would offer additional supervisory service to both levels.

The superintendent liked the proposal, and he said so. He was particularly impressed with the idea of capitalizing to a greater extent on the expertise that already existed within the teaching ranks. He knew that the program would be more costly and that he might find it difficult to persuade the school board to buy the plan, but he also recognized that significant steps had to be taken to improve the present situation. Of course, the proposed changes would first have to be sold to the principals, which would not be easy, and the actual implementation of the reorganization would have to wait until the next budget year. But he gave the assistant superintendent the green light to begin laying groundwork with the building principals.

The assistant superintendent was delighted by his superior's response, and immediately after the conference, he told his secretary to set up a meeting on Friday with all the building principals. At that time he would present his plan for administrative reorganization and try to persuade the principals that a change in their role would be in their own best interests.

On Friday morning he distributed to the assembled group of principals a copy of his proposal, which had since been amplified with supporting rationale, although not changed in basic concept. For the next 15 minutes he discussed his observations on the present role of the principal and the need for change. Then he paused and asked the principals for their reactions. He didn't have to wait long.

One principal after another objected to the proposed plan of administrative reorganization. No one spoke in favor of the idea. In fact, they were unanimously opposed to relinquishing the role of the principal as instructional and curricular leader of the school. They protested that this was the role they had been trained for and that this was the role their professional associations expected them to assume. Perhaps it was true that they were not subject matter experts, but, they argued, it was not absolutely necessary to be an expert in order to work with teachers in the improvement of instruction and curriculum. They felt the main problem was that principals were too bogged down with administrative detail and didn't have the time to function the way they would like to–as educational leaders. They were *not* managers, they were *educators,* and they rejected the analogy offered by the assistant superintendent comparing them with hospital administrators.

It was obvious to the assistant superintendent that he had stirred up trouble. As the principals waited for his reaction to their opposition, he debated his next move.

Suggested Learning Activities

Analyze the Case

1. What are your analysis and evaluation of the observations made by the assistant superintendent in regard to the role of the building principal?
2. What do you see as the strengths and limitations of the assistant superintendent's plan for administrative reorganization?
3. What is your assessment of the assistant superintendent's strategy for introducing change? What are some of the reasons he encountered resistance?
4. What assumptions or errors in logic might the principals be making in their defense of the role of the principal as an instructional leader?

Discuss the Larger Issues

1. Specifically, what do you feel should be the role of the principal with respect to improving instruction and curriculum in the school?
2. What barriers or handicaps must a principal overcome in order to make a real contribution as an instructional or curricular leader?
3. How can the principal best utilize the other sources of expertise within the school, the school district, or the community for the improvement of instruction and curriculum?

Be a Problem Solver The initial reactions of the principals to the assistant superintendent's proposal to change their role were negative. If you were the assistant superintendent in that situation, what would be your next step? What would be your long-range objective *and* strategy? Utilize appropriate administrative and social science concepts from Part I of the text in planning and implementing your approach.

Test Your Solution To test your proposed plan of action for dealing with the problem presented at the end of this case, create and role-play one or more of the following situations in class:

1. A continuation of the meeting between the assistant superintendent and the principals.
2. A conference between the assistant superintendent and the superintendent.

Investigate Further

1. How does your district define the role of the principal? What are the principal's responsibilities for instructional leadership? What system of evaluation exists for ascertaining whether the principal is, in fact, effectively carrying out leadership responsibilities?
2. How would the principals in your district feel about a change in their roles similar to that proposed in this case? How would the teachers react? The department heads?

59 IN-SERVICE OR DISSERVICE EDUCATION? PART I

The principal had been staring at the wall in his office for the past five minutes. He was trying to think about topics and guest speakers for the two days of in-service education the faculty was supposed to receive this year. One in-service day was to occur on Friday, the second week in November, and the other day to be set aside for in-service education was also a Friday, during the third week in April.

The problem was that it was now the latter part of October, and he had just begun to think about the need to plan something for the first in-service day. He knew that he probably should have initiated his planning early in the fall, but he had been busy with a number of other activities and the time had slipped by. Still, he figured that he had plenty of time to plan something worthwhile as long as he could line up a certain professor he knew who often gave talks about lesson planning.

The principal felt that lesson planning was a major deficiency on the part of many of his teachers, as evidenced by the lesson plans they submitted to his office, and that the morning of the first in-service should focus on this topic. The afternoon could be devoted to opportunities for teachers to practice the development of model lesson plans, and, later in the day, several of the better lesson plans might be presented to the entire faculty.

Having completed his planning for the first in-service day, the principal decided that he needed a break before planning the second one, so he left his office to go to the faculty room for a cup of coffee.

Suggested Learning Activities

Analyze the Case

1. What is your evaluation of the reason the principal gave for not planning earlier in the year for in-service education?
2. What is your assessment of the principal's planning for the first in-service day? What assumptions is he making? What unanticipated consequences might he encounter?

Discuss the Larger Issues

1. To what extent is there a need for teacher in-service education today? Why does the need exist?
2. Who should be involved in planning an in-service program? Why should these people be involved? What are the advantages and disadvantages of involving others?
3. What criteria and processes should be utilized in planning for and evaluating in-service programs?

Be a Problem Solver Assume that the principal in this case study proceeds with the first in-service day. Based on your answer to the second question under "Analyze the Case," how would you, as the principal in this situation, address the problems that you anticipate will occur during and after the in-service program?

Test Your Solution To test the approach you developed to deal with the problems you anticipate will arise during and after the first in-service program, you and your colleagues should create and role-play one or more of the following situations:

1. A faculty meeting in which the principal announces his plans for the November in-service meeting for teachers and asks whether there are any questions or reactions.
2. Reluctance or refusal by those members of the faculty whom the principal approaches in the afternoon of the in-service program with a request to present to the rest of the faculty the lesson plans that were developed.

Investigate Further

1. How does your school or school district develop plans for in-service education?
2. To what extent are in-service programs evaluated in your school or school district? What criteria and procedures are employed?
3. What is the attitude of administrators and teachers toward in-service education in your school or school district?

60
IN-SERVICE OR DISSERVICE EDUCATION? PART II

It was the last day in February, and the principal had set aside a block of time in the afternoon to plan an in-service day in April. He felt that as a result of his teachers' negative reactions to and poor participation during the November in-service program, he had learned *his* lesson about the importance of adequate planning and teacher involvement. It was essential that he allow himself more advance time to plan the next in-service program and that he conduct some sort of needs assessment of the teachers so the program would be relevant for them.

After instructing his secretary that he did not want to be interrupted for any reason during the next two hours, he entered his office after lunch to work on plans for the April in-service program. As the principal reflected on the planning that needed to take place, it seemed to him that the first priority was to construct some type of instrument to assess the perceived needs of his teachers. If he could find out what they were interested in or needed, then he could design a program tailored to those interests or needs.

For the next hour and a half the principal worked at his desk, attempting to develop a needs assessment instrument for his teachers. His basic approach was to jot down a number of needs that he believed his teachers felt–or, at least, *should* feel–and he added to that list a number of topics about which he thought teachers *might* be interested. He then organized the list into a survey format and added instructions for the teachers to follow in responding. Before giving the survey to his secretary to be typed and distributed to the faculty, he decided that he should look it over one more time.

In-Service Needs Survey

February 28

Dear Teacher:

To plan in-service programs that more closely meet your needs and that have a greater chance for practical application, it is necessary for me to know your interests and needs.

Listed are nearly 30 possible in-service activities. These have been categorized (rather roughly in some cases) into four major groupings. Please consider the items in each category and put a mark (X) opposite those in which you have a definite interest or need. *Please check no more than the number allotted for each category.*

It is very important that these be completed and returned to me no later than March 4. Please put your name on the form.

Sincerely,
Ed Bain, Principal

In-Service Interest Assessment

Name: ______________________________ *Date:* ______________

Category 1–You as a Person

Check Only 2:

_____ Stress management
_____ Time management
_____ Career alternatives for teachers
_____ Physical fitness and wellness
_____ Personal investments for educators
_____ Other (describe): ________________

Category 2–For Professional Background

Check Only 3:

_____ Identifying creativity
_____ Learning styles
_____ Use of student records
_____ Writing meaningful comments

_____ Structuring a parent conference
_____ Evaluating teaching resources
_____ Human growth and development
_____ Increasing school/home cooperation
_____ Other (describe): ______________________

Category 3—Improving Your Classroom Skills

Check Only 4:

_____ Teaching gifted/talented students
_____ Classroom motivation strategies
_____ Classroom discipline strategies
_____ Making interesting lessons
_____ Interpreting tests
_____ Time on task
_____ Creative bulletin boards and posters
_____ Computer-assisted instruction
_____ Computerized gradebooks
_____ Constructing good tests
_____ Using drama to teach
_____ Other (describe): ______________________

Category 4—Child Development and Adjustment

Check Only 2:

_____ Improving students' self-images
_____ Conferencing
_____ Brain growth in children
_____ Sensible approaches to individualization
_____ Support services for you and your students (special education/guidance)
_____ Alternative family styles (single parent, etc.)
_____ Other (describe): ______________________

Satisfied that the instructions were clear and the topics important, the principal gave the needs assessment questionnaire to his secretary to be typed and distributed, and then returned to his office to plan some of the other aspects of the in-service program. He didn't feel that he could begin selecting speakers for the program because he didn't know yet how the results of the needs assessment. One piece of planning that he could work on immediately, however, was the development of an evaluation for assessing the effectiveness of the in-service program. After the last in-service meeting, he had neglected to conduct a formal evaluation, and although he was able to conclude from the lack of participation during that day and the subsequent negative comments he had heard about the program through the grapevine that the program had not been a total success, he wanted to conduct a more systematic and more formal evaluation next time. He worked for the next half hour on a draft of a possible evaluation form. When it was finished, he looked over the form to see whether he had overlooked any aspect.

Evaluation of In-Service Program

Instructions

Teachers need not identify themselves in completing the form. Its primary purpose is to give me some feedback on what you saw as the strengths and weaknesses of the activities scheduled for the November in-service day. Please provide information that is as complete as possible, and then return the form to my secretary.

1. What did you think of the speakers?

Morning session	*Afternoon session*
______ Superior	______ Superior
______ Adequate	______ Adequate
______ Unsatisfactory	______ Unsatisfactory

2. How useful did you feel the handouts were?

Morning session	*Afternoon session*
______ Very useful	______ Very useful
______ Useful	______ Useful
______ Not useful	______ Not useful

3. To what extent were you satisfied with your involvement during the in-service program?

Morning session	*Afternoon session*
______ Very satisfied	______ Very satisfied
______ Satisfied	______ Satisfied
______ Not satisfied	______ Not satisfied

4. Was the time allocated to each session adequate?

Morning session	*Afternoon session*
______ Very adequate	______ Very adequate
______ Adequate	______ Adequate
______ Not adequate	______ Not adequate

5. Do you feel you learned very much from the in-service program?

Morning session	*Afternoon session*
______ A great deal	______ A great deal
______ To some extent	______ To some extent
______ Not at all	______ Not at all

Thank you!

The principal felt satisfied with the evaluation form he had designed, and he believed that it should provide him with useful feedback for making the in-service program in April effective. One addition, however, needed to be made. He needed to specify in the instructions a deadline for returning the completed form. He thought a couple of days ought to give the teachers sufficient time to think through their answers to the questions. If he allowed more time, some of the teachers would only misplace, lose, or forget about the form.

As the principal left his office to take the evaluation form to his secretary for typing, he felt pleased with himself. It had indeed been a productive two hours of planning with the development of a needs assessment form and an evaluation form. He recognized that there were some other aspects of planning for the in-service day that remained to be accomplished—such as lining up the speakers—but he still had plenty of time to work on that after collecting the needs assessment. *Now* seemed like a good time to take a well-deserved coffee break.

Suggested Learning Activities

Analyze the Case

1. Analyze the principal's planning and decision-making *process* in developing a needs assessment instrument for his teachers. What would you have done differently?
2. Evaluate the in-service needs survey that the principal developed. What are its strengths and weaknesses? What modifications would you recommend?
3. Analyze the principal's planning and decision-making *process* in developing an evaluation procedure and form for assessing the effectiveness of the in-service program. What would you have done differently?
4. What do you see as strengths and weaknesses of the in-service evaluation procedure and form that the principal has designed? What modifications would you recommend?

Discuss the Larger Issues

1. Are teachers' interests the same thing as teachers' needs? Who decides, and by what criteria?
2. To what extent should an in-service program for teachers focus on teachers' needs as compared to organizational needs?
3. To what degree should the evaluation of an in-service program focus on whether the participants actually acquired whatever knowledge or skill the program was designed to deliver? How would this type of evaluation be carried out?

Be a Problem Solver Assume that you are an administrator or a supervisor who has the responsibility for planning and evaluating two days of in-service education during the year. How would you proceed? Utilize administrative and social science concepts from Part I of the text in developing your approaches.

Test Your Solutions To test the approach you developed in response to "Be a Problem Solver," create and, if appropriate, role-play one or more of the following situations in class:

1. Write a report to the superintendent, describing your plans for the two days of in-service programs, including the method you used for developing those plans.
2. Present your plans to the faculty, including an evaluation procedure or form.

Investigate Further

1. Examine the educational literature for recommendations regarding how you should plan for and evaluate an in-service program.
2. Interview appropriate personnel in the state department of education and/or universities for their recommendations for planning and evaluating an in-service program.

61
SCHOOL CHOICE

In March the state legislature passed a law that would allow parents to send their school-aged children to any school of their choice in the fall, either within or outside the school district where the family resided. Included in the legislation was authorization for a transportation and tuition voucher, based on a rather complicated formula that considered the distance traveled and the financial well-being of the family.

There had been considerable opposition to the school choice bill while it worked its way through the legislative process. Nevertheless, once it was approved, most educators accepted the need to plan for its impact. One of the problems was that few people–even the so-called experts–were very certain or specific on what the precise nature or extent of the impact would be. One implication that almost everyone agreed on was that the schools would need to compete for students on a much greater scale than had been true in the past.

Katie Hernandez, principal of Cesar Chavez School, had been sitting in her office for the last hour on a Saturday morning in the first week of May, trying without much success to jot down some ideas about getting her school ready for the implementation of school choice. This was a new task for her, and she wasn't sure about everything that needed to be done. One thing she did know was that she had to put together some plan and implement it, or she might wind up with the school less than half full in September.

Suggested Learning Activities

Analyze the Case

1. What kind of plan is needed under these circumstances? What elements should be included in the plan?
2. Whom, if anyone, should the principal consult or involve in the development of her plan? Is there a particular planning process that should be followed?
3. Identify the concepts in Part I of the text that would be helpful to consider while developing and implementing the plan.

Discuss the Larger Issues

1. What variations might the school choice approach take? Identify the advantages and disadvantages of those variations.
2. Which individuals and groups are likely to favor a school choice approach, and which are likely to oppose it? To what extent is support or opposition based on the merits of school choice as opposed to other factors?
3. What are the short- and long-range implications of school choice? What should be the response by those educators who do not favor it?
4. What criteria and methods should be used to evaluate the effectiveness of school choice?

Be a Problem Solver Assume that you are the principal of this school. Agree on any additional details you will need in order to address the implementation of the school choice legislation in the school administered by Katie Hernandez. Prepare a plan for dealing with the school choice situation.

Test Your Solution To test your plan of action, you and the class should create and role-play one or more of the following situations:

1. A call from a local reporter who would like to learn the details of your proposed plan.
2. A presentation to the faculty of a rough draft of your plan. (Simulate different reactions to the plan being presented.)
3. A presentation to the PTA of your plan.

Investigate Further

1. Examine the educational literature on various school choice approaches.
2. Ascertain the type of school choice legislation, actual or proposed, in your state.
3. Determine what plans, if any, have been made in your school district to respond to school choice possibilities.
4. Investigate school choice plans and/or approaches by other school districts and states.

62
SCHOOL DISTRICT CHIPS AWAY AT STUDENT TECHNOLOGY LITERACY PROBLEMS

The superintendent had just finished reading her copy of *School Tech News.* The latest issue raised questions about how schools were incorporating the study of computers and technology literacy into the curriculum. These questions reflected concerns that the superintendent had developed recently about the use of computers in her own district. She hadn't expressed her concerns to anyone yet because she wasn't sure she was right. But after reading *School Tech News,* she decided to call a meeting of the district's principals and supervisors to address the issue.

The following Friday, the meeting was held at the district office. The superintendent had decided to begin the meeting by giving some background, expressing concern, and then asking the principals and supervisors to think about the problem and send her their recommendations.

The superintendent began the meeting by stating her views. "In recent years the school district has introduced computers into elementary school curriculum, and at the high school level several courses are offered in computer programming. In addition, our schools are using data processing more in the area of attendance and are using the computers to help with student scheduling. Still, I am not sure that we are making maximum, or even in some instances appropriate, use of the computer.

"For example, we study keyboarding, LOGO, and the history of the computer at the elementary schools. Is this the best way to introduce computers to children? I should also mention that I have heard that a number of elementary teachers still don't feel competent in teaching the use of computers and don't like taking time away from the other subjects.

"At the high school, I see computers and computer programming being utilized primarily by math and business education teachers, but what about the rest of the teachers and curriculum? And should we be placing such emphasis on teaching high school students how to program?

"I don't have answers to these questions, but I believe strongly that the school district *needs* answers. Therefore, I would like each of you to think about how computer education and utilization could best be improved in your building or subject area, and then forward your recommendations to me by the end of next week.

"Are there any questions?"

To the superintendent's surprise, no one responded with a question. So she proceeded to the next item on the agenda.

Suggested Learning Activities

Analyze the Case

1. What is your assessment of the process used by the superintendent to identify the need for change? What would you have done if you had been the superintendent in similar circumstances?
2. Assuming the superintendent is correct in her assumption about the need for change, what alternatives other than calling a meeting could she have pursued?
3. Assuming that calling a meeting was the best way to proceed in this case, how would you have planned and conducted the meeting differently?

Discuss the Larger Issues

1. How important is it for schools to incorporate computer education into their programs?
2. What is the most appropriate way for schools to introduce computer education?
3. What criteria and process should schools use to determine the extent to which their use of computers is effective?
4. To what degree should all teachers and administrators become literate and competent in the use of computers?

Be a Problem Solver The superintendent of schools in the case study has expressed her concerns about computer education and the use of computers in the schools. As a principal or supervisor in this district, how would you respond to the superintendent's concerns?

Test Your Solution To test your plan of action for dealing with the problems presented at the end of the case, create and role-play one or more of the following situations in class:

1. Continuation of the meeting at the point when the superintendent asks, "Are there any questions?"
2. A faculty meeting in which you present the superintendent's concerns and then discuss the matter.
3. A meeting of the superintendent's cabinet in which you present your recommendation on how to improve the use of computers in the school.

Investigate Further

1. Examine the educational literature for recommendations on the best use of computers; try to identify a description of exemplary programs.
2. Ascertain how computers are being used in your own school and district. How is their use being evaluated? By what criteria?
3. Review any concept chapter presented earlier in the book that would help you improve your skills for addressing the problems in this case, for example, Chapter 7.

63
WHEN NCLB MEETS YOU AT YOUR SCHOOL DOOR

Feeling overwhelmed, Principal Cynthia Foster returned to W.E.B. Dubois High School after attending a districtwide principals meeting with the superintendent. During this meeting, she was given more information about *No Child Left Behind* (NCLB) and the new initiatives to be instituted at the building level for accountability. She knew she had to meet with her "core content" department chairs but did not look forward to sharing the mountain of paperwork that would become part of their jobs. As she sat at her desk preparing the agenda for the meeting, she thought it best to create a script for at least the first part of the meeting. She wrote:

> Thank you all for attending this additional meeting, given the short notice. I want to express my appreciation for all the extra work that each of you does to help us make this a collaborative learning community and a place where academic achievement and high expectations yield results.

She thought this was maybe a little over the top, but she realized that she did not express her thanks and appreciation enough. She made herself a note to put something special in the school newspaper about the state science fair. The science department did good work with the students, she thought.

> I am sure you are wondering why I called this meeting. As you know, I have been out of the building two days this week at districtwide principals meetings. These meetings were called to discuss the district initiatives to meet the revisions to No Child Left Behind. Before I get into specifics, let me share some information with you that was new to me. Some of you may already know this, so chime in if you have some additional information.
>
> The Elementary Secondary Education Act (ESEA) was legislation introduced in 1965 by President Johnson to address the needs of students living in poverty. In 1994 President Clinton signed into law the Improving America's Schools Act (IASA). This statute amended the ESEA and included the reauthorization of Chapter I as the new Title I. The new law loosened some of the statutory and regulatory program requirements, discouraged pull-out programs, and demanded that all children, including the poor and educationally disadvantaged, develop the same knowledge, skills, and level of achievement once expected from only the top students.
>
> President Bush in 2002 signed into law the No Child Left Behind (NCLB) Act of 2001. This new law represents the most sweeping changes to the Elementary and Secondary Education Act since it was enacted in 1965. It changed the federal government's role in kindergarten through grade 12 education by asking America's schools to describe their success in terms of what each student accomplishes.
>
> NCLB has specific provisions that will directly affect our district in general and our school in particular: plans for new programs, personnel, spending, staff development, intervention strategies, and parental involvement.
>
> Our spending priorities and operating procedures drastically changed with new requirements for accountability, highly qualified staff, parental choice, student support, and staff development. It is the most demanding and comprehensive legislation enacted to this date.

Okay, she thought, now to let the other shoe drop:

> I have here a notebook for each of you. A big thank you to my clerical staff for getting these done so quickly. In these books you will find all the changed NCLB items that deal with content; these changes will be described as "core content." Let me say that I know that this is asking you to add

> another layer of paper—no, it is a mountain of paper—onto the already many forms that you must complete. I will assist in any way that I can and will provide the clerical support that you request.

Cynthia looked at the notebooks stacked on the table on the other side of her office. She decided not to take the notebooks to the meeting but ask each teacher to stop by her office to pick up the notebooks. That way she could talk to them individually when they came by, making it easier to deal with their reactions to so much paper work.

> There is one change to an NCLB item that we will need to address especially and that is Title X, repeals, redefinitions, and amendment to other status, Part C, homeless education. As you know in our school demographics, we have about 200 or so students who are classified as homeless. We are already under the Education for Homeless Children and Youth program and receive funds to support those efforts. In fact the grant money that was available to us from Title I funds increased as the subgrants awarded to our district increased. This helped us facilitate the additional clerical support for enrollment, attendance, and the overall academic support for our homeless students.
>
> We will need to work on making sure school records and guardianship issues are addressed, especially since a student who has reached the age of 16 and petitions the courts can become an emancipated minor. Overall we are doing an excellent job making sure these students are not "left behind" and have access to educational and other social services they need to meet the highest academic achievement.

Cynthia wondered if her staff could handle another round of accountability. She knew that NCLB requires that as principal she attest in writing to meeting the standards. However, just how much of this should she delegate to the teachers? The school operated in a context of shared governance, but she wondered at what point she may be asking for too much. She continued writing:

> As a school community, we have done what "highly qualified teachers" do. You are giving all of our student population 110%, and our students who are homeless benefit from the many academic supports you have in place. We are already in compliance with one of the NCLB requirements with our H.Y.L.P., Homeless Youth Liaison Program.
>
> We will, however, need to address changes in NCLB that have new implications for us: transportation. According to the changes, at the request of the parent or guardian, we must provide or arrange for transportation to a homeless student's school of origin. This will require, according to the district, a new method for sharing transportation responsibility and costs from our general fund.
>
> In addition, the only place we have flexibility in the general fund to date is in the "core content" allocations for supplies. This is not a final decision by any means. I would like us to sit with your line items in the general fund budget and see where we may be able to shift money. The district is firm on this item. As a school, if a student who is attending our school is moved or moves to a shelter across town, we must share cost with the district for his or her transportation. A decision does not have to be made today, but a decision on where this money is going to come from must be made by close of business Friday.

Cynthia stopped and could hear ringing in her ear, "Why not take it from athletics?" She wished it were that easy. The superintendent had stopped her on the way out of the meeting to congratulate her again on the basketball team winning the state championship. She cannot cut the generative part of the school budget. She continued to write:

> There will be subgrants on the state and federal level that will be awarded competitively and based on need. This will require a team to write the grants.

Cynthia thought, Great, a request for more teacher time. She felt overwhelmed. She didn't sign on for this. She loved being a high school principal, but the joy faded with each new policy and form as well as district, state, and federal report. There was a knock on the door. She opened the door. Two students from the school newspaper greeted her. She had forgotten she agreed to be interviewed for the new career choice column, "Why I Became ______."

As she stood there in the doorway, she thought maybe she should reschedule.

Suggested Learning Activities

Analyze the Case

1. Do you agree with principal's first plan of action? Why or why not?
2. What alternative measures could she have chosen to deal with the issue?

Looking at the Larger Issue

1. In what ways can principals ensure that faculty and staff do not feel overburdened with the local, state, and federal processes for accountability?
2. What leadership criteria should a principal use to determine when work should be delegated to faculty and staff?

Be a Problem Solver If you were the principal in this high school, what would you do? Utilize appropriate administrative and social science concepts from Part I of this text in planning and implementing your approach.

Test Your Solution To test your proposed plan for dealing with the circumstances in this case, create an agenda and a script for a meeting with the faculty to discuss the issues presented in this case.

Investigate Further Investigate your school and district initiatives related to meeting NCLB and the 2004 revisions. Review the history of the initiatives from creation, implementation, and budget implications.

64
DO EXTREME TIMES CALL FOR RADICAL ACTION? BE THE CHANGE! (A LEADERLESS GROUP ACTIVITY)

Background

According to the National Institute on Drug Abuse, approximately one-half of all high school seniors in the United States admit to having used alcohol or an illegal drug. Substance abuse among teens thus increases the risk of involvement in crime, high-risk sexual behavior, accidents, and injuries. In November the superintendent of schools sent the following memorandum to all administrators and supervisors:

> As you know, the drug problem in our schools has worsened (the rise of illegal prescription drug use, meth, GHB, and many others), and the school board and community are very concerned. In the last few weeks several ideas have been projected, and the school board and I would like your

reaction to them. I acknowledge that these items are controversial, but extreme times may call for radical action. In any case, I would like you to consider the following proposals and give me your most thoughtful analyses and recommendations. Also, I would like your own ideas on what we should do to address the problem if you judge any of the following ideas to be undesirable or not feasible.

1. Students would periodically be randomly searched for drugs prior to entering the school corridors.
2. In those schools with the most serious drug problem, trained dogs would be used to sniff lockers and, when needed, classrooms to detect drugs.
3. All students participating in athletics would be subject to random drug testing.
4. Any student who is suspected of using drugs would be required to undergo drug testing.
5. Any student caught using any kind of illegal drugs on the school grounds or at a school activity would be expelled. Present policy expels only drug sellers and chronic users.
6. Any student found to have known about (but failed to inform the proper authorities about) another student's engaging in the sale of drugs at the school would be suspended.

Although there would be financial considerations to many of these proposals, at this point I want you to consider them solely on their merit without regard to expense. Just give me your best thinking on the proposals themselves.

Instructions

1. Either the instructor will distribute additional information about the nature and extent of the drug problem in the school district or the members of the group will discuss these aspects and reach agreement on them prior to preparing a response to the superintendent's memo. As another alternative, it may be desirable to assume different scenarios regarding the nature and extent of the drug problem to see whether and how this would affect the response given to the superintendent.
2. Once the instructor and/or the group has further defined the drug problem, one or more of the following activities should be pursued:
   a. The group should attempt to reach consensus on a response to the superintendent's request.
   b. Each individual should prepare a written response.
   c. Members of the group should prepare for an oral presentation to the superintendent's cabinet. Each person who is not involved in making the presentation should assume the role of a member of the superintendent's cabinet.

65
TEACHER DIFFICULTY IN A MULTICULTURAL CLIMATE

Mr. Adkins is a first-year teacher of social studies at Westside Middle School, located in a large metropolitan area with diverse cultures represented in the enrollment. Westside is a magnet school for gifted and talented youngsters. Asian and Pacific Islander (A-PI) children are disproportionately represented and have parents, the majority of whom are involved in international careers. Eleven different languages are represented at Westside, and English as a second language (ESL) is taught extensively. Parents of the A-PI children place heavy pressure on them to excel at all times in all areas. The school curriculum is accelerated in addition to providing global connection by means of technology.

Mr. Adkins is a Caucasian from the Midwest with a degree from a small private men's college in the East. His achievements as a graduate student employed as a research analyst at the U.S. Department of Education paved the way for his employment by Westside.

Orientation provided to new staff members focuses on scheduling and other routine procedures. There is no staff development on multicultural interpersonal relations or instruction in ESL for teachers. Several new teachers of varying professional backgrounds join Westside faculty each year. The school is strictly managed with English as the oral and written language. All communication and visual materials are in English. No provisions are made for different cultural activities.

Mr. Adkins teaches a class in world history to a group of 12 students representing Thailand, Korea, Indonesia, the Netherlands, Bosnia, and the United States. His teaching style is 95 percent lecture, textbook-developed tests, and a minimum of discussion. Recently during a lecture concerning the history of events between 1945 and 1965, the students began to ask questions relative to the placement of U.S. troops in Korea. The discussion led to details of the Korean conflict, philosophical differences among those nations involved, impact on U.S. armed forces, and economic shift in South Korean lifestyle. Mr. Adkins shared his personal opinion about the conflict, most of which revealed strong negative feelings toward Koreans and Japanese. He elaborated on the economic war in the marketplace between Japan and the United States and emphasized the decline of U.S. jobs because of Japanese imports.

Most of the students expressed their thoughts, which were often contrary to Mr. Adkins's explanations. Realizing this was a high-interest topic to his students, Mr. Adkins decided to have them discuss these issues with their parents prior to writing a 250-word essay entitled "Factors Contributing to the U.S. Market Deficit Because of Far East Imports." The essays would be due in five days. Mr. Adkins sensed his students' stress and, therefore, assigned an essay as an opportunity for the students to objectively view historical happenings through oral history research. He realized his instructional comfort level declined as he moved away from lecturing, which caused discussion to escalate. "Just another show of opinionated youth behavior," he thought when class ended. During the next few days, students asked specific questions among themselves and occasionally a student would solicit comments from Mr. Adkins in preparation for the essay.

During the five-day assignment period, parents phoned the department's lead teacher to discuss Mr. Adkins's limited perspective on multicultural topics. Some parents sensed a strong feeling of bias and prejudice. Two parents requested a conference with Mr. Adkins, his lead teacher, and the principal to determine the effect his comments had had on the students. A conference was scheduled to be held one day following the assigned essay due date.

Each student completed the assignment on time, demonstrating extensive use of technology networking plus oral history. When Mr. Adkins assessed each paper, he discovered that most students had written opposing views to those he had presented. Most students expressed resentment toward his attitude by writing positive comments about other cultures. Additionally, the essays expressed an overtone of disfavor with Mr. Adkins's teaching style. The majority felt they were being stereotyped in addition to being deprived of an opportunity to interact with classmates. These students preferred to learn about other cultures through idea exchange with their classmates. Mr. Adkins became uncomfortably anxious about his students' writing. He did not dwell on the issues because he believe he would meet with the two parents and reassure them that he was a highly effective teacher and not in the least prejudiced.

On the following day, Mr. Kim, a Korean, and Mrs. Miskoski, from Bosnia, met with Mrs. Gusto, the principal, Mr. White, the lead teacher, and Mr. Adkins. Both parents presented journals their children had written daily over the seven months in Mr. Adkins's class. These journals highlighted approximately 200 comments that could be evaluated as prejudiced, stereotypical, or negative. Mrs. Miskoski shared with the group the fact that all the students realized that parental expectations demanded top scores with no leeway. Mr. Kim reinforced this by revealing a consensus among the students that their scores were too important to make waves with Mr. Adkins. As each student had gathered oral history data, however, it became apparent they should speak up to ensure free expression of thought. Both parents were adamant that the scores given to students on their essay work should not be affected by expression of philosophies or thoughts contrary to those of Mr. Adkins. Second, the parents requested that Mrs. Gusto and Mr. White monitor the world history class and prepare a report for each parent. Mr. Kim elaborated on the necessity for each student to achieve high marks on all tests. These scores determined the students' placement for transfer to the next school. This was critical because many of these students would transfer several times. He also requested an opportunity to visit Mr. Adkins's room at his convenience. Both parents mentioned that they had contacted other parents who were outraged about such instruction.

Mrs. Gusto struggled to mediate such a conference while sensing that a grave problem had surfaced, one for which she had no tolerance. She turned to Mr. Adkins, requesting his comments, only to hear: "I'm not overly concerned with this issue. It is more a display of rebellious youth plus a lack of a knowledge base."

Mrs. Gusto diplomatically shifted the focus and began to address both parents' requests by assuring them of her compliance. She asked Mr. White to cooperatively plan and teach with Mr. Adkins daily. She thanked them for their strong school support, and the conference ended.

Suggested Learning Activities

Analyze the Case

1. What orientation information and training could be provided to better prepare new teachers to work in a multicultural school environment?
2. Consider cooperative teaching strategies that a teacher could use to maximize cultural information the students may contribute to classes.
3. What proactive measures could be implemented to ensure positive communication with ethnic parents?

Discuss the Larger Issues

1. Relate contributing factors that had caused students to be intimidated by such instruction as described in this case.
2. What other options could students choose to diminish instructional overtones of prejudice?

Be a Problem Solver Assume that you are the principal in this situation. How would you handle Mr. Adkins's behavior? Consider professional development strategies.

Test Your Solution

1. Act as a facilitator with the teachers to move those culturally diverse negative emotions toward more positive ones.
2. Convince teachers at a faculty meeting to incorporate cultural diversity content in all of the classes.

Investigate Further

1. Investigate through interviews and school visits how administrators act as a catalyst to nurture teachers struggling with issues relative to cultural diversity.
2. Prepare a log of community events that represents various cultures to be available for teachers to use as resources.

BACKGROUND READING

The reader who would like to develop further background and understanding of the problems and issues associated with introducing and implementing change in the schools should see Chapter 7 in this book and pursue the following readings.

AIT School Leadership Institute: Voices of Challenge and Change (Bloomington, IN: Agency for Instructional Technology, 1996).

Alston, Judy A., "The Many Faces of American Schooling: Effective Schools Research and Border Crossing in the 21st Century," *American Secondary Education* (vol. 32, no. 9, 2004), pp. 79–93.

_______, "Tempered Radicals & Servant Leaders: Black Females Persevering in the Superintendency," *Educational Administration Quarterly* (vol. 41, no. 4, 2006), pp. 675–688.

Au, Wayne, "Social Justice and Resisting Neoliberal Education Reform in the USA," *FORUM* (vol. 58, no. 3, 2016), pp. 315–324. *Symposium Journals*, 2016.

Billingham, Chase M., and Matthew O. Hunt, "School Racial Composition and Parental Choice New Evidence on the Preferences of White Parents in the United States," *Sociology of Education* (vol. 89, no. 2, 2016), pp. 99–117.

Brewer, Dominic J., and Maryann Jacobi Gray, "Do Faculty Connect School to Work? Evidence from Community Colleges," *Educational Evaluation and Policy Analysis* (vol. 21, no. 4, Winter 1999), pp. 405–416.

Feiler, Amanda R., and Deborah M. Powell, "Behavioral Expression of Job Interview Anxiety," *Journal of Business and Psychology* (vol. 31, no. 1, 2016), pp. 155–171.

Fullan, Michael, *Change Forces: The Sequel* (Levittown, PA: Falmer Press, 1999).

Fullan, Michael, et al., *The Rise and Fall of Teacher Education Reform* (Washington, DC: American Association of Colleges of Teacher Education Publications, 1998).

Gordon, Hava Rachel, "'We Can't Let Them Fail for One More Day': School Reform Urgency and the Politics of Reformer-Community Alliances," *Race Ethnicity and Education* (vol. 19, no. 1), pp. 1–22.

Guskey, T. R., and K. D. Peterson, "The Road to Classroom Change," *Educational Leadership* (December 1995), pp. 10–17.

Jargowsky, Paul A., Zachary D. Wood, J. Cameron Anglum, and David N. Karp, "Expanding Educational Opportunity in Urban School Districts," in Susan M. Wachter & Lei Ding (Eds.), *Shared Prosperity in America's Communities* (Philadelphia, PA: Penn Press, 2016), p. 102.

Juchniewicz, Jay, "An Examination of Music Teacher Job Interview Questions," *Journal of Music Teacher Education* (vol. 26, no. 1, 2016), pp. 56–68.

Kaimal, Girija, and Will J. Jordan, "Do Incentive-Based Programs Improve Teacher Quality and Student Achievement? An Analysis of Implementation in 12 Urban Charter Schools," *Teachers College Record* (vol. 118, no. 7, 2016), p. 7.

McLeskey, James, Bonnie Billingsley, and Nancy L. Waldron, "Principal Leadership for Effective Inclusive Schools," in Jeffrey P. Bakken & Festus

E. Obiakor (Eds.), *General and Special Education Inclusion in an Age of Change: Roles of Professionals Involved* (Bingley: Emerald Group Publishing Limited, 2016), pp. 55–74.

Park, Toby J., David A. Tandberg, Shouping Hu, and Dava Hankerson, "One Policy, Disparate Reactions: Institutional Responses in Florida's Developmental Education Reform," *Community College Journal of Research and Practice* (vol. 40, no. 10, 2016), pp. 824–837.

Ravitch, Diane, *The Death and Life of the Great American School System: How Testing and Choice Are Undermining Education* (New York: Basic Books, 2016).

Rogers, George E, "The Perceptions of Indiana High School Principals Related to Project Lead the Way," *Journal of STEM Teacher Education* (vol. 44, no. 1, 2017), p. 5.

A Safe Place to Learn Video (Alexandria, VA: Association for Supervision and Curriculum Development, 1996).

Sattin-Bajaj, Carolyn, *Unaccompanied Minors: Immigrant Youth, School Choice, and the Pursuit of Equity* (Cambridge, MA: Harvard Education Press, 2016).

Shannon, Donna M., "Principals' Perspectives of School Librarians," *School Libraries Worldwide* (vol. 15, no. 2, 2009), p. 28. Skaalvik, Einar M., and Sidsel Skaalvik, "Teacher Stress and Teacher Self-Efficacy as Predictors of Engagement, Emotional Exhaustion, and Motivation to Leave the Teaching Profession," *Creative Education* (vol. 7, no. 13, 2016), p. 1785.

Tillman, Beverly A., and Lessie L. Cochran, "Desegregating Urban School Administration: A Pursuit of Equity for Black Women Superintendents," *Education and Urban Society* (vol. 33, no. 1, November 2000), pp. 44–59.

Tooms, Autumn, and Judy A. Alston, "(OUT)siders at the Gates: Administrative Aspirants' Attitudes towards the Gay Community," in A. H. Normore, (Ed.), *Leadership for Social Justice: Promoting Equity and Excellence through Inquiry and Reflective Practice,* sponsored by American Educational Research Association SIG Leadership for Social Justice (Charlotte, NC: Information Age Publishers, 2009).

White, Terrenda C, "Teach For America's Paradoxical Diversity Initiative: Race, Policy, and Black Teacher Displacement in Urban Schools," *Education Policy Analysis Archives* (vol. 24, 2016), p. 16.

Yu, Chien, and Debra Lindsey Prince, "Aspiring School Administrators' Perceived Ability to Meet Technology Standards and Technological Needs for Professional Development," *Journal of Research on Technology in Education* (vol. 48, no. 4, 2016), pp. 239–257.

WEB EXPLORATIONS

The Web links below contain more useful material related to Chapter 14.

"Catalog of School Reform Models," Northwest Regional Educational Laboratory. Accessed online at http://www.nwrel.org/sepd/catalog/index.shtml

"Comprehensive School Reform." Accessed online http://www.bestevidence.org/csr/elem_csrq/elem_csrq.htm

ERIC Clearinghouse on Educational Management, an excellent source of up-to-date information on school leadership trends, school choice debates, school safety, relationships with the community, and current reform issues. Accessed online at https://scholarsbank.uoregon.edu/xmlui/handle/1794/3111

"Evaluating Comprehensive School Reform Models at Scale: Focus on Implementation." Accessed online at http://www.aypf.org/forumbriefs/2011/documents/RandCSRstudy.pdf

"How Leadership Influences Student Learning." Accessed online http://www.wallacefoundation.org/knowledge-center/Documents/How-Leadership-Influences-Student-Learning.pdf

"Urban Education in America" Resources. https://nces.ed.gov/surveys/urbaned/resources.asp

"The Tech Savvy Administrator." http://www.ascd.org/Publications/Books/Overview/The-Tech-Savvy-Administrator.aspx

"What Does A Tech Savvy Administrator Look Like?" Accessed online https://www.aasa.org/SchoolAdministratorArticle.aspx?id=8566

INDEX